Anonymous

State of Labor in Europe

1878 - reports from United States Consuls in the several countries of Europe on rates of wages, cost of living to the laborers, past and present rates, present condition of trade, business habits and systems

Anonymous

State of Labor in Europe

1878 - reports from United States Consuls in the several countries of Europe on rates of wages, cost of living to the laborers, past and present rates, present condition of trade, business habits and systems

ISBN/EAN: 9783337291235

Printed in Europe, USA, Canada, Australia, Japan

Cover: Foto ©Suzi / pixelio.de

More available books at **www.hansebooks.com**

STATE OF LABOR IN EUROPE:

1878.

REPORTS FROM THE UNITED STATES CONSULS

IN THE

SEVERAL COUNTRIES OF EUROPE

ON THE

RATES OF WAGES; COST OF LIVING TO THE LABORERS; PAST AND PRESENT RATES; PRESENT CONDITION OF TRADE; BUSINESS HABITS, AND SYSTEMS; AMOUNT OF PAPER MONEY IN CIRCULATION, AND ITS RELATIVE VALUE TO GOLD AND SILVER; FOR THE SEVERAL CONSULAR DISTRICTS,

IN RESPONSE TO

A CIRCULAR FROM THE DEPARTMENT OF STATE REQUESTING INFORMATION UPON THESE SUBJECTS;

TOGETHER WITH

A LETTER FROM THE SECRETARY OF STATE TRANSMITTING THESE REPORTS TO THE SPEAKER OF THE HOUSE OF REPRESENTATIVES.

WASHINGTON:
GOVERNMENT PRINTING OFFICE.
1879.

46TH CONGRESS, 1st Session. } HOUSE OF REPRESENTATIVES. { Ex. Doc. No. 5.

STATE OF LABOR IN EUROPE.

LETTER

FROM

THE SECRETARY OF STATE,

TRANSMITTING

Reports from United States consuls in relation to the state of labor in Europe.

MAY 20, 1879.—Referred to the Committee on Education and Labor and ordered to be printed.

DEPARTMENT OF STATE,
Washington, May 17, 1879.

SIR: In compliance with section 208 of the Revised Statutes, I have the honor to submit herewith reports from the consuls of the United States in Europe on labor and labor statistics in their several districts, covering the following principal subjects: Rates of wages; cost of living to the laborers; past and present rates compared; present condition of trade; business habits and systems; character of paper money, the amount in circulation, and the relative value of paper money and coin to each other.

These reports are in response to a labor circular—a copy of which will be found immediately preceding said reports in this volume—issued by this Department under date of April 11, 1878.

These reports, covering, as they do, the labor question in all its aspects, in Belgium, Denmark, France, Germany, England, Ireland, Scotland, Wales, Italy, Holland, Spain, and Switzerland (which, with the United States, may be said to comprise the world of educated and progressive labor), embrace so vast and interesting a field of investigation, that, in order to exhibit as directly as possible the salient points relating to the several districts, I have arranged them into national groups, thereby presenting a compact yet comprehensive view of the present state of labor in the various countries of Europe, and at the same time a comparison between labor in those countries and in the United States.

To save repetition as much as possible, I may say that a perusal of the consular reports herewith submitted forces the painful impression upon the mind that low wages, enforced idleness, dear and scanty food, make the laborer's life, in a majority of the countries of Europe, a continual struggle with absolute want.

No American laborer or capitalist can read these reports without a feeling of the utmost commiseration for the toiling millions of Europe, and of heartfelt pride in, and appreciation of the blessings which Heaven, through a free government, has vouchsafed to the people of the United States.

BELGIUM.

Taking areas and populations into consideration, there is, perhaps, no other country in Europe whose labor statistics present so condensed a field for investigation, or whose workingmen have so clearly accepted their situation—putting their patient industry, and even continuity, against the almost limitless capital and capacity, but less reliable labor, of their more powerful neighbors—as those of Belgium.

Contentment among her working people, a fixed principle of living within their means, and a feeling of reciprocity between the employer and the employé, have made Belgium an important power in the commercial and manufacturing world. Perhaps necessity compels this mutual understanding, for it is only thereby that Belgian manufacturers are enabled to compete with English, French, and German manufacturers in foreign markets, and give employment to their workingmen. A few years of misunderstandings between capitalists and laborers, such as periodically convulse England, would paralyze Belgium and ruin both employers and employés. Therefore, the great wisdom displayed by the Belgian workingmen in accepting their peculiar situation is worthy of the highest commendation; whether this has been learned of necessity or whether it has been reached through a more patriotic channel, is of minor consequence.

Such is the reciprocity of feeling between capitalist and laborer, that manufactories or workshops are scarcely ever closed; the employers, in the dullest of times, preferring to run them even at a loss, rather than throw their employés out of work; and the latter, under such circumstances, cheerfully complying with a reduction in hours and wages, cutting down their already bare necessaries of life to tide over the dark hour, confident that when better times return their full time and wages will be again restored.

It must not be understood from this pleasing picture that the working people of Belgium are better off than their neighbors. On the contrary, their lives are continual struggles for meager subsistence, and nothing but that spirit of patience, kindness, and fortitude, which enables them to practice the severest economy, makes it possible for them to subsist themselves and supply the necessaries of life to their families. At the very best, the lot of the workingmen of Belgium is hard and unremitting toil, an unceasing battle with most adverse circumstances, but it would be immeasurably worse were they to resort to strikes and violence to better their condition; indeed, were it not for the reciprocal feeling which unites laborer and capitalist, Belgium would be scarcely known as a commercial or manufacturing country.

Rates of wages.—That you may be enabled to compare the rates of wages in Belgium with the rates in the United States, I herewith give a list of wages paid certain trades in Brussels and the rates paid to similar trades in New York and Chicago:*

Weekly wages paid in Belgium and in the United States.

Occupations.	Brussels.	New York.	Chicago.
Building trades:			
Bricklayers	$6 00	$12 00 to $15 00	$6 00 to $10 50
Masons	6 00	12 00 to 18 00	12 00 to 15 00
Carpenters and joiners	5 40	9 00 to 12 00	7 50 to 12 00
Gas-fitters	5 40	10 00 to 14 00	10 00 to 12 00
Painters	4 20	10 00 to 16 00	6 00 to 12 00
Plasterers	5 40	10 00 to 15 00	9 00 to 15 00
Plumbers	6 00	12 00 to 18 00	12 00 to 21 00
Blacksmiths	4 40	10 00 to 14 00	9 00 to 12 00
Bakers	4 40	5 00 to 8 00	8 00 to 12 00
Cabinet-makers	4 80	9 00 to 13 00	9 00 to 15 00
Saddlers and harness-makers	4 80	12 00 to 15 00	6 00 to 12 00
Tinsmiths	4 80	10 00 to 14 00	9 00 to 12 00
Laborers	3 00	6 00 to 9 00	5 50 to 9 00

It will be seen by the foregoing statement that the mechanics of Brussels do not receive anything like one-half the wages received by the mechanics of New York and Chicago.

To enable you to carry the comparison further, let me submit a statement showing the prices of the necessaries of life in both countries. I regret that the Belgian reports do not enable me to present as extended a list of articles as might be desirable, but the few articles given will enable you to apply the comparative rule to those not given:

Prices of the necessaries of life in Belgium and in the United States.

Articles.		Brussels.	New York.	Chicago.
		Cents.	*Cents.*	*Cents.*
Bread	per pound..	4 to 5	4½	5
Beef	do	16 to 20	8 to 16	4 to 12½
Veal	do	16 to 20	8 to 24	6 to 15
Mutton	do	16 to 20	9 to 16	5 to 15
Pork	do	16 to 20	8 to 10	4 to 12
Lard	do	20	10 to 12	6 to 10
Butter	do	20 to 50	25 to 32	16 to 40
Cheese	do	20 to 25	12 to 15	5 to 16
Coffee	do	30 to 40	20 to 30	15 to 40
Sugar	do	15 to 20	8 to 10	7 to 11

The foregoing statements show that while the Belgian workingman does not receive one-half the wages of the American workingman, the former pays more for the necessaries of life than the latter.

According to the report from Brussels, it appears that while the rates of wages in the mechanical industries have fallen off 25 per cent. during the last seven years, agricultural wages have been steadily on the increase. This has been due to the great development in manufactures, and to that desire, which seems to pervade all peoples more or less, for the excitement of city life, which continually draws off agricultural labor.

The consul at Ghent gives the rates of wages paid to agricultural laborers as from 17 to 20 cents per day to men, and from 15 to 17 cents

* For an explanation as to the sources of information which has enabled the Secretary to give the rates of wages and prices of the necessaries of life in New York and Chicago in the comparative forms in which they are used throughout this letter, see introduction to Appendix.

per day to women, and their food. When hired as servants, with food and lodging, they are paid $1.75 to $2 per month.

The consul at Brussels notes, as a consequence of the scarcity of agricultural laborers, that a man who is willing to remain upon strictly agricultural lands will receive from 40 to 60 cents per day, without food. A comparison of the foregoing rates with those paid to agricultural laborers in the United States will result even more favorably to the latter than in the case of mechanics.

Habits of the workingmen.—The consul at Ghent writes as follows concerning the habits of the workingmen in his district:

About 80,000 of this population (Ghent) are work people employed in the various manufactories situated here. The habits and customs of this large number of work people are particularly noticeable for frugality, exemplary behavior toward their employers and toward each other, and their strict attention to business. Drunkeness is almost entirely unknown among them, and, according to the police reports, charges against them for crimes are very rare.

Paper money.—The paper money in circulated in Belgium is confined to notes of issue of the National Bank, and is regulated by the law of 1850, which created the bank, and caused the withdrawal of all other circulating notes.

For a full explanation of the monetary system of Belgium, I refer you to Consul Wilson's very interesting report thereon. It may be here said, however, that the entire note circulation of the National Bank must be represented by securities which can be readily converted into money, and that the bank is required to keep an amount of coin in its vaults equal to one-third of its note circulation.

The notes of this bank are received by the Government for debts due the state, and they are legal tender for all private debts, although they have no forced currency further than that they receive from the foregoing facts.

The amount of paper money in circulation at the close of the year 1877 was 342,108,340 francs ($66,000,000), in denominations of 20, 50, 100, 500, and 1,000 franc notes. The bank-note circulation of Belgium is estimated at 661 francs to each inhabitant.

According to the tabulated statements accompanying the report from the consul at Brussels, the total coinage of gold and silver of the Belgian mints, from 1832 to 1878, deducting that which has been demonetized, was as follows: Gold, 522,442,520 francs; silver, 527,678,210 francs; but no correct estimate can be arrived at as to how much of this there is in circulation in the country, owing to the fact that Belgian coins circulate in all the countries forming the Latin Union, viz: Belgium, France, Italy, and Switzerland.

Permit me to call your attention to a peculiar fact noted by Consul Wilson, which is, that during the years 1874 and 1875 over 12,992,611 francs' value of United States gold coin was demonetized and converted at the mint at Brussels into Belgian coin. How much of our money was thus converted into Belgian money previous to 1874 the consul had no means of knowing; how much, if any, has been so converted since 1875 the consul does not say.

DENMARK.

According to the report of the consul at Copenhagen, the present rates of wages throughout Denmark are from 10 to 15 per cent. less than they were in 1872, while the cost of living is somewhat higher. Agricultural laborers are paid as follows, computing the daily wages and averaging summer and winter:

Men, without board or lodging, per week	$1 85
Men, with board and lodging, per week	1 00
Women, without board or lodging, per week	1 25
Women, with board and lodging, per week	72
Women house-servants, per year	19 00

Small as are these rates, they must be the maximum, for the consul says that, "as a general rule, farm hands are employed at from $2.16 to $2.70 per month, with board and lodging." This would give an average of only about $31 per annum as the wages of agricultural laborers.

The wages paid to the several trades in Copenhagen and the rates paid to similar trades in New York and Chicago will be seen by the following statement:

Weekly wages in Copenhagen, New York, and Chicago.

Occupations.	Copenhagen.	New York.	Chicago.
Building trades:			
Masons	$4 45	$12 00 to $18 00	$12 00 to $15 00
Carpenters and joiners	4 25	9 00 to 12 00	7 50 to 12 00
Painters	4 15	10 00 to 16 00	6 00 to 12 00
Blacksmiths	3 90	10 00 to 14 00	9 00 to 12 00
Bakers	4 25	5 00 to 8 00	8 00 to 12 00
Bookbinders	3 72	12 00 to 18 00	9 00 to 20 00
Shoemakers	3 30	12 00 to 18 00	9 00 to 18 00
Butchers	4 50	8 00 to 12 00	12 00 to 18 00
Coopers	4 10	12 00 to 16 00	6 00 to 15 00
Coppersmiths	3 85	12 00 to 15 00	15 00 to 21 00
Cutlers	3 85	10 00 to 13 00	....
Horseshoers	3 85	12 00 to 18 00	15 00 to 21 00
Millwrights	4 00	10 00 to 15 00	12 00 to 21 00
Printers	4 62	8 00 to 18 00	12 00 to 18 00
Saddlers and harness-makers	3 85	12 00 to 15 00	6 00 to 12 00
Sailmakers	4 85	12 00 to 18 00	12 00 to 15 00
Tinsmiths	3 90	10 00 to 14 00	9 00 to 12 00
Tailors	4 10	10 00 to 18 00	6 00 to 18 00
Brassfounders	4 20	10 00 to 14 00	8 00 to 15 00

The general complaint—running through all these labor reports—of commercial and trade depression, and consequent "hard times," is particularly emphasized by Consul Ryder in regard to the condition of affairs in Denmark. The consul enters at some length into the discussion of what he considers the causes of the depression and the necessary remedies for the prevalent evils. The disease being, however, universal, it may be safely asserted that the remedies therefor must be also universal, and that the restoration of commerce and labor to their former healthy condition must begin with the larger nations and flow outward to the branches, not from the branches to the trunk.

Paper money.—The National Bank of Copenhagen is the only bank permitted to issue paper money in Denmark. The notes of this bank are redeemable in gold coin, that being the legal tender; silver being legal tender only to the amount of $5.30.

The amount of National Bank notes in circulation on the 30th of April, 1878, was about $17,000,000. The amount of gold and silver coin and bullion held by the bank, on the same date, for the security and redemption of said notes, was about $9,500,000. The amount of gold coin in circulation in the country, including that held by the National Bank, is calculated at about $8,000,000; silver coin, $4,300,000; and copper coin, $134,000.

According to treaty stipulations, the coins of Denmark and Sweden-Norway circulate in all three countries as legal tenders.

FRANCE.

There is no country in Europe whose labor habits and systems are more worthy of careful investigation than are those of France.

The French working people have, more truly than any other working people, illustrated that commendable phase of political economy—getting the greatest possible result out of the most limited means. They look squarely and sensibly at their capital, and then limit their requirements within that capital; make the most and best of their lot, and fling a halo of sentiment about their lives of toil. For these reasons the work people of France, with as little remuneration and as scanty fare as those of almost any other country—much less than many of their neighbors—are the happiest and most contented labor population in Europe.

Rates of wages.—Although the reports herewith submitted may not afford in all cases an exactly correct view of the wages prevailing throughout France, in other respects—customs and habits of the people and their modes of living—they will be found full and interesting. In regard to agriculture—the greatest industry in France, comprising 10,000,000 land-owners, over 18,000,000 large and small of the population being engaged therein—the average rate of wages is computed from the reports from Bordeaux, La Rochelle, Lyons, Nice, and St. Etienne. The highest rates in any of these five reports are quoted for Bordeaux and La Rochelle, viz, $3.60 per week for men, without board or lodging; and the lowest from Lyons, $1.75 per week, without board or lodging.

The district of the Seine is not included in the rates here given, the agriculturists therein being engaged principally in market-farming for Paris. For this reason the agricultural wages given in the report of the consul-general are exceptionally high, and if given with the five other reports would result in showing an unfair average.

The weekly wages, therefore, paid to agricultural laborers throughout France may be set down as follows:

Men, without board or lodging	$3 15
Men, with board and lodging	1 36
Women, without board or lodging	1 10

There is scarcely any necessity for saying that the French farm laborer must practice the closest economy to enable him to support himself and family on the foregoing wages. Not only does he do this, but in many cases he saves enough to work himself into independent proprietorship in the land. How this is accomplished must be a matter of such general interest as to excuse a somewhat detailed account thereof.

The consul at Bordeaux, department of the Gironde, writes:

> The farm laborers are frequently economical to avariciousness, and many of them, in the course of time, become quite wealthy proprietors.

The consul at La Rochelle, where the French peasant still preserves his primitive manners and rural virtues, says:

> Upon these wages the agricultural laborer not only supports himself and family, but saves money. The steady increase of wealth and prosperity in the rural districts of this portion of France is a matter of general congratulation among the people themselves. *The country is free from tramps.* The laborer thrown out of employment, yet always willing to work, at once starts out, with his loaf of bread under his arm and his gourd of sour wine swung over his shoulder, confident of finding employmen promptly.

The consul at Lyons writes:

> I regard the condition of the agricultural classes of the United States as much superior to those of France, and, I may add from observation and study, to those of Germany, Italy, and Austria-Hungary; yet from the systematic and economic habits of the farmers of France, as a general rule, the French farmer, small as well as large, is better off than his brother agriculturist in the United States.

The consul at Nice writes:

The laboring man's food consists principally of Indian meal, vegetables, bread, and wine. Meat he seldom eats.

In many districts in France the laborers supplement their agricultural earnings by secondary employments, such as weaving, wood-cutting, sawing, wooden-shoe making, &c. The consul at Lyons says that from 8 to 10 per cent. of the agricultural laborers in his district are engaged in these secondary employments, which yield to each laborer about $40 per annum.

Not only must the husband labor for the support of his family, but the wife and children must also labor for the general fund in order to make ends meet. The Lyons report gives a most interesting insight into the economies which enter into the yearly subsistence of the French agricultural laborer's family, and one cannot help being struck with the amount of sobriety, patience, and mutual sacrifices which the insight displays. Had this same economy and patient industry the scope and plentifulness which the more generous agricultural opportunities of the United States afford, to what happy results would it not lead?

The married farm laborer, who supports and lodges himself, may earn in the Lyons district $150 per annum, divided as follows: Husband's wages, $80; wife's wages, $30; children's wages, $40.

The cost of living to such a family, per annum, is calculated as follows:

Rent	$10 50
Bread	55 00
Meat	10 00
Vegetables	8 25
Wine, beer, and cider	7 00
Milk	5 25
Clothing	25 00
Groceries	10 00
Fuel	8 00
Taxes	2 00
Total	141 00

An average struck from all the reports—seven in number—gives the following results in regard to the rates of wages paid to the several trades in France; the rates paid similar trades in New York and Chicago will help you to make comparison between both countries:

Statement showing the rates of weekly wages paid in France and in the United States.

Occupations.	France.	New York.	Chicago.
Building trades:			
Bricklayers	$4 00	$12 00 to $15 00	$6 00 to $10 50
Masons	5 00	12 00 to 18 00	12 00 to 15 00
Carpenters and joiners	5 42	9 00 to 12 00	7 50 to 12 00
Painters	4 90	10 00 to 16 00	6 00 to 12 00
Plumbers	5 50	12 00 to 18 00	12 00 to 21 00
Slaters	....	10 00 to 15 00	12 00 to 18 00
Blacksmiths	5 45	10 00 to 14 00	9 00 to 12 00
Bakers	5 45	5 00 to 8 00	8 00 to 12 00
Bookbinders	4 85	12 00 to 18 00	9 00 to 20 00
Shoemakers	4 75	12 00 to 18 00	9 00 to 18 00
Butchers	5 42	8 00 to 12 00	12 00 to 18 00
Cabinet-makers	....	9 00 to 13 00	7 00 to 15 00
Coopers	7 00	12 00 to 16 00	6 00 to 15 00
Coppersmiths	....	12 00 to 15 00	15 00 to 21 00
Cutlers	4 63	10 00 to 13 00	....
Horseshoers	5 40	12 00 to 18 00	15 00 to 21 00
Printers	4 71	12 00 to 18 00	12 00 to 18 00
Saddlers and harness-makers	5 00	12 00 to 15 00	6 00 to 12 00
Tinsmiths	4 40	10 00 to 14 00	9 00 to 12 00
Tailors	5 10	10 00 to 18 00	6 00 to 18 00

The foregoing statement shows that wages in New York and in Chicago are, on an average, nearly three times as much as the wages throughout France.

It is to be regretted that the reports do not give any very extended information concerning the articles and prices of the necessaries of life in the several districts of France. The following list, although very limited, may enable you to form an idea of the relative cost of food-supplies in France and the United States:

Statement showing the retail prices of certain articles of food in the cities of Bordeaux and La Rochelle and in the cities of New York and Chicago.

Articles.	Bordeaux.	La Rochelle.	New York.	Chicago.
	Cents.	*Cents.*	*Cents.*	*Cents.*
Bread .... per pound..	3	3	4 to 4½	4 to 4½
Beef .... do.....	16 to 20	16 to 24	8 to 16	4 to 12½
Mutton .... do.....	17 to 19	16 to 23	9 to 16	5 to 15
Veal .... do.....	17 to 20	15 to 24	8 to 24	6 to 15
Pork .... do.....	12 to 14	16	8 to 10	4 to 12
Flour .... do.....	....	4½ to 5	3¼ to 4½	2½ to 4½
Coffee .... do.....	....	30	20 to 30	15 to 40
Butter .... do.....	....	30	25 to 32	16 to 40

When the workingmen of France are able to buy the foregoing articles, it may be assumed that they purchase the lowest priced. There is no doubt, therefore, that articles of food of the same qualities are very much cheaper in the United States than in France. Thus, while wages are very much higher in the United States than in France, the necessaries of life are cheaper with us.

The report of the consulate-general at Paris gives the average daily wages throughout France as 45 cents and the average annual income of the typical French family—father, mother, and five children, one of the latter old enough to work—as $180. The annual expenses of this family are: Bread, $66.40; meat, $17.60; vegetables and fruit, $11; wine and beer, $20.60; milk and eggs, $5.40; sugar and salt, $4.40; rent and taxes, $13.20; fire and light, $7; clothing, $18; sundries, $10; total, $167.60.

Habits of the workingmen.—The habits of the French working classes may be summed up in the words "orderly and industrious." The consul at Bordeaux reports them patient, orderly, and prudent; their trade societies in that important district are entirely devoted to benevolent purposes. Unfortunately he has to record the increase of the demoralizing habit of resorting to cafés. It would seem that as times get bad and trade and commerce degenerate, drinking and drinking places increase. No less than 2,000 cafés are reported in and around Bordeaux, and when legitimate tradesmen have to close their doors on account of business depression, the same houses are certain to be reopened as cafés.

Paper money.—The reports herewith do not enable me to give you any very extended information regarding the paper money of France. The report from Lyons says that the Bank of France had, in May, 1878, bank-notes in circulation to the amount of $440,418,000, which was being retired at that time at the rate of from 5,000,000 to 30,000,000 of francs per week. As the foregoing notes are in large denominations, and as there are no small bank-notes in circulation, it may be said that gold and silver constitute the currency of France.

The report from Paris estimates the amount of gold and silver in circulation in France, since 1795, as follows: Gold, 8,435,427,000 francs;

silver, 5,287,966,000 francs; or a total circulation of gold and silver of 13,723,393,000 francs. Of this total, the amount in circulation at the present time is estimated by the consul-general at 8,000,000,000 francs.

GERMANY.

Germany may be considered *the* labor country of Europe. In all other countries there seems to be room for comparatively large populations which live without working, but the genius of the German mind affords no asylum for idleness. The labor reports herewith submitted from Germany are, therefore, worthy of the most careful analyzation, and, happily, they are very full and ably written, and cover the principal portions of the empire.

The ordeal through which the German labor market has passed, and through which it is still passing, will be painfully impressed upon the mind on the most cursory review of these reports. The commercial depression which has weighed so heavily on all countries during the last five years, and which, finally, fell with such crushing effect upon labor everywhere—for all disruptions and disarrangements, financial, commercial, or political, no matter what their origin may be, eventually fall heaviest on the workingmen—seems to have been more acutely felt in Germany than in any other country in Europe, and nothing but that patient fortitude, so characteristic of the people, subsidized by untiring industry and the most painful economy, has enabled the German workingmen to pull through these dark years.

That you may fully appreciate the condition of the German laborer, the straits to which he is subjected in order to supply the barest necessaries of life to his family, and also to enable the American laborer to compare his own condition with that of his fellow-workingman in Germany, I herewith give you some extracts from the consular reports covering the condition of the working classes in the various districts of the empire.

Barmen.—The condition of the laboring classes of the mining and iron industries is very distressing; the price of iron is so low that nothing can be earned, and coal is 40 per cent. below the average of the last twenty-five years. Wages are reduced and many hands discharged. In this district it is at present difficult, *if not impossible*, for a workingman to earn more than enough for his individual support, and every member of the family must contribute to the general fund; hence, from their earliest years, each member is inured to incessant toil and privation.—*From the report of Consul Stanton.*

Bremen.—In order to make life possible, at this rate, women in the country raise garden produce and work in the fields; in the towns, they keep shops, peddle, wash, sew, &c.—*From the report of Consul King.*

---

* The following extract from the annual commercial report for the year 1878 of Consul-General Fairchild, of Paris, successor to Consul-General Torbert, by whom the foregoing report was written, will be found interesting in connection with the subject of money in France:

"The circulation of bank-notes in France on the 28th December, 1876, amounted to $512,553,587; on the 27th December, 1877, $493,677, 202; decrease, $18,876,385: on the 27th December, 1877, $493,677,202; on the 22d November, 1878, $451,156,346; decrease, $42,520,856.

"The amount of paper money in circulation in France is limited by law to 3,000,-000,000 francs, or (5 francs to the dollar) $600,000,000.

"The amount in circulation on the 22d November, 1878, was, as above stated, $451,156,346.

"Cash and ingots on hand the 22d November, 1878, amounted to $414,840,038; amount of notes (paper money) in circulation, $451,156,436.

Brunswick.—With steady work and the assistance of each member of the household, the workingman can "make both ends meet."—*From the report of Consul Fox.**

Chemnitz.—At the present time large numbers are unable to obtain employment; the country is full of tramps, both honest and vagabondish; and almost every dwelling in this city is visited daily by at least a half a dozen beggars, although begging is prohibited by law. In this district (Saxony) labor is subdivided, giving one man's work to two, in order to employ the largest possible number. As the husband's earnings are not sufficient for the support of his family, the wife and older children must contribute their share of the weekly earnings. This is a general rule, and applies to all families whose support is dependent on labor.—*From the report of Consul Griggs.*

Frankfort-on-the-Main.—The condition of the laborer is not enviable; his opportunities are few; luxuries are almost unknown to him; and he is even obliged to use frugally the necessaries of life in order to live upon what he can earn. Butter and meat are luxuries. The American people would consider such a life bitterly hard and joyless.—*From the report of Consul-General Lee.*

Leipsic.—Females are largely employed in business houses, and a person traveling through the country receives the impression that all the work in the fields is done by women.—*From the report of Consul Stewart.*

Sonneberg.—The workingman rarely eats meat at all in any other form than sausage, and his wife and children scarcely know its taste, so little do they get of it. There is poverty in superabundance in the workingman's home, often verging upon squallor; his children are generally barefooted, and his wife looks haggard and weary of her lot.—*From the report Consul Winser.*

Rates of wages.—To enable you to compare the rates of wages paid in Germany with the rates prevailing in New York and in Chicago, I herewith submit a statement showing the weekly wages earned, as averaged from the several reports, in Germany, and the rates paid in those two cities.

Weekly wages in Germany and in New York and Chicago.

Occupations.	Germany.	New York.	Chicago.
Building trades:			
Bricklayers	$3 45	$12 00 to $15 00	$6 00 to $10 50
Masons	4 00	12 00 to 18 00	12 00 to 15 00
Carpenters and joiners	4 18	9 00 to 12 00	7 50 to 12 00
Gasfitters	3 95	10 00 to 14 00	10 00 to 12 00
Painters	4 60	10 00 to 16 00	6 00 to 12 00
Plasterers	4 35	10 00 to 15 00	9 00 to 15 00
Plumbers	3 90	12 00 to 18 00	12 00 to 21 00
Slaters	3 90	10 00 to 15 00	12 00 to 18 00
Blacksmiths	3 90	10 00 to 14 00	9 00 to 12 00
Bakers	3 90	5 00 to 8 00	8 00 to 12 00
Bookbinders	3 90	12 00 to 18 00	9 00 to 20 00
Shoemakers	4 32	12 00 to 18 00	9 00 to 18 00
Butchers	4 20	8 00 to 12 00	12 00 to 18 00
Cabinet-makers	4 95	9 00 to 13 00	7 00 to 15 00
Coopers	4 35	12 00 to 16 00	6 00 to 15 00
Coppersmiths	3 90	12 00 to 15 00	15 00 to 21 00
Cutlers	3 90	10 00 to 13 00	....
Engravers	4 00	15 00 to 25 00	9 00 to 30 00
Horseshoers	3 50	12 00 to 18 00	15 00 to 21 00
Millwrights	4 95	10 00 to 15 00	12 00 to 21 00
Printers	3 90	8 00 to 18 00	12 00 to 18 00
Saddlers and harness-makers	3 90	12 00 to 15 00	6 00 to 12 00
Sailmakers	3 90	12 00 to 18 00	12 00 to 15 00
Tinsmiths	3 60	10 00 to 14 00	9 00 to 12 00
Tailors	4 30	10 00 to 18 00	6 00 to 18 00
Brassfounders	5 50	10 00 to 14 00	8 00 to 15 00
Laborers, porters, &c	2 60	6 00 to 9 00	5 50 to 9 00

To enable you to carry the comparison still further, I submit a table showing the food-prices in Germany and in the United States.

*The figures presented in the report of Consul Fox do not show how the workingman can "make both ends meet," unless the members of his family earn an amount equal to that earned by the head of the family.

Statement showing the retail prices of the necessaries of life in Germany and the prices of similar articles in New York and in Chicago.

Articles.	Germany.	New York.	Chicago.
	Cents.	*Cents.*	*Cents.*
Bread .... per pound..	3 to 7	4 to 4½	4 to 4½
Flour .... do...	5½	4½ to 5	2½ to 4½
Beef:			
Roast .... per pound..	22	12 to 16	8 to 12½
Soup .... do...	14	6 to 8	5
Rump .... do...	14	14 to 16	8 to 12½
Corned .... do...	13	8 to 12	4 to 7
Veal .... do...	14	8 to 12	6 to 12
Mutton .... do...	14¼	9 to 14	5 to 15
Pork:			
Fresh .... per pound..	17	8 to 10	4 to 8
Salted .... do...	17	8 to 10	6 to 12
Bacon .... do...	20	8 to 10	7 to 12
Ham .... do...	20	8 to 12	7 to 15
Shoulder .... do...	19	8 to 10	4 to 10
Sausage .... do...	21	8 to 10	6 to 10
Lard .... do...	21	10 to 12	6 to 10
Butter .... do...	22	25 to 32	16 to 40
Cheese .... do...	24	12 to 15	5 to 16
Rice .... do...	9	8 to 10	5 to 10
Beans .... per quart..	10	7 to 10	5 to 9
Milk .... do...	4	8 to 10	3 to 6
Oatmeal .... per pound..	8	4 to 5	4 to 5
Tea .... do...	75	50 to 60	25 to 75
Coffee .... do...	35	20 to 30	15 to 40
Sugar .... do...	11	8 to 10	7 to 11
Soap .... do...	10	6 to 7	3 to 8
Starch .... do...	9	8 to 10	5 to 10
Coal .... per ton..	$4 25	$5 25	$3 00 to $6 75

It will be seen by the foregoing tables that while the rates of wages in New York and Chicago are, on an average, three times the rates in Germany, the prices of the necessaries of life in those two cities are much less than the average prices for all Germany. Assuming that, whenever the German workingman can buy the greater part of the articles mentioned in the foregoing list, he buys the cheapest, the difference in favor of the American workingman is very marked.

The average weekly wages of the agricultural laborers of Germany are as follows:

Men, without board or lodging $3 50
Men, with board and lodging 1 80
Women, without board or lodging 1 55
Women, with board and lodging 60

A few extracts from the consular reports will give you a better idea of the every-day life of the German farm laborer than any disquisition which might be indulged in.

In order to make life possible at these rates, women raise their own garden produce, and, when they can, work in the fields.—*Consul at Bremen.*

The laborers are really part and parcel of the estate. Wages in money are often merely nominal.—*Consul at Dresden.*

A large portion of the outdoor as well as the indoor work is performed by women, who receive from 20 to 50 per cent. less than men are paid for like services. The laborers are obliged to use frugally even the bare necessaries of life in order to live upon what they earn.—*Consul-general at Frankfort-on-the-Main.*

The agricultural laborers, as a class, are much inferior in point of intelligence and refinement to those of the United States; they are simple in manners, their wants are but few, and they cling with great tenacity to the customs of their ancestors. They are generally honest and law-abiding, very frugal and saving, even to parsimony, and always manage to live within their small earnings.—*Consul at Hamburg.*

A person traveling through the country receives the impression that all the field-work is done by women.—*Consul at Leipsic.*

The wages paid hardly cover the necessaries of life; many seldom taste meat more than once a week.—*Consul at Mannheim.*

It may be easily imagined from the foregoing figures, showing the wages of the laboring classes of Thuringia, that their daily fare is of the simplest sort, and that their life is, at best, a struggle for existence for themselves and families. Their principal food is rye-bread and potatoes.—*Consul at Sonneberg.*

Habits of the German workingmen.—The German workingmen have ever been noted for patience, industry, frugality, domestic affection, and love of rational enjoyment. While the accompanying reports bear evidence to the preservation of these characteristics, it cannot be denied but that a great disposition to run into excesses and recklessness—the latter considered so foreign to the German character—has recently manifested itself, especially among the workingmen in the large cities and trade centers.

Socialism and communism, taking advantage of the workingman's deplorable state during the last few years, seem to have appealed to his desperation with too much success. Would that the results attained, even at the cost of uprooting the old household virtues, gave promise of any improvement in the condition of the laborer and his family; but a few extracts from the accompanying reports will clearly show that socialism and communism only add demoralization and excesses to already existing evils, taking away from the laborer that respect for constituted authority and reverence for the moral law which were his strength and his hope without giving him anything in return.

The consul at Barmen, which is the great iron-mining and manufacturing district of Germany, says:

Whatever be the characteristics of the laborer in other parts of Germany, in this and in the adjoining districts he is, as a rule, improvident and quarrelsome. The towns are, in consequence, heavily burdened by poor-rates; the municipal assessments in this consular district being from five to seven times the amount of the imperial rates. A fearful cause of want and ruin among the laboring classes is the enormous increase of drinking saloons and dancing halls, and the complaint is universal as to the disposition of the laborers to indulge in excessive drink.

The consul at Brunswick, in referring to the deplorable condition of the German workingmen, says:

The general trouble seems to be that the workmen will not work at present prices, or at such work as is to be had. As far as I am able to learn, the Socialist-Democratic party is largely responsible for this state of things. This organization, through its machinations, has done much to interfere with the prosperity of this country.

The consul at Dresden says:

The cost of living to the laboring classes almost invariably goes *pari passu* with their wages. They seem to be generally improvident and regardless of the future, and spend in beer-drinking, dancing, and idleness all they earn.

While it is to be hoped that the growth of the principles so clearly referred to above is more apparent than real, the riotous and turbulent few always making more noise than the orderly many, it is pleasant to turn to the following from the report of the consul-general at Frankfort-on-the-Main, which, in addition to its local application, is thought to give the truer picture of the great body of the German working people:

Yet the German laborer can and does save from his earnings. He will not be idle if he can help it, and will rather work for a few pfennigs per day than do nothing. Strikes seldom or never occur, and nothing is lost, therefore, in costly and useless contentions with employers.

As an illustration at once of the condition of the working classes of Germany and their disposition to be happy under the most pinching circumstances, the following paragraph, from the interesting report of the consul at Chemnitz, in regard to the habits and customs of the Saxon working classes, is specially appropriate here:

The poorer classes in Southern Saxony fare very meanly indeed. For houses, they have generally a single room, which answers for workshop also. For household furniture, they have a few chairs or wooden stools, a table, stove, and sometimes a loom. For beds, they have the bare floors or straw pallets. For fuel, they have the dead branches fallen from the trees in the King's forest, carried home in their arms. For food, they have black bread, made of rye; coffee, made principally of chicory; a few boiled potatoes; sometimes a little cheese, butter, or goose-grease; and on Sundays a pound of meat for a family of five or six persons. But if "poor and content" is rich, no others within my knowledge can compare in wealth with the poor of this district. They live in villages and love company. When Sundays or holidays come, they meet at restaurants, smoke poor tobacco, drink poor beer, talk, sing, and dance, and seem as happy as if they had a thousand a year.

Such, in brief, are the characteristics of the German working classes, characteristics which, under more favorable circumstances in the United States, have helped so materially in the development of our vast resources, which have made the name of German-American synonymous with industry and good citizenship, and which have given to the agricultural and manufacturing mind of our country much of its solidity and perseverance.

Paper money.—In regard to the circulating medium in Germany, it may be said that paper money has the same value as gold and silver.

According to the report from the consul at Sonneberg, the Reichsbank and seventeen private banks are authorized to issue paper money. According to the bank act of 1875, the issue of notes uncovered by bullion or coin is limited to 273,875,000 marks for the Reichsbank, and 111,125,000 marks for the seventeen private banks; a total of 385,000,000 marks, or $92,630,000.

The actual issue of notes, covered and uncovered, was, on the 1st of April, 1878, 833,504,000 marks, and the amount of bullion and coin held by the banks on the same date was 623,896,000 marks; 75 per cent. of the entire note circulation being thus covered.

Besides the foregoing, there are 120,000,000 marks of state notes in circulation.

The entire note and coin system of Germany being based on the single (gold) standard, the bank-notes are on par with gold; all banks emitting paper money being required to redeem the same in gold on demand.

The consul-general at Frankfort-on-the-Main estimates the total amount of coin and notes in circulation in Germany, at the beginning of 1878, at 3,000,000,000 marks, or $714,000,000.

Silver is receivable as legal tender to the amount of not more than $23, but there is no limit to paper money as a legal tender unless by stipulation. Paper is the most popular currency, owing to its convenience and ready convertibility into gold; silver being used only as a medium for small transactions.

For further particulars concerning the paper money and coin circulation in Germany, and the laws and systems governing the same, I would refer you to the reports, herewith transmitted, from Consul Stanton at Bremen, from Consul-General Lee at Frankfort-on-the-Main, from Consul Stewart at Leipsic, and from Consul Winser at Sonneberg.

GREAT BRITAIN AND IRELAND.

ENGLAND.

The manufacturing supremacy of England has necessarily developed a great labor element in that country, and it may be said that, as England has led the nations in commerce and manufactures, her artisans, mechanics, and workingmen in general have also led the labor element of Europe.

The labor populations of the rest of Europe, although that of each country is seemingly distinct, have something in common in their tempers and habits. The English workingman stands out boldly alone. Lacking the *finesse* of the Frenchman, the patient industry of the German, the eternal evenness of the Dutch, the docility and adaptability of the Belgian, and the spirit which relies upon the climate for half their food and clothing, which makes the Italian and the Spaniard so happy in misfortune, he possesses attributes which in many respects make him the superior of all.

What is called "British pluck" is the predominating characteristic of the English workingman. This is the result of centuries of national training in a school from which all the softer attributes were excluded as tending to effeminacy; a school in which the so-called "manly exercises" (rightly or wrongly so called is not to the question) were practiced, developing the rough-and-ready give-and-take spirit of the Anglo-Saxon; that stubborn courage which displays itself sometimes in riot and violence and sometimes in that indomitable courage which has made the British flag feared and respected throughout the world—a long strike or a Waterloo.

These features, which have been so indelibly stamped, through a long series of years, into the English workingman's character, must be taken into consideration if we would seek to arrive at any approximate understanding of the present perplexing and unsatisfactory state of labor in England. It is evident to those who have marked the recent course of manufacturing and labor events in that country—the decline of manufactures and the uncompromising spirit of labor; a decline caused by foreign competition, and, in consequence thereof, less demand for manufactures, producing a contraction to which the employer and the employé might have gradually accommodated themselves by a sensible spirit of concession on the part of the latter, had the workingman been capable of appreciating the fact that his employer was forced to reduce his wages in order to sell at a profit, a reduction which the organized stubbornness of trades-unions have so long and at such fearful cost resisted,—it is evident to those who have noted these things of late that the British workingman has at length brought himself face to face with the inevitable. British manufacturers can go no further unless their workmen, by accepting less wages, assist them to maintain the foreign markets already being contested for by other nations.

Thus far the British workingman would seem to have believed that the British manufacturer sought a reduction of his wages in mere hostility to labor, not being capable, it would appear, to look beyond the narrow circle of his own interest to the broader fact that the manufacturer has sacrificed much already for British pride, and, to his honor be it noted, for the interest of the workman, in running his establishment often at a loss rather than cease manufacturing altogether.

The great aim, according to the reports herewith submitted, of the trades-unions has been to resist any attempted reduction of wages. It may be said that, thus far, they have been successful, but if it be a victory which has cost England her manufacturing supremacy, it is a victory which will destroy labor also; for if the factories are idle, so must labor go idle, and while capital may find profitable investment in channels not necessarily connected with manufactures, the laborer can only live by labor.

A few years more of strikes and disorganization in England, and it may be doubted whether any compromise between the employers and the employés will restore to that country her manufacturing supremacy.

As capital will not remain idle, nor permanently in unprofitable investments, it may be expected that English capitalists will seek new fields for investment, such as the transfer of the cotton manufacture to India, which may be said to have already begun.

Under such circumstances nothing will remain for the British workingmen but emigration. Thus, if they drive capitalists and manufacturers away, they must also go.

Already the British workingmen see the necessity of getting rid of their surplus labor so as to reduce it within the actual demand therefor, the greater portion of them being working at present, where they are working, on short time, to enable all to eke out an existence.

Premiums are being now offered to those workingmen who are willing to emigrate to Australia or to the United States by those very trade-unions which have divided capital and labor into hostile camps, brought ruin on the manufacturer, and poverty to the workingman's home, filled the land with strikes and resistance for years, made of the manly English workingman an organizer of reckless leagues, and which now offer the English people forced emigration.

There can scarcely be a doubt but that within the next five years half a million of English workingmen will emigrate; indeed, should the spirit of emigration once seize the English mind, there can be no reasonable limit set to the hegira.

That the greater number of these emigrants will seek "work and bread" in the United States, may be fairly assumed. We have, therefore, more interest in those people than even their own Government; they are Englishmen to-day; in ten years they will be American citizens. That they are as good material in physique, in pluck, and as workingmen as Europe has ever driven hither is undeniable, and if they will only rise up to the height of their new and more favorable surroundings, leave their trades-unions and strikes behind them, as well as their ruined manufactures, and fall into the ranks of the American workingmen proper, they will be a strength and an addition to our country.

These are questions, in connection with the present state of labor in England, to which I have considered it necessary to draw your attention before passing on to the review of the consular reports herewith submitted.

Although the reports from England are not as full nor as many as might be expected, it is thought that they are sufficient to enable you to reach a correct understanding of the present condition of labor in that country. A few consuls have written so fully in answer to the Department circular as to fill up the gaps which are so apparent in the reports of others, and the void which the total absence of reports from some districts has caused. In this connection I would refer you to the comprehensive and valuable report from Newcastle-upon-Tyne, and also to the reports from Leeds, Sheffield, and Liverpool.

Rates of wages.—In laying before you the following statement showing the rates of wages, as averaged from the reports herewith submitted, throughout England, as compared with those prevailing in New York and Chicago, it should be remarked that, in many cases, the English rates are more apparent than real, and that, while nominally the English workingman appears to receive a comparatively high rate of wages, he only works on half or two-third time, thus gratifying his desire to preserve a high rate of wages at the expense of time; a sentimental fiction which is neither profitable nor substantial:

Statement showing the weekly rates of wages paid the following trades in England and the rates paid to similar trades in New York and in Chicago.

Occupations.	England.	New York.	Chicago.
Building trades:			
Bricklayers	$8 12	$12 00 to $15 00	$6 00 to $10 50
Masons	8 16	12 00 to 18 00	12 00 to 15 00
Carpenters and joiners	8 25	9 00 to 12 00	7 50 to 12 00
Gasfitters	7 25	10 00 to 14 00	10 00 to 12 00
Painters	7 25	10 00 to 16 00	6 00 to 12 00
Plasterers	8 10	10 00 to 15 00	9 00 to 15 00
Plumbers	7 75	12 00 to 18 00	12 00 to 21 00
Slaters	7 90	10 00 to 15 00	12 00 to 18 00
Blacksmiths	8 12	10 00 to 14 00	9 00 to 12 00
Bakers	6 50	5 00 to 8 00	8 00 to 12 00
Bookbinders	7 83	12 00 to 18 00	9 00 to 20 00
Shoemakers	7 35	12 00 to 18 00	9 00 to 18 00
Butchers	7 23	8 00 to 12 00	12 00 to 18 00
Cabinet-makers	7 70	9 00 to 13 00	7 00 to 15 00
Coopers	7 30	12 00 to 16 00	6 00 to 15 00
Coppersmiths	7 40	12 00 to 15 00	15 00 to 21 00
Cutlers	8 00	10 00 to 13 00	....
Engravers	9 72	15 00 to 25 00	9 00 to 30 00
Horseshoers	7 20	12 00 to 18 00	15 00 to 21 00
Millwrights	7 50	10 00 to 15 00	12 00 to 21 00
Printers	7 75	8 00 to 18 00	12 00 to 18 00
Saddlers	6 80	12 00 to 15 00	6 00 to 12 00
Sailmakers	7 30	12 00 to 18 00	12 00 to 15 00
Tinsmiths	7 30	10 00 to 14 00	9 00 to 12 00
Tailors	$5 00 to 7 30	10 00 to 18 00	6 00 to 18 00
Brassfinishers	7 40	10 00 to 14 00	8 00 to 15 00
Laborers, porters, &c	5 00	6 00 to 9 00	5 50 to 9 00

That you may be able to make fuller comparison of the relative purchasing power of the wages of the English and American workingmen, I submit the following table, showing the food-prices as averaged from all the English reports and the prices in New York and Chicago:

Statement showing the retail prices of the necessaries of life in England and in the United States

Articles.	England.	New York.	Chicago.
	Cents.	*Cents.*	*Cents.*
Bread .... per pound	3½ to 4½	4 to 4½	4 to 4½
Flour .... do	3½ to 4½	3 to 4½	2½ to 4½
Beef:			
For roasting .... per pound	22	12 to 16	8 to 12½
For soup .... do	15	6 to 8	5
Rump steak .... do	26½	14 to 16	8 to 12½
Corned .... do	18	8 to 12	4 to 7
Veal:			
Fore quarters .... per pound	18	9 to 10	6 to 10
Hind quarters .... do	22½	12 to 14	10 to 12
Cutlets .... do	27	14 to 16	12½ to 15
Mutton:			
Fore quarters .... per pound	17	9 to 10	5 to 12½
Hind quarters .... do	22	12 to 14	5 to 15
Chops .... do	25	14 to 16	10 to 15
Pork:			
Fresh .... per pound	16½	8 to 10	4 to 8
Salted .... do	15	8 to 10	6 to 12
Bacon .... do	12 to 16	8 to 10	7 to 12
Ham .... do	13½ to 23	8 to 12	7 to 15
Shoulder .... do	12	8 to 10	4 to 10
Sausage .... do	18	8 to 10	6 to 10
Lard .... do	15 to 18	10 to 12	6 to 10
Codfish, dry .... do	8	6 to 7	5 to 9
Butter .... do	29 to 38	25 to 32	16 to 40
Cheese .... do	15 to 21	12 to 15	5 to 16
Potatoes .... per bushel	$1 12 to $2 00	$1 12 to $1 60	60 to 80
Rice .... per pound	3½ to 8	8 to 10	5 to 10
Beans .... per quart	9	7 to 10	5 to 9
Milk .... do	6 to 9	8 to 10	3 to 6
Eggs .... per dozen	19 to 30	25 to 30	10 to 24
Oatmeal .... per pound	3½ to 4	4 to 5	4 to 5
Tea .... do	43 to 88	50 to 60	25 to $1 00
Coffee .... do	28 to 42	20 to 30	15 to 40
Sugar .... do	5½ to 9	8 to 10	7 to 11
Soap .... do	5½ to 9	6 to 7	3 to 8
Starch .... do	10 to 12	8 to 10	5 to 10
Coal .... per ton	$3 20 to $4 10	$5 25	$3 00 to $6 75

It will be seen that while the wages in New York and Chicago are about twice the average wages throughout England, the prices of the necessaries of life are lower in those two cities than the average prices throughout England.

It is well that your attention should be specially drawn to the erroneous opinions which have more or less prevailed, especially in the minds of our working people, in the United States for the past few years, that wages were higher and the cost of living less in England than in this country.

At a time of unusual depression in all trades in the United States strikes of certain trades occurred in England. Some British manufacturers, taking advantage of the occasion, induced a number of workingmen from this side to go over and take the places of the English workingmen on strike. This gave rise to the idea that work was more easily obtained and that wages were higher in that country than in the United States.

It may be remarked that the principal portion of those workingmen were natives of Great Britain, many of them immigrants newly arrived in the United States, and all of them out of employment. The few Americans who did go were repaid for their venture by much humiliation and suffering, as the many reports from our consuls in England have testified; so that there is scarcely any need to refute the foregoing fallacy by any further consular testimony; but the consul at Bristol puts the question in so graphic a manner, that I cannot refrain from quoting his words:

> No laborer should allow himself to be enticed, by imagining that he could better his condition by leaving the United States to return to his native country, if born in Europe. A number of such laborers and also some mechanics have, during the last two years, called upon this consulate for help to get back to the United States, cursing the day when they left America for Europe, where neither milk nor honey is flowing. *Compared with Europe, the United States is a paradise for a sober and faithful workingman.*

In regard to the question of food-prices in England and in the United States, no stronger argument can be advanced to dissipate the idea that workingmen can live cheaper in that country than in this than the fact that Great Britain imported from the United States during a recent year, "necessaries of life" to the following amounts: Wheat, \$50,000,000; Indian corn, \$43,000,000; bacon and hams, \$34,500,000; cheese, \$10,300,000; flour, \$8,300,000; lard, \$6,800,000; pork, salted, \$3,000,000; butter, \$2,870,000; fresh beef, \$2,000,000; refined sugar, \$1,650,000; pease, \$1,500,000; canned and preserved meats, \$1,400,000; fruits, raw, \$1,243,000; molasses, \$653,000; coffee, \$516,000; oats, \$343,000; barley, \$264,000—a total food-supply of over \$171,000,000!

In regard to the food-living of the English workingman, it may be said that it is regulated solely by his ability to buy. He will have as much strong and wholesome food—and he is a good eater—as he can purchase, meat entering into his fare more plentifully than into the fare of any other workingman in Europe. The consul at Bristol says that the English workingman of to-day eats fully three times more meat than the English workingman of twenty years ago. It may also be remarked that American bacon is largely used by the English workingmen, as also other American meats when they can be purchased.

There would seem to be no disposition to lay anything by for the "rainy day," the English workingman never stinting himself in his food, as on the continent, for the purpose of laying by a reserve. This disposition of living each day in itself—coupled with the periodic strikes, which break up the even run of wages and bring so much suffering to his wife and children—renders the life of the English workingman a spasmodic struggle for existence; and it may be doubted whether the family of the average English laborer or mechanic is any better off, year in and year out, than the family of the German or French laborer or mechanic; it certainly has not that sentimental and musical enjoyment which throws such pictorial light about the poor man's home in the latter countries.

Habits of the English working people.—It is not necessary to dwell at any length upon the habits and customs of the English working people. The British press, with that bold honesty for which it is noted, has so often rebukingly published their vices, and approvingly their virtues, that the same are well known in the United States. I will, therefore, only quote, in this connection, from two of the accompanying reports—Newcastle-upon-Tyne and Sheffield—which show the best and, it is to be hoped, the worst of the habits and customs of the English workingmen. It is noteworthy that these two quotations reverse the generally conceived order of good and evil, all the refinement and sentiment being with the coal-miners of Northumberland, and all the brutality and vice with the operatives of Sheffield.

The miners of Northumberland.—John Stuart Mill says that "the majority of Englishmen have no life but in their work. The absence of any taste for amusement or enjoyment of repose is common to all."

This is not the case when applied to the Northumberland miners. They are great bird fanciers, and their skill as gardeners, under great difficulties, enables many of them to compete successfully at the local flower fairs. They are also enthusiastic sportsmen. Every Saturday afternoon, throughout the summer, the Newcastle town moor is visited by thousands of pitmen, who come to see their fellow-workmen playing matches at bowls for stakes varying from $25 to $125 a side. The fondness of the miners of this district for dogs is notorious throughout the country, and during the recent strike, when it became known that the pitmen were obliged to part with their pet dogs for want of money to pay their licenses, a gentleman in London sent a check for $125 to the secretary of the miners, with the request that the money be applied to procure licenses for the most deserving cases.—*Report of Consul Jones, Newcastle-upon-Tyne.*

It is not pleasant to turn from the foregoing to the following picture, showing the habits of the workingmen of Sheffield. It is to be feared, also, that the worst picture is the truer representation of the average workingman, especially in the large manufacturing centers, and that the ale-house has more attraction for him than the flower-garden:

The workingmen of Sheffield.—A bold recklessness as to earning and spending prevails among the Sheffield workingmen. Many a man who can easily earn his fourteen to nineteen dollars a week will be satisfied with earning half that sum, or just enough to provide him with his food, beer, and sporting, allowing his wife but a mere pittance of his wages for herself and children. Large numbers, who might make themselves independent, make no provision for the future, except to pay into their club a shilling or two a week, which assures them, if not in arrears, some aid in case of sickness. This method of insurance, good in itself, seems to operate here to paralyze the desire to save. One thing, however, seems evident, that, notwithstanding the great depression in the manfacturing interests of Sheffield, there would be but little destitution among the working people but for their drinking habits. Any one walking these streets will see at once where the earnings of the workingmen go, and, in many cases, the earnings of the workingwomen also; for there is in this town a far greater population of women employed in the heavier kinds of labor than will be found in the cities of the United States, excepting, it may be, the great cotton-manufacturing centers. This fact is to be considered in estimating the amount of earnings that go to the support of families, such earnings being larger than might at first appear. Were the same properly used, there would be comparatively little suffering or poverty.—*Consul Webster, Sheffield.*

Enough is shown in these reports to prove that the greater portion of the evils which afflict the laboring classes of England to-day, which have disorganized its manufactures and brought misery to the workingman's home, can be traced direct to strikes and drink.

The consul at Sheffield estimates the loss of time through drink to each workingman in that city at one day in each week. This would give a total loss in time alone—not counting the money spent for drink—to the workingmen of Sheffield of over $2,000,000 per annum, and this estimate the consul believes to be rather under the truth. The consul questions the ability of any nation, no matter how favorable other auspices may be, with an unreliable (drinking and striking) labor population to continue to compete successfully in the markets of the world with those countries whose working classes are temperate, industrious, and thrifty.

In regard to the agricultural laborers of England, it may be said that their condition has very materially improved within the last thirty years, the consul at Newcastle estimating the increase in their wages during that time at 35 per cent. The same consul notes a very interesting fact, that intelligence, good wages, and good farming go hand in hand, while ignorance, low wages, and poor farming are equally associated. In the north of England and in the southeast of Scotland—noted for the intelligence of their agricultural populations, owing to the early introduction of public schools therein—the farm laborers are paid $4.10 per week, while in the southern counties of England, where primitive ignorance and poor farming still prevail, the same class of laborers are only paid $2.75 per week.

The comfort and moral training of the laborers' families in the foregoing districts keep pace with the prevailing intelligence or ignorance.

The weekly wages, as averaged from these reports, of agricultural laborers throughout England are as follows:

Men, without board or lodging	$4 25
Men, with board and lodging	$1 50 to 2 40
Women, without board or lodging	1 80 to 3 25
Women, with board and lodging	60 to 1 00
Women, house servants, per annum	34 00 to 49 00

The currency of England.—According to the report from the Leeds consulate, the currency of England consists of: gold coins, $510,300,000; silver and copper coins, $87,480,000; Bank of England notes, $170,100,000 (on $97,200,000 gold bullion); provincial notes, $76,788,000; a total of $844,688,000.

The actual circulation, however, as given by the same report, is as follows: Gold coins, $510,300,000; silver and copper coins, $87,480,000; Bank of England notes on bullion, $97,200,000; bank-notes not issued on bullion, $92,340,000; total actual circulation, $787,320,000.

Gold is the only legal-tender standard in England, the tender of silver being limited to £2.

Notwithstanding the foregoing, it may be said that silver is still, to a great extent, the people's money in England; all the small business, wages, shopping, &c., being transacted principally through its medium. The workingman scarcely ever handles a bank-note; the lowest denomination issued being £5.

To enable you to make still further comparisons, I beg leave again to refer you to the principal reports from England, herewith submitted, drawing your attention to the special points of each report where questions outside of the general information requested by the Department Circular are discussed.

Leeds.—Interesting account of the constabulary system, and a report, principal and supplementary, on the currency, banking laws, and fixed issues of the United Kingdom.

Newcastle-upon-Tyne.—An exhaustive and interesting report on the following subjects: The nine-hour system, in connection with the great strike of the engineers in 1873; Northumberland coal mines, miners, and coal trade (valuable); agricultural laborers, a review of 100 years; seamen's wages; railway employés and their wages, &c,

Bradford.—Labor educational statistics, and the relations between capital and labor.

Manchester.—The public feeling in regard to, and the suffering caused by, strikes.

Sheffield.—Habits of the workingmen and workingwomen; time and money lost in drinking saloons.

IRELAND.

No country in Europe, perhaps, affords a better illustration of the commercial vigor and manufacturing activity which are ever the results of diversified industry than does Ireland by the almost total absence of the same, and the consequent monotony which is ever the accompaniment of such a commercial condition as prevails in that country.

With the exception of the linen manufacture—omitting local efforts for self-supply—Ireland may be said to have no national industry outside of agriculture; and as the great tendency of agriculture in that country is toward pasture-farming—over one-third of all the arable land being now given up to pasturage and meadow-land—and as the labor required to tend cattle and cut and save hay is comparatively little, it follows that even the requirements of this one industry, as far as labor is concerned, must be growing less year by year.

Emigration, however, would seem to draw off Ireland's surplus labor population, as the wages of farm hands in that country, according to the reports submitted, are very little less than the wages which prevail in England and Scotland, as may be seen by the following statement:

Weekly wages paid to agricultural laborers in Ireland, England, and Scotland.

Description.	Ireland.	England.	Scotland.
Men, without board or lodging	$3 40	$3 60	$4 25
Men, with board and lodging	1 30	2 60	$1 50 to 2 00
Women, without board or lodging	2 10	1 80	1 80 to 3 25
Women, with board and lodging	75	1 15	60 to 1 00
Women, house servants, per year	40 00	60 00	34 00 to 49 00

In a large number of cases the agricultural laborers of Ireland supplement their wages by the produce of small plots of ground attached to their cabins. As a general thing, a fair share of the field work is performed by women.

To enable you to compare the rates of wages paid to the trades in Ireland with the rates paid to similar trades in New York and Chicago, I submit the following table:

Statement showing the weekly wages paid by the board of public works throughout Ireland to the building trades and the general rates paid similar trades in New York and Chicago.*

Building trades.	Ireland.	New York.	Chicago.
Bricklayers	$7 58	$12 00 to $15 00	$6 00 to $10 50
Masons	7 58	12 00 to 18 00	12 00 to 15 00
Carpenters and joiners	7 33	9 00 to 12 00	7 50 to 12 00
Gasfitters	7 95	10 00 to 14 00	10 00 to 12 00
Painters	7 54	10 00 to 16 00	6 00 to 12 00
Plasterers	7 68	10 00 to 15 00	9 00 to 15 00
Plumbers	8 46	12 00 to 18 00	12 00 to 21 00

Food and food-prices.—In regard to the food-prices in Ireland and in the United States, it is enough to say that the principal part of the food used by the workingmen of Ireland comes from the United States.

In regard to the manner and cost of living of the working people, the consul at Cork says:

The food is made up of a selection from tea, bread, oatmeal, potatoes, dried fish, and among the poorer classes a coarse Indian meal instead of oatmeal, at an average expense to each person of 14 cents per day. The mechanic pays something more for his lodging, but in other respects his living is the same as the laborer.

The consul at Londonderry writes:

The food of all laborers here is Indian meal (principally), oatmeal, potatoes, and bacon next. Tea may be said to be in universal use.

With wages almost equal to those paid in England and Scotland, the food of the working people of Ireland is much inferior to the food of the English working people, lacking the solidity of meat, cheese, beer, &c., consumed in such comparatively large proportions by the latter. The English are also better clothed and lodged, the air of thrift and comfort which is so apparent in the homes of the English mechanic being almost totally unknown to the hard-working Irishman. Much of this undoubtedly arises from the diversity of industries in England, many members of the same family finding employment in mills and factories, &c., and thus helping to swell the general fund, while the single earning of the head of the family in Ireland as a general rule has to support the whole.

The consul at Belfast says that with the prevalent rates of wages the mechanic or laborer can save nothing.

In regard to the habits of the working classes, the reports are unanimously silent.

Paper money.—There are six banks authorized to issue notes in Ireland. The entire authorized circulation is about $31,000,000, although the bank returns for the four weeks ending March 16, 1878, as given in the report from Belfast, show that the average circulation for those four weeks was almost $34,000,000. The amount of coin held by the banks during the same period averaged about $15,000,000.

These banks have branches in the towns and villages throughout Ireland, and unbounded confidence is placed in them by the people.

The lowest denomination of bank-note being £1, the principal circulating medium among the working classes is silver, gold, and copper.

* The rates paid by the board of public works are somewhat higher than the general rates prevailing throughout the country; but, as the consuls have not specified the rates prevailing in their districts, and as the secretary of the board of public works very kindly gave the board rates for all Ireland, they are used in the above list. The rates of wages given by the consul at Cork for his district are doubtless nearer to the general rates for Ireland than those given by the board of public works.

Rates of weekly wages in Cork.—Masons, painters, and joiners, $7.25; gasfitters, $6.54. The consul at Belfast gives the rates of wages in his district as not more than $4.38 to $6.10 per week.

The consul at Dublin gives some interesting statistics concerning agriculture and postal savings institutions which are worthy of consideration.

SCOTLAND.

I take pleasure in calling your attention to the very interesting and comprehensive reports from the several consulates in Scotland, which have fully answered all the requirements of the Department Circular. The report from the consul at Leith is specially valuable for its treatment of the question of agriculture in the several districts of Scotland. His report upon the coal mines in his own district is equally interesting.

It would appear from the reports herewith submitted that the agricultural laborers of Scotland are as well paid as those of England, better paid than those of Ireland, and, on the whole, better off than their fellows in either of the sister countries.

The agricultural capacity of Scotland is, perhaps, more limited, according to area, than any other country in Europe, but it is doubtful whether the agriculture of any other country has been prosecuted with more educated skill and industry. The intelligence which was brought to the aid of agriculture in Scotland at a time when intelligence was the exception, and not considered essential to that industry, has made Scotch farming synonymous with all that is advanced in agriculture. This intelligence, common, as a rule, to employer and employé, makes these reports, where they treat of agriculture, specially interesting.

Rates of wages.—The average weekly wages of agricultural laborers in Scotland are as follows—although it is necessary to read the particular reports in order to arrive at a true understanding of the special advantages and disadvantages of Scottish rural life, no two districts being alike in habits and customs:

Men, without board or lodging	$3 60
Men, with board and lodging	2 60
Women, without board or lodging	1 80
Women, with board and lodging	1 15
Women, house servants, per annum	60 00

Agricultural wages in Scotland have increased 10 per cent. during the last five years and 25 per cent. during the last fifteen years.

In regard to the manner of life of the agricultural laborers, I would specially refer you to that part of Consul Robeson's report which treats upon this subject. Their food consists of oatmeal, milk, and potatoes, with a little meat and beer sometimes added. The consul remarks that were it not for extravagance in dress the Scotch farm laborers could save considerable money, and that, on the whole, they are the opposite of saving and thrifty.

In turning from the agricultural to the mechanical and manufacturing classes in the great trade centers of Scotland, it will be noted, by comparison, that wages seem to be a trifle higher than the rates prevailing in England; but if the great depression in the manufacturing interests of Scotland are taken into consideration, together with consequent short time and enforced idleness, it might be questioned whether the average rates of wages in Scotland would equal those of England.

Statement showing the weekly wages paid the following trades in Scotland and the rates paid to similar trades in New York and in Chicago.

Occupations.	Scotland.	New York.	Chicago.
Building trades:			
Bricklayers	$9 63	$12 00 to $15 00	$6 00 to $10 50
Masons	8 28	12 00 to 18 00	12 00 to 15 00
Carpenters and joiners	8 12	9 00 to 12 00	7 50 to 12 00
Gasfitters	8 40	10 00 to 14 00	10 00 to 12 00
Painters	8 16	10 00 to 16 00	6 00 to 12 00
Plasterers	10 13	10 00 to 15 00	9 00 to 15 00
Plumbers	7 13	12 00 to 18 00	12 00 to 21 00
Slaters	8 30	10 00 to 15 00	12 00 to 18 00
Blacksmiths	7 04	10 00 to 14 00	9 00 to 12 00
Bakers	6 63	5 00 to 8 00	8 00 to 12 00
Bookbinders	6 52	12 00 to 18 00	9 00 to 20 00
Shoemakers	7 35	8 00 to 12 00	9 00 to 18 00
Butchers	4 75	9 00 to 13 00	12 00 to 18 00
Cabinet-makers	8 48	12 00 to 16 00	7 00 to 15 00
Coopers	6 10	12 00 to 15 00	6 00 to 15 00
Coppersmiths	7 13	10 00 to 13 00	15 00 to 21 00
Cutlers	6 25	15 00 to 25 00	....
Engravers	8 75	12 00 to 18 00	9 00 to 30 00
Horseshoers	7 00	12 00 to 18 00	15 00 to 21 00
Millwrights	7 50	10 00 to 15 00	15 00 to 21 00
Printers	7 52	8 00 to 18 00	12 00 to 18 00
Saddlers and harness-makers	6 15	12 00 to 15 00	6 00 to 12 00
Sailmakers	6 33	12 00 to 18 00	12 00 to 15 00
Tinsmiths	6 00	10 00 to 14 00	9 00 to 12 00
Tailors	7 00	10 00 to 18 00	6 00 to 18 00
Brassfounders	6 92	10 00 to 14 00	8 00 to 15 00
Laborers, porters, &c	4 50	6 00 to 9 00	5 50 to 9 00

While the foregoing table shows the rates of wages in New York and Chicago to be on an average once and a half as much as the rates in Scotland, the prices of the necessaries of life are higher in Scotland than in the United States. The consul at Glasgow says that rent, clothing, bread, sugar, tea and coffee are about the same in that city as in New York.

The consul at Dunfermline notes that the importation of fresh meats from the United States has compelled a reduction in the price of domestic meats, while the consul at Leith says that the imports of cattle and meat have not diminished meat-prices in his district.

Habits of the workingmen.—In regard to the habits of the mechanical and manufacturing classes in the cities and trade centers of Scotland, it may be said that their besetting sin is whisky-drinking, and that to this, and to its great ally, strikes, may be attributed the greater part of the misery and degradation which afflict the labor population.

In speaking of the necessaries of life, the consul at Glasgow says:

Whisky, which is here considered a positive necessity by the great mass of laborers, and which costs about 300 per cent. more than in the United States, and beer, which is comparatively cheap and bad, absorb the larger portion of the laborers' earnings.

Of the evils resulting from strikes the consul at Leith writes:

Strikes are of frequent occurrence in all trades, but, as a rule, they result in impoverishing the workman, who has, in the end, to return to his previous wages or accept his employer's terms.

The rates of wages are at present 7 per cent. higher throughout Scotland than they were five years ago, but the increase in the cost of living has more than neutralized the increase of wages. The consul at Glasgow is inclined to the belief that, if the present stagnation continues, wages will recede to even less than the rates of five years ago.

Paper money.—According to the report from the Glasgow consulate, there are eleven banks of issue, with ten branches, in Scotland, each bank working under a special charter. The circulation is unrestricted; each bank is required to redeem its notes in coin on demand, and to hold an amount of coin equivalent to the excess of actual circulation over the authorized issue.

Only about five per cent. of the money in circulation in Scotland is coin, and four-fifths of this is silver coin. Paper is universally preferred. Gold coin is never called for, except for special purposes. Laborers of all classes are paid off in silver, which is in constant demand, for change, and sometimes commands a premium over gold and paper money, owing to the fact that a pound note is the smallest denomination of bank-note issued.

The average note circulation of the banks of Scotland, according to the statement of the consul at Dundee, during the four weeks ending March 16, 1878, was about $27,000,000, being $13,300,000 more than their authorized issue, and the average amount of gold and silver held by the banks during the same period was $16,000,000. This overissue is permitted by act of Parliament, provided the banks keep a reserve of gold and silver equal to the amounts so overissued.*

ITALY.

In the United States, and in the principal countries of Europe also, the idea of labor proper is, to a great extent, associated in the common mind with the Scandinavians, the British, the Germans, and the French; the Italians, and the Spaniards in that same mind being sentimentally connected with that labor which basks in the sun and resorts to agriculture only when forced by their necessities. The Italian in an especial manner is always associated with musical itineracy and all that lazy life which goes to complete the round of strolling vagabondage.

The better portion of Italian emigrants—especially the agricultural laborers—have sought homes in South America, while a large number of that class which at once suggests the name and the calling of the *padroné* have found a better field for their peculiar talents in the United States, thereby helping to confirm old errors in the public estimation.

That nothing can be more erroneous than the foregoing ideas in regard to the labor population of Italy will be duly appreciated by the most casual perusal of the reports from that country, herewith submitted.

These reports bear ample evidence to the fact that the working classes of Italy are as industrious, as frugal, and as patient under privations, as any peasant population in Europe, and that her artisans and mechanics stand on a par with their class elsewhere.

Rates of wages.—The weekly rates of wages paid to agricultural laborers in Italy, as averaged from the consular reports herewith submitted, are as follows:

Men, without board or lodging	$3 50
Men, with board and lodging	1 80
Women, without board or lodging	1 55
Women, with board and lodging	65

* In connection with the question of banking and currency in Scotland, a very interesting report from the consul-general at London on the failure of the City of Glasgow Bank will be found in the appendix. This report is the more necessary, in this connection, as the reports from the consuls in Scotland were all written previous to the foregoing failure.

The rates of wages paid to the trades in Italy, as compared with the rates paid to similar trades in the United States, are as follows:

Weekly wages in Italy, New York, and Chicago.

Occupations.	Italy.	New York.	Chicago.
Building trades:			
Bricklayers	$3 45	$12 00 to $15 00	$6 00 to $10 50
Masons	4 00	12 00 to 18 00	12 00 to 15 00
Carpenters	4 18	9 00 to 12 00	7 50 to 12 00
Gasfitters	3 95	10 00 to 14 00	10 00 to 12 00
Painters	4 60	10 00 to 16 00	6 00 to 12 00
Plasterers	4 35	10 00 to 15 00	9 00 to 15 00
Plumbers	3 90	12 00 to 18 00	12 00 to 21 00
Slaters	3 90	10 00 to 15 00	12 00 to 18 00
Blacksmiths	3 94	10 00 to 14 00	9 00 to 12 00
Bakers	3 90	5 00 to 8 00	8 00 to 12 00
Bookbinders	3 00	12 00 to 18 00	9 00 to 20 00
Shoemakers	4 32	8 00 to 12 00	9 00 to 18 00
Butchers	4 20	9 00 to 13 00	12 00 to 18 00
Cabinet-makers	4 95	12 00 to 16 00	7 00 to 15 00
Coopers	4 35	12 00 to 15 00	6 00 to 15 00
Coppersmiths	3 90	10 00 to 13 00	15 00 to 21 00
Cutlers	3 90	15 00 to 25 00	....
Engravers	4 00	12 00 to 18 00	9 00 to 30 00
Horseshoers	3 50	12 00 to 18 00	15 00 to 21 00
Millwrights	4 95	10 00 to 15 00	12 00 to 21 00
Printers	3 90	8 00 to 18 00	12 00 to 18 00
Saddlers and harness-makers	3 90	12 00 to 15 00	6 00 to 12 00
Sailmakers	3 90	12 00 to 18 00	12 00 to 15 00
Tinsmiths	3 60	10 00 to 14 00	9 00 to 12 00
Tailors	4 30	10 00 to 18 00	6 00 to 18 00
Brassfounders	5 49	10 00 to 14 00	8 00 to 15 00
Laborers, porters, &c	2 60	6 00 to 9 00	5 50 to 9 00

It will be seen by the foregoing table that the American tradesman receives more than three times as much wages as the Italian. It must not be inferred from this, however, that the Italian workingman cannot live comparatively well on his wages. The peculiar food on which he subsists—food which the American workman would not be satisfied with under any circumstances—can be purchased at such low rates as to enable him to do so. For instance, in Turin, according to the consul's report, the laborer's daily expenses are, say, 16 cents for food and 2 cents for lodging in a small room, where he has a family "all stowed away in a single room."

In regard to what are considered by the American workingman as the necessaries of life, but which are considered luxuries by the Italian—luxuries never to be enjoyed save on great festivals, and then very sparingly—it will be seen by the following statement that they cost more in Italy than in the United States. It would, therefore, be impossible for the Italian laborer or mechanic to purchase such food out of his low wages.

Food-prices in Genoa, New York, and Chicago.

Articles.	Genoa.	New York.	Chicago.
	Cents.	*Cents.*	*Cents.*
Flour ....per pound..	7	3 to 4	2½ to 4½
Beef ....do......	18	8 to 16	4 to 12½
Pork ....do......	20	8 to 12	4 to 12
Lard ....do......	28	10 to 12	6 to 10
Codfish ....do......	10	6 to 7	5 to 9
Butter ....do......	30	25 to 32	16 to 40
Cheese ....do......	28	12 to 15	5 to 16
Rice ....do......	7	8 to 10	5 to 10
Beans ....per quart..	8½	7 to 10	5 to 9
Milk ....do......	6	8 to 10	3 to 6
Coal ....per ton..	$11 00	$5 25	$3 00 to $6 75

The habits of the laborers.—The habits and manner of living of the Italian working people can be best shown by quoting from the consular reports:

Genoa.—The fare of the Italian laborer is usually very simple, consisting of bread, boiled chestnuts, mush, and ministrone, a substantial soup made of vegetables, olive-oil, and macaroni. This, with an occasional bottle of ordinary wine, a relish of stock-fish or cheese, and, at rare intervals, on great festivals and holidays, a dinner of fresh meat, constitutes the homely fare of the Italian peasant.—*From the report of Consul Spencer.*

Rome.—The ordinary laborer's fare is coarse bread and cheese and raw onions in the morning; at midday, a substantial soup of vegetables and macaroni, with fat pork or olive-oil, or a dish of polenta (mush); in the evening, bread and cheese, with onions or salad, as the case may be, sometimes varied with stockfish. On very rare occasions mutton or goat's meat and wine are indulged in.—*From the report of Consul-General McMillan.*

Turin.—The agriculturist, both farmer and laborer, lives very economically, hardly knows what fresh meat is, except half a dozen times a year, on state and church festivals. Sometimes he eats a little sausage, but his daily food consists of cornmeal mush, rice bread, soups of wheat-flour paste, rice, and sometimes a little lard in the soup by way of luxury, cheese, greens, and chestnuts in their season.—*From the report of Consul Noble.*

Messina.—The laboring classes are frugal and industrious. Contented with little, and living on what our workmen would despise, there is very little destitution among them.—*From the report of Consul Owen.*

The consul at Messina says that the condition of the working classes has very much improved under the present Government. The opening of public schools and the law which withholds the discharge of a soldier until he can read and write have been productive of good results.

The following extract from the report of Consul Potter, of Stuttgart, Germany, bears additional testimony to the frugality, steadiness, energy, and social virtues of the Italian laborers. As a picture of patient labor, thankfulness, and home-love it can scarcely be surpassed by the laborers of any other country:

ITALIAN LABORERS IN GERMANY.

A laboring population, heretofore unknown in Wurtemberg, is becoming now quite numerous. Reference is made to Italian laborers. They were at first employed only on railroad work, and as able miners and good diggers. In consequence of their industry and reliability, they have by degrees been employed to good advantage as a considerable element among workingmen in nearly all branches of laborious industry.

During the inflated period following the war between Germany and France the laborers of Wurtemberg demanded such a high rate of wages, that contractors were obliged, in order to fulfill their engagements, to import Italian laborers, and their services have proved highly satisfactory. They are also being extensively employed in Austria.

It is both interesting and instructive to become more closely acquainted with the ways of these people. Experience has proved that every one who contracts with these Italians for labor may be certain that they will adhere to their engagements. They will higgle about trifles, but as soon as a bargain is closed it can be relied upon.

From early morning until darkness they work industriously. No clamor for more "luncheon" and "more drink." It is astonishing how soberly and frugally they live. Their nourishment is "polenta," a porridge of mixed substances, in which fat is very scarce, and often wanting altogether. An additional luxury, not a daily one, however, consists of hard cheese. There are few men who are thus so easily satisfied. They generally manage to secure employment on large jobs, where they work in groups. One of them is selected to cook. The favorite and almost universal article of food referred to is a thick porridge, made of vegetables, flour, and coarse meal, and boiled in water. This porridge is an adhesive mass, of the consistency of clay, and is cut with a wire (like soap), each receiving an equal share. This food is consumed with great satisfaction, and the leavings of one is cheerfully handed over to another who has not, perhaps, had a sufficiency, or else it is put into a cloth and kept for the next meal. Water satisfies their thirst and aids digestion, and then they go again cheerfully to their work, and the energy with which they work is surprising to Germans. Any one who wishes to be quite clear as to their industry must examine the tunnels and the cuttings in rocks which Italians have blasted and wrought before dynamite was known.

Whenever any of the large contractors informs his agents in the different districts of some new work to be done, the latter take care to spread the news from village to village among the homes of the Italians. Men and able youths hastily prepare themselves for departure, whilst women, children, and old people stay behind. In this way isolated groups are formed who work in common. They are much attached to home and country, and during leisure hours delight to talk of their families, friends, and native land.

On Saturday evenings and also on Sundays and holidays they march in troops to the post-office to receive letters from home or to send greetings and money. As the younger generations of Italians are learning to read and write, a very extensive use is made of the post-office facilities.

The amount of money the Italian laborers contrive to save from their hard and comparatively small earnings is very surprising even to the economical German.

Paper money.—Paper money is a legal tender in Italy. According to the report of the consul-general at Rome, six credit establishments, by act of Parliament, form a syndicate for the emission of bank-notes. The syndicate guarantees the Government paper money with its united capital and reserve, and, in return, is authorized to issue a limited amount of paper money on its own account.

On the 1st of May, 1878, according to the same report, the total amount of paper money in circulation in Italy was as follows: Government notes, $182,000,000; syndicate notes, $122,155,396; a total of $304,155,396. It would seem, however, that all the foregoing guarantees, acts of Parliament, and syndicate endorsements are not sufficient to make this paper money equal to gold, for the premium on the latter in Italy during the first five months of 1878 (embracing the time up to the date of the report of the consul-general), ranged from 8 to 11 per cent.

The consul-general further notes that the small amount of coin reserve held by the syndicate—less than $26,000,000—renders it impossible that any immediate attempt at resumption can be entertained.

NETHERLANDS.

The two reports herewith from the Netherlands, although not as full and minute as might be desired, are sufficiently so to enable you to form a fair idea of the present condition of labor in that country.

According to the report from Amsterdam, agricultural laborers are paid from $50 to $60, with board and lodging, and usually two suits of common clothes, per annum. Hired by the day, they receive from 40 to 60 cents, without either board or lodging. The consul at Rotterdam says that the wages of farm hands in his district average about 40 cents per day, without food or lodging.

An average from both reports shows the weekly wages of mechanics and laborers to be as follows: Bricklayers, masons, carpenters and joiners, painters, and plasterers, $3.60 to $6; shoemakers, $3.60 to $6.60; tailors, $3.60 to $6.80; laborers, porters, &c., $2.40 to $3.60.

Low as are the foregoing rates of wages, the consul at Amsterdam says that they are from 25 to 35 per cent. higher than they were five years ago, but that the cost of living has increased in even greater proportion, so that, with all his patient frugality and practiced economy, the Dutch workingman has all he can do to maintain himself and family.

In regard to the food of the Dutch workingmen, the consul at Rotterdam says:

Meat, excepting sausage and chipped beef, is regarded by the mechanic and laboring man as a luxury, and is rarely indulged in. Bread, rice, fish, potatoes and other vegetables, constitute the staple articles of food for the laboring classes of the Netherlands.

For fuller particulars concerning this subject—the habits, customs, modes of living, &c., of the Dutch laborers and mechanics—I take pleasure in referring you to a report, which will be found in the Appendix to this volume, from Mr. Birney, our minister resident at the Hague. This report, although written in answer to the Department trade circular of 1877, treats of labor and labor statistics in such a comprehensive manner as to merit publication in its proper place among these labor reports.

Paper money.—According to the report of the consul at Rotterdam, the total amount of paper money in circulation in the Netherlands, on May 27, 1878, was about $81,000,000, as follows: Bank of the Netherlands, $77,000,000; notes of the Mint of the Netherlands, $4,000,000. The Bank of the Netherlands, on the above date, held a reserve of coin and bullion of $44,000,000.

The amount of paper money in circulation is less than the authorized maximum, and the reserve of coin and bullion is greater than the required minimum.

The amount of gold coins in circulation (10-florin pieces), as per last mint report, was about $57,000,000; silver coins, $38,500,000; copper coins, $650,000.

Paper money and silver are legal tenders, and are at par with gold.

SPAIN.

The reports herewith submitted from Spain are only four in number, viz, from Barcelona, Cadiz, Malaga, and Santander, and, although not as minute or exhaustive as many of the reports from other countries, will be found interesting and instructive, dealing as they do with a class of people whose habits and customs are not as clearly understood in the United States as are like classes in other countries of Europe.

Rates of wages.—The weekly rates of wages of agricultural laborers in Spain, as averaged from the submitted reports, are as follows:

Men, without board or lodging	$3 45
Women, without board or lodging	2 25
Women, house servants, per annum	40 00

The weekly wages paid the trades in Spain and the wages paid similar trades in the United States are as follows:

Occupations.	Spain.	New York.	Chicago.
Bricklayers	$5 25	$12 00 to $15 00	$6 00 to $10 50
Masons	4 80	12 00 to 18 00	12 00 to 15 00
Carpenters	4 88	9 00 to 12 00	7 50 to 12 00
Painters	4 80	10 00 to 16 00	6 00 to 12 00
Plasterers	7 20	10 00 to 16 00	9 00 to 15 00
Blacksmiths	4 65	10 00 to 14 00	9 00 to 12 00
Bakers	5 40	5 00 to 8 00	8 00 to 12 00
Bookbinders	3 60	12 00 to 18 00	9 00 to 20 00
Shoemakers	3 90	12 00 to 18 00	9 00 to 18 00
Cabinet-makers	4 20	9 00 to 13 00	7 00 to 15 00
Coopers	4 95	12 00 to 16 00	6 00 to 15 00
Tinsmiths	3 90	10 00 to 14 00	9 00 to 12 00
Tailors	3 90	10 00 to 18 00	6 00 to 18 00
Laborers, porters, &c	3 00	6 00 to 9 00	5 50 to 9 00

It will be seen by the foregoing statement that the Spanish workingmen scarcely average one-third the wages paid in New York and Chicago, while what are called the necessaries of life with us are much cheaper in the United States than in Spain.

Habits of the workingmen.—The consul at Barcelona says:

The Catalonian laboring classes are certainly very laborious, and the most sober and frugal I have seen. During my four years' residence here I have never met an intoxicated person belonging to that class, yet wine is constantly drunk by the men, women, and children. Not being drunk for enjoyment, it is considered beneficial to health, and taken regularly, but sparingly, at every meal. The Catalonian people live mostly on greens, beans, potatoes, onions, garlic, dried codfish, and wine.

Andalusia.—The farm laborers of Andalusia, fed by their employers, are allowed, daily, 3 pounds of bread, some oil, and a little vinegar. A portion of the bread is set aside, with the oil and the vinegar, to form the two meals of the "gaspacho," served to the farm hands. This gaspacho consists of bread, soaked in water, to which the oil and vinegar are added. In winter it is served hot, in summer cold. Any addition to this fare must be supplied by the laborer himself.—*Report from the consul at Cadiz.*

Malaga.—The laborer in the south of Spain is the most frugal of beings. He rarely, or never, eats meat. Indeed, it would be impossible for him to do so and live upon his earnings.—*From the report of the consul at Malaga.*

The consul at Malaga says that while the rates of wages have increased from 10 to 15 per cent. within the last five years, the cost of living has increased 40 per cent. within the same period.

The consul at Santander notes only a slight increase in wages in five years; the increase in the cost of living has more than counterbalanced any increase in the wages.

Paper money.—The consul at Malaga says that the circulating medium is gold and silver—chiefly silver. Paper money is, however, issued by the Bank of Spain at Madrid. These notes are at par, and convertible into specie.

According to the report from the consul at Cadiz, the average circulation of bank-notes during the year 1877 was as follows: In Madrid, $20,346,377; in the seventeen branches of the Bank of Spain, including such business centers as Barcelona, Valencia, Seville, Malaga, Jerez, Santander, and Cadiz, $11,228,977; total average circulation of bank-notes in Spain, $31,575,354.

RESUME.

Having given statements showing the rates of wages and the retail prices of the necessaries of life in the several countries, together with the wages and food-prices in New York and Chicago, I now submit two general statements, which will enable you, at a glance, to compare the wages and prices of food in the several countries with each other and all with the wages and prices in the United States. I also submit herewith two tables showing the wages and food-prices in the principal cities of Europe as compared with the wages and food-prices in New York and Chicago; also, a table showing the coinage and paper money of the principal countries.

Statement showing the weekly rates of wages in the several countries, compiled from the consular reports published herewith, and compared with rates prevailing in the United States.

Occupations.	Belgium.	Denmark.	France.	Germany.	Italy.	Spain.	United Kingdom.			United States.	
							England.	Ireland.	Scotland.	New York.	Chicago.
Agricultural laborers:											
Men, without board or lodging			$3 15	$2 87	$3 50		$3 60	$3 40	$4 25		
Men, with board and lodging			1 36	1 48	1 80		2 60	1 30	$1 50 to 2 40		
Women, without board or lodging			1 10	1 08	1 55		1 80	2 16	1 80 to 3 25		
Women, with board and lodging				75	60		1 15	75	60 to 1 00		
House-building trades:											
Bricklayers	$6 00		4 00	3 60	3 45	$5 12	8 12	7 58	9 63	$12 00 to $15 00	$6 00 to $10 50
Carpenters and joiners	5 40	$4 25	5 42	4 00	4 18	4 88	8 25	7 33	8 12	9 00 to 12 00	7 50 to 12 00
Gasfitters	5 40			3 65	3 95		7 25	7 95	8 40	10 00 to 14 00	10 00 to 12 00
Masons	6 00	4 45	5 00	4 30	4 00	4 80	8 16	7 58	8 28	12 00 to 18 00	12 00 to 15 00
Painters	4 20	4 15	4 90	3 92	4 60		7 25	7 54	8 16	10 00 to 16 00	6 00 to 12 00
Plasterers	5 40			3 80	4 35	7 20	8 10	7 68	10 13	10 00 to 15 00	9 00 to 15 00
Plumbers	6 00		5 50	3 60	3 90		7 75	8 46	7 13	12 00 to 18 00	12 00 to 20 00
Slaters				4 00	3 90		7 90		8 30	10 00 to 15 00	12 00 to 18 00
General trades:											
Bakers	4 40	4 25	5 55	3 50	3 90	5 40	6 50		6 60	5 00 to 8 00	8 00 to 12 00
Blacksmiths	4 40	3 90	5 45	3 55	3 94	4 65	8 12		7 04	10 00 to 14 00	9 00 to 12 00
Bookbinders		3 72	4 85	3 82	3 90	3 60	7 83		6 50	12 00 to 18 00	9 00 to 20 00
Brassfounders		4 20		3 20	5 49		7 40		6 90	10 00 to 14 00	8 00 to 15 00
Butchers	4 50	4 50	5 42	3 85	4 20		7 23		4 75	8 00 to 12 00	12 00 to 18 00
Cabinet-makers	4 80		6 00	3 97	4 95	4 20	7 70		8 48	9 00 to 13 00	7 00 to 15 00
Coopers		4 10	7 00	3 30	4 35	4 95	7 30		6 10	12 00 to 16 00	6 00 to 15 00
Coppersmiths		3 85		3 30	3 90		7 40		7 10	12 00 to 16 00	15 00 to 20 00
Cutlers		3 85	4 63	4 00	3 90		8 00		6 25	10 00 to 13 00	15 00 to 10 00
Engravers				4 00	4 00		9 72		8 75	15 00 to 25 00	9 00 to 30 00
Horseshoers		3 85	5 40	3 25	3 50		7 20		7 00	12 00 to 18 00	15 00 to 25 00
Millwrights		4 00		3 30	4 95		7 50		7 50	10 00 to 15 00	12 00 to 20 00
Printers		4 62	4 70	4 80	3 90		7 75		7 52	8 00 to 18 00	12 00 to 18 00
Saddlers and harness-makers	4 80	3 85	5 00	3 60	3 90		6 80		6 15	12 00 to 15 00	6 00 to 12 00
Sailmakers		4 85		3 30	3 90		7 30		6 33	12 00 to 18 00	12 00 to 15 00
Shoemakers		3 30	4 75	3 12	4 32	3 90	7 35		7 35	12 00 to 18 00	9 00 to 18 00
Tailors		4 10	5 10	3 58	4 30	3 90	$5 00 to 7 30		7 00	10 00 to 18 00	6 00 to 18 00
Tinsmiths	4 80	3 90	4 40	3 65	3 60	3 90	7 30		6 00	10 00 to 14 00	9 00 to 12 00
Laborers, porters, &c	3 00			2 92	2 60	3 00	5 00		4 50	6 00 to 9 00	5 50 to 9 00
Railway employés:											
Engineers, passenger trains			11 33	8 35	9 50		9 12	9 00	8 70		
Firemen, passenger trains			6 25	3 30	4 50		6 00	4 50	4 96		
Brakemen, passenger trains			3 60	3 22			5 50	4 00	4 69		
Signal-men			5 85	3 52	4 00		5 60	5 00	5 12		
Switchmen			5 50	3 41	4 00		5 60	5 00	5 19		
Porters			5 00	2 60	3 40		4 50	4 00	4 44		
Laborers			3 35	3 10	3 30		4 58	4 00	4 27		

Statement showing the weekly rates of wages in the principal cities of Europe, compiled from consular reports, and compared with rates in New York and Chicago.

Occupation.	Belgium.	France.	Germany.	Italy.	Spain.	Switzerland.	United Kingdom.	United States.	
	Brussels.	Bordeaux.	Dresden.	Rome.	Barcelona.	Geneva.	Liverpool.	New York.	Chicago.
House-building trades:									
Bricklayers	$6 00	$4 80	......	$3 00	$5 40	$4 80	$9 25	$12 00 to $15 00	$6 00 to $10 50
Carpenters and joiners	5 40	5 00	3 75	3 00	5 00	6 00	9 00	9 00 to 12 00	7 50 to 12 00
Gasfitters	5 40	......	......	......	......	4 60	7 80	10 00 to 14 00	10 00 to 12 00
Masons	6 00	5 40	3 75	3 00	6 00	4 80	8 70	12 00 to 18 00	12 00 to 15 00
Painters	......	......	......	......	7 00	4 60	8 50	10 00 to 16 00	6 00 to 12 00
Plasterers	5 40	......	......	......	7 00	4 60	9 72	10 00 to 15 00	9 00 to 15 00
Plumbers	6 00	6 00	......	......	......	4 60	9 00	12 00 to 18 00	12 00 te 20 00
Slaters	......	......	......	......	......	4 60	9 72	10 00 to 15 00	12 00 to 18 00
General trades:									
Bakers	6 00	4 80	3 50	......	5 40	4 80	......	5 00 to 8 00	8 00 to 12 00
Blacksmiths	6 00	4 80	4 00	3 30	4 50	4 80	8 90	10 00 to 14 00	9 00 to 12 00
Bookbinders	6 00	4 80	2 00	......	3·60	4 00	8 00	12 00 to 18 00	9 00 to 20 00
Brassfounders	......	......	3 00	4 75	6 00	......	7 20	10 00 to 14 00	8 00 to 15 00
Butchers	6 00	6 60	4 60	......	......	4 60	......	8 00 to 12 00	12 00 to 18 00
Cabinet-makers	4 80	......	......	......	4 20	6 00	8 00	9 00 to 13 00	7 00 to 15 00
Coopers	6 00	8 00	......	......	5 50	4 60	8 75	12 00 to 16 00	6 00 to 15 00
Coppersmiths	6 00	......	4 75	......	......	4 60	8 90	12 00 to 16 00	15 00 to 20 00
Cutlers	5 50	4 20	4 00	......	......	4 60	......	10 00 to 13 00	15 00 to 10 00
Engravers	6 00	......	......	......	......	4 80	......	15 00 to 25 00	9 00 to 30 00
Horseshoers	6 00	4 80	......	......	......	......	8 50	12 00 to 18 00	15 00 to 25 00
Millwrights	......	......	......	......	......	......	7 70	10 00 to 15 00	12 00 to 20 00
Printers	6 00	3 00	......	......	4 80	4 60	10 50	8 00 to 18 00	12 00 to 18 00
Saddlers and harness-makers	4 80	4 80	......	......	......	4 60	7 30	12 00 to 15 00	6 00 to 12 00
Sailmakers	6 00	......	......	......	......	......	......	12 00 to 18 00	12 00 to 15 00
Shoemakers	6 00	4 20	2 00	3 60	3 60	4 60	8 75	12 00 to 18 00	9 00 to 18 00
Tailors	6 00	4 80	3 00	3 60	3 60	4 80	......	10 00 to 18 00	6 00 to 18 00
Tinsmiths	4 80	4 80	3 00	......	4 00	4 80	7 50	10 00 to 14 00	9 00 to 12 00
Laborers, porters, &c	3 50	......	2 50	......	......	3 00	5 82	6 00 to 9 00	5 50 to 9 00

Statement showing the retail prices of the necessaries of life in the several countries, compiled from consular reports published herewith, and compared with prices in New York and Chicago.

Articles.	Belgium.	France.	Germany.	Italy.	Spain.	Switzerland.	United Kingdom. England.	United Kingdom. Ireland.	United Kingdom. Scotland.	United States. New York.	United States. Chicago.
	Cents.	*Cents.*	*Cents.*	*Cents.*	*Cents.*	*Cents.*	*Cents.*	*Cents.*	*Cents.*	*Cents.*	*Cents.*
Bread ... per pound	4 to 5	3	3 to 7	6	6¼ to 7½	4	3½ to 4½	4	4	4 to 4½	4 to 4½
Flour ... do		4	5½	10		7	3½ to 4½	4	4	3 to 4	2½ to 4½
Beef:											
Roasting ... per pound	20	22	22	20		30	22		22	12 to 16	8 to 12½
Soup ... do	16	16	14	12	18	18	15		16	6 to 8	5 to 8
Rump steak ... do	20	20	20	20		30	26½		26½	14 to 16	8 to 12¼
Corned ... do	16	16	13	12		18	18		20	8 to 12	4 to 7
Veal:											
Fore quarter ... per pound	16	16		15			18			8 to 10	6 to 10
Hind quarter ... do	18	20	14	20	25	18	22½		25	10 to 12	10 to 12
Cutlets ... do	20	22		22		20	27		30	20 to 24	12¼ to 15
Mutton:											
Fore quarter ... per pound	16	16		15			17		16	9 to 10	5 to 12¼
Hind quarter ... do	20	18	14½	18	14	18	22		20	12 to 14	5 to 15½
Chops ... do	20	20		18			25		24	14 to 16	10 to 15
Pork:											
Fresh ... per pound	16	14	17	13	24	18	16	10 to 12	13 to 16	8 to 10	4 to 5
Salted ... do	16	14	17	18		20	15	10 to 12	13 to 16	8 to 10	6 to 12
Bacon ... do	18	20	20	22			12 to 16			8 to 10	7 to 12
Ham ... do	25	25	22	25	45	28	13 to 23		25	8 to 12	7 to 15
Shoulder ... do	20	18	20	20			12			8 to 10	4 to 10
Sausage ... do	20	16	19	20			18			8 to 10	6 to 10
Lard ... do	20	20	21	22	21		15 to 18	12		10 to 12	6 to 10
Codfish ... do				0	10		8		6	6 to 7	5 to 9
Butter ... do	20 to 50	25	22	28	46	36	29 to 38	26½	32	25 to 32	16 to 40
Cheese ... do	20 to 25		24	26	28	23	15 to 21		20	12 to 15	5 to 16
Potatoes ... per bushel	56	50	50	$1 15	$1 10	60	$1 12 to $2 00	68	95	$1 40 to $1 60	60 to 80
Rice ... per pound			9	6	7		3½ to 8		5	8 to 10	5 to 10
Beans ... per quart			10	13	12		9			7 to 10	5 to 9
Milk ... do			4	7		5	6 to 9		5	8 to 10	3 to 6
Eggs ... per dozen	20 to 25	18	20	18	29 to 25	20	19 to 30	14	28	25 to 30	10 to 24
Oatmeal ... per pound			8				3½ to 4½	3½	4	4 to 5	4 to 5
Tea ... do			75		70	50	43 to 88	80	70 to 88	50 to 60	25 to $1 00
Coffee ... do	30 to 40	30	35	32	45	30	28 to 42		32 to 50	20 to 30	16 to 40
Sugar ... do	15 to 20		11	8¼	11	8	5¼ to 9	8	10	8 to 10	7 to 10
Molasses ... per gallon										60 to 70	40 to 80
Soap ... per pound			10	4	10		5½ to 9			6 to 7	3 to 8
Starch ... do			9	10	10		10 to 12		14	8 to 10	5 to 10
Coal ... per ton			$4 25	$11 80	$9 00		$3 20 to $4 10		$2 65	$3 00 to $5 25	$3 00 to $6 75

Statement showing the retail prices of the necessaries of life in the principal cities of Europe, compiled from consular reports, and compared with same in New York and Chicago.

Articles.	Belgium.	France.	Germany.	Italy.	Spain.	Switzerland.	United Kingdom.	United States.	
	Brussels.	Bordeaux.	Dresden.	Rome.	Barcelona.	Geneva.	Liverpool.	New York.	Chicago.
	Cents.	*Cents.*	*Cents.*	*Cents.*	*Cents.*	*Cents.*	*Cents.*	*Cents.*	*Cents.*
Bread .... per pound..	4 to 5	3 to 4	7	6	....	4	3⅓ to 4	4 to 4½	4 to 4½
Flour .... do.....	....	....	6	10	6¼	7	3⅛ to 5	3 to 4	2½ to 4½
Beef:									
Roasting .... per pound..	20	20	24	20	20	30	22	12 to 16	8 to 12½
Soup .... do.....	16	16	18	12	15	18	16	6 to 8	5 to 8
Rump .... do.....	18	18	19	15	18	25	18	14 to 16	8 to 12½
Corned .... do.....	16	16	18	12	....	18	16	8 to 12	4 to 7
Veal:									
Fore quarter .... per pound..	16	16	12	15	15	....	14	8 to 10	6 to 10
Hind quarter .... do.....	18	20	18	20	18	18	20	10 to 12	10 to 12
Cutlets .... do.....	20	22	18	22	22	20	20	20 to 24	12½ to 15
Mutton:									
Fore quarter .... per pound..	16	16	12	15	12	....	14	9 to 10	5 to 12½
Hind quarter .... do.....	18	20	18	18	15	18	20	12 to 14	5 to 15½
Chops .... do.....	20	20	18	18	18	....	20	14 to 16	10 to 15
Pork:									
Fresh .... per pound..	16	12	18	15	20	18	16	8 to 10	4 to 8
Salted .... do.....	16	14	18	18	20	20	16	8 to 10	6 to 12
Bacon .... do.....	18	20	30	25	30	....	20	8 to 10	7 to 12
Ham .... do.....	20	25	35	30	40	28	24	8 to 12	7 to 15
Shoulder .... do.....	16	16	30	25	30	....	16	8 to 10	4 to 10
Sausage .... do.....	18	16	20	20	....	....	20	8 to 10	6 to 10
Lard .... do.....	20	....	20	25	19	....	16	10 to 12	6 to 10
Codfish .... do.....	....	....	....	10	9	....	....	6 to 7	5 to 9
Butter .... do.....	20 to 50	....	16	30	40	36	24 to 36	25 to 32	16 to 40
Cheese .... do.....	20 to 25	....	33	28	25	23	12 to 20	12 to 15	5 to 16
Potatoes .... per bushel..	56	60	48	$1 20	$1 00	60	$1 20 to $1 50	$1 40 to $1 60	60 to 80
Rice .... per pound..	....	....	10	5	6¼	....	4 to 10	8 to 10	5 to 10
Beans .... per quart..	....	....	14	15	12	....	....	7 to 10	5 to 9
Milk .... do.....	....	....	....	4	12	5	6 to 8	8 to 10	3 to 6
Eggs .... per dozen..	20 to 25	10 to 15	....	20	20	20	14 to 18	25 to 30	10 to 24
Oatmeal .... per pound..	....	....	....	....	....	....	3½ to 4	4 to 5	4 to 5
Tea .... do.....	....	....	75	....	60	50	40 to 85	50 to 60	25 to $1 00
Coffee .... do.....	30 to 40	....	36	40	40	30	24 to 40	20 to 30	15 to 40
Sugar .... do.....	15 to 20	....	12	8	10	8	5 to 8	8 to 10	7 to 10
Molasses .... per gallon..	....	....	....	....	....	....	....	60 to 70	40 to 80
Soap .... per pound..	....	....	....	4	9	....	4 to 10	6 to 7	3 to 8
Starch .... do.....	....	....	....	10	9	....	....	8 to 10	5 to 10
Coal .... per ton..	....	....	$3 10	$11 00	$9 00	....	$3 65 to 4 38	$3 00 to $5 25	$3 00 to $6 75

Statement showing the coin and paper money of the several countries, compiled from consular reports, together with the same of the United States.

Countries.	Gold.			Silver.		
	Coined.	Demonetized.	In circulation.	Coined.	Demonetized.	In circulation.
France (coined and demonetized since 1795)	$1, 641, 756, 345 08	$13, 718, 990 98	$1, 628, 037, 353 10*	$1, 063, 455, 368 66	$42, 878, 096 72	$1, 020, 567, 271 94*
United Kingdom			510, 300, 000 00			87, 480, 000 00
Germany			385, 560, 000 00			93, 540, 989 82
United States (coined from 1793 to 1878)	1, 035, 958, 675 00		259, 353, 390 00	237, 163, 116 90		99, 090, 557 00
Belgium	103, 658, 089 18	2, 826, 682 82	100, 831, 406 36	105, 675, 749 96	3, 833, 855 43	101, 841, 894 53
Denmark			8, 000, 000 00			4, 300, 000 00
Italy						
Netherlands			56, 857, 227 25			38, 500, 000 00
Spain						

Countries.	Paper.			Population, estimated, 1879.
	Issued.	Redeemed.	In circulation.	
France			$440, 418, 081 21	38, 000, 000
United Kingdom	$160, 720, 102 16	$13, 025, 256 84	147, 894, 845 32	34, 000, 000
Germany			235, 382, 000 00	44, 000, 000
United States			688, 597, 000 00	49, 000, 000
Belgium			66, 026, 909 62	6, 000, 000
Denmark			17, 000, 000 00	2, 000, 000
Italy			304, 355, 396 00	27, 000, 000
Netherlands			80, 888, 731 00	4, 000, 000
Spain			31, 575, 354 00	17, 000, 000

NOTES.

* France.—These amounts cover all the gold and silver in circulation, less the amount demonetized since 1795; Consul-General Torbert says that the amount of gold and silver in circulation at present is estimated at about $1,600,000,000.

France has an issue of copper coins to amount of $12,101,637.50.

The United Kingdom has an issue of copper coins to amount of $6,648,300.18.

Germany has an issue of copper and nickel coins, amount not given; also an issue of thalers remaining in circulation of about $225,000,000.

United States has had an issue of copper and nickel coins to amount of $12,915,397.55. Amounts of demonetization each coin not given.

Belgium has an issue of copper coin; amount not given.

Denmark has an issue of copper coin to amount of $134,000.

Italy issues paper money through six (6) banks; secured by reserved coin.

The Netherlands has an issue of copper coin to amount of $650,000.

Spain issues paper money through Bank of Madrid; secured by reserve in coin of one-third amount of issue.

There are a number of most important points, deducible from these reports, which should be kept prominently and permanently in sight, in order that the relative conditions of labor in Europe and in the United States may be thoroughly appreciated. Some of these points are as follows:

1. The rates of wages in the United States, roughly estimated, are more than twice those in Belgium; three times those in Denmark, France, and Germany; once and a half those in England and Scotland; and more than three times those in Italy and Spain.

2. The prices of the necessaries of life are lower in the United States than in any of the foregoing countries; that is, the laboring people of Europe cannot purchase the necessaries of life, which are common to the American working people, as low as the same can be purchased in the United States; or, *vice versa*, if the working people of the United States lived on the same quality of food, or comparatively the same, and exercised the same frugality as the working people of Europe, they could live as cheaply as the working people of any country in Europe.

3. That while the present depression of trade in Europe has, undoubtedly, intensified the sufferings of its working classes, these reports but recite their normal condition; and while the present depression in the United States will eventually give way to better times, the working people of Europe have no "better days" to look forward to; as they are born to unremitting toil and scanty fare, so must they toil and mourn to the end, or emigrate.

4. That more misery is caused by strong drink in many countries in Europe than by dull times, and that more misery is caused by strikes than even by strong drink, for the workingmen may reform and recover from drink, but no community of workingmen can ever recover from a "long strike."

5. That some of the happiest working people in Europe may be said to be those whose wages are least, while some of the unhappiest may be classed among those whose wages are the highest. The former results from temperance and frugality, the latter from strong drink and strikes.

6. That the ruling classes of Europe look forward at all times to the destruction of this Republic at the hands of its workingmen; they see their own labor populations kept in order by force, and they cannot conceive how the working people of the United States can be a law unto themselves; hence all strikes and riots in this country are hailed in Europe as so many outbursts foreboding the final dissolution of the Republic. The report from the consul at Prague, which will be found in the appendix, giving an account of the feeling which prevailed in Europe in regard to the railroad strikes and riots of 1877, is a good illustration of this important point.

7. That the capitalists of Europe show more sympathy and kindly feeling toward their working people than the latter do toward the capitalists, and that all the bitterness and violence are on the side of the workingmen. On this point I quote from some of the reports:

Bradford, England.—Years ago, and for a long time, there was great reciprocity between the employer and the employé, the former looking after the latter in time of need, and the latter guarding religiously the interests of the former. Unhappily this mutual good feeling has died out in many parts of England. No doubt there is fault on both sides, but I am bound to say, from all I can learn, that the calamity must be laid more to the greed and exactions of the employed than to the selfishness of the employers.—*From the report of Consul Shepard.*

Newcastle-upon-Tyne.—The strike of 8.000 miners [against a reduction of $2\frac{1}{2}$ per cent. of their wages] lasted eight weeks, and was attended by much suffering and privation. While the coal-owners were stubborn in insisting upon the reduction, they were otherwise moved by the most generous feelings. None of the strikers were evicted from the houses [the property of the coal-owners] which they occupied *rent free.* At the end of the strike and the victory of the company, all the old hands were re-engaged.—*From the report of Consul Jones.*

Sonneberg, Germany.—The manufacturers are producing at unprofitable prices in order to keep their hands employed.—*From the report of Consul Winser.*

Brussels, Belgium.—The owners of these establishments have made it a point to identify the workmen as much as possible with the place of their employment, so as to secure permanence and uniformity of employed labor. Consequently, in such times as the present, employers make every possible concession to the workingmen.—*From the report of Consul Wilson.*

8. That the railroads of Europe, especially those of France and Germany, are so conducted as to make the interests of the employés as identical with the interests of the company as is possible—which will be seen by reading the very interesting reports from La Rochelle, Lyons, and Paris, where they refer to the subject, for France; and the reports from Bremen, Chemnitz, and Frankfort-on-the-Main, for Germany—the results of which wisdom on the part of the companies may be summed up in a few words: Good conduct and steadiness insure permanent employment at good wages, with the further incentive to the employés that economy and care in fuel and of the property of the companies brings the employés a good percentage, which increases their annual wages considerably.

The consul at La Rochelle, noting the good conduct of the French railway employés, says:

Brotherhoods, or other such organizations, are unknown. No strikes occur, and the relations between the employés and the companies are entirely harmonious.

The consul at Lyons, who writes at length on the railway systems of France, says:

On the whole, there appears to be no valid reason why our railway employés, of every rank and condition, should not, on comparing their pay and condition with those of their brethren in France, be every way contented and satisfied.

9. That the average American workman performs from one and a half to twice as much work, in a given time, as the average European workman. This is so important a point, in connection with our ability to compete with the cheap-labor manufactures of Europe, and it seems, on first thought, so strange, that I will trouble you with somewhat lengthy quotations from the reports in support thereof:

Denmark.—Another evil is the diminished worth of wages, the descending quantity and quality of work now obtained by employers for wages higher than those paid ten years ago.—*From the report of the consul at Copenhagen.*

France.—At his work the French laborer or mechanic lacks the energy of the American of the same class, and the amount of work executed by him is much less in the same number of hours. The hours of labor are from eleven to twelve, but an average American workman will accomplish as much in nine hours.—*From the report of the consul at Bordeaux.*

Germany.—I am satisfied that an ordinary workingman in the United States will do as much again as will one in this district in the same time.—*From the report of the consul at Chemnitz, Saxony.*

An active American workman will do as much work in a given time, at any employment, as two or three German workmen.—*From the report of the consul at Leipsic.*

There can be no question that, speaking in general terms, the quality as well as the quantity of the work of the German artisans is inferior to that produced by the Americans. The workman here is inclined to be sluggish, and what he accomplishes is relatively small.—*From the report of the consul at Sonneberg.*

For the first time our manufactures are now assuming international proportions. At a time of universal depression we have met those nations which held a monopoly of the world's markets, met them in their strongholds, and established the fact that American manufactures are second to the manufactures of no other nation, and that, with a proper and patriotic understanding between capitalist and laborer, we can command a fair share of the buying world's patronage, and command that patronage with larger profits to the capitalist and higher wages to the laborer than can be made or paid in any other country.

There is something in the Republic which gives an individuality to the people of the United States possessed by no other people to such a degree. Our inventive genius in mechanical appliances is original, and at least twenty-five years ahead of Europe. Our people accept innovation, are prepared for it by anticipation; Europeans do not. One workman in the United States, as will be seen from the foregoing extracts, does as much work as two workmen in most of the countries of Europe; even the immigrant from Europe attains this progressive spirit by a few years' association with American workmen. We have no oppressed and stupid peasantry, little more intelligent than the tools they handle. All are self-thinking, self-acting, and self-supporting.

Within the last fifteen years we have demonstrated our ability, by the brilliant development of our own resources, to exclude, by honest competition, foreign manufactures, to a large extent, from our shores. The question which now peremptorily challenges all thinking minds is how to create a foreign demand for those manufactures which are left after supplying our home demands. We cannot stand still, for the momentum of increase will soon become so great that it will push us outward anyway; to push us safely and profitably is of so much importance as to almost overtop all other public questions of the hour. This question appeals equally to the selfishness and patriotism of all our citizens, but to the laborer it appeals with tenfold force, for without work he cannot live, and unless we can extend the markets for our manufactures he cannot expect steady work, and unless our manufacturers can undersell foreign manufacturers we cannot enlarge our foreign market.

The first great truth to be learned by the manufacturers and workingmen is that the days of sudden fortunes and double wages are gone. We must realize the fact that ocean steam communication has annihilated distance and brought the nations face to face. This drawing together of the nations means equalization in trade, profits, wages, &c., the advantage being with those who soonest accept the situation, and show the most sensible continuity in the new paths of success.

The consul at Newcastle-upon-Tyne shows that that city is commercially nearer to New York than to London. If steam communication can thus bring one of the leading cities of a small island like England nearer to New York than to its own capital, it can work equal wonders with the leading seaport cities of all Europe in their commercial intercourse with the seaport cities of the United States. This is a question of great importance to both laborer and capitalist, for it must revolutionize all past theories of trade and commerce, by inaugurating international equalization.

In the near future, the workingman of New York cannot expect twice or thrice the wages of his fellow-worker in Europe, while all other things—food, rent, clothing, &c.—are on an equality; nor can the coalminer of Pennsylvania expect twice the wages of the Northumberland miner, while coal from the Northumberland mines can be landed in New York at less than the price of Pennsylvania coal.

Newcastle and New York.—During May, 1873, steamers were chartered from the Tyne to New York at $6 per ton to take gas-coals, which then cost $4.80 per ton, making the price of coals delivered in New York, including freight and insurance, $10.80 per ton.

Freights to New York have now reached the ridiculously low rate of 96 cents per ton, *being 36 cents lower than to London.* But Northumberland gas-coal may now be delivered in New York (price, freight, and insurance) for $2.88 per ton. If coals were admitted free of duty, New York and other of our Atlantic cities might be furnished with fuel at a lower price than London. And the impetus which the abolition of this duty would probably give to our American wheat export trade is, at all events, worthy of careful consideration.—*From the report of Consul Jones.*

In continuation of this question of international equalization, and what trade revolutions it can work when subsidized by steady and cheap labor, I shall quote from the report of the consul at Dunfermline an extract which, although only noting the building of an iron railway depot in Glasgow, is of great importance, and has astonished the iron-workers and manufacturers of Scotland.

Scotch vs. Belgian iron.—While all the industries of the country are at present more or less depressed, I am not aware of any of them being more so than the iron trade. One of the reasons assigned is the damaging effects of foreign competition. Within the last year or two a large railway station has been erected at Glasgow, and it is a well-known fact that all the iron required in its construction was brought from Belgium.

As Glasgow forms the center of the iron trade of Scotland, the circumstance above referred to is significant and startling.—*From a report of Mr. Walker, inspector of factories, on the iron trade of Scotland.*

When steam has brought New York nearer to Newcastle than the latter is to London, and the steady, common-sense, low-priced labor of Belgium can compete with Scotland in the very center of her iron industry, and erect a railway station in Glasgow of iron brought from Belgium, even while the Scotch founders are on half time, there remains but one safe course for us to pursue, viz: our American workingmen and their employers must go forward hand in hand, as in Belgium, if we would compete with the nations of Europe in the markets of the world.

Under no consideration must we have strikes; under no consideration must our factories lie idle. If our manufacturers cannot run their establishments profitably—and capital will no more remain permanently invested unprofitably than will labor work for nothing—and pay the prevailing wages, our working people must help them to make profit by consenting to a reduction of wages.

If our workingmen, native and naturalized, will only read these reports in that national spirit with which I have endeavored to point out some of the principal features therein, and drive from their midst communism, strikes, and drink—evil spirits born of oppression, and foreign to our country and our institutions, fatal to them should these vicious principles ever attain national proportions—labor faithfully and intelligently, like freemen; live within their means, like frugal and sensible men; and choke down all demagogical attempts to divide the American people into hostile ranks as capitalists and laborers, there can be no reasonable limit set to the development of our manufactures and commerce; but if our trade centers are to be thrown into confusion, accumulated capital dissipated, and honest labor impoverished and demoralized by periodic strikes, we shall simply follow in the wake of the greatest commercial nation in the world, whose workingmen have blindly and madly ruined their bread-source, and are now sorrowfully standing between their idle factories and the emigrant ships.

Let our workingmen read these reports and compare the fixed condition of the European labor populations, as graphically portrayed by our consuls, with the free and independent position of our American workingmen, not as special depression has made them at present, but as they have been and as they will be again.

The workingman of Europe is born to labor through life; in labor must he continue to the end. There, indeed, are capital and labor severely and eternally divided, unless when some great upheaval in its madness pulls all things down to a common level. But in the United States the workingman of to-day may be the capitalist of to-morrow. Labor and capital are only divided by intelligence, industry, and pluck, and all honest, steady, sensible laborers work to become capitalists.

It is unfortunate that so many who have escaped from the bondage and travail of European labor, and become citizens of the United States, should so soon forget the wages, food, and condition from which they sought release through emigration, and show such small appreciation of their new and superior surroundings and condition as to seek, by strikes and organized violence—European methods of remedying European evils, and totally foreign to and subversive of republican institutions—to introduce strife, where none of old existed, between employers and employés, where harmony and mutual reciprocity should alone prevail. It is equally deplorable, and more unaccountable, that so many native-born Americans should accept the teachings of the very worst school of Europe by countenancing or abetting strikes and communism.

Such things might be expected where the working people have no voice in the formation of the laws by which they are governed; but in a republic, where the people rule, resorts to violence to remedy existing evils only argue incapacity on the part of the violators of law.

But the great majority of American workingmen are intelligently true to the best interests of the Republic, and the noisy and demoralizing few—for in a republic vice and demagogism, taking advantage of that freedom which was meant but for virtue alone, are always agressive and violent—who keep irritating and goading this sensible majority, are public enemies, who eventually meet their merited punishment through the common sense of the people.

We are not a nation of capitalists and laborers; we are a nation of republican citizens. Let us, then, ignore these dividing lines, and, each accepting that position for which his capacity best fits him, work upward and onward in the scale of respectable citizenship, doing that which is best for all.

Let the workingman feel, as he should feel, that the man who employs him, who enables him to feed and clothe his wife and children, is his friend as well as his employer, and that all within and about the workshop are things to be protected, even with life if necessary, instead of being destroyed. Let the employer, on the other hand, as in Belgium and in Germany, look upon his workman as morally one of his family, to be treated with the dignity and sympathy which are his due, and in ten years we shall be known and felt in all the markets of the world, for under such circumstances neither cheap foreign labor nor the vast capital at its back could compete with the inventive genius, mechanical skill, and financial audacity of the workingmen and capitalists of the United States.

I have the honor to be, sir, your obedient servant,

WM. M. EVARTS.

Hon. SAMUEL J. RANDALL,
Speaker of the House of Representatives.

LABOR CIRCULAR.

DEPARTMENT OF STATE,
Washington, April 11, 1878.

To the consular officers of the United States in Great Britan, France, Germany, Belgium, Italy, Spain, the Netherlands, Sweden and Norway, and Denmark.

GENTLEMEN: With reference to the circular addressed to you in August, 1877, in respect of the trade of the United States with foreign countries, it is now deemed desirable that you should make inquiries and report in regard to the following points, viz:

1st. The rate of wages usually paid to laborers of every class, but with more especial reference to agricultural laborers, mechanical laborers, and those upon public works and railways.

2d. The cost of living to the laboring class, or the prices paid for what may be termed the necessaries of life.

3d. So far as practicable, a comparison of the present rates with those prevailing during the past five years, both as to wages and cost of living.

4th. Such information as may be obtainable touching the present state of trade, whether prosperous or otherwise; the amount and character of paper money, if any, as circulation; and the amount and character of coin, with the relation borne by paper and coin to each other.

5th. And, lastly, such information as may be obtainable as to the business habits and systems of your districts.

It is desired that the information which may come to your knowledge on the foregoing points should be embraced in a report to the Department, to be made as soon as may be practicable.

I am, gentlemen, your obedient servant,

F. W. SEWARD,
Acting Secretary.

Report, by Consul Wilson, of Brussels, on (1) labor and wages; and (2) the money of Belgium.

1. LABOR AND WAGES.

Depression of trade.—The general depression of trade that has prevailed in Europe for the last three or four years has reached its culminating point in Belgium within the last six months. All branches of industry are now realizing a degree of languor scarcely ever before experienced in the history of the country.

The Belgian labor system.—This general stagnation of business has resulted in throwing many of the laboring class entirely out of work, and entailing upon others much suffering. The daily earnings, however, of many of those who yet find employment are not so sensibly reduced as would be the case under similar circumstances in almost any other country. This fact results, I presume, from the better organization of the labor system in Belgium than in most other countries. In this country many of the public enterprises employing labor are either directly or indirectly under the control and supervision of the government, and the employés, as a rule, hold their places with more or less fixity of tenure, and are paid upon a scale of rates usually determined by length of service; consequently their wages are not subject to the same fluctuations as in a country like the United States, where individual enterprise largely substitutes that of the Government. Even in the large coal mines and iron and glass manufacturing establishments administered by individuals or companies, there is much less disposition on the part of employers to change and modify the price of labor than in the United States. The owners of these establishments have made it a point to identify the workmen as much as possible with the place of their employment, so as to secure permanence and uniformity of employed labor. Consequently, in such times as the present, rather than lose these advantages, employers make every possible concession to their woringmen.

Reduction of wages.—Such, however, has been the falling off in the foreign demand for Belgian manufactures within the last two years that, notwithstanding these politic and generous intentions on the part of employers, they have been forced to reduce considerably the wages of their workmen, and in some instances to stop operations entirely.

Depression in the glass manufactures.—The glass manufactures of the districts of Charleroi and Lodelinsart have suffered most severely from this depression of trade. In 1874, there were in these districts 167 furnaces in full operation; in 1875, 151; in 1876, 135; in 1877, 133; and in April of the present year the number had fallen to 117; thus showing no less than 50 furnaces out of an aggregate of 167 that have stopped operations entirely within the last four years for the want of profitable orders; and I am informed by the proprietors of some of the larger establishments yet in operation that, notwithstanding the fact that coal has fallen from 30 to 10 francs per ton and the price of labor from 25 to 40 per cent., they yet find the manufacture of glass unprofitable. There are but few iron mills in my consular district, yet I am convinced that the depressed condition of the glass trade is not much greater than that of the coal, iron, and other greater material interests of the country.

Agricultural labor.—Notwithstanding the fact that the price of labor has fallen off at least 25 per cent. within the last seven years in almost all branches of mechanical industries of the kingdom, the wages paid to agricultural laborers have been gradually but steadily growing up for a number of years. This improvement in the condition of the field laborer may justly be attributed to a number of influences, distinct in their character yet tending to the same results. The rapid development of steam and horse railroads, and the extraordinary increase of improvements, public and private, that have taken place in almost every city and town of the kingdom within the last few years have attracted the field laborer from the rural districts to these more populous centers, where he can not only get higher wages, but enjoy more social life with those of his own class.

There is another influence at work in the rural districts which is yearly tending to improve the condition of the laborer and change his relation to his employer. By the constitution of Belgium not only are all rights of primogeniture and entailment of estates prohibited, but the property of a Belgian subject dying intestate, or transmitted by testament, is required to be divided equally among the legal heirs. As a consequence of this constitutional provision, the great landed estates, upon which in former times large numbers of laborers were kept as mere retainers at nominal wages, are being gradually broken up, and the men employed upon them forced to seek employment elsewhere. Within late years many of the fractional parts of these former large estates have been purchased by rich and thrifty merchants and manufacturers, who, not compelled to obtain their revenue from the cultivation of the soil, build upon their property, from motives of pride as well as comfort, handsome *chateaux*, furnished with modern improvements, often involving a lavish expenditure of money; and this results in the employment of not only new men, but many of these old retainers, at wages often greatly above those formerly received on the old and larger estates. As a consequence of these influences, the field laborer in Belgium, who is willing to remain upon strictly agricultural lands, now receives from two to three francs per day, while but a few years since his wages ranged from but one to two francs.

Reduction of mill wages.—In the iron mills and other large establishments of mechanical industry the reduction in workmen's wages since the prosperous years of 1871, '72 and '73 will average about 25 per cent., while the cost of living has remained about the same.

Wages in the cities.—A careful inquiry of architects, builders, masterworkmen, and employers of unorganized labor in this and other cities of the kingdom has enabled me to give, in Table No. 1, a statement of the average wages now paid their workmen. On this subject I wish, however, to remark, that while ten hours are usually regarded as a day's work, carpenters, bricklayers, stonemasons, plasterers, plumbers, painters, paper-hangers, and all that class of labor not employed in large manufacturing establishments of organized labor, are employed and paid by the hour. Tailors, shoemakers, jewelers, and several other classes of special workmen are paid by the job, and usually gain from 80 cents to $1 per day, according to the character of their workmanship. In the large glass manufactories the chief workmen are employed by the month.

Table marked No. 2 will show approximatively the monthly earnings of workmen now employed in these establishments as compared with the wages received in 1872, '73, and '74.

Table No. 3, showing the wages paid by the Government to the employés on the railroads and other public works under the control of the state, has been compiled from information obtained directly from the ministry of public works.

2. MONETARY.

National Bank.—The circulation of Belgian paper money is regulated by the law of the 5th May, 1850, under which the National Bank was created. That law, while it especially provided for the issue of paper money by this bank, prohibited the creation of any other new bank of paper issue excepting upon the condition that the stockholders should be personally responsible to the fullest extent for the redemption of its currency; but up to this date no such bank has been chartered in the kingdom. Previous to 1850 several banks of paper issue existed in the kingdom, but it was provided in the law above referred to that they should all, after certain fixed dates, withdraw their notes from circulation and cease to issue paper money. The Bank of Liege, the last in this category, has ceased to be a bank of issue since the 4th February, 1875; consequently the notes of the National Bank of Belgium are now the only paper money of the kingdom.

The following are the provisions of the law of 1850 for the Government and regulation of this bank and for the issue and security of its currency:

1st. The aggregate amount of its notes, the mode of their emission, and their denomination by categories are determined by the government and the bank conjointly.

2d. Its notes are made payable at sight in Brussels, but any of the provincial branches may delay payment, in case of necessity, long enough to receive the requisite funds for payment, either from the central bank in Brussels, or from any of the other provincial branches.

3d. The notes of this bank are made receivable for all debts due the state, by an authorization of the minister of finance, but it is expressly stipulated that this authorization may at any time be revoked by him.

4th. The entire amount of its circulation is required to be represented by securities readily convertible into money, and the bank is obliged to keep constantly in its vaults coin equal to a third of its paper circulation and all its other obligations combined; nevertheless, by special authority of the minister of finance, the amount of reserve coin, under certain contingencies, may descend below this amount.

5th. So long as the Government continues to receive the notes of the bank for debts due the state, they are a legal tender for private debts, but have no forced currency excepting what is derived from this fact.

6th. The bank is strictly prohibited by law from the transaction, either directly or indirectly, of any affairs of a hazardous or doubtful character. Its operations are confined chiefly to the discount of commercial paper representing material value, maturing in one hundred days, and indorsed by three responsible names.

7th. It is directed by a governor and six directors, appointed by the King, and is under the surveillance of a Commissaire of the Government, who has the right to examine and supervise all its operations.

8th. The Government reserves the right to oppose and prevent the execution of any measure of the bank that may be deemed to conflict either with the laws or interests of the state.

Table No. 4 will show the denomination and aggregate amount of the notes of this bank in circulation at the end of each year from 1851 to 1877.

Gold and silver coin.—On the 25th December, 1865, France, Italy, Switzerland, and Belgium entered into a convention under the title of what is known as the "Latin Union," in which it was stipulated that the gold and silver coin of the contracting Governments should pass current at their nominal value within the territorial limits of this union; consequently it is now impossible to ascertain exactly the amount of metallic money of Belgium coinage that circulates in the kingdom.

The bank-note circulation of Belgium is estimated at about 661 francs per capita.

Table No. 5 gives the amount of gold and silver coined in Belgium from 1832 to 1876, and Table No. 6 the amount of coin demonetized and recoined into Belgian money from 1834 to 1877.

The reports of the minister of finance show that, in 1874, 3,248,484 francs' value of United States gold coin was converted by the mint at Brussels into Belgian money, and that, in 1875, this demonetization of our coin amounted to 9,744,126 francs in value, thus showing an aggregate of 12,992,610 francs' value of gold coin of the United States demonetized and converted into Belgian money within those two years. It may be proper here to remark that, previous to 1874, no registration was kept at this mint of the amount of foreign coin converted into the money of this country, otherwise it might be interesting to know to what extent the gold and silver coin of the United States has contributed to the metallic currency of this country.

MODES OF TRANSACTING BUSINESS.

Business systems.—The present depressed state of trade in Belgium, to which I have already referred, has so shaken and unsettled the commercial usages of prosperous times, that it is now almost impossible to give any reliable information on this subject.

Foreign orders and domestic demands for the products of the large manufactories of iron, steel, zinc, copper, glass, and woolen goods have so fallen off, and prices have been so reduced within the last year that owners, rather than close their establishments altogether, have been compelled to sell at rates for cash and grant lines of discount on unquestionable paper heretofore unknown in their commercial transactions. A few years since the glass manufacturers of Belgium entered into an agreement by which they bound themselves to sell at uniform rates and grant uniform rebates for cash, but at the present time all uniformity has disappeared, and the conditions of sales made are almost as various as are the necessities of the parties in the transactions; and so it is in almost every other department of trade in Belgium at the present time. Every man having anything to sell, in the hope of outriding the passing storm, consults but his pressing necessities in commercial transactions, without reference to what were formerly regarded as the usages of trade. The nominal rate of commission charged for buying or selling merchandise is usually about 2 per cent., and insurance on goods shipped to the United States five-eighths of 1 per cent. in summer and seven-eighths in winter; but so many modifying circumstances, depending upon advances made upon consignments and the character of the merchandise insured, enter into every transaction, that these figures can only be received as approximative in determining these features of the commercial usages of this country.

JOHN WILSON.

BRUSSELS, *June* 5, 1878.

No. 1.—*Wages paid workmen employed by the hour in the large cities and towns of Belgium.*

Occupation.	Average wages paid per hour.	Occupation.	Average wages paid per hour.
	Cents.		*Cents.*
Carpenters	9	Stonecutters	8
Bricklayers	10	Tinsmiths	8
Stonemasons	10	Cabinet-makers	8
Plasterers	9	Upholsterers	9
Housepainters	7	Locksmiths	10
Paper-hangers	8	Plumbers	10
Decorators	15	Carriage-makers	9
Machinists	10	Harness-makers	8
Marble workers	10	Gasfitters	9

No. 2.—*Monthly wages paid workmen in glass-factories in* 1878 *compared with* 1872, '73, '74.

Occupation.	Monthly wages, 1872, '73, '74.	Monthly wages, 1878.
Blowers	$100 to $100	$50 to $65
Assistants	24 to 30	26 to 45
Stokers	40 to 50	20 to 24
Flatteners	36 to 40	24 to 26
Cutters	24 to 30	20 to 24
Packers	26 to 30	15 to 24
Ordinary workmen	16 to 20	12 to 16

No. 3.—*Employés under the minister of public works, Belgium.*

Description of trade and administrative duties.	Rates of salaries per working day.		Rates of salaries monthly.	
	Minimum.	Maximum.	Minimum.	Maximum.
Blacksmiths	$0 48	$0 96	....	....
Blacksmiths' assistants	48	....	....	....
Model-makers	60	1 00	....	....
Joiners	32	80	....	....
Joiners' apprentices	24	28	....	....
Coopers	52	76	....	....
Supervisors	32	60	....	....
Sawyers	44	60	....	....
Letter-painters	56	84	....	....
Grinders	48	84	....	....
Painters	32	84	....	....
Upholsterers	86	76	....	....
Carpenters	35	1 00	....	....
Basket-makers	36	76	....	....
Adjusters	28	1 08	....	....
Adjusters' apprentices	20	52	....	....
Coppersmiths	48	96	....	....
Engineers	48	96	....	....
Engineers' assistants	40	48	....	....
Turners	40	80	....	....
Planers	52	64	....	....
Saddlers	44	80	....	....
Stretchers	40	56	....	....
Lampmakers	24	80	....	....
Porters	40	64	....	....
Porters' assistants	24	44	....	....
Evolutionists	32	64	....	....
Machinists	....	....	$22 00	$38 00
Water-heaters for passenger-cars	....	....	16 00	22 00
Chief workmen	....	....	....	60 00
Supervisors	....	....	18 50	22 00
Brigadiers	....	....	20 00	26 00
Diggers	38	42	....	....
Guards of public-road crossings	38	50	....	....
Guards of public tunnel	38	50	....	....
Guards of public switches	38	50	....	....
Billposters	....	....	24 00	26 00
Billposters for telegraphs	....	....	24 00	26 00
Letter-carriers	....	....	18 00	30 00
Messengers	....	....	14 00	26 00

No. 3.—*Employés under the minister of public works, Belgium*—Continued.

Officers and clerks.	Annual salary.		Allowance for traveling, lodging, &c.	
	Minimum.	Maximum.	Minimum.	Maximum.
Railroads.				
Clerks, third class	$200 00	$240 00	10 per ct.	....
Clerks, second class	300 00	360 00	10 per ct.	....
Clerks, first class	400 00	520 00	5 per ct.	....
Head clerks	600 00	750 00	5 per ct.	....
Chief clerk, second class	700 00	800 00	....	....
Chief clerk, first class	900 00	1,000 00	....	....
Chief of division, second class	1,100 00	1,200 00	....	....
Chief of division, first class	1,300 00	1,400 00	....	....
Inspectors	1,300 00	1,400 00	....	....
Directors	1,600 00	1,600 00	....	....
General inspectors	1,800 00	1,800 00	....	....
Managers	200 00	2,000 00	....	....
Guards	300 00	360 00	....	....
Ticket collectors	300 00	360 00	....	....
Department of bridges, mines, and highways.				
General inspectors	....	1,800 00	....	....
Chief engineers	....	1,600 00	$200	....
Principal engineers, first class	1,300 00	1,400 00	160	....
Principal engineers, second class	1,110 00	1,600 00	160	....
Engineers, first class	900 00	1,000 00	160	....
Engineers, second class	700 00	800 00	160	....
Underengineers	520 00	600 00	....	....
Principal conductors	700 00	800 00	20	....
Conductors, first class	600 00	600 00	20	....
Conductors, second class	440 00	520 00	20	....
Conductors, third class	360 00	360 00	....	....
Chief clerk	700 00	800 00	....	....
Writing clerk	540 00	600 00	....	....
Drawing clerk	240 00	480 00	....	....
Clerk, first class	420 00	480 00	....	....
Clerk, second class	300 00	360 00	....	....
Clerk, third class	240 00	300 00	....	....
Supervisors	320 00	480 00	....	....
Messengers	200 00	240 00	....	....

No. 4.—*Annual amount of bank-notes in circulation in Belgium at the end of each year from 1851 to 1877.*

Year.	Notes of 1,000 francs.	Notes of 500 francs.	Notes of 100 francs.	Notes of 50 francs.	Notes of 20 francs.	Total.
1851*	....	....	....	....	....	31,772,720
1858*	....	....	....	....	....	111,023,830
1859*	....	....	....	....	....	112,922,780
1860*	....	....	....	....	....	111,887,360
1864	55,476,000	12,323,500	32,398,900	5,138,650	5,097,180	110,434,230
1865	56,900,000	13,203,500	33,093,000	4,933,200	5,218,160	113,347,860
1866	60,857,000	13,258,000	34,164,500	5,984,450	5,292,400	119,556,350
1867	63,682,000	12,771,500	34,681,900	6,242,150	4,505,260	121,882,810
1868	75,036,000	15,034,500	42,367,600	7,777,950	6,610,720	146,826,770
1869	81,321,000	20,451,500	56,399,900	7,721,200	10,814,400	176,708,000
1870	79,811,000	18,123,500	65,283,200	7,109,300	15,220,100	185,607,100
1871	88,283,000	17,001,000	75,534,100	7,171,500	17,924,840	205,914,440
1872	108,464,000	16,018,000	96,347,500	4,784,150	25,701,760	251,315,410
1873	146,927,000	25,032,500	121,378,500	3,091,100	34,767,680	331,196,780
1874	119,127,000	18,852,000	126,381,900	2,082,800	38,416,420	304,860,120
1875	122,900,000	18,600,000	137,170,000	1,518,000	42,900,000	323,088,000
1876	151,942,000	28,437,000	136,334,600	24,282,400	23,563,260	364,559,260
1877	141,736,000	25,959,000	132,693,100	27,997,100	13,723,140	342,108,340

* The denomination of notes issued during these years cannot now be ascertained.

No. 5 A.—*Gold coined in Belgium from* 1848 *to* 1877.

Years.	10 francs.	25 francs.	20 francs.	Total.
1848		8, 037, 425		8, 037, 425
1849	371, 880	3, 749, 575		4, 121, 455
1850	633, 270	1, 853, 875		2, 487, 145
1865	Since demonetized.	Since demonetized.	20, 522, 060	20, 522, 060
1866	do	do	10, 639, 260	10, 639, 260
1867	do	no	26, 826, 140	26, 826, 140
1868	do	do	27, 634, 980	27, 634, 980
1869	do	do	24, 689, 480	24, 689, 480
1870	do	do	63, 824, 060	63, 824, 060
1871	do	do	45, 179, 440	45, 179, 440
1874	do	do	60, 927, 000	60, 927, 000
1875	do	do	82, 685, 060	82, 685, 060
1876	do	do	41, 393, 640	41, 393, 640
1877	do	do	118, 121, 400	118, 121, 400
Total	1, 005, 150	13, 640, 875	522, 442, 520	537, 088, 545

No. 5 B.—*Silver coined in Belgium from* 1832 *to* 1877.

Year.	¼ franc.	½ franc.	1 franc.	2 francs.	2½ francs.	5 francs.	Total.
1832						186, 760	186, 760. 00
1833		29, 175. 00	60, 836			5, 628, 330	5, 718, 341. 00
1834	188, 047. 00	789, 023. 50	481, 551	552, 712		1, 749, 880	3, 761, 213. 50
1835	160, 004. 75	402, 521. 00	830, 698	450, 110		1, 848, 840	3, 692, 173. 75
1838		275, 183. 50	525, 363	600, 610		26, 015	1, 427, 170. 50
1840		173, 685. 00	261, 041	472, 682			907, 408. 00
1843	2, 000. 00	182, 000. 00		1, 469, 000			1, 653, 000. 00
1844	241, 500. 00	792, 000. 00	2, 196, 400	966, 000		401, 000	4, 596, 900. 00
1847						3, 498, 005	3, 498, 005. 00
1848					1, 398, 537. 50	12, 581, 415	13, 979, 952. 50
1849			40, 602		5, 007, 115. 00	34, 610, 475	39, 658, 252. 00
1850	25, 209. 00	104, 785. 50	162, 016		397, 880. 00	26, 326, 480	27, 016, 370. 50
1851						18, 539, 610	18, 539, 610. 00
1852						23, 023, 380	23, 083, 508. 00
1853						12, 132, 990	12, 526, 000. 80
1858						90, 510	263, 560. 40
1865						4, 536, 800	4, 536, 800. 00
1866		3, 403, 000. 00	3, 041, 000	3, 884, 000			10, 328, 000. 00
1867		507, 000. 00	6, 652, 000	7, 578, 000		18, 465, 720	33, 202, 720. 00
1868		537, 932. 00	675, 000	4, 328, 460		32, 852, 820	38, 394, 212. 00
1869			1, 393, 608			63, 287, 710	64, 681, 318. 00
1870						52, 340, 375	52, 340, 375. 00
1871						23, 917, 170	23, 917, 170. 00
1872						10, 225, 000	10, 225, 000. 00
1873						111, 704, 795	111, 704, 795. 00
1874						12, 000, 000	12, 000, 000. 00
1875						14, 904, 705	14, 904, 705. 00
1876						10, 799, 425	10, 799, 425. 00
Total	616, 760. 75	7, 196, 305. 50	16, 320, 174	20, 301, 574	6, 803, 532. 50	495, 678, 210	547, 542, 745. 95

No. 6.—*Demonetization of Belgian coin from* 1832 *to* 1875.

Dates.	Description of specie.	Value of specie demonetized.
Dec. 1, 1852	Pieces of ¼ of franc	616, 760. 75
Aug. 11, 1854	Pieces of gold of 10 and 25 francs	14, 640, 025. 00
July 26, 1868	Pieces of 2.50 francs	6, 803, 532. 50
July 26, 1868	Pieces of 2.00 francs	4, 511, 114. 00
July 26, 1868	Pieces of 1.00 franc	4, 558, 566. 00
July 26, 1868	Pieces of 0.50 franc	2, 748, 373. 50
July 26, 1868	Pieces of 0.20 franc	626, 189. 20
Mar. 6, 1869	Pieces of 10 and 5 centimes in copper	2, 462, 832. 30
	Total	36, 973, 393. 25

GHENT.

Report, by Consul Millward, on the (1) *rates of wages;* (2) *cost of living;* (3) *business habits, for the district of Ghent.*

I have the honor to transmit herewith a report on the rates of wages prevailing; the cost of living to the laboring classes; the condition of labor and the laboring classes; the business habits and customs of this consular district.

1. *Rates of wages.*—Agricultural laborers: Males, 17 cents to 20 cents per day; females, 15 cents to 17 cents per day, besides their eating, which is supplied. When hired as servants, having eating and lodgment furnished, they are paid $1.75 to $2 per month.

Mechanical laborers and those employed upon public works earn from 60 cents to $1 per day.

2. *Cost of living.*—The cost of living to the laboring classes varies according to the locations they inhabit. For example, the cost of living to the laboring classes inhabiting cities, towns, and villages, averages, with rent included, 20 to 25 cents per day per person, and in the country from 15 to 20 cents per day.

The prices of the necessaries of life are as follows, per pound: White bread, 5 cents; rye bread, 4 cents; beef, veal, and pork, 16 to 20 cents; lard, 20 cents; potatoes, 1 cent; butter, best, 30 to 50 cents; butter, common, 20 to 22 cents; cheese, 20 to 25 cents; coffee, 30 to 40 cents; sugar, 15 to 20 cents; chickens, 50 cents to $1 each; eggs, per 13, from 20 to 25 cents.

The present rates, as compared with those prevailing during the last five years, both as regards wages and cost of living, are about 3 per cent. higher.

3. From all sources of information and personal observation, touching the present condition of trade throughout this consular district, I find that the depression is very great, and the general complaint is "hard times," with an apparently darker outlook for the immediate future.

The paper currency of this kingdom is at par with gold. The amount in circulation is 78,218,000, secured by reserve gold in the treasury.

4. *Business habits.*—For the business habits and systems prevalent throughout this district, I respectfully refer to my report of trade and commerce, sent to the department in February last.*

JAMES MILLWARD.

GHENT, *August* 20, 1878.

* The following extracts, from the report above referred to, illustrate the habits and customs of the laboring classes of Ghent: About 80,000 of this population (Ghent) are work people, employed in the various manufactories situated here, of which there are a large number. The habits and customs of this large number of work people are particularly noticeable for frugality, exemplary behavior toward their employers and toward each other, and their strict attention to business. Drunkenness is almost entirely unknown among them, and, according to the reports of the police department, charges against them for crimes are very rare. They, as a class, are a people who enjoy themselves in their own manner with each other in their innocent amusements, without broils or quarrels.

CANADA.

Report, by Consul-General Smith, of Montreal, on the rates of wages, cost of living, and currency of Canada.

LABOR AND WAGES.

The depression of business has, as in the United States, largely affected the price of labor. It is impossible to state with accuracy the extent of this depreciation, as I have received many varying statements. Different kinds of labor have been differently affected. I think it may be stated that, throughout the consular district of Montreal, farm labor is now about 25 per cent. lower than it was five years ago. The wages now usually paid seems to be at the rate of from $10 to $14 per month for the summer months, and from $100 to $120 per year, with board. During the present year a reduction has been made of from 5 to 10 per cent. on the salaries of officers of the city of Montreal. Day laborers employed by the city receive from 90 cents to $1 per day. In the country districts mechanics, carpenters, blacksmiths, &c., are receiving from 80 cents to $1.50 per day, or about 50 per cent. less than four years ago.

RAILWAY WAGES AND TARIFF.

The following table, kindly prepared for me by the officers of the Grand Trunk Railway, shows therein the rate of wages now being paid by that company to their employés; also, the tariff of freight charged by the Grand Trunk road between Chicago and Montreal for the year ending June 30, 1878; also, the tariff between Chicago and Portland for the same period.

GRAND TRUNK RAILWAY.

Rates of wages in Montreal and tariff on merchandise from Chicago to Montreal and to Portland during the year ending June 30, 1879.

RATE OF WAGES.

Traffic department.	Agents and cashiers.	Operators and clerks.	Yardmen and switchmen.	Conductors.		Brakemen.		Baggagemen.	Checkers.	Freight-porters.
				Passenger.	Freight.	Passenger.	Freight.			
Per annum	$900 to $1,000	$300 to $700	$390 to $580	$480 to $700	$420 to $540	$390	$313 to $390	$420	....	....
Per diem	....	....	....	....	....	....	....	....	$1.15 to $1.75	$1.00 to $1.15

ENGINEERS' DEPARTMENT.

Track foremen .... $1.62½ to $2.12½ per diem.
Track laborers .... $1 per diem.
Carpenters .... $1.40 to $1.60 per diem.
Painters .... $1.75 per diem.
Smiths .... 24c. per hour.
Helpers .... 14c. per hour.

MECHANICAL DEPARTMENT.

Boiler-makers	12c. to 23c. per hour.
Car-repairers	12c. to 20c. per hour.
Fitters	14c. to 23c. per hour.
Laborers	11c. to 24c. per hour.
Machinemen	12c. to 16c. per hour.
Painters	14c. to 16c. per hour.
Tinsmiths	13c. to 16c. per hour.
Turners	14c. to 20c. per hour.
Enginemen, first class	$2.25 to $2.75 per trip.
second class	$2 to $2.45 per trip.
Firemen, first class	$1.30 to $1.45 per trip.
second class	$1.15 to $1.25 per trip.

TARIFF ON MERCHANDISE FROM CHICAGO TO MONTREAL.

	1	2	3	4	Grain.	Flour.	Seeds.	Bulk meats.	Provisions.	Dressed hogs, &c.
On July 2, 1877 ....per 100 lbs..	$1 40	$1 00	$0 75	$0 30	$0 25	$0 50	$0 40	$0 35	$0 30	......
On April 1, 1878 ....do......	1 10	80	65	30	25	50	40	35	30	$0 70

TARIFF ON MERCHANDISE FROM CHICAGO TO PORTLAND.

	1	2	3	4	Grain.	Flour.	Seeds.	Bulk meats.	Provisions.	Dressed hogs, &c.
On July 2, 1877 ....per 100 lbs..	$1 60	$1 20	$0 90	$0 40	$0 35	$0 70	$0 50	$0 45	$0 40	......
On April 1, 1878 ....do......	1 30	1 00	75	35	30	60	45	40	35	$0 80
Live stock ....per car..	115 00	......	......	......	......	......	......	......	......	......

COST OF LIVING.

The cost of living in Canada is about 25 or 30 per cent. less, including house rent, food, fuel, and clothing, than it was a few years since. The general result seems to be that the wages now paid will procure about the same quantity of the necessaries of life as the wages paid four or five years ago would have procured. It is undoubtedly true, however, that a greater number of persons find difficulty in securing employment than formerly, and large numbers are either unemployed or employed only a portion of the time.

MONEY OF CANADA.

The money in circulation in Canada consists mainly of Canada bank-notes, American gold, and Canada silver subsidiary coin. American silver is not in circulation, and probably will not circulate in Canada to any considerable extent. United States legal-tender notes and United States national-bank notes, though not received by the banks, have been passing into circulation as they have approached par in value; and I see no reason to doubt that when the Government resumes specie payments both of these classes of notes will become current money throughout Canada for all commercial purposes. There is but little gold in use except that of American coinage.

BANKS AND FINANCES.

The banks acting under charter of the Province of Ontario and Quebec had, on the 30th of September last, according to the returns furnished by them to the department of finance, capital paid up of $58,075,683.42, with a note circulation of $19,929,229.00, with specie on hand at that date to the amount of $4,909,216.36. Their total liabilities were estimated at $89,657,317.82, and their total assets at $162,603,437.75. These banks, as a rule, have established credit, and there seems to be little disposition to demand gold in payment of their notes.

J. Q. SMITH.

UNITED STATES CONSULATE-GENERAL,
Montreal, November 21, 1878.

GODERICH, ONTARIO.

Report, by Commercial Agent Abbot, on the rates of wages, cost of living, &c., in the district of Goderich, Ontario.

I inclose tabular statement of wages paid at several ports in this commercial agency. The ports which I selected for inquiry are Goderich, Stratford, Kincardine, Owen Sound, Meaford, Collingwood, and Sault Ste. Marie.

At all these places workmen can live cheaply and comfortably. Neat frame houses, having from four to seven rooms, with an eighth or a quarter of an acre of ground attached thereto, rent for from $4 to $7 a month. These lots are quite sufficient, when carefully cultivated, to furnish the tenants with fresh vegetables, and most of them take great pride in cultivating flowers and vegetables and in making their lots of ground look neat and pretty.

The prices of food are very low. I annex a recent price-current of market rates at Goderich and some of the neighboring towns.

At Southampton, the next port above Kincardine, on Lake Huron, and distant from here 62 miles, I was told that the best roasting pieces of beef could be had at 7 cents per pound; mutton the same. In this town similar pieces are 10 to 12 cents per pound, or 5 cents by the quarter; chickens, 36 cents per pair; white fish and lake trout, 5 cents per pound. The usual rents paid by the railroad employés at Southampton for cottages are $4 to $5 per month.

Rents for comfortable cottages in Goderich, with an eighth to a quarter of an acre of ground, are from $5 to $7 per month. Handsome two-story houses, with stables, &c., can be had at from $100 to $200 per annum. Board in the best hotels in Goderich is from $8 to $12 per week, and for permanent lodgers a considerable reduction is made.

The proprietors of the largest flour and salt works here, who are also the owners of the only elevator in the harbor except the one owned by the Grand Trunk Railroad Company, and who have, besides, extensive works in Montreal and one or two other places, have found it for their interest to give their workmen and all persons employed by them, whether as bookkeepers, clerks, engineers, or laborers, in addition to their regular wages, a share in the profits of the works, which in good years amounts to a very considerable sum. In a recent year, the head bookkeeper at Montreal received, in addition to his salary, as his share of the profits, $4,000.

One of the proprietors informed me that by this plan every employé became interested in all the operations of the concern, as though he were really one of the proprietors, and all took care to prevent the least waste or theft in any part of the works, and great care was exercised in the running of the machinery to prevent breakage or injury in any way. One of the bookkeepers said that it was not only for their interest to do this, but it became a habit with them. Another good result from this plan was that the workmen remained a long time in the employment of the company, having no desire to leave the service or take part in strikes for increased wages.

All this region bordering on Lake Huron is very healthy, and invalids resort to it from many parts of the country. Many mothers with their children come here and pass the summers; also persons attacked with hay-fever. This latter disease is unknown here, and persons afflicted therewith find immediate relief on their arrival here. There are several mineral springs, which are found beneficial. Salt baths, hot and cold, for bathing and swimming, are open during the summer season.

GEORGE J. ABBOT.

COMMERCIAL AGENCY OF THE UNITED STATES,
Goderich, November 2, 1878.

Food prices in Goderich.

WHOLESALE.

GODERICH, *November* 5, 1878.

Wheat (fall, new)	per bushel	$0 80 to $0 87
Wheat (spring)	do	0 70 to 0 76
Flour	per barrel	4 60 to 4 50
Oats	per bushel	0 28 to 0 30
Pease	do	0 50 to 0 52
Barley	do	0 40 to 0 52
Potatoes	do	0 50 to 0 50
Pork	per cwt	4 00 to 4 50
Hay	per ton	7 00 to 8 00
Chickens	each	0 10 to 0 12
Butter	per pound	0 10 to 0 12
Eggs (unpacked)	per dozen	0 10 to 0 12
Wood	per cord	2 10 to 2 50
Corn	per bushel	0 55 to 0 60
Bran	per ton	12 00 to 13 00
Middlings	do	14 00 to 15 00
Wool	per pound	0 21 to 0 24

RETAIL.

Beef (best roasting pieces)	per pound	10 cents.
Beef (by the quarter)	do	5 cents.
Chickens	per pair	36 cents.
Geese, 25 to 50 cents each, or	per pound	7 cents.
Turkeys	do	8 cents.
Mutton	do	7 cents.
Lamb	do	10 cents.
Tea	do.	50 cents to $1.
Coffee (best Java)	do	40 cents.
Sugar (white, ground)	do	12 cents.
Milk	per quart	5 cents.

Meats can be bought from the market-wagons somewhat cheaper than the above.

Rates of wages at ports in the commercial agency of the United States at Goderich, Ontario, October, 1878.

Employés.	Goderich, Kincardine, Meaford, Sault Ste. Marie.	Stratford.	Owen Sound.
Sheriff	Fees, amounting to $4,000 per annum	Same as in Goderich	Same as in Goderich.
Clerk of the peace and crown attorney	Fees, averaging $2,500 per annum	do	Do.
Master in chancery	Fees, averaging $1,200 per annum	do	Do.
Clerk of the surrogate and law courts	Fees, averaging $2,500 per annum	do	Do.
County registrar	Fees, averaging $5,000 per annum	do	Do.
Chief justice of the supreme court of Canada	$6,000 per annum	do	Do.
Puisne judges	$4,000 per annum	do	Do.
Chief justice of court of error and appeal	$6,000 and an allowance of $1,000 per annum	do	Do.
Chief justice court of queen's bench	$6,000 per annum	do	Do.
Chief justice court of common pleas	do	do	Do.
Chancellor of the court of chancery	do	do	Do.
Managers of banks	$1,200 to $1,500 per annum	do	Do.
Cashier and teller	$400 to $800 per annum	do	Do.
Telegraph boys	$5 per month	do	Do.
Clerks in bookstore	$100 first year, $200 second year, and $400 third year of service.	do	Do.
Iron-foundery manager	$1,200 per annum	$1,000 to $2,000 per year	$1,000 per year.
Iron-foundery bookkeeper	$625 per annum	$500 to $800 per year	$600 per year.
Iron-foundery foreman	$2 per day	$1,000 per year	$800 per year.
Iron-foundery blacksmiths	do	$1.50 to $1.75 per day	$1.62 per day.
Iron-foundery boiler-makers	$550 per year	$1.75 to $2.00 per day	Do.
Iron-foundery molders	$400 to $600 per year	$1.50 to $1.75 per day	Do.
Iron-foundery machinists	$350 to $500 per year	$1.50 per day	Do.
Iron-foundery millwrights	$350 to $600 per year	$1.75 to $2 per day	Do.
Flour-mill head miller	$23 per week	$50 per month	$50 per month.
Flour-mill ordinary millers	$8 to $12 per week	$35 to $40 per month	$35 per month.
Flour-mill engineers	$15 per week	$35 per month	
Flour-mill bookkeeper	$750 per year, with a percentage on profits	$50 per month	$50 per month.
Flour-mill laborers	$1 to $1.20 per day	$1 to $1.10 per day	$1 per day.
Salt-works laborers	$6 to $7 per week		$1.25 per day.
Coopers	$1.50 per day	$1.25 per day	$1.50 per day.
Carpenters	do	$1.50 to $1.75 per day	$1.75 per day.
Hotel clerk	$475 per annum	$30 to $40 per month	$25 per month.
Hotel barkeepers	$375 per annum	$20 to $35 per month	$20 per month.
Hotel porters	$12 per month	$10 to $20 per month	$10 per month.
Hotel waitresses	$7 per month	$6 to $8 per month	Do.
Hotel male cooks	$15 to $30 per month	$12 to $30 per month	$35 per month.
Hotel female cooks	$10 to $12 per month		$15 per month.
Waiters	$15 per month	$10 to $20 per month	$15 per month.
Male servants	$20 per month	do	$20 per month.
Female servants	$6 to $7 per month	$4 to $8 per month	$5 to $8 per month.
Laundry women	90 cents per dozen, or $7 to $8 per month, with board.	$5 to $10 per month	$7 per month.
Hackmen	$15 per month	$15 per month	$15 per month.

Rates of wages at ports in the commercial agency of the United States at Goderich, Ontario, October, 1878—Continued.

Employés.	Goderich, Kincardine, Meaford, Sault Ste. Marie.	Stratford.	Owen Sound.
Stablemen	$10 to $12 per month	$10 to $15 per month	$10 per month.
Bricklayers	$2 per day	$2.25 per day	$1.75 to $2.50 per day.
Masons	do	$2 to $2.25 per day	Do.
Farm laborers	$132 per annum, with board	$1 per day	$10 to $12 per month and board.
Gardeners	$1.50 per day	$1.50 per day	$1.25 per day.
Printers	$8 to $10 per week	$1.25 per day	$8 per week.
Cabinet-makers	$1.50 to $1.75 per day	$1.40 to $1.50 per day	$1.50 per day.
Shoemakers	$9 per week	$1.15 to $1.35 per day	$1.50 per day; cutters $1,200 per year.
Tailor's cutter	$14 per week	$1.65 per day	$10 per week; cutters $1,200 per year.
Sewing girls	75 cents to $1 per day	80 cents per day	$5 per week.
Clerks in stores	$50 to $60 per month and from $150 to $720 per annum.	$500 to $700 per year	$400 to $600 per year.
Clerks in post-office	$375 per annum	do	$500 per year.
Telegraph operators	$200 per annum	$30 to $65 per month	$25 to $45 per month.
School teachers	Male, $500; female, $200 to $350	Female, $250; male, $600; principal, $1,100.	$250 to $1,200 per year.
County judges	$2,100 salary; traveling expenses, $200; fees, $300.	$2,500 per year	$3,000 per year.
County treasurer	$1,200	$1,200 per year	$1,200 per year.
County clerk	Salary and fees averaging $700 per annum	$400 per year	$600 per year.
Principal at high school	$700 per annum	$700 per year	
Railroad engineers	$15 to $20 per week, with extra allowance for over-time.	$1.50 to $2.50 per day	$2.50 per day.
Railroad firemen	$1 to $1.50 per day	$1 to $1.50 per day	$1.25 to $1.50 per day.
Railroad conductors	$60 per month. Commencing service in the railroad company, $45 per month.	$1.50 to $2 per day	$40 to $50 per month.
Railroad brakesmen	$1.25 per day	$1 to $1.25 per day	$1.25 per day.
Railroad detective	None here	$1.35 per day	
Railroad Pullman-car conductor	do		
Railroad Pullman-car porter	do		
Railroad switchmen	$1.25 per day	$1.15 to $1.25 per day	$1.25 per day.
Railroad laborers	$1 per day	90 cents to $1 per day	$1 per day.
Steamboat captain	$800 for the season of eight months		$800 per season of 8 months.
Steamboat first mate	$40 per month		$50 per month.
Steamboat second mate	do		$40 per month.
Steamboat first engineer	$800 for season of eight months		$800 per season of 8 months.
Steamboat second engineer	$400 for season of eight months		$400 per season of 8 months.
Steamboat purser	$500 for season of eight months		$600 per season of 8 months.
Steamboat steward	$40 per month		$40 per month.
Steamboat cook	$55 per month		$55 per month.
Steamboat waiters	$14 per month		$14 per month.
Steamboat firemen	$35 per month		$35 per month.
Steamboat wheelsmen	do		Do.

Steamboat deck-hands	$25 per month		$16 per month.
Hod-carriers	$1.25 per day		
Barrel-makers	11 cents per barrel		
Glaziers	$1.50 to $1.75 per day		
Barbers	10 cents for shaving; 15 cents for shaving and hair cutting; 25 cents for shaving, hair cutting, and shampooing head. No additional charge made for doing these operations in chambers not far distant from shop.		
Town clerk	$400 per year		
Chief of fire brigade	$240 per year, with free house		
Policeman, only one in town, on duty night and day	$400 per annum		
Bank accountant	$700 to $900 per annum		
Chief constable, county	$175 per annum		
Head master of high school	$1,000 per annum		
Male assistant in high school	$500 per annum		
Inspectors of county schools	$1,300 per annum		

Wages of laborers and employés at the port of Collingwood, in the district of Goderich.

Iron-foundery: manager	$800 to $1,200 a year.
bookkeeper	$300 to $500 a year.
foreman	$600 to $700 a year.
blacksmith	$1.50 per day.
boiler-makers	$1.75 per day.
molders	$1 50 per day.
machinists	$1.50 per day.
millwrights	$1.75 to $2 per day.
Flouring-mill: head miller	$600 to $1,000 a year.
ordinary millers	$300 to $400 a year.
engineers	$45 to $50 a month.
bookkeeper	$35 per month.
laborers	$1 per day.
Coopers	$1.25 per day.
Carpenters	$1.50 to $1.75 per day.
Hotel: clerk	$30 to $35 per month.
barkeepers	$26 and board per month.
porters	$12 to $18 and board per month.
waitresses	$5 to $7 and board per month.
male cooks	$20 to $26 and board per month.
female cooks	$6 to $8 and board per month.
waiters	$6 to $7 and board per month.
Male servants	$14 to $20 and board per month.
Female servants	$5 to $6 and board per month.
Laundry women	$6 to $7 and board per month.
Stable-men	$12 to $14 and board per month.
Bricklayers	$1.50 to $2.50 per day.
Masons	$1.50 to $1.75 per day.
Farm laborers	$12 to $18 and board per month.
Gardeners	$20 to $30 a month.
Printers	$6 to $8 per week.
Cabinet-makers	$30 to $50 per month.
Shoemakers	$1.50 to $1.75 per day.
Tailors	$1.75 to $2 per day.
Sewing-girls	$4 to $5 per week.
Clerks in stores	$30 to $50 per month.
Clerks in post-office	$30 to $50 per month.
Telegraph operators	$30 to $40 per month.
School teachers	$35 per month or $350 to $400 a year.
County judges	$2,000 to $2,500 a year.
treasurer	$1,600 a year.
clerk	$600 to $800 a year.
Railroad: engineers	$50 to $60 a month.
firemen	$30 to $35 a month.
conductors	$50 to $60 per month.
brakemen	$30 per month.
detectives	$30 per month.
Pullman-car conductors	$40 per month.
Pullman-car porters	$26 per month.
switchmen	$30 per month.
laborers	$1 per day.
Steamboat: captain	$600 to $1,000 for season.
first mate	$40 to $45 per month for season.
second mate	$35 per month for season.
first engineer	$50 to $60 per month.
second engineer	$40 per month.
purser	$300 to $500 for season.
steward	$25 per month and board.
cook	$40 per month.
waiters	$12 per month.
wheelsmen	$18 per month.
firemen	$16 per month.
deck-hands	$12 per month.

Seamboat hands all have board included.

HAMILTON.

Report, by Consul Leland, on the rates of wages in Hamilton, Ontario, and vicinity.

I have the honor to report that the following are the prices paid per day for services of mechanics and laborers in the city of Hamilton and its vicinity:

Molders	$2 25
Glassblowers	2 25
Bricklayers	2 25
Stovepolishers	2 25
Sewing-machine makers	2 00
Stonecutters	2 00
Wood-turners	2 00
Clerks, first grade	2 00
Clerks, second grade	1 00
Farm laborers	$1 25 to 2 00
Plasterers	1 75
Printers	1 67
Carpenters	1 50
Coopers	1 50
Trunkmakers	1 50
Cabinet-makers	1 50
Shoemakers	1 50
Harness-makers	1 50
Painters	1 50
Tinsmiths	1 50
Blacksmiths	1 50
Day laborers	1 00
Bridge carpenters	2 00
Bridge laborers	1 25
Switch repairers	1 87 to 2 12
Freight checkers	1 25 to 1 50
Foremen of laborers	1 75
Yardmen	1 20 to 1 50
Common railroad laborers	1 00 to 1 12

FRANK LELAND.

UNITED STATES CONSULATE,
Hamilton, August 30, 1878.

DENMARK.

Report, by Consul Ryder, of Copenhagen, on the (1) *rates of wages and cost of living;* (2) *present state of trade;* (3) *paper money; and* (4) *business habits and systems, with accompanying statistical tables; for Denmark.*

I have the honor to acknowledge herewith the receipt of your communication of the 11th of April last past, and beg to transmit annexed a statistical report, parts of which I have translated, issued by the department of the interior of the kingdom in 1872, giving the necessary information desired. I may call the attention of the Department to the fact that while wages on an average have been higher during the past five years in this country than in 1872, they are now about 10 to 15 per cent. less, while the necessaries of life are the same as in 1872, if not a trifle higher.

1. Rates of wages and cost of living.

Agricultural laborers are paid 37 cents per day, but as a general rule farm hands are employed at from $2.16 to $2.70 per month, including board and lodging. Mechanics earn on an average from 54 to 71 cents per day. Laborers on public works, such as railways, &c., earn from $135 to $162 per annum, without findings.

I may here add that there is a large surplus of labor at the time of my writing this dispatch and no employment for it.

The cost of living to the laboring class in this city is, on an average, for a grown person, at from 27 to 54 cents per day; for a family of adults and three children, from 61 to 81 cents per day. For the country and provincial cities the cost of living to the laboring class is less, say from 20 to 27 cents per day for a grown person, and from 33 to 40 cents per day for a family of two adults and two children.

I may here state that during the past years, including 1873 to 1876, of which no official reports pertaining to this matter can be obtained, wages were considerably advanced, say from 35 to 45 per cent. on an average, on all classes; but in 1877 a general reduction commenced, which has brought down the cost of production and labor to nearly the same figures as in 1872. The cost of living is about the same now as in 1872, if not a trifle higher.

2. Present state of trade.

The present state of trade in this country is very much depressed in every line of business. On looking for the cause of this general depression, I find that there have been several aggravations which have helped to bring about this present state of affairs, namely: Unfavorable harvests in 1875, 1876, 1877; overspeculation, and extreme uncertainty of all European politics.

The commercial distress may be explained in the following manner, namely, that the production and overspeculation in a large class of important commodities, requiring extensive capital and many workmen, is so much in excess of the real demand as to reduce the prices and leave no profit to the merchant or producer. In other words, the less wealthy are compelled to retire from the field ruined, and the wealth of the country is lessened by the aggregate of the capital they have lost, and by the cost of maintaining in some way or other the many workmen thrown out of employment. In this small country the cash demand for commodities has fallen off to a considerable extent, because, from some cause or other, the means of the consumers have considerably diminished, and in consequence of a larger amount of capital being applied to production or speculation than the actual facts and condition of the country justify.

With regard to the means of the consumers having been lessened here since 1874, it may be attributable to the following causes:

1st. From the great losses to investors in stocks and private enterprises, which in annual income amounts to many millions.

2d. From losses incurred in trade.

3d. From losses incurred by the maintenance of many workmen unable to procure employment.

It is very certain that the means of consumers, whether in this or in other countries, that is to say, the cash demand for commodities, can only be augmented by, 1st, greater frugality, harder work, and more invention; 2d, unusual productiveness of the seasons; 3d, the accumulation of savings over a considerable period of years. It is not a matter of confidence or credit, but a matter of hard positive capital; that is, of commodities or interest over and above consumption, applied to productive, useful, and dividend-bearing objects of expenditure.

Trade has been depressed here since 1874, because in this and in other countries there has been year by year little or no surplus of means over expenses, and trade will continue to be depressed until that surplus becomes considerable.

Among modern communities, and especially among the people of this country, there is no coyness or affection about expenditures as soon as the means for it exist. The disposition is not to leave money unspent, but to find plenty of it to spend.

Another evil more radical in its nature is the diminished worth of wages; so to say, the descending quantity and quality of work obtained by employers for wages not merely the same, but higher than they were ten and twelve years ago. This is a cause of dearness of production and of retarded accumulation of the most formidable character, to a great extent neutralizing the gain to the community from the increase of skill and the progress of mechanical invention.

Its effect on an entire country, if there are no sufficient compensations in the progress of invention or in other directions, is essentially as disastrous as would be a material reduction of the hours of daylight.

After a lapse of time, and that not a very long one, the severest and most hopeless sufferers by such a limitation of efficiency and progress are the working classes themselves. There can be no advancing welfare among the class of working people depending on weekly wages apart from the rapid accumulation of capital. It is the rapid accumulation of capital, arising from invention, skill, energy, and discovery, which has raised the wages and social standing of the humbler classes in this country within the last twenty-five years.

I am pleased to hear that everything in the United States is coming down in price; and I firmly believe from what I hear from home that one can live there cheaper than in Europe. If that is the case, labor, that is to say, the cost of production, will be cheaper; and as we can now manufacture many things cheaper than, and as well as in, Europe, I do not see any reason why we should not to a certain extent control the European market in a short time.

3. Paper money.

With reference to the currency of this country, I can inform the Department that on the 30th of April last about $17,000,000 of paper money were in circulation. On the other hand, the amount of gold coin and bars at the National Bank of this city for the security and redemption of said paper currency was $9,500,000.

The National Bank of Copenhagen is the only bank in this kingdom allowed to issue paper money; none being issued by the Government or by any other bank in Denmark. The notes of the National Bank are redeemable in gold coin, which is the legal tender; silver being used as fractional currency and only considered legal tender to the amount of $5.30. According to the treaty stipulations between Denmark and Sweden-Norway, the coins of the three countries are circulated in each of them as legal tenders.

It is impossible to give an exact statement of the amount of the gold in circulation in the kingdom of Denmark, but, including the amount held by the National Bank of this city, it may be said to be $8,000,000.

The circulation of silver amounts to about $4,300,000, and the amount of copper in circulation about $134,000.

4. Business habits and systems.

Regarding the business habits and systems of the commercial classes in the country, as far as I have been able to form an opinion, I should say that the majority of the Danish merchants is an honorable and respectable class, and a notable proof thereof can be brought forward. Not only is this opinion entertained, but also the wide-spread credit which is accorded them in all countries in Europe, namely: England, France, Germany, Russia, Holland, Belgium, and Sweden-Norway; in all of which countries several of the principal commercial establishments have had direct business connections with them, which has been kept up and strengthened both by constant personal visits of the parties, their traveling representatives, or by agents domiciled in Copenhagen. The general character of the merchants is that of strict probity in their transactions, but they are somewhat slow in their movements and difficult to be moved out of their old steady way of carrying on their business transactions. More especially do the wholesale merchants, as also a considerable class of the retailers, appear to be held in the highest estimation; and it is but very rarely that such confidence seems to have been misplaced, as in the whole manner of transacting business their chief desire seems to be the maintenance of the credit and high standing of their firms by a strict fulfillment of their engagements, rather than seek to obtain some profit by unreasonable reclamations or deductions; and one, therefore, in commercial intercourse with the Danish traders, does not run the risk of such tendency to chicanery which unfortunately in many other countries is but of too common occurrence in the present day, so long as their orders have been executed punctually and with proper exactitude.

Although a considerable part of the transactions, namely, in agricultural produce and colonials, is made in cash payments, that is to say, from three to thirty days, still the usual terms are a credit of ninety days, with or without bill of acceptance, and in many instances, more especially amongst the small retail dealers in the provincial towns, by an extension of credit to six months.

The style of the trade carried on with England, chiefly in manufactured goods, is on credit against remittance at the expiration of three months from date of shipment. The principal exports, namely, of cereals and fat goods, are chiefly made against direct orders for shipment, the consignments on merchants' account being to small extent. With live cattle, of which some 50,000 head are annually exported, I believe it is different, and that a large proportion of these shipments are made on speculation.

The beforementioned remarks have, of course, only reference to the high-toned, honorable, and respectable class of dealers, for naturally here, as well as in other countries, will be found some few who, looking less to their good name, will sacrifice the same for the sake of procuring some temporary profit.

Notwithstanding the increased facility of credit created by many years of considerable overspeculation in every branch of business, and obtained by incompetent and not in any way solvent traders and merchants, has tended to augment the number of bankruptcies, still these, when compared with what has taken place in other countries, are small in extent, and it is chiefly amongst this class of traders that the general and wide-spread stagnation seems mostly to be taking effect.

HENRY B. RYDER.

CONSULATE OF THE UNITED STATES,
Copenhagen, May 15, 1878.

1.—*Detailed statement of the average wages of the working people at Copenhagen.*

Occupations.	Number of hands employed.				Daily wages.	
	Men.	Women.	Youths.	Children.	Men.	Women.
Factory hands	1,615	535	217	275	$0 69	$0 28[5]
Joiners	359		31		75	
Carpenters	251		1		66	
Coopers	50		14		68	
Wheelwrights	128		8		67	
Turners	74	6	31	10	65	21
Blacksmiths	130		60		65	
Gunmakers	115		30	2	70	
Watchmakers	249	17	55		76	23
Glaziers	28	5	6	5	66	35
Shoemakers	120	14	12		56	30
Tailors	220	133	1		68	28
Millers	171		17		66	
Bakers	156		16		71	
Masons	476		55		79	
Tanners	175		3		61	
Hatters	53	12	12		89	22
Glovemakers	139	36	69		70	30
Saddlers	52	2	10		64	31
Dyers	66	15	3	2	58	23
Weavers	62	40	13	3	45	17
Brushmakers	6	7	6		71	45
Stonecutters	39		21		58	
Sailmakers	20	4	16		81	33
Basket-makers	22	73	11		63	31
Washing and bleaching	3	43			52	34
Painters	284		18		69	
Printers	238	27	98	9	77	26
Bookbinders	78	8	27		62	32
Butchers	42				75	
Sundry	187	30	39	20	64	30
Total	5,608	1,007	900	326		

2.—*Statement showing the annual income and cost of living of tradesmen's families in Copenhagen.*

Occupations.	Number in family.	Income.	General items.				Total.
			Rent.	Food.	Clothing.	Wine and tobacco.	
Metal-workers	7	$265	$32	$190	$21	$13	$245
Masons	5	261	42	180	18	22	249
Laborers	5	212	19	170	11	13	197
Carpenters and joiners	6	210	26	136	24	14	192
Tinsmiths	4	206	21	136	15	25	180
Sugar refiners	6	193	33	136	17	21	199
Porcelain workers	5	153	33	136	8	14	188
Tanners	......	227	31	150	14	27	213
Ropemakers	......	185	37	116	11	13	167
Cotton-house workers	......	150	26	127	13	14	173
Local workmen	......	......	21	105	15	13	153
Laborers	......	......	25	152	36	20	226
Average account of three journeymen painters	......	......	28	160	13	16	218

3.—*Average calculation for the city of Copenhagen.*

Nature of business.	Number of hands employed.				Daily wages paid.		Daily working time.			
	Men.	Women.	Youths.	Children.	Men.	Women.	Men.	Women.	Youths.	Children.
Manufactures:							*Hours.*	*Hours.*	*Hours.*	*Hours.*
Steam power	2,101	435	217	241	$0 75	$0 27	12.1	12.2	12.2	6.2
Without steam power	2,223	461	318	78	70	29	11.8	11.8	11.8	6.8
Total	4,324	896	535	319	72½	28	12.0	12.0	12.0	6.4
Mechanics:										
Joiners	189	......	56	......	69	......	12.3	......	12.6	......
Blacksmiths	83	......	44	......	62½	......	12.7	......	12.8	......
Shoemakers	77	2	10	......	51	25	13.5	12.0	12.8	......
Tailors	70	47	1	......	60	25	13.3	11.8	11.0	......
Bakers	144	......	16	......	70	......	13.3	......	12.9	......
Masons	19	......	......	......	75	......	11.7	......	......	......
Weavers	208	22	78	......	65	23	12.4	12.1	12.4	......
Painters	108	......	14	......	70	......	11.2	......	10.6	......
All others	416	40	146	7	69	28	12.1	11.6	11.3	......
Total	1,284	111	365	7	65	27	12.4	11.8	12.3	......
Grand total	5,608	1,007	900	326	70	28	12.1	12.0	12.1	......

4.—*Statement of the wages of agricultural laborers and servants throughout Denmark.*

Counties.	Daily average of earnings of agricultural laborers.										
	Summer.						Winter.				
	With board.		Without board.		By contract.		With board.		Without board.		
	Men.	Women.	Men.	Women.	Men.	Women.	Men.	Women.	Men.	Women.	Contract.
	Cents.	*Cents.*	*Cents.*	*Cents.*	*Cents.*	*Cents.*	*Cents.*	*Cents.*	*Cents.*	*Cents.*	*Cents.*
Copenhagen	20	13	37	24	53	30	14	10	29	17	38
Fredericksborg	18	12	34	22	45	26	13	10	28	17	33
Holbeck	18	12	30½	20	47	28	13	9	24	16	34
Soro	18	12¼	30	20	44	27	12½	9½	24	16	31
Præsto	17	10	30	19	41	24	13	8½	25	16	31
Bornholm	18	10	37	20	45	23	12	8	27	15	32
Maribo	19	12	33	21	45	26	14	9	26	16¼	32
Odense	18	15	31	24	43	28	13	10	24	18	31
Svendborg	18	14	30	20	39	26	13	10	23	16	31
Hjoring	18	14	37½	25	43	30	9	7	23	18	29
Thisted	18	13	35½	27	44	27	11	8	26	21	32
Aalborg	18	13	32	23½	44	28	10	8	22	16	30
Viborg	21	14	30½	25	47	29	12	8	25	17	31
Randers	21	14	39	24	43	27	12	9	29	17	30
Aarhuus	20	15	35	24	43	28	13	10	25	18	38
Veile	19	14	35¼	24	44	29	13	9	26	18	32
Ringkjobing	24	14	42	28	52	29	12	6	27	16	33
Ribe	25	14	41	25	49	28	13	8	26	18	32
Tjaelland	19½	12	32	22	46	27	13½	9	26	16	33
Fyen	19	14	30	22½	41	27	13½	10	23	16½	31
Oernes Amter	19	12	32	21	45	26	15	9	26	16	32
Jylland Amter	21	14	37	26	46	29	12	9	25	18½	31
Average of the whole kingdom.	20	14	35	24	45	28	14	9½	26	18	33

Counties.	Average half-yearly wages for servants, hired.									Average working time.			
	For the summer.					For the winter.				Summer.		Winter.	
	Adults.		Youths.			Adults.		Youths.					
	Men.	Women.	Boys.	Girls.	Children.	Men.	Women.	Boys.	Girls.	Work.	Rest.	Work.	Rest.
										Hours.		*Hours.*	
Copenhagen	$21 50	$11 50	$11 00	$7 50	$5 00	$14 00	$10 00	$8 00	$6 00	14	3	10	1
Fredericksborg	19 00	10 00	10 50	7 00	5 50	14 00	9 00	8 00	5 50	14	3	10	2
Holbeck	18 00	9 00	10 00	7 00	5 50	15 00	8 00	8 50	5 00	14	3	10	1
Soro	17 00	9 00	9 00	6 00	5 00	13 00	8 00	7 00	5 00	14	3	9	1
Præsto	18 00	9 50	9 00	7 00	5 50	13 00	8 00	8 00	5 00	13	3	9	1
Bornholm	19 00	8 00	10 00	6 00	6 00	14 00	7 00	6 00	4 50	15	3	13	2
Maribo	18 00	8 00	9 00	5 00	......	16 00	8 00	8 00	5 00	13	3	10	1
Odense	19 00	11 00	9 00	6 00	4 00	18 00	10 00	8 00	5 50	14	3	10	1
Svendborg	20 00	10 00	10 00	5 50	4 00	19 00	9 00	9 00	5 00	14	3	10	1
Hjoring	18 00	11 00	8 00	6 00	4 00	9 00	6 00	4 00	3 00	14	3	10	1
Thisted	18 00	10 00	7 00	5 00	4 00	12 00	7 00	5 00	3 50	14	3	10	1
Aalborg	20 00	12 00	9 00	7 00	4 50	10 50	7 00	5 50	3 50	14	3	10	1
Viborg	19 00	11 00	8 50	6 00	4 00	10 00	6 00	5 00	3 50	14	3	10	1
Randers	18 00	12 00	9 00	7 00	5 00	11 00	8 00	6 00	4 00	14	3	9	1
Aarhuus	19 00	12 00	10 00	7 00	5 50	11 00	7 50	6 50	4 00	14	3	10	1
Veile	20 00	12 50	10 50	7 50	5 00	13 00	7 00	9 00	4 50	14	3	10	1
Ringkjobing	24 00	13 00	11 00	7 50	4 50	9 00	5 00	4 00	3 00	15	3	10	1
Ribe	26 00	15 00	12 00	8 50	5 50	12 00	7 00	5 00	4 00	15	3	10	1
Tjaelland	19 00	10 00	10 00	7 00	6 00	14 00	9 00	8 00	6 00	14	3	10	1
Fyen	19 50	10 00	9 00	6 00	4 00	18 00	10 00	9 00	6 00	14	3	10	1
Oernes Amter	19 00	10 00	10 00	6 00	5 00	15 00	9 00	8 00	5 00	14	3	10	1
Jylland Amter	21 00	12 00	10 00	7 00	4 00	11 00	7 00	5 00	4 00	14	3	10	1
Average of the whole kingdom..	20 00	11 00	10 00	7 00	5 00	13 00	8 00	7 00	5 00	14	3	10	1

FRANCE.

BORDEAUX AND THE GIRONDE.

Report, by Consul Gerrish, of Bordeaux, on the laboring classes of the Gironde; the industries of Bordeaux; rates of wages and food-prices in Bordeaux; and the principal industries of the Gironde.

THE WORKINGMEN OF BORDEAUX.

Despite the agitation of the working classes in other large cities of France, Bordeaux, thus far, has remained exempt from reckless action by its industrial classes; not that they lack in desire or ambition to improve their condition, but they are patient, and, as a rule, more orderly and prudent in their conduct than men of their class in the large manufacturing districts. The industries of Bordeaux and the department are so numerous and so varied, that comparatively few men are employed in any one establishment, and no trades-unions or associations of any sort have attempted to dictate or fix their wages. There are upwards of 150 workingmen's societies here, existing through voluntary subscriptions, and designed to relieve such of their members as may become sick or disabled, but to the present time these societies have formed no union for any other purpose. The large majority of the workingmen barely earn sufficient for the necessaries of life. Their food, from month to month and year to year, consists of bread, soup, and wine. To this may be added grapes and other fruits when they are abundant and very cheap, and sometimes, but rarely, a little meat of the poorest quality. The married workman takes his meals with his family, but the unmarried takes his in cheap restaurants, which are found in every part of the city. Small as is the amount of wages received, and little as it will permit to be expended in food, the laborer often economizes on that for the entire six working days for the sake of indulging himself or his family in an extra bottle of wine or a more sumptuous repast on Sunday.

Formerly the better or more skillful class of workmen lived frugally the year round, and laid aside something for their future wants; but, although wages have increased somewhat, the savings of this class have diminished. The principal cause of this comes from the pernicious habit of spending their time in *cafés*. The number of these drinking-places in Bordeaux and its environs is upwards of two thousand. Wherever a shop remains empty for a fortnight it is almost invariably transformed into a *café*. Walk in any direction from the center of the city and you will pass some new *café* about to be opened.

The hard-earned money, as well as the time, uselessly lost in the these resorts of idleness and bad manners, it is impossible to calculate. Notwithstanding these *cafés* are such a universal resort for the workingmen, drunkenness is a rare exception; it is not the quantity drank there that is so prejudicial as the fascination of the place to seduce them from all serious occupation. Light wines and beer are the principal beverages indulged in. Although brandy, rum, gin, and other liquors are to be had at very low prices, no "prohibitory law" has yet led the workmen to consider them of prime necessity, and they are rarely used.

At his work the French laborer lacks the energy of the American of the same class, and the amount of work executed by him is much less in the same number of hours. It has frequently been amusing to me to watch these laborers at their tasks. A housepainter, for example, will perhaps work steadily for fifteen or twenty minutes, then descend from his scaffolding to the middle of the street, roll a cigarette, regard the work he has thus far accomplished, and for the next ten minutes enjoy his smoke with all the *nonchalance* of one living upon an ample income. In all other trades, the manufactures excepted, this slowness and instability in their manner of working is equally observable. The number of hours of labor per day is from eleven to twelve, but an average American workman would accomplish as much efficient work in nine hours.

To this improvidence and want of care for the future among the workmen there are, of course, many exceptions. Unquestionably a large portion is both industrious and economical, men of energy, capable of resisting the attractions of *cafés* and other resorts of idleness, who care for their families, and endeavor in every way to better their condition and make themselves somewhat independent; especially is this so where encouragement is offered them by those in better condition.

A striking example of this in Bordeaux is afforded by the efforts of one man, Mr. Lescarret, secretary of the city and professor of political economy, to whom I am indebted for many statistics herewith furnished. In 1872 he established in one of the lower quarters of the city, as an experiment, a provident savings society among fifty workmen, the poorest of the city. The average of their wages was from 50 cents to 60 cents per day. The suspension of work at the ship-yards in which they were engaged shortly after reduced their earnings from even this pitiable sum; they were actually brutalized by misery, without force, without courage, and without hope for the morrow, and with hearts filled with hatred against their employers.

Notwithstanding these discouraging circumstances they were induced to form a society, and to-day their savings, on which they are drawing interest, amount to upwards of $2,000. Their condition is in every way notably ameliorated. They make arrangements as an association with certain shopkeepers, all purchasing at the same places, and thus obtain such goods as are essential to them at a discount of 15 per cent. As Mr. Lescarret said to me, "they have no longer a hate for capitalists; they feel that they are capitalists themselves."

The farm laborers are frequently economical to the extreme of avariciousness, and many of them, in the course of time, become quite wealthy proprietors. They are hired either by the year, the month, or day. Those hired by the year are paid from $75 to $85 per year, lodged and boarded by the proprietor. When hired for a more limited period, they are paid according to the season of the year and the length of time engaged, but on an average, if lodged and not boarded, at the rate of from $160 to $170 per year; if engaged by the day, 30 cents per day from the month of November to March, and 45 cents from March to November, with board; without board, 45 cents to 60 cents per day and one bottle of wine. The cost of living to the agricultural laborers is slightly less than in the cities. The clothing used is the same as that of the workmen in the cities, and costs the same. It is of the cheapest material, and a suit is obtained for about $3 or $4.

Few of the workmen in Bordeaux are proprietors of the houses they inhabit. Some are making efforts towards becoming such, notably coopers and foremen in wine-cellars; these enjoy a certain independence and aspire to possess a small house of their own. Among the ship-carpenters, also, a few by long years of frugality have been enabled to save sufficient to make themselves independent of landlords.

The price of rent varies according to the location, but the tendency is to increase from year to year. It is difficult to fix with exactness the prices paid by workmen; but approximatively, for the majority, it can be stated as follows: For one unfurnished room, $1.60 to $2.40 per month; two rooms, $2.80 to $3.20; three rooms, $3 to $4.

The subjoined tables, compiled from the records of the bureau of statistics of this city, establish with sufficient exactness the wages actually paid to workmen in the various industries of Bordeaux, and also the price of provisions for the last five years. From these tables it will be seen that the average wages is from 80 to 90 cents per day, an increase of nearly 20 cents since 1873, and that the prices of such articles of food as form the principal nourishment of the laboring classes have not increased, but rather decreased within the last five years. This decrease was notable in 1875 on bread, meat, and potatoes.

INDUSTRIES OF BORDEAUX.

The mint.—Although there exist coins stamped at Bordeaux under the reign of Charlemagne, and even previous to his time, it appears that the veritable establishment of the mint was by a decree of Charles the Bald in the month of July, 864. After having been closed and re-opened at different times under the pressure of varying circumstances, it was re-established in 1455.

During the French revolution all mints were suppressed, and the mint at Bordeaux remained closed until 1795. It was also again closed in 1868, but the events of 1870, with Paris and Strasburg besieged, caused it again to be put in operation. The coinage of silver since 1795 has been as follows:

	Francs.
From 1795 to 1848	146,363,000
From 1848 to 1868	30,000,000
From 1868 to 1870	closed.
From 1870 to 1875	70,000,000
	246,363,000

The number of workmen employed varies from 50 to 80.

Government cigar manufactory.—This manufactory, established in 1816, is one of the largest and most important in France. Cigars of all kinds are manufactured, and for this purpose at least 1,500,000 kilos of tobacco (valued at about $3,000,000), are used annually, much of which is imported directly from the United States. Employment is given to about 150 men and 1,400 females. The wages of the former average about $1 a day and of the latter about 40 cents a day of ten hours' work.

Saltpeter refineries.—Bordeaux possesses two private refineries, producing about 3,000,000 kilos of saltpeter, and employing about 20 men; and one national refinery, employing about 50 men, with average wages of about $1 per day.

Cooperage.—The department of the Gironde counts upward of 700 cooper-shops, of which about 150 are established in the city of Bordeaux. More than 4,000 workmen are employed during the greater part of the year in the manufacture of pipes and wine-casks. A workman can make from eight to ten casks a week. He is paid by the dozen, and generally earns from $7 to $9 per week. The total number of casks manufactured is about 1,200,000 a year, valued at about $3,400,000. The staves of which these casks are manufactured come principally from the borders of the Baltic and Adriatic Seas. Some 18,000,000 to 20,000,000 are imported annually for this department. A few come from the United States; and, were any efforts made to prepare the staves there as desired by the French establishments, I doubt not large sales might be made here. Objections are made to the American staves: (1) To those that are sawed, which are rarely used here; and (2) to the thickness and the bungling way in which others are split. It is alleged that it takes a third longer time for a workman to prepare an American stave than it does one from the Adriatic.

Glass-works.—To-day there are seven large establishments in the city for the manufacture of bottles, employing about 700 workmen. The glassblowers and their assistants are paid by the 100 bottles, and their earnings vary from 70 cents to $2.40 per day, according to their skill. The other employés are paid from 40 to 60 cents per day. About 15,000,000 bottles are manufactured annually, valued at $600,000.

There are also four manufactories of white glass, preserve-jars, flasks, &c. Three hundred workmen are employed, and their wages vary from 60 cents to $1.20 per day. The average production annually is 1,600,000 bottles for oils and *liqueurs*, 1,400,000 fruit-jars, 400,000 perfumery bottles; but this number is not sufficient for the local demand, and a third as many more are imported from other departments.

Corks.—About 75 workmen are employed in this industry, who are paid by the piece: the cutters from 8 to 10 cents the thousand and the turners from 40 to 50 cents the thousand. Ten million corks are produced annually; a small fraction of the number required here. It is estimated that the number of corks brought to Bordeaux for local use and for exportation amounts to 110,000,000 per annum, valued at 4,000,000 francs.

Capsules for bottles.—There are three establishments, in each of which from 90 to 100 men, women, and children are employed, with average wages of 40 cents per day; 80,000,000 to 100,000,000 metal capsules are manufactured per annum, approximately valued at $220,000.

Sugar-refineries.—Bordeaux has five, refining about 25,000,000 kilos annually, valued at $7,200,000. They consume from 11,000 to 12,000 tons of coal and 1,500,000 kilos of animal black. From 425 to 450 men and 50 women are employed, receiving for wages, on an average—the men 80 cents, the boys 40 cents, and the women 25 cents per day. The sugar used in these refineries is imported from the islands of Réunion, Cuba, Guadeloupe, and Martinique.

Alimentary preserves.—The manufacture of preserves—fruit, vegetables, and meats—is one of the most important industries of Bordeaux, and these products deservedly hold a high rank. About 30 houses are engaged in preserving fruits. The number of workmen employed in these houses varies very much from year to year, according to the quantity and quality of the fruit. These preserves are prepared either with sugar or *eau de vie*, and rival all similar products of any other department or country.

For the preservation of vegetables there are about 20 houses, 10 of which also preserve meats; they employ about 500 men, women, and children, and furnish annually for local consumption and for exportation about $2,400,000 worth.

Chocolates.—The chocolate manufactories in the department of the Gironde employ about 350 persons; the average wage of the men is 80 cents per day and of the women 35 cents. Upwards of 800,000 kilos of chocolate are manufactured annually, valued at $560,000.

Liqueurs and confitures.—This industry can be said to equal almost that of any other in this department. Its products have a universal reputation, owing to the perfection attained in the manufacture of the *liqueurs*, and to the delicious fruit so thoroughly ripened by the warm sun of this favored region. There are upwards of 50 houses engaged in this manufacture in this department, employing in ordinary times about 1,200 persons. In the autumn months this number is sometimes doubled. Average wages: women, 30 to 40 cents; men, 60 to 80 cents per day. Annual value of the products, $2,000,000.

Tanneries.—Bordeaux possesses 5 tanneries, which give employment to 300 workmen. The value of their productions amounts to $800,000 per year.

Bricks and tiles.—In the manufacture of bricks and tiles in this department about 2,000 men are engaged from the 1st of April to the end of September, receiving for this period from $70 to $110 and board. In an ordinary season 100,000,000 bricks and tiles are made; the average value is, for tiles $6 per thousand, and for bricks $9 per thousand.

Accompanying this report, in addition to the statements showing the rates of wages and food prices in Bordeaux, will be found tables showing the industries of the department of the Gironde and the value of their products.

B. GERRISH, Jr.

UNITED STATES CONSULATE,
Bordeaux, July 17, 1878.

Daily wages of the laboring class in Bordeaux.

Occupations.	With board.			Without board.			Remarks.
	Common wages.	Maximum.	Minimum.	Common wages.	Maximum.	Minimum.	
Butchers	$1 00	$1 00	$1 00				
Bakers				$0 80	$1 00	$0 70	And one kilogramme of bread per day.
Brewers				1 00	1 20	90	
Brickmakers				80	1 20	70	
Boiler-makers				80	1 00	70	
Blacksmiths				80	1 00	50	
Barbers and hairdressers	$20 per month	$30 per month	$16 per month	70	1 00	60	
Bookbinders				80	1 00	60	
Basket-makers				60	80	60	
Carriage-makers				90	1 20	80	
Carpenters				1 00	1 20	80	
Corset-makers				30	50	25	
Cutlers				70	90	60	
Cabinetmakers				1 00	1 20	80	
Dressmakers				30	50	25	Earn from the second year.
Dyers				1 00	1 00	70	
Embroiderers				50	80	40	
Flower-makers				40	60	30	
Farriers				80	1 00	70	
Gardeners				80	90	70	
Glaziers				80	1 00	70	
Jewelers				1 00	1 40	80	
Joiners				80	1 00	70	
Laundresses	$1 00	$1 50	$1 00	30	50	25	Earn from the first year.
Lacemakers				40	50	25	
Masons				90	1 10	70	
Milliners	$4 per month	$6 per month	$3 per month	40	60	30	
Nightmen				70	90	60	
Pork-butchers	$1 00	$1 00	$0 80				
Printers				1 00	1 20	80	
Pastry-cooks	$4 per month	$8 per month	$3 per month				
Plumbers				1 00	1 20	80	
Potters				70	80	60	
Quarrymen				1 00	1 20	80	Earn from the first year.
Ropemakers				80	1 00	70	Apprentices earn 50 cents.

Daily wages of the laboring class in Bordeaux—Continued.

Occupations.	With board.			Without board.			Remarks.
	Common wages.	Maximum.	Minimum.	Common wages.	Maximum.	Minimum.	
Shoemakers				$0 70	$1 00	$0 50	
Seamstresses				30	50	25	
Silversmiths				1 00	1 40	80	
Shippainters				80	1 00	70	
Shoebinders				30	40	25	
Sik and felt hatters				1 00	1 40	80	In stores, $400 to $520 per year.
Stovemakers				1 00	1 20	80	
Sculptors				1 20	1 60	1 00	
Saddlers				80	1 00	70	
Locksmiths				80	1 00	70	
Stonecutters				90	1 00	80	Apprentices, after the first year, 40 cents per day.
Tilers, slators, and thatchers				1 00	1 40	90	
Tinsmiths				80	1 10	60	
Tailors				80	1 20	70	
Tanners				80	1 20	70	
Terrace-makers				70	90	50	
Upholsterers				80	1 00	70	
Vest and pantaloon makers				30	50	25	
Wheelwrights				80	1 00	70	
Watchmakers				1 00	1 40	80	
Woodsawyers				70	1 00	3 60	
Weavers				70	80	60	
Wood and metal turners				80	1 00	70	
Wood and metal engravers				90	1 60	80	Workmen by the piece can earn as high as $2.

THE PRINCIPAL INDUSTRIES OF THE GIRONDE.

By the census of the population in 1875, the number of persons living directly from the product of the divers industries of the department of the Gironde was 134,343 individuals; about one-fifth of the total population.

Industrial population of the Gironde.

Description.	Individuals following the profession below.		Their families supported by the labor or fortune of the foregoing.		Servants in the personal employ of the foregoing.		Number of individuals which each profession supports directly or indirectly.		
	Men.	Women.	Men.	Women.	Men.	Women.	Men.	Women.	Total.
Proprietors of—									
Mines and quarries....	448	20	354	511	41	22	843	553	1, 396
Factories for the preparation of raw materials...............	1, 219	231	1, 086	2, 054	312	286	2, 617	7, 571	5, 188
Cotton, woolen, and other manufactories.	2, 870	320	1, 466	3, 447	216	200	4, 552	3, 967	8, 519
Contractors, architects, and builders........	1, 902	61	1, 839	3, 941	257	342	4, 058	4, 344	8, 402
Principal workmen:									
Arts and trades	3, 150	861	2, 200	10, 588	248	1, 137	5, 598	12, 586	18, 184
Employés:									
Engineers, administrators, and clerks......	324	7	154	286	4	28	482	321	803
Workmen in mines and quarries	1, 517	175	920	1, 832	25	11	2, 462	2, 018	4, 480
Employed in factories .	2, 137	687	884	1, 968	31	1	3, 052	2, 656	5, 708
Light industries.......	12, 525	4, 884	9, 841	24, 663	2, 417	815	24, 783	30, 362	55, 145
Day-laborers, porters, cartmen, &c	15, 884	2, 690	3, 042	4, 833	49	20	18, 975	2, 543	26, 518
Total................	42, 036	9, 936	21, 786	34, 123	3, 600	2, 862	67, 422	66, 921	134, 343

Average price of bread, meat, eggs, and vegetables for the past five years in Bordeaux.

Articles.	1873.	1874.	1875.	1876.	1877.	June, 1878.
	Cts.	Cts.	Cts.	Cts.	Cts.	Cts.
Bread, first quality......per kilogramme.	8	$8\frac{1}{5}$	7	$7\frac{1}{5}$	8	$9\frac{3}{5}$
Bread, second quality..............do....	$6\frac{2}{5}$	$6\frac{1}{5}$	$5\frac{3}{5}$	$5\frac{1}{5}$	$6\frac{3}{5}$	$8\frac{3}{5}$
Beef, second quality ....do....	40 to 45	38 to 42	39 to 43	40 to 45	39 to 43	42 to 45
Mutton, second quality ....do....	42 to 46	40 to 45	39 to 43	42 to 46	40 to 45	42 to 44
Veal, second quality ....do....	44 to 50	40 to 42	41 to 43	42 to 45	40 to 42	46 to 50
Pork, second quality..............do ...	30 to 33	31 to 35	31 to 32	39 to 42	32 to 33	....
Chickens.......................per pair..	$1 00	$1 15	$1 20	$1 18	$1 24	$1 10
Eggs ....per dozen..	17 to 24	18 to 26	18 to 28	17 to 25	18 to 24	12
Potatoes ....per hectolitre..	$1 66	$1 35	$1 19	$1 88	$1 68	1 50
Beans...............................do....	2 82	3 36	2 49	3 20	3 05	3 20
French beans ....do....	5 00	5 10	4 96	4 75	5 29	5 10
Lentils.............................do....	10 10	11 25	10 00	9 25	10 75	10 50
Green pease.........................do....	4 44	4 97	4 75	4 25	4 92	4 55

Value of products manufactured, 1877.

National and municipal manufactories:

	Francs.
Mint..	14, 000, 000
Tobacco...	14, 650, 000
Aqueducts	410, 000
Gas...	1, 585, 000

	Francs.
Industries connected with the marine:	
Construction of vessels	2,800,000
Iron-works	1,000,000
Sailmakers	400,000
Rope manufacturing	1,800,000
Pulley manufacturing	70,000
Oar manufacturing	100,000
Industries connected with the wine trade:	
Cooperage, hoops, pegs, &c	21,000,000
Bottle manufacture	3,000,000
Cup manufacture	1,000,000
Corks, manufacture of	400,000
Straw wrappers	300,000
Metallic capsules for bottles	1,100,000
Cases, manufacture of	3,000,000
Crystallized tarter, manufacture of	750,000
Vinegar, manufacture of	1,000,000
Industries of alimentary substances:	
Refineries	36,000,000
Flour-mills	40,000,000
Decortication of rice	5,000,000
Codfish, drying of	8,000,000
Alimentary conserves, animal and vegetable	30,000,000
Alimentary pastes	400,000
Biscuits, manufacture of	800,000
Chocolate, manufacture of	2,800,000
Grain oil, manufacture of	5,000,000
Alcohol, manufacture of	2,500,000
Liqueurs and sweetmeats	10,000,000
Breweries	800,000
Fisheries	1,620,000
Oysters	3,000,000
Textile industries:	
Wool-cleaning, stripping sheepskins from La Plata	6,160,000
Wool-weaving	250,000
Woolen carpets, manufacture of	400,000
Hemp and cotton weaving	400,000
Hemp tissues	100,000
Clothing industries:	
Tanneries	4,000,000
Leather shoes, manufacture of	1,300,000
Shirts and undergarments	2,000,000
Ready-made clothing	3,200,000
Linen shoes	400,000
Silk and felt hats, manufacture of	800,000
Straw hats, manufacture of	700,000
Umbrellas, manufacture of	4,000,000
Metallurgical industries:	
Iron-founderies	3,000,000
Copper, brass, and zinc founderies	3,000,000
Machinery, manufacture of	1,500,000
Workshops of the Midi Railroad Company	3,200,000
Brazier's ware, manufacture of	1,200,000
Machinery and implements for agricultural purposes	5,000,000
Industries connected with architecture and public works:	
Stone-quarries	7,000,000
Brickyards, limekilns, and ceramic pavements	3,000,000
Hydraulic lime, manufacture of	150,000
Béton and cement	500,000
Plaster	500,000
Sawmills	2,100,000
Injected wood and mechanical fence-work	700,000
Cut-wood	100,000

	Francs.
Furnishing industries:	
Cabinet furniture and tapestry, manufacture of	1,200,000
Chairs, manufacture of, oil-cloth, and water-proof cloths	800,000
Matting, manufacture of	250,000
Brushes, manufacture of	100,000
Brooms, manufacture of	1,000,000
Flowers	800,000
Marble cutting and polishing and church furniture	500,000
Billiards, manufacture of	200,000
Carriages, manufacture of	3,500,000
Industries in mineral substances:	
Petroleum (refinery of)	1,750,000
Saltpeter-house	3,200,000
Porcelains and earthenwares	2,000,000
Potteries	600,000
Industries in vegetable substances:	
Resinous products	3,000,000
Paper, manufacture of	21,100,000
Pasteboard, manufacture of	60,000
Boarding of books	450,000
Dye-wood	200,000
Industries in animal substances:	
Leeches, raising of	770,000
Animal black	225,000
Wax candles	3,000,000
Soap	1,200,000
Candles	400,000
Printing and binding:	
Typographical printing	2,000,000
Lithographic printing	1,200,000
Bookbinding	125,000
Photographs	1,000,000

LA ROCHELLE.

Report, by Consul Catlin, on (1) price of labor; (2) cost of living; (3) past and present rates; (4) state of trade; (5) paper money; and (6) business habits and systems; for the consular district of La Rochelle.

In reply to the circular from the Department of State, under date of April 11, inquiring as to the prices of labor, cost of living, condition of trade, &c., in this consular district, I have the honor to state:

1. Price of labor.

The rate of wages paid to the average unskilled laborer in the towns varies from 60 to 90 cents per diem. Skilled labor, strange to say, commands wages but little, if any, higher than unskilled labor does. The following list, taken from various classes of employments, affords a fair idea of the prices received for a day of ten hours' labor viz:

Draymen	60 cents per day.
Masons	80 cents per day.
Carpenters	80 cents per day.
Joiners	80 cents per day.
Cabinet-makers	$1 per day.
Seamstresses	30 to 35 cents per day.
House-servants	20 cents per day.
Printers	$16 and $18 per month.
Chief of police	$720 per annum.
Policemen	$200 per annum.
Principal public schools	$600 per annum.
Male teachers of public schools	$200 per annum.

In the agricultural districts, owing to a prevalent tendency among the younger portion of the male population to seek employment in the cities, common farm labor has of late commanded better wages than heretofore, and a higher rate than in the towns, or what is practically a higher rate, inasmuch as the wages (60 to 90 cents per diem) paid in the towns will in the country purchase at least 25 per cent. more of the necessaries of life. Upon these wages the agricultural laborer not only supports himself and an average family, but saves money; and, in this connection, it may be stated that the steady increase of wealth and prosperity in the rural districts of this portion of France is a matter of general and unceasing comment and congratulation among the people themselves; and this, too, notwithstanding the comparative scarcity of farm laborers; a temporary evil, which in due season cannot but remedy itself, as the young men find city life unprofitable and return to cultivate the fields.

The country is free from "tramps." The laborer thrown out of employment, yet always *willing* to work, at once starts out with his loaf of bread under his arm and his gourd of sour wine swung over his shoulder, confident, and justly so, of finding other employment promptly. In brief, good wages, a demand for labor, and a steady accumulation of wealth are the noticeable features of the present situation in the agricultural portions of this district. And yet even this happy condition of affairs might be vastly improved upon could the farmers be prevailed upon to avail themselves of American labor-saving agricultural implements and machinery. The tenacity with which the laborious rural Gaul clings to the two-wheeled plow and the ancient harrow of his ancestors would be remarkable to the American observer, were not the same prejudice against innovation visible in the railway management, in house-building, and in almost every other department of labor here.

The following is a statement of—

Wages paid to railway employés.

Trackmen	40 cents per diem.
Brakemen	50 to 60 cents per diem.
Switchmen	$20 per month.
Firemen	$20 to $25 per month.
Baggage-masters	$20 to $25 per month.
Foremen	$25 to $30 per month.
Conductors	$25 to $30 per month.
Engineers	$35 to $66 per month.

Brakemen and trackmen, it will be observed, are employed by the day; all other employés by the year (though I have here reduced their rate of wages to that paid by the month). A system of bounties is offered by the companies for certain numbers of years of service, and during the sickness the wages of the employé continue, and medical treatment and medicines are furnished him at the company's expense. "Brotherhoods," or other such organizations, are unknown. No strikes occur, and the relations between the companies and their employés are entirely harmonious.

2. Cost of living.

The prices paid for "what are the necessaries of life" are—

Bread, first quality	4 cents per pound.
second quality	3 cents per pound.
third quality	2¼ cents per pound.
Flour	$9 to $10 per barrel.
Potatoes	35 cents per bushel.

Eggs	16 cents per dozen.
Coffee	20 cents per pound.
Butter	30 cents per pound.
Beef and veal	15 to 24 cents per pound.
Mutton	16 to 23 cents per pound.
Pork	16 cents per pound.

3. Past and present rates.

A comparison of the present rates with those which have prevailed during the past five years shows, as previously stated, an increase of, say, 50 per cent. in the wages paid farm hands, but no appreciable variation in the wages paid to common laborers, mechanics, railway employés, or those engaged in the public works. Neither has the cost of living perceptibly varied during the period, the grain crops and supplies of meat and vegetables having been so equable as to cause no serious fluctuation.

4. The state of trade.

The state of trade in the district varies somewhat according to localities and products. In the wine and grain growing regions in this vicinity the prospects are that this year's crops will be good ones, and producers are consequently hopeful, and indisposed to hoard; in this city, however, complaints that "trade is dull" are frequent among merchants and shippers, although retail dealers are but little affected. Foreign shipments lag, though it should be stated that at this season light shipments are the rule. There is no doubt, however, that the trade of this community, in common with other French cities, is experiencing, though perhaps in a less degree than that of many others, the results of that commercial crisis which has embarrassed France since 1875, and upon which a senatorial commission of eighteen members, after six months of inquiry, has recently reported, alleging the excess of production over consumption as primarily the cause of the existing evil. I inclose herewith a single copy (the only one, unfortunately, that I am able to secure) of an abstract made by a public print of the report of the commission referred to. Its allusion to the manner in which the American watch-making interest has supplanted the French will be found of especial interest.

From the portion of this consular district covered by the consular agency at Cognac come similar reports of anticipated good crops of grain, coupled with the surprising announcement *that fully one-half of the area formerly planted with grape-vines is now covered with wheat.* This singular change in the traditional habits of the agricultural laborer of that region is mainly attributable to the *possible* ravages of the *Phylloxera*, which, according to a recent careful official inquiry, has already made its appearance, to a greater or less extent, in thirty-three departments; but in the Charente (Cognac) and the Charente-Inférieure (La Rochelle) departments, it has thus far attacked only about one-sixteenth and one-thirtieth, respectively, of the areas under cultivation. Still, even this has sufficed apparently to frighten the vine-growers, in view of past years' experience, to such an extent, that they hasten to devote their acres to the less profitable, but more certain, wheat-culture.

In some sections war upon the *Phylloxera* has been vigorously declared; wherever practicable a submersion of the vineyard is found effective; fumigation of the vines is also tried. In other cases, sulphide of carbon is used; and in one instance a railway company, which is mutually interested with the vine-growers in the success of the crop, furnishes the preventive drug to the farmers from its depots at the nominal price of five cents per pound. The results of these remedial measures have yet to be seen.

Meanwhile, in the brandy trade of Cognac an unusual stagnation has been reported during the last quarter. One of the principal shippers of that place has stated that the dullness recently existing has been without a precedent during the last sixty years. The same establishment during May discharged a large number of its employés, only retaining others on the probable ground that, being to a certain extent skilled laborers, their services might be secured by rival houses when business should revive. Symptoms of such revival have already appeared, in fact, and sales during June and the present month have been better, though it cannot be denied that the brandy trade, in common with most other industries, seriously feels the present general prostration.

At Limoges the porcelain trade perhaps feels this prostration less than do most other industries. The impetus given of late years by various causes to the American interest in ceramics has served to counteract the depressing effects which, without doubt, would otherwise have made themselves here, as elsewhere, felt. In this connection a statement of the annual shipments of porcelain to the United States through the consular agency at Limoges since the year 1870 will prove of interest, viz:

In 1870	$440,600 08
1871	556,349 13
1872	672,370 11
1873	570,955 75
1874	512,699 86
1875	511,978 04
1876	349,212 46
1877	425,750 47
Total	4,039,915 90

To which may be added that the amount from January 1 to June 30, for the current year 1878, is $198,992.84, or at the rate of $397,985.68 for the entire year. Mr. Berthet, the consular agent at Limoges, whose long experience in that capacity fully qualifies him to judge, reports to me, under date of July 19, that the porcelain manufacturers at Limoges have recently received from the United States orders sufficiently large to justify the belief that a considerable revival in trade has begun.

During a recent visit of inspection to the consular agency at Limoges, I found that there exists in that city a museum of ceramics, containing an extensive, rare, and valuable collection of specimens of pottery, both ancient and modern, and comprising contributions from various parts of France, from Italy, Belgium, Russia, Germany, Austria, Great Britain, China, and Japan, but *none* from the United States. Learning upon inquiry that any specimens of American ceramics would be gladly received by the art committee (if consigned through our consular agent) and displayed side by side with the ceramic products of other nations, I take this opportunity of calling the attention of the Department, and through it, if deemed desirable, of our American potters at Trenton, N. J., and elsewhere, to the fact that they may, if they wish, be permanently represented by samples of their wares in one of the finest collections and at one of the principal ceramic centers of the world.

5. Paper money.

The only paper money in circulation in this district is that of the Bank of France, which is quoted at par, and which, for convenience of handling, may even command a slight premium.

6. Business habits and systems.

Long credits are the exception, and as a general thing business men are averse to contracting debts. Business obligations, however, when contracted, are generally met at maturity. Failures or assignments are seldom recorded. A due degree of caution characterizes capitalists and investors. Fortunes once made are not often lost, but are transmitted unimpaired, and oftener augmented, to the succeeding generations.

Remote from the main lines of travel, set off at one side in a quiet alcove into which only an occasional visitor or tourist finds time to step, La Rochelle feels but little of the throbbing which agitates the outer world. France may be convulsed with political throes, yet scarcely a ripple of excitement penetrates to this quiet spot. In short, it may be termed a counterpart of that peaceful Acadia which Longfellow has so beautifully described in Evangeline.

GEORGE L. CATLIN.

July 20, 1878.

LYONS.

Reports, by Consul Peixotto, on the rates of wages, condition of trade, &c., in the department of the Rhone.

1. Trade, money, and wages in Lyons.

Referring to your circular of the 11th of April, current, I have the honor to observe that—

1st. The rate of wages for working classes has increased in France since the Franco-German war 20 to 25 per cent., and that there has been little or no diminution during the last five years.

2d. The cost of living has increased in about the same proportion.

3d. The present state of trade is very depressed.

4th. Taxes have increased.

5th. The Bank of France has to-day (May 17) in circulation 2,281,958,970 francs (*billets au porteur*) of bank bills ($440,418,081); but these are of the denominations of 1,000, 500, and 100 franc notes, and very few of the latter are to be obtained. Of small bank-notes, as a currency for the masses, France has none. Gold and silver constitute the currency of France.

The Bank of France is retiring its currency circulation as fast as possible, the reduction being from 5,000,000 to 30,000,000 of francs per week; for example, it retired, for the weeks ending April 25, 33,142,890 francs; May 2, 5,057,400 francs; May 9, 29,061,265 francs; May 16, 6,252,000 francs.

In order, however, to answer more directly your inquiries and to show the changes which have taken place since and during the past five years (the period embraced in your questions), I have prepared and herewith beg to inclose a schedule, or table, showing the wages per diem of the principal working classes (including men, women, and children) employed in the department of the Rhone, in which this consular district is situated.

I shall in a few days supplement this report with statistics referring to the other branches of your inquiries, viz, agricultural laborers and those employed upon public works and railways.

Wages per diem of working classes at Lyons, May, 1878.

[Average working time, 10 hours.]

Classification.	Men.		Women.		Children.
	Range.	Average.	Range.	Average.	Average.
Masons	$0 60 to $1 60	$0 75			$0 30
Carpenters	1 00 to 1 80	1 00			20
House-painters	80 to 2 40	95			25
Silk-workers	50 to 2 40	90	$0 25 to $0 80	$0 50	12
Cotton-workers	50 to 1 20	65	25 to 60	35	15
Glovemakers	50 to 2 00	90	20 to 75	55	15
Dyers	60 to 1 80	90			12
Fine jewelers	80 to 2 50	1 00	20 to 1 00	60	15
Cheap jewelers	25 to 1 00	60	15 to 60	45	12
Shoemakers	50 to 1 60	1 00	40 to 1 00	55	18
Tailors	60 to 1 80	75	30 to 60	35	18
Shirtmakers	50 to 80	55	40 to 60	40	12
Shawlmakers	50 to 2 00	75	30 to 60	40	12
Lithographic printers	80 to 1 80	1 00	70 to 1 00	45	25
Gold-thread makers	80 to 1 20	85	50 to 60	55	12
Leather-dressers	60 to 1 00	80			35
Printing:					
Wool and cotton and silk	50 to 2 00	90	50 to 60	50	30
Shuttle-makers	1 00 to 1 60	1 00			15
Military equippers	80 to 1 20	1 00	40 to 60	50	10
Paper-hangers	80 to 1 20	1 00			20
Umbrella-makers	50 to 1 40	80	40 to 70	50	16
Piano-makers	60 to 2 00	90			15
Brushmakers	40 to 1 20	85	20 to 60	40	15
Pharmacists (druggists)	50 to 1 60	95			20
Church-ornament workers			35 to 50	40	10

2. Agricultural labor: wages and cost of living.

I have the honor to observe with reference to the department of the Rhone, in which this consular district is situated, that agricultural laborers are divided into two classes: those who are engaged by the year and live on the farms and those who work by the day.

Farm laborers who live in the farm buildings receive, in addition to food and lodging, wages, partly paid in money and partly in kind, amounting to about $30 per year.

Those who work by the day of fifteen hours (boarding and lodging themselves) receive—men, $80 to $100 per annum; women, $55 to $65 per annum.

It is estimated that the cost to the employer in supplying food and lodging is about $35 per capita per year.

The number of working days is as follows: Men, 200; women, 120; children, 80; working hours, 13 to 15.

There are certain laborers who supplement their revenues by the prosecution of secondary industries, such as weaving, wood-cutting, sawing, wooden-shoe making, cask-making, and building. Such secondary industry may increase their earnings by about $40 per year. It is calculated that 8 or 10 per cent. of the agricultural laborers are thus employed.

The married farm laborer, who finds himself, may earn $150 per annum, divided thus: husband's wages, $80; wife's wages, $30; three children's wages, $40; total, $150.

The cost of living to such a family is calculated as follows:

Lodging	$10 50
Bread	55 00
Meat	10 00
Vegetables	8 25

Wine, beer, and cider	$7 00
Milk	5 25
Clothing	25 00
Groceries	10 00
Fuel	8 00
Taxes	2 00
Total	141 00

It is estimated that there are 9,000,000 families in France; 1,000,000 of which are in easy circumstances. Of the 8,000,000 belonging to the industrial classes, 3,000,000 are inhabitants of towns and cities.

Land is very equally distributed among the bulk of the population, and the same is the case with personal property. The rural population is estimated at 70 per cent., the urban at 30 per cent.

In 1846 the rural population was 75.58 per cent., the urban 24.42; showing in France, as elsewhere on the continent, and in the United States, an increasing tendency of population toward cities. Since 1861 the urban population has augmented largely and the rural has decreased. There is some tendency the other way at present.

Broadly stated, I regard the condition of the agricultural classes of the United States as much superior to those of France, and I may add, from observation and study, to those of Germany, Italy, and Austria-Hungary.

The agricultural laborer of the United States is better fed and better educated. He is thus physically, mentally, and socially the superior of the same class in the countries above mentioned. The peasant classes of France, though as a rule ignorant, are remarkably independent. They cultivate the small economies; that is, they know how to save, and are, therefore, generally well to do. This is especially the case with small farmers.

If the American farmer would practice the same care, and clothe his family in the same plain and economical manner; if he would instil into the mind of his children the same love of nature and of his calling as does the French farmer, who, from father to son, and from generation to generation, continue the same avocation, the result would develop the finest race of agriculturists and the highest improvement in the economic cultivation of the soil that the world has ever witnessed.

From a comparison of tables made before the Franco-German war, and from information derived, as I believe, from reliable sources to day, I am of opinion that the farm laborer receives higher wages than five years ago, but the cost of living has increased in quite as large proportion. As a general rule, and viewed from a purely material standpoint, the French farmer, small as well as great proprietor, is better off than his brother agriculturist in America.

From such observation and opportunity as I have had, I believe there is more manual labor performed here than in the United States. Consequently it appears to me that there is a good field (I refer particularly to this and adjacent departments) in this portion of France for the introduction of agricultural machines and implements of husbandry, and our American manufacturers might do well to send their agents and cultivate this business.

3. WAGES OF RAILROAD EMPLOYÉS.

I have the honor to inclose a table showing the rate of wages paid to the employés of the principal railways in France.

I have derived my information from the most authentic sources, and therefore have no hesitation in declaring the same to be reliable.

On comparing these rates with those paid for like or similar labor in the United States, it will be seen that our employés and workmen are paid very much higher wages, and though the cost of living be greater in the United States, this difference is more than made up in the superior comforts which the American workmen possess.

On the whole, there appears to be no valid reason why our railway employés of every rank and condition should not, on comparing and contrasting their pay and condition with those of their brethren in France, be every way contented and satisfied.

BENJ. F. PEIXOTTO.

UNITED STATES CONSULATE,
Lyons, May 16 *and* 28, *and June* 5, 1878.

Rates of wages of employés of the principal railway companies in France, June, 1878.

Employés.	Employés.	Wages per year.
Engine-drivers (engineers on locomotives, passenger and freight trains), four classes.	Mécaniciens (ceux qui dirigent la locomotive pour trains de voyageurs et de marchandise), four classes.	$405 40 to $579 15
Stokers (firemen), those who fire the engines with coal, three classes.	Chauffeurs (ceux qui chauffent les locomotives), three classes.	289 58 to 347 49
Conductors (chiefs of the trains), three classes.	Conducteurs (chefs de train), three classes.	308 88 to 347 49
Chiefs of stations (in principal towns and villages).	Chefs de gare (aux chefs lieux et en province).	350 97 to 1,351 35
Deputy chiefs (in principal towns and villages).	Sous-chefs de gare (aux chefs lieux et en province).	289 58 to 694 98
Watchmen	Surveillants	231 66 to 318 53
Chiefs of baggage	Chefs à la reconnaissance	289 58 to 463 32
Baggagemen	Préposés à la reconnaissance	231 66 to 308 88
Chiefs of the gangs (workmen)	Chefs d'équipe	231 66 to 463 32
Chiefs of the porters	Facteurs-chefs	260 62 to 463 38
Porters and servants	Facteurs-porteurs	193 05 to 308 82
Overseers of workmen	Brigadiers (conducteurs d'équipe)	250 97 to 289 58
Chiefs of freight and engine depots, four classes.	Chefs des dépôts, four classes	888 03 to 1,158 30
Chiefs of bureaus and chief clerks	Chefs de bureau et commis principaux	386 10 to 772 20
Clerks	Commis	231 66 to 347 49
Auxiliary clerks	Commis auxiliaires	173 74 to 231 66
Telegraphy { Employés	Télégraphe { Stationnaires du télégraphe	231 66 to 318 53
Telegraphy { Employés stationnaires Tyer	Télégraphe { Stationnaires Tyer	212 35 to 250 97
Lampists	Lampistes	231 66 to 386 10
Switchmen	Aiguilleurs	231 66 to 308 88
Controllers	Contrôlleurs	289 58 to 579 15
Ticket-agents (men and women)	Distributeurs de billets (hommes et femmes).	260 62 to 637 06
Greasers	Graisseurs	193 05 to 250 97
Workmen	Hommes d'équipe	173 74 to 243 24

REMARKS.

I am principally indebted to the director of the Paris, Lyon and Mediterranean (the chief railway of France) Railroad for the prices of labor here given. It will be seen that they are much inferior to the wages received by similar employés in the United States. The system of labor and the general distribution is very different. The work is more subdivided. There are more laborers engaged. The *cost* of living, too, is much cheaper to the employé, but greatly inferior both in dwelling and food.

BENJ. F. PEIXOTTO.

NICE.

Report, by Consul Vesey, on the (1) *rates of agricultural and railroad wages;* (2) *cost of living;* (3) *wages of skilled artisans;* (4) *trade;* (5) *paper and specie money;* (6) *the business system; for the consular district of Nice.*

I have the honor to acknowledge the receipt of the Circular of the Department, dated the 11th ultimo, and beg leave to report:

1st. The rate of wages of workmen, such as laborers on roads, railroads, buildings, and similar work, is, in this district, the same as in most parts of France. Such labor is done by Piedmontese, who come from Italy, as do the Galegos from Spain to Portugal, in search of employment, and who, by their industry, frugality, and economical habits, have entirely monopolized all branches of rough manual labor. They earn from 30 cents to 40 cents a day.

Agricultural laborers earn from 50 cents to 60 cents a day, but are not very numerous in this part of France, agriculture being mostly carried on by the peasant proprietors themselves, or by the cultivators termed "metaillés," who work the land upon shares, half and half, with the owners.

The rate of wages earned by mechanical laborers is comparatively high. Thus, skilled plumbers get from $1.20 to $1.60 a day, and coopers $1.20 a day. Upholsterers are as well paid, while carpenters and blacksmiths earn somewhat less (from 90 cents to $1 a day). The wages of artisans in other branches of work vary considerably. The best journeymen tailors receive $1.60 per diem, while those of inferior skill receive $1, $1.20, or $1.40, according to their ability. Printers (compositors) earn about 80 cents a day, and shoemakers from 80 cents to $1 a day. Masons are paid by the hour, at the rate of 8 cents to 10 cents, never earning more than 90 cents a day.

2d. The cost of living to an ordinary laboring man here is from 30 cents to 40 cents a day. His food consists principally of Indian-meal, vegetables, bread, and wine; meat he seldom eats. The actual price of meal is 3 cents the pound, coarse bread 4 to 5 cents the pound, and wine about 6 cents the bottle.

3d. The wages of skilled artisans and laborers have not, I am informed, varied in any material manner at Nice during the past five years.

4th. The export trade of this consular district is exclusively confined to oils, perfumery, fruit, and flowers, for which there is always a good demand. At the present moment the trade in all these articles is healthy and prosperous, and shows signs of extension rather than diminution. Large quantities of perfumery are exported yearly to Germany, Russia, and Great Britain; no inconsiderable quantity going also to the United States.

The import trade consists merely in supplying this district with such articles as are not produced here, and is not, therefore, very extensive. It is mostly carried on overland, as the commercial importance of Genoa and Marseilles commands the maritime trade of this part of the Mediterranean.

5th. Paper money in France has the same value as gold coin. It consists of Bank of France notes of the denomination of 50, 100, 500, and 1,000 francs. The current gold coin consists of pieces of 5, 10, and 20 francs. During the French Empire large gold pieces of 40, 50, and 100 francs each were issued, but the present Government has discontinued coining them. The silver coin issued is in pieces of 20 centimes, ½ franc, 1, 2, and 5 francs. The copper coin in pieces of 5 and 10 centimes each.

6th. The manner of transacting business in this consular district is direct, from merchant to merchant, without the intervention of produce brokers, as is generally the case in other parts of France. In all commercial transactions the goods are invoiced, and delivered on board if sent by sea, or on the cars if by land; payment being made by drafts at 60 days against delivery of bill of lading or railway receipt.

W. H. VESEY.

UNITED STATES CONSULATE,
Nice, May 18, 1878.

PARIS.

Report, by Consul-General Torbert, on the (1) topographical, agricultural, and labor statistics of the department of the Seine; (2) French farming and farm-life; (3) wages and cost of living; (4) rates of wages in Paris; (5) wages paid by the city of Paris; (6) wages of railway employés; and (7) French money in circulation from 1795 to 1877.

In reply to circular from the Department of State, under date of 11th April, 1878, I have the honor to submit the following report:

In the absence of plans of statistics representing and detailing the various information for which it asks, I have made use of, as far as it has been practicable for the present, such compilations and individual instances as have been accessible and which might furnish the desired results.

1. DEPARTMENT OF THE SEINE.

That a comparative appreciation may be the more readily arrived at, I would respectfully beg to premise this report by giving some topographical and other statistics relating to the department of the Seine, in which this consulate-general is situated.

The department of the Seine is composed of 3 arrondissements, 28 cantons, 72 communes, 1,836 square miles, with a population (1876) of 2,400,849.

The 1st arrondissement is Paris; and is composed of 20 cantons, 1 commune, 132 square miles, with a population of 1,988,806.

The 2d arrondissement is St. Denis; and is composed of 4 cantons, 31 communes, 780 square miles, with a population of 237,852.

The 3d arrondissement is Lecaux; and is composed of 4 cantons, 40 communes, 924 square miles, with a population of 184,191.

a. Arrondissements and quarters of Paris.

No. of arrondissement.	No. of canton.	Quarters.	No. of quarters.	Acres.	Population in 1876.
1	......	St. Germain l'Auxerrois	1		9,114
		Halles	2		35,685
		Palais Royal	3		14,639
		Place Vendôme	4		12,460
	1	*Louvre*	......	469.50	71,898
2	......	Gaillon	5		9,786
		Vivienne	6		13,746
		Mail	7		21,713
		Bonne-Nouvelle	8		32,523
	2	*Bourse*	......	241	77,768
3	......	Arts et Metiers	9		26,670
		Enfants Rouges	10		21,025
		Archives	11		21,406
		Sainte Arvie	12		21,787
	3	*Temple*	......	286.50	90,797

a. Arrondissements and quarters of Paris—Continued.

No. of arrondissement.	No. of canton.	Quarters.	No. of quarters.	Acres.	Population in 1876.
4	......	Saint Merry	13		25, 617
		Saint Gervais	14		43, 216
		Arsenal	15		16, 219
		Notre Dame	16		13, 241
	4	*Hôtel de Ville*	......	387	98, 293
5	......	Sainte Victor	17		26, 621
		Jardin des Plantes	18		19, 501
		Val de Grâce	19		26, 702
		Sorbonne	20		31, 549
	5	*Panthéon*	......	615. 50	104, 373
6	......	Monnaie	21		19, 615
		Odeon	22		21, 326
		Notre Dame des Champs	23		40, 034
		St. Germain des Près	24		16, 156
	6	*Luxembourg*	......	521. 50	97, 631
7	......	St. Thomas d'Aquin	25		25, 257
		Invalides	26		13, 642
		Ecole Militaire	27		17, 606
		Gros Caillou	28		27, 167
	7	*Palais Bourbon*	......	995. 50	83, 672
8	......	Champs Elysées	29		8, 377
		Faubourg du Roule	30		18, 958
		Madeleine	31		25, 459
		Europe	32		31, 199
	8	*Elysées*	......	941	83, 993
9	......	St. Georges	33		34, 941
		Chaussée d'Antin	34		24, 137
		Faubourg Montmartre	35		23, 874
		Rochechouart	36		32, 737
	9	*Opera*	......	526. 50	115, 689
10	......	Saint Vincent de Paul	37		34, 140
		Porte Saint Denis	38		30, 361
		Porte Saint Martin	39		39, 316
		Hospital St. Denis	40		39, 147
	10	*Enclos Saint Laurent*	......	707	142, 964
11	......	Folie Mericourt	41		49, 595
		Saint Ambroise	42		40, 450
		La Roquette	43		59, 133
		Saint Marguerite	44		33, 109
	11	*Popincourt*	......	892	182, 287
12	......	Bel-Air	45		6, 369
		Picpus	46		30, 974
		Bercy	47		12, 976
		Quinze Vingts	48		43, 218
	12	*Reuilly*	......	1, 403. 50	93, 537
13	......	Salpêtrière	49		15, 119
		La Gare	50		24, 704
		Maison Blanche	51		23, 867
		Croulebarbe	52		8, 513
	13	*Gobelins*	......	1, 544. 50	72, 203
14	......	Mont Parnass	53		20, 123
		Santé	54		7, 385
		Petit Montrouge	55		15, 895
		Plaisance	56		32, 024
	14	*Observatoire*	......	1, 140. 50	75, 427

a. Arrondissements and quarters of Paris—Continued.

No. of arrondissement.	No. of canton.	Quarters.	No. of quarters.	Acres.	Population in 1876.
15	......	Saint Lambert	57		17,470
		Necker	58		27,980
		Grenelle	59		23,340
		Javelle	60		9,781
	15	*Vaugirard*	......	1,781.50	78,549
16	......	Auteuil	61		9,730
		La Muette	62		16,946
		Porte Dauphine	63		7,352
		Bassins	64		17,271
	16	*Passy*	......	1,752	78,599
17	......	Ternes	65		25,495
		Plaine Monceaux	66		15,708
		Batignolles	67		44,874
		Epinettes	68		30,605
	17	*Batignolles Monceaux*	......	1,099.50	116,682
18	......	Grand Carrieres	69		85,528
		Clignancourt	70		59,484
		Goutte d'Or	71		37,865
		La Chapelle	72		20,387
	18	*Butte Montmartre*	......	1,282.50	153,264
19	......	La Vilette	73		41,495
		Pont de Flandre	74		9,029
		Amerique	75		14,707
		Combat	76		33,136
	19	*Buttes Chaumont*	......	1,398.50	98,367
20	.....	Belleville	77		40,006
		Saint Fargeau	78		6,915
		Père Le Chaise	79		30,812
		Charonne	80		22,250
	20	*Meuilmontant*	......	1,287	100,083

b. Arrondissement, cantons, and communes of St. Denis.

Canton.	Population in 1876.	Communes.	Population in 1876.
Courbevoie	51, 850	Asnieres	8, 278
		Colombes	6. 640
		Courbevoie	11, 934
		Nauterre	4, 279
		Puteaux	12, 181
		Suresues	6, 140
		Geunevilliers	2. 389
Neuilly	82, 435	Boulogne	21, 556
		Clichy	17, 354
		Levallois Perret	22, 744
		Neuilly	20, 781
Pantin	35, 395	Bagnolet	2, 861
		Bobigny	972
		Bondy	2, 018
		Bourget (le)	1, 380
		Drancy	446
		Lilas (Les)	4, 411
		Noisy-le-Sec	3, 170
		Pantin	13, 065
		Pres St. Gervais (le)	4, 447
		Romainville	2, 025
Saint Denis	68, 172	Aubervilliers	14, 340
		Courneuve (La)	926
		Dugny	517
		Epinay	1, 698
		Ilé Saint Denis (d)	1, 350
		Pierrefitte	1, 151
		Saint Denis	34, 908
		Saint Ouen	11, 255
		Stains	1, 577
		Villetaneuse	450

Arrondissement, cantons, and communes of Sceaux.

Canton.	Population in 1876.	Communes.	Population in 1876.
Charenton	47, 068	Bonneuil	417
		Bry-sur-Marne	972
		Champigny	2, 813
		Charentin le Pont	8. 822
		Creteil	2, 965
		Joinville le Pont	2, 901
		Maisons Alfort	7, 619
		Nogeul-sur-Marne	7, 559
		Saint Mauer	8, 433
		Saint Maurice	4, 577
Sceaux	42, 636	Antony	1, 525
		Bagneaux	1, 509
		Bourg la Reine	2, 523
		Chatenay	982
		Chatillon	2, 060
		Clamart	3, 640
		Fontenoy aux Roses	2, 924
		Issy	9, 484
		Montrouge	6, 371
		Plessis Piquet	326
		Sceaux	2, 400
		Varnes	8, 812
Villejuis	47, 437	Arcueil	5, 209
		Chevilly	526
		Choisy le Roi	5, 821
		Fresnes	542
		Gentilly	10, 378
		Hay (L.)	671
		Ivry	15, 247
		Olly	689
		Rungis	232
		Thiais	1, 760
		Villejuij	2, 117
		Vitry	4, 155
Vincennes	47, 050	Fontenay sous Bois	4, 445
		Montreuil	13, 607
		Rosney	1, 924
		Sainte Maudé	7, 499
		Villemourble	1, 332
		Vincennes	18, 243

The total population of the department of the Seine is, as previously given, 2,410,849, of which 1,194,939 are males, and 1,215,910 are females; showing an excess of females over males of 20,971.

Table.

Males, unmarried	649,061
Males, married	497,412
Widowers	48,466
Total	1,194,939
Females, unmarried	563,347
Females, married	503,398
Widows	149,165
Total	1,215,910

Approximate area in acres of the agricultural territory of the department of the Seine, year 1875.

Farinaceous productions and grain	37,589
Market gardens	10,364
Manufactures	328
Meadows and pastures	6,726
Fallow land	32
Grape-vines	5,859
Woods and forests	3,457
Total	64,355
Uncultivated land	1,909
Agricultural territory	66,264
Area of roads	52,037

Approximate production of grain farinaceous products.

Wheat	cwt.	14,438
Mixed wheat and rye	do	48
Rye	do	5,483
Barley	do	108
Oats	do	18,021
Potatoes	do	85,113
Wine	gallons	2,509,005

Approximate number of farm animals, year 1875.

Horses	14,339
Mules	234
Asses	47
Bullocks and bulls	64
Cows and heifers	3,603
Calves	32
Sheep	4,390
Swine	2,699

Approximate animal production, year 1875.

Wool:		
Quantity	cwt.	846
Average price per pound		$0 18.16
Value		$17,520
Fat:		
Quantity	cwt.	14,204
Average price per pound		$0 09.8
Value		$144,320

Approximate production, year 1875.

Ordinary porcelain	$140,000
Fine porcelain	20,232
Chinaware	480,000
Glassware	2,400
Mirrors	208,000
Paper	277,080

Gas	$8,905,124
Candles	2,135,040
Soap	4,119,280
Refined sugar	43,692,000

Approximate force employed in spinning and weaving.

Description.	Number of establishments.	Number of work people.	Horse-power.
Cotton	9	844	372
Wool	8	296	34
Flax, hemp, and jute	3	153	45
Mixtures	13	273	39
Silk	1	148	61
Total	34	1,714	551

Of the number of salaried hands, about 75 per cent. of them have other trades and occupations, at which they work during the hours of the day and days of the year when they are not engaged in agricultural labor. Even those who are engaged permanently subserve their income by independent work, such as raising poultry, selling milk, eggs, and butter, and often by the produce of a garden or field spot which they cultivate in odd hours and in their own time.

In the department of the Seine, in the year of 1876, the average daily wages of an agricultural laborer was 90 cents, and in this same department the number of working days during the year is compiled as follows: Men, 275; women, 248; children, 173.

It should be noted that during the harvest months and vintage all agricultural hands receive greatly increased wages, in many instances double. The Government also permits the soldiers to help in the fields and vineyards during these seasons; this year their daily wages have been fixed at 34 cents per day.

FRENCH FARMING AND FARM LIFE.

In 1872 there were 18,513,325 individuals living upon the agricultural industry of France, divided as follows:

1. Proprietors cultivating or living upon their own lands	9,097,758
2. Planters or share farmers	1,428,881
3. Farmers, small owners	3,141,187
4. Hands permanently hired per annum	940,311
5. Temporary day laborers	3,255,618
6. Colliers and woodcutters	270,743
7. House-gardeners, market-gardeners, nurserymen	378,827
	18,513,325

The system of farming in France is unlike that pursued by the people in general in the United States. It may be stated as a communal system. Large land-owners rarely cultivate their own farms, but let them out to contractors, who in turn hire hands according to their wants, by the hour, day, or under contract for the season, or by the year, for their cultivation. Such demarkations as "line fences" are rarely seen in France, hence the properties of several land-owners are cultivated by the same contractors and by the same work people. The crops are not sown or planted according to dividing lines, but the whole property under contract is regarded as one farm, and cultivated accordingly. The lines of demarkation as to ownership of the land are usually made by stones set in the ground at fixed distances. It strikes the traveler as strange to see such vast areas of ground under cultivation with no dividing lines, and extending considerable distances from any habitation. In such localities there is usually a central village, which is, so to speak, entirely inhabited and supported by the various work people who have charge of the cultivation of these farms, and they radiate over them in every direction.

The life in these country (farm) villages is, in general, comfortable, well conducted, gay at times, and presents a good deal of picturesqueness at all seasons of the year. It is customary for families or bodies of farm hands to join together for the purpose of undertaking the sowing, planting, tending, or gathering of crops, which duties or occupation are called tasks, and for which they are paid by contract, either in kind or otherwise, as may be agreed.

Not only does the system of agricultural labor in France differ from that pursued by the people of the United States, but the existence of the agricultural laborer—that is to say, those who assist in the agricultural industry of France—is maintained, as before stated, by various other resources, so that there is a difficulty in establishing a complete comparison between the United States and French farm hands.

The department of the Seine can be scarcely regarded as an agricultural district, inasmuch as the produce of its fields and market-gardens, &c., is consumed at its own doors. Its commercial and industrial interests, which are mainly centered in the city of Paris, represent its importance.

The following information as to the wages of farm hands and their own expenses was received from a laboring hand:

3.—WAGES AND COST OF LIVING.

The average daily wages, without board, are as follows:

	Ordinary.	Maximum.	Minimum.
Men	$0 70	$1 00	$0 60
Women	50	60	25
Children, 12 to 16 years of age	30	45	20
Wages per month, with board.			
Men	$8 00	$10 00	$7 00
Women	6 00	7 00	5 00
Children, 12 to 16 years of age	4 00	5 00	4 00

The price of labor for men, without board, has advanced during the last five years about 40 per cent.; for women, about 40 per cent.; for children, 50 per cent. With board: For men, about 30 per cent.; for women, about 30 per cent.; for children, about 30 per cent.

For his necessaries of life he calculates as follows:

Bread	per pound..	3 cents.
Wine	per quart..	16 cents.
Beef	per pound..	12 cents.
Mutton	do......	12 cents.
Potatoes	do......	$1\frac{1}{4}$ cents.
Dried beans	per quart..	8 cents.
Cabbage	per piece..	2 to 3 cents.

His bill of fare per day:

First breakfast:

	Cents.
Wine	3
Bread	2
Total	5

Second breakfast:

	Cents.
Beef boiled in soup	8
One pint of wine	8
Bread	2
Cheese	2
Total	20

Dinner:

	Cents.
Ragout	8
One pint of wine	8
Bread	2
Cheese	2
Total	20
Total per day	45

It must be borne in mind that laborers in the vicinity of Paris are subject to greater expense than in more rural districts, and that they acquire a more expensive mode of living, eating and drinking at regular hours, and often supplementing their meals with plates according to their tastes, and with tobacco and coffee. Their further expense is estimated as follows: For room-rent, by month, 60 cents to $1.20; by year, $16 to $20. For washing, 20 to 25 cents per week; for clothing, $16 per year.

The foregoing information, having been received as individual, must not be regarded as local, and not as applying to the department of the Seine.

The nearest statistical information that I can arrive at gives the average daily wages in France at 45 cents, and the amount of the annual revenue of the typical French family, composed of father, mother, and five children, one of which is old enough to work, at $180. Their average annual expense is estimated as follows:

Bread	$60 40
Meat	17 60
Vegetables and fruit	11 00
Wine and beer	20 60
Milk and eggs	5 40
Salt and sugar	4 40
Rent and taxes	13 20
Fire and light	7 00
Clothing	18 00
Sundries	10 00
Total	167 60

The government statisticians are divided in opinion as to the per cent. of advance that has taken place during the past five years on the aggregate of wages and articles of consumption in France. The material for arriving at the precise average per cent., as well as the per cent. in individual instances, is not yet in hand. It is variously assumed to be 11.50 per cent., 15 per cent., and 20 per cent. Of course neither of these opinions can be proven until the statistics are in hand.

In different parts of France different modes are adopted for regulating both the value and expenses of the hired farm-hand. For instance, instead of calculating so much per annum in equal parts, the parts are calculated according to their value, but upon the rates of the annual amount, so that at the end of the year the agreed annual amount of wages is obtained.

4. *Statement showing the rates of wages of the several trades in Paris* (1875).*

Different industries.	Workmen's daily wages—						Length of time of apprenticeship.
	With board.			Without board.			
	Ordinary.	Maximum.	Minimum.	Ordinary.	Maximum.	Minimum.	
							Months.
Jewelers and goldsmiths	....	....	....	$1 30	$2 20	$1 10	60
Washing-women	†$0 80	†$1 40	†$0 40	60	70	50	30
Butchers	‡7 00	‡8 00	‡3 00	1 20	1 40	1 00	24
Bakers	....	....	....	1 33	2 00	68	....
Brewers	....	....	....	85	1 00	70	....
Bricklayers and tilemakers	....	....	....	66	99	55	....
Embroiderers	....	....	....	60	80	50	48
Quarrymen	....	....	....	80	90	70	....
Coachmakers	....	....	....	1 10	1 40	1 00	48
Charcoal-makers	‡7 00	‡8 00	‡6 00	80	1 00	70	....
Pork-butchers and dealers in cooked meats.	‡9 00	‡12 00	‡3 00	....	....	....	24
Hatters	....	....	....	1 30	1 80	80	6
Carpenters	....	....	....	1 20	1 30	1 10	....
Wheelwrights	50	54	40	1 00	1 10	80	36
Coppersmiths	....	....	....	1 10	1 80	90	48
Shoemakers of list and carpet matting	....	....	....	45	1 60	40	12
Ropemakers	....	....	....	80	1 00	60	....
Shoemakers	....	....	....	70	1 20	50	36
Corset-makers	....	....	....	40	70	30	24
Cutlers	....	....	....	1 10	1 50	90	36
Dressmakers	....	....	....	40	80	30	36
Slaters, tilers (roofmen)	....	....	....	1 20	1 25	1 10	36
Trousers-makers	....	....	....	80	1 20	60	24
Lacemakers	....	....	....	60	90	40	48
Cabinet-makers	....	....	....	1 00	1 10	90	48
Tinsmiths, lampmakers	....	....	....	80	2 00	60	36
Florists, or artificial flower-makers. — Men	....	....	....	1 00	1 60	80	36
Florists, or artificial flower-makers. — Women	‡10 00	‡20 00	‡5 00	60	70	30	36
Blacksmiths	....	....	....	1 30	1 80	60	....
Waistcoat-makers	....	....	....	60	80	40	24
Clock and watch makers	....	....	....	1 00	1 20	80	48
Printers	....	....	....	1 20	1 30	1 10	36
Gardeners	30	40	25	75	80	70	24
Lingéres, or needle-women	....	....	....	40	65	30	24
Masons	....	....	....	1 00	1 10	85	24
Horseshoers	50	50	40	1 00	1 10	80	....
Joiners	....	....	....	1 00	1 10	90	42
Milliners	‡12 00	‡30 00	‡5 00	....	....	....	24
Pastry-cooks	‡20 00	‡30 00	‡4 00	....	....	....	6
House-painters	....	....	....	1 20	1 30	1 00	....
Barbers and hairdressers	‡6 00	‡9 00	‡5 00	60	90	40	....
Stitchers of gaiter-boots	....	....	....	60	90	40	12
Plumbers	....	....	....	1 20	1 30	1 10	....
Stove and pipe makers	....	....	....	1 05	1 10	1 00	60
Potters	....	....	....	77	1 10	55	....
Bookbinders	....	....	....	1 10	1 20	1 00	....
Woodsawyers	....	....	....	1 00	1 05	90	....
Sculptors, ornamental	....	....	....	1 40	1 60	1 37	48
Saddlers and harness-makers	....	....	....	90	1 00	50	48
Locksmiths	....	....	....	90	1 20	80	36
Tailors, coatmakers	....	....	....	1 00	1 60	60	48
Stonecutters	....	....	....	1 20	1 40	1 10	....
Tanners	....	....	....	1 00	1 20	80	....
Carpet-makers	....	....	....	1 00	1 40	80	48
Dyers	‡15 00	‡20 00	‡10 00	90	1 40	70	42
Excavators for foundations, &c	....	....	....	77	80	70	....
Weavers	....	....	....	77	80	70	24
Coopers	‡8 00	‡10 00	‡6 00	1 00	1 20	80	24
Turners in wood	....	....	....	97	1 00	90	36
Turners in metals	....	....	....	1 20	1 40	1 10	36
Basket-makers	....	....	....	90	1 00	80	....

* This table of wages is taken from the Annuaire Statistique de la France, issued by the department of agriculture and commerce. One of the most striking features shown in this statement is the low wages paid to female labor—wages which makes it, in many cases, almost impossible for women to secure the bare necessaries of life. It may, however, be remarked that an improvement is going on in this regard, the difference between the wages of men and women in 1871 being 49 per cent., while in 1875 it had fallen to 28 per cent.—A. T. A. T.

† Per week. ‡ Per month.

4. *Statement showing the rates of wages of the several trades in Paris,* (1875)—Continued.

Different industries.	Workmen's daily wages— With board. Ordinary.	Maximum.	Minimum.	Without board. Ordinary.	Maximum.	Minimum.	Length of time of apprenticeship.
							Months.
Night-workmen (emptying water-closets, &c.)	....	....	....	$1 00	$1 40	$0 80	....
Glaziers	....	....	....	1 05	1 10	1 00	....
Men, average	....	....	....	80	1 01$\frac{3}{8}$	66	....
Women, average	....	....	....	56	82	40	....
General average	....	....	....	79$\frac{1}{8}$	1 01$\frac{3}{8}$	65$\frac{1}{8}$	....

Commercial and domestic annual salaries, 1875.

Description.	Paris. Ordinary.	Maximum.	Minimum.	Other cities in France. Ordinary.	Maximum.	Minimum.
Commercial						
Clerks in shops and stores, males	$240 00	$360 50	$200 00	$158 20	$255 60	$101 00
Cashiers in shops and stores, females, dames de comptoir	160 00	300 00	120 00	105 00	156 40	74 40
Clerks in shops and stores, females, demoiselles de boutique	80 00	120 00	40 00	81 40	118 60	55 60
Domestic.						
Men:						
Valets	120 00	200 00	80 00	73 80	101 80	57 10
House-servants	120 00	200 00	80 00	73 80	101 80	57 10
Coachmen	120 00	200 00	80 00	60 20	110 40	63 00
Women:						
Femmes de chambre	100 00	120 00	60 00	52 80	71 60	39 80
Maids, housemaids	100 00	120 00	60 00	52 80	71 60	39 80
Cooks	100 00	120 00	60 00	59 00	80 40	45 80
Maids of all work	100 00	120 00	60 00	60 00	77 80	46 20

5. WAGES PAID BY THE CITY OF PARIS.

The following tables are taken from the Série Officielle des Prix de la Ville de Paris, 1877–1878, issued by the Department of the Prefecture of the Seine. The government of the city of Paris, with rare exceptions, hires all labor by the hour, and not by the day, and it is also exacted that all workmen shall possess the tools and equipage or furniture of their trade. The prices which follow are termed Elementary and Composed. Elementary is an established base of price, and Composed is the price with what is called the "False expenses," "Profit," and "Advance of funds." The Composed price is the "Regulation price," and the foregoing added expenses are indifferently applicable, sometimes to labor, other times to tools, and again to equipage or furniture, which must be furnished by the workmen in their different branches of different trades.

Description.	Elementary price.	Composed price.
Foundations and other earth-works:	*Per hour.*	*Per hour.*
Excavation	$0 90	$0 10
Foreman	17	20
Drainer	13	16
Help to drainer	10	12
Masonry:		
Stonecutters, ornamental	16	20
Stonecutter	13	16
Stonelayer	14	18
Stonesetter (aid to stonelayer)	11	14
Mortar-man	10	13
Crowbar-laborers	10	15
Hand-barrow laborers	10	13
Mason or bricklayer (master)	13	16
Rough bricklayer, or aid to mason (journeyman)	08	10
Brickmaker (master)	15	19
Rough brickmaker, or aid to brickmaker (journeyman)	09	11
Rough-wall builder	10	13
Paving or pavement:		
Paving-man (master)	13	19
Paving-man, his aid (journeyman)	09	13
Carpenter-work:		
Carpenter	14	19
Sawyer	25	34
Roofing:	*Per day.*	*Per day.*
Roofer (master)	1 40	1 90
Roofer's aid (journeyman)	95	1 29
Man in the street to warn passers	70	95
Plumber:		
Plumber (master)	1 30	1 77
Plumber's aid (journeyman)	90	1 22
Borer, adjuster, &c	1 30	1 77
Introducing gas-pipes:		
Plumber	1 30	1 95
Plumber's aid	90	1 35
Setter	1 45	2 17
Joiner:		
Joiner	1 20	
Maker of inlaid floors	1 40	
Locksmiths:		
Blacksmith (large forge, furnace)	1 50	2 40
Striker or bellows-blower (large forge)	1 00	1 44
Blacksmith (small forge, furnace)	1 30	1 87
Striker (small forge, furnace)	90	1 30
Adjuster	1 20	1 73
Hanger of bells	1 30	1 87
Carpenter in iron-work	1 15	1 66
General aid	1 10	1 58
Borer	90	1 30
Ordinary workman	80	1 15
Heater	1 30	1 87
Fumistes:		
Fumistes, workers at chimneys (master)	1 20	1 66
Fumistes, workers at chimneys (journeymen)	70	97
	Per hour.	*Per hour.*
Fumistes, brickmaker for furnaces and factory chimneys (master)	13	18
Fumistes, brickmaker for furnaces and factory chimneys (journeyman)	09	12
Marble-work:	*Per day.*	*Per day.*
Marble-cutter	1 40	1 86
Marble-polisher	1 20	1 60
Stucco:		
Composition layer and cutter	1 50	1 95
Polisher	1 30	1 66
Painters:	*Per hour.*	*Per hour.*
Painter, summer and winter	13	17
Painter, night-work, from 10 p. m. to 6 a. m	19	26
Glaziers:		
Glaziers, summer and winter	14	19
Glaziers, night-work, from 10 p. m. to 6 a. m	21	28
Gilders:		
Gilders, summer and winter	16	20
Gilders, night-work, from 10 p. m. to 6 a. m.	32	40
Paper-hanging (wall-papering, &c.):		
Hanger, summer and winter	13	17
Hanger, night-work, from 10 p. m. to 6 a. m	18	26

NOTE.—The prices per day are average prices. A day's work is ten working hours; no difference between winter and summer. The workmen are paid by the hour at the rate of one-tenth of the price per day.

Description.	Elementary price.	Composed price.
Placing looking-glasses:	*Per day.*	*Per day.*
For workman, summer and winter	$1 20	$1 60
For workman, night-work, from 10 p. m. to 6 a. m.	....	2 40
Paving:	*Per hour.*	*Per hour.*
Paver (master)	12	15
Paver (journeyman)	08	10
Stone-chiseler	14	17
Granite:		
Granite-cutter	15	18
Granite-layer	12	14
Help to granite-layer	09	10
Asphalt bitumen:		
Workman who applies compressed asphalt	11	14
Workman who applies the flowing asphalt	11	14
Workman who helps to apply asphalt	08	10

6. Wages of railway employés.

I addressed a communication to the Compagnie des Chemins de Fer de Paris et Lyon et á la Mediterranée asking details upon the question of railway laborers. I received the following table, which I copy; but it appears to me that the information which it contains, for want of more detail and precision, is of limited practical use:

Wages paid to those employed by the Compagnie des Chemins de Fer de Paris et Lyons et á la Mediterranée.

Employés.	Annual wages.	Employés.	Annual wages.
Engine-drivers	$420 to $600	Freight and engine depot-masters	$920 to $1,200
Firemen	300 to 360	Heads of bureaus and chief clerks	400 to 800
Conductors	320 to 360	Clerks	240 to 360
Station-masters	260 to 1,400	Assistant clerks	180 to 240
Substation-masters	300 to 720	Telegraph clerks	240 to 330
Watchmen	240 to 330	Telegraph-station tenders	220 to 260
Baggage-master	300 to 480	Lamplighters and care of lamps	240 to 400
Man employed in the baggage department	240 to 320	Switchmen	240 to 320
Foremen over workmen	240 to 480	Controllers	300 to 600
Chief porters	270 to 480	Ticket-agents, men and women	270 to 600
Porters and servants	200 to 320	Greasers	200 to 260
Overseers over foremen of workmen	260 to 300	Ordinary workmen	180 to 252

I regret that more satisfactory statistics have not been found respecting agricultural labor, but from inquiries made I have reason to believe that the Government statisticians charged with this department will give the matter more interest in its details. The Government is in course of altering its manner of publishing its statistics, and it is possible that many branches of industry which have not been subjects of sifting inquiry may now receive its practical attention.

Before closing this report, which is already too lengthy to admit of more than a few brief reflections on my part, I would beg to call your attention to the disparagement which exists between the skilled labor of females and their domestic labor. Besides the wages of the domestic servants, they all receive a "pour bois." The "pour bois" of France has become a recognized "tax." A cook claims and receives from those with whom she deals a per cent. equal to 1 pound in 20 pounds, or 5 per cent., and on articles under 1 franc she usually receives 1 sou. The purchases made by the maid, the valet, the gardener, the coachman alike allow their "pour bois." Of course these remarks apply only where the servants have the charge of supplying their respective departments, and this they do in a majority of families well to do in Paris In many houses the amount received in "pour bois" becomes a handsome income and in all it is an item of importance. An inquiry made into this question would reveal how very much more the domestic "servant" acquires in her situation than does the average skilled female "laborer" acquire in her position.

FRENCH MONEY.

It is first remarked that the fundamental pieces of one centime, ten centimes, one franc, ten francs, one hundred francs advance in a tenfold manner; and, secondly, that they admit of only 5 and 2 as divisors. So that for francs the decimal multiples are the pieces of 2 francs, 5 francs, 10 francs, 20 francs, 50 francs, 100 francs; and for the centimes, the pieces of 1 centime, 2 centimes, 5 centimes, 10 centimes, 20 centimes, 50 centimes.

The ancient pieces of money, which were not decimal, the pieces of 25 centimes, 75 centimes, and 1 franc 50 centimes have been withdrawn from circulation. The piece of 40 francs, which is not decimal, is no longer manufactured, and the piece of 3 centimes has not been made.

The monetary convention concluded between France, Belgium, Italy, and Switzerland provides that they will not manufacture or allow to be manufactured any money in gold of any other standards than pieces of 100, 50, 20, 10, and 5 francs.

The foregoing pieces of money are received by the banks of contracting parties with the reservation to refuse them when their weight shall have fallen half per cent. below the recognized tolerance, or when the "impression" shall have disappeared.

Gold and silver in circulation from 1795 *to December* 31, 1877, *and of copper money from* 1852 *to December* 31, 1877.—The copper money issued according to the law of May 6, 1852, has been of the metal produced by the melting of the ancient copper which was withdrawn from circulation.

a. Amount of money in gold coined in France from 1795 *to December* 31, 1877.

(Gold value nominal.)

	Francs.
100-franc pieces	44,346,400
50-franc pieces	46,568,700
40-franc pieces	204,432,360
20-franc pieces	6,708,899,220
10-franc pieces	1,013,641,610
5-franc pieces	233,440,130
Total	8,251,328,420

b. Amount of silver coined from 1795 *to December* 31, 1877.

	Francs.
5-franc pieces	5,058,784,820.00
2-franc pieces	152,088,526.00
1-franc pieces	193,547,902.00
50-centime pieces	89,785,394.00
25-centime pieces	7,671,101.25
20-centime pieces	8,232,700.60
Total	5,510,131,443.85

RECAPITULATION.

Gold and silver.

	Total amount manufactured.	Amount deducted, demonetized.	Balance in circulation since 1795.
	Francs.	*Francs.*	*Francs.*
Gold	8, 506, 509, 560. 00	71, 082, 860. 00	8, 435, 426, 700
Silver	5, 510, 131, 443. 85	222, 166, 304. 25	5, 287, 965, 139
Total	14, 016, 641, 003. 85	293, 249, 164. 25	13, 723, 391, 839

The 71,082,860 francs gold money were retired from circulation in pieces of small coins. The 222,166,304.25 francs silver money were retired from circulation in pieces of 25 centimes, 2 francs, 1 franc, 50 centimes, and 20 centimes.

c. Amount of copper money manufactured since the melting ordered by the law of May 6, 1852.

	Francs.
10-centime pieces	33, 236, 024. 20
5-centime pieces	26, 470, 607. 25
2-centime pieces	1, 848, 646. 52
1-centime pieces	1, 147, 517. 43
Total to December 31, 1877	62, 702, 785. 40

Of the sum of 13,723,391,839.60 francs in circulation since 1795, it is estimated that, in round numbers, 8,000,000,000 francs are now in circulation.

A. T. A. TORBERT.

UNITED STATES CONSULATE-GENERAL,
Paris, June 21, 1878.

ROUEN.

Report, by Commercial-Agent Rhodes, on labor and wages in the district of Rouen.

The daily wages paid in the manufactories of Rouen and vicinity are as follows:

Workers.	Ordinary.	Maximum.	Minimum.
Cotton-spinners:			
Men	$0 75	$1 04	$0 60
Women	40	60	35
Children under 15	25	35	20
Cotton-weavers:			
Men	65	80	45
Women	47	64	40
Children under 15	25	30	20
Wool-spinners:			
Men	80	1 00	60
Women	40	50	30
Children under 15	19	25	14
Shawl-weavers:			
Men	1 00	1 30	80
Oil-cloth:			
Men	55	60	40
Women	30	40	25
Children under 15	20	25	15
Linen and hempen goods.			
Spinners:			
Men	60	75	50
Women	40	50	30
Children under 15	12	25	10
Weavers:			
Men	46	60	35
Women	40	57	31
Children under 15	20	25	16

The manufacture of cotton goods is the principal one of Rouen, and the wages paid the employés thereon represent the average. The salary of a day laborer is, when fed and lodged, ordinary, 29 cents; maximum, 33 cents; minimum, 22 cents. When not fed nor lodged, ordinary, 55 cents; maximum, 70 cents; minimum, 45 cents. The labor is generally done by those who provide their own board and lodging. As will be observed, the wages of those who board and lodge themselves is about double that of those who are boarded and lodged by their employers.

The average wages in the trades is as follows, per diem:

	Cents.
Jewelers	66
Butchers	54
Bakers	64
Brewers	61
Brickmakers	53
Tinsmiths	60
Gardeners	52
Blacksmiths	58
Plumbers	65
Coachmakers	64
Carpenters	69
Hatters	62
Tanners	58
Cutlers	52
Printers	66
Masons	63
Painters	64
Bookbinders	54
Dyers	56

These figures are gathered from town, village, and country, and are low when compared to the wages paid in Paris. For instance, the wages paid in Paris to the following mechanics are as follows: Bakers, $1.33; brewers, $1.05; brickmakers, 66 cents; hatters, $1.30; carpenters, $1.18.

The same difference exists in the other trades, and is accounted for by the difference in the cost of living between Paris and the provinces and in the more intelligent demands for the comforts of life of the Parisian workmen.

Workwomen receive as follows, per diem: Washwomen, 32 cents; seamstresses, 30 cents; corset-makers, 30 cents; tailoresses, 31 cents; laceworkers, 34 cents; artificial florists, 35 cents. In consequence of these very inadequate wages, these women are poorly fed and housed.

Shoptenders.—The wages in the retail shops of Rouen, per annum, are as follows, ordinary, maximum, and minimum: Men, $110, $160, and $60; women accountants, $80, $130, and $50; saleswomen, $70, $110, and $50.

Domestics.—The annual wages of domestics, lodged and fed, are as follows, ordinary, maximum, and minimum: Valets and footmen, $100, $150, and $60; coachmen and grooms, $120, $160, and $70; chambermaids, $70, $92, and $40; women cooks, $80, $85, and $50; general house-women, $80, $90, and $50.

I propose, in a future communication, to speak of the condition of the cotton interest of Rouen, which is called the Manchester of France.

ALBERT RHODES.

UNITED STATES COMMERCIAL AGENCY,
Rouen, September 13, 1878.

ST. ETIENNE.

Report, by Commercial-Agent Grinnell, on the rates of wages and condition of trade in St. Etienne.

Referring to the circular letter of the Department, dated April 11, I have been careful in collecting and sifting information from such sources as were open to me. I have labored under certain disadvantages, as, for example, the prefet will not recognize or show common civility to a "commercial agent." It is through the prefet and the bureaus under his control only that I could have obtained official figures for the laborers on public works and the manufacture of arms.

I have, however, from several sources gathered the following, comprising all the information demanded by the circular letter with the above exceptions:

1. *Farm hands* get 45 to 60 cents per day, boarding themselves; their lodging costs $2.50 to $3 per month, and food and wine $9 to $10 per month. Average received, $15.60; average cost living, $12.75; surplus, $2.85.

2. *Mechanical laborers.*—Weavers of plain common ribbons, 40 to 50 cents per day; weavers of plain better grade ribbons, 60 to 70 cents per day; weavers of fancy ribbons, 80 to 90 cents per day; and weavers of novelties, the best, $1.40 to $1.80 per day.

3. Women, who do most of the work in the manufacture of ribbons other than weaving, receive for work in finishing and preparing for market 50 to 65 cents per day, and the less skillful 30 to 40 cents per day.

4. *Miners.*—Those working under ground receive from $1.05 to $1.15 per day, and those above ground from 65 to 75 cents per day.

Business is very good in this district (business with the United States excepted), especially so with Paris and France, also with Germany and England.

There is an appreciation in the cost of living of about 10 per cent. as compared with five to seven years ago. No progress whatever is made toward improvement. Everything remains as it has been. No improvement in looms, or in manner of doing business, or in anything.

WILLIAM F. GRINNELL.

UNITED STATES COMMERCIAL AGENCY,
St. Etienne, June 19, 1878.

GERMANY.

BARMEN.

Report, by Consul Stanton, on the (1) *condition of the laboring classes;* (2) *rates of wages;* (3) *cost of living;* (4) *state of trade;* (5) *current money of the Empire; and* (6) *the business habits and systems; and a supplemental report on agriculture and railway labor; for the district of Barmen, embracing Westphalia and a portion of the Rhine provinces.*

1. CONDITION OF LABORING CLASSES.

The condition of the laboring classes of the mining and iron industries is very distressing; indeed, could not well be otherwise when the price of iron manufactures is so low that nothing can be earned, and the cost of coal is more than 40 per cent. below the average of the last twenty-five years. In consequence whereof wages were reduced and many hands discharged. Many mines were worked but four or five days per week, and miners in an eight hour shift were unable to earn enough to procure the necessaries of life. Many struggle daily with bitter want. Of the hands discharged the less skillful and the communistically inclined were the first to go, but in many districts even the more skillful had to be discharged, and many manufacturers were forced by circumstances to sever a connection with their workmen of over twenty-five years' standing.

A fruitful cause of want and ruin among the laboring classes is the enormous increase of the drinking saloons and dancing halls, and the complaints are universal as to the disposition of the laborers to indulge in excessive drink. In general, the present condition of the laboring classes in Germany is an unenviable one. Notwithstanding the efforts made by manufacturers to retain them, and the great sacrifices to the factories running, the long-continued depression has put a limit even to the greatest generosity, and large numbers of laborers are without work. In this district it is at present difficult, if not impossible, for a workingman to earn more than he needs for his individual support, and his weekly receipts are, on the average, by no means adequate for the support of a family. It is, consequently, essential that every member of the family should contribute to the common fund, and hence, from their earliest years, each member is raised to incessant toil and every privation.

The diet of the workingman is scant, and meat is a luxury seldom indulged in more than once a week, whilst the daily allowance for beer and spirits too often curtails that which should furnish a wholesome meal. The workingmen are also inveterate smokers, and the pipe or cigar is seldom out of their mouths. So wide-spread has this habit become, particularly among the youthful members of society, that the authorities of a number of cities have passed ordinances forbidding the use of tobacco in public places to youths under sixteen years.

Whatever be the characteristic of the laborer in other parts of Germany, in this and the neighboring districts he is, as a rule, improvident and quarelsome. The towns are, in consequence, heavily burdened by poor-rates; the municipal assessments within this consular district ranging from 5½ to 7 times the amount of the imperial rates.

2. Rates of wages.

German Empire.—For agricultural laborers the rate of wages varies greatly throughout the German Empire, rising or falling according as the locality is near to or remote from manufacturing centers. To exemplify this, I give below the present (1878) rate of wages for various parts of Germany, viz:

	Daily wages.
Bremen and vicinity	Cts. 56
Bavarian Highlands	53
Upper Rhine Valley	41
Lower Rhine Valley	31
Lake Constance and environs	40
Lower Highlands	33
Upper Alsace	45
Oppeln, Silesia	18

The wages now paid throughout this consular district, embracing Westphalia and a portion of the Rhine provinces, are as follows, viz:

Barmen and Crefeld.

Machinists, lock, wagonsmiths	daily	$0 51 to	$0 71
Navvies and day laborers	do		47
Saddlers and shoemakers	do		47
Journeymen tailors	do		52
Coppersmiths, plumbers, and plasterers	do	59 to	71
Carpenters, joiners, and masons	do	59 to	71
Bakers, with board and lodging	weekly	1 42 to	2 14
Bakers, without board and lodging	daily		59
Butchers, without board and lodging	do		59
Butchers, with board and lodging	weekly	1 66 to	2 14
Brewers, with board and lodging	do		2 14
Brewers, without board and lodging	do		4 28
Master brewers	do	6 42 to	10 71
Malsters, with board and lodging	do		3 57
Farm hands, with board and lodging (males)	yearly	107 00 to	215 00
Farm hands, with board and lodging (females)	do	28 00 to	36 00
Cooks, with board and lodging (female)	do	36 00 to	43 00
Cooks, with board and lodging (male), from $107 on (yearly), according to merit.			
Housemaids, with board and lodging	yearly	28 00 to	35 00
Painters and glaziers	daily		59
Hack-drivers	do.		71
Hack-drivers, with board and lodging	weekly		2 14
Furriers and tanners	do		3 57
Weavers and factory hands	do	2 50 to	3 57
Chimney-sweeps	daily		59

The Rhenish Railway pay the following wages for work now (1878) in course of construction:

Common laborer on day work	daily	$0 56 to	$0 64
Common laborer on piece work	do	71 to	83
Masons and miners on tunnel work	do	71 to	83
Masons and miners on tunnel work, piece work	do		95

Crefeld-Düsseldorf.

Mechanics, blacksmiths, and miners	daily		$0 65
Carpenters, bricklayers, and plasterers	do	$0 70 to	85
(Wages are about 24 per cent. less than formerly; working time from 10 to 12 hours daily.)			
Painters	per hour		05
Shoemakers are paid by the piece, and can earn with 12 hours daily work	per week		3 60
Agricultural laborers get—			
Male servants, with board and lodging	yearly	63 00 to	70 00
Female servants, with board and lodging	do	43 00 to	50 00
Day hands, with meals	daily	28 to	38
Day hands, without meals	do	48 to	60

(The present rates are about 20 per cent. under those of former years.)

Silk-weavers earn from $2.15 to $2.85 per week per loom. Married weavers have generally more than one loom, and in such cases receive one-third of the earnings of the extra looms for their supervision, the other two-thirds being the wages of those working the looms.

The wages of silk-weavers are at present extremely low, they being able to earn double the present amount in good times. Female operatives in factories earn weekly $2.15; children, $1; in good times the earnings are 80 per cent. higher.

Münster and agricultural districts.

Factory hands earn daily	$0 65
Day laborers earn daily	59
Field-hands earn daily	53
Artisans and mechanics earn daily	71

3. FOOD PRICES AND COST OF LIVING.

a. Food prices.

The cost of the various articles of food are shown in the following table during the years 1865–1877, in the district of Barmen-Elberfeld:

Average food-prices in Barmen-Elberfeld during the last thirteen years.

Article.		1865.	1866.	1867.	1868.	1869.	1870.	1871.	1872.	1873.	1874.	1875.	1876.	1877.
Wheat	per cwt.	$2 15	$2 60	$3 39	$3 14	$2 49	$2 73	$3 11	$2 97	$3 32	$3 17	$2 48	$3 45	$3 45
Rye	do.	1 61	1 90	2 52	2 47	2 09	2 16	2 41	2 16	2 40	2 50	2 14	2 02	1 95
Barley	do.	1 56	1 98	2 29	2 20	2 00	2 07	2 24	2 02	2 38	2 61	2 30	2 38	2 38
Oats	do.	1 59	1 84	2 04	2 22	2 07	2 01	2 15	1 66	2 13	2 38	2 20	1 90	2 38
Pease	do.	1 95	2 02	2 53	2 64	2 64	2 69	2 93	2 63	2 73	3 40	3 50	3 14	3 14
Beans	do.	......	......	......	3 02	2 85	3 01	3 21	2 90	2 97	3 57	3 57	3 14	3 14
Lentils	do.	......	......	......	2 97	2 98	3 27	......	3 33	3 21	4 76	5 35	3 57	3 69
Potatoes	do.	64	71	96	88	73	91	1 00	90	95	95	95	77	83
Straw	do.	62	67	56	73	81	74	06	71	83	95	83	83	95
Hay	do.	1 03	83	71	91	1 05	1 23	1 12	83	83	95	1 19	70	1 31
Beef, rump cuts	per pound.	12¾	12¾	13¼	13¼	12¾	13	14	16⅓	19	19	17¾	17¾	18
Beef, belly cuts	do.	......	......	......	......	......	......	......	15¼	15½	16	16	17	17
Pork	do.	13	14¾	16¾	17	16½	16⅓	16½	16½	17½	19	19	19	19
Mutton	do.	10	10½	11	9½	12	12	12	13	14⅓	15¼	14½	15	16¾
Veal	do.	10½	10	10¼	9¾	9½	10½	10¾	12	14	13	12	12 to 16	12 to 17
Bacon	do.	......	......	......	......	......	......	......	19	20	19	19	20	20
Butter	do.	24	23	22¾	25	27	25	28	28	33	33	32	35	35
Hog's lard	do.	......	......	......	......	......	......	......	19	20	20	20	20	21
Eggs	per 25.	24	27	28	31	32	33	37	39	40	40	28	35 to 45	35 to 45
Wheat-flour, prime	per pound.	......	......	......	......	......	......	......	04½	05	04¾	04	04	04
Rye-flour, prime	do.	......	......	......	......	......	......	......	03¾	04	03¾	03½	03	03
Scotch barley	do.	......	......	......	04	03½	03½	......	04¾	05	05¼	05¾	05¼	05¾
Pearl barley	do.	......	......	......	......	......	......	......	04¾	05	04¾	05	04¾	05
Buckwheat groats	do.	......	......	......	......	......	......	......	04	03⅘	04	04	......	......
Millet	do.	......	......	......	......	......	......	......	05	05	05	05	......	......
Rice, Java	do.	......	......	......	05	04½	04½	04	06	06	06	05	05 to 09	05 to 09
Coffee, medium Java	do.	......	......	......	31	33	31	30	28	32	33	32	32	32
Cooking-salt	do.	......	......	......	......	......	......	......	02	02	02	02	02	02
Oaten groats	do.	......	......	......	......	......	......	......	04¾	04¾	05¾	05¼	05⅛	05¼
White bread	do.	......	......	......	......	......	......	......	03⅗	04	04	03	05	05

Food-prices in Münster, April, 1878.

Pease	per cwt	$3 54	Beef	per kilo	$0 27
Beans	do	3 42	Suet	do	33
Rice	do	95 5	Mutton	do	24
Barley	do	5 95	Bacon	do	40
Potatoes	do	1 17			

b. Cost of living.

For a man and wife, with two or three children, the yearly cost is about $275. Such a family would live in two or three rooms, and would naturally live in a poor and comfortless manner. As many of the family as are able would be obliged to work ten to twelve hours daily.

The following detailed estimate of the expenses of a family of six persons, viz, man, wife, and four children, is, I think, rather high; for, as will be seen from the accompanying tables, few families would be in a position to gain a weekly income of $7.

Estimate of the expenses of a family of six—viz, two adults and four children—per week.

Flour and bread	$0 90	Fruits, green and dried	$0 07
Meat, fresh, corned, salted, and smoked	1 09	Fuel	23
Lard	19	Oil and light	23
Butter	56	Sundries	12
Cheese	7	Spirits, beer, and tobacco	35
Sugar and sirup	7	House rent	90
Milk	12	Religious objects (schools are free)	12
Coffee	28	Total weekly expenditure	6 19
Fish, fresh and salted	7		
Soap, starch, salt, pepper, vinegar	12	Clothing for year	55 00
Eggs	9	Taxes for year	2 50
Potatoes and other vegetables	70		

By way of comparison, I subjoin the estimate of a factory inspector in Silesia of the expenses of a family of five persons, two adults and three children under fourteen years, which I think is more correct than the preceding one, viz:

Bread		$33 55	Shoes	$16 66
Potatoes		38 55	Furniture	14 28
Vegetables		17 13	Taxes	2 85
Meat and fat		59 79	Club and burial-society subscriptions, &c	6 66
Coffee and sugar		25 70	Rent	14 28
Luxuries: beer, spirits, and tobacco		17 13	Lights and fire	5 00
Clothing, husband	$13 09			
wife	8 33		Total yearly expenses	283 65
children	10 47		Total weekly expenses	5 47
		31 89		

This estimate is as low as it is possible to make it, and, as will be seen by a reference to the table of wages, few of the men earn enough to pay the expenses of such a family. The amount allowed for rent in the above estimate is much too small for Barmen, where for $14.28 only two small garret chambers could be obtained. Here, according to the location in house, the rent of one to three rooms would be from $14.28 to $60.

For the purpose of comparison, I inclose the following tables of the wages paid in Barmen during the eleven years, 1865–1875. The tables are full, and explain themselves.

The cost of living has not varied much in the last few years, the chief difference being that the weekly receipts of the laborer do not suffice to meet his expenses, not because the wages are reduced, or living costs more, but owing to the extensive depression in all branches of trade, which prevents him doing *a full week's work.*

Family wages.

The following tables show the earnings of workmen's families, whose several members were employed in one and the same factory, either on factory or house work. The wages are exactly what was paid, and have been taken from the wages-books of factories in Barmen:

Description.	1873.			1874.	
	Family.			Family.	
	A.	B.	C.	A.	B.
First week:					
Man	$3 92	$3 92	$5 82	$3 92	$5 12
Wife	....	2 97	....	3 57	2 85
Daughter	3 21	3 33	3 09	4 16	3 09
Do	1 78	....	2 85	....	2 38
Do	....	....	2 50	....	....
Total income	8 91	10 22	14 26	11 65	13 44
Second week:					
Man	3 92	3 92	3 57	3 92	5 83
Wife	....	3 57	....	4 52	3 39
Daughter	2 30	3 21	3 09	4 28	3 09
Do	2 30	....	2 85	....	3 03
Do	....	....	2 50	....	....
Total income	8 52	10 70	12 01	12 72	15 34
Third week:					
Man	3 92	3 92	2 61	3 92	5 00
Wife	....	1 90	....	3 92	3 33
Daughter	2 15	3 35	3 33	4 04	3 21
Do	1 50	....	3 33	....	3 39
Do	....	....	2 50	....	....
Total income	7 57	9 17	11 77	11 88	14 93
Fourth week:					
Man	3 92	3 92	5 00	3 92	4 28
Wife	....	2 50	....	4 64	3 09
Daughter	3 33	3 21	2 85	4 16	2 97
Do	2 38	....	2 85	....	3 09
Do	....	....	2 85	....	....
Total income	9 63	9 63	13 55	12 72	13 43

The total income in 1873 in a branch which had but little demand was for—

Family B:

Man	$222 76
Wife	162 07
Daughter	149 94
Do	....
Do	....
Total income	534 77

Family C:

Man	242 76
Wife	....
Daughter	160 75
Do	149 94
Do	124 95
Total income	678 40

Branch of business.	Weekly					
	1865.	1866.	1867.	1868.	1869.	1870.
Turkey-red yarn-dyers:						
I. Journeymen	....	....	....	....	....	....
II. Journeymen	$3 09	$3 45	$3 21	$3 21	$3 21	$3 57
Apprentices	1 42	1 66	1 78	1 78	1 78	1 90
Female hands	1 42	1 66	1 78	1 78	1 78	1 90
Color-dyers:						
Journeymen	3 09	3 57	3 57	3 57	3 57	3 92
Apprentices	1 42	1 78	1 78	1 78	1 78	2 14
Female hands	1 42	1 78	1 78	1 78	1 78	2 14
Do	2 14	2 14	2 14	....	....	....
Finishing works and piece dyers:						
Finishers	4 28	5 00	5 00	5 00	5 00	5 35
Assistants	2 50	2 85	2 85	2 85	2 85	3 09
Piece dyers	2 73	2 85	3 09	3 21	3 33	3 57
Apprentices	1 42	1 78	2 14	2 14	2 14	2 38
Bleaching-works:						
Journeymen	2 66	2 85	3 21	3 21	3 21	3 57
Apprentices	1 25	1 42	1 60	1 60	1 60	1 90
Knitting, sewing, and glazed yarn works:						
Journeymen	4 28	4 28	4 28	4 28	4 28	4 64
Do	3 80	3 80	3 80	3 80	3 80	4 04
Female operatives	2 14	2 14	2 14	2 14	2 14	2 38
Do	1 78	1 78	1 78	1 78	1 78	2 14
Youthful operatives	1 78	1 78	1 78	1 78	1 78	2 14
Silk manufactories:						
Operatives on Jacquard looms	2 85–4 28	2 85–4 28	2 85–4 28	2 85–4 28	2 85–4 28	2 85–4 28
Operatives on pedal looms for plain work.	1 42–2 85	1 42–2 85	1 42–2 85	1 42–2 85	1 42–2 85	1 42–2 85
Zanilla and lasting weavers:						
Journeymen	2 85	3 21	3 57	3 92	3 92	4 28
Do	2 85	2 85	2 85	3 57	3 57	3 80
Female operatives	2 50	2 50	2 50	2 50	2 50	2 50
Girls	2 14	2 14	2 14	....	....	....
Silk and woolen braid and binding works:						
I. Masters—						
On ordinary articles	5 71	5 71	5 71	5 71	5 71	5 71
On medium articles	8 56	8 56	8 56	8 56	8 56	8 56
On best fashionable articles	14 28	14 28	14 28	14 28	14 28	14 28
II. Small-braid makers:						
Journeymen	2 50–3 57	2 50–3 57	2 50–3 57	2 50–3 57	2 50–3 57	2 85–3 92
Female operatives	2 14	2 14	2 14	2 14	2 14	2 50
Do	2 50	2 50	2 50	2 50	2 50	2 61
III. Factory hands:						
Male	2 50–2 85	2 50–2 85	2 50–2 85	2 50–2 85	2 50–2 85	2 85–3 21
Female	2 14	2 14	2 14	2 14	2 14	2 14–2 50

IV. Small-braid makers, with their own braiding-machines.

Cost of loom, $1,285.20.		
Weekly earnings		$17 85
Expenses:		
Assistants	$2 85	
One-third reeler	71	
Rent and power	1 78	
Oil	71	
	1 07	
		7 12
Remains for master		10 73
From which interest and amortisation of capital must be paid.		

REMARKS.—The great wear on the machines, the frequent change in the article, together with the erecting looms on their own premises. Wages vary largely with the state of business.

Branch of business.	Weekly					
	1865.	1866.	1867.	1868.	1869.	1870.
Cotton and linen braids and bindings:						
I. Master's on own looms or braiding-machines.	$2 85–4 28	$4 28	$3 92	$3 92	$3 92	$4 28
II. Factory hands:						
Journeymen	2 14–2 61	2 14–2 61	2 14–2 61	2 85	2 85	2 85–3 57
Female operatives	1 78	1 78	1 78	1 90	1 90	2 14
Youthful hands	71–1 42	71–1 42	71–1 42	....	....	....

wages.					Remarks.
1871.	1872.	1873.	1874.	1875.	
....	$4 28-5 00	$4 28-5 35	$4 28-5 71	$5 64-6 42	For piece-work; 10 hours' actual work.
$3 92-4 28	4 28	4 52	4 52	4 52	Weekly wages; 11 hours' actual work.
2 14-2 50	2 50	2 50-2 85	2 50-2 85	2 50-2 85	
. 2 14	2 50	2 50-2 85	2 50-3 21	2 50-3 92	
4 28	4 28	4 52	4 64	4 64	Weekly wages; 11 hours' actual work.
2 14-2 85	2 38-2 85	2 38-2 85	2 38-2 85	2 38-2 85	
2 38	2 14-2 85	2 14-2 85	2 14-2 85	2 14-2 85	
....	....	....	....	....	Piece-work.
5 35	4 40	4 52	5 18	5 71	Weekly wages. Hours of work from 6 a. m. to 8 p. m., with 2 hours' pause.
3 33	3 33	3 09	3 80	3 80	
4 28	....	....	....	....	
2 50	....	....	....	....	
3 92	4 28	4 52	4 64	4 64	Weekly wages; 11 hours' actual work.
2 02	2 02	3 14	2 14	2 14	
4 64	4 64	4 64	4 64	4 64	Piece-work. Hours of work from 6 a. m. to 8 p. m, with 2 hours' pause.
4 04	4 04	4 04	4 04	4 04	Weekly wages.
2 38	2 50	2 85	2 85	2 85	Piece-work.
2 14	2 14	2 50	2 50	2 50	Weekly wages.
2 14	2 14	2 14	2 14	2 14	Weekly wages. If under 14 years, half a day.
2 85-5 00	2 85-5 00	2 85-5 00	2 85-5 00	2 85-5 00	Piece-work; time uncertain, since men work on own looms at home. Combs, reeds, Jacquards, &c., are furnished by manufacturer.
1 42-3 21	1 88-3 57	1 88-3 57	1 88-3 57	1 88-3 57	
4 28-6 42	3 92-7 14	3 92-7 14	3 92-7 14	3 92-7 14	Piece-work. Hours of work from 6 a. m. to 7 p. m., with 1½ to 2 hours' pause.
3 92-5 00	3 21-4 28	3 21-4 28	3 21-4 28	3 21-4 28	Weekly wages.
2 85-4 28	2 50-4 28	2 50-4 28	2 50-4 28	2 50-4 28	Piece-work.
....	....	....	....	....	Weekly wages.
5 71	5 71	5 71	5 71	5 71	Piece-work. The journeymen participate, with 40 p.c., and the reeler, earning on the average $2.14 to $2.50 weekly, are also to be paid. One can tend 2 and 3 looms.
8 56	7 14	7 14	7 14	7 14	
14 28-17 25	8 56	8 56	8 56	8 56	
3 21-3 92	3 57-4 04	3 57-4 04	3 57-4 04	3 57-4 04	Weekly wages; 12 hours' actual work.
2 50-2 85	2 50-2 85	2 50-2 85	2 50-2 85	2 50-2 85	
2 85	2 85	2 85	2 85	2 85	
3 21-3 92	3 92-4 04	3 92-4 04	3 92-4 04	3 92-4 04	Weekly wages; 10½ hours' actual work.
2 50-2 85	2 50-2 85	2 50-2 85	2 50-2 85	2 50-2 85	

Cost of loom, $1,428.

Weekly earnings		$17 85
Expenses:		
Assistants	$3 57	
One-third reeler	83	
Rent and power	2 14	
Oil	71	
	1 07	
		8 32
Remains for master		9 53

From which interest and the amortisation of capital must be paid.

amount of capital necessary, are gradually ruining the small masters, so that the larger firms are now

wages.					Remarks.
1871.	1872.	1873.	1874.	1875.	
$4 64	$4 28-4 64	$4 28-4 64	$4 28-4 64	$4 28-4 64	Piece-work; 12 hours' actual work; wages for reeling woof, paid therefrom, amount to about $0.71 weekly.
2 85-3 57	3 21-3 92	3 21-3 92	3 21-3 92	3 21-3 92	Weekly wages; 12 hours' actual work.
2 32	1 00-2 50	1 00-2 50	1 90-2 50	1 90-2 50	
....	....	....	....	....	

Statement showing the rate of wages paid in Barmen

Branch of business.	Weekly					
	1865.	1866.	1867.	1868.	1869.	1870.
Elastic webbing works:						
I. Laborers in mechanical weaving—						
Journeymen	$3 21	$3 33	$3 39	$3 57	$3 57	$3 92
Weekly wages for adjusting	3 21	3 21	3 21	3 21	3 57	3 57
Lowest piece-work wages	3 57	3 57	3 57	3 57	3 57	4·64
Highest piece-work wages	7 85	7 85	7 85	5 00	6 06	6 42
	2 50–3 03	2 50–3 03	2 50–3 03	2 61	2 73	2 73–2 97
Female operatives	2 14	2 14	2 14	2 50–3 21	2 50–3 21	2 50–3 21
Youthful hands	1 78–2 14	1 78–2 14	1 78–2 14	1 78–2 26	1 78–2 26	1 78–2 26
II. Factory hands—						
Journeymen (Bindstube)	2 85–4 28	2 85–4 28	2 85–4 28	2 85–4 28	2 85–4 28	2 85–5 00
Journeymen, warp-room (Scheerkammer.)	2 14–3 21	2 14–3 21	2 14–3 21	2 14–3 21	2 14–3 57	2 14–3 57
Female reelers	1 78	1 90	2 14	2 14	2 14	2 14
III. Outside hands—						
Masters	5 71–11 42	5 71–11 42	5 71–11 42	5 71–11 42	5 71–11 42	5 71–11 42
Journeymen reelers (Handspuler.)	1 06–1 78	1 06–1 78	1 06–1 78	1 06–1 42	1 06–1 42	1 06–1 42
Journeymen reelers (Spuler mit Spulemachine.)	1 42–2 85	1 42–2 85	1 42–2 85	2 14–3 21	2 14–3 21	2 14–3 21
Soap and candle works:						
Male hands	2 85	2 85	2 85	2 85	2 85	2 85
Female hands	1 66	1 66	1 66	1 66	1 66	1 66
Chemical works:						
Men at smelting furnace	4 76	4 76	4 76	4 76	4 76	4 76
Men at iron pyrites furnace	3 92	3 92	3 92	3 92	3 92	3 92
Men at sulphur furnace	3 92	3 92	3 92	3 92	3 92	3 92
Men on other apparatus	3 33–3 92	3 33–3 92	3 33–3 92	3 33–3 92	3 33–3 92	3 33–3 92
Mechanics	3 57–3 68	3 57–3 68	3 57–3 68	3 57–3 68	3 92	4 04
Carters	3 21	3 21	3 21	3 21	3 21	2 21
Laborers	2 91	2 91	2 91	3 03	3 03	3 03
Boiler and machine shops:						
Turners and locksmiths	3 57	3 57	3 57	3 57	3 57	3 92
Boiler-smiths	3 57	3 57	3 57	3 57	3 57	3 92
Blacksmiths	3 92–4 28	3 92–4 28	3 92–4 28	4 28	4 28	4 64
Welders	2 85–3 21	2 85–3 21	2 85–3 21	3 21	3 21	3 57
Apprentices	1 78–2 50	1 78–2 50	1 78–2 50	1 78–2 50	1 78–2 50	1 90–2 61
Iron and steel ware factories:						
Smiths	3 57	3 57	3 57	3 92	3 92	4 28
Benchhands	2 85–3 57	2 85–3 57	2 85–3 57	2 85	....	....
General workmen	2 85	2 85	2 85	....	....	....
Day-laborers	2 56	2 56	2 56	2 85	2 85	3 57
Apprentices	1 06–2 14	1 06–2 14	1 06–2 14	1 42–1 78	1 42–1 78	1 78–2 14
Smiths	....	....	....	4 64	4 64	5 00
Benchhands	....	....	....	4 28	4 28	4 64
General workmen	....	....	....	4 28	4 28	4 64
Metal-turners	....	....	....	4 64	5 00	5 35
Brassfounders	....	....	....	4 64	4 64	5 00
Brassmolders	....	....	....	3 57	3 57	4 28
Iron founderies:						
Casters, molders	3 57	3 57	3 57	3 57	3 80	3 87
Day-laborers	2 61	2 61	2 61	2 61	2 85	2 97
Percussion-caps:						
Male hands	3 92	3 92	3 92	5 00	5 00	5 00
Do	....	....	....	3 87	3 57	3 57
Female hands	1 90	1 90	1 90	2 14	2 14	2 14
Button works:						
Children	71	88	1 00	1 06	1 19–1 42	1 42–1 78
Youths and girls from 17 to 20 years.	1 42	1 78	2 02	2 14	2 50–2 85	2 85–3 21
General workmen	2 38	2 61	3 09	3 09	3 09	3 09–3 57
Formers, polishers	3 21	3 80	4 28	....	....	....
Turners	4 28	5 00	5 71	5 71	6 90	7 14
Metal-plating works:						
Youthful hands	1 19	1 42	1 54	1 54	1 60	1 66
Adults	3 57	3 75	3 80	3 80	3 92	4 04
Whipmakers:						
Youthful hands (under 18)	1 42	1 53	1 53	2 14	2 50	3 57
Adults (over 18)	2 50	2 65	2 65	3 21	3 57	4 28
Lithographic works:						
Laborers	3 57	3 57	3 57	3 92	4 28	4 40
Piano and organ factories:						
Piano hands, carpenters	}	}	}	3 45	3 63	3 63
joiners	3 57	4 10	4 00	3 92	4 04	4 04
finishers	}	}	}	5 00	5 23	5 35
Organ hands	3 45	3 75	4 10	3 57	3 80	3 92
Other laborers	2 95	3 21	3 57	....	....	....
Book-printers:						
Typesetters	3 92	3 92	4 28	4 28	4 28	4 28–5 71
Day-laborers	2 85	2 85	2 85	2 85	2 85	3 21

wages.					Remarks.
1871.	1872.	1873.	1874.	1875.	
$4 16	$4 46	$4 64	$4 70	$4 76	Weekly wages.
3 57	3 57	3 57–4 28	3 57–4 28	3 57–4 28	Pay nothing for reeling.
4 64	4 28	4 28	4 28	4 28	
6 42	6 42	6 42	6 42	6 42	
2 73–2 97	2 97	3 09	3 09	3 09	Weekly wages. Lowest rates for hands from 16 to 20 years old, gradually increasing.
2 50–3 21	2 50–3 21	2 50–3 21	2 50–3 21	2 50–3 21	Piece-work.
1 78–2 26	1 78–2 50	1 78–2 50	1 78–2 50	1 78–2 50	Do.
2 85–5 35	2 85–5 00	2 85–5 00	2 85–5 00	2 85–5 00	Weekly wages. Hands from 16 to 20 get lowest wages.
2 14–4 28	3 21–3 92	3 21–3 92	4 28–5 00	4 28–5 71	
2 14	2 14–2 85	2 14–2 85	2 26–3 57	2 26–4 28	
5 71–11 42	8 56–11 42	8 56–11 42	8 56–11 42	8 56–11 42	Piece-work. Masters pay assistants from 40 to 50 per cent. of wages as well as the cost of reeling. Actual working time 10 hours daily.
1 06–1 42	1 06–1 42	1 06–1 42	1 06–1 42	1 06–1 42	
2 14–3 21	2 14–5 00	2 14–5 00	2 14–5 00	2 14–5 00	
3 21	3 21	3 57	3 57	3 92	Weekly wages; 11 hours' daily work.
1 90	1 90	2 14	2 14	2 50	
5 00–7 85	5 00	5 00	5 00	5 00	Weekly wages, except for furnace-men, who generally work by contract. Day and night hands are employed, each working from 7 to 7, with 2 hours' pause.
4 04–4 28	4 64	4 64	4 64	4 64	
4 04–4 28	5 00	5 35	5 35	5 35	
3 57–4 28	3 92	4 04	3 75	3 75	
4 28–5 00	4 28	4 28	4 28	4 28	
3 33–3 57	4 28	4 28	4 28	4 28	
3 03–3 33	....	....	....	....	
4 28	4 28	4 28–4 64	4 28–5 00	4 28–4 64	Weekly wages for 11 hours' daily work.
4 28	4 28	4 28–4 64	4 28–5 00	4 28–4 64	
4 64–5 35	4 64–5 35	5 00–5 71	5 00–5 71	5 00–5 71	
3 57–3 92	3 57–3 92	3 57–3 92	3 57–3 92	3 57–3 92	
1 90–2 85	1 78–2 85	1 78–2 85	1 78–3 09	1 78–2 85	
4 64	4 64	5 00	5 00	5 00	Weekly wages; 11 hours' work daily.
....	5 00	5 00	5 00	4 76	
....	5 00	4 76	4 52	4 52	
3 57	3 57	3 92	3 92	3 80	
1 78–2 14	1 78	1 78	1 78	1 78	
5 35–5 71	6 42	6 42	6 42	6 42	Piece-work; 11 hours' work daily.
4 64	5 71	5 71	5 71	5 71	
4 64	5 71	6 42	6 42	6 18	
5 35–5 71	6 42	5 71	5 71	5 71	
5 35–5 71	6 42	6 42	6 42	6 42	
4 28	5 00	5 00	5 00	5 00	
4 04	4 04	4 64	4 64	4 64	Weekly wages for 11 hours' daily work.
3 21	3 57	3 92	3 92	3 92	
5 00	5 00–8 56	5 00–8 56	5 00–8 56	5 00–8 56	Piece-work; hours of work varying.
3 57	3 57–4 28	3 57–4 28	3 57–4 28	3 57–4 28	Weekly wages; 10½ hours' daily work.
2 14	1 78–2 85	1 78–2 85	1 78–2 85	1 78–2 85	
1 78–2 14	1 42–1 78	1 42–1 78	1 78–2 14	1 78–2 14	Piece-work; hours of work about 10 daily.
3 57	2 50–3 21	2 50–3 21	3 21–3 57	5 71	
4 28–5 35	4 28–5 00	4 28–5 00	5 00	5 71	
....	....	....	....	....	
7 14–8 56	7 14–8 56	7 14–8 56	7 14–8 56	9 28	
1 83	2 02	2 02	2 02	2 02	Weekly wages; 10 hours' daily work.
4 28	4 64	4 64	4 64	4 64	
3 57	2 83	2 85	2 85	2 85	Weekly wages; 11 hours' daily work.
4 64	4 76	5 00	5 00	5 00	
4 52	4 64	4 64	4 76	4 88	Weekly wages for 10 hours' work.
4 28	4 64	5 95	6 42	6 42	Piece or contract work. Actual time of work 10 to 11 hours daily.
4 64	4 76	6 18	6 66	7 02	
6 07	6 18	6 66	7 14	7 61	
4 28	4 28	4 76	5 00	5 00	
....	....	....	....	....	
4 28–7 14	5 00	5 00–5 71	5 71	5 71	Weekly wages; 10 hours' daily work.
3 57	3 57	3 92	3 92	3 92	

Statement showing the rate of wages in Barmen

Branch of business.	Weekly					
	1865.	1866.	1867.	1868.	1869.	1870.
Book-binders:						
Binders of books, sample-cards, &c }	$2 85	$2 85	$2 85	$3 57	$3 57	$4 28
Cartoon-makers }				2 85	2 85	3 02
Apprentices	1 19	1 19	1 19	1 42	1 42	1 78
Masons, builders, and brickmakers:						
Journeymen masons	2 85	3 17	3 45	2 45	3 57	3 92
Hodmen	2 14	2 30	2 50	2 61	2 85	3 03
Carpenters, rough	2 85	3 21	3 45	3 57	3 75	3 92
house	....	....	....	3 57	3 92	3 92
Welldiggers	3 57	3 57	3 57	3 57	3 57	4 28
Brickmakers	....	....	....	....	....	....
Joiners:						
Journeymen	2 50	2 85	3 21	3 21	3 21	3 45
Do	....	....	....	....	....	....
Painters and glaziers:						
Journeymen	2 50	2 61	2 85	2 85	2 85	3 21-3 57
Turners (wood):						
Journeymen	71	71	95	95	95	1 06
Tinsmiths and japanners:						
Journeymen	1 06	1 19	1 19	1 19	1 19	1 19
Capmakers:						
Journeymen	1 06	1 19	1 42	1 42	1 42	1 42
Coppersmiths and brassfounders:						
Journeymen	1 06	1 19	1 42	1 42	1 42	1 78
Do	2 50	2 61	2 85	2 85	2 85	3 21
Tailors:						
Journeymen	1 06	1 19	1 42	1 42	1 42	1 42
Do	2 85	3 21	3 57	3 57	3 57	3 57
Shoemakers:						
Journeymen	71	88	1 06	1 06	1 19	1 42
Do	1 42	1 60	1 78	1 78	1 78	1 90
Saddlers:						
Journeymen	96	96	1 06	1 06	1 06	1 42
Bakers:						
Journeymen	83	96	1 06	1 06	1 06	1 19
Beer-brewers:						
Journeymen	1 06	1 19	1 42	1 42	1 42	1 78
Coopers:						
Journeymen	95	95	95	95	95	1 19
Slaters:						
Journeymen	95	1 42	1 78	1 78	1 78	2 14
Do	....	....	....	....	....	....
Millers:						
Journeymen	2 85	3 03	3 03	3 03	3 03	3 57
Ropemakers:						
Journeymen	83	83	83	83	83	95
Wheelwrights:						
Journeymen	71	71	83	83	83	1 06
Watchmakers:						
Journeymen	*4 28	*5 00	*5 71	1 42	1 42	1 60
Jewelers:						
Journeymen	1 42	1 42	1 42	1 42	1 42	1 42
Barbers:						
Journeymen	71	71	71	71	71	76
Carriers:						
Carters, drivers	1 06	1 19	1 42	1 42	1 42	1 60
Gardeners:						
Journeymen	05	05	05	05	05	06
Locksmiths:						
Journeymen	1 06	1 19	1 42	1 42	1 42	1 78
Do	2 85	3 03	3 21	3 21	3 21	3 57
Tanners:						
Journeymen	2 85	3 03	3 09	3 21	3 21	3 57

* Monthly wages.

during the eleven years, 1865 *to* 1875—Continued.

wages.					Remarks.
1871.	1872.	1873.	1874.	1875.	
$5 00–5 71	$4 28	$4 28	$4 28	$4 28	Weekly wages. 10½ hours' daily work. Wages for 1865–'67 include board and lodging.
3 21	3 57	3 57	3 57	3 57	
1 90	1 90	1 90	1 90	1 90	
4 28	4 64	5 35	5 71	5 71	Masons wages less in winter.
3 21	3 57	4 28	4 64	4 64	Weekly wages; 12 hours' actual work.
4 28–5 00	4 64	5 35	5 71	5 71	
4 28–5 00	4 64	5 00	5 35	5 35	
5 00–5 71	4 64–7 14	5 35–7 85	5 71–8 21	5 71–8 56	
....	4 28–5 00	5 00–5 71	5 71	5 83	
3 57	3 92	3 92	5 00	5 35	Weekly wages for 12 hours' work.
....	5 00–5 71	5 71–6 42	6 42–6 78	7 14	Piece-work.
3 92–4 28	4 28	5 00	5 35–5 71	5 71	Weekly wages; 11 hours' daily work.
1 19	1 42	1 42	1 42	1 42	Weekly wages, with board and lodging; 11 to 12 hours' daily work.
1 42	1 42	1 78	1 78	1 78	Weekly wages, with board and lodging; 11 to 12 hours' daily.
1 60	1 60	1 78	1 78	1 78	Weekly wages, with board and lodging; 13 hours' actual work.
1 78–2 14	2 14	2 50	2 85	2 85	Weekly wages, with board and lodging; 12 to 13 hours.
3 57–4 28	4 28	5	5 71–6 42	6 42	Weekly wages, without board and lodging; 12 to 13 hours.
1 60	1 60	1 78	1 78	1 78	Weekly wages, with board and lodging; 13 hours.
3 92–4 28	4 28	5	5 71	5 71	Piece-work.
1 78	1 78	1 78	1 78	1 78	Weekly wages, with board and lodging; 13 hours.
2 14	2 14	2 85	2 50	2 85	Piece-work, with board and lodging.
1 42–1 78	1 78	1 90	2 14	2 14	Weekly wages, with board and lodging; 13 hours.
1 42	1 42	1 78	2 14	2 14	Weekly wages, with board and lodging; 13 hours.
2 14	2 14	2 50	2 85	2 18	Weekly wages, with board and lodging; 13 to 14 hours daily.
1 42–1 78	1 78	1 78	2 14	2 14	Weekly wages, with board and lodging; 12 hours' daily work.
2 50	2 61	2 85	3 21	3 21	Weekly wages, with board and lodging; 12 hours.
....	5	5 71	6 42–7 14	7 14–8 56	Piece-work.
3 57–4 28	3 57–4 28	4 28	4 64	4 64	Weekly wages; 13 hours' daily work.
1 19	1 42	1 78	1 78	1 78	Weekly wages, with board and lodging; 13 hours' daily work.
1 42	1 42	1 78	2 14	2 14	Weekly wages, with board and lodging; 13 hours' daily work.
1 78	1 78	1 90	1 90	1 90	Week. and monthly wages, with board and lodging; 11 to 12 hours.
1 60	1 60	1 60	2 14	2 14	Weekly wages, with board and lodging; 12 hours daily.
1 06	1 42	1 78	2 14	2 14	Weekly wages, with board and lodging.
1 78	1 78	2 14	2 14	2 14	Weekly wages, with board and lodging.
07½	07½	07½	07½	07½	Per hour; some varying.
1 90	1 90	2 14	2 14	2 14	Weekly wages, with board and lodging.
4 28	4 28	4 28	4 64	4 64	
3 57–4 28	4 28	4 28	4 28	4 28	Weekly wages; 12 hours daily.

4. State of trade.

The state of trade throughout this district is one of great depression; in fact, without resulting in total ruin, it could not be worse.

All textile branches are and have been for years suffering from stagnation of trade. There is, excepting for button stuffs and ribbons, actually no demand for silk manufactures.

All thoughts of profit are put aside, and goods are continually sold for less than it costs to manufacture them.

With large investments in factories and raw materials, and great numbers of work people dependent upon them, to close their works would be to cast away the business acquired during a long series of years, and in many cases would be irretrievable ruin.

Hence, all manufacturers are living on their capital, working away with yearly losses, waiting for the arrival of better times.

Of failures, as yet there are comparatively few, since the accumulation of a long series of good business years have enabled manufacturers to bear the losses of the last three years; but, unless the reaction in business soon sets in, the disasters of the immediate future must necessarily be great and wide-spreading.

All sales of any magnitude are made at a loss; and, though small ones may be made at a profit, they disappear in the total of the year's business.

The retail trade seems better off, for, whilst the manufacturer must sell his wares at prices cheaper than they have been for twenty years, there is no appreciable difference in the prices of articles purchased at retail now from those of former years.

This prosperity is in a great measure, however, apparent only, since the retailer does not buy directly from the manufacturer, and the wholesale and retail cost is swallowed by the number of hands an article passes through before reaching the consumer.

In the iron branches, such as hardware and cutlery, nail and wire works, there is the same depression, and the above remarks are quite as applicable to those branches as to the textile branches of manufacture.

5. The current money of the German Empire.

The current money or legal tender of the German Empire consists of coin and notes of the character described below, viz:

a. Gold coins.

The value and number of gold coins are—
$69\frac{3}{4}$ pieces of 20 marks, or double-crowns, to the pound of gold.
$139\frac{2}{4}$ pieces of 10 marks, or crowns, to the pound of gold.
279 pieces of 5 marks, or half crowns, to the pound of gold.
These pieces are composed of $\frac{900}{1000}$ gold and $\frac{100}{1000}$ copper.

b. Silver coins.

20 pieces of 5 marks to the pound of fine silver.
50 pieces of 2 marks to the pound of fine silver.
100 pieces of 1 mark to the pound of fine silver.
200 pieces of 50 pfennige to the pound of fine silver.
500 pieces of 20 pfennige to the pound of fine silver.

c. Nickel coins.

Pieces of 5 and 10 pfennige.

d. Copper coins.

Pieces of 1 and 2 pfennige.

According to the provisions of the law of July 9, 1873, the amount of silver shall not exceed 10 marks, nor copper 2½ marks, per head of the population.

e. Notes.

The Imperial Bank, or Bank of Germany, and a number of private banks (see table), are authorized to issue notes at par in denominations of 1,000, 500, 200, 100, 50, 20, and 5 marks.

According to paragraph 2 of the law of 1875, the imperial notes excepted, bank-notes are not legal tender, and their acceptance in payment of debts due in coin is in no way obligatory.

On presentation, each note must be redeemed at once in the coin of the realm.

Each of the banks, which in 1875 issued notes, has been permitted to emit a certain amount of notes without coin security.

For all notes which shall be circulated in excess of this sum 5 per cent. interest per annum must be paid to the Imperial Bank as long as they are in circulation, and in *all cases* one-third of the amount of notes issued must be secured by coin deposits.

Circulation.

About 170,000,000 marks of the notes of the Imperial Bank were in circulation up to April 20, 1878, and there has been coined to same date of—

	Marks.
20-mark pieces	1,190,847,520
10-mark pieces	365,296,020
5-mark pieces	27,969,845
Total gold coined	1,584,113,385

The amount of silver coined to same date is—

	Marks.
5-mark pieces	71,652,415.00
2-mark pieces	97,810,530.00
1-mark piece	148,847,743.00
50-pfennige pieces	71,486,388.00
20-pfennige pieces	35,717,718.20
Total silver coined	425,514,794.20

There are, moreover, several hundred millions—about 400,000,000 marks—of the old thaler pieces, equal to 3 marks, in circulation, which, however, like all other silver coins, are legal tender only for sums not in excess of 20 marks.

There was, therefore, at the beginning of 1878 (estimating the German population at 42,000,000), to each person—

		Marks.
1. In fractional silver coins		20.00
2. In legal-tenders:		
a. Gold	37.72	
b. Notes of the Imperial Bank	4.00	
		41.72
3. Notes of private banks		19.83
Total to each person		81.55

Up to April, 1878, the Imperial Bank has issued altogether notes to the amount of 595,968,000 marks, of which coin security existed for 495,672,000, the unsecured issue being 100,296,000.

The 15 banks, including the Imperial Bank, had, on the 30th of March, 1878, notes in circulation to the amount of 833,500,000 marks, of which were secured by coin 641,610,000; the total unsecured issue being 191,890,000.

In February, 1870, 31 German banks had in circulation notes to the amount of 614,000,000 marks, with coin deposit of 381,000,000, leaving an unsecured issue of 233,000,000.

There has, therefore, been an increase of the amount of notes in circulation in the German Empire since 1870 of 219,000,000 marks, with a decrease in the amount of unsecured notes of 41,110,000 marks.

No.	Name of bank.	Authorized to issue unsecured notes in 1876.	Imperial Bank can issue in 1878 unsecured notes.
		Marks.	*Marks.*
1	Imperial Bank	250, 000, 000	250, 000, 000
*2	Ritterschaftliche Privatbank, Pommern	1, 222, 000	1, 222, 000
3	Städtische Bank, in Breslau	1, 283, 000	
*4	Bank des Berliner Cassenvereins	963, 000	963, 000
5	Kölinsche Bank	1, 251, 000	
6	Magdeburger Privatbank	1, 173, 000	
7	Danziger Privat-Actien-Bank	1, 272, 000	
8	Provinzial-Actien-Bank des Gross Herzogthums Posen	1, 200, 000	
*9	Kommunalständische Bank (Görlitz)	1, 307, 000	1, 307, 000
10	Hannoverreche Bank	6, 000, 000	
11	Landgräfliche hessische Landesbank	159, 000	
12	Frankfurter Bank	10, 000, 000	
13	Bayerische Bank	32, 000, 000	
14	Sächsische Bank zu Dresden	16, 771, 000	
*15	Leipziger Bank	5, 348, 000	5, 348, 000
16	Leipziger Cassenverein	1, 440, 000	
17	Chemnitzer Stadtbank	441, 000	
18	Würtembergische Notenbank	10, 000, 000	
19	Badische Bank	10, 000, 000	
20	Bank für Süddeutschland	10, 000, 000	
21	Rostocker Bank	1, 155, 000	
*22	Weimarsche Bank	1, 971, 000	1, 971, 000
*23	Oldenburgische Landesbank	1, 881, 000	1, 881, 000
24	Braunschweigische Bank	2, 829, 000	
*25	Mitteldeutsche Creditbank (Meiningen)	3, 187, 000	3, 187, 000
*26	Privatbank zu Gotha	1, 344, 000	1, 344, 000
*27	Anhalt, Dessanische Landesbank	935, 000	935, 000
*28	Thüringische Bank (Landershausen)	1, 658, 000	1, 658, 000
*29	Geraer Bank	1, 631, 000	1, 631, 000
*30	Niedersächsiche Bank (Bückeburg)	594, 000	594, 000
*31	Lübecker Privatbank	500, 000	500, 000
32	Commerz Bank (Lübeck)	959, 000	
33	Bremer Bank	4, 500, 000	
	Total	385, 000, 000	272, 501, 000

*The banks in the table which are marked (*), having renounced their rights of issue, the same have been transferred to the Imperial Bank, increasing the amount which this bank is authorized to issue, viz, 250,000,000 marks, by 22,561,000; so that the Imperial Bank may issue 272,561,000 of unsecured notes in 1878.

6. BUSINESS HABITS AND SYSTEMS.

In most if not all branches of manufacture it is more or less the custom of the manufacturer, who has either no factory or but a small one, to give out raw materials to the so-called masters, who, with their assistants, work the raw material up at their own shops.

In many branches the goods are traveling back and forth between workman and principal, involving naturally a much greater loss of time than if the workmen were united in one or two large factories.

The manufacturers are conscious of all the disadvantages of the present system, but are unable to overcome the workmen's prejudices to the factory system.

Under present arrangements the workman enjoys much more liberty, working or not as he pleases, and generally being his own master; all of which questionable privileges he would be obliged to forego if working in a factory.

Business is done chiefly on the credit plan, and here in Germany bills run from nine months to a year. For instance, raw silks are paid in two months' bills, either nine months after date of invoice without discount, or on receipt of invoice with 5 per cent. discount.

Cotton yarns are paid in two months' bills on receipt of invoice with 5 per cent. discount, or three months after date of invoice with $3\frac{1}{2}$ off.

Chappe silk is paid in two months' bills on receipt of invoice with 6 per cent. discount, or three months after date of invoice with 4 per cent.

Silk manufactures are generally paid six months after date of invoice. The discounts vary with the promptness of the buyer's payments and are too varying to specify.

The hours of business are generally from 8 a. m. to 7 p. m., but there is an interval for the principals of three hours (from twelve to three) for dinner and siesta (the latter is a universal practice), which to strangers and buyers is a continual source of annoyance and delay.

Business is carefully done and for very small profit, risky speculations being the exception and not the rule.

Generally speaking the German business people are utterly devoid of that liberality which in their business transactions characterize the American and English merchant. Their integrity and industry, however, abundantly compensate for this trait of "meanness" or littleness in their national character.

EDGAR STANTON.

UNITED STATES CONSULATE,
Barmen, May 23, 1878.

Supplement to Mr. Stanton's report.

AGRICULTURE AND RAILWAY LABOR IN THE RHENISH PROVINCES.

[Translation of a letter received by Consul Stanton from the president of the Agricultural Society for the Rhenish provinces.]

LAUERSFORT, *May* 31, 1878.

SIR: I beg to submit the following remarks in reply to your favor of the 18th ultimo:

After a standstill of about two years, when the wages of farm-hands and journeymen, during the years 1871–1874, had been rapidly driven to such a height that agricultural pursuits yielded a profit in but very few instances, resulting generally in severe losses to tenants and to owners with mortgaged lands, there is a slightly falling tendency in wages, so that rise, which was about 50 per cent. above the normal rates of 1860–1870, now stands but about 20 or 25 per cent. above them.

In North Germany we are accustomed to measure the rate of agricultural wages by the price of rye, as being the chief necessary of life. According to this rule the average daily wage of the Rhenish field-hand equaled in 1874 the average price of 18.1 pounds of rye during the last ten years.

The agricultural daily wages in Germany vary in proportion to the ten years' average price from 23 to 10.8 pounds of rye. Of the twenty-five districts therein the Rhine province occupies the tenth position.

Within the Rhenish province the relation between the rate of daily wages and the average price of rye varies to such an extent that in 1874 the day's wages would purchase 17.7 pounds rye in the district of Düsseldorf, 15.7 pounds rye in the district of Cologne, 16.4 pounds rye in the district of Aix la Chapelle, 15.5 pounds rye in the district of Treves, 13.3 pounds rye in the district of Coblentz.

This difference arises partly from the difference in the price of rye and partly from the competition which in various districts agriculture suffers from manufacturing industries.

The prices of the necessaries of life have not fallen at the same rate that wages have retrograded. True, grain and bread prices have fallen slightly, but all other necessaries remain to a great extent at their former height.

This is particularly true of the products of the dairy and the herd. Milk, butter, cheese, meat, and leather have more than doubled in price during the last twenty-five years, so that the rise in wages at the beginning of the last decade but just enabled the laborer to indulge in a little more liberal enjoyment of these articles.

If, however, wages, in consequence of the depression in trade, should fall once more, the laborer will be forced at once to limit greatly the use of dairy products.

But aid is at hand. The progress made in the manner of feeding and in the treatment of milk are effecting, if slowly, plainly perceptible increase in the products of butter, cheese, and meat, so that we may hope that, in conjunction with the increasing import of cheap dairy products and preserved meats from foreign countries, the laborer will not be compelled in the future to renounce a diet which is essential to his health.

H. VON RATH,
President of Agricultural Society of Rhenish Prussia.

To E. STANTON, Esq.,
United States Consul, Barmen.

Statement of the wages and food-prices in the district of Lennep.

Articles.	1876.	1877.	1878.
Rye ... per 2 cwts.	$4 64	$4 40	$4 28
Oats ... do	4 28	3 92	3 57
Pease ... do	7 14	6 87	6 66
Potatoes ... do	2 38	2 14	1 78
Beef ... per 2 lbs.	43	36	28
Pork ... do	38	36	28
Veal ... do	28	28	23
Mutton ... do	33	33	28
Wheat flour ... do	12	09	09
Butter ... do	71	71	57
Wages of field-hands:			
Male ... per day	71	71	57
Female ... do	48	36	23

The wages of laborers on public works have fallen from 20 to 30 per cent. as compared with former years.

Iron and metal workmen earn at present, in this district, on the average, from $2.38 to $3.57 weekly; the laborers in cloth factories from $1.90 to $2.85 the week.

Total exhibit of the number of workmen employed on the Bergish-Märkischen Railway, and their wages on the 1st of January, 1878, as compared with those of October 1, 1877.

Name.	I.									
	a. Car-recorders.						*b.* Manager of car-reporting bureau.			
							Not according to estimates.			According to estimates.
	October 1, 1877.			January 1, 1878.			October 1, 1877.			
		Daily wages received.			Daily wages received.			Daily wages paid.		
	Number.	Total.	Average.	Number.	Total.	Average.	Number.	Total.	Average.	Number.
Aix la Chapelle	8	$3 43	$0 43	8	$3 43	$0 43	4	$2 42	$0 60	......
Düsseldorf	14	5 61	40	13	5 18	39	......	......	......	......
Hagen	8	3 43	43	9	3 86	43	1	89	89	......
Essen	22	9 71	43	23	9 86	43	4	2 64	66	......
Cassel	14	5 75	41	14	5 73	41	2	1 07	53	......
Altena	10	4 09	41	10	4 09	41	......	......	......	......
Total	76	32 02	42	77	32 15	41	11	7 02	64	......

Name.	*b.* Manager of car-reporting bureau.				*c.* Assistant telegraphist, and telegraphist's assistants.					
	Not according to estimates.			According to estimates.						
	January 1, 1878.				October 1, 1877.			January 1, 1878.		
		Daily wages paid.				Daily wages paid.			Daily wages paid.	
	Number.	Total.	Average.	Number.	Number.	Total.	Average.	Number.	Total.	Average.
Aix la Chapelle	4	$2 42	$0 60	......	7	$3 92	$0 56	8	$4 52	$0 57
Düsseldorf	......	......	......	......	15	7 85	52	15	7 65	50
Hagen	1	89	80	......	12	6 02	50	12	6 27	52
Essen	4	2 64	66	......	9	4 79	53	9	4 79	53
Cassel	2	1 07	53	......	19	9 28	48	16	7 85	49
Altena	......	......	......	......	6	3 11	52	6	3 16	52
Total	11	7 02	64	......	68	34 97	51	66	34 24	51

Number of workmen employed on the Bergish-Märkischen Railway, &c.—Continued.

Name.	II.							
	a. Night-watchmen, laborers (wages exclusive of that earned by day-work).						b. Night-watchmen (official).	
	October 1, 1877.			January 1, 1878.			October 1, 1877.	October 1, 1878.
	Number.	Daily wages paid.		Number.	Daily wages paid.		Number.	Number.
		Total.	Average.		Total.	Average.		
Aix la Chapelle	16	$6 06	$0 37	16	$5 99	$0 37	20	20
Düsseldorf	22	8 15	37	22	8 25	38	17	17
Hagen	5	1 73	34	5	1 70	36	9	9
Essen	21	7 47	35	20	7 12	36	11	11
Cassel	9	2 82	31	2	64	32	7	4
Altena	6	1 99	33	3	99	33	5	8
Total	79	28 22	35	68	24 78	36	69	69

Name.	III.											
	a. Railway hands (exclusive of those mentioned under other heads).						b. Bahnhofs-Vorarbeiter (preparatory laborers in station).					
	October 1, 1877.			January 1, 1878.			October 1, 1877.			January 1, 1878.		
	Number.	Daily wages paid.		Number.	Daily wages paid.		Number.	Daily wages paid.		Number.	Daily wages paid.	
		Total.	Average.		Total.	Average.		Total.	Average.		Total.	Average.
Aix la Chapelle	90	$37 73	$0 42	87	$36 54	$0 42	6	$2 96	$0 49	7	$3 50	$0 49
Düsseldorf	108	45 83	42	109	46 36	43	...	.....	.....	...	.....	.....
Hagen	48	19 62	41	48	19 54	41	...	.....	.....	...	.....	.....
Essen	46.50	20	43	45.50	19 59	43	...	.....	.....	...	.....	.....
Cassel	83.50	33 53	40	82	33 06	40	2	1 07	53	2	1 08	55
Altena	32.25	15 07	47	32.25	15 07	47	...	.....	.....	...	.....	.....
Total	408.25	171 78	42	403.75	170 16	42	8	4 03	50	9	4 58	51

Name.	IV.					
	a. Warehouse hands, employed only as such.					
	October 1, 1877.			January 1, 1878.		
	Number.	Daily wages paid.		Number.	Daily wages paid.	
		Total.	Average.		Total.	Average.
Aix la Chapelle	5	$2 30	$0 46	5	$2 30	$0 46
Düsseldorf	.....	.....	.....	.....	.....	.....
Hagen	3	1 55	52	3	1 55	52
Essen	.....	.....	.....	.....	.....	.....
Cassel	3	1 76	59	3	1 74	58
Altena	1	64	64	1	64	64
Total	12	6 25	52	12	6 23	52

Number of workmen employed on the Bergish-Märkischen Railway, &c.—Continued.

Name.	V.					
	a. Coal-heavers, used only as such.					
	October 1, 1877.			January 1, 1878.		
	Number.	Daily wages paid.		Number.	Daily wages paid.	
		Total.	Average.		Total.	Average.
Aix la Chapelle	7	(*)	(*)	7	(*)	(*)
Dusseldorf	†19	†$9 36	†$0 49	†20	†$10 43	†$0 52
Hagen	13	(‡)	(‡)	15	(‡)	(‡)
Essen	16.50	8 23	50	16	§8 62	54
Cassel	19	9 91	52	19.50	8 61	44
Altena	8	4 10	51	8	4 78	60
Total	82.50 —20= 62.50	31 60	51	85.50 —20= 65.50	32 44	49

* By the piece. † Also locomotive cleaners at several stations. ‡ Piece-work.
§ By contract mostly, per cart, 4 cents.

Name.	VI.													
	a. Freight-porters in warehouse.						*b.* Vorarbeiter (preliminary laborers.)						*c.* Weigh-masters.	
	October 1, 1877.			January 1, 1878.			October 1, 1877.			January 1, 1878.			Oct. 1, 1877.	Jan. 1, 1878.
	Number.	Daily wages paid.		Number.	Daily wages paid.		Number.	Daily wages paid.		Number.	Daily wages paid.		Number.	Number.
		Total.	Average.		Total.	Average.		Total.	Average.		Total.	Average.		
Aix la Chapelle	131	$61 29	$0 47	131	$61 29	$0 47	10	$5 52	$0 55	10	$5 52	$0 55	73	60
Düsseldorf	227	103 43	45	228	103 88	45	....	......	......	....	......	......	131	131
Hagen	98	89 27	40	96	42 81	43	5	2 76	55	4	2 00	50	61	60
Essen	132	63 62	48	135	64 76	48	....	......	......	....	......	......	98	98
Cassel	75	31 14	41	71	29 43	41	8	4 17	52	8	4 17	52	40	40
Altena	59	27 06	46	59	27 18	46	....	......	......	....	......	......	22	23
Total	722	325 81	45	720	329 35	46	23	12 45	54	22	11 60	53	425	421

Number of workmen employed on the Bergish-Märkischen Railway, &c.—Continued.

Name.	VII.					
	a. Baggage-porters, employed only as such.					
	October 1, 1877.			January 1, 1878.		
	Number.	Daily wages paid.		Number.	Daily wages paid.	
		Total.	Average.		Total.	Average.
Aix la Chapelle	19	$2 79	$0 15	19	$2 61	$0 14
Düsseldorf	17	2 16	13	18	2 26	12
Hagen	11	3 30	30	11	3 30	30
Essen	10	1 96	19	10	1 96	19
Cassel	10	3 77	37	10	3 78	38
Altena	3	83	24	3	83	24
Total	70	14 81	21	71	14 74	20

Name.	VIII.									
	a. Switchmen for making up trains (exclusive of hour-money), used for no other work.						b. Station brakemen.		c. Switch-masters for making up trains.	
	October 1, 1877.			January 1, 1878.			Oct. 1, 1877.	Jan. 1, 1878.	Oct. 1, 1877.	Jan. 1, 1878.
	Number.	Daily wages paid.		Number.	Daily wages paid.		Number.	Number.	Number.	Number.
		Total.	Average.		Total.	Average.				
Aix la Chapelle	32	$14 37	$0 4[illegible]	35	$15 66	$0 45	27	26	11	11
Düsseldorf	46	20 58	4[illegible]	49	21 91	45	39	40	16	15
Hagen	49	20 70	4[illegible]	56	24 05	43	21	17	9	9
Essen	126	53 48	4[illegible]	131	55 39	42	44	41	36	34
Cassel	22	8 54	3[illegible]	23	8 93	39	9	9	2	2
Altena	7	2 99	4[illegible]	6	2 55	42	7	8	9	9
Total	282	120 66	43	300	128 49	43	147	141	83	80

Name.	IX.								
	Classification of lines with respect to employment.						a. Tracklayers.		
	Class I.		Class II.		Class III.		October 1, 1877.		
	Main lines.	Side lines.	Main lines.	Side lines.	Main lines.	Side lines.	Number.	Daily wages paid. Total.	Daily wages paid. Average.
	Kil.	*Kil.*	*Kil.*	*Kil.*	*Kil.*	*Kil.*			
Aix la Chapelle	167.89	55.80	104.10	34.	75.15	38.25	313	$123 22	$0 30
Dusseldorf	208.994	150.234	81.711	47.852	40.167	10.800	430	192 29	45
Hagen	125.20	83.32	112.52	64.93	31.63	13.56	398	159 99	40
Essen	167.5	182.3	147.7	134.5	19.6	0.5	408.24	181 64	44
Cassel	275.09	63.71	241.80	34.16	21.40	9.51	621	221 92	36
Altena	43.52		185.83		32.01		262	104 69	40
Total	.....	.....	.....	.....	.....	.....	2,432.24	983 75	40

Name.	a. Tracklayers.			b. Gangmasters.					
	January 1, 1878.			October 1, 1877.			January 1, 1878.		
	Number.	Daily wages paid. Total.	Daily wages paid. Average.	Number.	Daily wages paid. Total.	Daily wages paid. Average.	Number.	Daily wages paid. Total.	Daily wages paid. Average.
				*26	*$12 11	*$0 47	*26	*$12 11	*$0 47
Aix la Chapelle	313	$123 22	$0 30	35	18 73	53	35	18 70	53
Düsseldorf	398	167 41	42	54	32 92	61	50	28 91	58
Hagen	411	158 89	38	41	24 30	59	41	24 22	59
Essen	386	170 42	44	47.18	27 63	59	47.50	27 90	59
				*6.32	*3 10	*49	*3.99	*1 97	*49
Cassel	521	188 37	36	83	42 27	51	72	36 23	50
Altena	275	108 36	39	47	22 89	49	29	15 11	52
							*24	*10 49	*44
Total	2,304	916 67	40	307.18	168 76	55	274.50	151 07	55
				*32.32	*15 21	*47	*53.99	*24 57	*45

* Laborers on preliminary work.

Number of workmen employed on the Bergish-Märkischen Railway, &c.—Continued.

Name.	IX—Continued.											
	c. Permanent sworn laborers for guarding line.						*d.* Permanent sworn switchmen.					
	October 1, 1877.			January 1, 1878.			October 1, 1877.			January 1, 1878.		
	Number.	Daily wages paid.		Number.	Daily wages paid.		Number.	Daily wages paid.		Number.	Daily wages paid.	
		Total.	Average.		Total.	Average.		Total.	Average.		Total.	Average.
Aix la Chapello	0. 56	$4 34	$0 45	9	$4 11	$0 46	21	$9 38	$0 45	19. 50	$8 69	$0 44
Düsseldorf	52	14 47	46	34	16 23	48	22	10 01	47	18	8 21	46
Hagen	12	5 45	45	2	88	44	3	1 38	46	2	93	46
Essen	71. 44	33 63	47	77. 71	36 59	47	10. 61	4 93	46	17. 20	7 79	45
Cassel	65	28 11	43	58	24 78	43	11	5 02	46	16. 25	6 83	40
Altena	......	......	......	......	......	......	......	......	......	......	......	......
Total	209. 94	86	45	180. 71	82 59	46	67. 61	30 72	45	72. 95	32 45	44

Name.	*e.* Railway-keepers.		*f.* Switchmen.	
	October 1, 1877.	January 1, 1878.	October 1, 1877.	January 1, 1878.
	Number.	Number.	Number.	Number.
Aix la Chapello	239	233	170	168
Düsseldorf	259	249	289	281
Hagen	217	216	196	194
Essen	268	267	324	316
Cassel	423	421	221	214
Altena	161	159	87	86
Total	1, 567	1, 545	1, 287	1, 259

Name.	X.							
	a. Laborers permanently employed as brakemen.						*b.* Brakemen (quasi officials).	
	October 1, 1877.			January 1, 1878.			Oct. 1, 1877.	Jan. 1, 1878.
	Number.	Daily wages paid.		Number.	Daily wages paid.		Number.	Number.
		Total.	Average.		Total.	Average.		
Aix la Chapello	15	$6 42	$0 43	15	$6 42	$0 43	165	140
Düsseldorf	49	20 77	43	51	21 53	38	149	153
Hagen	56	22 84	41	53	21 58	41	130	126
Essen	50	21 40	43	51	21 84	43	215	224
Cassel	65	27 85	43	77	30 65	40	163	163
Altena	1	40	40	......	......	......	85	83
Total	236	99 68	42	247	102 02	41	907	900

Number of workmen employed on the Bergish-Märkischen Railway, &c.—Continued.

Name.	XI. a. Locomotive-cleaners. October 1, 1877. Number.	Daily wages paid. Total.	Average.	January 1, 1878. Number.	Daily wages paid. Total.	Average.
	*1	*$0 52	*$0 52	*1	*$0 48	*$0 48
Aix la Chapelle	63. 50	29 38	46	64. 50	29 86	46
Düsseldorf	†87	†46 76	†54	†86	†47 12	†55
Hagen	72	(‡)	(‡)	‡78	(‡)	(‡)
Essen	†118	†60 75	†51	†123	†63 99	†52
Cassel	83	36 38	44	85. 50	37 69	44
Altena	32	16 51	52	33	17 17	52
Total	455. 50 —72= 383. 50 §1	189 78 §52	40 §52	470 —78= 392 §1	195 83 §48	50 §48

*Preliminary workmen in M. Gladbachs. †Also coal-heavers at several stations. ‡By contract. §Preliminary workmen.

Name.	XII. a. Car-cleaners. October 1, 1877. Number.	Daily wages paid. Total.	Average.	January 1, 1878. Number.	Daily wages paid. Total.	Average.
Aix la Chapelle	20	$8 54	$0 43	21. 50	$9 21	$0 43
Düsseldorf	31. 75	14 33	45	31 75	14 29	45
Hagen	17	7 56	44	16	7 06	44
Essen	16	7 11	44	17. 50	7 77	44
Cassel	7. 7	2 99	39	8	3 09	38
Altena	5	2 07	41	5	2 07	41
Total	97. 45	42 60	44	99. 75	43 40	43

Number of workmen employed on the Bergish-Märkischen Railway, &c.—Continued.

Name.	XIII.							
	a. Laborers used as machine-stokers.						b. Quasi-official stokers.	
	October 1, 1877.			January 1, 1878.			Oct. 1, 1877.	Jan. 1, 1878.
	Number.	Daily wages paid. Total.	Daily wages paid. Average.	Number.	Daily wages paid. Total.	Daily wages paid. Average.	Number.	Number.
Aix la Chapelle	1	$0 64	$0 64	1	$0 64	$0 64	11	11
Düsseldorf	9	4 61	51	8	3 85	48	8	9
Hagen	5	2 95	59	5	2 95	59	6	6
Essen	5	2 80	56	6	3 40	57	4	4
Cassel	9	4 38	49	8	3 86	48	2	3
Altena	4	2 38	59	4	2 38	59	3	3
Total	33	17 76	54	32	17 08	53	34	36

Name.	XIV.							
	a. Car-masters' assistants (journeymen in workshops).						b. Car-masters (quasi-official).	
	October 1, 1877.			January 1, 1878.			Oct. 1, 1877.	Jan. 1, 1878.
	Number.	Daily wages paid. Total.	Daily wages paid. Average.	Number.	Daily wages paid. Total.	Daily wages paid. Average.	Number.	Number.
Aix la Chapelle	4	$2 40	$0 60	4	$2 40	$0 60	15	15
Düsseldorf	5	2 97	59	7	4 16	59	18	18
Hagen	5	2 83	57	5	2 83	57	11	11
Essen	8	4 73	59	8	4 76	59	22	23
Cassel	21	10 45	50	20	9 99	50	13	13
Altena	4	2 33	58	4	2 33	58	5	5
Total	47	25 71	55	48	26 47	55	84	85

Name.	XV.							
	a. Workshop-porters (laborers).						b. Workshop-porters (quasi-officials).	
	October 1, 1877.			January 1, 1878.			Oct. 1, 1877.	Jan. 1, 1878.
	Number.	Daily wages paid. Total.	Daily wages paid. Average.	Number.	Daily wages paid. Total.	Daily wages paid. Average.	Number.	Number.
In all workshops	3	$1 66	$0 55	2	$1 19	$0 59	5	5

Number of workmen employed on the Bergish-Märkischen Railway, &c.—Continued.

Name.	XVI.							
	a. Laborers employed as watchmen for workshops at night.						*b.* Night-watchmen for workshops (quasi-officials.)	
	October 1, 1877.			January 1, 1878.			October 1, 1877.	January 1, 1878.
	Number.	Daily wages paid.		Number.	Daily wages paid.		Number.	Number.
		Total.	Average.		Total.	Average.		
In all workshops	11	$4 19	$0 38	11	$4 30	$0 39	1	1

Name.	XVII.					
	a. Workshop journeymen.					
	October 1, 1877.			January 1, 1878.		
	Number.	Daily wages paid.		Number.	Daily wages paid.	
		Total.	Average.		Total.	Average.
In all workshops	2,648	$1,769.76	$0 67	2,648	$1,721.85	$0 65

Name.	XVIII.					
	a. Workshop laborers.					
	October 1, 1877.			January 1, 1878.		
	Number.	Daily wages paid.		Number.	Daily wages paid.	
		Total.	Average.		Total.	Average.
In all workshops	379	$185.84	$0 49	355	$166.90	$0 47

RECAPITULATION.

	Laborers.	October 1, 1877. Number.	October 1, 1877. Daily wages paid. Total.	October 1, 1877. Daily wages paid. Average.	January 1, 1878. Number.	January 1, 1878. Daily wages paid. Total.	January 1, 1878. Daily wages paid. Average.
I.	*a.* Car-recorders	76	$32 02	$0 42	77	$32 15	$0 41
	b. Managers of car-recording office	11	7 02	64	11	7 02	64
	c. Assistant telegraphist and telegraphist's assistants	68	34 97	51	66	34 24	51
II.	*a.* Night-watchmen	79	28 22	35	68	24 78	36
III.	*b.* Station-workmen	408.25	171 75	42	403.75	170 16	42
	c. Station-workmen, preliminary	8	4 03	50	9	4 58	51
IV.	*a.* Warehouse workmen	12	6 25	52	12	6 23	52
V.	*a.* Coalheavers	62.50	31 60	51	65.50	32 44	49
VI.	*a.* Warehouse freight-porters	722	325 81	45	720	329 35	46
	b. Warehouse preliminary workmen	23	12 45	54	22	11 69	53
VII.	*a.* Baggage-porters	70	14 81	21	71	14 74	20
VIII.	*a.* Trainmakers	282	120 66	43	300	128 49	43
IX.	*a.* Tracklayers	2,432.24	983 75	40	2,304	916 67	40
	b. Gangmasters	307.18	168 76	55	274.50	151 07	55
	c. Preliminary workmen	32.32	15 21	47	53.99	24 57	45
	d. Trackmen	209.94	86 00	45	180.71	82 59	46
	e. Switchmen	67.61	30 72	45	72.95	32 45	44
X.	*a.* Brakemen	230	99 68	42	247	102 02	41
XI.	*a.* Locomotive-cleaners	383.50	189 78	49	392	195 83	50
	b. Preliminary workmen	1	52	52	1	48	48
XII.	*a.* Car cleaners	97.45	42 60	44	99.75	43 49	43
XIII.	*a.* Stokers	33	17 76	54	32	17 08	53
XIV.	*a.* Car-masters' assistants	47	25 71	55	48	26 47	55
XV.	*a.* Workshop porters	3	1 66	55	2	1 19	59
XVI.	*a.* Workshop night-watchmen	11	4 19	38	11	4 30	39
XVII.	*a.* Workshop journeymen	2,648	1,769 76	67	2,648	1,721 85	65
XVIII.	*a.* Workshop laborers	379	185 84	49	355	166 90	47
	Total	8,708.99	4,411 01	....	8,547.15	4,281 83	....
		1	52	....	....	....	....
		8,709.99	4,411 53	....	....	....	....

	Officials.	No. October 1, 1877.	No. January 1, 1878.
II.	*b.* Night-watchmen	69	69
VI.	*c.* Weighmasters	425	421
VIII.	*b.* Station-brakemen	147	141
	c. Master trainmakers	83	80
IX.	*e.* Railway hands	1,567	1,545
	f. Switchmen	1,287	1,259
X.	*b.* Brakemen	907	900
XIII.	*b.* Stokers	34	30
XIV.	*b.* Master carmen	84	85
XV.	*b.* Workshop porters	5	5
XVI.	*b.* Workshop night-watchmen	1	1

Comparative table of the wages paid by the Bergisch-Märkischen Railway during the years 1871–1875, *inclusive.*

Class of laborers.	1871.	1872.	1873.	1874.	1875.
Navvies employed in repairing line and keeping same in order	$0 43 / 45	$0 48	$0 55	$0 48	$0 45
Journeymen in the workshops:					
a. Daily wages	51	64	55	58	56
b. Piece-work wages	91	95	1 05	97	89
c. Average wages	66	71	77	76	71

Class of laborers.	Jan. 1, 1876.	Jan. 31, 1877.
Navvies	$0 43	$0 42
Gangmasters	58	57
Laborers in workshops:		
a. Journeymen	70	68
b. Day-laborers	53	51
Locksmiths	61	61
Car-recorders	46	45
Night-watchmen	38	37
Station-laborers	45	44
Trainmakers	46	45
Oilers and warehousemen	53	53
Locomotive-cleaners	52	50
Car-cleaners	48	46
Stokers	58	57
Workmen in freight-depots	49	47
Baggage-porters	23	23

BAVARIA.

Report, by Consul Wilson, of Nuremberg, on the rates of wages, cost of living, labor systems, condition of the working classes, and industrial museums of Bavaria.

Referring to the circular of the Department of State, dated Washington, April 11, 1878, wherein information is called for respecting the ruling rates of wages, cost of living to the laboring classes, &c., I have to report that at once I attempted to obtain reliable information, but without satisfactory results; so I deferred the matter until the present, hoping to be able to furnish fuller information. My labors in this direction have not met with gratifying success.

The workmen and manufactures of Nuremberg were once so universally known and prized in all parts of the world as to give rise to a proverb:

Nuremberg's hand
Goes through every land.

The same founderies and workshops are still famous. Yet, perhaps more than any other German city, Nuremberg has peculiar views and prejudices respecting the question of capital and labor. She glories in her long pedigree of toil, and clings with wonderful tenacity to the ways and customs of a remote ancestry, of "ye mediæval times," and to the memory of her great artists and inventors and manufacturers. She retains in a marked degree the ancient notions respecting the relations of employer and employé. Apparently the manufacturers of this neighborhood look with suspicion and distrust upon all who would find out anything pertaining to their business or their manner of employing their help. Indeed, it is something quite beyond the reach of the newspaper reporter or other gatherer of statistics. The Government does not publish such information even if it obtains it. If one applies to the different manufacturers for the rates of wages, &c., if he receives any information at all, the probability is it will not be reliable. If the representatives of two different newspapers should make the attempt for such information, from the same sources, I am quite certain there would be a ludicrous difference in their figues. Under these circumstances, I cannot give a labor report obtained from official sources. However, I have watched this question closely, and base my conclusions upon personal observations and the little data I have been able to obtain.

RATES OF WAGES.

I find that the question of wages generally, in both workshop and field, is largely a matter of personal contract, and that no two employers pay exactly the same wages, even for the same kind of work; then, again, a large proportion of the labor of this district is known as "piece-work," in which the laborer is paid according to the amount he accomplishes. Whenever practicable, this custom is regarded the most desirable to all concerned, except to the drones and those who are evil-disposed. All honest workmen, here and elsewhere, must admit that this plan stimulates industry and ambition, and then it is fairer to pay for results than by hours. By this means the lazy and vicious laborer soon finds his proper level.

I think it safe to say that laborers, such as mechanics and others, receive from 50 to 75 per cent. less wages than they did five years ago, and the wages now earned vary from 25 cents to $1 per day (without board), according to capacity. And where one man earns $1 per day, probably twenty receive less than fifty cents. At the present time not so much complaint is made of the low price paid for labor as for the want of work. As business now is, the mechanics are not employed more than two-thirds of the time.

As in other countries, the industries here have been much paralyzed during the past three or four years, and the future outlook is not cheerful. Not until the long hard times in the United States and the consequent falling off in American orders did this people know how important a customer our country had been to them in the years gone by. And now, while they admit that our home manufacturers will supplant them largely in the future, they hope for increased orders as prosperity returns to our country. In this it is presumed they will not be disappointed.

COST OF LIVING.

Respecting the cost of living to the laboring class, or the prices paid for what may be termed the necessaries of life, I have to report that this is also largely a matter of personal contract or self-denial.

The lodgings of most of the laboring classes are such as the same class of laborers in the United States would not think of occupying. For the most part they are two or three dark, comfortless rooms for a family of a half-dozen persons, more or less. These quarters vary in price according to locality and desirability, and command from, say, $15 to $25 per annum. There are many lodgings, if such they may be called, occupied by the very poor, where the rent is very low, corresponding to the accommodations; but they resemble dungeons more than the habitations of human beings. Such "homes" are found located within the recesses of the old inner feudal walls of the town, in dilapidated towers and turrets, and in the dark and dismal lanes. Sometimes the same roof may cover a family luxuriously lodged and also a family living in squalid poverty. And this is explained in this way: The houses of Nuremberg were constructed for the accommodation of business, manufacturers generally, and were built of hewn stone, for eternity, *i. e.*, in the most massive as well as artistic manner. The private buildings, such as the mansions of the nobility and "merchant princes," were planned after the same style, though, of course, more highly ornamented, such as rich decorations with carving and stucco. Throughout the city most of the buildings are still inhabited by the families whose forefathers originally constructed them. Though built in the fashion of the mediæval ages, with high, narrow, ornamented fronts, pointed gables, &c., they are mostly of large size, and from the exterior one can form no idea of the immense business facilities contained in the parterre and inner courts or yards, sometimes containing as many as two or three large, deep courts.

These buildings are usually of six to eight stories high, and constructed with an eye to economy of space and capital invested, the buildings having been constructed for a double or triple purpose. The ground story, or first floor, being low and vaulted, was, and is, usually occupied as a warehouse, with packing-rooms, offices, &c., for a commission and export business, with, perhaps, workshops in the rear for their own business. Then came the habitations, being arranged in flats, to accommodate four, five, or six families, quite distinct and independent of each other, with outside covered stairs leading thereto from the inner courts. The first, second, and sometimes third flats, or etages, were usually quite elegantly ornamented, and occupied by the different members of the firm. Indeed, so fine were these lodgings for the period in which they were built, that an ancient author, when writing of the splendor of this city, once declared that a simple Nuremberg citizen was better lodged than a king of Scotland.

Of course, these were the warehouses and lodgings of the burgher "merchant princes" already adverted to, who in the fifteenth century, before Vasco de Gama had discovered the route around the Cape of Good Hope, dictated in a measure the commerce of Continental Europe.

The same author did not refer to the fact that the third, fourth, fifth, and sixth stories (flats) of these buildings were filled, like bee-hives, with human beings, who toiled in the same groove from generation to generation. It often happened that the floors above the second or third stories were used as workshops or lodgings for the employés, or both. These were the better class of manufacturers and also workmen.

Apparently most of the laborers of this country only expect or care to "make ends meet," there being not the same chance to acquire property, such as homestead, &c., as in our more favored country. It often happens that the wife of the mechanic can earn enough by going out washing, scrubbing, sawing wood, &c., to pay for the lodgings, and the poor woman may be the mother of many children to look after at the same time.

Also, it is quite impossible to make a correct estimate of the cost of families' supplies, since about everything in the line of marketing, groceries, &c., have different prices. Even in the markets there are different grades of vegetables, and, as a rule, the poor laboring man's family has to put up with the poorer qualities of meat, vegetables, &c. Good meat and fish are higher than in American markets; other marketing about the same as with us. Not all of the working people can afford meat every day, but must content themselves with black bread and beer, the latter being often regarded as both victuals and drink.

In fine, I am of the opinion that the same class of laborers in the United States are much better paid, lodged, and fed than in this country. And those interested in the labor question here, who have visited our country and carefully investigated this subject, are of the same opinion. In the first place, it would be quite out of the question to expect an American mechanic to put up with the same poor living and other discomforts that have to be borne with here.

TRADE, PAST AND PRESENT.

Notwithstanding the comparative hardships of the laborer, there has been much done by the Government and their employers in Bavaria during the last few years to ameliorate their condition. Less than four decades ago trade was hemmed in with the most illiberal and absurd restrictions. The producers and others of the most useful classes of society, such as the mechanics, had no liberty of trade. All the trades were divided up into different parts and each mechanic was restricted to a particular branch in the same trade. The law did not permit the man who made the wagon to paint the same; nor could a blacksmith proper shoe a horse, or a cabinet-maker employ a woodcarver, nor the man that shaved you cut your hair. So, too, not until within the same period of time could a Jew remain in the city overnight. They (the Jews) were allowed to enter the gates of the city after the sun was up in the morning. A registry of their names and description of their persons was kept. All were required to leave the city before the going down of the sun, when their names were checked off, and if one was found not to have left, the police were required to hunt him up, and, when caught, he was punished.

In those days the Jews were cruelly denied all privileges. They were not permitted to become merchants or enter the learned professions. They were compelled to learn some trade, although against their natural inclination, and from the labors of which they could scarcely subsist. The result was that, in order to make ends meet, they took to peddling clandestinely, since the laws prohibited their doing even this. Under such circumstances, it is not to be wondered at that they flocked to our hospitable shores by the tens of thousands, and canvassed all our populous States, with their packs upon their backs, where they not only acquired wealth, but came to be recognized as among the very best of our adopted citizens. So, too, in Bavaria, all the barriers have been removed, and to-day, even in old Jew-hating Nuremberg, a Jew can marry a Christian, and the Israelites are not only the leading bankers and merchants, but rank among the first in all the learned professions.

THE ARISTOCRACY OF TRADE.

Among the quaint customs of this people with their industries I have found that certain families have not only conducted their factories and other business for many generations, but have given employment to certain families during the whole time. For instance, one, two, or three hundred years ago the family of Sachs were distinguished as manufacturers of Dutch-metal or as goldbeaters, and at the commencement had in their employ certain workmen by name of Schmidt. To-day the same business is conducted upon the same spot and by the descendants of the family Sachs, and to be found among the employés are descendants of the family Schmidt; and I am told that such circumstances are by no means infrequent. It is interesting to know that time and circumstances have created hereditary interests and labor rights, so to speak, between these families. At any rate, the family Sachs feel in duty bound to give employment to the family Schmidt before employing outsiders; and, perhaps, they pay them a little more and give them certain privileges or perquisites, such as their fathers may have received before them. On the other hand, the Schmidts prefer to follow the well-beaten track of their ancestors, and, possibly, would prefer to work for the house of Sachs for a little less than for other people. When capital and labor blend together by the ties of age and mutual interest, the relations of employer and employé are more than interesting. On the one side the manufacturer shows a friendly interest not only in the workman personally, but in all his affairs, such as the personal comfort of his family, the education of his children, &c.; on the other, the laborer evinces a reciprocal interest in the welfare and prosperity of his principal, as well as a proper appreciation of the dignity of labor. Should it become necessary to reduce the hands, as now is the case, those that have the least claim upon the firm are first dispensed with, and sometimes even they receive some slight assistance, and are encouraged with the promise that so soon as times improve they shall be the first employed.

This class of laborers feel themselves above the common herd, who cannot show so long a pedigree. The noble families, of course, affect to look with disdain upon all producers; and, strange as it may seem, there is no class of laborers in the cities but have a contempt for the farmer, or man that tills the soil; the word "*bauer*" (farmer) being a word of reproach. Perhaps it may be owing partly to the fact that the peasant farmers have been always treated like stupid creatures, and have lived such ambitionless lives for so long a period as to have degenerated them into a very inferior class of human beings, as they really seem to be. However, a few years' residence among the more intelligent, spirited, and thrifty farmers of the United States produces a marvelous change for the better with this class.

As may be well supposed, this class of high-toned employers and employed look wich unfriendly eyes upon all laborers not to the Nuremberg manor born. This is especially so respecting the foreigner in the persons of German-American citizens who may have become so reduced while temporarily visiting their fatherland as to be obliged to seek work here, as I personally know from having interested myself in behalf of some such unfortunates.

THE HOUSE OF FABER & CO.

Adverting once more to the mutual interest existing among some of the old capitalists and employés, wherein the hapiness and general welfare is studied by both parties, thereby explaining the absence of all discontent and the presence of harmony, sympathy, and good feeling, I will mention that the world-renowned A. W. Faber Pencil Company is located and originated at Stein, in this neighborhood; the head of the present firm being Lothar von Faber, who succeeded his father, A. W. Faber, in the year 1839.

From a very small beginning the present Mr. Faber has, with the assistance of his brothers (John at Stein and Eberhard at New York), built up an immense business, having two large factories in Bavaria and one in New York.

In each of the factories here several hundred men and women are employed, each hand having their daily piece-work, or "stint." Whenever it is possible, the work is paid by piece.

The Messrs. Faber are distinguished for their philanthropy and for their close attention to the moral and physical welfare of their employés. At their own expense they have established schools and kindergartens, built churches, founded libraries, archer clubs, and other games of recreation for the improvement and amusement of their workmen. The Messrs. Faber evince a most commendable interest in the temporal wants and necessities of their employés, having adopted the union or corporation system for their laborers.

All the actual necessaries of life are purchased by the firm by the wholesale, and the employés can obtain their meat, groceries, vegetables, &c., at wholesale cost prices (same as our Army officers can obtain their supplies from the commissary), care being taken that no unhealthy food is furnished to them, and their sanitary condition closely watched.

These workmen have stronger inducements for saving their wages than their fellows elsewhere in Bavaria; for the Messrs. Faber sell them small parcels of land and build houses for them, giving them a term of years to make their payments, charging 4 per cent. for money on mortgage. Also, they established a savings-bank for their hands, which at present contains $42,000 of the laborers' money; and a hospital, which is supported by allotment from the weekly wages of all the workmen as a reserve or hospital fund; so that, if any of the hands become disabled, their pay goes on, and when old age overtakes them they can rely upon a small pension. In other ways there is evidence of mutual respect and sympathy between this firm and their workmen. When the present company took the establishment, they adopted for their motto the irresistible device, "Truth, Respectability, Industry." Their well-earned fame, both at home and abroad, redounds to the honor of Bavarian industry.

I may mention that a large proportion of the graphite, or black lead, used by the Messrs. Faber comes from the summit of the mountain of Batougal, Eastern Siberia, which now on the Russian maps of the country is designated by the name of Alibertsberg, in honorable remembrance of the discoverer of the black-lead mine. The Fabers have a complete monopoly of this mine, by contract made in 1856, "now and for all time." The cedar-wood used for the pencils, not only by the company Faber, but by all of the many other pencil manufacturers of this neighborhood, comes from our Florida swamps. After being thoroughly dried, it is brought to the importers here, who sell it by the hundred-weight, many thousand hundred-weight being yearly consumed. The export of the world-renowned Faber pencil to the United States has fallen off very largely, now that the firm manufacture extensively in the United States. Also the justly-celebrated "Eagle" pencil, which was formerly made at Fürth, in this consulate, is now manufactured in New York.

I do not know of any other establishments here conducted upon the same plan of the Messrs. Faber, but I have referred to this one at such length as one, in my judgment, worthy of imitation wherever labor and capital are brought into contact. Indeed, this principle and practice seems to be the best solution of the labor question. It shows how labor and capital can best harmonize. Under such arrangements it is quite impossible for such pernicious characters as the destructive "strikers" and lazy "tramps" to exist. With such model regulations, there evidently must be mutual sympathy and interest between employer and employed. And when such harmony exists, there can be no antagonism between those who should be partners.

INDUSTRIAL MUSEUMS.

In connection with the question of labor, I think it pertinent to refer to the Gewerbe (industrial) museums as promoters of science, literature, and the arts.

While the magnificent display made by our inventors and manufacturers at the late Philadelphia and Paris Expositions called forth loud praise from the industrial critics of the old European countries, the same critics were compelled to declare that our exhibits were conspicuous for the absence of works of high art. But, at the same time, they have admitted that, since the taste and spirit for art requires age and much study, in time our people will not be behind the older nations even in this evidence of culture and refinement. I may state that in all of the manufacturing centers of Europe the industrial museums are regarded indispensable adjuncts to the development and improvement of mechanical skill, and I believe these institutions, unlike our mechanical institutes, are all under the fostering care of the different governments.

As may be well supposed, the Gewerbe Museum of Nuremberg is one worthy of the city that in earlier times produced such eminent artists as Albrecht Dürer, Adam Kucht, Peter Vischer, and their contemporaries of the mediæval age. The rapid development of the industries, especially since the first International Exhibition at London, has made it evident that an education beyond the apprenticeship in the workshop is indispensable for the artificer, and industrial museums have proved to be the most effectual means for this purpose.

The South Kensington Museum, in London, may be designated as the prototype of all such institutions. In their collections they furnish the artificer a select number of ready-made articles of all imaginable materials, such as textile fabrics, tapestries, books, book-bindings, works of graphic art, of decorative painting, glass and earthen ware, works in stone, wood, and metal, which can by form, style, and other qualities be assigned as models, and ought to show the inquirer "how to do."

For this purpose it is a matter of indifference from what time or country the objects originated. But since a great many articles cannot be procured in originals because they are too rare or too expensive, drawings of these are collected, which form a so-called "Collecton of models," while the collection of original articles is designated "Collection of samples."

A library in which the literary material regarding the works of arts, inventions, and general industry can be found belongs to the museum as a necessary supplement thereto.

To guide the public in the use of these departments and to furnish information in technical, commercial and juridical matters and questions, a "Bureau of information" is attached to the same, and to facilitate the use of the "Collection of models" a "Drawing-room" is opened; also a "Reading-room" is connected with the library.

These arrangements in the museum proper are used by the artisans in the manner that blacksmiths, joiners, architects, sculptors, bookbinders, engravers, metal and earthenware manufacturers, come to seek technical and artistical advice for the works ordered of them by the public, to make drawings and take notes, so as to give their executions tasteful forms in addition to reliable workmanship. Young men can, under the guidance of professionals, practice drawing from models, samples, or nature. Weekly public lectures, by professors of the museum, treat on the historical, technical, or scientific part of industry. To stimulate industries, a permanent exhibition of modern productions is established, and ready to receive from local and foreign manufacturers such works as are worthy of being exhibited.

Besides these institutions, which at certain hours of the day and evening are open to the public free of charge, exhibitions and lectures are held at stated times in other neighboring cities, in order to instruct those who cannot be at the seat of the museum so as to partake in its benefits. The influence of those industrial museums cannot naturally show itself immediately, but requires some time and a generous outlay of money to make itself felt. Only such artisans will visit the museum as have an earnest desire to improve their manufactures. Only by the advantages realized by these will it be likely that the others, indifferent and unambitious manufacturers, will be obliged to avail themselves of the same privileges if they would not be left far behind.

In countries like England, France, and Austria, where such institutions have also existed for some time, their influence is acknowledged and generally apparent. The prominent position held in the markets of the world by the industrial productions of these countries, especially by the works of art-industry, is due, in no small degree, to the influence of the industrial museums, the foster-mothers of technical and artistical education.

JAMES M. WILSON.

UNITED STATES CONSULATE,
Nuremberg, October 15, 1878.

BREMEN.

Report, by Consul King on the (1) *rates of wages;* (2) *cost of living;* (3) *past and present rates;* (4) *present condition of trade;* (5) *specie and paper money;* (6) *the habits and customs; for the district of Bremen.*

I have the honor to acknowledge the receipt of the Department Circular dated April 11, 1878.

During my absence on leave, Mr. Gruner, vice-consul, collected the following information, which I now beg leave to lay before the Department by way of compliance with instructions contained in said circular. I have numbered the answers to correspond with the questions in the circular:

1. RATES OF WAGES.

Agricultural laborers, without board, per day	$0 48
Agricultural laborers, with board, per day	30
Shoemakers, per week	$2 40 to 3 60
Tailors, per week	4 80 to 6 00
Blacksmiths, per week	2 40 to 2 88
Carpenters, per week	3 60 to 4 80
Masons, per week	3 60 to 4 80
Joiners, per week	2 40 to 2 88
Laborers on public works, daily	36 to 60

2. COST OF LIVING.

Unmarried men, about $1.92 per week; families, consisting of husband, wife, and three children, from $3.60 to $4.32 weekly.

In order to make life at this rate possible, women in the country raise their own garden produce and, when they can, work in the fields. In town the women keep small shops, peddle fish or fruit, knit, wash, scrub, or sew.

3. PAST AND PRESENT RATES.

	Present weekly wages.	Wages five years ago.
Agricultural laborers	$2 88	$4 32
Shoemakers	$2 40 to 3 60	$3 60 to 4 80
Tailors	4 80 to 6 00	6 00 to 7 20
Carpenters	3 60 to 4 80	7 20 to 8 40
Masons	3 60 to 4 80	7 20 to 8 40
Joiners	2 40 to 2 88	6 48 to 8 40
Blacksmiths	2 40 to 2 88	6 48 to 7 20

The rent of small houses is a little less at present than it was five years ago; otherwise the cost of living is about the same now as then.

4. Present condition of trade.

Trade at present is not prosperous, and all tradesmen complain of a scarcity of work and of hard times generally. Failures are of almost daily occurrence, especially among small shopkeepers and mechanics. The general badness of the times is best shown by the forced judicial sales of about a hundred houses weekly in this city, which have been taking place for nearly three years past; one of the results of which sales has been a depreciation of about 50 per cent. in the value of real estate.

5. Specie and paper money.

The coin in circulation here is the Reichsmark in use throughout the German Empire, and the paper used is at par value with the coin There are two sorts of paper money in use in Bremen. One is the notes issued by the German Reichs- (Imperial) Bank at Berlin, under the control and management of the Imperial Government, and I believe unlimited as to the amount of issue; the other is the notes issued by the Bremen Bank, a private local institution, which has the legal right to issue 4,500,000 marks of uncovered notes; any excess of this amount being taxed 5 per cent. If the amount be covered, however, its issue is unlimited. It cannot issue notes of less than 100 marks.

6. Customs and habits.

Workingmen, mechanics, &c., usually commence work in summer at 6 o'clock, stop half an hour for breakfast at 8, an hour for dinner at noon, half an hour at 4, and quitting at 7. In winter the hours are the same, except in the case of bricklayers, carpenters, and such others as cannot easily use artificial light, who work from dark to dark, at one-third less wages than in summer. Many, however, work according to contract or agreement.

It is the custom to pay mechanics and laborers weekly on Saturdays. The law requires fourteen days' notice to be given before quitting work.

Especial courts, called trade-courts, have been established by law for settling disputes. Each court consists of one employer, one employé, and one of the judges from the law courts.

A credit of six months, or even of a year, is given by tradesmen, but an allowance of 4 per cent. for cash is customary.

In wholesale business mostly all transactions are finally settled at the exchange, which meets at 1 o'clock each day.

Every one dines at 2, and business is usually suspended until after 4 o'clock, when business is resumed until 7 or after.

WILSON KING.

United States Consulate,
Bremen, June 17, 1878.

BRUNSWICK.

Report, by Consul Fox, on the (1, 2, *and* 3) *rates of wages;* (4) *cost of living;* (5) *monetary affairs;* (6) *present state of trade; for the district of Brunswick.*

I have the honor to acknowledge the receipt of the Department Circular of the 11th ultimo, and, in reply to the same, I beg to report the following as the result of my inquiries and investigations:

In regard to the German laborers and the rates of wages paid, I have arranged them into three classes, giving the minimum and the maximum price paid to each class.

1. Mechanics and skilled laborers of all kinds receive from 48 to 75 cents per day, without board.

2. Ordinary laborers, including farm and field hands, receive from 36 to 48 cents per day, without board. In the country the custom is to pay more in land products than in cash, similar to the American "on share" plan. To these two classes only belong those who are employed by the day.

3. Railway hands, laborers on public works, and all such as are employed for a period of time receive from 38 to 60 cents per day, without board.

4. The family of the laboring man, consisting of himself, wife, and three children, can live very comfortably on $216 per annum; therefore, with steady work, such a man can make both ends meet.* In most cases the wife and elder children contribute to the general support by performing other work. Such work is to be found in abundance in Brunswick.

5. In regard to German monetary affairs, I beg to say that the German Reichsbank has the privilege of issuing about 270,000,000 marks more of bank-notes than she has specie in her vaults. Should the circulation of these notes exceed the amount of coin by more than the above-named sum, the bank must pay a yearly tax of 5 per centum on the surplus.

The Bank of Hanover can issue 6,000,000 marks; the Bank of Brunswick about 3,000,000 marks on the same conditions.

At the last statement the Reichsbank had 80,000,000 marks; the Bank of Hanover, 3,000,000 marks; and the Bank of Brunswick, 1,600,000 marks of notes, uncovered by coin, in circulation. Paper money is equal in value to coin, since it is at all times redeemable in coin.

6. Trade in general is very dull all over Germany; in this consular district especially. Work, however, of many kinds is readily to be obtained. The great trouble seems to be that workmen will not work at present prices or at such work as is to be had. As far as I am able to learn, the Social-Democratic party is largely reponsible for this state of things.

The rapid increase of German industry, especially in 1871 and 1872, had a most extraordinary influence on wages. This, coupled with the success of the German arms, led the German laborer to believe that his position would henceforth be one of ease and affluence; and he there-

* Taking the minimum rates of wages given above into consideration, and even multiplying the per-diem compensation by 313 days, the maximum of working days in the year, it is not possible for the laborer to make "both ends meet," unless his family earns an amount equal to or more than he earns himself.—NOTE BY THE DEPARTMENT.

fore accustomed himself to indulge in various luxuries previously to him unknown.

In 1874, when the grand reaction came, exchange turned against Germany; her industries declining, wages, of course, declined in proportion, and the working hours were increased. The workman then was in a worse condition than ever before, and, becoming disgusted and discontented, would not work.

I am well aware that the Department is fully posted on this point, and I only desire to refer to it in connection with the fact that the German Government is endeavoring to enact new and stringent laws for the control of this organization, which through its machinations has done so much to interfere with the prosperity of this country.

WILLIAM C. FOX.

UNITED STATES CONSULATE,
Brunswick, May 23, 1878.

CHEMNITZ AND SAXONY.

Report, by Consul Griggs, of Chemnitz, on (1) *the condition of labor;* (2) *cost and manner of living;* (3) *taxes;* (4) *business habits and customs, together with tables showing the rates of wages, food prices, &c.; for Chemnitz and all Saxony.*

1. LABOR IN SAXONY.*

Saxony is so densely populated that, at all times, the labor supply is greatly in excess of the demand. At the present time large numbers are unable to obtain employment; the country is full of tramps, both honest and vagabondish, and almost every dwelling in Chemnitz is visited daily by at least a half dozen beggars, notwithstanding that begging is strictly prohibited by law. In this district labor is subdivided so as to give employment to the largest number possible, this giving one man's work to two. This, coupled with the fact that the future holds forth no promise of better days, is naturally productive of slowness and idleness. An American mechanic or laborer would be astonished to see two men at work where but one was needed, but he would be still more astonished to see the small amount of work which the two would perform. However, these people claim, perhaps justly, that their work is fully equal to their pay, and that they would not be justified in moving faster, as there is not enough to do to give all employment even when they work at their present speed. I remember to have seen some statistics in a continental paper, which went to show that in a given length of time 900 factory hands in England do as much work as 1,200 in Saxony. Whether this statement is true or not I cannot say, but I am satisfied that an ordinary laborer in the United States will do almost as much again as will one in this district in the same length of time, and there can be no doubt that our mechanics are at least as skillful as those in Saxony.

The hosiery and glove makers, as well as a few others, are idle but very little for want of work. With these exceptions, the laboring classes of this consular district lose a large portion of their time owing to their inability to find employment. If the time lost by reason of the holi-

*For rates of wages for the years 1873 to 1878, inclusive, see Tables A, B, and C, accompanying this report.

days, of which there are about twenty during the year, and this enforced idleness is considered, the average amount of wages earned by each workman will be found to be only about $2.50 per week; surely a very small sum with which to pay rent and taxes and purchase food and clothing for a family.

During the past five years the decrease in the average amount of wages paid to the women of this district has been very slight. This is partly owing to the fact that in 1873 the price paid for female help was too insignificant to admit of much reduction, but more to the increased demand in the United States for fancy embroidered hosiery and gloves.

A comparison of the average amount paid to the workingmen five years ago with the average amount paid now will show that they received about 9 per cent. more then than at present. This reduction is due partly to the general stagnation of trade since the panic, partly to the not unlooked-for collapse of the overgrown machine-shops and founderies, but more to the fact that men are generally employed to make such articles only as can be manufactured by machinery. As such goods can be produced in England or America at least of as fine a quality, and almost as cheaply as in Saxony, foreign competition drove prices down, and as they fell, so also decreased wages in nearly the same ratio.

For a number of years past the crops in this district have been all that could be desired. During the past year trade was better here than in any other part of Germany; the exports to the United States showing an increase of 12.7 per cent. over the previous year and 2.2 per cent. over 1873. With good crops and increased trade we should expect good times and but little want. While the times have been fair for some classes of workmen, others have been kept from starvation alone by public charity. This singular state of affairs, although foreseen, was unavoidable. A large number of the inhabitants of Southern Saxony—Voigtland—formerly made their living by weaving lace curtains. Her superior machinery has enabled England quite recently to drive the Saxon goods so completely from the market, that they cannot now be sold even at home. As the Voigtlanders had no means save what their business brought them, when it was ruined they were at once reduced to want and a few are said to have died of hunger. A famine of considerable magnitude was prevented alone by the generous people of this kingdom coming promptly to their assistance. Notwithstanding that the hand-made curtains of these people are so superior that they are being sold now in the English and American markets as the *finest French* goods, still, in order to produce them at sufficiently low figures to find purchasers, a grown person must work fourteen hours per day to earn *forty-seven cents* per week. Unable to live upon this small pittance, and without means to purchase new machinery with which to regain their lost trade, the future of a large portion of the Saxon lace-weavers is a cheerless one indeed.

For making hosiery and gloves the workmen received more per dozen in 1873, but notwithstanding this, thanks to improved machinery, their earnings have not seriously decreased. Machinists and foundery men still receive as much per hour as before the panic, but diminished trade has decreased their hours of labor and consequently their annual earnings about 30 per cent.

Formerly many of those employed in the postal and telegraph service were allowed "extras," but retrenchment has done away with nearly all of such perquisites. Until lately the railroad employés were given "free coffee" after performing certain service. Now, not only is this withheld, but three men are required to do the work previously assigned to four. Five years ago the embroidery and silk-fringe makers earned no more than was necessary to provide them with the most common necessaries of life; now, to earn 40 per cent. of their former earnings, they must work, in summer from 5 o'clock a. m. to 8.30 p. m., and in winter from daylight to dark. At night they cannot afford to work, as their wages would not purchase lights. While the men, who generally use machinery, are able to earn from $1.50 to $2.50 per week, many of the women, especially makers of hand-made embroidery, make no more than one-third part of that amount. That the general depression of trade has had much to do in bringing about the present condition of the embroidery makers of this district there can be no doubt, but that our market and our importers are also largely responsible I am equally certain. As the makers of such goods are paid for their work by the thousand stitches, they must necessarily earn less now, when our market requires heavy work and coarse stitching, than they did in 1873, when the demand was for finer work and finer stitching. A few years since all of the embroideries exported from this district, as well as from St. Gall, Switzerland, were manufactured by local firms for their own account. Of late years the majority of our large importers have furnished the materials, and, through agents, employed workmen to make them such goods as they wanted; thus getting them at cost price. The home firms, in order to hold any of the American trade, had to sell at reduced rates, and, to do so, had to cut down the wages of their workmen, most of whom had to submit, as the importers did not require the services of all. The importers, in turn, paid less and less to those whom they, through their agents, employed; and thus, for two or three years past, have the workmen's earnings been gradually diminishing. The result of this is, that the business of the local firms is almost ruined and the laborers are working at starvation wages.

Postal and telegraph service.—The imperial postal and telegraph service extends to all parts of Germany except Bavaria and Würtemberg. These kingdoms, although under the same system, are entirely independent of the general government in this regard. Table B is based upon the latest official report of the imperial office, that of 1875. Since that time the service and numbers of the employés have been slightly increased, but the official salaries still remain unchanged.

In 1875 there were employed in the post-office general at Berlin 191 officials, with salaries aggregating $176,393.70; an average of about $923.53 each. Of the 191 officials, 25 received more than $1,000 per annum; the postmaster-general, in addition to free dwelling, was given $5,735.80; the director of the post, $3,570; and the director of the telegraph the same. In the year 1875 the employés in the general postal and telegraph service numbered 36,527, with salaries aggregating $10,267,910.58; an average of about $281.11 each. At the principal cities, 41 in number, the postmasters received $1,904 each, with the exception of the one at Berlin, whose salary was $2,499. Telegraph operators of the first class received $392.70 each; those of the second class, $285.60; women, $214.20. The places of the latter are shortly to be given to men. The letter-carriers of the first class, 700 in number, received $285.60 each; those of the second class, 11,500 in number, only $128.42. These salaries are slightly increased by the Christmas present of from 50 cents to $1.50, which custom requires each person to give to the carrier who delivers him mail during the year.

Railroads.—The Saxon Government, either by virtue of ownership or rental, controls all the railroads in this kingdom with the exception of three or four. The latter will be purchased by it as soon as satisfactory arrangements can be made with the corporations now owning and operating them.

In Germany the railways are admirably managed. Here there is no confusion, no delay, no accident. The neatly-uniformed officers, many of whom are pensioned soldiers, not only understand their duties, but discharge them with the precision of military discipline. A rule is prescribed for everything, and everything is done by rule. No one steps on the car when it is moving, and no one opens the door but the conductor. One tap of the bell says "Start shortly"; two, "Be seated"; three, "Go." As the train moves away from one station the fact is announced at the next by a bell which is rung by telegraph. That we travel faster, have finer engines and cars, and better accommodations in the United States than in Germany is true, but that the railway management is far better and life much safer here than in our country is just as undeniable.

There are at least three grades of each class of railway employés, the first receiving about 14 per cent. more than the second, the second about 14 per cent. more than the third. Five years' service in one grade advances the person serving to the next higher; hence at least ten years' service is necessary to attain to the first rank. In this city, of eight railroads, only four officials receive more than $1,000 annually, the superintendent's salary, $1,513.68, being the highest. Section-hands are paid per year from $144.80 to $174.45.

A certain sum is allowed all railway employés for clothing, and some are furnished dwellings and servants; but, with the exception of the commission of the ticket-agent and the savings of the engineer and fireman, the salaries given in Table C are not only *first class*, but are inclusive of all extras of every kind whatever. The ticket-agents, in addition to salary, receive a commission of $\frac{1}{100}$ per cent. on money received by them from the sale of tickets; and if the engineer and fireman run their engine with a less quantity of coal and oil than the government provides, they are allowed for such savings at a certain fixed rate, three-fourths going to the engineer, the other fourth to the fireman. The sum realized from such "savings" is no mean part of these men's earnings, and certainly the arrangement is to be commended on the score of economy.

2. Cost and manner of living in Saxony.*

Since 1873 the cost of living in this district has increased about 10 per cent., and is now fully as great as in the large cities of the United States. When the price of labor in Saxony is compared with the cost of what may be termed the necessaries of life, one unacquainted with the working classes will naturally wonder how they manage to exist; but to know their habits, see their homes, and behold their spread tables solves the mystery. As the husband's wages are insufficient to support a family, the wife, as also the older children, must contribute a share of the weekly earnings. This is a general rule, and applies to all families whose support is dependent upon labor. The women and children residing immediately south of this city embroider fancy hosiery or manufacture staple goods upon small hand-looms; those residing in the hilly country, still farther south, make embroideries, laces, fringes, musical goods, &c.; those in this city of the lower classes are glad to obtain any kind of menial employment which will bring them from twenty to twenty-five cents per day. Thus by them are manufactured fully one-half of the

* For prices of groceries in June, 1878, see Table D.

goods which are exported from this market, and to them a large proportion of the laborers' earnings may be accredited.

Plain living is the universal rule in this part of Europe. Very few in this country ever saw such a meal as the hotels of ours furnish daily. To order such an one would astonish the landlord; to pay for it would dumfound the guest. That plain food is healthy no one can doubt after having seen the robust people of Germany.

Owing to the demand for hosiery and gloves in America, the makers of such goods are able to earn more and consequently live better than the other working people of this district.

The poorer classes in Southern Saxony fare very meanly indeed. For homes, they have generally a single room, which answers for workshop as well. For household furniture, they have a few plain chairs or wooden stools, a table, stove, and sometimes a loom. For beds, they have the bare floor or straw pallets. For fuel, they have the dead branches which fall from the trees, and which are carried by them in their arms from the king's forests. For food, they have black bread made of rye, coffee made principally of chicory, a few boiled potatoes, sometimes a little cheese, butter, or goose grease, and on Sundays a pound of meat for a family of five or six persons. Their clothes are of the coarsest material, and their shoes are generally wooden-soled slippers. If "poor and content is rich," then no others, within my knowledge, can compare in wealth with the poor of this district. They live in villages, and love company. When Sunday or a holiday comes, they meet together at a restaurant, smoke poor tobacco, drink "Einfach" beer, talk, sing, and dance, and are as happy as if they "had a thousand a year."

3. Taxes assessed in the city of Chemnitz for the year 1878.*

By the laws of Saxony a certain sum is named as a "single rate." As many times this single rate is collected each year as the necessities of the Government may require. For the purposes of taxation, individuals and property are divided into classes. There are four taxes levied annually, viz: municipal, royal, taxes on personalty, and taxes on realty. The tax last named is based upon the rental value of the property. Personal property is assessed according to actual value. The municipal and royal taxes are levied upon the income. The law providing for income taxes was made in the interest of the poorer classes: Thus, an income of $100 pays $2.04; $500, $17.46; $1,000, $54; $1,500, $107.14; $2,000, $168.32; $3,000, $251.60, &c.

The municipal tax is $14\frac{1}{2}$ times the single rate, and is applied as follows: $\frac{77}{145}$ to city uses, $\frac{53}{145}$ to school purposes, $\frac{15}{145}$ to the support of the churches.

The royal tax, first collected in 1877, is six times the single rate, and is applied to the uses of the Saxon Government.

The personal-property tax is about the same in amount as the royal. It will probably be omitted from the tax-list after next year, and the income taxes correspondingly increased.

The real-estate tax is an assessment based upon the rental income of the property charged. The single rate is $3\frac{1}{2}$ mills on the dollar. The amount levied for 1878 is $14\frac{1}{2}$ times the single rate, or $5\frac{3}{40}$ per cent. of the rental income. Realty is classified thus: Class A is property renting for 10 marks ($2.38) or less; class B, 10 to 20 marks, and so on up to 100 marks. After that classes increase by 100 marks each.

* See Tables E and F.

4. Business customs in the city of Chemnitz.

In no country is the law of custom more strictly obeyed than in this. For many years past the rich as well as a majority of poor parents have bound their sons to a master to have them taught some trade or business. This custom has become so much a law that places of honor or profit are given to those only who have served this indispensable apprenticeship. At fourteen years of age the youth leaves the common school. If his parents are poor, he is at once articled to a master. If rich, he continues his studies two or three years, and then begins his service. The apprenticeship must end at twenty, for then comes the army, which, if the young man is able to pass an examination in certain branches of education, is for one year only; otherwise for three. If the apprentice has taken a course of studies in the Royal Workmaster's School, his term of apprenticeship is generally for two years; if not, then it is for three or four years, and in some cases even longer. Some apprentices are boarded and clothed by their masters; others are boarded or clothed only. The majority receive nothing whatever, while many pay from $50 to $200 for the privilege of learning certain kinds of business. They cannot be required to work more than ten hours per day, and in all cases must be permitted to attend the schools which are provided for them by the Government. These schools are held two or three evenings each week, but were formerly held on Sundays.

Office hours are from 7 to 12 and from 2 to 7. Here it is very common to work on Sundays. Women do light work at home, and usually crochet or knit at Sunday concerts. The butcher-shops and bakeries are open from early morn until 9 o'clock, the hour for church service, has arrived. All business must then be suspended. At 11 o'clock the majority of the stores are opened, and kept open for the remainder of day. Even the workshops are frequently kept busy on Sundays, but leave to operate them must first be obtained from the city authorities.

The offices are most plainly furnished. The counter of the leading bank in this city is a rather rough board about 2 feet wide. The bank has no desk for the convenience of its customers, no carpets, no curtains, no ornaments, and although about a dozen clerks are employed, its entire furniture would scarcely cost $500. The cashier is receiving as well as paying teller. No deposit-checks are used, hence when he receives money he at once enters it in two books, the bank's and the depositor's. A check will not be honored unless the depositor's book is also presented, so that the amount can be entered in it at the time of payment. The bank alluded to is sound, and does a large and extended business. It is one of the most important in this district, and in every respect may be said to fairly represent Chemnitz banks and banking.

Loans by banks or private persons usually run from one to five years' time, the interest charged is from 5 to 6 per cent. per annum, and the security required is usually real estate worth from three to four times the amount loaned. Banks allow interest on deposits at the rate of 2 per cent. when subject to check, and at the rate of 3 per cent. when left a certain length of time.

Before 1873 long credits were given and bills rendered annually; then money was plentiful, interest low, and chances for speculation numerous. The panic wrought as great a change here as in the United States. The stoppage of trade ruined many and injured all of Saxony's great workshops. Bills were withdrawn, and stocks, which had previously circulated as money, became worthless. As the volume of the circulating medium thus decreased and money became scarcer the rate of interest became higher. To obtain cash, manufacturers gladly sold their goods at greatly reduced rates, and thus was established the present custom of selling at low rates on three months' time, with a small discount for cash.

The Saxon exporters deserve great credit for their business enterprise and energetic efforts to secure foreign customers. They now send their goods to every part of the world, and if a new article makes its appearance in any other country, they will duplicate and export it in a very short time, provided they can profit by so doing. Not so much can be said for the other business-men of this district, a large majority of whom contentedly transact their affairs in the same manner as did the generation before them; they sell their wares in the same little shops, office in the same cheerless rooms, sit on the same old chairs, write on the same rude desks, dry their ink with the same abominable sand, pay their debts in the same old-fashioned honest way, and move quietly along, seemingly unconscious of the fact that this is the day of fine offices, bazaars, railroads, telegraphs, and bankruptcies.

N. K. GRIGGS.

UNITED STATES CONSULATE,
Chemnitz, June 19, 1878.

A.—*Wages, per week, in the district of Chemnitz for the years* 1873 *to* 1878.

Occupations.	1873.	1874.	1875.	1876.	1877.	1878.
Accordeon-makers	$2 38	$2 85	$2 85	$2 85	$2 61	$2 38
Artificial-flower makers, women	1 42	1 90	2 38	2 49	2 38	2 38
Bakers	3 92	3 92	3 92	3 92	3 92	3 92
Barbers	3 21	3 21	3 21	2 85	2 85	2 85
Basket-makers	3 45	3 33	3 21	2 92	2 92	2 92
Beltmakers	2 85	2 85	2 85	2 85	2 85	2 85
Bleachers	3 57	3 21	2 85	2 38	2 14	2 14
Bleachers, women	2 14	1 90	1 66	1 42	1 42	1 42
Bookbinders	3 30	3 92	4 40	4 40	4 28	4 28
Bookbinders, women	1 38	1 42	1 60	1 60	1 60	1 60
Braziers	4 28	4 28	4 28	4 28	4 28	4 28
Brickmakers	3 68	3 68	3 68	3 09	2 86	2 53
Brickmakers, women	2 55	2 55	2 26	2 08	1 85	1 85
Brushmakers	3 32	3 32	3 03	2 90	2 87	2 80
Butchers	3 57	3 68	3 92	3 68	3 68	3 68
Button-makers	3 80	3 80	3 57	3 33	3 10	2 87
Car-builders	4 04	4 16	3 92	3 92	3 92	3 92
Carders	4 28	4 28	4 28	4 28	4 28	4 28
Carders, women	1 88	1 84	1 90	1 90	1 90	1 90
Cardmakers	3 56	3 56	3 56	3 56	3 56	3 56
Cardmakers, women	1 37	1 37	1 49	1 49	1 49	1 49
Carpenters	3 64	3 64	3 64	3 64	3 14	2 85
Cement-makers	5 71	5 71	5 00	5 00	4 77	4 77
Chairmakers	3 57	3 80	3 80	3 80	3 57	3 57
Chemical makers	3 50	3 50	3 50	3 50	3 50	3 50
Chimney-sweeps	2 14	2 14	2 38	2 85	2 38	2 38
Cigar-makers	3 21	3 21	2 61	2 61	2 61	2 61
Cigar-makers, women	2 61	2 61	1 78	1 78	1 78	1 78
Clerks	7 14	7 14	6 44	6 44	6 44	6 44
Clerks, women	4 76	4 76	4 28	4 28	4 28	4 28
Clothfinishers	3 21	3 56	3 41	3 27	3 04	3 04
Clothfinishers, women	1 60	1 72	1 72	1 72	1 72	1 72
Combmakers	2 80	2 80	2 80	2 80	2 80	2 80
Compositors	7 14	7 00	6 88	6 45	6 21	6 06
Confectioners	3 92	3 92	3 92	3 92	3 92	3 92
Coopers	2 61	2 61	2 73	2 73	2 61	2 61
Designers	2 85	3 21	3 57	3 57	3 34	3 34
Distillers	3 78	3 78	3 61	3 63	3 61	3 61
Dyers	3 56	3 56	3 56	3 56	3 56	3 56
Embroidery-makers (machine)	5 71	5 23	4 76	4 28	3 09	2 38
Embroidery (hand-work), women	1 66	1 42	1 19	95	83	53
Engravers	4 76	4 76	3 57	3 92	3 57	3 57
Filecutters	4 27	3 57	2 85	1 90	1 90	1 90
Fringemakers	3 33	2 97	2 61	2 25	1 90	1 67
Fringemakers, women	2 61	2 37	2 14	1 90	1 66	1 43
Furniture-makers	5 47	4 52	4 52	3 57	3 24	3 04
Furniture-makers, women	1 42	1 36	1 36	1 36	1 36	1 36
Furriers	3 09	3 32	3 56	3 87	3 56	3 56

A.—*Wages, per week, in the district of Chemnitz for the years* 1873 *to* 1878—Continued.

Occupations.	1873.	1874.	1875.	1876.	1877.	1878.
Furriers, women	$1 42	$1 60	$1 90	$2 08	$1 90	$1 90
Gardeners	3 56	3 80	4 04	4 04	3 80	3 80
Glaziers	4 28	4 28	3 93	3 93	3 70	3 70
Glovemakers, women	1 78	1 78	1 78	1 78	1 66	1 66
Goldsmiths	3 39	3 39	3 75	4 44	4 11	4 11
Hairdressers	4 36	4 70	4 70	4 70	4 47	4 47
Harness-makers	3 03	3 03	3 03	3 03	3 03	3 03
Hatters	3 50	3 56	3 56	3 56	3 10	3 10
Hosiery-finishers, women	1 42	1 66	1 54	1 54	1 48	1 48
Iron and steel workers:						
Blacksmiths	4 52	4 76	4 64	4 28	4 05	4 05
Founders	4 28	4 04	3 98	3 78	3 78	3 78
Hosiery-loom builders	3 45	3 45	3 45	3 45	3 45	3 45
Locksmiths	3 75	3 75	3 45	3 39	3 27	3 27
Machine-builders	4 75	3 91	4 32	4 39	4 17	4 17
Nailmakers	3 09	3 09	3 09	2 97	2 97	2 97
Planers	3 80	4 28	4 76	4 28	4 28	4 28
Safemakers	4 09	4 00	4 00	4 00	4 00	4 00
Job-printers	5 91	5 68	5 00	4 76	4 53	4 28
Joiners	3 56	3 56	3 44	3 32	2 85	2 85
Laborers, servants, &c	2 14	2 14	2 14	2 14	2 14	2 14
Laborers, servants, &c., women	1 42	1 42	1 42	1 42	1 42	1 42
Laborers, per year, with board	31 00	31 00	31 00	31 00	31 00	31 00
Laborers, per year, with board, women	23 80	23 80	23 80	23 80	23 80	23 80
Lacemakers, women	1 66	1 42	1 19	95	80	47
Lithographers	4 28	4 28	4 28	4 28	4 28	4 28
Lithographers, women	1 42	1 42	1 42	1 42	1 42	1 42
Mechanics	4 40	4 40	4 40	4 40	4 05	3 70
Millers	4 16	4 40	4 52	4 22	4 22	4 22
Milliners	1 90	1 90	1 90	1 96	1 96	1 96
Musical-instrument makers	3 33	3 33	3 33	3 33	3 33	3 33
Musical-instrument makers, women	1 60	1 60	1 60	1 60	1 60	1 60
Oilcloth makers	3 53	3 57	3 68	3 21	3 21	3 21
Painters	4 34	4 46	4 58	4 28	4 28	4 28
Photographers	3 57	3 57	3 57	3 57	3 57	3 57
Plasterers	4 34	3 92	3 86	3 63	3 28	3 00
Potters	5 00	5 00	4 28	3 51	3 51	3 51
Printers of cotton, wool, &c	3 57	3 21	2 85	2 38	2 38	2 38
Printers of cotton, wool, &c., women	2 14	1 90	1 66	1 42	1 42	1 42
Roadmakers	3 45	3 45	3 27	3 21	3 21	3 21
Saddlers	3 21	3 27	3 80	3 74	3 57	3 57
Sculptors	5 35	4 28	5 00	3 80	3 80	3 80
Shoemakers	2 08	2 38	2 38	2 38	2 38	2 38
Shoemakers, women	1 78	1 78	1 78	1 78	1 78	1 78
Slaters	4 82	4 82	4 82	4 88	4 88	4 88
Soapmakers	3 57	3 92	4 40	4 40	4 40	4 40
Spinners of cotton	3 57	3 57	3 57	3 43	3 43	3 43
Spinners of wool	2 50	2 74	2 97	2 97	2 97	2 97
Stone-quarrymen	2 50	2 50	2 14	2 14	2 14	2 14
Stone-masons	4 04	4 04	4 04	3 69	3 14	2 85
Sugar-makers	2 71	4 04	3 63	3 49	3 37	3 37
Sugar-makers, women	1 26	1 26	1 36	1 38	1 38	1 38
Tailors	4 40	4 40	3 57	2 97	2 97	2 97
Tanners	3 39	3 57	3 57	3 57	3 57	3 57
Tinners	4 16	4 16	4 10	3 92	3 92	3 92
Trunkmakers	4 10	3 75	3 75	3 75	3 75	3 75
Umbrella-makers	4 28	4 28	4 28	4 28	4 28	4 28
Umbrella-makers, women	2 14	2 14	2 14	2 14	2 14	2 14
Watchmakers	4 46	4 58	4 82	4 46	4 46	4 46
Weavers of damasks	3 93	3 93	3 93	3 93	3 93	3 93
dress-goods	3 57	3 57	3 03	2 73	2 73	2 73
dress-goods, women	2 38	2 26	2 14	1 90	1 66	1 66
hose in factories	3 21	3 21	3 21	2 98	2 98	2 98
hose, home labor	2 50	2 50	2 50	2 26	2 26	2 26
wire cloth	2 85	2 85	2 85	2 85	2 85	2 85
Wheelwrights	2 97	3 09	2 97	2 85	2 85	2 85

B.—*Salaries at post-offices and stations.*

Officials.	No. employed in 1875.	Annual salary.
Chief of newspaper department	....	$1,285 20
Inspector of newspaper department	....	1,071 00
Comptroller of newspaper department	....	999 60
Cashier of newspaper department	....	928 20
Chief of station, first class	542	833 00
second class	566	464 10
third class	2,070	221 34
Chief of telegraph station	43	833 00
railroad postal station	35	833 00
Cashier postal and telegraph station	60	714 00
Secretary postal and telegraph station, first class	480	678 30
second class	4,222	547 40
Telegraph operators, first class	1,700	392 70
second class	1,138	285 60
third class, ladies	93	214 20
Overseer newspaper and packet depot	96	290 38
Postal and telegraph employés	8,806	249 90
Letter-carriers, large cities, first class	760	285 60
second class	11,500	128 42
Carriers of dispatches	120	285 60
packages	1,590	183 26
Carriers for emptying mail-boxes	680	183 26

B.—*Salaries of postal and telegraph officials in Germany.*

Officials.	No. employed in 1875.	Annual salary.
Postmaster in Berlin	....	$2,499 00
Postmasters at other large cities	40	1,904 00
Commissioners of postal service, first class	8	1,213 80
second class	77	1,073 38
Assistants (extra fees allowed)	40	214 20
Architects of postal buildings	13	1,071 00
Inspectors, postal and telegraph service	113	749 70
Inspector at Berlin, postal and telegraph service (extra fees)	....	142 80
Clerks at postal treasury, first class	38	928 20
second class	79	678 30
Cashiers	18	785 40
Accountants, first class	309	678 30
second class	172	535 50
Clerks, first class	87	535 50
second class	118	285 60
third class	8	228 48

B.—*Salaries at post-office general, Berlin.*

Officials.	No. employed in 1875.	Annual salary.
Postmaster-general (dwelling free)	....	$5,735 80
Director postal department	....	3,570 00
Director telegraph department	....	3,570 00
Commissioners postal telegraph	16	2,070 60
Assistants	4	1,356 60
Register money-order department	....	1,428 00
Assistants	5	573 58
Engineer telegraph department	....	1,285 20
Auditors	52	999 60
Chief money-order department	....	999 60
supply department	....	999 60
of office department	2	999 60
Cashier money-order department	....	999 60
Postal-building architects	2	535 50
Architects' clerks	2	357 00
Bookkeepers	8	749 70
Private secretaries	25	606 90
Accountants, first class	39	678 30
second class	28	464 10

C.—Salaries and wages paid by the Saxon Government to railway officials and employés.

	Per annum.
Superintendent, passenger department	$1,513 68
Master-machinist	1,313 76
First assistant	714 00
Second assistant	499 80
Chief division engineer	1,285 20
First assistant	979 08
Second assistant	642 60
Third assistant	471 24
Master-mechanic	1,056 72
Assistant	257 04
Manager, freight department	980 32
Custodian, heavy freight	980 32
light freight and baggage	680 44
Station inspector	956 76
Assistant	471 24
Telegraph inspector, district	746 13
division	628 32
Paymaster	737 56
Cashier, freight department	730 42
Ticket agent, first class	723 28
second class	609 04
Custodian, railroad supplies	714 00
Assistant	599 76
Overseer, round-house	714 00
depot and freight-yard	460 53
Auditor, repair-shop	714 00
Freight-master	571 20
First assistant	456 96
Second assistant	364 38
Locomotive engineer, freight	535 50
passenger	514 55
Foreman, repair-shop	528 36
Assistant	456 96
Foreman, engine-house	416 76
Track inspector	519 79
Track-master	440 53
Assistant	337 00
Chief telegraph operator	514 79
Telegraph operator	379 13
Assistant	364 85
Weigher	505 51
Register, machine-shop	499 80
Clerks, freight and passenger departments	494 80
superintendent's office	456 96
Baggage-master on train	474 80
Assistants	366 28
Messenger, freight department	462 67
Conductor, chief	444 10
Second class, acting brakeman	274 17
Third class, acting brakeman	257 04
Brakeman on freight-train	291 31
Draughtsman	357 00
Foreman, freight unloaders	322 01
Freight unloaders	251 18
Foreman, baggage-carriers	322 01
Baggage-carriers	252 75
Porter, passenger-depot	306 30
ordinary	253 47
Fireman, locomotive	299 88
at depot	253 47
night	242 76
Advertiser	287 26
Switch-tender	274 17
Coal-measurer	271 32
Assistant	234 19
Engine-cleaner	248 47
Bell-ringer	232 76

Watchman at railroad crossing in city	$231 81
country	227 05
Assistant in country	188 49
Night-watchman	231 33
Section-hands, first class	174 45
second class	159 65
third class	144 80

D.—Statement showing the price, in June, 1878, of groceries, produce, &c., in Chemnitz.

Beef	per pound	$0 18.5
sirloin	do	23.8
Bread	do	06
rye	do	02.3
Butter	do	16.1
Cheese	do	33.3
Coffee, Rio	do	30
Java	do	38.3
Dried currants	do	10.9
Flour	do	05.7
Hams	do	32
Lard	do	21.4
Pork, salt	do	17.8
fresh	do	18.5
Rice	do	09.5
Salt	do	02.3
Sugar, white	do	14
brown	do	09.5
Tea	do	75
Canned peaches, from the United States	per can	35.7
tomatoes, from the United States	do	35.7
Coal-oil, from the United States	per gallon	30
Apples, in fall or early winter	per bushel	1 90
Potatoes	do	45
Coal	per ton	3 15

E and F.—*Taxes in the city of Chemnitz.*

Municipal tax for 1878.				Royal tax for 1878.			
Class.	Income.	Single rate, mills on the dollar.	Amount of tax.	Class.	Income.	Single rate.	Amount of tax.
a	$71 40	1	$1 03	1*a*	$95 20	......	$0 07
b	95 20	1.4	1 38	1*b*	119 00	$0 02	14
c	119 00	1.4	1 90	2	154 70	04	21
h	238 00	1.4	4 31	3	190 40	06	36
1	261 80	1.5	5 18	4	226 10	10	57
2	285 60	1.55	5 86	5	261 80	14	86
3	309 40	1.6	6 54	6	297 50	20	1 21
5	357 00	1.6	7 76	7	333 20	26	1 57
6	380 80	1.65	8 02	8	380 80	33	2 00
7	404 60	1.7	9 32	9	452 20	41	2 43
8	428 40	1.75	10 35	10	523 60	51	3 07
10	476 00	1.85	12 62	11	595 00	64	3 86
15	595 00	2.1	17 43	12	666 40	77	4 64
20	714 00	2.35	23 46	13	785 40	92	5 50
25	833 00	2.6	30 52	14	904 40	1 17	7 00
30	952 00	2.85	38 30	15	1,234 00	1 45	8 71
35	1,071 00	3.1	46 87	16	1.142 40	1 76	10 57
40	1,190 00	3.35	56 60	17	1,285 20	2 07	12 42
50	1,428 00	3.85	78 34	18	1,499 40	2 49	14 92
70	1,951 60	4.75	131 13	20	1,999 20	3 90	23 42
75	2,189 60	5	155 29	24	3,332 00	7 14	42 84
80	2,427 60	5	172 35	26	4,284 00	9 52	57 12
90	3,641 40	5	250 08	28	5,236 00	11 90	71 40

DRESDEN.

Report, by Consul Wilson, on (1) *rates of wages;* (2) *cost of living;* (3) *present state of trade;* (4) *coin and paper money of Germany;* (5) *business habits and systems; for the district of Dresden, in Saxony.*

I have the honor, in reply to circular dispatch from State Department of April 11 ultimo, to report as follows:

My seeming delay has been occasioned by my inability to obtain sooner from the Royal Saxon Government answers to several interrogatories I was unable to gather elsewhere. The courtesies of the Government in all its departments I wish to acknowledge in this, as in all other instances. Where I have had occasion to ask information, it has been accorded with dispatch and politeness, evidencing the good-will entertained for the United States.

1. Rates of wages.

The rates of wages usually paid to the laborer of every class will be found in Table A, with the percentage of unemployed.

This consular district, from various causes, can scarcely be taken as an index of the agricultural districts of Saxony, containing the capital, Dresden, and the numberless villages clustering around for miles in every direction. The lands are attached to the old castles of their ancient nobility, while all that could be purchased in the past have been beautifully improved and built upon by people from all parts of Europe, to be near the fashion and art of this elegant capital.

The laborers are really part and parcel of the estate. Wages in money are often merely nominal, and no index to such wages as are usual and general to the agricultural districts of Saxony.

On the lands of the chateaus and country seats of people above alluded to the prices of labor are fancy, according to their proficiency in elegant gardening, or getting such parts or whole of proceeds from the garden farming after furnishing the family table.

Where land is let on shares, laborers of the renter are often paid by subshare of the crop, and that varying with fertility of soil and proximity to market.

Very little of this district is agricultural; its great interests centering in the extensive Government forests, coal and silver mines. I might in general terms put the price of ordinary agricultural labor at $4 per month for men and $2.50 for women, plain lodging and simple food included.

I subjoin the following extract from report of the Chamber of Commerce of Dresden to the city council:

> In general, we are able to state that wages in the various industrial branches in the city of Dresden continue to be decidedly adequate to the cost of living, as the recent reduction from the high rates, which five years since rose from 20 to 60 per cent. above those previously paid, has by no means brought them to their former level.

2. Cost of living.

The cost of living to the laboring classes almost invariably goes *pari passu* with their wages. They seem to be generally improvident and regardless of the future, and spend in beer-drinking, dancing, and idleness all they earn. In general terms, I should say the actual cost of living was quite as much as with us for similar food. Our people (in the United States) of all classes, live far better than the people here in Saxony. The wages being so much less than with us, it requires the labor of each one that is to be provided for, because the wages of the head of a family cannot support a wife and children in idleness. So it is common for every one in a family, so soon as they are old enough, to learn some little art or trade by which he or she may contribute his or her part to the family support. The *etages*, or flats, in which they live are not unfrequently very unhealthy and uncomfortable, sparsely furnished and very plainly; and in cities, generally in the cellars or immediately next to the roof of the tall houses found here. Their food is mostly of potatoes and black (rye) bread, a coffee made of chicory, gruel or broth, very little meat, and very seldom too.

You will find in Table B the cost of the principal articles of food, and in Table C a comparison of the present rates with those prevailing during the past five years.

3. The present state of trade.

The present state of trade is deplorably depressed; universal complaint is heard on all sides, and I would say the depression and contraction experienced with us since 1873 have been more severely felt in Germany; and their rally is not to be so soon as with us. Emerging from their victorious wars with such eclat, and from their last one with France with millions of indemnity, speculation ran riot and wild, and the collapse was so sudden and unexpected, as to cause universal losses in all trades and operations, and too often complete ruin. I would respectfully refer on this branch of the subject to my dispatch No. 44, dated October 12, 1877.*

4. Coin and paper money of Germany.

Table D is a statement of amount and character of coin and paper money, as well as their circulation, in Germany. In regard to the relation borne to each other, I have to state that both have the same value, there being no discount on paper.

5. Business habits and systems of Saxony.

The business habits and systems of Saxony are fixed, and I might add unchangeable; all branches of trade and labor tread the same paths as those who preceded them.

Banks open at 9 a. m. and stores at 8 a. m., the former closing at 7 p. m., with two hours' rest from 1 until 3 o'clock.

Stores generally remain open until 9 o'clock p. m.; the latter observe the same hours of work on the Sabbath, only closing during the hours of morning church worship. Sunday is always remarkable for the crowds of people moving in all directions in pursuit of pleasure, such as beer drinking, dancing, concert music, excursions by boat and rail. The same love of pleasure and the same indifference to labor seem to animate all classes of society, no one working who is independent of labor, and those who do work perform just as little as possible for the small wages they obtain. The army absorbs the flower of the youth of Germany, and is officered by the youth of the nobility and wealth of the land. It is the only stepping-stone to distinction in the Government or to posi-

* See Commercial Relations for 1877, page 291, a report upon the results of the Franco-German war as they affected the commerce and industries of Germany, 1872 to 1877.

tion in the society of the *elite*. So the best years of early manhood, when the mind is in its plastic state and receiving its impressions for future usefulness, are prostituted to arms, to the detriment of trade in all its branches, and the higher professions are deprived of that talent and position from which their ranks should be recruited.

The future of Germany, with such tastes, habits, and customs, is an enigma, when we contemplate the competition of the Anglo-Saxon race in the various parts of the world, heretofore affording a market for their cheap hand labor, now confronting them; a successful competition in many branches of trade, and threatening her everywhere with their intelligence, activity, enterprise, and industry, and with machinery in a thousand forms laboring against their handwork or primitive machinery. A great revolution must be at hand.

The order and discipline of the Saxon people are admirable; always obedient, never malevolent, respectful to all constituted authority, order and security are seldom threatened or invaded.

Love of country, its traditions, and for the reigning houses is marked on every hand, while a listless disregard of religion and its teachings are equally discernable. They are an interesting people, often enigmatical, and one is often astonished as amused with their customs and eccentricities.

Many of the social customs of the highest classes would appear very peculiar and *outré* to our people, while they are refined and highly cultured and educated.

Accompanying this dispatch you will please find such documents and reports furnished me by the Saxon Government. I send them as they may be of use to the Department.

JOS. T. MASON.

UNITED STATES CONSULATE,
Dresden, July 31, 1878.

A.—*Statement showing the rates of wages in Dresden*, 1878.

Occupation	Per week.
Bakers (including food and lodging, many unemployed)	$3 00 to $3 75
Brewers (including food and lodging, many unemployed)	4 50 to 5 00
Butchers (including food and lodging, 10 per cent. unemployed)	3 75 to 4 57
Blacksmiths (33⅓ per cent. without employment)	3 75 to 4 50
Coppersmiths (exclusive of food and lodging, 10 per cent. unemployed)	4 50 to 5 00
Joiners (25 per cent. without employment)	3 75 to 4 00
Locksmiths (25 per cent. without employment)	3 75 to 4 00
Stonecutters (good employment)	3 75 to 4 00
Shoemakers (33⅓ per cent. without employment)	2 00 to 2 00
Stocking-makers (almost entirely unemployed)	2 00 to 3 00
Tailors (75 per cent. without employment)	2 50 to 3 00
Tinners (many unemployed)	3 75 to 4 00
Tin-founderymen (many unemployed)	3 00 to 3 00
Workers in paper manufactories (many unemployed)	2 00 to 2 00
Workers in large iron industries (many unemployed)	2 50 to 3 00
	Per hour.
Carpenters (well employed, 10-hour shift)	06¼ to 06½
Masons (well employed, 10-hour shift)	06¼ to 06¾
Common workmen in house-building (well employed, 10-hour shift)	05½

In some trades, such as the blacksmith's and shoemaker's, the present time of the year is the most unfavorable.

B.—*Statement showing the prices of the necessaries of life at Dresden.*

Beef	per pound..	$0 19
Bread	do......	07
Butter	do......	16½
Cheese	do......	33½
Coffee	do......	36
Flour	do......	06
Hams	do......	33
Lard	do......	21½
Pork	do......	18
Rice	do......	10
Salt	do......	02½
Sugar, white	do......	15
Sugar, brown	do......	10
Tea	do......	75
Coal-oil	per gallon..	31
Potatoes	per bushel..	48
Coal	per ton..	3 20

C.—*Statement showing rates of wages in Dresden—1873–1877.*

Rates of wages.		1873.	1874.	1875.	1876.	1877.
Bakers	per week..	$3 92	$3 92	$3 92	$3 92	$3 92
Bookbinders	do......	3 30	3 92	4 40	4 40	4 28
Butchers	do......	3 57	3 68	3 68	3 68	3 68
Blacksmiths	do......	4 52	4 70	4 28	4 28	4 05
Button-makers	do......	3 80	3 80	3 33	3 33	3 10
Braziers	do......	4 28	4 28	4 28	4 28	4 28
Carpenters	do......	3 64	3 64	3 64	3 64	3 14
Cigar-makers	do......	3 21	3 21	2 61	2 61	2 61
Gardeners	do......	3 56	3 80	4 04	4 04	3 80
Glovemakers, women	do......	1 78	1 78	1 78	1 78	1 66
Hatters	do......	3 56	3 56	3 56	3 56	3 10
Joiners	do......	3 56	3 56	3 44	3 32	2 85
Locksmiths	do......	3 75	3 75	3 45	3 39	3 27
Lacemakers, women	do......	1 66	1 42	1 19	95	80
Mechanics	do......	4 40	4 40	4 40	4 40	4 05
Musical-instrument makers	do......	3 33	3 33	3 33	3 33	3 33
Painters	do......	4 34	4 46	4 58	4 28	4 28
Photographers	do......	3 57	3 57	3 57	3 57	3 57
Shoemakers	do......	2 08	2 38	2 38	2 38	2 38
Stone-masons	do......	4 04	4 04	4 04	3 69	3 14
Tailors	do......	4 40	4 57	3 57	2 97	2 97
Tinners	do......	4 16	4 10	4 10	3 92	3 92

TABLE D.

Up to the 18th of May, 1878, have been coined in all the mints of Germany—

	Marks.	
Marks in 20-mark pieces	1,200,190,220	
Marks in 10-mark pieces	365,296,020	
Marks in 5-mark pieces	27,969,845	
Marks in gold coin		1,593,456,085
Marks in silver 5-mark pieces	71,652,415	
Marks in silver 2-mark pieces	97,810,530	
Marks in silver 1-mark pieces	148,847,743	
Marks in silver ½-mark pieces	71,486,388	
Marks in silver ⅕-mark pieces	35,717,718	
Marks in silver coin		425,514,794
Marks in gold and silver coin		2,018,970,879

In addition to this sum there has been coined about 800,000,000 marks in thaler or 3-mark pieces; making the entire gold and silver coins in circulation in Germany, in round numbers, 2,819,000,000 marks.

Some millions must be deducted from this sum, as a large amount of coin has left the country, especially in 1875.

The paper issue is as follows:

NATIONAL BANK.

	Marks.
Issue of the National Bank	584,873,000
Issue of the private banks	780,020,000
Total	1,364,893,000

[Inclosures in Consul Mason's report.—Translations.]

Mr. Steglich to Mr. Mason.

CHAMBER OF COMMERCE AND MANUFACTURES,
Dresden, June 28, 1878.

JOS. T. MASON, Esq.,
United States Consul at Dresden:

Referring to the four points of inquiry made by your Government, and transmitted to me with your communication of the 28th instant, I have the honor to inform you that it would be totally impossible for me to give even an approximately exhaustive reply to these inquiries within the limits of a letter.

Moreover, I have not all the necessary data just now at my command to enable me to perform such a task. Abundant material, though much scattered, will be found in the late annual reports of the five Saxon chambers of commerce and manufactures, as also to some extent in the periodical publications of the board of agriculture of the Kingdom of Saxony, which documents will, in all probability, be cheerfully furnished to you by the corporations referred to.

In inclosure A I note the figures which come into question of the latest printed report of our board, which was sent to you in November of last year. Some further information with regard to points 1 and 4, section I, you will be able to obtain from the reports of our board of the 13th and 28th of September of last year, a copy of which is inclosed. No important changes have taken place since then in the labor market (except the more steady employment of mechanics employed in building during the summer).

Information on point 2 is just now not at my command.

On point 4, I submit the following data for your use, which are taken from official sources:

Up to May 18, 1878, the governmental coinage at all German mints was as follows:

	Marks.	
Marks in double-crowns (20-mark pieces)	1,200,190,220	
Marks in crowns (10-mark pieces)	365,296,020	
Marks in half-crowns (5-mark pieces in gold)	27,969,845	
Making a total of marks in gold coin		1,593,456,085
Marks in 5-mark pieces of silver	71,652,415	
Marks in 2-mark pieces	97,810,530	
Marks in 1-mark pieces	148,847,743	
Marks in 50-penny pieces	71,486,388	
Marks in 20-penny pieces	35,717,718	
Marks in silver coin		425,514,794
Total of gold and silver coin		2,018,970,879

The value of the German thaler pieces still in circulation is estimated by competent judges at eight hundred millions of marks in round numbers. The total value of German gold and silver coin is thus about 2,819,000,000 marks.

In making further computations, however, it would be necessary to subtract a number of millions from this sum total, it being well known that, particularly in 1875, a considerable drain was made upon the coin of Germany for transmission to foreign countries.

The entire amount of paper money issued by the Government in pursuance of the law of April 30, 1874, was one hundred and twenty millions of marks, issued in sums of 5, 20, and 50 marks. All the paper money of the various German States has been withdrawn.

To the foregoing must be added the notes of the German banks according to the official statements of the middle of May; the notes then in circulation amounted to 584,873,000 marks of the Government bank, 780,020,000 marks of the other German bill banks; making a total of 1,364,893,000 marks in bank-notes.

Other data relative to the banking and coinage question could be furnished by Professor Soetbeer, who is a recognized authority in such matters, or they might be obtained from his writings on this subject, which have been published both in book form and in the financial newspapers.

I take pleasure in furnishing the foregoing information for your consular report, and sign myself,

With the highest consideration, your obedient servant,

E. STEGLICH,
Secretary of the Board of Trade and Manufactures.

[Inclosure 2.]

Messrs. Rülke & Steglich to the city council of Dresden.

To the City Council of Dresden:

As a supplement to our communications of the 13th instant, relative to the condition of the working classes in the city of Dresden, we now lay before the honorable city council a statement lately received by us from well-informed sources concerning the amount of wages now paid in various mechanical trades, remarking, at the same time, that the accompanying statements concerning mechanics out of employment have been prepared by us taking into consideration the large numbers now occupying the trades lodging-houses and the numbers of those applying to master-workmen for assistance or employment.

We refer, moreover, to our previous report, and have the honor to be—

THE BOARD OF TRADE AND MANUFACTURE,
ERNST RÜLKE,
EDM. STEGLICH, *Secretary.*

[Inclosure 3.]

Messrs. Rülke & Steglich to the city council of Dresden.

To the City Council, present:

In reply to your inquiry of the 26th ultimo, relative to the present condition of manufactures and industry, with special reference to the situation of mechanics, we beg leave to say that special data of the kind required for the current month are not at our command.

In general, however, we are able to say that the prices paid for labor in the city of Dresden are very liberal when the price of provisions is considered, inasmuch as the rates of wages, which were increased from 20 to 60 per cent. about five years ago, have been reduced only in a few branches, and in those by no means to their former level.

It is proper to state that a greater amount of work is now required of the mechanic, as also an improved quality of work, while no increase of wages, as was the case a few years since, is allowed him. It is known, for instance, to the chamber that the wages paid in the sewing-machine factories of this city have been reduced during the past year or two about 20 per cent., while no appreciable diminution of the average wages of other workmen has taken place. The amount of their pay is now almost equal to what it was in 1873, namely, 24 marks per week, on an average (the number of operatives in one factory in this city now being 250), in which connection it is to be remarked that among these operatives there are many young persons who are employed on automatic machines, and who earn only from six to eight marks per week; from which it appears that the average earnings of skilled and capable workmen in iron and wood in the sewing-machine branch are still higher than the above-mentioned average earnings of other workmen.

It is to be remarked, in general, that competent mechanics are in demand for almost all kinds of work, that they are well paid, and that there is no lack of work in Dresden even for ordinary laborers, so far as we are aware.

It is also known to the chamber that the wages of ordinary operatives in factories, &c., which were increased out of proportion, have here and there again been reduced of late years from 10 to 25 per cent., the temporary scarcity of hands having come to an end, and a normal state of things again prevailing in the labor market. The building department of the honorable council has doubtless observed the same phenomena, so far as the wages paid in the various branches of building are concerned.

We would remark, in conclusion, that the difficulties that have now prevailed for several years in industrial affairs have thus far affected the working classes in a very slight degree, while they have very sensibly affected the so-called well-to-do classes, the owners of manufacturing establishments and those engaged in manufactures on their own account.

THE CHAMBER OF COMMERCE AND MANUFACTURES,
ERNST RÜLKE.
EDM. STEGLICH.

DRESDEN, *September* 13, 1877.

[Inclosure 4.]

Mr. Lehman to the Chamber of Commerce and Manufactures.

To the Chamber of Commerce and Manufactures, Dresden:

The rates of wages paid to mechanics employed in the following trades in the city of Dresden are as follows: Bakers, from 12 to 15 marks per week, with board, &c.; many unemployed. Brewers, from 18 to 20 marks per week, with board, &c.; many unemployed. Butchers, from 15 to 18 marks per week; ten per cent. unemployed. Coppersmiths, from 18 to 20 marks, without board, &c.; ten per cent. unemployed. Masons, from 25 to 27 pfennige per hour; abundant employment (ten hours per day). Carpenters, from 25 to 26 pfennige per hour; abundant employment (ten hours per day). Stonecutters, from 15 to 20 marks per week, mostly by contract; abundant employment. Tailors, from 10 to 12 marks per week; three-fourths of the entire number unemployed. Shoemakers, from 8 to 10 marks per week; one-third unemployed. Locksmiths, from 15 to 18 marks per week; one-fourth unemployed. Blacksmiths, from 15 to 18 marks per week; one-third unemployed. Cabinet-makers, from 15 to 18 marks per week; one-fourth unemployed. Turners, from 15 to 16 marks per week; many unemployed. Stocking-knitters, from 8 to 12 marks per week; scarcely anything doing. Pewterers, from 12 to 15 marks per week. Laborers employed in building, 22 pfennige per hour; employment tolerably abundant. Operatives in paper factories, from 8 to 10 marks per week. Iron-founders, from 10 to 12 marks per week; very little employment.

In some trades, such as tailoring and shoemaking, this is the dullest time of the year, and will be offset by the busy season. The average weekly earnings of tailors the whole year round are from 14 to 15 marks per week; those of shoemakers from 12 to 15 marks.

OTTO LEHMANN.

DRESDEN, *September* 14, 1877.

FRANKFORT-ON-THE-MAIN.

Report, by Consul-General Lee, on the rates of wages; labor customs; food-prices; business systems; currency, banking, and coinage (of Germany), and the present condition of trade; for the consulate-general of Frankfort-on-the-Main.

In pursuance of Department Circular Letter, dated April 11, 1878, desiring information with reference to various topics therein stated, I beg to report as follows:

In my annual report, forwarded to the Department during the month of November last, the subjects of labor, wages, and laborers' living expenses were discussed at considerable length, and a careful compilation was given of the rates of wages then prevailing in Western and Southern Germany.* The statements made then are applicable, without material variation, to the present time. The labor market has not improved during the last six months. In this city, where a great accumulation of capital creates a continual temptation to building and other improvements, employment is more abundant, perhaps, and labor more remunerative than in most German cities; but here, as in other parts of the empire, wages are extremely low as compared with those which prevail in the United States. The rates paid per week here and in this vicinity, at the present time, are about as follows:

RATES OF WAGES IN FRANKFORT.

	Per week.
Bakers, board and lodging	$1 40 to $1 90
Beltmakers, without board	4 70 to 7 00
Building-joiners, without board	4 70 to 5 70
Locksmiths, without board	4 95
Blacksmiths, with board	1 40 to 1 90
Bookbinders, without board	3 50 to 4 70
Brewers, without board	4 25 to 4 70
Carpenters, without board	3 80 to 4 25
Coopers, without board	4 25 to 5 65
Cutlers, without board	4 70
Day-laborers, without board	2 80 to 3 50
Dyers, without board	3 50 to 4 25
Field-laborers, men, board and lodging	1 20
Field-laborers, women, board and lodging	95
Glaziers, without board	4 70 to 5 65
Gardeners, without board	3 50 to 4 70
Hatmakers, without board	8 50
Jewelers, with board	2 35
Lithographers, without board	8 25 to 9 40
Masons, without board	3 78 to 4 25
Machinists, without board	7 00 to 8 50
Printers, without board	4 70 to 7 00
Roofmakers, without board	4 70 to 5 64
Shoemakers, without board	3 50 to 4 70
Tinners, without board	3 80 to 5 90
Tailors, with board	1 00
Tailors, without board	3 50 to 4 20
Tin-founders, without board	3 50 to 4 25
Type-setters, without board	4 70 to 5 90
Type-founders, without board	4 70 to 7 00
Watchmakers, without board	4 70 to 5 90
Whitewashers, without board	4 23
Wagoners, brewer, without board	4 25 to 4 70
Wagoners, ordinary, with board	1 40 to 1 90
Wagoners, ordinary, without board	3 80 to 4 25

LABOR CUSTOMS.

The custom is for all laborers to work ten hours per day; that is, from 6 o'clock a. m. to 6 p. m., with two hours of intermission, and to receive from 5 to 6 cents per hour for extra time.

To most classes of laborers it is the practice to bestow small gratuities, known as drink-money, and these gratuities are so customary and so universal, that they may be considered as a part of the regular wages.

A large amount of the outdoor as well as indoor work is performed

*The statements above referred to have been incorporated into this report at the Department of State, and will be found in their proper places herewith.

by women, who receive from 20 to 50 per cent. less than men are paid for like service.

The condition of the laborer is not enviable, his opportunities are few, luxuries are almost unknown to him, and he is obliged to use frugally even the necessaries of life in order to live upon what he can earn. The German laborer expects to eat not less than four times a day, but his food is usually of the plainest description. Butter and meat are luxuries to a large proportion of the working people; their clothing is coarse and cheap, and except upon the holidays, which are numerous, they have little relaxation from the perpetual struggle for daily bread. Few American working people but would consider such a life bitterly hard and joyless.

Yet the German laborer can and does save from his earnings; he will not be idle if he can help it, and will work for a few pfennige per day rather than do nothing. Strikes seldom or never occur, and nothing is lost, therefore, in costly and useless contentions with employers.

Written contracts with laborers are rarely if ever made. Engagements for service are almost invariably entered into with the simple verbal understanding, based upon the custom of the country, that either employer or employed may terminate the arrangement at fourteen days' notice. Instances have come to my knowledge in which individual workmen have been employed in this way for forty years successively in the same establishment.

For a full statement as to the terms of service of railway employés and the bounties and wages paid them, I beg to refer the Department to my annual report for the year 1877.* I would also respectfully refer to the same report for a statement as to the influence of the co-operative

---

* Wages of railway employés in Germany.—The following is the extract concerning the wages of railway empolyés referred to above, as published in Commercial Relations for 1877, page 284: "Report upon the railroads, telegraphs, &c., of Germany for 1876 and 1877:

"All railways of Germany are subject to the police supervision of the empire, which is applied more especially to the general security of traffic. The tariffs for passengers and freights are determined by a board of commissioners of such railway companies as agree to be guided by its decisions, subject to the revision of the imperial and local governments. All questions between the railways and the Government are referred to a central bureau for the empire, but no general railway law has yet been enacted. The different lines are subject to the control of the local sovereignties within whose territory they lie in all matters with which the empire is not concerned. A new road cannot be built without the consent of the state through which it extends.

"The wages paid to railway employés are as follows:

"*Wages of railroad employés.*—Locomotive engineers, $222 @ $343 per year; 2 cents mileage per kilometer; 35 per cent. premium on coal saving, averaging $130 per year; 15 per cent. premium on oil saving, averaging $3.50 per year; allowance for work done in shops, averaging $14 per year, and lodging allowance of 27 cents per night when detained from home.

"Conductors, $160 @ $180 salary per year; 1 cent mileage per ten kilometers, and 27 cents per night for lodging when detained from home.

"Brakemen, $140 @ $165 salary per year; 1.5 cents mileage per ten kilometers, and 27 cents per night for lodging when detained from home.

"Road-keepers or watchmen, $130 @ $150 salary per year; 1.5 cents mileage per ten kilometers, and 27 cents per night for lodging when detained from home.

"Switchmen, $130 @ $180 salary per year, and 3.5 cents per hour for night service.

"Common laborers, 48 @ 82 cents per day.

"The mileages paid are the actual distance traveled while on duty. The percentages on coal and oil which are paid to engineers are bounties for the amount of those materials saved by their economical management. For example, a certain weight of coal is allowed to an engineer for running his engine a certain distance within a given time, and if he saves on this allowance, a premium is paid him on the amount saved.

"No labor-unions exist among the employés of German railways, and no strike of any importance has ever taken place on any German road."

system upon labor in Germany, and especially as to the influence and operations of co-operative savings societies.*

The best testimony concurrently leads to the opinion that the general cost of living for all classes has much increased during the past five years, and that the rates of wages have at the same time declined. For further discussion of this subject, also, I beg to refer the Department to my annual report.

In that report, and in my subsequent dispatch No. 56, dated the 26th of November last, the condition of trade then prevailing in Germany was treated as fully as space would permit. The general depression at that time complained of in all branches of business has continued until now. Indeed, the added uncertainties of European politics have rather increased this depression, and until the existing complications shall be finally and conclusively solved, capital will be timid, production languid, and business conservative.

[The extracts from the report referred to by the consul-general are herewith republished.—*Commercial Relations*, 1877, pp. 309–312.]

FOOD-PRICES.

The prices of food have somewhat advanced during the past year, though not universally. The following are sample expressions on this subject from well-informed persons in many different localities: 1. Cost of living one-third greater than a few years ago. 2. Cost of living never so high as now. 3. Cost of living greater than last year. 4. Food costs more than last year; meat two and a half cents a pound more, and so of butter. 5. Cost of living a little cheaper. 6. Cost of living growing greater and greater. 7. Cost of living unchanged. 8. Meat costs more than last year; bread is cheaper; potatoes and other vegetables 10 @ 20 per cent. cheaper. 9. Cost of living same as last year. 10. Living 25 per cent. cheaper than last year.

These expressions as to the cost of subsistence have special reference to the laboring and middle classes, but are equally applicable to all.

The country generally, while reasonably fertile, is not profuse in its agricultural resources, and its dense population will doubtless, in spite of the bountiful crops of this year, be obliged to draw largely upon external resources for food essentials. Meat and wheat bread are considered luxuries by the ordinary laborers, and butter is but little used by them. Indeed, the great majority of working people, in the present prices of provisions, are limited to the plainest food. Rents have somewhat declined, owing to the amount of unemployed capital that has been invested in buildings and the protracted stringency of the times, but the general cost of living has greatly advanced of late years, and the tendency is still decidedly in that direction.

LABOR AND WAGES.

There has been a palpable decline in wages during the year. The following expressions of large employers, in as many different localities and districts, are taken from an extensive correspondence, and are significant of the condition of the labor market: 1. Wages unchanged; fewer workmen employed. 2. Wages same as last year. 3. Wages relatively higher than in preceding years. 4. Wages about the same as last year; 50 per cent. more idle workmen. 5. Wages same as last year. 6. Wages unchanged, but workmen employed only four days of the week. 7. Must employ fewer workmen if depression continues. 8. Wages generally lower than last year; factories have dismissed 10 per cent. of their employés, and have economized by taking poorer workmen. 9. Wages and number of employés same as last year. 10. General wages greatly reduced during last four years; few unemployed. 11. Wages generally reduced; few unemployed; manufacturers continually discharging operatives. 12. Wages about 15 per cent. lower than in 1875; 30 per cent. fewer workmen employed than during that year. 13. Wages and number employed same as last year; working hours reduced one-third.

These observations cover nearly every variety of occupation, skilled and unskilled. Increase of wages has been exceptional, and is reported only by manufacturers of

* *Co-operative societies in Germany.*—That these labor reports may be as full and comprehensive as possible, the above report on the co-operative societies of Germany (Commercial Relations, 1877) is herewith republished, and will be found in the Appendix to this volume.

specialties which require rare qualifications. The decided tendency has been toward lower pay and reduced employment. A table of the current rates of wages paid in the various districts of Southern and Eastern Germany is appended hereto.

It will be observed from the foregoing that, while a large proportion of laborers has been discharged from the factories, there are yet few or no idlers. The explanation given is, that the discharged workmen have sought and found other employments. It is not the disposition of the German laborer to refuse to work at all because he cannot command wages to suit him. No matter how dull the labor market, he will have occupation, though it may bring him only a few pfennige per day. This commendable trait is encouraged by the severity of the police regulations against all manner of vagrancy. These regulations make voluntary idleness not only unprofitable but inconvenient, and at the same time afford a certain protection to the laborer who is willing and anxious to be employed.

The discharged laborer has also been helped by the heavy drafts made upon the male population for military services. The avenues of employment which might otherwise have been glutted have thus been kept open, and the prices of labor have been preserved from wholesale decline. The places of men absent in military service have been supplied to a great extent by women, a fact which has added perhaps both to the variety and the recompense of female occupations.

In their general effect, however, these demands of the army are not beneficial to labor interests. Their tendency is to break up fixity of occupation and destroy steadiness in the aims of life. Time given to the army is lost to business and production, and, what is more important, is also lost to the business and industrial training which is so essential to success in civil occupations.

For these and other reasons the prices paid for labor in Germany are not an exact indication of its relative value. Wages are proportionately not quite so low as they may seem. Where less is paid than elsewhere, it often happens that more persons are employed, or persons who are less skillful. Machinery, which facilitates production and reduces the number of workmen required for a particular purpose, is regarded with much jealousy by the unskilled classes. When machinery takes the place of hand-labor, the equilibrium is often restored by the liberal requirement of hand-laborers to operate the machine.

The wages paid vary greatly in different districts and occupations, as may be seen by the appended table of current rates, carefully compiled from many different sources.

Statement of wages paid to laborers and artisans in Eastern and Southern Germany during the year ending September 30, 1877.

[From Commercial Relations for 1877, p. 313.]

Place.	Kind of labor.	Time.	Amount in United States gold.
Barr	Tanners	Day	$0 56 to $1 13
Eisenach	Color fabricants	do	42 to 70
	Field-hands	do	35 to 42
	Field-hands (women)	do	21 to 28
	Masons	do	59 to 61
	Carpenters	do	50 to 61
Schwabach	Bronze powder and metal fabricants	Week	3 29
	Same (women)	do	1 64
	Field-hands	Day	35 to 47
Rudolstadt (Thuringen)	Porcelain fabricants, best	Week	4 23 to 4 70
	Painters of porcelain	do	5 87½
	Field-hands	do	2 82 to 3 52
	Masons and carpenters	Day	82
	Common laborers	do	59
Mayence	Field-hands (without board)	do	59 to 94
	Field-hands (with board)	do	23½ to 47
	Mechanics	Week	3 52 to 4 22
Offenbach	Leather fabricants	Day	82 to 1 42
Lürth	Glassgrinders	Week	4 23 to 5 64
	Same (women)	do	1 88 to 2 35
	Field-hands	Day	47 to 70
Culmbach	Workmen in brewery	Month	12 69
	Coopers and brewers	do	18 80
	Field-hands	Day	35 to 59
	Mechanics	do	47 to 70
Bayreuth	Housemaids	Year	9 40 to 23 50
	Porters (without board)	Week	2 35 to 3 52
	Salesmen	Year	141 00 to 423 00
	Factory operatives	Week	2 82 to 3 52
	Same (women)	do	1 17 to 2 35
Höchst	Aniline-color fabricants	Day	47 to 94

Place.	Kind of labor.	Time.	Amount in United States gold.
Bielfeld	Common laborers	Day	$0 33 to $0 47
	Factory laborers	...do	41 to 59
	Mechanics	...do	59 to 94
	Flax factory (girls)	...do	23½ to 35
	Field-hands (summer)	...do	41 to 47
	Field-hands (winter)	...do	23½ to 35
	Field-hands (with board)	Year	70 50 to 82 25
Wurzburg	Sparkling-wine fabricants	Day	
Hof in Bavaria	Weavers	...do	47 to 70
	Field-hands	...do	70 to 1 17½
Saarguemines	Plush and silk fabricants (men)	Month	13 16 to 23 50
	Same (girls and women)	...do	6 05 to 18 80
Nüremberg	Cabinet-makers	Day	80
Nüremberg and vicinity	Tailors	...do	1 00
	Masons	...do	75
	Glaziers	Week	3 75
	Carpenters	Day	85
	Locksmiths	Week	6 75
	Printers	Day	80
	Blacksmiths	...do	75
	Street-pavers	...do	1 10
	Brewers (with board)	Week	1 50 to 2 50
	Bakers (with board)	...do	1 75
	Butchers (with board)	...do	1 25 to 1 50
	Confectioners (with board)	Month	6 00 to 6 50
Sonneberg and vicinity	China factories:		
	Modelers	Day	1 50
	Decorators	...do	0 75 1 25 to 1 50
	Formers and turners	...do	75 to 1 00
	Formers (women)	...do	37½ to 62½
	Firemen	...do	62½ to 75
	Packers	...do	50 to 62½
	Day-laborers (women)	...do	37½ to 50
	Gunmakers	...do	37½ to 1 00
	Papier-maché fabricants (men)	Week	2 75 to 3 50
	Papier-maché fabricants (women)	...do	1 75 to 2 25
	Lampmakers (men)	...do	3 00 to 4 52
	Kid-glove makers:		
	Common workmen	...do	3 00
	Skilled workmen	...do	3 75 to 4 50
	Women	...do	1 50 to 3 00
	Cotton-hosiery fabricants	...do	2 50 to 6 00
	Fancy woodenware fabricants	Day	50 to 62½

Current prices of provisions in the city of Frankfort-on-the-Main, October 31, 1877.

Articles.	Quantity.	Price in United States gold.
Beans, white ... pounds	222. 8	$5.88 to $6.58.
Butter ... do	1. 114	18 to 29 cents.
Cabbage ... per 100 heads		$2.82 to $3.52.
Eggs ... dozen		15 to 22 cents.
Hay ... pounds	111. 4	61 to 77 cents.
Lentils ... do	222. 8	$7.05 to $8.93.
Meat:		
Beef ... do	1. 114	14 to 20 cents.
Bacon ... do	1. 114	26 cents.
Mutton ... do	1. 114	11 to 16 cents.
Pork ... do	1. 114	18 to 20 cents.
Veal ... do	1. 114	15 to 17 cents.
Potatoes ... do	222. 8	$1.32 to $1.41.
Pease, shelled ... do	222. 8	$6.58 to $7.75.
Rye-meal ... do	222. 8	$5.82 to $5.95.
Rye-meal, coarse ... do	222. 8	$5.34 to $5.58.
Straw ... do	111. 4	51 to 56 cents.

MANUFACTURERS AND MANUFACTURES.

Manufacturers who are able to gain a net profit of 5 per cent. on the capital invested are considered as doing very well, and are quite content. Generally, manufacturing is rather a losing than a profitable business at the present time. Many large establishments have for some time past declared no dividends at all, though there are also many exceptional cases where net profits have ranged as high as 7 to 10 per cent.

The manufacturing industries are widely distributed throughout the empire. Berlin is the leading commercial metropolis, and also produces largely and variously; Chemnitz manufactures heavy machinery, knitted woolens and cottons; Cologne supplies perfumery, paints, carpets, furniture, confectionery, and starch; Crefeld manufactures silk goods; Elberfeld, woolens, cottons, and hardware; Remscheid, files and skates; Aachen and Düren, fine cloths; Solingen, cutlery; Hagen and Dortmund, heavy cast-iron ware; Bielefeld, linen and silk goods and sewing-machines; M. Gladbach, cotton and shirtings; Hanover, velvets; Suhl, in Thuringia, fire-arms and boots and shoes. Leipsic is the metropolis of the German book trade. Cloths are manufactured in Saxony, and in the Prussian Lansitz, Görlitz, Collbus, and Guben. Ir Osnabrück and Essen are manufactured steel and steel goods. Bremen manufactures cigars, and supplies the country with tobacco. Nuremberg manufactures toys, pencils, steel wire, and porcelain. Augsburg and Ettlingen make shirtings and cotton yarn. The Black Forest produces clocks, boots and shoes, and wooden carved ware. Würtemberg furnishes lace goods, corsets, and jewelry. Printed shirtings and sheetings are made extensively in Alsace and Lorraine. Jewelry is largely produced at Hanau, Idar, and Oberstein; and leather at Mayence. Offenbach manufactures fancy leather goods, wagons, carriages, machinery, and patent leather. Frankfort owns large and varied manufacturing interests, many of which are located in neighboring towns.

BUSINESS SYSTEMS.

Capital continues to be abundant in Germany, and respectable manufacturers, dealers, and business houses can always obtain good bank accommodations. In most parts of the empire it is the custom for banks to grant what is called blanco credit to manufacturers and merchants, amounting in many cases to 25 to 35 per cent. of the amount of capital invested in business. To this extent cash is advanced without security, but the rate of interest in such transactions is always 1 per cent. higher than the current rate of discount at the German Reichsbank.

Perhaps the most noticeable feature of the general method of conducting business in Germany is the system, or rather want of system, of credits. Manufacturers and wholesale dealers habitually dispose of their wares and fabrics against time. Three, four, and six months are allowed to buyers. If cash payment is agreed upon, a discount on the original prices of 2 to 3 per cent. in wholesale and 5 per cent. in retail trade is generally granted. The terms and discounts differ somewhat in the various branches of trade, but in general a much longer time is allowed than is customary in France, England, or the United States. An exception to this is made in the trade in raw materials and agricultural products, which are usually sold for cash.

Three months may be considered the shortest time for payment; oftener, especially in retail trade, it is six months or longer. Dealers seem to have the idea that credit stimulates purchases and increases sales. Accounts instead of being promptly squared from month to month go on accumulating, until at length large discounts are made to secure settlements.

In many cases invoices are balanced by acceptances after receipt of the goods, or a draft is set in course at least three months before the account falls due. But generally collections are made by runners and traveling clerks, who visit the retailers annually from two to three times. This business of traveling has been enlarged to excess, and the expense it incurs often amounts to five, or even ten, per cent. of the annual sales.

As might be supposed, the losses incident to this method of doing business are considerable. The longest credits are given in the eastern provinces, and there also the losses are largest. The average rate of loss throughout the empire is believed to be not less than three to five per cent. of the sales. In a recent lecture at Leipsic, Professor Rouleaux, one of the most sagacious and practical economists of the empire, stated that the practice of extended credit causes in some cases a loss of 18 per cent. interest on the capital invested in an article before it finds its way from the manufacturer to the consumer. During the last five years of business stagnation the amount of loss has been much greater than before that period, dullness of trade having increased the temptation to sell on time.

Realizing the injury done to commerce by the credit abuse, chambers of commerce and corporations of merchants have endeavored to reform the evil, and have vigorously urged the adoption of short time or cash payment, but without material success. The pernicious custom is so deeply rooted as to have defied, thus far, all efforts to disturb it.

Manufacturers dispose of their wares either directly to retailers or consign them to intermediaries on commission. The larger manufacturers mostly deal directly with retailers, but the smaller concerns, not having means to employ traveling clerks, sell through brokers, agents, and commission merchants. The trade with Russia, Austria, Italy, and other neighboring countries is carried on, for the most part, through agents who reside at the business centers of those countries, and who visit their customers at certain periods. The trade with more distant countries, as, for instance, South America, Africa, and Asia, is effected through Hamburg exporters, who have branch houses to receive and dispose of their goods at their place of destination. Articles exported are mostly sold for cash, or, if the purchase is made through a German house, the latter is allowed the same facilities as are customary here.

CURRENCY, BANKING, AND COINAGE.

With reference to the subjects of currency, banking, and coinage, I beg to refer the Department to my annual report,* wherein these topics

---

*GERMAN BANKS AND BANKING SYSTEM.

[From annual report referred to.—From *Commercial Relations* for 1877.]

The recent and disastrous failure of the great Ritterschaftliche Privatbank, at Stettin, has drawn attention to some of the defects of the German banking system, and will perhaps lead to important legislation. The Stettin institution was formerly a joint-stock bank of issue, and as such its administration was vested in a board of managers, nominally under control of the directors or council of supervision (*Sufsichtsrath*). The fact that the council was in ignorance of the perilous condition of the bank and of the nature of its transactions until it was obliged to suspend, shows, it is thought, that there is great imperfection in the requirements as to scrutinizing the management of joint-stock banks, and also in the limitations placed upon the scope and nature of their business. A large proportion of German banks are not held to strictly legitimate banking, but may, if they choose, launch into all sorts of irregular schemes. Such are some of the criticisms which the Pomeranian failure has given rise to, and which may lead to beneficial results.

As a rule, deposits are not received by either joint-stock or private banks in Germany, and the check system is therefore not generally used. Only the Reichsbank can issue notes of less than 100 marks, and the number of banks of issue, other than national, is therefore only about fifteen in the whole empire. Many which had the are treated at some length. A few additional statements may now, however, be made.

The total amount of money coined in the empire during the fiscal year 1877 was 2,013,029,369 marks. Of this sum, about four-fifths (1,620,000,000 marks) was gold coin, the remainder silver and copper. The amount of paper in circulation at the end of 1876 was 989,000,000 marks. The total of coin and currency in circulation at the beginning of the present year may be approximately estimated at 3,000,000,000 marks, equivalent to $714,000,000.

Silver is receivable as a legal tender to the extent of not more than 100 marks ($23), but there is no limit to the amount of paper money so receivable, unless there be a special stipulation for payment in gold. Paper is the most popular currency, owing to its convenience and ready convertibility into gold coin. Silver, gold, and paper circulate freely together, but silver is used as a medium for small transactions only, and especially for small change. The copper and nickel coins are very small, representing values ranging from about a quarter of a cent to, say, 2½ cents. The smallest silver coin is the 20-pfennig piece, equivalent to about 5 cents, and the largest the 5-mark piece, equivalent to, say, $1.20. The 5-mark pieces are large and inconvenient, and are much less used than the 5-mark paper bills. The gold pieces, ranging from 5 marks upwards, are very popular, especially the 10 and 20 mark pieces.

The new coinage and currency system is undoubtedly one of the greatest blessings the empire has conferred, and its influence in consolidating the German people is great and continuing.

The National, or Reichsbank, continues to grow in popular favor. The total of its transactions during the last year amounted to the enormous sum of 5,494,826,000 marks. Its principal business consists in discounting bills of exchange and making loans on collaterals. Its accommodations are conservative, yet within the reach of all, when perfect security is afforded. Its paper, redeemable in gold only, is everywhere equivalent to gold, and preferred to coin. The branches of the Reichsbank are scattered throughout all parts of the empire, and perform a service very similar to that of the national banks in the United States.

On the 1st of May, 1875, the paper money of the empire superseded that of the separate States. The Imperial Government has reserved the exclusive right to issue bills of less denomination than 100 marks, and its issues consist of 5, 10 and 50 mark bills, redeemable in gold, and limited in aggregate amount to 120,000,000 marks. This paper is receivable for taxes, and at the post, telegraph, and all other government offices.

Bank issues of paper, including those of the Reichsbank, are limited to denominations of 100, 500, and 1,000 marks.

---

privileges of issue have surrendered it to the government as an unprofitable franchise.

The National, or Reichsbank, formerly the Bank of Prussia, now has branches in all parts of Germany, and has given the utmost satisfaction. Its paper, redeemable at sight in gold only, and receivable for all debts, public and private, is everywhere current, and is preferred to coin for money transactions. The bank exacts, as it gives, the most perfect security, and affords the best facilities for discounts and exchange. Reaching out through its branches to all the centers of commerce, it has the best possible means of knowing the reliability and value of the paper presented, and the surest safeguards against loss.

The new imperial coinage has also gained in popularity, and has apparently subdued all desire to return to the mixed and inconvenient system, or rather want of system, which it superseded. Indeed, scarcely anything has done more to nationalize the German people than the acknowledged advantages of the imperial coin and currency system.

The Reichsbank is obliged to purchase bar-gold at the rate of 1,392 marks per pound against its notes.

The circulation of all German banks, not covered by coin or bullion, has been limited since the first of January, 1876, to 385,000,000 marks, of which amount 250,000,000 is awarded to the Bank of the Empire. Any trespass upon this limitation is taxed 5 per cent. per annum.

The banks of issue other than national are now only nineteen in number, and their importance as regards the circulation of paper money has greatly declined, the government giving its entire influence to the Reichsbank, of which it shares the profits.

The commercial depression has been unfavorable to the prosperity of the private banks, many of which, established during the years 1871–'73, have been forced to enter into liquidation, while others have been unable to pay any dividends. The principal business of such banks consists in carrying accounts current and in drawing and buying domestic and foreign drafts.

Deposits are not, as a rule, received by either joint-stock or private bankers in Germany, and the check system is not generally used.

Extended reference having been made in my annual report to the operations of the co-operative credit banks, they perhaps need not now be further discussed.

There are also many savings institutions in Germany, controlled by the municipal authorities, and which loan money on real estate to the extent of 50 per cent. of its taxable valuation, at from 3½ to 5 per cent. interest.

PRESENT CONDITION OF TRADE.

In conclusion, I may say that at the present moment all business in Germany, financial and commercial, is more or less in abeyance of a settlement of the existing political complications. Should peace come, with an appearance of permanency, there is every reason to believe that a greatly-improved condition of trade, commerce, and production will supervene. Business will at least be more healthful and buoyant, if not more profitable. The present condition of the crops is promising, and an ample harvest is expected. Should this hope be realized, and with it the still more ardent desire for political tranquillity, an era of renewed prosperity can hardly fail to dawn upon this people and this continent.

ALFRED E. LEE.

UNITED STATES CONSULATE-GENERAL,
Frankfort-on-the-Main, May 3, 1878.

HAMBURG.

Report, by Consul Wilson, on the (1) *rates of wages;* (2) *cost of living;* (3) *past and present rates;* (4) *present state of trade;* (5) *paper money;* (6) *business habits and systems; for the district of Hamburg, including the cities of Harburg, Kiel, Lubeck, and Cuxhaven.*

The Department circular-letter, dated April 11, 1878, desiring certain information, is at hand. In answer thereto, I have the honor to submit the following report:

1. RATES OF WAGES.

Agricultural laborers.—In this consular district, including the agencies of Harburg, Kiel, Lubeck, and Cuxhaven, agricultural labor is principally performed by males, but few females being so engaged. This class of laborers is usually hired by the year, and the wages paid to first and second class hands are as follows:

For first, from $85.70 to $114.25; for second, from $57.12 to $85.70 per year, with board and lodging included.

During the harvest months, when extra agricultural labor is required, the same is paid for by the day, and the wages range from 50 to 68 cents per day, including board and lodging.

In some instances agricultural labor is paid for by the day, and in such cases the wages are, during the winter and fall months, 47 cents, and during the summer months, 59 cents, with board and lodging.

The number of working hours per day for the above-mentioned class of laborers is, during the winter and fall months, from daylight until dark, or from 4½ o'clock in the morning until 5 o'clock in the evening; during the spring and summer months, from 5 o'clock in the morning until 7 o'clock in the evening. The time allowed for breakfast is half an hour; for dinner during the fall and winter months, an hour; for dinner during the spring and summer months, two hours, and usually half an hour in the afternoon, say at 4 p. m., for lunch.

The agricultural land in this consular district is principally owned by large landed proprietors, under whose management and control the farming is conducted.

Laborers who are married and have a family usually obtain from the landowner a house and a small quantity of ground ranging from one to three acres, for which they pay a rent, which is usually paid in work. Upon this land, which is principally cultivated by the female members of the family, enough vegetables, &c., are raised to support them.

The agricultural laborers, as a class, are much inferior in point of intelligence and refinement to those of the United States; they are simple in their manners and their wants are but few, and they cling with great tenacity to the old customs and habits of their ancestors. They are generally honest and law-abiding, very frugal and saving even to parsimony, and always manage to live within their small earnings.

Mechanical laborers.—This class of labor is paid for by the day or week, and board and lodging is not included. The present daily wages in this consular district are as follows:

Occupation	From		To
Blacksmiths	$0 65	to	$0 83
Butchers	71	to	95
Barbers and hairdressers	71	to	95
Carpenters	83	to	1 07
Cabinet-makers and joiners	83	to	1 07
Cigar-makers	83	to	1 07
Locksmiths	83	to	1 07
Machinists	76	to	99
Masons, brick	86	to	1 07
Masons, stone	90	to	1 13
Plasterers	83	to	1 07
Painters	76	to	95
Piano-makers	71	to	95
Paper-hangers	71	to	95
Shoemakers	65	to	83
Stevedores	83	to	1 00
Saddlers and harness-makers	71	to	95
Tailors	65	to	75
Upholsterers	71	to	95

Commercial employés.—Clerks in stores, offices, banks, bookkeepers, chiefs of bureaus, cashiers, &c., receive from $714 to $1,428 per year.

Labor on public works.—The following tables give the kind of mechanical and other labor employed by the Hamburg Government, the time of working during the different months, and the prices paid per day. The labor is performed on the streets, public roads, promenades, harbor, docks, water-works, &c.

1. *Statement showing the regulations as to working-time and wages paid to workmen by the board of public works of the city of Hamburg.*

	Time employed.	Breakfast.	Dinner.	Lunch.	Working-time.	Wages paid per day.
a. MASONS AND CARPENTERS.						
(*i. e.* If engaged direct, which, however, is not often the case, generally the hands are obtained from a master-mechanic, to whom an extra of 75 pfennige, or 18 cents per day, is paid, in addition to the following wages for each man):						
From January 1 to January 11	From 7½ a. m. until 4 p. m	½ hour	1 hour		7 hours	$0 83
From January 12 to February 9	From 7 a. m. until 4½ p. m	do	do		8 hours	95
From February 10 to February 24	From 6½ a. m. until 5 p. m	do	do		9 hours	1 07
From February 25 to March 9	From 6 a. m. until 5½ p. m	do	do	½ hour	9 hours	1 07
From March 10 to October 5	From 6 a. m. until 6 p. m	do	do	½ hour	10 hours	1 19
From October 6 to October 20	From 6½ a. m. until 5½ p. m	do	do	½ hour	9 hours	1 07
From October 21 to November 2	From 6½ a. m. until 5 p. m	do	do		9 hours	1 07
From November 3 to December 1	From 7 a. m. until 4½ p. m	do	do		8 hours	95
From December 2 to December 31	From 7½ a. m. until 4 p. m	do	do		7 hours	83
b. STREET PAVERS.						
(These have to furnish their own tools for splitting, cutting, and setting stone.)						
a. STONECUTTERS.						
From the first Tuesday in March until the first Monday in October.	From 6 a. m. until 6 p. m	¼ hour	½ hour		10 hours	1 10
From the first Tuesday in October until the first Monday in November.	From 6 a. m. until 5½ p. m	½ hour	1 hour		10 hours	1 10
From the first Tuesday in November until the first Monday in March.	From daylight until sunset	½ hour	1 hour		7-9 hours	1 03
STONESETTERS.						
First class	Working-time the same as with the stonecutters.					92 85
Second class						85 78
STONESETTER'S HANDS.						
First class						78 71
Second class						74 64
c. COMMON LABORERS.						
Engaged on roads						53 to 71
Engaged on promenades						45 to 64
Engaged on the water-works						71 to 78

2. *Mechanics and laborers engaged on harbor and quay work.*—Masons and carpenters, brick and lime carriers, firemen of pile-driving engines, hands on pile-driving engines, shipcarpenters and wheelwrights, laborers and assistants on earthworks, according to kind of work, receive from 67 to 70 cents per day of 10 to 11 hours. Watchmen receive from 28 to 42 cents per night.

The above wages are calculated for the time from 6 a. m. until 6 p. m., with one-half hour rest for breakfast (from 8 to 8.30 o'clock), 1 hour rest for dinner (from 12 to 1 o'clock), and one-half hour rest for afternoon lunch (from 3.30 to 4 o'clock), making the actual working time 10 hours per day.

Hands on earthwork work until 7 p. m. (working-time 11 hours per day).

Extra work is paid at the rate of 12 cents per hour to mechanics and 7 cents to laborers and assistants. At the same rates the wages are reduced during winter and bad weather.

Night-work (from 9 p. m. until 5 a. m.) is paid at the rate of 14 cents per hour to mechanics and 10 cents to laborers and assistants.

At contract work the daily wages may increase to 86 cents for laborers, and hands engaged on earthwork and at very hard work, such as dredging and similar work, from $1.09 to $1.19 can be earned.

Railway laborers receive from 59 to 85 cents, exclusive of board and lodging. The usual working-time is, in the winter 8 hours and in summer 10 hours per day.

2. The cost of living.

Agricultural laborers employed by the year, board and lodging included, cost their employers from $41.65 to $59.50 per year for each person employed; agricultural laborers, with families of from three to five children, from $119 to $166.60 per year, including rent of house.

The cost of living to mechanical laborers, for single men, is from $2.83 to $3.57 per week; with family, from one-third to one-half more per week. Commercial employés pay for living expenses from $285.60 to $714 per year, and about one-half more when they have a family. The cost of living to mechanics and laborers engaged upon the public works, quays, harbors, and railways is the same as that of other mechanics and laborers.

3. Past and present rates.

The present rate of wages is from 10 to 20 per cent. higher than the rates prevailing five years ago.

The following table gives the wages paid prior to 1873:

3. *Statement showing the wages paid by the board of public works at Hamburg prior to* 1873.*

1. Masons and carpenters:	
From beginning of January until beginning of February	$0 71
From beginning of February until beginning of March	78
From beginning of March until beginning of April	85
From beginning of April until end of October	92
From beginning of November until middle of November	85
From middle of November until end of December	78

*The working hours were generally the same as those now existing and mentioned in statement 1, except that then the men worked in the summer months (from March until October) from 6 a. m. until 7 p. m., for the season; the street-pavers at that time were allowed only 1 hour for dinner and one-half hour (4 to 4.30 p. m.) for afternoon lunch.

1a. Brick and lime carriers for same time	50 53 60 64 60 60
2. Streetpavers:	
a. Stonecutters, in summer	85
in March and October	82
in winter	78
b. Stonesetters, first class, as above	71 67 65
second class, in summer	64
in March and October	60
in winter	57
c. Stonesetters' hands, in summer	53
in March and October	50
in winter	46
3. Common laborers:	
a. Engaged on roads and promenades, in summer	$0 50 to $0 42
in March and October	46 to 39
in winter	42 to 35
b. Engaged on water-works, &c., in summer	60 to 57
in March and October	57 to 53
in winter	53 to 50

The cost of living has also increased in a greater ratio, so that the laboring classes are in no better condition financially than they were formerly. Since the consolidation of the German Empire, and more especially since the close of the war with France, all the necessaries of life have greatly advanced, and the actual living expenses have doubled in the last ten years. The price of labor has not, however, made a corresponding advance, and, as a natural result, it requires the greatest frugality, saving, and industry on the part of the laboring classes to enable them to obtain sufficient means for their proper support.

4. Present state of trade.

During the last two years business of every kind has been very dull, and trade in a languid condition. Want of confidence, the unsettled and warlike condition of affairs in Europe, and the general disinclination on the part of merchants, business men, and capitalists to engage in any business of a speculative character, is assigned as a principal reason for this general depression.

Within the last three months, however, business has been on the increase, and in general a more confident feeling prevails among business men, and it is thought that the worst has passed.

5. Paper money.

As to the amount of paper money in circulation and the relation borne by paper and coin to each other, I have been unable to obtain any definite or specific information. This information can only be obtained from the Government officials at Berlin. Up to the 6th of July, 1878, there had been coined of the new coinage in the different mints of the German Empire 1,612,678,685 marks in gold, and 425,716,076 marks in silver.

The paper money in circulation in Germany is all issued by the Imperial Bank in Berlin and branches thereof in other parts of the empire, and consists of notes of the value of 5, 20, 50, 100, 500, and 1,000 marks.

The silver coin issued is 20 and 50 pfennige, and 1, 2, and 5 marks. No difference is made between gold, silver, and paper; all circulate alike, and are received at their full stamped value for all debts, public or private.

6. BUSINESS HABITS AND SYSTEMS.

The manner of conducting business in Hamburg is similar to that prevailing in other large commercial cities of Europe, and is generally transacted at the exchange, which is held daily between the hours of 1 and 3 p. m., and is visited by from 5,000 to 6,000 business men, representing every branch of business, trade, and industry.

Sales made and contracts entered into are on three months' time, unless cash sales are specially contracted for. In the latter case, it is customary for a discount of from 1½ to 4 per cent. to be given. In smaller transactions, such as purchases in stores, shops, &c., it is customary to render bills twice a year for such purchases. If cash payments are made, a discount of from 2 to 4 per cent. is always given. The manner of payments of debts incurred in large business transactions is by means of an authorized transfer from the bank account of the purchaser to that of the seller. Bank-checks and clearing-houses as existing in the United States are commercially unknown. Within the last few years there have been several attempts on the part of business men to introduce the American system of bank-checks, but it has been steadily opposed by the banks, who allege that this innovation on old and long-established customs would revolutionize their whole system of banking and bookkeeping and open the way for questionable bank transactions, which their present system does not permit.

JOHN M. WILSON.

UNITED STATES CONSULATE,
Hamburg, July 10, 1878.

LEIPSIC.

Report, by Consul Steuart, on the past and present rates of wages; American and German workingmen compared; business habits and systems; food of the laboring classes; rates of wages; money (gold, silver, and paper of the empire); commissions, credits, and discounts, &c., for the district of Leipsic.

In making this report upon the rate of wages paid to workmen and the cost of the necessaries of life in this district, I have availed myself largely of the resources of the "statistical bureau" of this city, whose means of procuring information in this channel are of the best and widest range. From their records I have compiled a table, which I hand herewith, giving the average yearly income of the workmen employed in the different trades and vocations mentioned therein, gathered from the reports received in the years 1875 and 1877. The highest and lowest wages are given for 1877, and the average is made up from the number of cases specified. Other of the facts herein stated I have obtained from the same reliable source.

PAST AND PRESENT RATES.

During the short season of activity and prosperity that Germany enjoyed after the close of the Franco-Prussian war, rents, provisions, and all the necessities of life advanced so rapidly, that an increase in wages of from 10 to 30 per cent. became a necessity and was granted to the workmen; but the present heavy commercial depression is gradually drawing both back from the high point they reached, and they will probably go still lower unless there is an early revival in trade.

AMERICAN AND GERMAN WORKMEN.

The prices paid for labor, as here quoted, may seem low, viewed from an American standpoint, but they are fully equal to the value of the services rendered. An active American workman fills the place, or, in other words, will do as much work in any employment in a given time as two or three German workmen; he is able to do this from his quicker and wider powers of comprehension, from being naturally more rapid in his movements, and from the superiority of the tools with which he works.

In this country the supply of persons needing employment is very great, and the work to be done must be so meted out that it will contribute to the support of the largest number. They work very leisurely and with the least inconvenience to themselves. Females are largely employed by retail and often by large business houses both in the office and sales department, and a person traveling through the country receives the impression that all the work in the fields is done by women.

BUSINESS HABITS AND SYSTEMS.

It is the custom in this city and in the small towns and villages through this district for all banks, factories, and business houses to close up two hours for dinner in the middle of the day, say from 12 to 2 or from 1 to 3 o'clock.

Formerly, all the retail establishments observed this custom, but they are gradually working out of it, and now some of the enterprising retail merchants, beginning to appreciate the value of time, keep open all day, but with a small force to attend any customers that may come in during the hours above stated; in this connection, and to show how rigidly old customs are adhered to in this country, I will mention a circumstance related to me recently by a gentleman who visits Europe at least once every year to make purchases for the firm with which he is connected in America.

Two American buyers, wishing a large quantity of the goods made by a certain manufacturer, decided to go direct to his factory, although it was some distance from the railroad, and make their purchases. They arrived about 11 o'clock in the morning and, after the usual courtesies, wished to commence work; but the manufacturer, looking at his watch, said "It is nearly 12 o'clock, we will go into my house, have a glass of wine and something to eat, and then to business"; but the merchants replied, "It is not possible; our time is limited, and we must leave early this afternoon." Well, in a word, the manufacturer could not violate his custom of closing his factory and taking his lunch at 12, and the buyers, not being able to lose the time, had to depart without making any purchases, and thoroughly disgusted with such an experience; but I am sure that the circumstance did not in the least affect the appetite of the manufacturer.

I must think this an isolated case, but that it could happen once seems strange to a business man in America.

FOOD OF THE LABORING CLASSES.

In looking at the prices of the necessaries of life as given, it must be remembered that the habits of the laboring man here are very different from those in America. There the workman has three meals every day of good strengthening food, while here he eats much oftener, but of food not so nourishing. For instance, on rising in the morning he will have a cup of common black coffee and a slice of black bread with butter; about 9 or 10 o'clock he makes his breakfast of a glass of beer with bread and sausage; then dinner at 12, and this consists generally of some vegetables, such as beans, potatoes, carrots, rice, &c., stewed together, sometimes with the addition of a small piece of meat; then at 4 o'clock he must rest and have his cup of coffee, and in the evening a supper of beer and cheese or sausage, always with black bread. About once a week, generally on Sundays, they have a good meat dinner.

A single workingman can live on from $2 to $3 per week, and one with a family from $5 to $6 per week.

RATES OF WAGES.

In giving the following quotations for wages and provisions in American currency, I have valued the mark at twenty-five cents.

Book-printing: In a printing establishment the lowest wages are paid to folders, about $1.35 per week, and the highest to foremen, about $11.25 per week. From statistics carefully gathered for the years specified below an average has been made from the wages paid to printers, including all, the highest and the lowest, with the following result: In 1870–'71, an average of $2.90 per week; in 1871–'72, $2.93; in 1872–'73, $3.25; in 1873–'74, $3.76; and in the last half of 1874, an average of $4.08 per week was paid; in 1875, $3.94; in 1876, $3.99; in 1877, $3.94, and at the present time same rate continues.

Bookbinders: In the year 1862 there were employed in this city 82 masters and 252 workmen (no females were employed at that time), and from the last census, taken on the 1st of December, 1875, we find the number increased to 1,101 males and 484 females. Good binders receive from $5 to $6 per week, and gold printers as high as $10 per week. Workmen employed by the hour receive from 5 to 10 cents.

Clerks: For salaries paid to clerks in business houses in 1877, an average, made up from the number of cases cited, shows the following figures: Clerks who hold a power of attorney to sign and act for the firm are called procurists. Procurists, in 149 cases, received an average of $880 per annum, 8 per cent. less than in 1875.

Bookkeepers, in 83 cases, received an average of $527, being 5 per cent. less than in 1875.

Salesmen, in 1,250 cases, received an average of $340, being 2 per cent. more than in 1875.

Office-clerks, in 46 cases, received an average of $236, being 5 per cent. more than in 1875.

Porters, in 629 cases, received an average of $195 per annum, being 5 per cent. less than in 1875.

In the wool-combing factory in this city there were employed, on the 1st January, 1876, 84 males, at an average weekly pay of $3.89; 121 females, at an average weekly pay of $1.91. On the 30th September, 1877, 161 males receiving, weekly, an average of $4; 253 females receiving, weekly, an average of $1.92.

In the worsted-yarn establishment, on the 30th September, 1877, there were 17 master workmen, weekly pay $7.50 to $12; 80 spinners, weekly pay $5.25 to $6.75; 327 females, weekly pay $2.25; 10 day laborers, weekly pay $3.75.

Cabinet-makers receive, as foremen, about $1 per day; as workmen, 70 cents; and as laborers, 55 cents per day.

Employés in essential-oil factories receive from $4 to $5 per week.

Cigar-makers: Wages in this branch of trade have not varied in four years. Males receive, weekly, from $3 to $5; females receive, weekly, from $2 to $2.75.

Engravers on stone: Ordinary workmen receive from $4.50 to $5, and the best from $9 to $11.50 per week.

Stonemasons receive, as foremen, about $1.10 per day; masons, 90 cents to $1; laborers, 55 to 65 cents; and as mortar-makers, 70 to 75 cents per day.

Farm-laborers: In 1873 men received about 50 cents and women 38 cents per day, with plain food and lodging; in 1878, for the same labor, the wages are, for men about 40 cents, and women 35 cents per day, with board and lodging.

Female kitchen-servants receive about the same wages now that they did in 1873. Cooks receive from $50 to $80 per annum; chambermaids, from $40 to $60 per annum; and common servants, from $25 to $30 per annum; but, in addition to these wages, they must have at each of the three fairs held here a present of from $1 to $3, and at Christmas a sum of money equal to about one-fourth of their yearly wages, besides a dress and other small presents.

There are certain police regulations governing the relations between these servants and their employers. Each servant is furnished with a book, numbered and registered, in which these regulations are printed. One month's notice must in all cases be given before they are sent away. They must report to the police whenever they change their places of service, and must show an indorsement of character written in their book by their last employer.

Railways: Station-masters received in 1873 from $900 to $1,000, and in 1878 from $600 to $900. Passenger-conductors, in 1873, from $500 to $600, and in 1878 from $450 to $525, with from $50 to $75 for clothing. Freight-conductors, in 1873, from $450 to $500, and in 1878 from $375 to $450, with the same allowance for clothing as passenger-conductors. Engine-drivers receive from $450 to $600 per annum, and about $40 for clothing. Firemen receive from $150 to $225 per annum.

Police: Captains of police receive about $700 per annum, with an allowance of $75 for dwelling. Lieutenants receive from $390 to $420 per annum. Men receive $275 to $320 per annum.

FOOD PRICES.

The prices of some of the necessaries of life are about as follows:

		Cents.
Black bread	per pound..	2
Butter	do	15 to 16
Cheese	do	8 to 12
Candles	do	13 to 23
Petroleum	do	3½
Rice	do	8 to 12
White bread	do	3
Flour	do	5 to 6
Sugar	do	10 to 12
Starch	do	8
Coffee	do	28 to 50
Dried beans	do	4½

Eggs, about 13 cents per dozen; milk, from 4 to 4¼ cents per quart;

salted herrings, from 2 to 2½ cents each; potatoes, from 85 to 90 cents per American bushel.

		Cents.
Beef, inferior	per pound..	15
Beef, best	do	18
Pork	do	14 to 16
Mutton	do	15
Veal	do	14
Sausage-meat	do	18 to 27

Pigeons cost from 18 to 25 cents per pair; chickens, $1 to $1.25, and capons $1.50 to $2.25 per pair; but the goose is to the German market what the turkey is to the American, the favorite and most plentiful fowl. They cost from $1 to $2.50, and when a poor family are so fortunate as to have a goose for their Sunday dinner, the fat therefrom is made to serve the place of butter during the following week.

MONEY.

Paper money has the same value as gold and silver. I have obtained from a banker in this city the following facts and figures regarding the coinage and the amount of paper money issued in the German Empire to the 12th October of this year:

Gold.—Twenty-mark piece; weight, 7.9650 grammes; $\frac{9}{10}$ fine; amount coined, 1,233,459,100 marks. Ten-mark piece; weight, 3.9825 grammes; $\frac{9}{10}$ fine; amount coined, 381,513,840 marks. Five-mark piece; weight, 1.9912 grammes; $\frac{9}{10}$ fine; amount coined, 27,969,845 marks.

Silver.—Five-mark piece; weight, 27.77 grammes; $\frac{9}{10}$ fine; amount coined, 71,652,415 marks. Two-mark piece; weight, 11.11 grammes; $\frac{9}{10}$ fine; amount coined, 98,509,686 marks. One-mark piece; weight, 5.55 grammes; $\frac{9}{10}$ fine; amount coined, 149,423,211 marks. Fifty-pfennig piece; weight, 2.77 grammes; $\frac{9}{10}$ fine; amount coined, 71,486,388 marks. Twenty-pfennig piece; weight, 1.11 grammes; $\frac{9}{10}$ fine; amount coined, 35,717,718 marks.

Nickel.—Ten-pfennig and five-pfennig pieces; weight, 4 grammes and 2.5 grammes; composed of one-quarter part nickel and three-quarter part copper.

Copper.—Two-pfennig and one-pfennig pieces; composed of 95 per cent. copper, 4 per cent. tin, and 1 per cent. zinc.

The amount of nickel and copper coins is not published, but there are probably about 100,000,000 marks of these coins in circulation in the German Empire.

In addition to the coins enumerated above, the old silver thaler is still in circulation. Its weight is 18.52 grammes, and is about 10 per cent. better than the silver of the new currency. None have been coined since 1872, and as they are being retained by all government offices, a large amount has already been taken out of circulation. It is not possible to make any reliable estimate of the amount now in circulation.

PAPER MONEY.

The Government has issued about 138,000,000 marks in 5, 20, and 50 mark notes, and these must be received at all the government offices.

The following 18 banks issue notes for 100, 200, 500, and 1,000 marks to the amounts placed opposite their names:

	Marks.
Reichsbank, Berlin	640,815,000
Städtische Bank, Breslau	2,297,400
Kölnische Bank, Coln	2,283,220
Magdeburger Privatbank, Magdeburg	2,926,800

	Marks.
Danziger Privatbank, Danzig	2,020,200
Provinzial-Actien-bank, Posen	2,124,300
Sächsische Bank, Dresden	38,903,300
Leipziger Cassenverein, Leipzig	2,949,500
Chemnitzer Stadtbank, Chemnitz	510,000
Hannoverische Bank, Hannover	5,006,200
Kommerz Bank, Lübeck	800,300
Bremen Bank, Bremen	5,167,100
Frankfurter Bank, Frankfort-on-the-Main	11,127,900
Bayerische Notenbank, München	66,353,000
Würtembergisch Notenbank, Stuttgart	21,896,800
Badische Bank, Mannheim	9,914,100
Bank of Süddeutschland, Darmstadt	11,450,300
Braunschweigische Bank, Braunschweig	2,616,700
Total issue	829,162,120

The issue of the Brunswick Bank is limited in circulation to the Duchy of Brunswick. The notes of all the other banks circulate freely over the whole German Empire.

COMMISSION, CREDITS, AND DISCOUNTS.

Commission-houses charge from 1½ to 3 per cent. on purchases for America. The rate of discount and length of credit are matters of agreement, as also whether the goods are delivered in Leipsic or free on board ship at Bremen or Hamburg. Charges for packing are calculated at from 1 to 2 per cent. on the value of the goods. On cloth, from ½ to ¾ per cent. on the value; on furs, the actual cost is charged; and on drugs no charge for packing is made.

JOHN H. STEUART.

UNITED STATES CONSULATE,
Leipsic, October 26, 1878.

MANNHEIM.

Report, by Consul Smith, on the (1) *rates of wages;* (2) *cost of living;* (3) *past and present rates;* (4) *paper and specie money of Baden and Germany; and* (5) *business habits and systems; for the district of Baden.*

A delay on the part of my informant has prevented an earlier reply to the questions asked in circular dated April 14.

1. Rates of wages paid to laborers, especially agricultural, mechanical, and those employed upon public works and railways:

Agricultural laborers, summer	per day		$0 50
winter	do		40
Mechanical laborers	do	$0 60 to	1 44
Public works and railways (night-work extra)	do		50
Locksmiths	do		84
Carpenters	do		72
Brick and stone layers	do		78
Masons	do	60 to	72
Cabinet-makers	do		72
Cooks	per month	4 80 to	8 40
Chambermaids	do	2 50 to	4 80
Coachmen	do		8 40
Man-servants	do		7 20
Hotel-servants, porters	do		6 00
waiters	do	12 20 to	19 20
porter (boots)	do		3 88
Physicians	per visit		72
Clergymen	per annum		*480 00

* And upward.

School-teachers, men	per annum..	$360 00
women	do	192 00
Governesses	do	96 00
Sewing-women	per day..	48

2. Cost of living.

The wages paid hardly cover the necessaries of life; many seldom taste meat more than once a week:

Rent, two to four rooms	per annum..	$33 60 to	$60 00
Bread, white	per pound..		3
Bread, black	do		2¼
Beef, steaks	do		25
roast	do		25
common	do	10 to	14
Chickens	each		48
Mutton	per pound..		14
Pork	do		14
Veal	do		14
Eggs	per dozen..	12 to	14
Butter	per pound..	24 to	30
Cheese	do	10 to	24
Coffee	do	20 to	38
Tea	do	72 to	1 20
Sugar	do		9½
Potatoes	per cwt..	82 to	96
Turnips	per pound..		1
Beets	do		1
Cabbages	each..		1½

3. Past and present rates.

Five years ago agricultural laborers were paid in summer 72 cents, and in winter 60 cents per day. Mechanical laborers were paid 62 cents to $1.44; laborers on public works and railroads, 72 cents; masons, $1.20; and other trades in proportion.

During the last five years there has been an increase in the cost of living and a gradual decrease in the price of labor. This fact has alarmed the Government and people of Germany, and earnest efforts are being made to ascertain the reason and, if possible, to remedy the evil. It is mainly attributed to overtrading and overproduction, which have led to disastrous terms of credit and not wise methods of business. Long terms of credit are given—three, six, and nine months—without acceptances on the part of the buyer, depressing natural industry and embarrassing the manufacturer both by the uncertainty of the time of payment and the character of the funds received in payment; the seller often receiving long-sight bills of exchange or foreign coin at a high rate. This necessarily raises the price of manufactures beyond foreign prices, and prevents stability either on the part of the buyers or sellers. The seller has no means of judging of the solvency of his customer, and the buyer is induced to make indirect purchases.

The present state of trade is, in this district, at a low point, and a gloomy spirit exists among all classes of merchants and manufacturers.

4. Paper and specie money.

There is no paper money issued in Baden, except the emission of the Badische Bank, a bank established in 1871, with special privileges from the Government. At the expiration of its charter, some fifteen years hence, it is expected that it will be absorbed by the Reichsbank of

Berlin, which is similar in its functions to the Bank of England and that of France. Its issues are in bills of 100 marks, which are at par in all business transactions, and are redeemed at the bank and its agencies in gold. The German Government reserves to itself the issue of notes of 5, 20, to 50 marks.

The gold issues of Baden, sanctioned by the German Government, are 5, 10, and 20 mark pieces; silver, 1, 2, and 5 marks, and 20 and 50 pfennige; nickel, 5 and 10 pfennige; copper, 1 and 2 pfennige.

The present amount of the gold and silver issue of Germany (August 10, 1878) is, gold, 1,624,253,425 marks; silver, 426,205,662 marks.

The returns of German banks of issue, as exhibited June 30, 1878, were as follows:

Banks.	Joint-stock capital.	Cash.	Bills.	Deposits.	Bank-note circulation.
	Marks.	*Marks.*	*Marks.*	*Marks.*	*Marks.*
German Imperial Bank	120, 000, 000	546, 249	379, 167	59, 405	672, 898
The five old Prussian private banks	15, 000, 000	5, 423	28, 887	6, 219	11, 321
The three Saxon banks	33, 510, 000	26, 609	48, 615	7, 282	43, 825
The remaining five North German banks	46, 907, 000	5, 925	58, 127	5, 448	14, 476
The Bank of Frankfort-on-the-Main	17, 142, 900	5, 662	28, 981	2, 161	12, 344
Bavarian Bank	7, 500, 000	36, 771	36, 523	1, 548	67, 048
The three remaining South German banks	49, 389, 000	18, 695	47, 403	3, 094	41, 099
Total	289, 448, 900	645, 334	627, 703	85, 157	863, 011

5. Business habits and systems.

The business habits and systems of this district are conservative; no large purchases or investments are made without very extensive investigation. Few changes are made in the business rules of the past, and few in firm names. Business descends from father to son, and families retain their investments therein from generation to generation. In depressed times expenses are reduced both in the business place and in the family. It being almost impossible for a person who has once failed, or who has been discredited, to resume business or re-establish himself; consequently an American merchant who has once failed to meet his engagements here is always regarded with suspicion.

EDWARD M. SMITH.

United States Consulate,
Mannheim, August 22, 1878.

SONNEBERG.

Report, by Consul Winser, on the (1) *rates of wages*; (2) *cost of living*; (3) *past and present rates*; (4) *present state of trade*; (5) *business habits and systems*; (6 *and* 7) *paper money and coin* (*German Empire*); *for the district of Sonneberg* (*Thuringian Duchies and Principalities*).

I have the honor hereby to acknowledge the receipt of Department Circular, under date of the 11th ultimo, which calls upon consular officers in Europe to make inquiries and report, respectively, upon the following subjects:

1. The rate of wages paid to agricultural laborers and mechanics.
2. The cost of living to the laboring classes, or the prices paid for what may be termed the necessaries of life.

3. A comparison of the present rate of wages and cost of food with the same during the past five years.

4. The amount and character of the currency.

5. The business habits and systems in vogue in their respective districts.

1. Rates of wages.

In regard to the rate of wages usually paid to laborers of every class, but with more especial reference to agricultural laborers, mechanical laborers, and those upon public works and railways, I confine my reply to the rates which are paid in the Sonneberg consular district, embracing the Thuringian Duchies and Principalities, which cover an area of 3,300 English square miles, and contain a population of over one million.

The wages paid to day-laborers of every class is as follows:

	Cents.
Agricultural laborers in villages, per day, males (not found)	28 to 48
Agricultural laborers in villages, per day, females (not found)	24 to 28
Agricultural laborers in villages, per day, males (found)	16 to 20
Agricultural laborers in villages, per day, females (found)	8 to 10
Day-laborers in towns, per day, males (not found)	50 to 55
Day-laborers in towns, per day, females (not found)	25 to 37½
Day-laborers in towns, per day, females (found)	12½ to 25
Railway-station laborers and those employed on public works (not found)	40 to 57

Laborers, male and female, living in villages in the neighborhood of towns, earn the same wages as those who live in towns, always finding employment in the latter.

In the summer the working hours are from 6 a. m. to 6 p. m. During this time there are three rests allowed—half an hour in the forenoon, one hour at noon, and half an hour in the afternoon—for the purpose of taking food. Ten hours constitute a day's work.

For three months of the summer, when there is an average of 16 hours of daylight, laborers make overtime and are paid therefor from 5 to 7 cents per hour.

In winter the working hours are necessarily shorter and wages are reduced from 10 to 30 per cent. For instance, the burgomaster at Coburg employed 200 laborers during the winter and early spring of this year in laying out and grading an addition to the city cemetery, and paid each man a daily wage of 26 cents upon which to keep body and soul together.

Working on Sundays is quite the rule.

Railway-station laborers (freight-handlers and car-shiftsrs) on the Werra Railroad, which is a private corporation, are compelled to be on duty from 5.30 a. m. to 10.30 p. m., working more or less during all these 15 hours as the demand for their services presents itself.

On the State railways wages are much higher. It may not be amiss, in connection with the foregoing, to add a statement showing the average wages in the Thuringian States paid for a day's work at the principal trades and occupations.

The piece-work system, however, is generally followed, and, in this case the earnings average about 20 per cent. more.

Daily wages in the Thuringian States.

Cabinet-makers		$0 75
Carpenters	$0 55 to	62½
Blacksmiths	55 to	62½
Chinaware-makers:		
Modelers and chief decorators		1 50
Decorators	75 to	98

China-ware makers:	
Formers and turners, males	$0 75 to $0 98
females	36 to 60
Firemen	60 to 75
Packers	50 to 60
Day-laborers, males	40 to 60
females	36 to 45
Doll and toy makers, males	49 to 98
females	24 to 49
Glassmakers	50 to 75
Glaziers	60 to 86
Gunmakers	$1 and upward.
Kid-glove makers, males	$0 50 to 75
females	24 to 36
machine-sewers	33 to 50
Lampmakers	50 to 75
Letter-carriers	75 to 80
Locksmiths	50 to 60
Masons and bricklayers	55 to 63
Painters	60 to 75
Paintmakers	30 to 50
Papier-maché workers, males	50 to 55
Polishers, French	70 to 75
Railway conductors, exclusive of uniform and mileage	45 to 50
brakemen	40 to 45
switchtenders	45 to 50
telegraph-operators	75 to 80
Tailors	45 to 50
Tobacco-pipe makers, males	50 to 95
females	25 to 50
Upholsterers	75
Weavers	40 to 50

It will be seen by this statement that the daily rates of wages in this district are fabulously small in comparison with those paid to craftsmen and employés in the United States, and that the amount paid varies very little in the different trades and occupations. There can be no question that, speaking in general terms, the quality as well as the quantity of the work of the German artisan is inferior to that produced by the American.

The workman here is inclined to sluggishness, and what he accomplished is relatively small.

Railway conductors and brakemen on the Werra Railway receive mileage in addition to their regular wages. This mileage amounts on the average to $7.50 a month for conductors and $5 for brakemen.

The present rate of wages in the various mechanical occupations is from 10 to 15 per cent. lower than in the year 1876, and is about as high as that paid for some years prior to 1873.

2. The cost of living.

As to the cost of living to the laboring class, or the prices paid for what may be termed the necessaries of life, it may be easily imagined from the figures which show the earnings of the laboring and manufacturing classes of Thuringia that the workman's daily fare is of the simplest sort, and that his life is, at best, a struggle for existence for himself and family.

The principal food is rye bread and potatoes. He is, perforce of circumstances, a vegetarian in diet, as all his forefathers were. He rarely eats meat at all in any other form than sausage, and his wife and children scarcely know its taste, so little do they get of it. The ordinary bill of fare is rye bread and chicory coffee, without sugar, for breakfast; rye bread without butter for lunch; potato soup, potatoes, rye bread, and home-made cheese, with a glass of beer, for dinner; again, rye bread at four o'clock in the afternoon, and still rye bread and beer in the evening. There is little variety in the standard fare, except on Sundays and festival days, when, perhaps, sausage is substituted for the cheese, more beer is consumed, and a few eggs and a potato salad are added to the evening meal. The laborer himself, without exception, is in the habit of taking a dram of spirits more or less often during the day, but drunkenness is a vice rarely known here. From immemorial ages the Thüringian workman, be he a day-laborer, a mechanic, or a manufacturer, engaged in any of the cottage industries, has laid the greatest value upon the control of a piece of ground, either as owner or lessee, which his wife and children may cultivate while he is employed at his calling. This plot of garden or field not only supplies him with potatoes and other vegetables, but generally enables him to keep a goat or two, raise poultry, and sometimes to have a cow.

This small husbandry is an important factor in the problem of making both ends meet. Indeed, if the garden consists only of a stony acre on a steep hillside and is capable of yielding potatoes, it appears to be sufficient to tide the family of a laboring man over the oft-recurring periods of lack of work which have marked recent years, and at no time is its cultivation neglected. In order to possess this mainstay of a garden the married workman, although employed in the town, prefers to live in the country, and spend an hour or more every morning and evening in walking between his cottage and place of occupation.

This cottage, it must be said, is always of primitive construction, with unsightly mottled walls, and seldom contains more than two small rooms and a kitchen, and is furnished in the barest manner. For such a shelter and the garden plot the rent is from $12 to $15 per annum, unless the occupant happens to own the property, which not unfrequently is the case.

There is poverty in superabundance in the workman's home, often verging upon squalor; his children are generally ragged and barefooted; his wife looks haggard and weary of her lot; but cases of absolute destitution are not common. The unmarried laborer fares somewhat better than the man of family. He usually finds a lodging in the town if his occupation takes him there, and pays for his bed, a breakfast of coffee and black bread, and a very plain dinner at the rate of 25 to 30 cents per day. The supper he provides for himself at a beer-house.

The following statement shows the present average retail prices of what are ordinarily termed the necessaries of life, although most of the articles enumerated are only exceptionally to be found on the table of the laboring man:*

Article	Unit	Cents
Apples, sliced	per pound	$0 14
Bread, white	do	9
rye, according to quality	do	$0 2½ to 4
Butter	do	26 to 32
Cheese, Swiss	do	20 to 25
handkase	each	2
Brandy 48 per cent. Tealles	per liter	15 to 20
Coffee, Java, raw	per pound	33
roasted	do	38
Chicory, substitute for coffee	do	6
Grains, &c.:		
Barley, large	do	5
hulled	do	6½
Rice, Java	do	6

*In this statement the quantities are given in German pounds (½ kilogram), and a German pound is equal to 1.1 pounds avoirdupois. Where a liter is the measure used, it is equal to 1$\frac{1}{18}$ liquid quarts.

Grains, &c.:		
Rice, broken	per pound..	$0 05
Flour, white	do	7
Farina	do	7
Oatmeal	do	8
Potato-meal	do	7
Vermicelli	do	9
Pease, hulled	do	5
Beans, white	do	4¾
Lentils	do	5
Herrings, Scotch	each..	2½
Meats:		
Beef	per pound..	$0 15 to 16
Veal	do	12 to 14
Pork	do	16 to 17
Mutton	do	13 to 14
Milk	per liter..	4 to 5
Oil (salad), poppy	per pound..	20 to 22
olive	do	30 to 33
rapeseed, refined	do	12½
petroleum	do	5½
Acohol	per liter..	20 to 25
Potatoes	per 5 liters..	6¼ to 7½
Sugar, refined loaf	per pound..	13½
powdered	do	12
crude brown	do	11
Salt, coarse	do	2½
Starch	do	9 to 10
Soda, washing	do	3
Soap	do	8 to 12½
Sauerkraut	do	3 to 3½
Eggs	each..	1¼ to 2
Candles, stearine	per pound..	25
tallow	do	14
Vinegar	per liter..	5
Coal	per ton..	6 50 to 7 00
Wood, hard	per cubic meter..	4 25 to 5 00
pine	do	2 25 to 3 00
Fowls, old	each..	25 to 40
Pigeons	per pair..	20 to 22

Excepting in the case of meats and a few other articles, such as butter and eggs, the supply of which depends upon the season of the year, there has been little variation in the retail price of the aforementioned provisions during the past five years, the average difference per pound on any given article scarcely exceeding one-half of a cent during the entire period.

The price of beef per pound in the markets of Coburg and Sonneberg, which may be taken as the criterion for the entire Thuringian district, has ranged as follows during the years named: 1874, 13 cents; 1875, 12½ cents; 1876, 12½ cents; 1877, 14 cents; 1878, 16 cents.

The price of veal per pound in the same markets during the same years ranged as follows: 1874, 11 cents; 1875, 12½ cents; 1876, 11 cents; 1877, 11½ cents; 1878, 15½ cents.

The price of pork per pound during the same period was: 1874, 15½ cents; 1875, 15½ cents; 1876, 17 cents; 1877, 17 cents; 1878, 16 cents.

The price of mutton per pound during the same period was: 1874, 13 cents; 1875, 10 cents; 1876, 13 cents; 1877, 14 cents; 1878, 14½ cents.

The extraordinary high prices of meat at present is attributed to a scarce supply, farmers having decreased their stock materially during the past few years in consequence of the continued distrust which has prevailed in political and commercial affairs, and the markets are now affected as a result of this course of the stock-raisers. The price of pork has fallen lately in consequence of an existing scare from recent fatal cases of trichinosis in various parts of the country.

The price of the following-enumerated articles per hectoliter (equal to 2 bushels and 3.35 pecks American standard measure) in the markets of the eleven garrison towns of Thuringia, during the years 1873–1878, has averaged as follows: Wheat, $4.28; rye, $3.39; barley, $2.70; oats, $1.70; potatoes, $1.30.

The price of rice and barley per centimeter (equal to 100 pounds avoirdupois) in the eleven garrison towns of Thuringia during the years 1873–1878 has averaged as follows: Rice, $6.37; barley (hulled), $5.62.

3. Past and present rates.

So far as practicable, a comparison of the present rates with those prevailing during the past five years, both as to wages and cost of living, have been made under the headings 2 and 3.

4. Present state of trade.

From all the indications now visible it does not appear that trade will be able very soon to shake off the incubus which has depressed it for so many years. An improvement is scarcely to be expected until the European political horizon becomes clearer.

Industrial establishments in this region are now filling the comparatively small orders which were given in the early spring, but great complaint is made of the low prices which are obtained for goods, and which from necessity must be accepted.

In fact, the manufacturers are producing at unprofitable prices, for the most part, in order to keep their hands employed and their machinery in operation, hoping for an improvement in affairs as the season advances. The bulk of the orders to the trade in this district is given after the Easter fair at Leipsic, which is just about to close, and it would, therefore, be premature at this moment to express a positive opinion upon the prospects of business during the summer.

At present, the daily reports from the exchanges in the principal financial centers of Germany tell of small transactions and a general tendency to refrain from engagements for any extended period.

The public has become very cautious, and will only invest in first-rate securities.

The returns of the great railway companies for the first quarter of the year show again diminished receipts both for goods and passengers, and the stockholders in some cases will receive no semi-annual dividend.

5. Business habits and systems.

It is difficult to define clearly the business habits of the merchants and manufacturers of this district. There is no general standard nor system governing commercial transactions. The principal characteristic of trade is excessive competition.

There are, certainly, a great many business men here who base their operations upon sound principles, but the mass of traders, in their eagerness to push sales, are accustomed to take great risks in view of a very small profit.

The smaller manufacturers are not satisfied with keeping their own regular customers, but seek to take away from their competitors every other customer, even when there is no profit in prospect. The larger manufacturers to some extent also are guilty of the same fault. They are not content with selling to wholesale buyers, but endeavor to draw away the heavier customers of the latter class by offering goods to the smaller dealers at the same if not lower prices, as those which they get from their larger customers. The only excuse for this breach of commercial ethics is to be found in the fact that trade in all parts of the world remains in a state of depression, and there is a constant overproduction in almost all the articles which are manufactured in this district.

A grave error has been committed during the past few years in granting credits altogether too freely and imprudently. The result of this laxity has recently been demonstrated by great losses to many traders in this district in the suspension of several business firms in the United States and elsewhere, who have bought very largely on credit with what appears to have been a premeditated intention to defraud the manufacturers.

The larger the orders which were given by the alleged swindling firms, the greater was the temptation of the manufacturer to take large risks. In these cases, cash payment was promised very often for the first shipment, in order that the cash discount (generally 5 per cent. on six months' time, and 2 to 3 per cent. on three month's time) might be obtained; but it frequently has happened that the goods purchased on these terms were paid for only after a year or more had expired, and sometimes have not been paid for at all. In many cases extensions have been gained by the payment of interest on transactions which were made on a cash basis. Under these circumstances, large and prompt-paying buyers have been made to suffer greatly, while small and unscrupulous competitors have gained an advantage.

I believe it to be the habit of some American importers to buy their goods here in March, have them shipped in May and June, and pay for them only in January and February of the following year.

For this class of custom a cash discount is very often deducted, and interest reckoned from the date of the invoice in the account current, in violation of the declaration which is made by the exporter to the consular officer. But proof of this allegation is difficult to obtain.

In England at present, owing to the stagnation of commerce, prices are altogether nominal, and English consumers and jobbers of the goods manufactured in this district now buy next to nothing.

Consequently, a large number of manufacturers have accumulated stocks of china, "knickknacks," glass and stone, marbles, &c., on hand, which they are willing to sell very often below the cost of manufacture to American customers in order to raise money. I have recently heard of stone marbles being offered at 70 pfennige per thousand; a decrease of 30 per cent. on the low prices which were paid a few months since.

I scarcely think, however, that the manufacturers in this district, as a class, would themselves declare to undervalue invoices of goods, but I suspect that some invoices of merchandise shipped from this district are sent to agents of American buyers at other places and are authenticated at other consulates.

Practices of this sort a consul can neither control nor prevent.

Toys in general cannot be bought, packed, boxed, and forwarded, even for cash payment, on a bare commission of 10 per cent. A much larger margin is necessary to compensate for labor, loss of interest, and outlays. Most of the toys sent hence to the United States are manufactured upon special order according to sample (they are not kept on hand in the warerooms as stock), and prices generally tend upward from the month of July to December in each year.

From December, ordinarily, to April of the following year, and exceptionally, as at present, goods may be bought at the lowest figures. In former years new and saleable toys which any manufacturer devised and produced would generally be imitated by his competitors and sold at lower prices before the first shipment of any new article had reached its destination. The novelty very often would be shown by the foreign buyer to a competing manufacturer with the direct purpose in view of creating an unfair emulation. This underhand mode of business has been checked recently to some extent by the German patent and registry laws, which have been in force about three years.

A great many of the manufacturers of this district are greatly in debt, their small accummulated capital having disappeared during the past three or four unprofitable years. Credits have also been shortened, and new mortgages on factories are not easily obtainable, and foreclosures are frequent.

Large losses have been suffered during the past few months by the failures and compromises of several importing houses in America.

Perhaps these sad experiences of the late years will teach the manufacturers and merchants of this consular district good and sound business principles. Such principles heretofore to a very great extent have been unobserved.

6 AND 7. PAPER MONEY AND COIN.

The Reichsbank and seventeen private banks are at present entitled to issue 100, 200, 500, and 1,000 mark notes, as well as 5, 10, 20, and 50 mark notes.

According to the bank act of March 14, 1875, the issue of notes uncovered by bullion is limited to 273,875,000 marks for the Reichsbank and 111,125,000 marks for the seventeen private banks; making 385,000,000 marks.

The actual issue of notes, both covered and uncovered, was on the 1st of April, 1878, 833,504,000 marks against an amount of bullion and coin in the cellars of the banks of 623,896,000 marks, which shows that 75 per cent. of the issued notes were covered by bullion.

Besides the above-mentioned bank-notes, there are 120,000,000 marks of State notes (Reichscassenscheine) of 5, 20, and 50 mark denominations in circulation.

The coins of the German Empire are of gold, silver, nickel, and copper. All the gold coins, according to the law of July 9, 1873, are of one purity, 9 parts of pure metal and 1 part of copper alloy. Out of 500 grammes of pure gold are coined 69¾-twenty-mark pieces, 139½ ten-mark pieces, 279 five-mark pieces.

All the old German gold coins were demonetized on the 1st of April, 1874, and have not been redeemed since the 1st of July of the same year.

All the German silver coins are also of one purity, 9 parts of pure silver and 1 of alloy. Out of one pound of pure silver is coined 20 five-mark pieces, 50 two-mark pieces, 100 one-mark pieces, 200 fifty-pfennig pieces, 500 twenty-pfennig pieces.

The nickel coinage consists of ten pfennig-pieces and five-pfennig pieces, each containing 25 parts nickel and 75 parts copper.

The copper or bronze coinage is confined to pieces of one and two pfennige, which contains 95 parts copper, 4 parts tin, and 1 part zinc.

The entire amount of the imperial silver coinage is limited by law to 10 marks per head of the population, and the issue of nickel and bronze coins shall not exceed 2½ marks per head.

Nobody is compelled to take in payment more than 20 marks in silver and 1 mark in nickel and bronze, excepting only the imperial and state treasuries, which must receive the silver coinage to any amount which may be offered.

The small coins of the old thaler currency have been already demonetized, but the currency reform is still incomplete, and will remain so until the thaler pieces are called in from circulation.

The imperial chancellor is empowered by law to call in the old thaler coins at any moment which may appear to him advisable. Until this is done, the thaler is declared to be worth three marks and remains a legal tender.

Professor Soetbeer, of Hamburg, an authority on finance, estimates the amount of thalers still in circulation to be not less than 300,000,000. The conversion of this large sum into the proper currency will enhance the cost of the money reform to the empire by many an additional million of marks.

As to the relation of paper money and coin to each other, it may only be said that as the entire note and coin system is based upon the gold standard, the bank-notes are at par with gold, and all the banks which emit notes are required to redeem the same with gold upon demand.

H. J. WINSER.

UNITED STATES CONSULATE,
Sonneberg, May 9 and 31, 1878.

WÜRTEMBERG.

Report, by Consul Potter, of Stuttgart, on the condition of the laboring classes in the kingdom of Würtemberg, viz: Manufacturing and agricultural classes; views of mechanics and laboring men; amount of wages received and how it is expended; what they eat and drink and what it costs to live; taxes, national, state, and municipal; women and children's labor; charitable societies and benevolent associations; dwellings of the laboring classes; political sentiments of the laboring classes of Germany; causes of their discontent; Italian laborers in Würtemberg—their characteristics; rates of wages in different branches of industry; price of provisions in different cities of Würtemberg and hours of labor.

MANUFACTURING AND AGRICULTURAL CLASSES.

Within the last few years one who has mingled among the more intelligent portions of the laboring classes of Würtemberg has been accustomed to hear them complain that their lot in life was hard to bear; that the taxes levied by the Government were burdensome; that they did not receive proper compensation for their labor; that they were compelled to work too many hours each day; that the cost of the necessaries of life were so high that, living in even comparative comfort was impossible; that women were drudges, and obliged to do the work that naturally belonged to men; that children were sent into the fields and workshops too early in life, and were there kept at work during their tender years, and as soon as their services became useful to their families the boys were forced into the army, where they became consumers instead of producers, &c. In order that the true situation of matters connected with the laboring classes of Würtemberg may be understood by those who may chance to read these lines, and themselves be able to judge as to whether or not there is ground for such complaints, I will endeavor to give substantially the facts bearing upon the subject, first, however, referring briefly to the manufacturing and agricultural condition of the kingdom.

It has been often said that those countries were most prosperous where the employments of the people were equally divided between agriculture and other mixed industries, and that where one-half of the people were engaged in producing food and clothing, the other half could safely engage in mechanical, artistic, and scientific pursuits, and by such equitable division of the duties of mind and muscle the national wealth would be promoted and the happiness of the people secured. Were this a substantial truth instead of a declaration, the kingdom of Würtemberg might be considered a prosperous country, for about half of its people are employed in a productive agriculture, that yields plenty of wheat, oats, barley, rye, legumes, potatoes, turnips, carrots, hemp, flax, hops, &c. Wine grows abundantly on the hillsides and slopes that overlook the picturesque valleys of the Neckar, the Tauber, the Rems, and the Kocher. Fruit-trees are extensively cultivated all over the country, and the Black Forest and other woods supply the people with timber and fuel. Much of the heavier timber of the Black Forest is exported, principally to Holland, whilst coals, mainly from Saarbrücken, in Prussia, are easily and cheaply brought into the country over its net-work of well-managed railroads, or upon the Neckar, which is navigable to the interior of the kingdom. Thus, if a harvest is only an average one, Würtemberg satisfies, from her own agricultural productions, the natural wants of a population of about two millions of people, who occupy only 365 square miles of territory. When compared with other German States, her industries may be regarded as in a flourishing condition. It is claimed that every able-bodied person, not employed in agriculture or in the army, may easily find occupation in a factory or a workshop, or in some other calling, the duties of which he may be competent to discharge.

The industry of the country is improving so far as the introduction of new sources of mechanical employment are concerned. This is a necessity, for the reason that the field of agriculture is fully occupied. All the arable acres of the kingdom being under cultivation, that source of employment cannot be extended. During the period between 1871 and 1875 there was a considerable rush of the working classes to the various manufacturing establishments, on account of the higher rate of wages there paid; but the slight inconvenience which the farmer experienced from this cause soon disappeared. The principal manufactures are in cotton, linen, wool, wooden ware, leather, and metals. The commerce of the country, which is not extensive, has considerably increased since the formation of the German Zollverein. Its trade with neighboring States is actively maintained through the instrumentality of the excellent highways of the country, its navigable rivers, the Neckar and Danube, the Lake of Constance, and by its extended railroad system.

This degree of apparent prosperity would seem to justify the opinion that the complaints of the laboring classes were without foundation, unless, perhaps, in exceptional cases. Most of the wealthy, titled, and favored portions of society think that the laboring man has no cause for dissatisfaction, while others with more sensitive and humane feelings, even in high circles, entertain the view that much can and ought to be done, by way of legislation or otherwise, to better the condition of the laboring classes, and help them up to a higher level in the scale of manhood. The fact is indisputable that a laboring man in Würtemberg who has to support a family of 3 to 4 children upon the proceeds of his daily wages is utterly unable to save anything for old age, sickness, or loss of employment. To obtain the plainest food and clothing from day to day is the acme of his hope in life. And yet the intelligent mechanic or laboring man will frankly say that he sees no possible remedy that will much improve the condition of things which now makes life a tug for the toiler; and, believing that contentment is better than a contest with the inevitable, he wisely seeks happiness only in those things that are possible to him:

In order that the feelings and views of a workingman of average ability and education may be better understood, a strict translation is here given of a conversation had with an intelligent mechanic, a Mr. A. G. This interview will fairly represent many others had with mechanics and laborers in different parts of the kingdom:

Question. How old are you?—Answer. I am thirty-six years old.

Q. What is your business?—A. I am a house-carpenter.

Q. Have you a family?—A. I have a wife and three children; the oldest is 11 and the youngest 3 years old.

Q. What wages do you receive per day?—A. I receive 3 marks and 30 pfennige. The average wages paid to house-carpenters is from 2 marks 80 pfennige to 3 marks per day (68 to 73 cents).

Q. How many hours per day are you required to work for such wages?—A. During the entire year we begin work at 6 o'clock in the morning and quit at 7 o'clock in the evening. In the winter season we begin our work with gas or candle light.

Q. How much time are you allowed for your meals?—A. We have half an hour for breakfast, at 9 o'clock in the morning; one hour for dinner at noon; and half an hour at 4 o'clock vespers. We take our supper after the day's work is done.

Q. Can you support your family upon such wages?—A. What I must do I must do. Part of the time my wife earns 60 pfennige (15 cents) a day, and with our joint earnings we manage to live.

Q. What does the united earnings of yourself and wife amount to in a year?—A. With general good health we earn about 1,050 marks ($252) per year.

Q. Will you explain in detail the uses you make of this money?—A. O, yes. I pay per annum—

For rent of two rooms in fourth story, 206 marks	$49 44
For clothing for self and family, 160 marks	38 40
For food and fuel per day, 1.75 marks (43¾ cents), or per year, 638 marks	153 12
This makes an average for each member of my family per day of 35 pfennige (8¾ cents).	
For residence tax, 4 marks	96
For school tax, three children, 13.50 marks	3 24
For dues to mechanics' aid society, 7.20 marks	1 73
For tax on earnings of self, 5 marks	1 20
Leaving for school-books, doctor's bills, and incidentals, 16.30 marks	3 91
Per annum, 1,050 marks	252 00

Q. Of what kind of food do your daily meals consist?—A. For breakfast, bread and coffee; for dinner, soup and the meat of which the soup is made, and one kind of vegetables; at four o'clock, beer and bread; and for supper, white bread and potatoes.

Q. Are you able to save any portion of your earnings for days of sickness or old age?—A. Saving is only possible to a man who has no family. In case I am myself sick, I receive one mark per day from the mechanics' aid association of which I am a member. I do not think of old age, for I expect to work until I die.

Q. Are you contented with the conditions of life which you describe?—A. I am contented, because I have no reason to hope for anything better. I am as well off as others of my class, many of whom scold and fret a good deal, because to sustain life requires an apparent never-ending struggle; but I see no sense in fretting and finding fault, unless there is a practical remedy and a power to apply it which is withheld from us; and I can discover neither. The Government itself is poor and can't help us, because the resources of the country are not adequate.

Q. If the vast number of able-bodied men now in the great armies of Germany were employed on the farms and in the workshops, thus becoming active producers instead of idle consumers, don't you think the condition of the laboring classes would be thereby bettered?—A. No, I think not; for then we should have more competition for the work there is to do, and that would cheapen wages. The fact is, there are too many of us. Every hectare of land in Würtemberg that can produce anything is now thoroughly cultivated, and there are plenty of people to do the work. If the men in the army should come home, they would add nothing to the productions of the country. It would simply be, perhaps, four men doing the work which two could better perform. This surplus population must be fed and clothed, and we think the Government can do that more cheaply by keeping them in the army, where they are not in our way.

This is the view of one of the hard-working mechanics of Würtemberg, and the views expressed in his last answer are entitled to more than a passing thought.

TAXES.

Taxes here, as in all other parts of the world, constitute the most prolific theme of the laboring man's sorrowful complaints. It is, however, the slight direct tax which gives him most annoyance. That he can see and feel, and it appears like an unbearable incubus. The greater burden which comes to him through the insidious indirect tax does not seem to bother him, because it comes in the dark and steals upon him unawares. At the present time there is an indirect tax on salt and different kinds of beverages. After much trouble, and after years of careful study, the attempt has been successfully made of assessing real estate, buildings, capital, income, and business as nearly just as possible. But these direct taxes have been raised from year to year until they have become really burdensome to poor laborers, mechanics, and to men doing a small business, and are even regarded as oppressive at this time, when all branches of industry are so depressed. Yet it may in truth be said that since the tax reform the assessments upon the richer portion of society are proportionately heavier than upon the poorer class. State taxes are not generally as high as the local taxes. The town of Heilbronn, for instance, with 24,000 inhabitants, pays 149,658 marks and 4 pfennige State taxes, and 222,000 marks city tax (4 marks=$1, and 4 pfennige=1 cent).

But however high the taxes may be, it must be admitted that they are justly distributed between rich and poor. Often, however, groundless complaints are made regarding high taxes. For instance, the other day a man was charged with a verbal offense which he uttered against His Majesty the Emperor of Germany, and he offered as an excuse for the offense that his taxes were unjustly heavy. An examination proved that the man was assessed only for the small sum of 1 mark and 46 pfennige (36 cents). Of course, instances might be quoted showing how a poor laborer or mechanic was obliged to deprive himself and his family even of the necessaries of life in order to meet the demands of the tax-gatherer. By far the greatest amount of taxes paid are consumed by the Imperial German Government for military purposes. The army at the present time is reduced to a peace footing and embraces only 401,000 soldiers, who are supported at an estimated daily expense of 3,500,000 marks. For the time being, there is nothing to indicate that the army expenses will be diminished. On the contrary, there is every reason to believe that they will be still further increased, for the Imperial Government proposes to impose an indirect tax upon tobacco, coffee, petroleum, and other articles of daily use. That this method of taxation is more burdensome for the poor and laboring classes than direct taxation there can be little doubt. But experience proves that heavy taxes thus levied are more cheerfully paid than lighter direct taxes. It is difficult to forecast the effect upon the laboring classes if they are obliged to pay an extra tribute to the Government for every pound of sugar, coffee, tea, and salt they buy, for every glass of beer they drink, and every cigar they smoke.

Rate of State taxation.—The following data will exhibit the sources of income by taxation in the kingdom of Würtemberg:

On buildings, $12\frac{13}{100}$ pfennige on each 100 marks of value.

On land, $1.20\frac{28}{100}$ marks on each 100 marks of value.

On income from industries, trades, &c., $2.98\frac{46}{100}$ marks on each 100 marks of value.

On all bonds, mortgages, and stocks, 4 per cent. of the interest received on the same.

Municipal tax.—Cities and towns impose a tax of $1.44\frac{70}{100}$ marks for every 1 mark of general State tax. The tax, therefore, for municipal expenses is about 45 per cent. higher than for general State expenses.

WOMEN AND CHILDREN'S LABOR.

That the labor which the women of the working classes in all Germany, including Würtemberg, have to perform, so far as kind and amount are concerned, is in a large degree wholly unfit for their sex, cannot be disputed. In all parts of Würtemberg may be seen women splitting and sawing wood in the streets; carrying heavy burdens of fuel, stone, and water, or earth, upon their heads; thrashing with the flail the whole day long with men; plowing, hoeing, mowing in the hay-field, and gathering the crops; mounting the ladder with bricks and mortar for the builder, and performing the duties of scavenger in the great cities. Such labor is, in the broadest sense, unfit for women, yet this kind of work is every day performed in Würtemberg by women; and it is believed that the condition of the women of the laboring class is still worse in the northern parts of the empire. It may, perhaps, be not entirely correct to say that the military system of Germany is responsible for the position which women occupy with respect to their occupations; but it is safe to say that it would be difficult, if not impossible, to maintain her magnificent armies unless women performed the work which naturally belongs to the vigor and muscle of the young men, who, in times of peace, to the number of more than 400,000, constitute the martial force of Germany.

This unnatural state of affairs does not appear to be confined to the poorer class of women, for the wife of a mechanic, or of a farmer who is in comfortable circumstances, is obliged to take the entire care of three or four children, and perform all the household work, besides assisting her husband upon the farm or in the workshop. The condition of such hard-working women is made still worse by the fact that in many, if not in most, of the larger German towns nearly every fifth house is a place where intoxicating beverages of some kind are abundantly sold. If there is anywhere a class of persons who can justly complain of a hard lot in life, it is the poor laboring women in Germany.

Not so well founded are the statements sometimes made regarding children being forced to work in the fields and workshops too early in life or beyond their strength. This complaint is perhaps groundless, at least as far as Würtemberg is concerned. There may be a slight pretext for such statements in some parts of North Germany, or in the merely manufacturing districts of Saxony, but not in Würtemberg. In this kingdom the employment of children at hard labor too early in life is already prohibited by the excellent educational laws, which are fully enforced. These laws provide that no normally constituted child at the age of fourteen is permitted to leave the common school without being able to read, write, and cipher, and understand the main articles of his religious faith. Hence in Würtemberg, perhaps throughout the empire, no laborer, however poor, can be found who has not acquired these accomplishments at school. The law of June 21, 1869, provides that "children under the age of twelve years are not permitted to work regularly in any kind of factory. Children from twelve to fourteen can only be employed for six hours per day for any regular work in a manufactory. Before being so employed, their parents or guardians must prove that the children receive at least three hours' daily instruction at a school recognized and approved by the Government. Young people between fourteen and sixteen years of age are not allowed to be employed for any regular work over ten hours a day."

The Board of Trade of Würtemberg reports upon this subject as follows:

> The number of children from twelve to fourteen years of age employed in factories is very limited, for the reason that they are obliged by law to attend school until their fourteenth year, and because, also, their labor is by many not regarded as profitable. The greatest proportion of children employed in any establishment were found in a cotton factory, where, among 791 laborers, 15 boys and 13 girls under the age of fourteen were at work. They were paid from 98 pfennige to 1 mark per day.

CHARITABLE SOCIETIES, BENEVOLENT ASSOCIATIONS, AID SOCIETIES, &C.

Such societies are very numerous all over the country. Yet, strange as it may seem, most of these institutions are not enjoyed or used by the majority of the laboring classes whom they were intended especially to benefit. This statement is particularly true in regard to the so-called "People's Kitchen" (Volksküche). There are three causes for this seemingly strange fact, viz:

First. Very many laborers, conscious of the value of the services they render to society at large, are utterly unwilling to receive public alms. A man of some pride feels that he will in some way be degraded by accepting the benefits which these establishments offer.

Second. Deeply-rooted distrust on the part of the laboring classes of the wealthy members of society, who are generally the founders of these institutions.

Third. Many laborers look upon such institutions as being the outcome of some sort of a speculation on the part of those whose generosity established them. The first-mentioned reason is the only one entitled to any notice.

Perhaps the more frequented institutions of this kind are the so-called "Krippen." The object of these "Krippen" is to receive, for general care and protection during the entire day, children from six weeks to three years old, so that the mothers, who are obliged to labor in the field or elsewhere, may pursue their occupations without interruption or anxiety. Another object of these "Krippen" is, "by proper care and nourishment, to prevent, as far as possible, great mortality among children." The average cost for a child is 10 pfennige ($2\frac{1}{2}$ cents) per day. The children are brought in the morning and must be taken home again in the evening. Experience has proved the great utility of these institutions, and their excellence is now acknowledged on all sides, not alone for the advantages which the mothers derive from them, but also for the superior mental and physical care and training which the chil dren receive. They are, however, only to be found in the larger cities, where, as at Stuttgart and Heilbronn, handsome buildings have been erected for this purpose. For children from three to fourteen years of age there are also many other institutions which have proved to be great public blessings, among which may be mentioned the orphan asylums, asylums for poor and neglected children, asylums for poor and sick children, asylums for deaf and dumb children, &c. These institutions are generally maintained by the Government. The "Krippen" are, however, under the special protection of Her Majesty the Queen of Würtemberg. For the support and aid of grown-up laboring people, the following institutions may be mentioned. These are maintained partly by the Government and partly by private associations: "Associations for the protection of young women working in factories," "Young Men's Association," and "Journeymen's Association." These three are private benevolent institutions, and have for their object not only the furnishing of cheap lodgings and food, but also proper amusement and instruction for leisure hours. Only such women and men are admitted as members of these associations as can, by proper testimony, prove a good standing in society. After the labor of the day is over the journeymen meet in their society-rooms, where they listen to an instructive lecture or read in books taken from the library of the association. In the "Journeymen's Association" at Stuttgart the members pay for their board as follows:

For breakfast	9 pfennige = $2\frac{1}{4}$ cents.
For dinner	40 pfennige = 10 cents.
For supper	30 pfennige = 7 cents.

If the members are on a journey, they receive at the rooms of any similar association in other cities, after having proved their membership, refreshments and fair lodging free of charge. As another benevolent institution for the laboring class, I have already mentioned the "People's Kitchen." These are maintained by local authorities. They provide board at the following reduced rates:

Breakfast, 1 cup of coffee with bread	12 pfennige = 3 cents.
without bread	9 pfennige = $2\frac{1}{4}$ cents.
Dinner: soup, vegetables, and meat	30 pfennige = $7\frac{1}{2}$ cents.
without soup	25 pfennige = $6\frac{1}{4}$ cents.
soup alone	10 pfennige = $2\frac{1}{2}$ cents.
Supper: only soup	10 pfennige = $2\frac{1}{2}$ cents.

For these prices the applicant receives one-half liter (1 pint) of soup, one-half liter of vegetables, and a piece of good meat, weighing, before being cooked, 100 grammes (about 4 ounces). These prices, of course, could not be made without a loss to the city treasury, if the provisions were not bought in large quantities and, therefore, at reduced rates.

There is also in Würtemberg, in the village of Fellbach, a so-called "Maid Servant Institution"; the object of which is to provide a comfortable home for such female servants as can prove by proper testimony that they have been in service a certain number of years and are either sick or too old to serve any longer. It also may be mentioned in this connection that such male and female servants as have satisfactorily served a certain number of years in one place receive a handsome premium at the agricultural fair of their place. Another institution which has the welfare of the laboring classes for its object may be mentioned, viz, certain "Building Associations," which are formed in the larger towns. These endeavor to provide laborers with small but healthy dwellings at reduced rates of rent. In enumerating the various arrangements which are designed to ameliorate the condition of the laboring classes, it would be ungenerous to forget all the noble private efforts made by the owners of some of the large manufactories in Würtemberg. Among these, the Messrs. Staub & Co., at Kuchen, deserve to be especially remembered. In 1867, at the Paris Exhibition, this firm received the first prize for the best arrangements for laborers' dwellings. In their great establishment care is taken that every laborer has a good lodging, and good schools are there provided for the education of the children of the employés. Bath-rooms are provided, and various provisions are also made for the proper amusement of children and adults.

DWELLINGS OF THE LABORING CLASSES.

"How do the laboring classes live?" The answer to this question represents, perhaps, the most unpleasant feature in the condition of the laboring community. If the laborer is a single man, the case is very simple. If he cannot hire some sort of a chamber up in the highest or down in the lowest story, he pays from 10 to 20 pfennige (2½ to 5 cents) for a bed overnight in a more or less comfortable room. Upon the latter he has no claim during the daytime, and during the night he shares it often with two, three, or four fellow-laborers, as the case may be. Often he sleeps with one of his friends in the same bed, and they share alike in the expense. Often, also, two or three single workmen have a room in common at the factory or workshop. Single persons can manage the matter of house-room with comparative ease. Altogether different is the case of families, where there are children who are wholly dependent for their support upon the daily wages of father or mother. Married laborers who have wages enough to enable them to rent lodgings in houses belonging to building associations obtain comforts in a comparative degree. But the class of workmen so favored is small, as such associations exist only in the largest cities. By far the greatest number of married laborers are obliged to seek their lodgings in basements or in the higher stories, and pay, on an average, 100 marks yearly for one room. Hence a lodging with three rooms costs 300 marks ($72) annually. Such a lodging, however, includes, besides a kitchen, a small apartment in a cellar, a place for wood and washing, and also the stoves in rooms and kitchen. Thus here, as elsewhere, house-rent devours the largest part of the wages of a laborer who has a family, and the unsolved problem of "how to furnish cheap homes for the laboring classes" is ever being presented for the consideration of the philanthropist.

THE POLITICAL SENTIMENTS OF THE LABORING CLASSES IN GERMANY

Are at present neither republican nor monarchical. Expressed in the most general form, the political sentiments of the laboring classes in Würtemberg, as in all Germany, may be summed up in the following sentence: "The laborers complain that their lot in life is unjustly hard as compared with that of the rich," and questions of governmental policy, which formerly divided all classes, are now forgotten by laboring men in their efforts to discover a leveling-out process by which the rich and the poor shall enjoy an equality of ease and social happiness. Their sentiments upon this subject have brought into active existence the organization of the so-called "Social Democratic party," which represents, under various forms, names, claims, principles, views, &c., the political sentiments of a great, if not the greatest, part of the laboring classes of Germany. In Würtemberg, to judge by outward demonstrations, the "Social Democrats" are not very strong. Those, however, wise in such matters declare them to be much stronger than it is generally supposed. The names, "Communists," "Anarchists," "Nihilists," "Workingmen's Union," &c., are merely different terms meaning the same thing. Upon questions relating to the causes of these complaints there is such a variety of answers, and so many proposed remedies for this social sickness, that it is difficult to separate confused reasoning from sound argument.

The nobility and wealthy aristocracy are greatly exasperated at the pretensions of the Social Democrats in claiming an equality of rights and privileges, socially and otherwise, and very intemperate speeches are sometimes made, in which the laboring classes are bitterly denounced, and the sentiments they now hold are declared to be the natural outcome of a condition of "growing laziness," and remedial measures are proposed which are very harsh and extreme in character.

Statesmen do not appear inclined to discuss the cause of the labor movement, and confine their efforts to devising means for summarily suppressing it. The great middle and well-to-do class of Germany have little to say upon the subject, and take the comfortable view that the Government's policy, whatever that may be, will be satisfactory to them. Labor strikes in Würtemberg have been small affairs and of rare occurrence, and have only taken place in those localities where manufacturers paid very low wages, while it was known they were making large profits. In Würtemberg, as a general rule, laborers obtained highest wages at those times which were most favorable to the manufacturer. This was particularly the case in 1872, after the Franco-German war. But a large portion of the laborers did not live economically, and their high wages were soon squandered.

It is quite safe to predict that the Social Democratic, or Labor, party organization is of a more lasting character than has yet been generally supposed. It should not be forgotten that it comes into existence at a time when the laboring classes throughout the world have attained a higher degree of education than ever before known. They fully understand that all power and wealth, whether wielded by nations or individuals, is the outgrowth of labor, and the higher and more numerous the educational institutions of a country are, precisely in the same ratio of advancement will the social distinctions created by wealth and position weaken, and bring men nearer together upon the platform of merit.

It cannot be justly said that the laboring men and women of Würtemberg envy the wealth of those who are higher up on the ladder of fame and fortune. But, with their perceptions brightened through the excellent educational institutions of the country, they cannot look without irritation upon the assumed individual superiority which in a thousand different forms the wealthy and favored classes are daily parading before those whose lot in life compels them to toil for bread and clothing. Ladies will pay from 12,000 to 20,000 marks for a dress to wear but once at an imperial ball, and, with this waste of wealth and assumed hauteur, roll in magnificent equipages by poor women, better educated perhaps, but who, in rags, are sawing wood in the streets. A glance from the humiliated toilers and the vain show vanishes, and the women continue to saw and think and think and saw till their work is done, and then go home to poverty, and over scanty meals husband, wife, and children tell of the day's experience.

If one may judge by what is heard among the laboring people, the public display, extravagance, and waste of those who accumulated wealth rapidly during the money-making days of the war and the years immediately following, have had much to do in creating the discontent which at present exists in Germany among the working classes. If, instead of such imprudent and tantalizing exhibitions, a demeanor had been maintained which was in true harmony with the dignity which naturally attaches to wealth, and a part of the money which was wasted in frivolity and show had been wisely used in the interest of the poor, political labor unions and Social Democracy would not, in this kingdom at least, have had an existence.

The measures proposed by the Social Democratic party are impractical, and for that reason are more dangerous, for they regard a refusal to concede any of their demands as designed oppression. If a single legislative step could be taken toward meeting their wishes, they would have some excuse for retiring from their hostile attitude toward the Government. Until that is done, the party bitterness is likely to remain and *grow with covert agitation.*

ITALIAN LABORERS IN GERMANY.

A laboring population heretofore unknown in Würtemberg is becoming now quite numerous. Reference is made to Italian laborers. They were at first employed only on railroad work and as able miners and good diggers. In consequence of their industry and reliability, they have by degrees been employed to good advantage, as a considerable element among workingmen, in nearly all branches of laborious industry. During the inflated period following the war between Germany and France the laborers of Würtemberg demanded such a high rate of wages, that contractors were obliged, in order to fulfill their engagements, to import Italian laborers, and their services have proved highly satisfactory. They are also being extensively employed in Austria. It is both interesting and instructive to become more closely acquainted with the ways of these people. Experience here proves that one who contracts with them for labor may be certain that they will adhere to their engagements. They will higgle about trifles, but as soon as a bargain is closed, it can be relied upon.

From early morning until darkness they work industriously. No clamor for more "luncheon" and "more drink." It is astonishing how soberly and frugally they live. Their nourishment is "polenta," a porridge of mixed substances, in which fat is very scarce, and often wanting altogether. An additional luxury, not a daily one, however, consists of hard cheese. There are few men who are thus so easily satisfied. They generally manage to secure employment on large "jobs," where they can work in groups. One of them is selected to cook. The favorite and almost universal article of food referred to is a thick porridge, made of vegetables, flour, and coarse meal, and boiled in water. This porridge is an adhesive mass, of the consistency of clay, and is cut with a wire (like soap), each receiving an equal share. This food is consumed with great satisfaction, and the leavings of one is cheerfully handed over to another, who has not, perhaps, had a sufficiency, or else it is put into a cloth and kept for the next meal. Water satisfies their thirst and aids digestion, and then they go again cheerfully to their work, and the energy with which they work is surprising to Germans. Any one who wishes to be quite clear as to their industry must examine the tunnels and the cuttings in rocks which Italians have blasted and wrought before dynamite was known. Whenever any of the large contractors informs his agents in the different districts of some new work to be done, the latter take care to spread the news from village to village among the homes of the Italians. Men and able youths hastily prepare themselves for departure, while women, children, and old people stay behind. In this way isolated groups are formed, who work in common. They are much attached to home and country, and, during leisure hours, delight to talk of their families, friends, and native land.

On Saturday evenings, and also on Sundays and holidays, they march in troops to the post-office to receive letters from home or to send greetings and money. As the younger generation of Italians are learning to read and write, a very extensive use is made of the post-office facilities. The amount of money the Italian laborers contrive to save from their hard, and comparatively small, earnings is very surprising even to the economical German.

RATE OF WAGES PAID AND PRICES OF PROVISIONS.

The following tables are prepared from information obtained from authentic and reliable sources, and show the rate of wages paid per day (October 1, 1878), as compared with the years 1872, 1873, 1874, and 1875:

Kinds of labor.	Hours of labor.	Wages paid during the years—				
		1872.	1873.	1874.	1875.	1878.
	Hours.	*M. Pfg.*	*M. Pfg.*	*M. Pfg.*	*M. Pfg.*	*M. Pfg.*
Day-laborers	11 to 12	2 00	2 00	1 50	1 70	1 70
Masons	10	3 00	3 00	2 70	2 80	3 00
Stonecutters	10	4 80	6 00	5 80	5 20	5 20
Carpenters	10	3 45	4 30	4 30	3 80	3 50
Railroad laborers	10	2 00	2 25	2 00	....	2 25
Farm help	12	2 50	2 50	2 00	....	2 00
In sugar manufactories:						
Female hands	10	1 00	1 20	1 00	1 00	1 00
Male hands	10	1 50	2 20	2 00	1 50	2 20
Mechanics	10	2 20	3 50	3 80	3 00	3 50
Boys from 14 to 16	10	1 00	1 20	1 20	....	....
In paper-mills:						
Female hands	10	1 00	1 20	....	....	1 40
Male hands	10	1 85	2 25	....	....	2 25

In other manufactories, sugar-mills, &c., the rates of wages are about the same. It should be remembered that the wages referred to in the foregoing table do not include board. Sometimes, however, day-laborers and farm hands receive, at 10 a. m. and 4 p. m., some kind of a light lunch. Sewing-girls doing plain sewing in tailor-shops, or elsewhere, receive from 80 pfennige to 1 mark (20 to 25 cents) per day. A shirt-maker receives 1 mark to 1 mark 20 pfennige (25 to 30 cents) a day. Journeymen mechanics receive from 3 to 12 marks (75 cents to $2.80) per week, including board and lodging. A good dressmaker receives from 1.80 to 2.20 marks per day (45 to 55 cents).

PRICES OF PROVISIONS.

The prices for provisions are somewhat higher now than they were previous to the Frenco-German war of 1870-'71, or during its progress. At present (October 1) the average prices in three cities in different parts of Würtemberg are as follows:

Table showing the price of certain articles of provisions in different parts of Würtemberg October 1, 1878.

Kind of provisions.	Heilbronn.		Stuttgart.		Ulm.	
	M.	*Pfg.*	*M.*	*Pfg.*	*M.*	*Pfg.*
1 kilo of black bread costs	0	24	0	29	0	26
1 kilo of white bread costs	0	27	0	31	0	29
1 kilo of beef costs	1	27	1	41	1	34
1 kilo of veal costs	1	22	1	33	1	10
1 kilo of pork costs	1	27	1	40	1	31
1 kilo of butter costs	2	30	2	41	1	88
50 kilo of potatoes costs	3	50	3	57	3	52
1 egg costs	0	6	0	6	0	6

Wood and coal average about 45 cents per 100 English pounds.
1 kilo (kilogramme) is equal to about two pounds; 1 mark = 24 cents; 4 pfennige = 1 cent.

JOSEPH S. POTTER.

UNITED STATES CONSULATE,
Stuttgart, November 9, 1878.

GREAT BRITAIN AND IRELAND.

ENGLAND.

BIRMINGHAM.

Report, by Consul Gould, on the state of trade, cost of living, and rates of wages; for the district of Birmingham.

In reply to the Department circular dated April 11, 1878, in reference to wages, cost of living, &c., I beg to say that I have carefully investigated the subject, and have to report in the accompanying statements the result of my inquiries.

Business of every description is dull in this district; not more than one-third the goods are now sent to the United States that were sent five years ago. But the American trade is not exceptional; all other branches are equally depressed.

American goods of many descriptions are gradually being introduced here, and with the revival of business there will probably be an increased demand therefor.

I am not aware of any peculiarities in the manner of conducting business in this district, the credit being but short for safe customers, and cash or guaranty for those unknown or doubtful. It is customary with buyers to make deposits with bankers to be drawn upon as the goods are sent forward.

None of the banks in this town issue paper money, and the law of England does not allow the issue of notes of less value than £5; so that all the wages and living expenses of the working people are paid in gold, silver, and copper. Notes are only used in large transactions, and soon find their way back to the banks.

The Bank of England notes are available in all parts of the country, but the notes of provincial banks are only of use in the immediate neighborhood where they are issued. The poorer class of people seldom handle or see a bank-note of any description.

J. B. GOULD.

UNITED STATES CONSULATE,
Birmingham, May 20, 1878.

Comparison of wages and cost of living in Birmingham and neighborhood in the years 1878 *and* 1873.

1. FOOD PRICES.

Articles of consumption.	1878.	1873.
Flour:		
Fine wheat .... per barrel..	$8 75	$8 50
Extra wheat .... do......	9 75	9 00
Beef:		
Good roasting .... per pound..	22	21
Soup pieces .... do......	12	12
Rump steak .... do......	28	26
Corned beef .... do......	18	18

Comparison of wages and cost of living in Birmingham, &c.—Continued.

Articles of consumption.	1878.	1873.
Veal:		
Forequarters .... per pound..	$0 17	$0 16
Leg .... do......	20	18
Cutlets .... do......	28	26
Mutton:		
Forequarters .... per pound..	16	16
Leg .... do......	22	21
Chops .... do......	24	24
Pork:		
Fresh .... per pound..	16	15
Corned .... do......	15	14
Bacon .... do......	$0 15– 0 22	$0 15– 0 20
Hams, smoked .... do......	24	24
Shoulders .... do......	12	10– 12
Sausages .... do......	18	18
Lard .... do......	16– 18	14– 18
Butter .... do......	28– 32	24– 28
Cheese .... do......	18	18
Potatoes .... do......	2	2
Rice .... do......	8	6
Beans, white .... do......	5	6
Milk .... per quart..	8	6
Eggs .... per dozen..	16– 0 24	16– 0 24
Tea, good black .... per pound..	50– 0 70	60– 0 72
Coffee:		
Rio, green .... per pound..	28	24
Rio, roasted .... do......	36	32
Sugar:		
Brown .... per pound..	6	8
Yellow .... do......	7	7
Coffee B .... do......	8	8
Molasses:		
New Orleans .... per pound..	6	6
Porto Rico .... do......	4	4
Soap, common .... do......	6	6
Starch .... do......	8	10
Coal .... per ton..	4 50	4 36
On the foregoing articles of provision there is an average increase of about 7½ per cent.		
Shirtings:		
Brown, 4-4 .... per yard..	8	10
Bleached, 4-4 .... do......	11	13
Sheetings:		
Brown, 9-8 .... do......	12	14
Bleached, 9-8 .... do......	15	17
Cotton-flannel .... do......	9	10
Ticking	26	30
Prints	11	13
M. de laine	20	21
Boots, elastic sides .... per pair..	2 50	2 50
On the foregoing fabrics there has been a decrease of about 14½ per cent.		

2. RATES OF WAGES.

	1878.	1873.
Carpenters (54 hours per week) .... per hour..	$0 17	$0 15
Joiners (54 hours per week) .... do......	17	15
Bricklayers (54 hours per week) .... do......	17	15
Stonemasons (54 hours per week) .... do......	18	16
Plasterers .... do......	17	15
Painters .... do......	15	14
Plumbers .... do......	17	15
Fitters .... do......	17	15
Blacksmiths .... do......	17	15
Strikers .... do......	12	10
Navvies, masons, laborers, &c .... do......	12	9½
Agricultural laborers, average per week	4 25	3 75
On the foregoing there has been an increase of about 14 per cent. in five years.		
House-rent in towns, front, per room, per week	36	....
House-rent in towns, back, per room, per week	30	....
Agricultural laborers, cottages per week, average	50	....

In the item of house-rent there has been very little change.

Report, by Consul Shepard, on the rates of wages, cost of living, past and present rates, present state of trade, and business habits and systems of the district of Bradford.

With respect to the Department circular of April 11, 1878, I have the honor to transmit a tabulated statement, which will, I think, pretty fully answer the first and second inquiries.

THE WORKINGMEN'S FOOD.

Fifteen or twenty years ago the farm-laborer, the navvy, the factory-hand, &c., in fact, nearly all the lower orders, ate but little meat and lived largely upon oatmeal and vegetables; but at present they consume fully four times as much flesh-meat as formerly, and not unfrequently purchase the choicest cuts; hence, the cost of living is enhanced pretty much in accordance with the patronage they give the butcher. Of the articles of food mentioned in the accompanying "food price-list," the laboring classes consume more or less.

LABOR EDUCATIONAL STATUTES.

The law allows children between the ages of ten and thirteen to work but half-time, the employers being by the same statute ("Factory act," inclosure No. 2*) obliged not only to provide instruction for the other half of the time, but are prohibited from employing these children unless certified by the schoolmaster (inclosure No. 3*) to have attended school the requisite number of years. At thirteen all children are freed from compulsory school attendance.

I have not unfrequently met the statement that this education is an injury, rather than a blessing, to all concerned; to the laborers, because it makes them discontented with their lot, and leads them to seek easier and more genteel occupations, such as writing and shop-tending; to the employers, because it makes them the target of the workingman's jealousy and envy, the workman looking upon the capitalist as a natural enemy, and upon the employer's profits as more largely his by right. I draw attention to this reasoning not because of its significance, but as a unique and, strange to say, rather prevalent specimen of logic.

RELATIONS BETWEEN LABOR AND CAPITAL.

Years ago, and for a long time, there was great reciprocity between the employer and the employé, the former looking after the latter in time of sickness and need, and the latter guarding religiously the interests of the former; in fact, it is still so to a large extent in Yorkshire; but, unhappily, this mutual good feeling has nearly or entirely died out in many other parts of England. No doubt there is fault on both sides, but I am bound to say, from all I can learn, that the calamity must be laid much more to the greed and exactions of the employed than to the selfishness of the employers.

PAST AND PRESENT RATES OF WAGES.

In prosecuting query No. 3, I find that for three years previous to the middle of 1877 but little variation had taken place in the rates of wages

**Factory act.* (See Appendix to this volume.)

among the working classes; in fact, so little as to be hardly worthy of note. About June, last year, however, a general reduction was made in nearly all trades, and from time to time since still further curtailment has been found necessary. Strikes and disastrous riots in some localities have been the result, accounts of which have, of course, reached the Department through the newspapers. It may be seen, therefore, that America does not monopolize the riotous element of the world.

The last great advance in wages was about 1871—an increase of from 25 to 30 per cent. This increase was, however, more the result a system by which one hand could attend additional machines than in consequence of a direct augmentation of per-diem compensation. All that advance has, however, been lost since last year.

PRESENT CONDITION OF TRADE.

In meeting the fourth question, I can only make the answer which must reach the Department from every quarter, namely, that trade in all branches is extremely bad. In this district, interested so largely in American trade, the fictitious demands following our civil war and the Franco German war led manufacturers into large outlays for extensions and additional plant, which they now find double what are needed to meet the demand. It is hard perhaps, because unpleasant, for Yorkshire merchants and manufacturers to realize that, on account of largely-increased home manufacture, the demand from the United States, Germany, and other countries can never again be what it has been, and they *almost* feel that by our manufacturing we are infringing upon their prerogative, and that in failing to buy of them we fail to perform our bounden duty.

BUSINESS HABITS AND SYSTEMS.

In each manufacturing center there is an open market or exchange, and each center has its "market days." Bradford, for instance, has its market days on Mondays and Tuesdays. On these days extra trains come from all directions, bringing a great number of dealers, who visit the centers not only to buy the finished article, but to sell the raw material.

I may say that the foreign buyer, or customer, scarcely ever purchases direct from the manufacturer, but that he almost invaribly buys through a merchant. Sometimes, to be sure, the merchant is a manufacturer, but not generally. Frequently the manufacturers invent their own designs and patterns, and submit them to the merchant, stating the prices, he adding a profit and forwarding them to his foreign customers. Still more frequently, however, the merchat purchases cloth "in the gray," and sends it to the dyer and finisher, to be completed according to his own ideas and patterns; but so vigilant are the merchants, that the manufacturer actually *fears* and generally *refuses* to deal directly with the foreign buyer, lest he lose through the merchant's antagonism more than he gains by direct sale to the purchaser.

Again, but few manufacturers take wool in the bale and turn it out finished cloth. Oftener the wool is bought of the woolstapler by the woolcomber, or "topmaker"; he sells to the spinner, and the spinner to the manufacturer; the latter disposes to the merchant, who, as I have said, sends the cloth on his own account to the dyer and finisher. It is claimed for this division of labor that it insures a better article at a cheaper price, upon the principle that a man who makes a specialty of any particular branch of manufacture can work best and most economically. Certainly the practice tends to localize certain industries and build up manufacturing centers.

C. O. SHEPARD.

UNITED STATES CONSULATE,
Bradford, June 14, 1878.

Statement showing the rates of wages in Bradford and vicinity.

Railway employes:				
Station-master, with house	per year..	$350 00	to	$500 00
Guards	per week..	5 00	to	7 50
Engine-driver	per day..	1 37	to	1 87
Pointsman	per week..	5 00	to	6 00
Stoker	per day..	87	to	1 00
Porter	per week..	4 50	to	5 00
Navvy	per day..	75	to	87
Farm-hands:				
Skilled hand	per week..	5 00	to	6 25
Common hand	do....	3 75	to	4 50
Factory-hands:				
General foreman for works of any kind	per day..	3 00	to	5 00
Foreman	do....			1 50
Skilled hand, man	do....			1 25
Skilled hand, woman	do....			75
Common hand, man	do....			87
Common hand, woman	do....			50
boy over 13	per week..			2 25
boy, 10 to 13	do....			1 12
girl over 13	do....			2 50
girl, 10 to 13	do....			1 25
Mechanic	per day..			1 25
Artisan	do....			1 25
Cartman	do....			1 00
Warehouseman	per week..	6 00	to	8 00
Collier (average 50 cents per ton, and at that rate usually make)	per day..			1 50
Police force:				
Chief superintendent, with house	per year..			2,500 00
Superintendents of division	do....	700 00	to	750 00
Inspectors	per week..	8 75	to	10 00
Sergeants	do....	7 25	to	8 75
Policemen	do....	6 00	to	6 50
Public works:				
Streetsweepers	per day..			83
Laborers	do....	87	to	95
Repairers of street-paving	do....			1 10
Gas-meter inspectors	do....			1 00
Gas-stokers	do....	1 00	to	1 25

Food-prices at Bradford.

Beef, inferior parts	per pound..	$0 12	to	$0 14
best joints	do.....	18	to	22
Mutton, according to joint	do.....	12	to	22
Pork, inferior parts	do.....	10	to	12
better parts	do.....	14	to	18
Bacon	do.....	16	to	20
inferior	do.....	12	to	16
Veal, according to joint	do.....	16	to	25
Geese	do.....	16	to	25
Fowls	each..	62	to	75
Ducks	do.....	62	to	75
Salmon	per pound..			32
Cod	do.....			10
Turbot	do.....			28
Soles	do.....			20

Haddock	per pound..	$0 04 and	$0 06
Flour	do.......		4½
Potatoes, old	per stone (14 lbs.)..		37
new	per pound..		5
Eggs, cooking	per dozen..		18
fresh	do.....		25
Butter	per pound..	33 to	35
Cheese	do.....	16 to	20
Cauliflowers, according to size	each..	4 to	12
Cabbages		2 to	4

Notes on the foregoing statement.

All factory hands, artisans, and mechanics have half-holiday (from 1 o'clock) on Saturdays. On other days they work from 6 a. m. to 5.30 p. m., with half an hour for breakfast and one hour for dinner (56½ hours per week).

Warehousemen, 8 a. m. to 6 p. m.; Saturdays 8 a. m. to 1 p. m.

The farm laborer is frequently allowed a house and a small bit of land, upon which he raises what vegetables he uses; he works from 6 a. m. to 6 p. m. (with eating-time).

A workingman (single) can live for from $2 to $2.50 per week, and with a wife and five children may live (frugally) for from $5 to $6 per week.

The police work 9 hours per day.

Streetsweepers work 54 hours in summer and 53 hours per week in winter. (Time for eating.)

Laborers and repairers of street-paving work 49½ hours per week. (Time for eating.)

Gas-meter inspectors work 49½ hours in winter and 52½ hours per week in summer.

Gas-stokers 12 hours a day on duty, but actual time working about 7 hours per day, with time for eating.

BRISTOL.

Report, by Consul Canisius, on the rates of wages, cost of living, and general condition of the laboring classes of Bristol, Gloucestershire, Wiltshire, Somersetshire, and Devonshire.

In conformity with your instructions, dated April 11, I have the honor to report, in a condensed form, all the facts which I have gathered in relation to agricultural laborers, mechanical laborers, and those upon public works and railways. My inquiries have extended to Bristol, Gloucestershire, Wiltshire, Somersetshire, and Devonshire.

LABOR AND COST OF LIVING.

For all practical purposes, I deem it sufficient in my statement to divide the laborers into five kinds. No reasonable space would suffice to give the different rates paid in my consular district to each kind of labor, because I find that in the same locality different rates according to ability, and in different localities there are different wages paid. I also give you the prices of necessaries of living at the present time, and have compared them with those of 1872, when all kinds of laborers found employment very readily and were eagerly sought for in all parts of the country. Since then prices have slightly advanced, but not to any noteworthy extent. The general food of the class of people here referred to consists of bread, bacon, cheese, salt, butter or lard, potatoes, tea, and sugar, all of the cheapest sort. As a rule, the laborers eat meat but twice a week, and that consists of the very cheapest kinds.

PAST AND PRESENT RATES.

Wages for the last five years have not undergone any marked alteration. In several places in some occupations they have increased slightly, while in others they have within the last two years gone down. Of the former, I should instance the agricultural laborers and the builders' laborers, who may be said to have on an average 2 shillings per week more than they received in 1872. The wages of quarrymen and navvies have remained stationary, while mechanical laborers get 2*s* 6*d* to 3*s* less per week than in 1872. The causes of these variations are numerous and complicated to the unobservant. Giving you my opinion of them will, I think, answer your fourth question.

In giving this opinion, I would like to say, first, that the counties of Gloucester, Wilts, Somerset, and Devon, although considered the worst-paid parts of England, produce the best agricultural laborers, excavators, and quarrymen in the world: hence there is always a large emigration of these classes of men to the north and midlands, where they are better paid. Besides, large numbers constantly emigrate to the colonies, particularly of navvies and agricultural laborers. All contractors for large works in the colonies wishing to take men out invariably come to the southwest of England for them. To give an instance, last summer a large contractor of railroads at the Cape of Good Hope took out many hundreds of picked men. This large immigration and emigration constantly going on has, doubtlessly, caused the preventing of the downward tendency of wages here on account of the slack trade, from which at present this country suffers so much. No large public works whatever are going on at present in my consular district, such as docks, canals, or railroads, with the exception of the Portishead docks and the Severn tunnel, both near Bristol, but on these works only a very small force of hands is kept employed. This extreme slackess, together with the very large number of able men discharged from time to time during the last two years from iron and coal works, has resulted in more unskilled labor being out of employment than has been the case for many years past. If it were not for the emigration mentioned, the suffering of the laboring classes in this part of the country would be very great indeed.

WORKING HOURS.

In regard to the fifth question, I have to state that in all cases men work by the hour, day, or week, and in some instances by the piece. As a rule the day consists of 10 hours; a week of 56 hours, some few of 54 hours; this chiefly among mechanical laborers. Some work 60 hours per week.

In the statement which I now subjoin I have given you the average of each agricultural laborer's working-time 60 hours per week, except harvest season; excavators, quarrymen, and builders' laborers, 56 hours; mechanical laborers, 54 hours. All men are paid weekly in cash, and not in kind or perquisites.

LABOR IN THE UNITED STATES.

I beg to remark, in conclusion, that no laborer should allow himself to be enticed by imagining that he could better his condition by leaving the United States to return to his native country, if born in Europe. A number of such laborers, and also some mechanics, have, during the last two years, called upon this consulate for help to get back to the States, cursing the day when they left America for Europe, where neither milk nor honey is flowing, as some impatient mechanical and unskilled laborers in the United States may suppose. Compared with Europe, the United States is a paradise for a sober and faithful workingman.

RATES OF WAGES.

In the following carefully-prepared statement I have only given the maximum of wages of the best men in Somersetshire, and the minimum in Wiltshire and Devonshire, and also the average of wages paid in my consular district:

Kind of laborers.	Highest per week.	Lowest per week.	Average per week.
Agricultural	$3 66	$2 16	$2 91
Excavator or navvy	5 10	3 36	4 23
Quarryman	5 34	3 60	4 47
Mechanical	6 54	3 84	5 19
Builder	5 34	3 66	4 50

Cost of living.

	Year.	
	1878.	1872.
Bread per quartern (4 lbs.)	$0 13	About same.
Meat, beef and mutton	$0 14 to 20	Somewhat cheaper.
Bacon or pork	12 to 24	Same.
Cheese	10 to 20	Slightly cheaper.
Sugar	06	Do.
Butter, salted	20 to 32	Cheaper.
Potatoes, per 10 lbs	12 to 24	Much cheaper.
Rents, per week	24 to 96	Considerably cheaper.

THEODORE CANISIUS.

UNITED STATES CONSULATE,
Bristol, May 13, 1878.

CHESHIRE AND NORTH WALES.

Report, by Consul Fairchild, of Liverpool, on the wages of agricultural laborers in Cheshire, and the general rates of wages in the mining districts of Flintshire, North Wales.

CHESHIRE.

In Cheshire the average wages of agricultural laborers are $3.60 a week, and have been the same during the last five years. Previous to that time they rose gradually from $2.40 in 1855 to $3.60 in 1872.

The rate of wages in the agricultural districts is only relative, as very much depends on the cottage rents, and also on the perquisites received from the farmers, which go to balance a larger amount of money paid in other localities.

These perquisites are food and beer in harvest time, straw for pigs, milk or whey for children, and in a few instances potato ground almost gratis, also an increase of 72 cents to 96 cents per week for the harvest month.

The cost of living is regulated by the foregoing wages.

No increase during the past five years has taken place in the cost of provisions, clothing, or rent, except in meat, eggs, butter, and milk. More meat is now consumed, which necessarily adds to the expense of living; but the provident farm-laborers feed their own pigs, and consequently buy little.

Cottages are rented to the laborers at about $21.84 per annum, with a good garden, in many instances, of 14 to 15 roods in extent.

The gardens vary from ⅛ to ½ a statute acre, and are generally productive and well stocked with fruit-trees, and are even a source of profit.

Throughout Cheshire many cottages have, in addition to the garden, an acre or two of land, and keep cows; such land is rented at $24.30 to $29.16 an acre.

These are the usual wages paid in this consular district, namely:

Farm-foreman, $4.08 a week and a house; head plowman, $4.86 and a cottage and garden; second head plowman, $4.56 and no house; plowman, $4.08, no house; head cowman, $4.86, no house; cowmen, $3.84, and lodge in the buildings; shepherd, $3.60 a week and a cottage; ordinary laborers, $3.60 and $4.32, and no house; women, $2.16 a week; boys, $1.44 and $1.92, according to age.

In the salt-mining district the wages of agricultural laborers are from $3.60 to $4.32 a week, and during the last five years have varied from $3.60 to $4.86. Cottage rents are from $24.30 to $38.88 a year.

NORTH WALES.

The following is a comparison of present wages and those paid five years ago in the coal and iron mining districts of North Wales (Flintshire) per day:

Description.	Present wages.	Old wages.
Mechanics, smiths, and carpenters	$1 20	$1 00
Common laborers	$0 80 to 84	64
Agricultural laborers	72 to 80	64
Railway-navvies	80 to 88	72
Masons	1 32	1 20
Colliers	1 80	96
Engine-men	1 12	96

Of the $1.80 paid colliers, about 60 cents is spent by them in beer.

The following are the average earnings of men employed in the collieries of North Wales during the month of February, 1878:

	Per day.
Colliers, underground	$1 02
smelt-work	1 02
Holers, hewers	82
Fillers (men filling up coal in pit)	74
smelt	72
Wagoners and hookers	70
Bymen, day-laborers	70
contract-work	74
Firemen, overlookers	90
Pitmen (men repairing the pit)	82
Furnace-men	64
Horsekeepers	64
Bankmen, contract-work, at the surface	90
day-work	68
smelt-work	6[illegible]
Engine-workers, winders	90
deep winders	82
Stokers	66
Smiths	92
Smith-strikers	58
Fitters, mechanics	1 04
Boiler-makers	80
Carpenters	98
Sawyers	80
Laborers about surface	66

The average wages paid to joiners in the counties of Lancashire and Yorkshire at the present time are 16 cents and 17 cents per hour, the working hours being from 49 to 54½ per week.

Proceeding southward, wages vary from $4.26 to $4.86 per week in the agricultural districts, and the working hours are from 54½ to 60 per week.

In 1874 wages were 14 and 15 cents per hour and the work hours 55 per week.

Bricklayers receive 18 cents per hour and work 54 hours. Masons receive 18 cents per hour and work 49 hours. Five years ago bricklayers were paid 16 cents an hour and masons the same.

The following wages were paid by the railways from 1867 to 1874: Mechanics, $7.74 for 54 hours; laborers, $4.56 for 54 hours. From 1876 to 1878: Mechanics, $8.22 for 54 hours; laborers, $4.86 for 54 hours; engine-men, $1.44 per day first year, $1.56 per day second year, $1.68 per day after; firemen, 84 cents per day first year, 90 cents per day second year, 96 cents per day after, $1.08 per day firing five years; porters, $4.08 to $5.58 per week; goods guards, $6.06 to $7.26 per week; passenger guards, $5.58 to $6.54 per week; ticket-collectors, $5.10 to $5.58 per week; shunters, $4.56 to $5.58 per week; signal-men, $4.32 to $5.82 per week; station-master, $4.86 per week to $972 a year.

LUCIUS FAIRCHILD.

UNITED STATES CONSULATE,
Liverpool, July 27, 1878.

FALMOUTH.

Report, by Consul Fox, on the (1) rates of wages; (2) cost of living to the laboring class; (3) past and present rates; (4) condition of trade; (5) paper money; (6) the business habits and systems; for the Falmouth consular district.

I beg to submit the following report, embracing the information I have been enabled to obtain on the several points specified in the Department circular, dated April 11, 1878.

1. RATES OF WAGES.

The rates of wages per diem in this district are as follows:

Agricultural laborers	$0 60
Navvies, and other laborers on railways and other public works. (These are only few in number)	84
Engine-drivers	$1 20 to 1 68
Steam-crane drivers	96
Donkey-engine drivers	72
Iron-foundery men:	
Molders	1 20
Fitters	1 32
Iron-ship builders	1 20
Furnacemen	84
Laborers	60
Stonemasons and smiths	1 08
House carpenters and joiners, plasterers, bricklayers, sailmakers, carpenters, plumbers, painters, coopers, cabinet-makers and upholsterers	96
Ropemakers, printers, tailors, bakers, and gardeners	84
Tin and copper miners, per month	12 00 to 15 00
China-clay laborers	84
Unskilled laborers of other kinds in towns	72

The foregoing are the general rates, but superior workmen of all classes earn more.

The hours of labor of the laboring classes vary from 8 to 10½ hours.

2. Cost of living to the laboring class.

Beef and mutton, 15 cents per pound; pork, 14 cents per pound; milk, per quart, 6 cents; eggs, 17 cents a dozen; bread, 14 cents per quartern 4½ pound loaf.

In towns, twenty shillings a week (for a family) would be little enough to put as the approximate cost of living to the laboring class (rent included), but in the country districts, where house-rent is usually lower, eighteen shillings a week would probably cover it.

3. Past and present rates.

The present cost of living and rates of wages do not differ very materially from those which prevailed five years ago. On the whole, animal food (or, at least, beef and mutton) is a little dearer. On the other hand, wages are generally somewhat higher; the latter, I think, being quite equivalent to the former.

4. Condition of trade.

In common with almost every other part of this country, the trade of this district is generally in a very depressed state.

5. Paper money.

The only paper money in circulation are notes issued by the Bank of England and certain local private banks established before the year 1844. All of these are, and always have been, taken by the public at par. The amount of the latter is restricted by an act of Parliament passed in that year to the circulation which each of those banks then had, and banks established after the passing of that act are not permitted to issue paper money. I have no means of ascertaining the extent of the circulation of Bank of England notes in this district, but full information on this point will probably be furnished from London. The amount of paper money issued by the private banks bears no fixed relation to the amount of coin in circulation; it being in fact quite independent thereof, and of the same value as gold coin.

6. Business habits and systems

There is scarcely anything that can be said to be peculiar in the business habits and systems of this district. Merchants generally buy and sell at credit varying from three to six months, with discounts for cash payment ranging from 2½ to 10 per cent. per annum. Retail dealers usually supply goods for cash or for half-yearly payment.

HOWARD FOX.

United States Consulate,
Falmouth, June 14, 1878.

Report, by Consul Dockery, on the (1) *rates of wages;* (2) *cost of living;* (3) *past and present rates;* (4) *business habits and systems;* (5) *the currency of England;* (6) *the present condition of trade; for the district of Leeds; with a supplementary report on the fixed issues in Great Britain and Ireland.*

In answer to your circular requiring information upon various matters connected with the industries of this district, I have the honor to submit the following report:

1. Rates of wages.

The rates of wages in the various industries of this consular district have not materially varied during the past four or five years.

Generally speaking the reduction of wages has been greatest in the coal and iron districts of the United Kingdom, but here only a slight change has taken place, even in these industries. Although the employers have in many instances been compelled to shorten the time of work, yet the rate of pay has always been maintained.

Latterly most of the "strikes" have been made not for higher wages, but against a contemplated reduction, and have often accomplished their purpose.

In the linen trade there has been no alteration whatever in the price of labor during the past four years. This trade, however, is being practically driven out of this district to more favorable localities.

Agricultural laborers, who five years ago received an average wage of from $4.32 to $5.75 per week of 60 hours, now receive only $3.84 to $5.28 for the same work.

The following statement may be said to fairly represent the rate of wages usually paid to persons employed in woolen mills in this consular district. The week comprises 54 work hours:

Woolsorters	per week..	$6 24 to $6 72
Scourers and dyers	do	4 80 to 5 75
Dyers (not foremen)	do	5 25 to 5 75
Teasers	do	4 32 to 5 25
Scribblers (foremen)	do	9 60 to 14 40
Fitters	do	4 32 to 5 75
Feeders	do	1 92 to 2 88
Spinners	do	7 70 to 9 69
Piecers	do	1 92 to 2 40
Weavers, men	do	6 00 to 8 40
women	do	3 60 to 4 80
Millers	do	4 80 to 5 75
(foremen)	do	9 60 to 14 40
Raisers and cutters	do	6 00 to 7 20
(boys)	do	1 92 to 2 88
Burlers	do	1 92 to 2 40
Pressers	do	5 75 to 6 72
Laborers	do	4 32 to 5 25

In the large foundry of Messrs. Greenwood & Batley the wages of skilled artisans range from $6.72 to $10.08 per week of 54 hours; $8.64 being regarded as a fair, good price.

Leeds constabulary.—The following are the rates paid to the constabulary of Leeds per annum: Chief constable, $1,944; superintendent of detectives, $730; superintendent, first class, $594; second class, $556. Per week: Court inspector, $10.70; hackney-carriage inspector, $10.70; inspectors, first class, $10; second class, $9.50; sergeants, first class, $8;

second class, $7.50; constables, good-conduct class, after eighteen months' service in first class free from fine for misconduct, $6.50; first class, after twelve months' service in second class free from fine for misconduct, $6.25; second class, after six months' service in third class without fine for misconduct, $6; third class, on appointment, $5.75.

Uniform clothing provided gratis, and 12 cents per week given as boot-money; detective officers allowed 75 cents per week in lieu of clothing; ordinary night and day duty, eight hours per diem.

Constables of the good-conduct class receive, in addition to their ordinary pay, 2 cents per diem for five years, and 4 cents per diem (including the 2 cents for five years) for seven years' service, dating from their original appointment in the force, making the maximum pay of a constable $6.80 per week.

If a constable in the good-conduct class is convicted and fined for misconduct, he will be reduced to the rank of first class, and rendered ineligible for good-conduct pay until he regains his rank in the good-conduct class.

Rates of wages of the various classes of skilled artisans per week of 54 hours.

Boiler-plate makers	$8 64
Riveters	7 32
Engineers	$7 20 to 7 68
Machinemen	6 72 to 7 68
Blacksmiths	7 20 to 7 68
Pattern-makers	8 16
Shipcarpenters	7 92 to 8 64
Bricklayers	7 64
Coopers	8 64 to 9 10
Carpenters	9 12 to 9 62

Ordinary laborers per week of 56 hours.

Cement-works' laborers	$5 10
Stonedressers	6 30
Oil-mill laborers	5 85
Bricklayers' laborers	5 68
Pattern-makers' laborers	4 86
Boiler-makers' laborers	5 34
Holders-up laborers	5 98
Strikers' laborers	5 34
Railway-pulley laborers	5 58
Platform laborers	5 34
Permanent-way laborers	4 62
Agricultural laborers	4 08

Dock-side laborers receive 10 cents per hour.

In regard to the cost of living to the laboring class in this district, it may be stated as a general rule that, in families, 22 cents per day per head for adult members and 12 cents for children will provide the food consumed; necessaries alone being taken into account. When families are large this rule is subject to some modification, as regard must be paid to the greater cheapness of providing for a goodly number in the same house in proportion than for a smaller number.

2. Cost of living.

The cost of living to the laboring classes (or the prices paid for what may be termed the necessaries of life) is as follows:

2½ stone (stone = 14 pounds) flour, at 48 cents per stone	$1 20
8 pounds bacon (American), 96 cents; 1¼ pounds butter, 42 cents	1 38
3 pounds sugar, 18 cents; tea or coffee, say, 24 cents; rice, 8 cents	50
1 pound soap, 6 cents; candles or paraffine, 12 cents; vegetables, 24 cents	42

Salt, vinegar, pepper, mustard, starch, baking-powder, blacking, black lead, firewood	$0 18
Coals, 24 cents; milk, 12 cents; tobacco, 12 cents; clothing, 24 cents; shoes, 24 cents	96
3 children to school (board school) 4 cents per week each	12
Sick club, 12 cents; funeral club, 6 cents	18
House-rent	60
Cost per week	5 54

3. Past and present rates.

In regard to a comparison of present rates as to wages and cost of living per week with those prevailing during the past five years, I am informed by good authority that this district has earned about the same wages for a period of years, commencing about 1872, when wages were considerably increased throughout the district. Previous to the commencement of this period rather smaller wages were paid in most departments of the woolen business and in the woolen mills. Likewise but little change has occurred in the cost of living; for while beef and mutton have advanced 20 per cent., this has been met by a similar decline in the price of American bacon. And the people manifest a noteworthy aptitude in adapting their diet to circumstances, a forcible example of which is noted in their eating American bacon because of high-priced fresh beef.

4. Business habits and systems.

In regard to business habits and systems, I must remark that they vary very much in different sections of this district. For instance, Huddersfield, being a *fancy* woolen district, for the most part makers work for orders and very little for stock, except in a few plain black and blue goods. Consequently heavy stocks of goods are seldom found there, and makers have, beyond their mills, very little warehouse accommodation, often only offices where they show samples and sample prices. Quite the reverse is the case in the heavy woolen district lying between Huddersfield and Leeds, at Dewsbury and Batley. There the bulk of the production is of such a plain staple kind (consisting of pilot and president cloths, and the same "friezed or napped") that makers work as much to stock as to order, and large, handsome warehouses full of stock are the rule. At the present day the manufacturers are in direct contract with wholesale houses and large ready-made clothing establishments in the large towns throughout these kingdoms, and in many of the principal commercial centers on the continent the intermediary, or middleman, having been displaced from his former important position as regards the markets alluded to above, and having left as his only field of operation the second-rate towns and the less easily accepted markets abroad and in the colonies.

The mode of doing business is by means of new styles of fancy goods being prepared almost a year in advance of the season when the goods will actually come into consumption, and being submitted for the collection of orders to the wholesale trade, they in their turn are furnished with samples of the goods they order for the use of their commercial travelers. The basis of settlement is generally understood to be a monthly one, but is of course subject to many modifications according to the varying circumstances of this or that transaction, and as between manufacturer and merchant this basis of settlement is naturally frequently arranged for special reasons differently from the general rule.

The rate of discount allowed thoughout the woolen district is usually 2½ per cent., but this again depends upon the extent of the transactions, on which, when very large, a greater discount is allowed.

5. THE CURRENCY OF ENGLAND.

The currency of England consists at this time of—

Gold coin	£105,000,000
Silver and copper coin	18,000,000
Bank of England notes on £20,000,000 of gold bullion	35,000,000
Country notes	15,800,000
	173,800,000

Of which are in circulation £162,000,000; there being bank-notes of £11,800,000 not in circulation.

The actual circulation, therefore, consists of—

Gold coin	£105,000,000
Silver and copper	18,000,000
Bank of England notes on bullion	20,000,000
In metallic basis	143,000,000
In bank-notes not issued on bullion	19,000,000
Good currency in circulation	162,000,000

England in 1816 adopted gold as the only legal standard, assigning to silver coins the office of change or divisionary coin, limiting its tender to £2 in amount. The characteristic of this gold valuation as regards silver is that, for the purpose of making gold the effective legal tender, the tender of payment in silver must be restricted. The effect of this limitation is that comparatively little silver can be used, and so, while the total circulation is £162,000,000, there are but £15,000,000 of silver; and more must not be coined for the time, because the circulation cannot take more under the above condition of tender. It is often the case now that large sums in silver collect in the hands of bankers, and lie there idle at a loss of interest to them. At the same time such surplus amounts cannot be exported, because, just in order to avoid any exportation of the already limited amount to the great inconvenience of trade, the silver coin is issued under value; that is to say, it is coined at 66 pence per ounce, standard, whereas the proportion of 15½ to 1 in gold gives 60⅞ pence; so that there would be a heavy loss on export. Hence, silver coinage is merely token money, and at the present price of silver, of 52½ pence, a shilling of the nominal value of 12 pence is worth about 9¾ pence in metal.

Most people seeing that the English use both gold and silver coin, as is done elsewhere, imagine that the conditions of their use and value are alike, and derived from the natural laws of value implied. But silver coin not only lacks the element of legal tender beyond the payment of £2, but must of necessity become undervalued; and what is more important still, its use is limited to a percentage of but 10 per cent. in the total circulation. At the first glance this result, viz, the proportion of 10 per cent. to which silver can come into use in the gold valuation, appears to be a natural settlement by way of the ordinary laws of supply and demand. But this easy view requires a modification, for it will be seen that the laws of supply and demand, as they are generally understood to be free of shackles, are here hampered by an actual law in the legislative sense, which forcibly restricts the use or demand, and deliberately deteriorates the quality of the supply of silver coin.

The English metallic system, therefore, consists of—

Gold valuation.

Gold coin of full value and legal tender.

Silver coin of debased value and restricted tender; besides the copper-token coinage, of which no note may be made, as it forms only about 1½ per cent. of the amount of the total circulation.

6. Present condition of trade.

The present state of trade is very bad, and stagnation exists in very nearly all branches. In fact, the trade of this district is in quite a languishing condition, caused by an uncertain and expensive system of labor, coupled with keen competition from sources hitherto deemed only worthy of contempt; and until some great remedy shall have been discovered and applied, little improvement may be expected. These people appear to be determined not to see that their monopoly is declining, and perhaps they will wake up from their apparent lethargy when it is too late. Although labor is expensive, it cannot now be made cheaper, because the very essence of existence—meat and bread—is so costly. A reduction in the tariffs of various foreign countries would undoubtedly stimulate a revival of the industries of this district, but those new markets, as it were, would be quickly glutted, and, in my opinion, the relief would be only temporary in its nature, as I think there is some more serious cause of the present depression than hostile tariffs. In this connection it is a significant fact that some other nations have begun to manufacture articles hitherto purchased here, and the success of these experiments has led to an extension of their scope of trade, until they find themselves able to enter the list of competitors for a share of the profits derivable from markets that were formerly monopolized by English manufacturers. Perhaps this accounts for the decline in British trade. Chiefly among the nations referred to above is the United States. Emboldened by fair profits, and encouraged by the Department of State in these efforts to find new and remunerative markets, it need not be surmised that the American manufacturers will quickly despair of establishing a pre-eminence and maintaining it despite all competitors. It is true that America has not planted colonies in every quarter of the world with people not unnaturally predisposed in favor of her manufactures; nor does she conquer trade into obsequiousness by a selfish system of coercion of innumerable distant islands and weakly countries, where, with a handsome establishment of rulers from the home country, trade is forced into the desired channels; but America must and will extend her commerce by means of the cheapness and excellence of her various products. Competition, which is the "soul of trade," will still go on; so that, if we wish to keep (where we must soon be) at the head of the great commercial nations, we must never forget that intelligence and moderation are absolutely necessary; intelligence in adapting our trade system and our taste and style of goods to those of other nations as well as in progress and improvement; moderation in our profits and in the display of undue selfishness or contempt for our competitors.

A. V. DOCKERY.

United States Consulate,
Leeds, July 25, 1878.

LEEDS (SUPPLEMENTARY).

Financial report, by Consul Dockery, on the fixed issues in Great Britain and Ireland.

As a supplement to my report recently forwarded, I have the honor to make the following statement with regard to state of the fixed issues in Great Britain and Ireland as at present existing:

Amounts authorized by the acts of 1844 and 1845:		
England: Bank of England		£14,000 000
207 private banks		5,153 407
72 joint-stock banks,		3,495 446
Scotland: 12 joint-stock banks		3,087 209
Ireland: 6 joint-stock banks		6,354 494
		32,090 556
Add increase since, in authorized amount of Bank of England:		
1855. Dec. 7	£475,000	
1861. July 10	175,000	
1866. February 21	350,000	
		1,000 000
		33,090 556
Deduct lapsed issues:		
England: 91 private banks	1,434,261	
20 joint-stock banks	907,895	
Scotland: 1 joint-stock bank combining two issues, namely:		
Ayrshire Bank £53,656		
Western Bank of Scotland 284,282		
	337,938	
		2,680 094
		30,410 462

Summary of present fixed issues.

England: Bank of England	£15,000 000
110 private banks	3,719 146
52 joint stock banks	2,587 551
Scotland: 11 joint stock banks	2,749 271
Ireland: 6 joint-stock banks	6,354 494
	30,410 462

The principle involved in the act of Parliament of 1844, better known as the Peel act, was to fix a limit to the issuing powers of the banks of the United Kingdom, the *gist* of the act being to limit the issue of paper to the amount outstanding at that time, and prohibiting any other banks than those *in esse* from hereafter issuing any paper whatever. The act further provided, that as any of the various private and joint-stock banks contemplated in its scope should become defunct from whatever cause, the Bank of England becomes the residuary legatee, as it were, of the issuing privileges possessed by the defunct bank or banks, but this benefit is to be limited to the issue of only two-thirds of the whole amount of the authorized issue of the said defunct bank; the remaining one-third going out of circulation forever. So it will be seen that the general tendency of the act has been to greatly contract the paper currency, and will ultimately draw towards the Bank of England the entire privilege of issuing notes; yet, while the issuing power of this bank is gradually increasing, still it can never absorb the whole amount of outstanding issue authorized in 1844, because the act provides that one-third shall be withdrawn from circulation upon the contingency above noted.

In the tables herewith it will be observed that, in accordance with the provisions of the said act, the bank has availed itself of the privilege since 1844 to the extent of £1,000,000; but since then the national, provincial, and other banks have surrendered a considerable amount, so that the Bank of England is at this moment entitled to apply for an order in council for the extension of the note issue against securities from £15,000,000 to £15,750,000; the effect of which would be a permanent increase of £750,000 in the reserve, and, furthermore, to raise the total authorized issue to an amount nearly equal to that of all the other banks combined.

A. V. DOCKERY.

UNITED STATES CONSULATE,
Leeds, July 31, 1878.

LIVERPOOL, LANCASHIRE, AND NORTH WALES.

Report, by Consul Fairchild, on labor, rates of wages, cost of living, and state of trade in Liverpool, Lancashire (St. Helens and Warrington and vicinities), and North Wales (Holyhead and vicinity).

Referring to the Department circular of April 11, 1878, directing report to be made of the rates of wages usually paid to laborers of every class, but with especial reference to agricultural and mechanical laborers and those upon public works and railways, together with the cost of living or prices paid for what may be termed the necessaries of life, I beg leave to report the following as the result of careful inquiry made by me in this and other towns in this consular district:

RATES OF WAGES IN LIVERPOOL.*

(Per week of 54 hours, 9 hours constituting a day's work.)

Engineering:	
Millwrights and fitters	$7 70
Pattern-makers	8 42
Turners	8 42
Smiths, in all branches	8 90
Molders	8 90
Brassfounders and coppersmiths	7 22
Shipbuilding trades:	
Shipcarpenters, wood and iron	10 20
Joiners	9 50
Sailmakers	8 75
(Sailmakers work only 8 hours during the four winter months, so called.)	
Mast and block makers	9 00
Painters, in summer	8 22
(Painters work 9½ hours in summer and 9 hours in winter.)	
in winter	7 74
Boiler-makers	7 30
platers	10 20
riveters	8 75
Building trades:	
Joiners	9 00
(Joiners: Previous to May 1, 1877, the rate was 15½ cents per hour; May 1, 1876, and for the three preceding years, 13¼ cents per hour.)	

* Where no remarks are made the hours of labor and the rates of wages have undergone no change in five years. The local regulations and agreements in regard to overtime, &c., will be found in the Appendix to this report.

Building trades—Continued:

Stonemasons (February 1 to November 10, $8\frac{1}{4}$ hours per day) $9 00

(Stonemasons: Reduction of $5\frac{1}{2}$ hours per week two years ago.)

(November 11 to December 4, $7\frac{5}{6}$ hours per day) 8 60

(December 5 to January 10, $6\frac{11}{12}$ hours per day) 7 50

(January 11 to February 1, $7\frac{5}{6}$ hours per day) 8 60

Bricklayers (in summer, $9\frac{1}{6}$ hours per day) 10 00

(in winter, November 1 to March 1, $7\frac{11}{12}$ hours per day) 8 67

Slaters and plasterers ($8\frac{1}{4}$ hours per day) 9 72

(Slaters and plasterers: In 1875, and perhaps 1874, the working hours were $9\frac{1}{6}$ per day and the wages $8.25 per week; in 1876, $9\frac{1}{6}$ hours per day and wages $8.75 per week; in 1877, present hours and wages.)

Brickmakers (estimated) 10 25

(Brickmakers: No correct average of hours or wages in this trade can be obtained. If working 60 hours per week, a man can earn probably from $12.15 to $19. Owing, however, to interruptions by the weather, &c., brickmakers are not employed more than two-thirds' time during the year. Taking the average between $12.15 and $19, and reducing the working time as herein given, the wages above estimated will be found approximately correct.)

Plumbers, in winter 8 65

(Plumbers: In winter 8 hours and in summer 9 hours constitute a day's work. Present wages were obtained three years ago. During the previous two years the wages were $15\frac{1}{2}$ cents per hour in summer and 17 cents per hour in winter. No change in hours of labor.)

Plumbers, in summer 9 50

Painters and paper-hangers ($9\frac{1}{6}$ hours per day) 8 50

Grainers and decorators ($9\frac{1}{6}$ hours per day) 8 50

(Paper-hangers, painters, grainers, and decorators: An advance of a penny per hour was secured three years ago. At the time this dispatch was written they were on a strike for another advance of a penny per hour.)

Gilders ($9\frac{1}{6}$ hours per day) 7 30

Gasfitters ($9\frac{1}{4}$ hours per day) 7 80

Tinplate-workers 7 53

(Tinplate-workers: During the last five years the working hours have been reduced 6 hours and the wages increased 72 cents per week.)

Cabinet-makers 8 00

(Cabinet-makers: Same hours for the last five years, but an increase in wages of 50 cents per week.)

Upholsterers 8 75

(Upholsterers: Same hours for the last four years, but an increase of 72 cents per week in wages.)

Wood turners 7 75

French polishers 7 53

Coopers 8 75

(Coopers, skilled hands, can earn $10.70 on piece-work.)

Wheelwrights 7 80

(Wheelwrights: An advance in wages in five years of $1.20 per week.)

Coachbuilders 8 25

Farriers 8 53

Printers, daymen ($8\frac{1}{4}$ hours per day) 10 68

(Printers: In 1876 daymen's hours were reduced 3 per week, and nightmen's 1 per week, while the daymen received an advance of 18 cents per week and the nightmen 48 cents. Overtime: Daymen, 20 cents per hour, nightmen, 24 cents.)

Printers, nightmen ($8\frac{1}{4}$ hours per day) 10 68

Bookbinders:)

(In 1876 an advance of 24 cents per week was obtained.)

Finishers 9 25

Forwarders 7 80

Paper-rulers 7 80

Saddlers 7 30

Pavers ($9\frac{1}{4}$ hours per day) 8 25

Watchmakers (rough estimate) 8 75

Piano tuners and repairers (8 hours per day) 9 25

Shoemakers (9¼ hours, piece-work)	$8 75
Teamsters (11 hours per day)	7 05
Carters	6 30
Laborers (roughly averaged)	5 82

Cost of living in Liverpool.

Article	Unit	From	To
Tea	per pound	$0 40 to	$0 85
Coffee	do	24 to	40
Sugar, moist	do	05 to	08
Sugar, lump	do	07 to	08
Rice		04 to	10
Sago			08
Tapioca	per pound	12 to	20
Beef	do	16 to	22
Mutton	do	16 to	22
Lamb	do	24 to	28
Veal	do	14 to	20
Ham	do	16 to	24
Bacon	do	12 to	20
Pork, fresh	do	14 to	18
Butter	do	24 to	36
Cheese	do	12 to	20
Lard	do		16
Eggs	per dozen	14 to	18
Potatoes	per peck	30 to	36
Flour	per 6 pounds	20 to	28
Oatmeal	do	21 to	24
Pease, white	per quart	05 to	06
Pease, green	do	08 to	10
Bread	8-pound loaf	24 to	32
Milk	per quart	06 to	08
Rib pork	per pound		08
Tongues, ox	do		11
Tongues, pig	do		12
Cocoa	do	12 to	48
Corn-flour (farina)	do		16
Candles	do	12 to	24
Barley	do	04 to	06
Biscuit	do	08 to	32
Soap	do	04 to	10
Coal	per ton	3 65 to	4 38
Rent, 3 to 4 small rooms, in courts	per week	60 to	1 08
Rent, artisans' cottages, 5 rooms and attic		1 32 to	2 04
Rent, laborers' cottages, 4 or 5 rooms		1 20 to	1 68
Laborers' and artisans' working suits		7 30 to	9 20
Sunday suits		14 60 to	19 50

ST. HELENS, LANCASHIRE.

Rates of wages in St. Helens and vicinity, Lancashire.

Plate-glass works, per week:

Laborers	$4 48
Mechanics' laborers	5 34
Mechanics	8 50
Glassgrinders	10 92
Women, experienced	3 60
Polishers, boys	3 36
Casting-hall mixers	6 96
Furnace and table men	9 36
Potmakers	7 68
Glassgrinders, boys	2 40
Women, young	1 20
Warehouse-packers	$4 32–6 00
Blacksmiths	8 16
Sandmen	6 72
Plaster-turners	8 64
Smoothers and overlookers	10 92
Polishers, men	7 92

Iron-works, per week:

Engineers		$8 25
Fitters		7 90
Turners		7 80
Pattern-makers		8 25
Molders, loam		8 75
Molders, greensand		8 25
Smiths		8 75
Strikers		5 82
Joiners		8 50
Boiler-makers		8 50
Platers and anglesmiths	$9 25 to	9 72
Holders-up		6 78
Riveters		7 86
Laborers		4 62
Planers		6 78
Grinders		6 78

Agricultural laborers.—The wages paid to agricultural laborers vary from $4.40 to $5.35 per week.

Navvies.—The navvies employed on public works and railways earn from $6.54 to 7.30 per week, according to the work on which they happen to be employed.

Colliers.—It is a very difficult matter to arrive at a correct average of colliers' wages, as some men can earn so much more than others in the same mine during the same hours; but I am informed that $5.80 per week is considered at the present time a good week's earning; that there are not many men who earn more, but that there are very many who do not earn so much.

Chemical works.—In the chemical works most of the men are employed on piece-work, and in the various works there are different regulations, so that, as in the case of colliers, it is not easy to arrive at the average weekly earnings of the men. The best estimates I can obtain are as follows, per week: Laborers, $4.40; soda-panmen, $6.30; black-ashmen, $8; white-ashmen, $8.50; alkali-finishers, $9.72 to $12.75; salt-cake-men, $9.25.

Building trades.—The builders pay the men in their employ, who work 54 hours per week, as follows: Bricklayers (18 cents per hour), $9.72; bricklayers' laborers, $6.50; joiners, $9.

Past and present rates.

The wages now paid, as compared with those paid five years ago, are very much the same in the cases of ordinary and agricultural laborers. The list I have given of wages paid to workmen in plate-glass works is, I believe, exactly the same. The wages in the iron-works, in some branches, have undergone some reduction, and the chemical workmen and colliers have been very considerably reduced.

Prices of food.

Flour	per 5 and 6 pounds..		$0 24
Bread	per pound..		05
Butter	do....	$0 24 to	36
Cheese	do....	16 to	24
Meat	do....	20 to	24
Bacon, home-cured	do....		20
American	do....	10 to	16
Rice	do....	03 to	04
Oatmeal	do....		04
Sugar	do....	05 to	09
Tea	do....	60 to	88
Potatoes	per bushel..	1 56 to	1 92
Coffee	per pound..		36
Milk	per quart..		08

The cost of living has varied very little; if anything, it is perhaps a little more expensive now than five years ago.

The population is almost entirely composed of workingmen, who work six days or nights per week, as dayshifts and nightshifts; that is, a portion of the men work at night during one week and by day during the next week. Some of them have also to be at the works on Sundays to attend the furnaces and save them from going out. They are all paid weekly, except the colliers, who are paid fortnightly or ever three weeks. A large proportion of the work is piece-work.

The state of trade could hardly be in a more depressed condition than it is at present. The chemical, coal, and glass trades are all suffering severely; in fact, trade has never before been so depressed in this district. The manufacturers have been looking for an improvement for the last two years, but matters, instead of improving, seem to be getting worse.

WARRINGTON, LANCASHIRE.

Rates of wages in Warrington and vicinity.

Brewers, porter and beer, unskilled hands ....per week..		$4 62
Chemical workers, unskilled hands ....do....		4 86
Cotton-mills, men skilled ....do....	$4 40 to	$9 72
women ....do....	2 90 to	4 86
children ....do....		1 44
Filemakers ....do....		6 30
Flint-glass makers* ....do....	9 72 to	22 30
Iron-puddlers† ....do....		7 30
† superior ....do....		9 72
Fitters, molders, &c.† ....do....		7 80
Laborers in iron-works, unskilled† ....do....		4 86
Wiredrawers, about ....do....		9 72
Wireworkers ....do....		7 30
Soapboilers ....do....		6 30
Tanners, skilled ....do....		7 80
unskilled ....do....		4 86
Laborers ....do ...	4 40 to	4 86

The prices of articles which may be termed the necessaries of life, and house-rent and clothing are about the same as those given for Liverpool.

NORTH WALES.

Rates of wages for North Wales.

Holyhead and vicinity:		
Agricultural laborers, and found ....per week..		$2 43
Navvies on principal works ....do....	$5 40 to	5 75
Mechanical laborers ....do....	4 40 to	5 60
Blacksmiths ....do....	6 80 to	7 75
Boiler-makers ....do....	6 80 to	8 25
Platers ....do....	7 30 to	8 75
Fitters ....do....	6 80 to	8 25
House-joiners ....do....		6 54
Shipcarpenters ....do....		7 30
Stonemasons ....do....		8 75

The necesaries of life cost about the same as at Liverpool.

Rent of small cottages for laborers, from 72 cents to $1.30 per week. House-rent has increased 20 per cent. during the past two years.

The state of general trade and commerce at Liverpool is so well under-

* *Flint-glass makers:* An advance in wages within five years of 10 to 15 per cent.

† *Iron-works:* A decrease in five years of 15 per cent., with the exception of fitters and molders, who have received an advance of 5 per cent.

stood by the mercantile community in the United States, that I can probably say nothing which is not already known. The whole story can be told in a very few words; that is to say, general trade and commerce are in almost as bad a condition as is possible without bringing many engaged therein to utter ruin.

WORKING RULES.

I inclose the working rules of some of the trades in this consular district. To any one investigating the condition of labor in this country I think these rules will afford much valuable information.*

LUCIUS FAIRCHILD.

UNITED STATES CONSULATE,
Liverpool, May 29, 1878.

LONDON.

Report, by Consul-General Badeau, on the (1) *rates of wages;* (2) *cost of living;* (3) *past and present rates of wages and cost of living;* (4) *present state of trade;* (5) *business habits and systems; for the district of the consulate-general of London.*

Referring to your circular of April 11, ultimo, calling for information in regard to the wages of laborers, the cost of living to the laboring class at the present time, and also for a comparison with the rates prevailing during the past five years; also, for information in regard to the present state of trade; the amount and character of paper money in circulation and its relation to coin; and for general information in regard to business habits and systems, all with reference to the district of this consulate-general, I have the honor to submit—

1. A list of the rates of wages of laborers and artisans of every class, including agricultural laborers, mechanical laborers, and those upon public works and railways, compiled from original sources and after extensive and careful inquiry.

2. A statement of the cost of living, that is to say, of the prices paid for the necessaries of life.

3. A comparison of the present rates of wages with those prevailing during the past five years shows a gradual increase of about 10 per cent. within that period; the cost of living has also increased about 25 per cent. The prices of separate articles of clothing can, of course, not be generalized, but they have also risen about 30 per cent. Fuel has not advanced in price within the last five years.

4. The state of trade, as described in my annual reports for 1877 and subsequent dispatches, is greatly depressed, no change for the better being yet apparent. The markets for staple commodities are very dull. The strikes in the north of England are indications that cannot be mistaken of the unprosperous condition of manufactures, and the prospects of war contribute to unsettle all commercial operations.

5. The business habits and systems in this consular district—the commercial center of the world and the market for the products of every known country—are naturally cosmopolitan in character. The magnitude and variety of the operations render it necessary to maintain

---

* These working rules of the trades will be found in the Appendix to this volume.

separate markets for special purposes, such as the colonial market, the corn-market, coal-market, tea-market, as well as separate markets for coffee, leather, wool, hides, meat, cattle, hay, wood, &c. This is, of course, in addition to the markets for stocks and shares, and the ordinary, or rather extraordinary, banking business. The systems according to which business is transacted in this community are as numerous and different as the articles for which London is the mart. Some idea of the universality of the trade may be gathered from the enumeration of only a portion of the articles invoiced at this consulate-general for America, made by me in my dispatch No. 360, to which I respectfully refer.

Wages of laborers and artisans in the consuler district of London, 1878.

Occupation		Wages
Agricultural laborers (beer found, rent about 24 to 36 cents per week for families)	per week..	$1 92 to $2 88
Agricultural laborers, children on farms	do......	24 to 1 20
Laborers (builders)	do......	4 38 to 5 10
Gardeners	do......	4 38 to 7 26
Bricklayers (day of 9 hours)	do......	7 30 to 9 72
Carpenters and joiners (day of 9 hours)	do......	7 30 to 9 72
Masons, stone	do......	8 46 to 10 94
Masons, marble	do......	8 46 to 14 58
Engineers (working)	do......	7 30 to 9 72
Cabinet-makers (often by piece-work)	do......	8 46 to 12 15
Pianoforte makers (often by piece-work)	do......	8 46 to 12 15
Printers and lithographers	do......	8 70 to 12 15
Bookbinders	do	8 22 to 12 15
Jewelers	do......	8 46 to 14 58
Silversmiths	do......	7 30 to 10 93
Bootmakers	do......	4 86 to 8 46
Tailors	do......	6 10 to 8 46
Tinmen	do......	4 86 to 7 30
Smiths (various)	do......	4 86 to 14 58
Butchers	do......	6 10 to 8 46
Butchers, boys	do	2 43 to 3 35

Bakers, with partial board, from $4.38 to $7.30 weekly.

Linendrapers' assistants, with board and lodging, from $97.20 to $729 per annum.

Grocer's assistants, the same, with board and lodging.

Porters and messengers receive from $4.38 to $6.08 weekly, with partial board.

Dressmakers, with board and lodging, from $73 to $243 per annum; if out of the establishment, from $1.93 to $6.08 per week, with dinner.

Clerks, from $97.20 to $1,458 per annum; principal clerks, up to $4,860, but these are rare exceptions. Bankers' clerks begin at a salary of $243 per annum.

Hatters, from $6.08 to $12.15 per week.

Omnibus drivers and conductors, from $1.20 to $1.92 per day.

Cabmen hire their carriages, paying from $2.80 to $3.86 per day for said hire.

Domestic servants, per annum, with board and lodging:

Housekeepers, from $97.20 to $486.

Cooks, $87.48 to $243.

Housemaids, $64 to $97.20.

Parlor-maids, $64 to $97.20.

Nursery-maids, $48.60 to $97.20.

Butlers, from $97.20 to $486.

Footmen, from $77.75 to $145.80, with livery.

Coachmen, from $243 to $379, with livery.

Grooms, from $87.48, in house, to $379 out of house, with livery, without lodgings.

Railway employés, porters, oilmen, ticket-collectors, &c., from $4.38 to $7.30 per week.

Railway guards and inspectors, from $5.10 to $12.15 per week.

Engine-drivers, from $1.44 to $1.93 per day.

Stokers, from 96 cents to $1.44 per day.

Chemists' and druggists' assistants receive from $243 to $486 per annum, with board and lodging.

Laborers on public works, roadmakers, &c., receive from $4.32 to $7.30 per week, according to skill and ability.

COST OF LIVING.

The cost of living for the working classes has increased in London very much during the last five years; rents have risen nearly 30 per cent., and food of every description is much dearer.

The present prices are—

Article	Unit	Price
Beef	per pound..	$0 16 to $0 32
Mutton	do	14 to 32
Pork	do	14 to 24
Veal and lamb	do	20 to 32
Bread	the 4-pound loaf..	14 to 17
Butter	per pound..	24 to 48
Cheese	do	16 to 28
Flour	per quartern of 3½ pounds..	13 to 18
Sugar, raw	per pound..	6 to 12
Sugar, refined	do	8 to 14
Tea	do	40 to 1 20
Coffee, pure	do	32 to 56
Potatoes	do	2 to 4

Rent in London, for artisans, from $1.20 to $2.40 per week for one or two rooms; more for better accommodations. Respectable lodgings for clerks or warehousemen, from $122 to $242 per annum. Small houses can be had for $175 per annum, with taxes, which amount to about one-fifth of the rental.

ADAM BADEAU.

UNITED STATES CONSULATE-GENERAL,
London, May 18, 1878.

MANCHESTER.

Report, by Consul Shaw, on the (1) *rates of wages, and* (2) *strikes, for the district of Manchester.*

In answer to the Department circular of April 11, 1878, I have the honor to submit the following report, and premise the same by offering as an apology for any shortcomings which may be apparent the fact of my so recently entering upon the discharge of my official duties at this consulate.

1. RATES OF WAGES.

I have found it extremely difficult to procure full particulars as to wages received by operatives in the various manufacturing establishments in and about Manchester, inasmuch as those in authority refuse particulars.

The following extract from a letter from one of the first manufacturers of this city illustrates:

I cannot accede to your request, because I think it militates against the interests of English spinners and manufacturers to do so.

The following table is believed, however, to be an accurate statement of the rates of wages paid per diem to operatives in this district:

Statement showing the rate of wages paid per diem to the mill-operatives of Manchester.

Pickers:	
Man	$0 90
Openers	55
Pickers	55
Carding-room:	
Overseer	1 75
Grinders	90
Stickers	95
Oilers	95
Lapboys	60
Cardboys	50
Strippers	65
Drawing-girls	75
Slubber-girls	75
Intermediate girls	75
Flyframe girls	75
Roving-boys	65
Sweeper	30
Warp spinning:	
Overseer	1 30
Second hand	65
Oiler and rover	50
Doffer	55
Assistant doffer	35
Girls (400 spindles each)	45
Mule-spinning:	
Overseer	1 70
Second hand	70
Buck boys	35
Spinners	1 70
Dressing-room:	
Overseer	1 40
Second hand	95
Spooler	60
Warper	90
Drawing-girl	70
Weaving-room:	
Overseer	1 70
Second hand	1 30
Section-hand	1 00
Weaver	62
Yard and watch:	
Watchman	84
Fireman	88
Shop:	
Foreman	2 00
Wood-workers	75
Iron-workers	75
Cloth-room:	
Overseer	1 70
Man	60
Folder	1 00
Inspector	1 00

2. Strikes.

There have been numerous strikes among operatives in this consular district during the past year. These were caused, as a rule, by the reductions made in the rates of wages, and, while a better feeling on the whole now prevails, yet there is still great discontent and dissatisfaction existing among them. The press and the pulpit dwell upon this subject, counseling great patience and necessary sacrifices in order that wide-spread suffering may be avoided, which might arise if mills and factories should be closed on account of the heavy losses incurred in running them.

The plea that the factory operatives in Manchester are now receiving higher wages in proportion to the time they work than American operatives is urgently made by manufacturers here, and this, together with the increasing financial distress among mill-owners, is gradually allaying the discontent among operatives.

The present outlook in Manchester is, however, far from being hopeful or assuring, either to manufacturers or operatives, and the unavoidable friction between poorly remunerative capital and dissatisfied operatives will, I am convinced, soon become alarming to the former and distressing to the latter, unless the cloud of business depression which now hovers over both is speedily lifted by the advent of better times.

ALBERT D. SHAW.

UNITED STATES CONSULATE,
Manchester, October 2, 1878.

NEWCASTLE-UPON-TYNE.

Report, by Consul Jones, on the labor, wages, cost of living, and condition of the working classes in the north of England.

The circular letter issued by the Department under date of April 11, 1878, calling for information upon the questions of the price of labor and the cost of living, has been the subject of careful inquiry. I now have the honor to report upon the questions submitted by the Department.

The nine-hour system.—In the summer of 1873 the engineers of Newcastle-upon-Tyne, numbering over 8,000, turned out on strike for a reduction of the hours of labor from 59 to 54 hours per week. The men were successful, and on the 12th of October, after a strike of twenty weeks, they returned to their labor under the nine-hour system. National importance was given to the struggle then going on between capital and labor on the Tyne. The victory of labor was submitted to all over England, and nine hours became a day's work throughout this country. Without asserting or denying the cry of many, that depression of trade followed as a consequence of "the nine-hour movement," we are quite entitled to take the period of the great engineers' strike, 1873, as the high-water mark of commercial prosperity in England. In the north of England, but more especially on the banks of the Tyne, this prosperity was without precedent in the history of the district, and extended to every branch of industry.

The Northumberland Miners.—During the period of prosperity the efforts of trades-unions toward securing advance of wages were felt in every branch of the labor market, and were uniformly successful. The power of the unions also reached the culminating point of success in the victory of the Newcastle engineers in 1873. Since that time we have had unsuccessful strikes against a reduction of wages in various parts of this country.

The Northumberland miners, under the able secretaryship of Thomas

Burt, esq., M. P., are the best organized, though not the most powerful, body of workmen in England. But the proposition that "strikes against a falling market must fail" has again been established by the recent failure of this organization to avoid a reduction of 12½ per cent. insisted upon by the coal owners, who positively refused to submit the question to arbitration.

The coal of Northumberland and Durham is the foundation of the commercial and manufacturing importance of this district. A glance at the depression of that trade from the commencement of 1874 until the present time, as indicated by prices, gives a faithful representation of the general decline in the north of England.

During the prosperous year, leading up to 1874, coals had doubled in value, reaching the extraordinary price of $5.50 per ton. Coal-hewers, participating fairly in the extra profits of the coal-owners, were then receiving 9*s.* per day of 6 hours (at face of working), with coals and houses free. The several advances obtained by the men—amounting in all to 50 per cent.—were always decided by arbitration, and when the decline set in, the amount of reductions were settled in the same friendly manner.

More than thirty years had elapsed since a general strike or lockout had occurred in the Northumberland coal-trade. Confidence, good feeling, and mutual respect were shared by masters and men alike, and the principles of arbitration seemed firmly established. The tide of prosperity turned with 1873; and during the spring of 1874 the first reduction of wages, amounting to 6¾ per cent., took place. Four more reductions followed, and in the autumn of last year a request was made by the coal-owners for a still further reduction of 12½ per cent. The first step in a controversy which ended in a "strike" (as the coal-owners style it) or "lockout" (as the miners call it), was taken in the following letter, sent by Mr. Bunning, secretary of the Coal Owners' Association, to Mr. Burt, M. P., secretary of the miners:

NOVEMBER 26, 1877.

DEAR SIR: We regret to have to inform you that the exigencies of the trade require us immediately to apply to you for a reduction in wages. We wish as much as possible to act with all courtesy towards your association, and ask you to send a deputation to meet us here on Saturday, the 1st December, at 11.30 o'clock, to receive our request, and to hear the reasons that have compelled us to make it.

A deputation representing the miners met the coal-owners, according to the terms of the above letter, when a reduction of 12½ per cent. was demanded. This was rejected. The representatives of the men urged that the question should be referred to arbitration; but the coal-owners had evidently decided, before open action was taken, not to submit to that mode of settlement.

A two-weeks' notice was served upon the men. At the expiration of that time they came out on strike against the reduction. Ultimately the representatives of the men proposed to accept a reduction of 10 per cent.; but the owners declined the offer, and advertised in the daily papers "that the pits were open to any man who would accept 12½ per cent. reduction."

The difference between employer and employed was only 2½ per cent., and it was proposed on behalf of the men that the difference should be referred to an umpire. This offer, however, was rejected by the coal-owners, who were determined to carry every point and the full reduction of 12½ per cent.

This strike of 8,000 men lasted eight weeks, and was attended by much suffering and privation. The men and their familes displayed great fortitude and good feeling, and the absence of crime from the district of the strikers during so long a time and at a period of great depression reflects additional credit upon the high moral character of the Northumberland miners.

While the coal-owners were firm, if not stubborn, in insisting upon the whole of the reduction demanded, they were otherwise moved by generous feelings. None of the strikers were evicted from the houses which they occupied free of rent; and the old hands were re-engaged when the struggle was ended by the complete victory of capital.

The following table shows the number and amounts of the reductions in the wages of the Northumberland miners from the commencement of 1874 to the present time (June, 1878):

Number.	Time.	Amount.
1	April, 1874	6¾ per cent.
2	October, 1874	10 per cent.
3	March, 1875	8 per cent. steam-coal, 10 per cent. manufacturing coal.
4	January, 1876	7 per cent.
5	October, 1876	Do.
6	February, 1878	12½ per cent.

The great extent of the depression in the coal trade since 1873 will be seen at once by the following comparative table:

Northumberland coal trade.

	1873.	1878.
Number of men working underground	16,000	12,000.
Hours worked by coal-getters (at face of working)	6 hours	6½ hours.
Wages earned per day by coal-getters	9*s.*	5*s.* 4*d.* steam-coal, 4*s.* 10*d.* manufacturing coal.
Wages earned per day by off-handed men	7*s.*	3*s.* 6*d.*
Hours worked per day by off-handed men (from bank to bank)	8 hours	8 hours.
Days worked per week by coal-getters	5 days	3½ days.
Days worked per week by off-handed men	6 days	5 days.

During the period of prosperity, the great demand for men to work in the pits and the high wages paid induced a large number, especially of agricultural laborers, to seek employment in the coal trade; and in 1873 the number of men working underground reached 16,000; but when the depression of trade set in, and was followed by reduced wages, 4,000 of these men were obliged to return to their former employment or look to some other branch of industry for means of livelihood. The number of men working underground now (June, 1878) is 12,000. The average wages during the good times was $2.16 per day. The hewers worked five out of the six working days, thus earning $10.80 per week. Three days and a half is the average number of days worked in the Northumberland collieries now, which, at, say, $1.20 per day, reduces earnings now to $4.20 per week against $10.80 per week in 1873. The depressed state of the coal trade is further illustrated by the fact that during the last two years and a half several collieries have stopped working, and during the same period the sum of $73,000 has been distributed by the Northumberland Miners' Association to support men thrown out of employment or in furnishing them with transportation to other parts of the kingdom.

A single reference to the habits of the miners and I have done with this part of my report. Mr. John Stuart Mill says that "the majority of Englishmen have no life but in their work; that alone stands between them and *ennui*. The absence of any taste for amusement or enjoyment of repose is common to all classes." This is not true when applied to the Northumberland miners. They are great bird-fanciers, and their skill as gardeners, under great difficulties, enables many of them to compete successfully at our local flower-shows. They are also enthusiastic sportsmen. Every Saturday afternoon throughout the summer the Newcastle town moor is visited by thousands of pitmen, who come to witness their fellow-workmen playing matches at the very stupid game of bowls, for stakes varying from $25 to $250 a side. This, I may explain, is not the game generally known as bowls, but consists simply of throwing a stone ball, varying in weight from 10 to 18 ounces, in successive throws over a straight mile-course. The fondness of the miners of this district for dogs is notorious throughout the country, and during the recent strike, when it became known that the pitmen were obliged to part with their pet animals for want of the money to pay for the licenses, Mr. Peacock, of London, sent a check for $125 to the secretary of the miners, with the request that the money should be applied to procure licenses in the most deserving cases.

AGRICULTURAL LABORERS.

The position of the agricultural laborer in Great Britain has been very much improved within the last thirty years; his remuneration has increased about 35 per cent. during that time. It is a noteworthy fact that wages in Scotland and the northern counties of England are at least 30 per cent. higher than they are in the southern counties.

To illustrate this fact I will here introduce a table of comparison:

	1850.	1873.	1878.
Average weekly wages paid in the southeastern parts of Scotland, and northern counties of England	$2 75	$4 35	$4 10
Average weekly wages paid in the southern counties of England	2 12	2 90	2 75

The excellence of agriculture in Scotland over the South of England is to a great extent due to the superior intelligence of her peasantry, arising from the early establishment of parochial schools in Scotland. The northern English counties have been able to draw upon the country beyond the Tweed, and thus participated in the advantages.

The difference in the system of the northern and the southern counties of England contributes to the advantage of the former. In many of the southern districts of England the cottages adjacent to the farms occupied by the laborers, under the system prevailing 100 years ago, have been pulled down by landlords and tenants in order to lessen their share of the poor rates. This is a short-sighted policy. The laborers are thus forced to reside in the adjoining towns and villages, and pay extravagant prices for wretched apartments in crowded situations; they are thrown into the way of temptation to the national weakness for drink, and both time and energy are wasted in going long distances to and from their work. It may be interesting to show here that in 1770, many years before the system of housing the laborers was done away with, the average weekly wages paid in the southern counties were in advance of those paid in the northern counties:

	1770.
Average weekly wages paid in the southern counties	$1 80
Average weekly wages paid in the northern counties	1 62

In the north of England and the southeastern counties of Scotland the very opposite policy is carried out. The majority of farms are provided with as many cottages as will accommodate all the people statedly required to work them. The farmers are thus enabled to secure a permanent staff of laborers upon whose services they can rely. On the other hand, the men are secure in their situations against slack times, bad weather, and casual sickness, and they are removed from the pernicious influence of the village taverns and public houses of the towns, which take away the limited means sadly required towards procuring the necessaries of life, and often leave the men exhausted and unfit to perform a fair day's work.

It is generally acknowledged by those who are authority upon the subject that the northern English counties and the southeastern districts of Scotland, in which this system of housing the men prevails, have an agricultural population superior for intelligence, good conduct, and general well-being to any in Great Britain.

As the result of personal inquiries among the farmers, I give the following table showing the prices paid to agricultural laborers as well as the system under which farming is conducted in Northumberland and Durham.

Character of employment.	Wages.		Remarks.
	1873.	1878.	
Hinds (stewards, generally married men), per week.	$5 52 to $6 68	$5 28 to $6 25	With house and firing; also privilege of planting 10 stone of potatoes and 4 to 6 bushels of wheat.
Ordinary laborers (men), per week.	4 32 to 5 04	4 20 to 4 80	Harvest wages, with bed and board.
Do	6 72	6 56	Harvest wages, without bed and board.
Men servants, per annum	83 00 to 102 00	78 00 to 98 00	With bed and board.
Women servants, per annum	39 00 to 54 00	34 00 to 49 00	Do.
Women (ordinary), per day	30	30	Without board, while preparing land for crops, and doing other small work.
Do	48 to 60	48 to 60	Harvest wages, without board.

There is no doubt but good farming and high wages go together. Ignorance and insubordination generally characterize the badly paid agricultural laborer.

SEAMEN'S WAGES.

The following table of wages paid by the Tyne Steam Shipping Company to men employed on their steamers during the years 1873 and 1878 shows a reduction during the last five years. But the falling off in the business done and profits made by the company is much greater than the reduction in the wages of their seagoing men would indicate.

It would, perhaps, be worth while noticing, under this head, that the cost of labor is not always determined by the rate of wages. The pay of seamen in France is much more moderate than in England, and yet it costs 25 per cent. more to sail a French ship than an English ship of equal tonnage. The cheaper labor is, the more prodigal is it used. The American sailors receive the highest wages and the best rations of any seamen in the world, but they work harder. The average proportion of seamen to an American ship is one man to every twenty-five tons, while in English ships it is one man to every fifteen tons.

Scale of wages paid by the Tyne Steam Shipping Company, limited, during the years 1873 and 1878.

Rank.	Navigating.		Laid up.	
	Seven days per week.		Six days per week.	
	1873.	1878.	1873.	1878.
Master	$19 20	$19 20	$15 40	$15 40
Chief mate	10 80	10 80	7 44	7 44
Second mate	8 40	8 16	6 48	6 24
Carpenter	8 64	8 64	8 16	8 16
Boatswain	7 24	6 96	5 76	5 52
Seamen, A, B	7 20	6 72	5 76	5 52
Seamen, ordinary	5 04	4 56	4 32	3 84
Cook and steward	7 08	6 72	6 60	6 72
Cook	5 75	5 52	5 76	5 52
Chief engineer	15 60	15 60	12 00	9 60
Second engineer	10 20	9 60	8 40	7 20
Third engineer	7 92	7 92	6 24	6 24
Firemen	7 20	6 72	6 72	5 52
Trimmers	6 72	6 24	6 00	5 52
Watchmen	*5 28	*5 28	†5 76	†5 76

* Night only. † Constant.

The wages of seagoing engineers at north of England ports, as recommended by the committee in steamships of a hundred horse-power nominal and upwards, 1878, were as follows:

Home trade, without provisions, per week: First engineer, $13.58; second engineer, $9.72.

Baltic, Mediterranean, American, with provisions, per month: First engineer, $68; second engineer, $43.74; third engineer, $34.

India, with provisions, per month: First engineer, $77.76; second engineer, $53.46; third engineer, $38.88.

In the Baltic, Mediterranean, and American trades no engineers' stewards are allowed.

Wages paid by the principal manufacturers and railway companies in the north of England.

The difficulties attending the compilation of wages tables can scarcely be appreciated by those unacquainted with the work. The compiler is both astonished and puzzled, not only by the difference paid for the same class of work in different towns, but also at the want of uniformity in the various workshops of the same towns. Trades-unions have endeavored during many years to regulate and equalize the rate of wages. Their want of success is most marked. If we take as an example members of the Amalgamated Society of Engineers, the most powerful of all the unions, we find the average rate of wages for engineers to be, in Lancashire, about $7.68 per week; on the Tyne, $6.96 per week; on the Wear (only 12 miles south of the Tyne), $7.92; in London, about $9.60 per week.

Among iron-founders we find wages varying in single towns from $5.76 to $10.80 per week. It is held that a greater degree of uniformity exists in the building trades than in others, and yet the wages of carpenters and joiners vary from $5.16 per week in Litchfield to $9.72 in London. The cost of living is much less in Litchfield than in London; therefore men are willing to work there for lower wages; for the degree of comfort to be procured by the day's wage bears an important relation to the price of labor. But it is beyond the pretensions of this report to consider economic propositions at length.

It is a remarkable fact that the great engineering firm of Robert Stevenson & Co., on the Tyne, are paying their men about 7½ per cent. higher wages now than in 1873, while in the chemical trade a falling off equal to 20 per cent. has taken place since 1873. One thing is, however, clear, beyond a doubt, the tendency of wages in every department of labor is downward.

The table of wages paid to men employed on the railways of the north of England treats of the years 1870 and 1878. The prices paid for labor before the advances commenced are thus obtained. No reductions of the wages prevailing during 1873–'74 have as yet taken place on the railway systems; therefore the full extent of the increase may also be ascertained.

Consequent upon the great stagnation in the coal and iron trade of the north of England, the earnings of the Northeastern Railway Company fell off $202,395 during the last half year of 1877, as compared with the corresponding period of 1876; and that, too, with 18¾ extra miles of line brought into the working account. Northeastern stocks have, under the influence of the reduced dividends, gone down; and, with a view to improving the financial position of the road, a general reduction in the wages of the employés is, I have reason to believe, under consideration.

Average rates of wages paid by the principal manufacturers and others to skilled and unskilled workmen at Newcastle-upon-Tyne, England.

Occupation.	Wages per week.			
	1859.*	1869.*	1873.†	1878.†
Braziers	$6 84	$6 84	$6 84	$7 20
Bricklayers	5 88	7 20	7 20	6 96
Brickmakers	6 66	6 66	8 40	7 92
Boilersmiths	7 62	7 32	6 96	7 44
Carpenters	7 68	7 68	8 36	8 16
ship	....	....	8 64	8 16
Fitters	6 78	6 84	6 84	7 14
Forgemen	8 22	8 28	8 40	8 40
Grinders	6 60	6 92	6 84	6 16
Horseshoers	6 84	7 00	7 44	7 20
Joiners, pattern-makers, and sawyers	5 88	5 86	7 44	7 20
Painters	5 48	5 56	6 84	6 24
ship	....	....	7 68	7 20
Molders	7 04	6 84	6 96	7 36
Plasterers	6 90	6 96	7 20	6 96
Platers	7 92	8 28	8 64	8 40
ship	7 68	8 16	8 88	8 64
Plumbers	6 72	6 84	7 20	6 96
ship	6 96	6 90	8 64	8 28
Riveters	....	....	8 16	7 68
Holders-up	5 52	5 76	6 00	5 76
Holders-up, ship	5 52	5 76	5 76	6 24
Saddlers	4 72	4 86	6 72	6 56
Sailmakers	....	....	7 20	7 20
Smiths	6 96	6 44	6 58	7 06
Stonemasons	6 60	6 84	7 20	6 06
Strikers	4 56	4 80	4 80	4 56
Turners	6 80	6 84	6 72	7 16
Watchmen, night	4 80	5 04	5 76	5 52
Laborers in ship-yards	....	....	5 52	5 76
Laborers in brick-yards	4 56	4 80	5 76	5 04

* Hours worked, 59 per week. † Hours worked, 54 per week.

Wages paid to railway employés in the north of England during the years 1870 and 1878.

Character of employment.	Rate per week.		Hours per week.	
	1870.	1878.	1870.	1878.
Engineering department:				
Inspectors	$6 48 to $8 40	$6 72 to $9 60	......	......
Gaugers	5 28	5 76	61	56
Navvies (pickmen)	4 32	5 28	61	56
(shovelers)	4 08	5 04	61	56
Plate-layers	3 84 to 4 56	5 04	61	54
extra gang	3 84 to 4 08	4 56	61	54
Joiners	4 80 to 6 24	5 76 to 7 44	61	54
laborers	4 32	5 28	61	54
Masons	5 76 to 6 72	7 68	61	54
laborers	4 32	4 80	61	54
Bricklayers	6 12	6 96	61	54
Plumbers	6 72	7 20	61	54
Gas and signal fitters	6 72	7 20	61	54
Gasmakers	4 56 to 5 76	5 76	61	54
Painters	6 24	6 96	61	54
Smiths	4 80 to 7 20	6 72 to 8 16	61	54
Strikers	2 88 to 4 56	3 84 to 5 76	61	54
Locomotive department:				
Foremen	9 60 to 17 28	10 08 to 18 00	61	54
Chargemen	7 68	8 16	61	54
Fitters	4 56 to 7 20	5 04 to 7 68	61	54
Boilersmiths	5 52 to 6 96	5 52 to 8 64	61	54
Tin and copper smiths	5 76 to 7 68	8 88	61	54
Blacksmiths	4 80 to 7 20	6 72 to 8 16	61	54
Turners and machinemen	4 56 to 7 20	5 04 to 8 16	61	54
Brassmolders	6 24	5 76 to 7 92	61	54
Brassfinishers	6 24 to 7 20	7 44 to 7 92	61	54
Carriage-builders	4 32 to 7 20	4 32 to 7 68	61	54
Wagon-builders	4 32 to 6 72	4 32 to 7 68	61	54
Carriage-painters	4 32 to 5 76	4 32 to 6 24	61	54
Painters	6 24	7 44	61	54
Pattern-makers	6 24 to 7 20	7 68 to 8 64	61	54
Sawyers	3 84 to 5 76	4 32 to 7 68	61	54
Laborers	3 36 to 5 04	3 60 to 6 00	61	54
Engine-drivers	7 20 to 10 08	7 92 to 10 80	72	60
Firemen	4 32 to 5 76	4 32 to 5 76	72	60
Mineral guards	4 80 to 5 76	5 04 to 5 76	72	60
Engine-cleaners	2 88 to 4 32	2 88 to 4 32	61	54
Boiler-cleaners	4 32 to 6 00	5 28 to 7 20	61	54
Lighters-up	3 84 to 5 28	4 32 to 6 00	61	54
Stationary-engine drivers	5 28 to 6 24	6 48 to 7 20	61	54
Coke and coal fillers	4 32 to 4 80	4 80 to 7 20	61	54
Wagon-greasers	2 16 to 4 08	2 16 to 5 04	61	54
Passenger department:				
Inspectors	6 56 to 6 96	8 16 to 9 60	......	......
Station-masters	4 32 to 23 00	4 32 to 27 60	......	......
assistants	4 80 to 9 24	5 52 to 9 60	......	......
Booking and parcel clerks	1 20 to 8 40	1 20 to 9 00	......	......
Telegraph clerks	1 20 to 6 48	1 20 to 9 60	......	......
Guards	4 80 to 6 24	6 12 to 7 20	......	......
assistants	4 80	5 28 to 5 64	......	......
Foreman-porters	4 32 to 5 28	5 28 to 6 60	......	......
Parcel-porters	4 32 to 4 92	4 80 to 5 76	......	......
Excess porters	4 32 to 5 04	6 00 to 6 60	......	......
Porters	3 84 to 4 32	3 84 to 4 80	......	......
Lampmen	4 08 to 5 40	4 32 to 6 36	......	......
Carriage-cleaners	4 08	4 80	......	......
Ticket-collectors	4 80 to 6 24	5 04 to 7 20	......	......
Signal-men	4 32 to 5 28	4 80 to 7 20	......	......
Gate men	1 20 to 2 40	1 20 to 3 60	......	......
Water-closet attendants	....	3 12 to 4 32	......	......
Goods department:				
Inspectors	4 80 to 6 72	5 28 to 8 40	......	......
Goods-agents	9 60 to 20 16	12 00 to 25 20	......	......
guards	4 80 to 6 00	5 28 to 7 20	......	......
Foremen	5 76 to 8 40	6 48 to 9 72	......	......
Porters	4 08 to 6 00	4 32 to 6 00	......	......
Timber-loaders	3 84 to 4 80	4 80 to 5 76	......	......
Shunters	4 56 to 5 28	4 56 to 6 56	......	......
Rolley-men	4 80 to 5 04	4 80 to 5 76	......	......
Horsemen	4 36 to 4 80	4 80 to 5 76	......	......
Number-takers	2 40 to 3 36	2 40 to 3 84	......	......

Night-work upon daily papers.

Description.	1870.	1878.
	Cents.	*Cents.*
Ruby, per 1,000 ems	17	18
Nonpareil, per 1,000 ems	16	17
Long Primer to Emerald, per 1,000 ems	15	16
Pearl	15	19

Weekly prices are less—12 cents per 1,000 minion instead of 15 cents. The prices for day-work are 2 cents per 1,000 less than night-work.

Domestic servants.

Occupation.	Wages.		Remarks.
	1873.	1878.	
Cooks	$97 00 to $146 00	$68 00 to $122 00	Per annum.
Housemaids	78 00 to 97 00	68 00 to 87 00	Do.
Waiting-maids	87 00 to 107 00	78 00 to 97 00	Do.
Kitchen-maids	58 00 to 73 00	48 00 to 68 00	Do.
Butlers (single)	170 00 to 228 00	146.00 to 194 00	Per annum, with bed and board.
Coachmen	7 20	6 00	Per week. with house and firing.
Footmen	97 00 to 146 00	87 00 to 122 00	Per annum.

THE COST OF LIVING.

The cost of living is considerably less now than it was in 1873, and the tendency of prices in what may be termed "the necessaries of life" continues to be downward. The greatest reduction has taken place in fuel. The best house coals may now be bought for from $2.88 to $3.60 per ton. The price in 1873 ranged from $4.80 to $6 per ton. The change in the price of groceries, provisions, and staple articles in the dry-goods or drapery department is inconsiderable, and, in spite of the great importation of American beef and mutton during the last five years, butchers' meats still command the prices of 1873. Should the foreign-cattle bill, which is at present receiving the attention of Parliament, become law in its present form, the clause which provides that cattle imported from Continental Europe must be slaughtered at the port of debarkation, will probably have a tendency to enhance the price of meat. This stringent clause does not apply to America. Lord Salisbury and other advocates of the bill maintain that a voyage across the Atlantic, occupying, say, fourteen days, will prove an efficient guarantee against disease. Infected cattle would show the plague within that time. The passage of the bill would not only encourage the importation of live stock from our country, but it would give a stimulus to the "dead meat" and "tinned meat" trade, in which we are more deeply interested as exporters than any other people.*

* The act has, since the consul wrote the above, become a law without any exception in favor of the United States. After the passage of the act, however, the exception was made by an order of the Council.

Prices paid for the necessaries of life at Newcastle, 1873 *and* 1878.

Articles.		1873.	1878.
Provisions:			
Wheat flour, superfine	per barrel	$6 17	$7 56
extra family	do	6 70	7 92
Rye flour	do	4 90	5 64
Beef:			
Fresh roasting pieces	per pound	22	20
soup pieces	do	14	14
rump steaks	do	24	24
Corned	do	16	16
Veal:			
Fore quarters	per pound	18	18
Hind quarters	do	20	20
Cutlets	do	24	24
Mutton:			
Fore quarters	per pound	16	18
Leg	do	20	20
Chops	do	22	22
Pork:			
Fresh	per pound	16	16
Corned or salted	do	16	16
Bacon, American	do	18	14
Hams, smoked, Wiltshire	do	24	24
Shoulders, American	do	16	10
Sausage	do	18	18
Lard	do	20	16
Codfish, dry	do	08	....
Butter	do	$0 24–$0 32	$0 24–$0 32
Cheese	do	18	$0 16–$0 22
Rice	do	04	$0 03–$0 10
Beans	per quart	08	08
Milk	do	08	07
canned, condensed, pint tins	per tin	15	15
Eggs	per dozen	22	....
Groceries, &c.:			
Tea, Oolong and other good black	per pound	$0 48–$0 72	$0 32–$0 60
Coffee:			
Rio, green	per pound	24	22
roasted	do	28	32
Sugar:			
Good brown	per pound	07	05
Yellow C	do	08	07
Coffee B	do	09	07
White A	do	....	08
Molasses:			
New Orleans	per gallon	36	40
Porto Rico	do	48	48
Sirup	do	60	60
Soap, common	per pound	08	07
Starch	do	12	10
Coal (retail)	per ton	$4 80–$5 28	$2 88–$3 60
Oil, petroleum	per gallon	54	48
Domestic, dry goods, &c.:			
Shirtings:			
Brown, 4-4, standard quality	per yard	09	09
Bleached, 4-4, standard quality	do	16	15
Sheetings:			
Brown, 72 inch, standard quality	per yard	18	18
Bleached, 98 inch, standard quality	do	24	21
Cotton flannel, good quality	do	16	16
Ticking, good quality (single linen)	do	20	24
(double linen)	do	....	60
Prints	do	14	10
Mousseline de laines	do	24	24
Cloth, all wool, suitable for workingman's clothes	do	76	72
Cloth, unions	do	52	48
Boots, men's heavy	per pair	$2 64	$2 52
House rent:			
Four-roomed tenements	per week	$1 25	$1 20–$1 80
Two-roomed tenements	do	....	$0 84–$1 20
Six-roomed tenements	do	$1 75	$1 92–$2 40
Boarding and lodgings:			
For men	per week	....	$2 88–$3 65
For women	do	....	$2 16–$2 88

THE CONDITION OF TRADE.

The condition of trade on the Tyne may be stated in a single sentence. It is in a deplorably bad state. A glance at the following table, which gives the prices of the leading products of this district in May, 1873, and at the date of this report, will show the extraordinary falling off that has taken place during the last five years. Many of the manufacturers of this district are working at a loss.

Chemicals are lower now than they have been at any time since the foundation of the trade on the Tyne. The leading manufacturers are striving to reduce the cost of production. They are making extra efforts to turn out more material, with the same working staff and capacity, than they did in the prosperous times. It is their "last ditch."

During May, 1873, steamers were chartered from the Tyne to New York at $6 per ton to take gas-coals, which then cost $4.80 per ton, making the price of coals delivered in New York (price, freight, and insurance) $10.80 per ton. Freights to New York have now reached the ridiculously low rate of 96 cents per ton, *being 36 cents lower than to London.* Best Northumberland gas-coals may be delivered in New York (price, freight, and insurance) *for $2.88 per ton.* If coals were admitted free of duty, New York and other of our large Atlantic cities might be furnished with fuel at a lower price than London. And the impetus which the abolition of this duty would probably give to our American wheat export trade is at all events worthy of careful consideration.

Hopes were entertained that trade would revive when it became known that a congress for the settlement of the Eastern question was to meet; this has proved groundless. The bountiful harvest which is reasonably expected in the United States is far more likely to bring about better times in Europe than even the permanent and satisfactory settlement of the affairs of Turkey and her provinces.

Comparative price-list of the products of the Tyne for 1873 *and* 1878.

Articles.	Price.		Remarks.
	1873.	1878.	
Alkali, white ... per cent. per cwt.	$0 07	$0 03½	Strength 48 to 52 per cent.
Alkali ... do ... do	07	03¼	Strength 36 to 40 per cent.
Bleaching powder ... per ton	56 72	24 30	
Brick, fire ... per M	16 98	$9 72 to 13 32	
Coals, gas ... per ton	$4 56 to 4 80	1 68 to 1 92	
steam ... do	6 00	2 28 to 2 40	
Cannel ... do	7 68	4 32	
Iron, Cleveland pig, No 1 ... do	30 96	10 32	
No. 2 ... do	30 36	9 72	
No. 3 ... do	29 16	9 42	
No. 4 ... do	28 86	9 18	
Iron, manufactured bars, ordinary size ... do	65 58	26 70	
best ... do	68 04	29 16	
best best ... do	72 90	34 02	
Lead, orange ... per cwt.	8 46	6 60	
red (refined) ... do	5 70	4 38	
white ... do	6 66	5 37	
red (glassmakers') ... do	6 18	4 86	Ordinary size cask (excepting paint cask) free.
Litharge, flake ... do	5 94	4 62	
ground ... do	6 06	4 50	
Paint (white lead) ... do	7 24	5 79	
Soda crystals ... per ton	32 76	14 58	
ash ... per cent. per cwt.	05¼	02¾	Strength 48 to 52 per cent.
bicarbonate ... per ton	92 34	72 90	
hyposulphite ... do	72 90	46 14	
Venetian red ... per cwt.	1 60	96	Ordinary size casks (excepting paint casks) free.

EVAN R. JONES.

UNITED STATES CONSULATE,
New Castle O. T., June 7, 1878.

NOTTINGHAM.

Report, by Consul Smith, on the (1) *rates of wages ;* (2) *cost of living ;* (3) *present condition of trade, &c., in the district of Nottingham.*

In compliance with the requirements of the circular of the Department of State, dated April 11, ultimo, I forward my report on the wages of labor, cost of living, &c., within my district.

1. Rates of wages.

Inclosure No. 1 is a tabular presentation of the average earnings of laborers employed in the lace and hosiery trades in this district, those being the principal industries here, as will be seen by reference to the annual reports of the exports from this district to the United States. The table is made up from returns to the board of trade of this city, and, having been compiled with care, may be taken as reliable.

Inclosure No. 2 is a statement of the wages paid by one of the largest lace manufacturers in the district.

2. Cost of living.

Inclosure No. 3 gives the prices of provisions, groceries, and other leading articles of consumption.

3. Present condition of trade.

There is great complaint here, as in all parts of England, of the very depressed state of trade. Manufacturers complain that their business is small and falling off, and there is a general cry of hard times. The employers of labor claim that they are losing money, or doing business at so small a profit as to make it necessary to reduce the wages of laborers. The latter are not disposed to submit to reductions. The consequence is a great uncertainty as to the future of trade. In Lancashire a great strike is now prevailing, accompanied with violence and arson, and there seems little prospect of a settlement. In this district there is much talk of the necessity of reducing wages, especially in the hosiery factories. The manufacturers complain that the competition is so sharp, especially from Germany, that a reduction of wages here is absolutely necessary. Of course the laborers resist. There has not yet been any decisive action on the part of the employers, but there is a very uneasy feeling on all sides. Therefore, the state of trade may be characterized as extremely depressed, with much anxiety for the future. Shippers have been hoping for a revival of business with the United States, and they are still looking to our country for the beginning of better times. Up to this time there has been no increase of orders from our country, which is a liberal buyer in prosperous times.

JASPER SMITH.

United States Consulate,
Nottingham, June 8, 1878.

1. *Rates of weekly wages paid in the lace and hosiery manufacture at Nottingham.*

Occupation.	Males.				Females.			
	Men.		Lads and boys.		Women.		Girls.	
	Wages.	Hours.	Wages.	Hours.	Wages.	Hours.	Wages.	Hours.
A.—LACE WORKERS.								
Leaver's machines for fancy lace:								
Lacemakers	$6 06 to $19 44	57						
Winders			$2 16 to $2 40	Very variable				
Menders							$2 10 to $2 64	
Threaders			1 20 to 2 16	Very variable				
Warpers	4 86 to 7 30	57						
Designers and draughtsmen	9 72 to 24 30	57						
Curtain and other classes:								
Makers	7 30 to 19 44							
For cotton, average about	6 06 to 9 72							
For silk	7 30 to 10 92							
Winders, silk			2 43 to 3 65	Very variable				
cotton			1 92 to 2 88					
Menders							1 92 to 3 84	
Threaders, cotton			1 44 to 2 43	Very variable				
silk			2 43 to 3 30	Very variable				
Warpers	7 30 to 9 72							
Designers	14 58 to 29 16							
Draughtsmen	9 72 to 24 30							
Plain net:								
Makers, cotton	4 86 to 9 72							
silk	7 30 to 10 92							
B.—HOSIERY MANUFACTURE.								
Cotton and silk hosiery:								
Narrow hand-frames	4 38 to 5 82				All piece-work			No limit.
Wide hand-frames	5 82 to 6 78		2 43 to 3 60		do			50
Rotary frames	6 06 to 12 15		3 66		do			54
Circular frames	6 06 to 8 52				do			54
Winders					$2.88 by time	54	$2.16 by time	54
Employed in cutting					$4 86			54
stitching, mending, sewing, and folding					$3 60 to 5 82			54
Superintendents					4 86		By time	54

2. *Wages paid by one of the largest lace manufacturers in Nottingham.*

Average of men (piece-work ....per week..	$10 92
Highest wages..........do......	18 70
Second-class workmen 25 per cent. less.	
Average earnings of young women (winders, menders &c.)..do......	2 64
Average wages of girls (half-time)..........	1 08
Good fitters, average wages ....do......	$10 44 to 11 88

3. *Prices of provisions, groceries, and other leading articles of consumption.*

Articles.		1878.
Flour:		
Superfine	per barrel..	$8 00
Extra family	do......	8 06
Beef:		
Fresh roasting pieces	per pound..	$0 22– 24
soup pieces	do......	14– 16
rump steak	do......	28
Corned	do......	19– 22
Veal:		
Fore quarters	per pound..	18
Hind quarters	do......	24
Cutlets	do......	28
Mutton:		
Fore quarters	per pound..	16– 18
Leg	do......	22– 24
Chops	do......	24
Pork:		
Fresh	per pound..	17
Corned or salted	do......	17
Bacon	do......	12– 20
Hams	do......	13– 26
Shoulder	do......	14
Sausages	do......	20
Lard	do......	16– 18
Butter	do......	35– 48
Cheese	do......	14– 20
Potatoes	per bushel..	1 60
Rice	per pound..	05– 08
Beans	per quart..	....
Milk	do......	08
Eggs	per dozen..	*22– 48
Tea (Oolong and other good black)	per pound..	60– 96
Coffee:		
Rio, green	per pound..	36
roasted	do......	40
Sugar:		
Good brown	per pound..	06
Yellow C	do......	07
Coffee B	do......	08
Soap, common	do......	06– 09
Starch	do......	10– 12
Coal	per ton..	2 20– 3 90
Oil, coal		(†)
Gas	per 1,000 feet..	73
Domestic dry goods, &c.:		
Shirting:		
Brown 4-4, standard quality	per yard..	07– 12
Bleached 4-4, standard quality	do......	08– 16
Sheeting:		
Brown 9-8, standard quality	per yard..	17– 32
Bleached 9-8, standard quality	do......	20– 45
Ticking, good quality	do......	24– 42
Prints	do......	08– 16
House rent:		
Four-room tenement	per month..	3 25– 4 50
Six-room tenement	do......	6 00– 7 00

* According to season. † Very variable.

SHEFFIELD.

Report, by Consul Webster, on (1) rates of wages; (2) cost of living; (3) present state of trade; (4) habits of the workingmen and workingwomen; for the district of Sheffield.

Referring to the Department circular of April 11, 1878, requiring information upon certain subjects, I beg to present the following report:

1. RATES OF WAGES.

The rates of wages in most of the Sheffield trades have been kept up to the standard of five years ago, and in many cases they have been advanced, notwithstanding the great depression in business. But, although the rates have advanced, the amounts actually earned are much diminished, from the fact that there is so much less work to be done. The fact must be considered, however, that men can now earn larger amounts in a given time than in former years on account of the increased facilities, which enable them to work more rapidly. For instance, the steel for round, half-round, flat, and three-square files was formerly made square, and the fileforger was obliged to hammer it into the required shape. The same was true of steel for cutlery, including razors, edge-tools, and many other articles. Now, the steel comes to the hand of the forger from the manufacturer already rolled into shapes suited to the various purposes for which it is designed, thus saving much time and trouble to the forger. The use of machinery also—the use of steam power, instead of leg power, for instance—in many operations which were formerly done by "hand labor," is greatly to the advantage of the workman, since he now receives as much per dozen for the articles he makes as he did formerly, when he could only turn out one-half or two-thirds as many in a day. In such cases machinery has been the friend of the workingman, although he has been in the habit of looking upon it as his enemy.

The following table gives a fair average of what men in the various trades can earn, if working full time, at the present rates of wages:

Railway employés:*	
Engine-drivers, 12 hours per day	$1 20 to 1 80
Firemen, 12 hours per day	72 to 1 32
Passenger guards, per week	4 86 to 9 72
Goods guards, per week of 72 hours	6 06 to 7 30
Pointsmen, per week of 72 hours	5 68 to 7 30
Watchmen, per week of 72 hours	4 86 to 6 06
Passenger porters, per week of 72 hours	3 66 to 4 38
Goods porters, per week of 72 hours	4 38 to 5 01
Engine-fitters, per week of 66 hours	6 06 to 8 52
Examiners, per week of 72 hours	6 06 to 7 30
Oilers (boys), per week of 72 hours	1 20 to 1 92
Laborers, per week of 72 hours	3 90 to 4 86
Workers in iron (founderies, machine-shops, &c.,) per week:	
Puddlers	7 83
assistants	5 34
Shinglers	12 79 to 14 58
assistants	8 76 to 9 72
Ball-furnace men	12 79
assistants	6 06 to 8 76

*Men in goods department work six days per week, while those in passenger department work seven days. Engine-drivers, working 18 hours, get pay for two days; 16 hours, one day and a half; 14 hours, one day and a quarter.

Workers in iron (foundries, machine-shops, &c.,) per week:	
Charcoal-lumpers	$14 58
Rollers	$9 96 to 14 58
assistants	6 66 to 9 12
Metal-refiners	10 92
Plate-rollers	14 58 to 19 44
Furnacemen	13 38 to 18 24
Firemen	7 30 to 10 92
Scalemelters	8 52
Forgemen	12 15 to 18 24
Levermen	7 89
Bogiemen	6 06
Hammer-drivers	7 30
Pattern-makers	8 26 to 8 74
Molders	8 74 to 9 72
Fettlers	6 78 to 7 77
Laborers	4 86 to 6 18
Irontrailors	3 00 to 5 10
Springfitters	9 72
assistants	4 86
Tirerollers	9 72
Machinists	5 82 to 8 76
Joiners	7 30
Turners (same as machinists)	5 82 to 8 76
Engine-fitters	8 25
Blacksmiths	8 50
Millwrights	8 00
Apprentices	1 20 to 3 36
Brassfounders	8 25
Brassfinishers	7 77
Boiler-makers:	
Riveters and bulkers	7 53
Holders-on	5 82
Blacksmiths	7 02
Flangers	8 00
Apprentices	1 20 to 2 64
Rivet-boys	1 20
Laborers or helpers	4 86
Enginemen	6 78
Steelworkers:	
Melters	19 50
Teemers	9 72
Pullers-out	8 76
Cokers	5 82
Potmakers	9 48
Collar-lads	3 60
Fileworkers:	
Forgers	8 52
Strikers	8 52
Hardeners	7 30
Grinders	10 94 to 13 38
Cutters	8 52
Sawmakers:	
Long and circular saw smiths	12 12
Short and circular saw smiths	8 04
Grinders	12 12 to 14 58
Handle-makers	9 72 to 12 12
Edge-tool workers:	
Forgers	13 38
Strikers	12 12
Grinders	14 50
Hardeners	6 30 to 7 30
Pocket cutlery:	
Forgers	5 82 to 10 92
Grinders	9 72 to 14 58
Hafters	4 86 to 9 72
Table cutlery:	
Forgers	7 30 to 9 72
Strikers	6 06 to 8 52
Grinders	8 52 to 9 72
Hafters	5 10 to 8 28

Razors:	
Forgers	$13 38
Strikers	10 92
Grinders	14 58
Hafters	9 72
Putting-up women	$1 44 to 3 40
Scissors-makers:	
Forgers	12 12
Grinders	12 12
Filers	7 30
Fitters	7 30
Holders and hardeners	6 82
Burnishers, women	3 36
Dressers, women	3 84
Electroplaters:	
Stampers	7 78 to 8 52
Piece-workers	7 78 to 8 52
Braziers	8 52 to 9 72
Buffers	7 30 to 7 78
Buffers, women	3 66 to 4 38
Chasers	9 72
Engravers	9 72
Burnishers, women	2 40 to 2 88
Britannia-metal workers:	
Spinners	9 72 to 14 58
Stampers	7 30 to 9 72
Casters	7 30 to 9 72
Makers-up	8 52 to 9 72
Burnishers, when plated	2 40 to 2 88
Rubbers, girls	2 40 to 2 88
Building-trades:	
Carpenters and joiners	8 10 to 8 62
Masons and bricklayers	9 12
Hod carriers	6 06
Slaters	9 12 to 9 62
Plasterers	7 78 to 8 26
Painters	7 30 to 8 52
Grainers	9 72 to 10 92
Paper-hangers	8 52 to 9 72
Agricultural laborers, with small cottage and garden	4 14 to 4 86

2. Cost of living.

The prices of provisions have advanced in some cases, but in other cases they have receded sufficiently to make the average cost of living very nearly the same at present as in any time in the last five years.

American fresh meats and American and Australian canned meats are extensively sold, and have tended to keep down the prices. These are now so abundant and so cheap, that the poor can have an ample supply; yet it is a fact that there is a stronger prejudice against American fresh and canned meats among the ignorant poor than among the better and more intelligent classes.

The following are the prices of the principal necessaries of life at the present time in Sheffield:

a. Provisions.

Flour, superfine	per 14 pounds	$0 54
biscuit	do	50
best bakers'	do	46
Oatmeal	per 8 pounds	$0 32 to 34
Beef, roasting	per pound	22
soup	do	19
rump steak	do	30 to 32
Veal, fore quarter	do	18
hind quarter	do	19
cutlets	do	24

Article	Unit	From	To
Mutton, fore quarter	per pound..		$0 21
leg	do		22
chops	do		24
Pork, fresh	do		20
bacon	do	$0 06 to	14
ham	do	11 to	14
sausage	do		14
Lard	do	12 to	18
Fish, fresh	do	05 to	24
Butter *	do	32 to	36
Cheese	do	16 to	20
Potatoes	per peck of 20 pounds		32
Rice	per pound	03 to	08
Pease, dried	per quart		06
Milk	do		80
Eggs	per 16		24

b. Provisions.

Article	Unit	From	To
Tea, good black	per pound	36 to	96
Coffee	do	24 to	44
Sugar	do	05 to	10
Molasses	do	05 to	06
Sirup	do		06
Kerosene	per quart		08
Soap, common	per pound	05 to	09
Coal	per ton	2 88 to	4 15
Gas	per 1,000 feet		68
Benzine	per quart		12

c. Dry goods, &c.

Article	Unit	From	To
Shirtings, brown	per yard	06 to	14
bleeched	do	06 to	14
woolen	do	28 to	36
cotton and wool	do	13½ to	28
Sheetings	do	21 to	42
Flannel, medium	do	19 to	24
Flannel, red	do	23 upwards.	
Prints	do	07 to	19
Serges and reps	do	15 to	60
Satin cloths (so-called)	do	24 to	70
Boots, men's heavy	per pair	2 04 to	6 06

d. House rent and board.

Article	Unit	From	To
Four-roomed tenements, clear of rates	per week	96 to	1 20
Six-roomed tenements, with rates to pay	per annum	78 00 to	97 50
Board for men, mechanics	per week	2 88 to	3 60
women employed in factories	do	1 44 to	1 92

3. Present state of trade.

The present condition of trade is anything but prosperous in this district, which has heretofore furnished so large a share of the exports of England.

4. Habits of the working men and women.

I fear I may not be able to give as definite information on the "business habits and systems" of this district as was intended. Here, as everywhere else, men differ greatly in their willingness and ability to work. A bold recklessness as to earning and spending prevails among the Sheffield workingmen. Many a man who can easily earn his $14 or $19 a week will be satisfied with earning half that sum, or just enough to provide him with his food, beer, and sporting, allowing his wife but

* 12 cents per pound more in winter.

a mere pittance of his wages for herself and children. Large numbers who might make themselves independent make no provision for the future, except to pay into their club a shilling or two per week, which insures them, if not in arrears, some aid in case of sickness. This method of insurance, good in itself, seems to operate here to paralyze the desire to save. Whether this indifference as to any provision that exists so largely among the workingmen has any connection with the certainty that there is the workhouse for them as a last resource is a question that will suggest itself; a question that is answered in the affirmative by many; a very important question as bearing upon the best methods of dealing with the poor. One thing, however, seems evident, that, notwithstanding the great depression in the manufacturing interests of Sheffield, there would be but little destitution among the working people but for their drinking habits. Any one walking our streets will see where the earnings of the workingman go, and in very many cases the earnings of the workingwomen also; for there is in this town a far greater proportion of women employed in the heavier kinds of labor than will be found in the large towns of the United States, excepting, it may be, the great cotton-manufacturing centers. This fact is to be considered in estimating the amount of earnings that go to the support of families, such earnings being larger than might at first appear. Were these sums properly used, there would be comparatively little suffering from poverty.

The amount spent in intoxicating drink in Great Britain during the year 1877, according to the excise returns, was more than \$700,000,000. Sheffield's share of this expenditure would amount to more than \$5,000,000. A considerable part of this sum would not come from the earnings of what are termed the laboring classes; but a sufficient amount comes from that source, if saved, to place a great proportion of them above want. The waste of money on drink implies, also, a very great loss of time. This amounts, at a moderate estimate, to one day a week, on an average, to the workingmen of Sheffield. The loss of one day a week to 40,000 workingmen means the loss of \$40,000 per week at the low estimate of \$1 per day each; this gives a total loss to the workingmen of Sheffield per year, by lost time alone through drink, of \$2,180,000, and the better the times the greater the loss.

Making all allowances, the foregoing estimates are thought to be under than over the truth. There is but little doubt in the minds of those who know the working population of Sheffield that almost the whole of this loss of time is fairly chargeable upon the drink habit.

This subject could be followed out to startling results. It is introduced here as being in part an answer to the fifth inquiry, and as bearing upon the question of Sheffield's—and England's—ability to continue to compete successfully in the markets of the world with any nation whose producing classes are temperate, and, therefore, industrious and thrifty, a subject to be considered in the discussion of the means by which our country can, by an honorable rivalry, attain to commercial superiority.

C. B. WEBSTER.

UNITED STATES CONSULATE,
Sheffield, July 16, 1878.

IRELAND.

Report, by Consul Barrows, of Dublin, on the rates of wages, cost of living, postal savings-banks, &c.; for Ireland.

In obedience to the instructions contained in Circular from the Department of State dated April 11, 1878, the following report and accompanying returns are respectfully submitted:

AGRICULTURE AND AGRICULTURAL LABORERS.

The earnings of agricultural laborers in Ireland are usually supplemented by the produce of a small plot of ground attached to their cabins. The return marked No. 4 shows 120,557 holdings under 5 acres, and a more recent abstract of landholders in Ireland (May, 1878) is as follows:

Leinster	10,043, holders of one acre and upwards. 15,684, holders of less than one acre.
Munster	7,679, holders of one acre and upwards. 8,101, holders of less than one acre.
Ulster	11,946, holders of one acre and upwards. 10,036, holders of less than one acre.
Connaught	2,944, holders of one acre and upwards. 2,322, holders of less than one acre.

Total of Ireland, 32,612 holders of one acre and upwards; 36,143 holders of less than one acre; 68,755 holders in Ireland with an acreage of 20,162,000, at a total valuation of £13,420,022.

The great majority of the holders of one acre and a considerable percentage of holders of over one acre may be fairly classed as agricultural laborers; *i. e.*, working for neighboring farmers as laborers and cultivating their small holdings in overtime. During the months of August and September there is yearly a migration of a large portion of this class from the west of Ireland to England, where they obtain speedy and remunerative employment in harvesting the crops; returning to their homes with the proceeds of their trip carefully preserved to meet their rents and to procure necessaries for the coming winter. It is most probable that this annual migration will gradually decrease until it ceases, practically, altogether, which it must do when the rates of wages in the more remote agricultural districts in this country are higher than at present and nearer to an equality with the wages prevailing in England.

The following table gives the territorial divisions and acreable extent of each province in Ireland, according to ordnance survey and census reports 1871, the last issued:

Provinces.	Land.	Water.	Tillage.	Pasture.	Plantation.	Towns, waste bogs, &c.
	Acres.	*Acres.*	*Acres.*	*Acres.*	*Acres.*	*Acres.*
Leinster	4,824,498	52,435	1,612,116	2,482,661	102,567	627,154
Munster	5,915,561	152,161	1,362,664	3,326,035	168,752	1,118,110
Ulster	5,273,107	210,100	1,911,545	2,179,427	63,678	1,118,457
Connaught	4,179,020	213,065	755,732	2,083,162	49,993	1,290,133
Total	20,192,186	627,761	5,642,057	10,071,285	384,990	4,153,854

It is most difficult, with any accuracy to estimate in money the cost of living to the agricultural laborer, and the percentage such cost bears to his total earnings. As before stated, the agricultural laborer in this country usually cultivates a small plot of ground, the produce of which costs the sum paid for seed and the value of the occupant's labor in his overtime, with perhaps the assistance of some portion of his family. There is usually, in this class of cases, a pig or two reared and sold to assist in supporting the family.

The returns of agricultural produce for 1876 give the total of land in

Ireland under cereal crops at 1,848,788 acres, and under green crops, such as turnips, potatoes, &c., at 1,363,692 acres; flax, mainly produced in Ulster, at 132,938 acres; meadow and clover, 1,861,128 acres. It appears, therefore, from these figures that over one-third of the entire agricultural surface of Ireland is given up to meadow and pasture; hence the number of men living on the wages earned as hired laborers is comparatively small, as grazing farms require little more labor than need be given by the herdsmen necessary for the safekeeping of the cattle. Indeed, the marked tendency of Irish farming is, in my opinion, to pasture. Farmers here find it more profitable to breed and fatten oxen, sheep, and pigs for the English market than to raise cereals. Considerable attention is given by the landed gentry and by many of the smaller proprietors to improving the breed of horses. There is annually a large show of horses held here, and I am informed that each successive exhibition is an improvement on those previously held, in the breed and character of the animals exhibited. Prizes are given in the various classes of horses, and every effort made to promote the objects of the agricultural society under whose auspices these meetings are held. The following is an abstract return of the number of horses and cattle in Ireland for 1876 and 1877:

1876. Total number of horses in Ireland	534,833
1877. Total number of horses in Ireland	486,165
1876. Total number of cows and heifers in Ireland	1,532,546
1876. Other cattle in Ireland	2,581,147
1877. Total number of cows and heifers in Ireland	1,521,260
1877. Other cattle in Ireland	2,474,767

The general dependence of this population on agricultural rather than manufacturing industry renders the foregoing figures of considerable interest.

The following meteorological report bears on these statistics: "The mean temperature in Dublin is 40°.4′ Fahr.; total fall of rain, 28¼ inches; mean height of barometer, 29°.93" (for year 1877). The climate is temperate and moist, the crops being more frequently injured by excess of moisture than of aridity. This peculiarity of climate is not prejudicial to health. The average of life is much the same as in Great Britain; longevity much greater.

POSTAL SAVINGS-BANKS.

There are 32 post-office savings-banks in the city of Dublin, and in Ireland over 700. These offices are open daily. Interest at the rate of 2½ per cent. is allowed, and depositors have direct government security for their money. A depositor in any one of these banks can continue his deposits in any other of such banks without change of book, and can withdraw his money at any post-office bank. "In these banks you may make deposits to the amount of one shilling, or of pounds and shillings, provided you do not deposit more than £30 in any one year."

The number of depositors in the post-office savings-banks in Great Britain and Ireland is estimated at over 2,000,000. I have been unable to ascertain the exact number in Ireland.

The postmaster-general is empowered (act 27 and 28 Victoria, cap. 43) to insure the lives of persons of either sex, between the ages of sixteen and sixty, for not less than £20 or more than £100. He is also empowered under the same act to grant immediate or deferred annuities of not more than £50 on the lives of persons of either sex and of the age of ten years and upwards. I believe a large number of persons have availed themselves of the provisions of this act, but in the absence of returns as to Ireland, I am unable to give the figures.

The object of the promoters of the act of Parliament above referred to seems to me to have been mainly to provide a safe place of deposit for the poorer classes of the population. The restrictions as to the amount of deposits in post-office savings-banks and the limits named for immediate and deferred annuities indicate the intention of the Government; *i. e.*, that persons of small means should have the opportunity of saving trifling sums, and have government security for their deposits, and to afford opportunities to the same class for the purchase of annuities; at the same time not to interfere with the business of bankers and insurance offices.

RATES OF WAGES ON PUBLIC WORKS.

Through the very kind courtesy of the board of public works, I am enabled to forward the rate paid by that department to its employés in the seven districts of Ireland.

The tables furnished me by the secretary are extremely valuable, as an index of the wages earned by the industrial classes. They are thoroughly reliable, and were specially prepared by the secretary from the records in his office, in accordance with my request for data to meet the requirements of the Department circular.

B. H. BARROWS.

UNITED STATES CONSULATE,
Dublin, July 3 and 24, 1878.

List of tables sent with Consul Barrows's report.

1. Rates of wages, A. Guinness, Son & Co.
2. Rates of wages of agricultural laborers.
3. Prices of agricultural produce.
4. Number and classification of holdings.
5. Annual averages of note circulation.
6. Joint-stock banks.
7. Post-office savings-banks.
8. Trustee savings-banks.
9. Distilleries and inland duty.
10. Wages paid by the board of public works: 7 tables.

1. *Rate of wages paid by Messrs. A. Guinness, Son & Co., Dublin.*

Skilled labor, mechanics	per day	$1 56
Unskilled labor, carters, &c	per week	4 25
Boys	per week	2 43

NOTE.—Messrs. A. Guinness, Son & Co., brewers, Dublin, are reported to be, for a private firm, the largest employers of skilled (mechanical) labor in Ireland.

2. *Return of wages paid to agricultural laborers in Ireland.*

	Per day, without board.		Yearly, with board.
	Permanent.	Busy seasons.	
Males:			
Ploughmen	$0 28 to $0 60	$0 60 to $0 88	$58 00 to $97 00
General men	24 to 48	60 to 88	48 00 to 88 00
Boys	12 to 24	24 to 36	39 00 to 58 00
Females:			
Dairy-maids			58 00 to 97 00
Farm-servants			29 16 to 48 60
Women for field-work	24 to 36	36 to 60	
Girls (weeding)	12 to 24	24 to 36	

NOTE.—The rate of wages paid to laborers in Ireland varies very much according to locality and seasons. Near large towns the rate is much higher than in the country districts; also in spring and harvest the rate is higher than at other seasons.

3. *Return of prices of agricultural produce in Ireland in 1851 and 1876, with the average increase of prices per cent. between 1851 and 1876.*

Distribution.	Wheat, per 112 lbs.		Oats, per 112 lbs.		Barley, per 112 lbs.		Potatoes, per 112 lbs.		Butter, per 112 lbs.		Beef, per 112 lbs.		Mutton, per 112 lbs.		Pork, per 112 lbs.	
	1851.	1876.	1851	1870.	1851.	1870.	1851.	1870.	1851.	1870.	1851.	1876.	1851.	1870.	1851.	1870.
Leinster: Average of six principal markets	$2 04	$2 47	$1 37	$1 87	$1 40	$2 19	$0 05	$0 90	$18 03	$33 30	$10 23	$17 90	$11 09	$19 32	$9 23	$13 12
Munster: Average of six principal markets	1 80	2 35	1 32	1 81	1 35	2 09	1 01	80	17 09	32 04	10 39	17 03	12 18	19 34	9 54	13 58
Ulster: Average of seven principal markets	2 04	2 30	1 37	1 83	1 44	1 90	92	81	18 54	32 76	10 03	16 84	11 68	18 58	9 51	12 21
Connaught: Average of five principal markets	1 80	2 18	1 26	1 64	1 11	1 82	81	81	15 04	28 98	9 30	16 38	11 40	16 74	None.	11 28
Average prices, Ireland	1 93	2 33	1 33	1 75	1 40	2 01	91	85	17 16	31 76	9 09	17 06	11 80	18 50	9 42	12 54
Increase, per cent., between 1851 and 1876	20		35		45		....		70½		71		50		41¼	

4. *Number and classification of holdings in each province of Ireland in 1874 and 1875.*

Provinces.		Not exceeding 1 acre.	1 to 5 acres.	5 to 15 acres.	15 to 30 acres.	30 to 50 acres.	50 to 100 acres.	100 to 200 acres.	200 to 500 acres.	Above 500 acres.
Leinster	1874	17,753	20,401	26,013	23,210	15,709	13,950	6,725	2,730	367
	1875	17,603	20,176	26,720	23,057	15,778	14,051	6,718	2,718	369
Munster	1874	11,574	11,575	19,658	25,300	22,475	22,359	8,855	2,727	349
	1875	11,101	11,377	19,641	25,218	22,386	22,362	8,955	2,735	360
Ulster	1874	13,580	22,537	71,276	56,460	24,046	13,042	3,261	971	273
	1875	14,841	22,069	71,228	56,518	24,131	13,195	3,268	968	292
Connaught	1874	7,360	15,512	49,603	32,971	10,723	6,034	2,098	1,791	508
	1875	7,914	15,470	49,364	32,876	10,750	6,010	2,068	1,770	508
Total of Ireland	1874	50,267	70,023	107,450	137,956	73,043	55,385	21,839	8,225	1,497
	1875	51,459	69,098	166,950	137,669	73,045	55,618	21,909	8,197	1,529

5. *Annual average amount of the note circulation of the six banks of issue in Ireland in each year, 1865 to 1876, inclusive, showing the amount under or over the issue fixed by act, with the average amount of coin held by the banks.*

Years.	Notes issued. Certified circulation, 1845, £6,354,494.			Certified circulation, 1845.		Coin held by the banks of issue.		
	£5 and upwards.	Under £5.	Total.	Less.	More.	Gold.	Silver.	Total.
1865	£2, 958, 049	£3, 028, 900	£5, 986, 950	£367, 544	....	£1, 912, 625	£275, 750	£2, 188, 375
1866	2, 912, 450	2, 972, 038	5, 884, 488	470, 006	....	1, 982, 999	254, 648	2, 237, 647
1867	2, 968, 437	2, 842, 739	5, 811, 176	543, 318	....	2, 046, 711	285, 173	2, 331, 884
1868	3, 216, 999	2, 971, 654	6, 188, 653	165, 841	....	2, 018, 644	271, 129	2, 289, 773
1869	3, 480, 912	3, 126, 815	6, 607, 727	....	£253, 233	2, 158, 640	263, 197	2, 421, 847
1870	3, 574, 170	3, 305, 404	6, 879, 574	....	525, 080	2, 314, 137	223, 416	2, 537, 553
1871	3, 975, 376	3, 568, 760	7, 544, 136	....	1, 189, 642	2, 921, 920	209, 151	3, 131, 071
1872	4, 187, 957	3, 486, 260	7, 674, 217	....	1, 319, 723	2, 918, 265	243, 177	3, 161, 442
1873	3, 925, 059	3, 151, 854	7, 076, 913	....	722, 419	2, 534, 835	285, 653	2, 820, 488
1874	3, 746, 314	3, 026, 083	6, 772, 397	....	417, 903	2, 502, 093	296, 183	2, 798, 276
1875	3, 847, 406	3, 216, 597	7, 064, 004	....	709, 509	2, 661, 765	274, 065	2, 936, 430
1876	4, 155, 943	3, 343, 240	7, 499, 183	....	1, 136, 996	2, 962, 064	310, 519	3, 272, 583
1877*	....	....	....	....	....	....	....	....

* Returns not available.

6. *Return of joint-stock banks doing business in Ireland, the number of their branches, number of shares, amount of subscribed and paid-up capital, rate of dividend, reserve fund, &c.*

Bank and year when established.	Number of branches.	Subscribed capital.			Capital paid up.		Last annual dividend.	Reserve fund after last dividend.	Note circulation November 24, 1877.	Certified issue of notes by 8 and 9 Vic., cap. 37.
		Number of shares.	Per share.	Amount.	Per share.	Amount.				
							Pr. ct.			
Bank of Ireland, 1783	56	Stock.	£100	£2, 769, 230	£100	£2, 769, 230	12	£1, 064, 000	£3, 342, 175	£3, 738, 428
Belfast Banking Company, 1827	36	5, 000 5, 000	100 100	500, 000 500, 000	25 25	125, 000 125, 000	8 20	218, 890	540, 957	281, 611
* Hibernian Joint Stock, 1824	38	20, 000	100	2, 000, 000	25	500, 000	11½	251, 430	....	....
* Munster Bank (limited), 1864	42	100, 000	10	1, 000, 000	3½	350, 000	14	165, 452	....	....
National Bank, 1835	00	50, 000	50	2, 500, 000	30	1, 500, 000.	12	120, 000	1, 642, 228	852, 209
Northern Banking Company, 1824	47	5, 000 5, 000	92 6 2 100	961, 538	30 30	300, 000	15 7½	127, 500	561, 120	243, 440
Provincial Bank, 1824	44	20, 000 4, 000	100 10	2, 040, 000	25 10	540, 000	15	198, 477	950, 678	927, 067
* Royal Bank, 1836	5	30, 000	50	1, 500, 000	10	300, 000	15	200, 000	....	....
Ulster Banking Company, 1836	51	120, 000	10	1, 200, 000	2½	300, 000	20	300, 000	881, 392	311, 079
Total	409	....	....	14, 970, 768	....	6, 809, 230	....	2, 645, 755	7, 918, 550	0, 354, 494

* Not a bank of issue.

NOTE.—There are only three private banks carrying on business in Dublin, viz: Ball & Co., Boyle, Low, Murray & Co., and Guinness, Mahon & Co. Paper money circulated by banks of issue is in the form of promissory notes, for sums of £1, £3, £5, £10, £20, £25, &c., usually extending to £100. Occasionally larger amounts are issued in the form of a note, especially by the Bank of Ireland.

7. *Amount of deposits in the Irish post-office government savings-banks since the foundation, in* 1862.

Year ended—	Amount.	Increase.	Rate of yearly increase.
			Per cent.
December 31, 1862	£78, 696	....	....
December 31, 1863	143, 521	£64, 825	82
December 31, 1864	176, 619	33, 098	23
December 31, 1865	207, 045	30, 426	18
December 31, 1866	220, 637	13, 592	6
December 31, 1867	260, 053	39, 416	18
December 31, 1868	355, 631	95, 578	37
December 31, 1869	458, 148	102, 517	29
December 31, 1870	583, 165	125, 017	27
December 31, 1871	643, 000	59, 835	10
December 31, 1872	727, 000	84, 000	13
December 31, 1873	750, 000	23, 000	3
December 31, 1874	788, 000	38, 000	5
December 31, 1875	845, 000	57, 000	7
December 31, 1876	939, 000	94, 000	11
December 31, 1877	1, 052, 000	113, 000	12

8. *Number of depositors and amount of deposits in the trustee savings-banks in Ireland in the years* 1847 *to* 1876.

Years.	No. of depositors.	Amount.	Years.	No. of depositors.	Amount.
1847	80, 351	£2, 410, 720	1862	67, 468	£2, 088, 370
1848	48, 512	1, 334, 296	1863	66, 652	2, 071, 523
1849	45, 548	1, 200, 273	1864	63, 957	1, 973, 446
1850	47, 987	1, 291, 798	1865	59, 733	1, 836, 862
1851	49, 554	1, 347, 617	1866	51, 583	1, 540, 578
1852	52, 142	1, 447, 315	1867	53, 006	1, 633, 018
1853	55, 630	1, 586, 010	1868	56, 702	1, 813, 984
1854	54, 008	1, 579, 490	1869	59, 401	1, 974, 750
1855	54, 547	1, 616, 126	1870	60, 164	2, 064, 907
1856	57, 508	1, 723, 726	1871	63, 073	2, 220, 575
1857	57, 726	1, 775, 915	1872	61, 746	2, 221, 852
1858	59, 893	1, 804, 163	1873	58, 745	2, 124, 487
1859	65, 504	2, 005, 318	1874	55, 455	2, 017, 561
1860	69, 294	2, 143, 284	1875	55, 505	2, 061, 193
1861	70, 214	2, 153, 211	1876	56, 849	2, 178, 266

NOTE.—Trustee savings-banks are in the process of being superseded by the post-office savings-banks.

9. *Number of distilleries and number of gallons of proof spirits on which duty was paid for consumption in Ireland, and rate of duty charged in each year ended December 31, from 1834 to 1867, and for years ended March 31, 1868 to 1876.*

Years.	No. of distilleries.	No. of gallons entered for home consumption.	Rate of duty, per proof-gallon. £ s. d.
1834 ..	89	9,708,462	0 3 4 2 4
1835 ..	93	11,381,223	2 4
1836 ..	90	12,248,772	2 4
1837 ..	90	11,235,635	2 4
1838 ..	87	12,296,342	2 4
1839 ..	89	10,815,709	2 4
1840 ..	86	7,401,051	2 4 2 8
1841 ..	75	6,485,443	2 8
1842 ..	70	5,290,650	2 8
1843 ..	64	5,546,483	2 8
1844 ..	62	6,451,137	2 8
1845 ..	57	7,605,196	2 8
1846 ..	54	7,952,076	2 8
1847 ..	51	6,037,383	2 8
1848 ..	55	7,072,933	2 8

Years.	No. of distilleries.	No. of gallons entered for home consumption.	Rate of duty, per proof-gallon. £ s. d.
1849..	53	6,973,333	0 2 8
1850..	51	7,408,086	2 8
1851..	52	7,550,518	2 8
1852..	46	8,208,206	2 8
1853..	40	8,136,362	2 8 3 4
1854..	40	8,440,734	3 4 4 0
1855..	39	6,228,856	6 0 6 2
1856..	38	6,781,068	6 2
1857..	37	6,920,046	6 2
1858..	36	6,402,142	8 0
1859..	35	6,538,448	8 0
1860..	31	5,336,313	8 0 8 1 10 0

Years.	No. of distilleries.	No. of gallons entered for home consumption.	Rate of duty, per proof-gallon. £ s. d.
1861..	30	5,022,894	0 10 0
1862..	27	4,653,773	10 0
1863..	26	4,623,242	10 0
1864..	27	4,845,160	10 0
1865..	25	5,285,232	10 0
1866..	23	5,910,061	10 0
1867..	22	4,676,704	10 0
1868..	22	4,842,055	10 0
1869..	24	5,024,976	10 0
1870..	30	5,212,746	10 0
1871..	30	5,749,811	10 6
1872..	30	6,090,534	10 0
1873..	30	6,176,501	10 0
1874..	30	6,094,038	10 0
1875..	30	6,697,435	10 0
1876..	30	6,982,896	10 0

NOTE.—The total number of distilleries in England in 1870 was 9, in Scotland 113, and in Ireland 30. The number of detections for illicit distillation in 1876 was 8 in England, 1 in Scotland, and 796 in Ireland.

10. *Wages paid by the board of public works throughout Ireland.*

Description.	1873.	1874.	1875.	1876.	1877.	Time.
Northwestern district.						
Carpenters	$0 84 to $0 66	$0 99 to $1 08	$0 90 to $1 03	$0 96 to $1 12	$0 96 to $1 12	Per day.
Masons and bricklayers	80 to 88	80 to 88	88 to 96	96 to 1 08	1 08 to 1 20	Do.
Stonecutters	1 20 to 1 26	1 20 to 1 26	1 26 to 1 32	1 32 to 1 40	1 38	Do.
Plasterers	80 to 88	80 to 88	88 to 96	96 to 1 08	1 08 to 1 20	Do.
Painters and glaziers	6 42 to 6 90	6 42 to 7 62	6 42 to 7 62	7 29 to 8 50	7 29 to 8 50	Per week.
Plumbers, in town	6 06	6 54	6 78	6 78	6 78	Do.
Gasfitters, in town	6 06	6 54	6 78	6 78	6 78	Do.
Smiths	84 to 90	84 to 90	90 to 96	96 to 1 08	96 to 1 02	Per day.
Fitters	1 44 to 1 56	1 44 to 1 56	1 44 to 1 56	1 44 to 1 62	1 44 to 1 62	Do.
Laborers, attending masons, &c	3 12	3 12	3 12	3 36	3 60	Per week.
ordinary	2 16	2 16	2 40	2 40	2 88	Do.
on engineering work (navvies)	3 60	3 60	4 38	4 38	4 38	Do.
agricultural, ordinary	2 16	2 16	2 40	2 40	2 88	Do.
superior	3 60	4 38	4 38	4 86	4 86	Do.
Northeastern district.						
Carpenters	7 62	7 62	7 62	8 38	8 38	Per week.
Masons and bricklayers	7 96	8 20	8 20	8 44	8 56	Do.
Stonecutters	15	15	15	15	16	Per hour.
Plasterers	7 62	7 62	7 62	8 44	8 44	Per week.
Painters and glaziers	7 29	7 29	7 29	7 77	7 77 to 8 44	Do.
Plumbers	7 29	7 29	7 77	7 77	7 77	Do.
Gasfitters	7 29	7 29	7 77	7 77	7 77	Do.
Smiths	5 82				*8 44	Do.
Fitters	6 78				*9 12	Do.
Laborers, attending masons, &c	4 08	4 08	4 32	4 32	4 32	Do,
ordinary	3 12				*3 60	Do.
on engineering works (navvies)	3 60				*4 32	Do.
agricultural, ordinary	2 88				*3 60	Do.
superior					*4 32	Do.
Eastern district.†						
Carpenters	5 94	6 06	6 60	6 90	6 90	Per week.
Masons and bricklayers	6 30	6 30	6 66	6 90	7 02	Do.
Stonecutters	6 60	6 78	6 98	7 39	7 41	Do
Plasterers	5 94	5 94	6 30	7 02	7 14	Do.
Painters and glaziers	5 46	5 82	6 06	6 30	6 52	Do.
Plumbers	7 56	7 56	8 28	8 76	8 76	Do.
Gasfitters	8 52	8 52	9 72	9 72	9 72	Do.
Smiths	6 30	6 66	6 90	7 82	7 82	Do.
Fitters	7 29	7 29	8 01	8 25	8 76	Do.

Laborers, attending masons	2 64	2 64	2 88	3 66	3 66	Do.
ordinary	2 16	2 16	2 40	2 88	2 88	Do.
on engineering works (navvies)	3 66	3 66	3 88	3 88	3 88	Do.
agricultural, ordinary	2 16	2 16	2 40	2 64	2 64	Do.
superior	2 40	2 40	2 64	2 88	2 88	Do.
Western district.						
Carpenters	6 30	6 30	6 78	7 29	7 29	Per week.
Masons and bricklayers	6 30	6 30	6 78	7 29	7 29	Do.
Stonecutters	7 29	7 29	7 29	8 01	8 01	Do.
Plasterers	7 29	7 29	7 29	8 01	8 01	Do.
Painters and glaziers	6 30	6 30	6 78	7 29	7 29	Do.
Plumbers	10 20	10 20	10 20	10 92	10 92	Do.
Gasfitters	7 29	7 29	7 29	8 01	8 73	Do.
Smiths	7 29	7 29	7 29	8 01	8 73	Do.
Fitters	10 20	10 20	10 20	10 92	10 92	Do.
Laborers, attending masons, &c	2 88	2 88	3 12	3 36	3 36	Do.
ordinary	2 40	2 40	2 88	2 88	2 88	Do.
on engineering works (navvies)	3 00	3 36	2 36	3 60	3 60	Do.
agricultural, ordinary	2 16	2 16	2 40	2 64	2 88	Do.
superior	2 88	2 88	3 12	3 36	3 60	Do.
	59 hours.	59 hours.	59 hours.	59 hours.	59 hours.	
South-western (Waterford) district.						
Carpenters	$6 30	$6 30	$6 30	$6 30	$6 30	Per week.
Masons and bricklayers	6 78	6 78	6 78	6 78	7 26	Do.
Stonecutters	6 78	6 78	6 78	6 78	7 26	Do.
Plasterers	6 78	6 78	6 78	6 78	7 26	Do.
Painters and glaziers	6 78	6 78	6 78	6 78	7 26	Do.
Plumbers	7 98	7 98	7 88	7 98	7 98	Do.
Gasfitters	7 98	7 98	7 98	8 76	8 76	Do.
Smiths	7 98	7 98	7 98	8 76	8 76	Do.
Fitters	7 98	7 98	7 98	8 76	8 76	Do.
Laborers, attending masons	3 12	3 60	3 60	3 60	3 60	Do.
ordinary	3 12	3 36	3 36	3 36	3 36	Do.
(navvies) on engineering work	3 12	3 36	3 36	3 84	3 84	Do.
agricultural, ordinary (and two meals per diem each)	1 44	1 44	1 44	1 68	1 68	Do.
superior (and two meals per diem each)	1 92	1 92	1 92	2 16	2 16	Do.

* Increased irregularly to.

† Dublin is not included in the eastern district; if added the average would be increased by about 48 cents per week on tradesmen and 24 cents on laborers.

10. *Wages paid by the board of public works throughout Ireland*—Continued.

Description.	1873.	1874.	1875.	1876.	1877.	Time.
	60 hours.	60 hours.	58 hours.	58 hours.	58 hours.	
Southwestern (Limerick) district.						
Carpenters	$7 26	$7 26	$7 20	$7 26	$7 74	Weekly.
Masons and bricklayers	7 26	7 26	7 26	7 26	7 74	Do.
Stonecutters	7 26	7 26	7 20	7 26	7 98	Per week.
Plasterers	7 26	7 26	7 26	7 26	7 74	Do.
Painters and glaziers	6 30	6 78	7 26	7 26	7 26	Do.
Plumbers	6 78	7 26	7 26	7 74	8 76	Do.
Gasfitters	$6 78 to 7 26	$5 82 to 7 74	$6 78 to 7 74	$6 30 to 7 74	$6 78 to 7 74	Do.
Smiths	7 26	7 26	7 26	7 26	7 26	Do.
Fitters	7 26	7 26	7 26	7 26	7 26	Do.
Laborers, attending masons, &c	2 88	2 88	3 36	3 36	3 84	Per week.
ordinary	2 88	2 88	2 88	2 88	3 84	Do.
on engineering work (navvies)	2 88	2 88	2 88	2 88	3 84	Do.
agricultural, ordinary	2 40	2 40	2 40	2 88	2 88	Do.
superior	2 88	2 88	2 88	3 36	3 36	Do.
Southern district.						
Carpenters	7 26	7 74	7 98	7 98	7 98	Per week.
Masons and bricklayers	7 74	7 74	7 98	7 98	7 98	Do.
Stonecutters	7 26	7 98	7 98	7 98	8 76	Do.
Plasterers	7 26	7 74	7 98	7 98	7 98	Do.
Painters and glaziers	6 54	6 54	7 26	7 20	7 26	Do.
Plumbers	7 26	7 26	7 26	8 22	8 22	Do.
Gasfitters	6 54	6 54	6 54	6 78	7 26	Do.
Smiths	6 78	7 26	7 98	7 98	8 22	Do.
Fitters	7 98	7 98	8 22	8 70	8 70	Do.
Laborers, attending masons, &c	2 88	2 88	2 88	3 36	3 60	Do.
ordinary	2 40	2 88	2 88	2 88	2 88	Do.
on engineering work (navvies)	2 88	3 60	3 60	3 60	3 60	Do.
agricultural, ordinary	2 88	2 88	2 88	3 60	3 60	Do.
superior	2 88	3 60	3 60	$3 60 to 3 60	$3 60 to 4 32	Do.

Report, by Consul Donnan, on the (1) *rates of wages;* (2) *cost of living;* (3) *bank returns (all Ireland);* (4) *business habits and systems; for the district of Belfast.*

I have the honor to acknowledge the receipt of the Department circular of April 11, 1878, and will now proceed to answer the same as fully as I am able.

1. Rates of wages.

Agricultural laborers, with board and lodging	per week..	$1 92
Railway and other laborers, without board and lodging	do.....	4 38
Mechanics	do.....	$4 38 to 6 06

At these rates the workingmen are not able to accumulate anything, as all their wages are expended in living.

The rates of wages remain about the same as five years ago.

2. Cost of living.

The necessaries of life may be quoted, at retail, about as follows:

Flour	per stone (14 pounds)..	$0 56
Oatmeal	do......	40
Lard	per pound..	12
Butter	do......	34
Potatoes	per 14 pounds..	24
Indian-meal	do......	28
Tea	per pound..	80
Sugar	do......	08
Rent and taxes, according to location	per annum..	$30 00 to 82 00

3. Irish bank returns.

An account, pursuant to the act 8 and 9 Vic., cap. 37, of the amount of bank-notes authorized by law to be issued by the several banks of issue in Ireland and the average amount of bank-notes in circulation and of coin held during the four weeks ending Saturday, the 16th day of March, 1878:

Name and title, as set forth in license.	Circulation authorized by certificate.	Average circulation during four weeks ending as above.	Average amount of coin held during four weeks ending as above.
The Bank of Ireland	£3, 738, 428	£3, 010, 600	£548, 909
The Provincial Bank of Ireland	927, 667	850, 606	395, 794
The Belfast Banking Company	281, 611	469, 879	202, 834
The Northern Banking Company	243, 440	493, 040	339, 432
The Ulster Banking Company	311, 079	745, 300	568, 006
The National Bank	852, 269	1, 376, 308	848, 652

4. Business systems and habits.

As regards the business habits and systems of the district, the rule prevails in the linen mills to begin work at 6 o'clock a. m. and stop at 6 p. m., with an intermission of two hours for meals.

The merchants do not generally appear at their places of business before 10 o'clock a. m., but the business places are usually opened at from 7 to 9 o'clock a. m. The banks open at 10 o'clock a. m., and close at 3 p. m., except on Saturday, when they close at 1 p. m.

All mills, founderies, &c., close at 2 p. m. on Saturdays.

JAS. M. DONNAN.

UNITED STATES CONSULATE,
Belfast, May 3, 1878.

CORK.

Report, by Consul Richmond, on (1) *the rates of wages;* (2) *cost of living;* (3) *past and present rates;* (4) *present state of trade;* (5) *paper money* (*all Ireland*); (6) *business of the district; for Cork and vicinity.*

Referring to the circular from the Department calling for information as to the wages of laborers and the particulars as to the working classes and the business of this district, I have the honor to report as follows:

1. RATES OF WAGES.

Agricultural laborers	per day..	$0 48
Boatmen	do....	73
Coalheavers	do....	1 09
Machinists	do....	1 09
Gasfitters	do....	1 09
Bakers	do....	1 09
Masons	do....	1 21
Shoemakers	do....	1 21
Printers	do....	1 21
Joiners	do....	1 21
Engineers (steamers)	per week..	12 16
Firemen......do	do....	6 68
Sailors.......do	do....	6 07

Public works.—The laborers in the Hawlbowline Extension Works, where large royal naval locks are being constructed, are paid as follows, per day: 48, 54, and 60 cents, according to class; boys, 24, 32, 36, and 40 cents, according to class; excavators and quarrymen, 73 cents.

Railways.—On the Great Southern and Western Railway, the principal line in this country, the employés are paid as follows:

Guards	per week..	$4 38 to $7 29
Head-porters	do....	4 13 to 4 86
Porters	do....	3 40 to 3 89
Engineers	per day..	1 21 to 1 70
Firemen	do....	60 to 85
Cleansers and steam-raisers	per week..	2 92 to 4 38
Gaugers	do....	4 13
Milesmen	do....	3 40

The gaugers and milesmen receive a gratuity of $4.86 at Christmas. These men have charge of the repair of the permanent way. In the summer of 1877 they struck for a slight advance on the above pay, but, after holding out for some two months, were obliged to come back at the old rates.

2. COST OF LIVING.

The food of the above classes, with the exception of engineers and guards, is made up of a selection from tea, milk, bread, oatmeal, potatoes, dried fish, and, among the poorer people, a coarse Indian-meal, which is used instead of oatmeal. The cost of this subsistence varies slightly in different localities, the highest, 14 cents per day, being about the expense in Cork, Queenstown, and their neighborhoods. Rent and clothing cost about $35 a year, making a total of about $85.

The mechanic pays something more for a better lodging, but in other respects his living is the same as the laborer.

3. PAST AND PRESENT RATES.

The cost of living is believed to have increased about one-sixth in the last five years, and wages have advanced in about the same proportion.

4. PRESENT STATE OF TRADE.

Trade in this district is much depressed, as it has been for some years past, and many failures have taken place among the grain and dry-goods merchants.

5. PAPER MONEY OF IRELAND.

The amount of paper money in circulation in this district cannot be obtained by itself, neither can the amount of coin, and I therefore give the latest published report for the whole of Ireland, which shows an issue of £7,208,453 ($35,079,943), and the amount of coin held in the banks as £2,940,468 ($14,306,589). The paper money is made up of notes from one pound upwards; the gold coins are ten shillings and one pound; the silver coins, five shillings, two shillings and sixpence, two shillings, sixpence, fourpence, and threepence. Paper money and coin are on a par.

6. BUSINESS OF THE DISTRICT.

Trade in Queenstown, where the consulate is situated, consists in the supplying of vessels with their various stores; while at Passage, a mile or two above, are the Royal Victoria Locks, where vessels are repaired, the money for the expenses being furnished by the shipping agents, who draw for their disbursements on the owners or bankers.

Cork is the principal port in the south of Ireland for the importation of wheat and Indian corn, for distribution throughout the district for distilling, feeding, and milling purposes. The grain-trade is nominally conducted on cash principles, but in reality short notes are usually received for the cargoes.

The distilling of whisky is a large business, the last available report showing an export for the year of 3,516 puncheons and 6,931 hogsheads. This is also sold on short time.

The district is, however, essentially agricultural and stock-raising, and large quantities of pigs, sheep, cows, and calves are bought by the farmers for cash and sent over to the English markets. Butter, to the amount of nearly five hundred thousand firkins, passes annually through the butter exchange of Cork, and is sent to England and Scotland; the farmers usually selling their prospective crops for a cash sum in the beginning of the season, leaving a margin for the risk taken by the buyer, which has proved very profitable to the butter merchants.

All the branches of trade and industry in this district are seriously affected by the falling off of business with the United States.

LEWIS RICHMOND.

UNITED STATES CONSULATE,
Cork, June 27, 1878.

LONDONDERRY.

Report, by Consul Livermore, on the (1) *rates of wages;* (2) *cost of living;* (3) *past and present rates;* (4) *present state of trade;* (5) *the paper money; for the district of Londonderry.*

In compliance with the circular of the Department of State, dated the 11th day of April last, I have to report:

1. RATES OF WAGES.

It has long been the custom of young persons of both sexes desiring employment on farms to present themselves in this town on or near the 15th days of May and November for half-yearly engagements, and a crowd numbered by thousands at this moment occupy some of the largest streets. Upon inquiry, I find the rate of wages to be about $34.02 for the six months embracing the summer, and a little less for the other half-year. Girls get nearly as much, and perform much of the same kind of work as that performed by the men. These are all kept by their employers.

The cotter is a more desirable man, and commonly lives for years upon the soil of his employer, with cottage, garden, and a small patch for potatoes rent free, and deems himself well paid at $1.92 or $2.16 a week.

The day-laborer gets from 24 cents to 36, and at harvest-time 48 cents a day.

A teamster in the town is paid $3.60 a week, with no perquisites whatever.

A girl in the factory, who is so much valued as to be paid a steady rate of wages, obtains $1.68 a week; which is better than the irregular gains of the larger number working by the piece.

2. COST OF LIVING.

The food of all laborers here is Indian-meal principally; oatmeal, potatoes, and bacon next. Tea may be said to be in universal use in liberal supplies. The Indian meal and, to some extent, the bacon are derived from the United States, and their cost depends of course upon prices there. Potatoes are of uncertain and fluctuating prices. The present, which is about 22 cents per stone (14 pounds), is nearly double the average; 8 cents in the autumn, equal to 32 cents the bushel of 56 pounds, being usual.

I append a quotation of prices for the current week at the country market of Strabane, May 14, 1878:

Oats	per 14 pounds..	$0 24
Oatmeal	per cwt..	3 36
Indian-meal	do..	1 80
Flour, first quality	do......	4 32
second quality	do......	4 08
American	per barrel..	7 98
Bran	per cwt..	$1 80 to 2 16
Potatoes	do......	1 08 to 1 20
Pork	do......	10 56 to 12 00
Butter, in kegs	per pound..	24 to 27
in lumps	do......	20 to 25
Eggs, hen	per dozen..	14
duck	do......	16

The mildness of this climate causes fuel and clothing to be a light charge in comparison with like commodities in colder countries. Peat is in the country a mere perquisite to the cotter. Coal is brought from England and Scotland, costing the consumer from $3.12 to $4.86 a ton. I am unable to gain any valuable information as to the cost of clothing. In Donegal the fabrics are made up in the cottages, where also the garments are shaped with such skill and fancy as may by chance pertain to the untaught shapester.

3. Past and present rates.

I am convinced, upon inquiry, that little or no change has taken place in the prices which I have named during the last five years. But the wages of domestic female servants have materially advanced, and may now be set down at from $43.74 to $77.76 a year, with weekly allowance for their breakfast and tea. Exceptional cases of both higher and lower wages may be found in that class of servants whose aptitudes are so widely variant and command accordingly so great differences in the rates of compensation.

4. The present state of trade.

The manufacture of underclothing is the largest of the industries at this place. But the establishments are merely the shops, to which the materials are brought from English and Scotch ports, and to which they are at once returned on being manufactured. It is therefore at those ports and not here that inquiry should be made as to the prosperity of the business. It is, however, most pertinent to remark that the mills are at work, and afford apparently undiminished employment for the large numbers who have for a considerable time derived subsistence therefrom. The basis of most of the business of this port is agriculture, which is, and during the last seven years has been, prosperous; and consequently the trade and commerce, ministering to its wants, have been and continue to be in a fair degree prosperous. In this category may be named the manufacture of various artificial manures; the cure of bacon and hams; the importation of corn and the grinding of it, and distribution of its products; the importation and manufacture of timber, mainly from British America, but to some extent from the Southern States of the Union; a small but growing importation from the United States of agricultural and other tools of wood and hardware. Flax holds a good place among the products of the farm, and is always, I think, grown from imported seed.

5. Paper money.

The money in circulation is mainly the notes of the chartered banks of the denomination of one pound and upwards. These institutions are not numerous, but their branches, with managers under the control of the directors of the principal bank, are found in every town and village in Ireland. Unbounded confidence is reposed in them. I have not succeeded in my endeavors to ascertain the ratio between coin and paper in the actual circulation.

ARTHUR LIVERMORE.

CONSULATE OF THE UNITED STATES,
Londonderry, *May* 15, 1878.

SCOTLAND.

Report, by Consul Robeson, of Leith, on labor, rates of wages, cost of living, and paper money in Scotlvnd.

I had the honor duly to receive your Circular of date 11th April last; and, in accordance with the directions therein contained, in reference to certain points connected with the extension of the trade between the United States and foreign countries, I have now to report as follows:

RATES OF WAGES OF AGRICULTURAL LABORERS.

Between 1865 and 1873 the wages of agricultural laborers in Scotland advanced about 15 per cent.; and naturally, with such a large increase in such a short period, the rise since 1873 has been more moderate; about 10 per cent. The exact rate of wages paid to farm laborers varies slightly in different parts of the country. Estimates referring to different districts, for one year, are as follows:

The Lothians and east of Scotland.

1873.		1878.	
Free cottage, garden, and allowances of fire, food, &c., amounting to about	$105 60	Free cottage, &c., and allowances, slightly increased to	$108 00
Money wages	112 80	Money wages	134 40
	218 40		242 40

Increase since 1873, $24.

Day-laborers in the Lothians receive from 40 to 84 cents per day, according to the quality of the labor and the exigencies of the time. In 1873 they had fully 10 per cent. less than at present.

Southwest of Scotland.

I. MARRIED MEN.

1873.		1878.	
Allowance of meal and potatoes, with free cottage and garden, valued at	$67 20	Allowance of meal and potatoes, with free cottage and garden	$67 20
Money wages	144 00	Money wages	163 20
	211 20		230 40

Increase since 1873, $19.20.

II. SINGLE MEN.

1873.		1878.	
Board and lodging, equal in value to	$74 80	Board and lodging, &c., equal to	$74 80
Money wages	136 80	Money wages	153 60
	211 60		228 40

Increase since 1873, $16.80.

III. WOMEN.

1873.		1878.	
Board and lodging, &c., equal to	$67 20	Board and lodging, &c., equal to	$67 20
Money wages	60 00	Money wages	76 80
	127 20		144 00

Increase since 1873, $16.80.

Day-laborers received from 36 to 48 cents per day in 1873; now they receive about 72 cents per day.

Central counties, Perthshire, &c.

In these counties the rate of remuneration is about the same as in the southwest; rather less money and more perquisites being given in this case. The increase since 1873 is estimated at over 12 per cent.

Northeastern counties.

(From Aberdeen to Inverness.)

I. MARRIED MEN.

1873.		1878.	
1. Cottage	$14 40	1. }	
2. 6½ bolls oatmeal *	31 20	2. }	
3. Pint of milk per day, at 8 cents.	29 12	3. } Same	$89 12
4. Four loads peat, at $1.20	4 80	4. }	
5. Allowance of potatoes	9 60	5. }	
6. Money wages	108 00	6. Money wages	132 00
	197 12		221 12

Increase since 1873, $24.

II. SINGLE MEN.

1873.		1878.	
1. 6½ bolls oatmeal	$31 20	1. }	
2. Pint milk per day, at 8 cents	29 12	2. } Same	$67 52
3. Fire and houseroom	7 20	3. }	
4. Money wages	127 20	4. Money wages	153 60
	194 72		221 12

Increase since 1873, $26.40.

Female kitchen-servants, in addition to board and lodging, got about $55.20 in 1873, and now they get about $76.80 per annum. Women working outside got 36 cents per day in 1873, now they get 44 to 48 cents. Male day-laborers got 68 cents per day in 1873, and now they get 80 cents.

Extreme northern counties.

MARRIED MEN.

1873.		1878.	
1. Cottage	$9 60	1. }	
2. 10 to 12 bolls oatmeal	52 80	2. }	
3. Milk, say	21 60	3. } Same	$110 40
4. Potatoes	14 40	4. }	
5. 2½ tons coals	12 00	5. }	
6. Money wages	64 80	6. Money wages	76 80
	175 20		187 20

Increase since 1873, $12.

There is a slight difference in the form in which single men are paid, but the value of the remuneration is about the same as that received by married men. Day male laborers get from 48 cents to 72 cents a day, without any allowances; the increase to this class since 1873 being about 12 per cent.

*A boll equals four American bushels.

WOMEN.

(For housework.)

1873.		1878.	
Board and lodging	$62 40	Board and lodging	$62 40
Money wages	28 80	Money wages	38 40
	91 20		100 80

Increase since 1873, $9.60.

Some women employed by the day at field-work get about 24 cents per day.

These figures represent the *average* rate paid in the different districts named.

Many skilled or specially trustworthy servants receive considerably more than the rates specified, while a few inferior hands have to content themselves with a little less. Grieves, or farm managers, frequently receive as much as $288 per annum including perquisites, while specially capable foremen and cattlemen sometimes get $172.80 to $192 a year, with the usual allowances. As a rule, in the districts where cattle-feeding or cattle-breeding, or both, are carried on extensively, the better class of cattlemen are paid higher wages by from $5 to $10 per annum than horsemen. This is particularly the case in the northern counties, where plowmen are paid with about 20 per cent. less wages than in the neighboring counties of Moray, Banff, and Aberdeen and farther south. The main cause of this great difference in two parts so closely situated is probably to be found in the fact that the servants of the northern counties are natives of the districts in which they serve, being born perhaps on the very farm on which they are engaged, and attached to their native spot with all the characteristic clannish devotion of the Celtic race. Taking Scotland as a whole, the following is about as reliable an estimate as can be given of the average yearly rate of wages paid to plowmen now and five years ago.

1873.		1878.	
Allowances in kind	$74 40	Allowances in kind	$74 40
Money	129 60	Money	148 80
	204 00		223 20

Increase since 1873, $19.20.

HOW THE AGRICULTURAL LABORERS LIVE.

With regard to the hiring of agricultural servants, the practice most general in Scotland is half-yearly engagements entered into at feeing or hiring markets held at convenient centers in May and November. From many circumstances the system is regarded as unsatisfactory, and at the present time efforts are being made to abolish it. In many places engagements are effected through "registers," which are gradually superseding the feeing markets. In the majority of cases married men are paid monthly and single men half-yearly.

There are three systems of "putting up" servants on Scottish farms, viz: in kitchens, bothies, and cottages. The "kitchen" system was at one time very general in most parts of Scotland, but the widening of the breach between master and servant in the social scale has made it less popular, and it is now confined mainly to two opposite angles of Scotland—the southwest and northeast. The "bothy" system is fortunately also on the wane, its headquarters being now in a few central counties, notably Perth and Forfar. The "cottage" system abounds principally in the extreme northern counties, in Fifeshire and the three Lothians, while it exists to a lesser or greater extent all over Scotland.

Of these three systems, the "cottage" or family system is beyond all comparison the best, and it is pleasing to be able to say that it is on the increase. In districts where there are no cottages, servants must either remain single or send their wives and families away to live in towns and villages, perhaps five or ten miles distant from the scene of their labors, and where they can visit them only every third or fourth Sunday. And the moral tone which pervades these "bothies," institutions free from all sort of restraint, is anything but satisfactory.

Married servants who occupy cottages with their families, as a rule, live a comfortable, happy, and contented life, giving their children a good elementary education, and also, in most cases, a healthy moral upbringing. It is scarcely necessary to say that children brought up in these cottages on farms are far more likely to make good farm-laborers than the children of farm-servants whose wives and families are compelled to live in towns and villages.

There is little variety in the food of the Scottish peasant; it is plain but substantial, consisting almost wholly of oatmeal in various forms, potatoes, and milk, with a little meat and beer added in harvest. With plain oatmeal, milk, and potatoes it is possible for a man to feed himself at about $1.15 per week.

No class of workmen in this country is more handsomely remunerated for their labor than farm-servants. While the artisans in towns and cities have had their wages greatly advanced during the past few years, the corresponding increase in the cost of living in towns and the increased expensiveness of the customs of life among artisans have so counterbalanced the rise in wages, that their free balance at the end of the year is very little, if any, larger than when their wages were barely two-fifths of what they are now. With farm-servants the case is different. Their board and lodging have always been included as part of their wages, and thus the great increase in the money portion of their remuneration is in no way affected by any advance that may have taken place in the cost of living; and as to clothing, it can hardly be said that the really necessary cost is higher, to any appreciable extent, than thirty or forty years ago. The principal articles of clothing were almost as costly when wages were barely one-third of their present rate as they are now, and therefore the only increase in the expenditure under this head arises from the altered tastes of the people, or a sort of craving that has arisen among peasants, as among other classes, for greater display and variety of dress. This is especially the case in regard to women-servants, the majority of whom spend every spare shilling in dress or on ornaments.

But for this extravagance in dress a very large amount of money might be saved among Scotch farm-servants. A married man with a family dependent upon him of course needs to exercise strict economy to make ends meet; but an unmarried plowman if thrifty and temperate in his habits, might save as much money as any other workman in the country. Out of his $144 or $154 a year he has only to clothe himself and pay for washing and such necessaries, purchase a little tobacco, and meet "incidental" or two or three holidays during the year, all of which, without going to excess in any case, should not cost him more than $57.60 at the most. Indeed, a careful plowman can clothe himself decently and comfortably at about $30 per annum, so that the above estimate of $57.60 may be taken as on the safe side. It will thus be seen that an unmarried plowman might very easily save from $86 to $96 a year. It is pleasing to be able to say that a good many do lay by a little; but it cannot be denied that the majority of young plowmen in Scotland squander almost the whole of their earnings. On the whole, Scottish farm-laborers are the opposite of saving and thrifty.

Servant girls might dress respectably and be provided with all other necessaries, exclusive of food, at about $40 a year; and thus they also ought to store up a little of their earnings. Their surplusses, however, melt away in dress.

TRADES' WAGES.

Railways and railway-shops.—The following are the rates of wages paid to the various classes of workmen employed upon railways in Scotland in 1873 and at the present time:

Description.	1873.	1878.
	Per week.	Per week.
Passenger department:		
Passenger guards	$4 80 to $6 00	$5 04 to $6 48
Goods guards	5 28 to 6 96	5 76 to 7 20
Block signal-men	4 56 to 5 04	5 00 to 5 50
Pointsmen	4 32 to 4 56	4 32 to 4 80
Ordinary station-porters	4 00 to 4 20	4 00 to 4 20
Porters in Edinburgh	4 32 to 4 56	4 32 to 4 56
Goods porters	4 32 to 4 56	4 32 to 4 80
Goods porters in Edinburgh	4 80	5 04
Foremen in goods department	4 80 to 5 57	4 80 to 5 76
NOTE.—Sunday duty is paid for in addition to the above.		
Engineer's department:		
Chief foremen	5 76 to 6 48	6 76 to 6 48
Second foremen	5 28 to 5 52	5 04 to 5 28
Ordinary surfacemen	4 56	4 32
Special squads	4 80 to 5 04	4 56 to 4 80
	Rate per day of 12 hours.	Rate per day of 12 hours.
Locomotive department:		
Passenger-engine drivers	$1 44 to $1 68	$1 44 to $1 68
Goods engine drivers	1 08 to 1 56	1 20 to 1 56
Passenger firemen	72 to 84	84 to 96
Goods firemen	72 to 84	76 to 84
Cleaners	56 to 64	Usually 04
Running shop-fitters	1 08 to 1 16	1 08 to 1 28
Molders	1 00 to 1 28	1 08 to 1 28
Dressers	80 to 1 00	1 00 to 1 10
Laborers	70	72
Pattern-makers	1 00 to 1 25	1 06 to 1 35
Blacksmiths	1 06 to 1 20	1 06 to 1 25
Strikers	72 to 76	76
Boltmakers	1 08 to 1 20	1 12 to 1 25
Springmakers	1 00 to 1 15	1 15 to 1 25
Turners	1 00 to 1 25	1 00 to 1 25
Brassfinishers	1 10 to 1 10	1 15 to 1 20
Slotters	1 00 to 1 10	1 00 to 1 10
Planers	80 to 1 00	88 to 1 05
Fitters	95 to 1 20	95 to 1 25
Tinsmiths	1 15	1 10 to 1 20
Engine-fitters	1 00 to 1 15	1 00 to 1 25
Erectors	1 00 to 1 25	1 00 to 1 32
Boiler-makers	1 00 to 1 25	1 10 to 1 25
Joiners	1 00	1 00 to 1 25
Woodturners, sawyers, &c	1 00	1 00 to 1 10
Carriage-builders	1 05 to 1 10	1 15 to 1 30
Carriage-painters	1 05	1 15 to 1 30
Carriage-trimmers	88 to 1 00	1 05 to 1 25

Linen-weavers.—In the linen trade no important change has been made in the scale of wages paid to workmen during the last five years.

For the past few months, however, there appears to be a tendency toward reduction; but at present the following is the average wages paid now and for the last five years:

Male workers (mechanics)	per week..	$5 75 to $6 00
(ordinary)	do.....	4 30 to 4 56
Female workers (age 16 to 30)	do.....	2 05 to 2 65
(age 13 to 16)	do.....	1 30 to 1 70

NOTE.—56½ hours one week.

WAGES IN LEITH.

The following are the number of workmen employed at the docks in Leith since 1874 and the wages paid to them since that time:

Description.	1874.		1875.		1876.		1877.		1878.	
	Number of men.	Per day.	Number of men.	Per day.	Number of men.	Per day.	Number of men.	Per day.	Number of men.	Per day.
Carpenters and joiners	20	$1 40	18	$1 40	18	$1 30	21	$1 30	20	$1 25
Blacksmiths	5	1 30	5	1 30	5	1 15	6	1 10	6	1 05
Hammermen	5	80	5	85	5	85	6	85	6	80
Fitters	4	1 36	4	1 40	4	1 40	6	1 40	8	1 30
Engine-drivers	......	......	3	1 10	6	1 20	12	1 15	16	1 10
Engine-shinters	......	......	3	1 00	4	1 10	6	1 05	6	1 05
Masons	3	1 44	30	1 70	52	1 62	32	1 62	69	1 50
Laborers of all kinds	58	90	204	90	450	90	662	84	844	80

The above wages are per day of 10 hours, except in the case of the masons, whose day is only 9 hours.

Taking the various classes of laborers within my district in their order, the following are the rates of wages paid to them respectively:

Blacksmiths, per week of 51 hours, receive $4.55 to $7.68. The average weekly wage of the trade is $6.36, and during the last five years has risen about $1.25 per week.

Bookbinders, per week of 54 hours, get $8.50. The increase for the last five years has been about $1 per week.

Bookfolders, per week of 54 hours, get $2.50. The workers here are chiefly women and boys and girls.

Brassfounders, per week of 51 hours, get from $3.70 to $8.50. The average is $6.15 per week, and the increase for the past five years has been 10 per cent.

Boot and shoe makers, per week of 60 hours, earn $6 on an average. As a rule, however, they work by piece-work.

Builders, per week of 51 hours, $8.88.

Cabinet-makers, per week of 51 hours, earn on an average $7.20. They work by piece-work to a great extent and can make from 15 to 17 cents per hour. There has been no appreciable rise here during the last five years.

Coachmakers, per week of 51 hours, receive from $4.50 to $9.12. There are many branches of this trade, but the average wage is $6.75 per week, and has risen $1 in the last five years.

Compositors make varying wages. Those on the night shift of newspapers make from $11 to $18 per week, and even more sometimes. As an instance of weekly wages, those on the day-shift of the *Scotsman* receive $7.80 per week and on the night-shift $9.60. The day-hands work 51¼ hours per week and the night-hands 48 hours. Those in publishing establishments receive for a week of 54 hours $6.75.

Engineers, per week of 51 hours, $4.55 to $7.68; average $6.36 per week. Increase for preceding five years $1.25.

Horseshoers, per week of 51 hours, $4.80 to $7.20; average per week $6.25. No appreciable increase.

Ironmolders, per week of 51 hours, get from $7.20 to $9.50; increase, about 25 cents in a week during the last five years.

Joiners, per week of 51 hours, receive $8.65; being an increase of $1.50 during the previous five years.

Laborers, per week, receive from $4.50 to $6.20; being an increase of about $1.20 in five years.

Lathsplitters, per week of 51 hours, get $8.40; showing an increase of $1 in a week.

Masons, per week of 51 hours, get $8.20. There has been a rise here in mason's wages, but latterly they have been reduced.

Millwrights, per week of 51 hours, get $6.65. No appreciable increase for some years.

Painters, per week of 51 hours, get $7.65; a rise of about $1.45 in a week in the last few years.

Plasterers, per week of 51 hours, get $10.20; being an increase in five years of $2 in a week.

Plumbers, per week of 51 hours, get $6.25 to $7.20; being an increase since 1873 of $1.25 in a week.

Press and machine winders, per week of 56 hours, get $5.50 to $6.50; a rise of 25 cents in a week.

Printers (machine), per week of 54 hours, receive $8; a rise of $1 in a week in five years.

Saddlers, per week of 51 hours, get $4.80 to $8, the average $6; the increase being $1 in a week in five years.

Stereotypers, per week of 54 hours, get $7.70; being an increase of 50 cents since 1873.

Tailors.—These work generally by the piece. Fine workers get $6.75 per week of 56 hours; and this may also be taken as the average of the piece-workers. Increase 72 cents.

Tinplate-workers, per week of 51 hours, get $4.80 to $9; average $6.90. Many work by the piece.

Turners, per week of 51 hours, get $6.40; a rise of about 30 cents since 1873.

Typefounders.—These are all on piece-work, and earn from $5.60 to $9.50 per week of 56 hours. Increase 5 per cent. in five years.

Typographical printers are mostly on piece-work, and earn $5.30 to $6.25 per week of 56 hours. Time-workers receive about $6.70 per week; a rise of 60 cents since 1873.

Warehousemen receive from $6 to $9 per week; a rise of from 50 cents to $1 since 1873.

Slaters, per week of 51 hours, receive $8.66; being a rise of $1.60 since 1873.

PAPER MONEY.

In this country paper money is equal in value to gold or silver. The following shows the amount of paper in circulation by the various Scotch banks for the month ending 8th June, 1878, with the amount of gold and silver held in reserve:

Paper circulation in Scotland.

Name of bank.	Head office.	Authorized circulation.	Average circulation during the four weeks ending June 8, 1878.			Average amount of coin held during the four weeks ending June 8, 1878.		
			£5 and upwards.	Under £5.	Total.	Gold.	Silver.	Total.
Bank of Scotland	Edinburgh	£343, 418	£273, 195	£499, 095	£772, 290	£458, 268	£76, 044	£534, 312
Royal Bank	Edinburgh	216, 451	305, 013	498, 609	803, 622	599, 377	82, 642	682, 019
British Linen Bank	Edinburgh	438, 024	205, 993	419, 269	625, 262	191, 917	55, 729	247, 646
Commercial Bank	Edinburgh	374, 880	285, 146	584, 392	869, 539	548, 178	44, 665	592, 844
National Bank	Edinburgh	297, 024	217, 662	450, 003	667, 665	388, 371	53, 456	441, 827
Union Bank	Edinburgh	454, 346	311, 692	555, 068	866, 760	444, 738	80, 200	524, 938
Aberdeen Town and County Bank	Aberdeen	70, 133	141, 496	135, 261	276, 757	213, 781	17, 138	230, 919
North of Scotland Bank	Aberdeen	154, 319	219, 820	198, 711	418, 531	273, 462	12, 646	286, 108
Clydesdale Bank	Glasgow	274, 321	222, 543	363, 896	586, 440	314, 172	68, 446	382, 618
City of Glasgow Bank	Glasgow	72, 921	234, 436	391, 327	625, 763	563, 235	44, 535	607, 770
Caledonian Bank	Inverness	53, 434	50, 893	89, 555	140, 448	90, 665	7, 439	98, 104

COST OF LIVING.

In regard to the cost of the necessaries of life to the laboring classes other than agricultural, this depends always upon the number of the family. Within my district these classes live in towns, where rents are very high and the style and necessities of life involve a large expenditure for people of all trades and professions. In the case of a family of five persons (husband and wife and three children, on an average), with an income of $6 per week, the cost of living is as follows:

Income, $6 per week			$312 00
Rent		$62 40	
Taxes, gas, fuel, school-fees, &c		19 60	
Clothing		48 00	
Leaving for food $3.50 per week; used thus:			
Bread ......per day	$0 16		
Milk ......do	04		
Meat ......do	12		
Butter and eggs ......do	10		
Potatoes ......do	06		
Vegetables ......do	02		
	50=182 00		
			$312 00

It is therefore impossible for the average ordinary workman to save, as each lives up to his income. It may fairly be estimated that within the last five years the income of all classes of workmen has increased by about 10 per cent., and the cost of living has, in the same time, risen about 15 per cent. Previously, the average workingman had the opportunity of saving about 25 cents per week, when his income was $5.50 per week and the cost of living about $5 or $5.15 per week; but the rise in the cost of the necessaries of life beyond the advance in income has rendered this impossible at the present time. In connection with this, it is somewhat surprising that though there has been a system of great importation of cattle and dead meat into this country for some time, this has not in the least diminished the cost of meat or of any other article of the necessaries of life.

Strikes are of frequent occurrence in all trades, but as a rule they result in impoverishing the workman, who has in the end to return to his previous wage or accept the employer's terms.

JOHN T. ROBESON.

UNITED STATES CONSULATE,
Leith, July 1, 1878.

DUNFERMLINE.

Report, by Vice-Consul Scidmore, on the rates of wages, cost of living to the laboring classes, state of trade, and banks and banking (for Scotland), in Dunfermline and vicinity.

In conformity with the Department Circular of April 11, 1878, I have now the honor to submit the following report upon the subjects therein referred to.

First. The rates of wages and the hours of labor in various avocations in Dunfermline and vicinity are set forth in the statement marked No. 1.

Second. The cost of living to the laboring classes, or the prices paid for what may be termed the necessaries of life, will found in the statement herewith, marked No. 2.

Third and Fourth. So far as I can learn, the present remuneration of labor, as compared with rates prevailing five years ago, is very low, there having been a steady decline in this respect in nearly all trades during the succeeding years.

The coal trade.—In coal-mining, which is one of the leading industries of this district, the depression is very marked, miners now receiving not one half the wages obtainable in 1873.

In this connection, Mr. Ralph Moore, inspector of mines for the eastern district of Scotland, in his report for the year 1877, says:

During the past year the mining industry has been in a most depressed state, and fewer coals were sold than in 1876. Many of the new collieries which were projected during the period when high prices prevailed—1871, 1872, 1873—have now been sunk, and are turning out large quantities of coal notwithstanding this dull trade. The result is that many of the older collieries have had to give way, and prices, in the competition for trade, have been reduced to the lowest point, and miners' wages were reduced in some instances, but not to any extent. In the counties of Fife and Clackmannan, where the output is about one-sixth of the whole district, there was a strike and lock-out which lasted fifteen weeks, and the output was only 1,566,635 tons in 1877 against 2,022,635 tons in 1876. There were no other strikes. Twenty-four pits have been abandoned and the plans sent to the Home Office, and ten pits have been commenced.

The linen trade.—In this important industry the condition is almost as equally cheerless as in the coal trade. Overproduction and a slackening in the demand in the United States have, during the past five years, brought the linen trade to sore straits.

Mr. Walker, inspector of factories, in his report for the half-year ending October 31, 1877, says:

It is very distressing, in visiting the manufacturing districts throughout the country, to hear complaints of the bad state of trade so general. Of course, many persons have been thrown out of employment, although the number is not so great as might be expected, even in the manufacturing districts, where the trade is worst. The flax and jute trades in this immediate district are suffering much from present depression, and it is unfortunate that as yet there is no immediate prospect of improvement. As an evidence of the present bad state of trade, I may mention that, while some works were in operation near a railway station in the north of England, the revenue at that station averaged about $2,000 a month. These works have been standing idle for some time; and I am informed, on good authority, that now the receipts at that station are barely sufficient to pay the wages of the station-master and porter.

The iron trade.—Particular note is made of the depression in the iron trade. Mr. Walker says:

While, as I have stated, all the industries of the country coming under my observation are at present more or less depressed, I am not aware of any of them being more so than the iron trade in the north of England and Scotland. One of the reasons assigned is the damaging effects of foreign competition. Within the last year or two a large railway station has been erected at Glasgow, and it is a well-known fact that all the iron required in its construction was brought from Belgium. As Glasgow forms the center of the iron trade in Scotland, the circumstance above referred to is significant and startling.

The pictures presented by these gentlemen in their official reports have not been improved since the time of their writing, and the prospect for the future presents as little encouragement. While there has been a considerable decline in wages during the past five years, the prices of the necessaries of life have not generally been reduced in the same proportion. The only notable exception to this statement that now occurs to me is in the matter of butchers' meat, which during the last two years has been supplied in such steadily-increasing quantities from the United States and Canada at such low prices as to compel a reduction in the price of domestic meat.

Inclosures 3, 4, 5, 6, and 7, herewith, cover the quotations of discounts, banks and banking, and railway statistics of Scotland.

For much of the statistical information contained in the statements herewith following I am indebted to the Dunfermline agent of the Bank of Scotland, Mr. John Barclay, and to the yearly reports by Messrs. Oliver & Boyd, of Edinburgh, and Mr. G. B. Weiland, secretary of the North British Railway Company.

GEO. H. SCIDMORE.

UNITED STATES CONSULATE,
Dunfermline, June 1, 1878.

---

1. *Statement showing the rates of wages and the number of hours of labor in various occupations at Dunfermline and in the surrounding district.*

Occupations.	Wages.	Hours of labor.
Blacksmiths ... weekly ..	$6 56	9 per day.
Bleachers (women) ... do ...	3 04	9½ per day.
Bricklayers ... daily ..	1 62	9 per day.
Bookbinders ... weekly ..	6 08	56 per week.
Cabinet-makers ... minimum weekly ..	6 08	9 per day.
Do ... maximum weekly ..	7 29	Do.
Compositors ... weekly ..	6 08	56 per week.
Carpenters and joiners ... minimum daily ..	1 26	9 per day.
Do ... maximum daily ..	1 44	Do.
Coachmen ... minimum weekly ..	3 88	
Do ... maximum weekly ..	4 86	
Cooks ... minimum yearly ..	77 86	
Do ... maximum yearly ..	121 65	
Coopers ... weekly ..	6 08	Do.
Dyers ... minimum weekly ..	6 80	Do.
Do ... maximum weekly ..	7 30	Do.
Engineers, not railway ... minimum weekly ..	6 32	Do.
Do ... maximum weekly ..	6 80	Do.
Firemen, not railway ... minimum weekly ..	4 38	Do.
Do ... maximum weekly ..	4 86	Do.
Footmen ... minimum weekly ..	3 64	
Do ... maximum weekly ..	4 14	
Founders, brass ... minimum weekly ..	6 32	56 per week.
Do ... maximum weekly ..	6 56	Do.
Factory hands:		
Cardlacers (women) ... weekly ..	2 67	Do.
Clothpickers (women) ... do ...	2 67	Do.
Cloth-inspectors (men) ... do ...	5 58	Do.
Dressers (men) ... do ...	6 32	Do.
Drawers (women) ... do ...	2 67	Do.
Engine-keepers (men) ... do ...	5 82	Do.
Firemen (men) ... do ...	5 82	Do.
Joiners (men) ... do ...	6 32	Do.
Mechanics (men) ... do ...	8 27	Do.
Tenters (men) ... do ...	6 56	Do.
Warpwinders (women) ... do ...	3 16	Do.
Warpers (women) ... do ...	3 76	Do.
Weavers (women) ... minimum weekly ..	96	Do.
Do ... maximum weekly ..	4 86	Do.
Weftwinders (women) ... minimum weekly ..	3 28	Do.
Do ... maximum weekly ..	4 14	Do.
Yarnstorekeepers (men) ... weekly ..	4 38	Do.
Gardeners ... minimum weekly ..	4 38	
Do ... maximum weekly ..	5 82	
Laborers ... minimum daily ..	60	9 per day.
Do ... maximum daily ..	84	Do.
Laborers, agricultural (women) ... minimum daily ..	30	Do.
Do ... maximum daily ..	48	Do.
Laborers, agricultural (men) ... minimum weekly ..	3 88	10 per day.
Do ... maximum weekly ..	4 86	Do.
Lithographers ... weekly ..	6 16	56 per week.
Masons ... daily ..	1 44	9 per day.
Machinists ... weekly ..	6 56	Do.
*Miners, coal ... minimum daily ..	84	7 per day.
Do ... maximum daily ..	1 08	Do.
Molders ... minimum weekly ..	8 27	9 per day.
Do ... maximum weekly ..	9 24	Do.

* The miner supplies his own tools and oil, and works four or five days per week.

I.—*Statement showing the rates of wages, &c.*—Continued.

Occupations.	Wages.	Hours of labor.
Painters ... daily..	$1 35	9 per day.
Plasterers ... minimum daily..	1 62	Do.
Do ... maximum daily..	1 80	Do.
Plumbers ... minimum weekly..	5 82	10 per day.
Do ... maximum weekly..	6 80	Do.
Policemen ... minimum weekly..	4 86	12 per day.
Do ... maximum weekly..	5 34	Do.
Pressmen ... weekly..	6 32	56 per week.
Quarrymen ... minimum daily..	72	9 per day.
Do ... maximum daily..	84	Do.
Railway hands:		
Passenger drivers ... minimum daily..	1 56	12 per day.
Do ... maximum daily..	1 68	Do.
Passenger firemen ... minimum daily..	84	Do.
Do ... maximum daily..	96	Do.
Goods drivers ... minimum daily..	1 20	Do.
Do ... maximum daily..	1 50	Do.
Goods firemen ... minimum daily..	72	Do.
Do ... maximum daily..	92	Do.
Cleaners ... minimum daily..	48	Do.
Do ... maximum daily..	64	Do.
Pointsmen ... minimum weekly..	4 62	
Do ... maximum weekly..	4 86	
Passenger guards ... minimum weekly..	5 11	
Do ... maximum weekly..	6 56	
Passenger porters ... minimum weekly..	4 14	
Do ... maximum weekly..	4 38	
Goods guards ... minimum weekly..	5 82	
Do ... maximum weekly..	7 29	
Goods porters ... minimum weekly..	4 86	
Do ... maximum weekly..	5 11	
Mechanics ... minimum daily..	1 00	8¼ per day.
Do ... maximum daily..	1 20	Do.
Laborers ... weekly..	4 38	Do.
Surfacemen, foremen ... minimum weekly..	5 11	
Do ... maximum weekly..	5 34	
Surfacemen, special ... minimum weekly..	4 62	
Do ... maximum weekly..	4 86	
*Seamen, 1st mates ... monthly..	26 76	
*2d mates ... do ...	21 89	
*cooks and stewards ... do ...	21 89	
*A B's ... do ...	14 59	
*ordinary ... do ...	10 94	
†Stevedores ... minimum daily..	1 32	
Do ... maximum daily..	1 80	
Servants, domestic maid ... minimum yearly..	48 66	
Do ... maximum yearly..	87 59	
Shepherds ... weekly..	4 86	
Turners ... minimum weekly..	6 56	9 per day.
Do ... maximum weekly..	6 80	Do.
Wheelwrights ... minimum daily..	1 26	Do.
Do ... maximum daily..	1 44	Do.

* Usually receive one month's advance wages.
† For "trimming" coal at port of embarkation, threepence per ton.

2.—*Statement showing the retail prices of certain household necessaries, as prevailing at Dunfermline.*

Bread	4-pound loaf..	$0 14 to $0 16
Butter	per pound..	28 to 40
Barley	do ...	04
Cheese	do ...	14 to 40
Coffee	do ...	40 to 48
Currants	do ...	10
Coal	per ton..	2 40 to 2 91
Chickens	per pair..	96 to 1 32
Ducks	do ...	96 to 1 20
Eggs	per dozen..	24 to 26
Flour, corn	per pound..	12
Wheat	per peck..	30 to 36
United States	per barrel..	6 54 to 9 24
Canadian	do ...	7 25 to 9 24

Gas	per 1,000 cubic feet..		$1 03
Hares	each..		96
Marmalade	per pound..	$0 12 to	14
Meat, boiling beef	do	12 to	22
steak	do	24 to	34
mutton	do	20 to	24
lamb	do		36
veal	do	24 to	30
pork	do	14 to	16
smoked ham	do	24 to	28
Milk	per pint..		06
Mustard	per pound..		40
Meal, barley-meal	per peck..		30
brosemeal	do	28 to	32
oatmeal	do	30 to	36
Peas, green	per pound..		05
Pickles	per quart bottle..	18 to	22
Potatoes	per stone..	24 to	30
Pigeons	per pair..	28 to	32
Rabbits	each..	20 to	30
Raisins	per pound..		12
Rice	do		06
Sugar, brown	do	07 to	08
white	do	09 to	12
Soda, baking	do		08
washing	do		02
Starch	do		14
Sirup	do		06
Sago	do		10
Tapioca	do		16
Tea	do	40 to	96

NOTE.—House-rent can be approximately estimated by calculating, as the landlord's net profit, 4½ per cent. of the value of the property.

3. *Table showing the fluctuations in the rate of discount charged by the banks in Edinburgh and Glasgow and interest allowed on deposits since August 1, 1873.*

Date.	Minimum rate per cent. of—		Interest, per cent. allowed on—			Number of days at which rate continued.
	Discount on bills of three months currency.	Interest on cash credit accounts.	Daily balances.	Minimum monthly balances.	Deposit receipts.	
1873—Aug. 1	*4	5	1	1½	2½	21
Aug. 22	*3½	4½	1	1½	2	35
Sept. 26	*4½	5	1	1½	3	3
Sept. 29	*5½	6	1	2	4	16
Oct. 15	6	6½	1½	2½	4½	5
Oct. 20	7	7	2	3	5	14
Nov. 3	8	8	2½	3½	5½	5
Nov. 8	9	9	2½	3½	6	12
Nov. 20	8	8	2½	3½	5½	8
Nov. 28	6	6½	1½	2½	4½	7
Dec. 5	*5½	6	1	2	4	6
Dec. 11	*5	5½	1	1½	3½	28
1874—Jan. 9	*4½	5	1	1½	3	6
Jan. 15	*4	5	1	1½	2½	105
May 1	*4½	5	1	1½	3	28
May 29	*4	5	1	1½	2½	6
June 4	*3½	4½	1	1½	2	63
Aug. 6	*4½	5	1	1½	3	14
Aug. 20	*4	5	1	1½	2½	7
Aug. 27	*3½	4½	1	1½	2	50
Oct. 16	*4½	5	1	1½	3	31
Nov. 16	*5½	6	1	2	4	15
Dec. 1	6	6½	1½	2½	4½	37
1875—Jan. 7	*5½	6	1	2	4	7
Jan. 14	*4½	5	1	1½	3	14
Jan. 23	*3½	4½	1	1½	2	21
Feb. 18	*4	5	1	1½	2½	140
July 8	*3½	4½	1	1½	2	36
Aug. 13	*3	4½	1	1½	2	55
Oct. 7	*3½	4½	1	1½	2	7
Oct. 14	*4	5	1	1½	2½	8
Oct. 22	*4½	5	1	1½	3	27
Nov. 18	*3½	4½	1	1½	2	42
Dec. 30	*4½	5	1	1½	3	7
1876—Jan. 6	*5½	6	1	2	4	21
Jan. 27	*4½	5	1	1½	3	56
Mar. 23	*4	5	1	1½	2½	14
April 6	*3½	4½	1	1½	2	546
1877—Oct. 4	*4½	5	1	1½	3	7
Oct. 11	*5½	6	1	2	4	31
Nov. 10	*5	5½	1	1½	3½	19
Nov. 29	*4½	5	1	1½	3	42
1878—Jan. 10	*3½	4½	1	1½	2	25
Feb. 4	*3	4½	1	1½	2	24
Mar. 28	*3½	4½	1	1½	2	62
May 30	*3	4½	1	1½	2	....

* Bills on London one-half per cent. lower.

4. *Balance-sheets of Scottish banks for the year 1877.*

Established.	Name of bank.	Liabilities.								Assets.			
		Capital paid up.	Rest.	Dividends and balances.	Deposits.	Acceptances.	Drafts.	Notes.	Total liabilities.	Banking advances.	Buildings.	Banking reserves.	Total assets.
1695	Bank of Scotland	£1, 250, 000	£750, 000	£102, 081	£10, 409, 120	£2, 097, 162	£195, 159	£639, 156	£15, 442, 678	£10, 541, 733	£207, 755	£4, 693, 190	£15, 442, 678
1727	Royal Bank of Scotland	2, 000, 000	500, 000	133, 426	10, 549, 326	429, 185	175, 022	738, 941	14, 525, 900	10, 581, 493	249, 315	3, 695, 092	14, 525, 900
1746	British Linen Company Bank.	1, 000, 000	350, 000	206, 741	7, 611, 751	222, 282	243, 313	510, 639	10, 174, 726	7, 547, 742	136, 726	2, 490, 258	10, 174, 726
1810	Commercial Bank of Scotland	1, 000, 000	421, 333	88, 000	9, 197, 794	*445, 890	....	839, 759	11, 902, 776	8, 319, 905	155, 931	3, 517, 340	11, 992, 776
1825	National Bank of Scotland ...	1, 000, 000	500, 000	103, 465	11, 057, 841	1, 502, 756	184, 559	659, 986	15, 068, 607	10, 960, 035	131, 400	3, 977, 172	15, 068, 607
1825	Aberdeen Town and County Bank.	252, 000	126, 000	40, 193	1, 881, 172	....	....	217, 378	2, 516, 743	1, 912, 069	30, 512	565, 162	2, 516, 743
1830	Union Bank of Scotland	1, 000, 000	300, 000	154, 529	9, 666, 687	190, 182	197, 322	839, 317	12, 348, 037	8, 133, 421	167, 692	4, 046, 924	12, 348, 037
1836	North of Scotland Banking Company.	393, 780	202, 601	35, 075	2, 593, 442	....	....	342, 801	3, 567, 090	2, 791, 306	58, 982	716, 811	3, 567, [illegible]
1838	Clydesdale Banking Company	1, 000, 000	500, 000	148, 084	6, 625, 117	473, 205	154, 655	646, 441	9, 547, 502	7, 235, 594	148, 929	2, 162, 979	9, 547, 502
1838	Caledonian Banking Company	158, 000	75, 000	25, 166	1, 154, 818	....	....	123, 604	1, 528, 588	1, 007, 796	28, 262	492, 530	1, 528, 588
1839	City of Glasgow Bank	1, 000, 000	450, 000	148, 501	8, 382, 712	*1, 350, 335	....	763, 894	12, 095, 442	8, 758, 839	†257, 689	3, 078, 914	12, 095, 442
	Totals, 1877	10, 045, 780	4, 174, 334	1, 245, 261	79, 159, 780	6, 710, 997	1, 150, 030	6, 321, 016	108, 808, 098	77, 789, 533	1, 582, 193	20, 436, 372	108, 808, 098
	Totals, 1876	9, 795, 600	3, 833, 231	1, 193, 594	80, 142, 463	5, 707, 448	1, 791, 844	6, 297, 776	108, 761, 956	76, 899, 605	1, 506, 779	30, 355, 572	108, 761, 956
	Increase, + ; decrease, −	+250, 180	+341, 103	+51, 667	−982, 683	+‡1, 003, 549	−‡641, 814	+24, 140	+46, 142	+889, 928	+75, 414	−910, 200	+46, 142

* Including drafts. † Including advances. ‡ In 1876 the city bank separated acceptances and drafts.

5. *Statement showing the fluctuations in the prices of stocks and shares of the principal Scottish banks as publicly quoted in December of the years* 1873, 1874, 1875, 1876, 1877, *and on May* 31, 1878.

Name of bank.	Price, per £100 stock, and per share of those marked (*).					
	1873.	1874.	1875.	1876.	1877.	May 31, 1878.
	£ s. d.	£ s. d.	£ s. d.	£ s. d.	£ s. d.	£ s. d.
Bank of Scotland	292 0 0	303 0 0	313 0 0	308 0 0	319 0 0	322 0 0
Royal Bank of Scotland	106 0 0	230 15 0	228 0 0	235 0 0	232 0 0	225 0 0
British Linen Company Bank	272 0 0	291 0 0	295 0 0	300 0 0	306 0 0	311 10 0
Commercial Bank of Scotland	300 0 0	319 0 0	314 0 0	318 0 0	320 0 0	322 10 0
National Bank of Scotland	300 0 0	319 0 0	315 10 0	315 10 0	319 0 0	321 0 0
Union Bank of Scotland	285 0 0	292 0 0	269 0 0	280 0 0	277 10 0	268 10 0
Aberdeen Town and County Bank*	15 7 6	17 10 0	18 10 0	21 15 0	23 0 0	21 11 0
North of Scotland Banking Company*	9 5 0	11 0 0	11 17 6	12 15 0	13 15 0	13 10 0
Clydesdale Banking Company	263 10 0	284 0 0	275 0 0	277 0 0	281 0 0	273 0 0
City of Glasgow Bank	219 0 0	240 0 0	228 0 0	228 0 0	243 2 6	237 0 0
Caledonian Banking Company*	7 5 0	8 2 0	7 7 0	7 7 6	7 12 6	7 11 0

*The capital of banks marked with an asterisk is in shares. The Aberdeen Town and County Bank, £7 paid; the North of Scotland Banking Company, £4 paid; the Caledonian Banking Company, £2 10*s.* paid.

6. *Statement showing the number, the face-value, and the amount paid up of shares of the leading Scottish insurance companies, together with the market value of said shares from the year* 1873 *to date.*

Companies.	Number of shares.	Amount of each share.	Amount paid up.	Price per share.					
				1873.	1874.	1875.	1876.	1877.	May 31, 1878.
		£	£ s. d.	£ s. d.	£ s. d.	£ s. d.	£ s. d.	£ s. d.	£ s. d.
Caledonian Fire and Life	3,000	100	10 0 0	69 0 0	70 0 0	73 0 0	76 0 0	91 10 0	92 0 0
City of Glasgow Life	24,000	25	2 10 0	4 10 0	4 10 0	4 17 6	5 2 6	5 10 0	4 16 0
Edinburgh Life	5,000	100	15 0 0	31 10 0	31 10 0	30 0 0	38 0 0	40 0 0	....
English and Scottish Law Life	20,000	50	3 10 0	5 7 6	5 10 0	6 2 6	6 2 6	6 12 6	7 0 0
Life Association	10,000	40	8 15 0	27 10 0	25 0 0	25 10 0	29 0 0	32 7 6	....
North British and Mercantile	40,000	50	6 5 0	26 0 0	28 10 0	37 10 0	41 12 6	44 5 0	42 17 6
Northern Assurance	30,000	100	5 0 0	19 0 0	22 5 0	33 0 0	38 15 0	38 15 0	41 15 0
Scottish Commercial	100,000	10	1 0 0	1 6 0	1 18 0	2 10 0	2 17 0	2 18 0	2 10 0
Scottish Imperial	50,000	10	1 0 0	10 6	1 4 0	1 9 0	1 4 0	1 7 0	1 0 0
Scottish National Insurance	20,000	10	3 0 0	7 5 0	8 0 0	8 17 6	10 15 0	13 12 6	13 5 0
Scottish Provincial	20,000	50	3 0 0	6 7 6	6 10 0	7 10 0	9 17 6	11 2 6	....
Scottish Union Fire and Life	207,571	20	1 0 0	2 16 0	2 17 0	3 0 0	3 5 0	3 12 6	....
Standard Life	10,000	50	12 0 0	75 5 0	71 15 0	76 2 6	71 5 0	73 0 0	....

7. *Table showing the amount of paid-up capital, as at the 31st of December*, 1876, *and dividends on ordinary stock for the years* 1873 *to* 1877 *of the principal railways of the United Kingdom, with the prices of their shares, as publicly quoted in Edinburgh in December* 1873, 1874, 1875, 1876, 1877, *and on May* 31, 1878.

Railways.	Capital.		Dividends on ordinary stock.								Price per £100, ordinary stock.					
	Ordinary paid-up stock, including preferred and deferred ordinary stocks.	Guaranteed preference and debenture stocks and loans.	Second half of 1873.	First half of 1874.	Second half of 1874.	First half of 1875.	Second half of 1875.	First half of 1876.	Second half of 1876.	First half of 1877.	1873.	1874.	1875.	1876.	1877.	May 31, 1878.
			Pr. ct.	*Pr. ct.*	*Pr. ct.*	*Pr. ct.*	*Pr. ct.*	*Pr. ct.*	*Pr. ct.*	*Pr. ct.*						
Caledonian	£11, 337, 725	£19, 868, 229	4¼	2	5½	6¼	7½	6¼	7	6¼	£104½	£97½	£132¾	£120	£121½	£112
Glasgow and Southwestern	4, 777, 710	4, 255, 383	4	2½	3½	4	3¾	4	4½	4½	113½	99½	110¼	109¼	104	98¼
Great Northern of Scotland	877, 915	2, 604, 174	½	1⅛	½	3	2	3	1½	2¾	45¼	60	86	84	76¼	64½
Highland Railway	1, 470, 270	1, 794, 607	4	5	5	2	4¾	5	5	5	109	165	107	105½	105¼	105½
North British	6, 281, 691	20, 892, 050	None.	None.	1½	4	4½	3½	4	2	72¾	66½	123¼	106	87¾	84
Great Eastern	10, 942, 573	19, 579, 895	1	None.	None.	None.	1	None.	1⅛	None.	50¾	39¾	47⅞	49¼	49½	49⅞
Great Northern	10, 051, 777	17, 272, 348	8½	5½	8¼	5½	7½	4¼	6¾	4	138	139	137	134	116	113⅞
Great Western	14, 957, 211	44, 717, 497	6¾	4	5	3¼	3¾	4¾	4¼	3½	126¾	112¼	114¾	104½	90	100
Lancashire and Yorkshire	14, 116, 594	14, 353, 214	7	6	6½	6	6	5½	6¼	5¾	145	143	142	135	134½	132¼
London and Northwestern	31, 344, 578	37, 481, 560	8	6½	7¼	6¼	7¼	6	7¼	6	155½	148	146	145¼	144	147¾
London and Southwestern	8, 650, 263	11, 424, 122	6¼	4½	6¼	4¼	6½	4¾	6	4¾	108	114	124	128	130	138
London, Brighton and Southern Coast	6, 839, 943	12, 629, 959	5	1½	6¼	2¼	7¼	2¾	7¼	3	88¾	92¼	118	118	128	138½
London, Chatham and Dover	10, 190, 188	11, 426, 677	None.	None.	None.	None.	None.	None.	None.	None.	24¼	23	25½	21½	22	25¼
Manchester, Sheffield and Lincolnshire	5, 492, 553	15, 594, 202	3	½	3	1	4	¾	3¾	1	80¾	76½	84¼	70½	82½	82¾
Metropolitan	4, 158, 370	4, 033, 765	2	2½	3	3¾	4	4	4½	4½	69¾	73¼	101¼	106½	116¼	116¼
Midland	18, 809, 388	40, 605, 599	6½	5½	6½	6	6	5	5¾	5	138	135¼	143	130¾	126	127¼
Northeastern	19, 583, 294	33, 511, 370	10	7½	9¼	8½	8¾	7	7¾	6½	174½	165¾	166	155	149¾	140¼
Southeastern and Dover	8, 077, 949	11, 403, 055	6½	3½	6⅛	3¼	7½	3¾	7½	3½	108	112	130½	126	129	127⅞

GEO. H. SCIDMORE,
Vice-Consul and Consular Clerk.

UNITED STATES CONSULATE,
Dunfermline, Scotland, May 31, 1878.

DUNDEE.

Report, by Consul McDougall, on the (1) rates of wages; (2) cost of living; (3) present condition of trade; (4) currency of Scotland; and (5) business habits and systems; for the district of Dundee.

Referring to the Department Circular dated April 11, 1878, I now beg to reply to the points first, second, and third of said circular, by giving you—

1. Comparative statement of the number of hours worked per week by, and the rate of wages paid to, laborers of every class at Dundee during the past five years (1878 back to 1874 inclusive).

2. Statement showing the average value of commodities that may be termed the necessaries of life during the past five years. I have been most careful to get these particulars exact in every way, and have given you the rates of wages embraced in statement No. 1 and the prices of articles mentioned in statement No. 2 in United States gold.

1. *Comparative statement showing the number of hours worked per week by, and the rate of wages paid to, laborers of every class at Dundee during the past five years* (*1878 back to 1874, inclusive.*)

Occupation.	1878.			1877.			1876.			1875.			1874.		
	Wages per hour.	Per week.		Wages per hour.	Per week.		Wages per hour.	Per week.		Wages per hour.	Per week.		Wages per hour.	Per week.	
		Hours of labor.	Wages.		Hours of labor.	Wages.		Hours of labor.	Wages.		Hours of labor.	Wages.		Hours of labor.	Wages.
House-building trades:															
Bellhangers	$0 14	51	$7 14	$0 14	51	$7 14	$0 14	51	$7 14	$0 13	51	$6 63	$0 13	51	$6 63
Bricklayers	20	51	10 20	20	51	10 20	18	51	9 18	16	51	8 16	16	51	8 16
Bricklayers' laborers	13	51	6 63	13	51	6 63	13	51	6 63	12	51	6 12	12	51	6 12
Masons	16	51	8 16	17	51	8 67	18	51	9 18	20	51	10 20	16	51	8 16
Masons' laborers	12	51	6 12	13	51	6 63	13	51	6 63	13	51	6 63	12	51	6 12
Carpenters and joiners	15	51	7 65	16	51	8 16	15	51	7 65	14	51	7 14	13	51	6 63
Gasfitters and plumbers	17	51	8 67	16	51	8 16	15	51	7 65	14	51	7 14	13	51	6 63
Glaziers	14	51	7 14	14	51	7 14	13	51	6 63	13	51	6 63	12	51	6 12
Lathsplitters	14	51	7 14	14	51	7 14	13	51	6 63	13	51	6 63	13	51	6 63
Painters	15	51	7 65	15	51	7 65	14	51	7 14	14	51	7 14	13	51	6 63
Plasterers	20	51	10 20	20	51	10 20	22	51	11 22	20	51	10 20	18	51	9 18
Slaters	16	51	8 16	15	51	7 65	14	51	7 14	14	51	7 14	14	51	7 14
Stonecarvers	24	51	12 24	24	51	12 24	24	22	12 24	22	51	11 22	20	51	10 20
(Foremen or overseers in these trades get from 2 to 3 cents more per hour, equal to $1.02 to $1.53 per week more than the ordinary workmen.)															

1. *Comparative statement showing the number of hours worked per week, &c.*—Continued.

Occupation.	1878. Per week.		1877. Per week.		1876. Per week.		1875. Per week.		1874. Per week.	
	Hours of labor.	Wages.	Hours of labor.	Wages.	Hours of labor.	Wages.	Hours of labor.	Wages.	Hours of labor.	Wages.
Ship-building trades:										
iron riveters, piece-work	51	$7 00 to $8 50	51	$7 00 to $8 50	51	$7 00 to $8 50	51	$7 00 to $8 50	51	$7 00 to $8 50
workers, piece-work, various	51	6 00 to 7 50	51	6 00 to 7 50	51	6 00 to 7 50	51	6 00 to 7 50	51	6 00 to 7 50
laborers	51	4 50 to 5 00	51	4 50 to 5 00	51	4 50 to 5 00	51	4 50 to 5 00	51	4 50 to 5 00
carpenters	51	7 00 to 7 50	51	7 00 to 7 50	51	7 00 to 7 50	51	6 50 to 7 00	51	6 50 to 7 00
wrights or joiners	51	7 25 to 7 50	51	7 25 to 7 50	51	7 00 to 7 50	51	7 00 to 7 25	51	7 00 to 7 25
carvers	51	7 50 to 8 00	51	7 50 to 8 00	51	7 50 to 8 00	51	7 50 to 8 00	51	7 50 to 8 00
smiths	51	6 50 to 7 00	54	6 50 to 7 00	51	6 50 to 7 00	51	6 00 to 6 50	51	6 00 to 6 50
(Foremen or overseers in these trades get from 75 cents to $1.50 per week more than ordinary workmen.)										
Coach-building trades:										
body makers	51	6 50 to 7 00	51	6 50 to 7 00	51	6 50 to 7 00	51	6 50 to 7 00	51	6 50 to 7 00
smiths	51	7 00 to 8 00	51	7 00 to 8 00	51	7 00 to 8 00	51	7 00 to 8 00	51	7 00 to 8 00
painters	51	6 25 to 7 00	51	6 50 to 7 00	51	6 25 to 6 75	51	6 25 to 6 75	51	6 25 to 6 75
wheelwrights	51	6 75 to 7 50	51	6 75 to 7 25	51	6 75 to 7 25	51	6 75 to 7 25	51	6 75 to 7 25
upholsterers	51	6 25 to 6 75	51	6 25 to 6 75	51	6 25 to 7 00	51	6 50 to 7 00	51	6 25 to 6 75
workers, other branches	51	6 00 to 6 50	51	6 00 to 6 50	51	6 00 to 6 50	51	6 00 to 6 50	51	6 00 to 6 50
(Foremen or overseers in these trades get from $1 to $1.50 per week more than the ordinary workmen.)										
Engine and machine making trades:										
Pattern-workers	51	7 00 to 8 00	51	7 00 to 8 00	51	7 00 to 8 00	51	7 00 to 8 00	51	7 00 to 8 00
Molders	51	7 00 to 7 50	51	7 00 to 7 50	51	7 00 to 7 50	51	7 00 to 7 50	51	7 00 to 7 50
Engine fitters and finishers	51	6 00 to 6 50	51	6 00 to 6 50	51	6 00 to 6 50	51	6 00 to 6 50	51	6 00 to 6 50
Machine fitters and finishers	51	6 00 to 6 25	51	6 00 to 6 25	51	6 00 to 6 25	51	6 00 to 6 25	51	6 00 to 6 25
Ironturners	51	6 50 to 6 75	51	6 50 to 6 75	51	6 50 to 6 75	51	6 50 to 6 75	51	6 50 to 6 75
Blacksmiths	51	6 50 to 7 00	51	6 50 to 7 00	51	6 50 to 7 00	51	6 50 to 7 00	51	6 50 to 7 00
Boiler-makers	51	6 75 to 7 25	51	6 75 to 7 25	51	6 75 to 7 25	51	6 75 to 7 25	51	6 75 to 7 25
Laborers	51	4 00 to 4 75	51	4 00 to 4 75	51	4 00 to 4 75	51	4 00 to 4 75	51	4 00 to 4 75
(Formen get from $1 to $1.50 per week more than the ordinary workmen.)										
Miscellaneous trades:										
Bakers	51	6 25 to 7 00	51	6 25 to 7 00	51	6 25 to 7 00	51	6 25 to 7 00	51	6 25 to 7 00
Basket-makers	51	6 00 to 7 00	51	6 00 to 7 00	51	6 00 to 7 00	51	6 00 to 7 00	51	6 00 to 7 00
Bleachers	51	4 00 to 4 75	51	4 00 to 4 75	51	4 00 to 4 50	51	4 00 to 4 50	51	4 00 to 4 50
women	51	2 25 to 3 00	51	2 25 to 3 00	51	2 25 to 2 50	51	2 25 to 2 50	51	2 25 to 2 50
Blockmakers	51	5 00 to 6 00	51	5 00 to 6 00	51	5 00 to 6 00	51	5 60 to 5 90	51	5 60 to 5 90
Boatbuilders	51	6 25 to 7 00	51	6 25 to 7 00	51	6 25 to 7 00	51	6 25 to 7 00	51	6 25 to 6 90
Bookbinders	54	6 50 to 7 00	54	6 50 to 7 00	54	6 50 to 7 00	54	6 00 to 7 00	54	6 00 to 7 00
women	54	2 25 to 3 00	54	2 25 to 3 00	54	2 25 to 3 00	54	2 25 to 3 00	54	2 25 to 3 00
Shoemakers, by machinery, piece-work	56	7 00 to 8 00	56	7 00 to 8 00	56	7 00 to 8 00	56	7 00 to 8 20	56	7 00 to 8 20

1. *Comparative statement showing the number of hours worked per week, &c.*—Continued.

Occupation.	1878. Per week.		1877. Per week.		1876. Per week.		1875. Per week.		1874. Per week.	
	Hours of labor.	Wages.	Hours of labor.	Wages.	Hours of labor.	Wages.	Hours of labor.	Wages.	Hours of labor.	Wages.
Miscellaneous trades:										
Shoemakers, by hand, piece-work	56	$5 25 to $5 75	56	$5 25 to $5 75	50	$5 25 to $5 75	56	$5 25 to $5 75	56	$5 25 to $5 75
by machinery, women	56	2 00 to 3 25	56	2 00 to 3 25	56	2 00 to 3 25	56	2 00 to 3 25	56	2 00 to 3 25
Bottlers	56	4 25 to 5 25	56	4 25 to 5 25	56	4 25 to 5 25	56	4 25 to 5 25	56	4 25 to 5 25
Brewers	56	4 75 to 5 50	56	4 75 to 5 50	56	4 75 to 5 50	56	4 75 to 5 50	56	4 75 to 5 50
Brushmakers, piece-work	54	5 75 to 6 25	54	5 75 to 6 25	54	5 75 to 6 25	54	6 00 to 6 50	54	6 00 to 6 50
Butchers	50	4 50 to 5 00	59	4 50 to 5 00	59	4 50 to 5 00	59	4 50 to 5 00	50	4 50 to 5 00
Cabinet-makers	51	6 75 to 7 25	51	6 75 to 7 25	51	6 75 to 7 25	51	6 75 to 7 25	51	6 00 to 6 25
Chairmakers, piece-work	51	6 50 to 7 00	51	6 50 to 7 00	51	6 50 to 7 00	51	6 50 to 7 00	51	6 50 to 7 00
Confectioners	51	7 00 to 7 50	51	7 00 to 7 50	51	7 00 to 7 50	51	6 75 to 7 00	51	6 75 to 7 00
Coopers	51	5 50 to 6 00	51	5 50 to 6 00	51	5 50 to 6 00	51	5 25 to 5 75	51	5 25 to 5 75
Coppersmiths	51	7 00 to 7 25	51	7 00 to 7 25	51	7 00 to 7 25	51	7 00 to 7 25	51	7 00 to 7 25
Corkcutters, piece-work	56	5 75 to 6 25	56	5 75 to 6 25	56	5 75 to 6 25	56	5 75 to 6 25	56	5 75 to 6 25
Curriers, piece-work	56	7 00 to 8 50	56	7 00 to 8 50	56	7 00 to 8 50	56	7 00 to 8 50	56	7 00 to 8 50
Cutlers	51	6 00 to 6 50	51	6 00 to 6 50	51	6 00 to 6 50	51	6 00 to 6 25	51	6 00 to 6 25
Dyers	56	4 75 to 5 75	56	4 75 to 5 75	50	4 75 to 5 75	56	4 75 to 5 75	56	4 75 to 5 75
Engravers	51	7 50 to 10 00	51	7 50 to 10 00	51	7 50 to 10 00	51	7 50 to 10 00	51	7 50 to 10 00
Flaxdressers, piece-work	56	3 50 to 4 50	56	3 50 to 4 50	56	3 50 to 4 50	56	3 50 to 4 50	56	3 50 to 4 50
French polishers	51	6 00 to 6 50	51	6 00 to 6 50	51	6 00 to 6 50	51	6 00 to 6 50	51	6 00 to 6 50
women	51	2 50 to 3 25	51	2 50 to 3 25	51	2 50 to 3 25	51	2 25 to 3 00	51	2 25 to 3 00
Gardeners, nurserymen, and florists	56	3 75 to 4 50	56	3 75 to 4 50	50	3 75 to 4 50	56	3 75 to 4 50	56	3 75 to 4 50
Hackle-makers	56	5 00 to 5 50	56	5 00 to 5 50	50	5 00 to 5 50	56	5 50 to 5 75	56	5 50 to 5 75
boys	56	2 00 to 2 50	56	2 00 to 2 50	56	2 00 to 2 50	56	2 00 to 2 50	56	2 00 to 2 50
Horseshoers	51	6 50 to 7 50	51	6 50 to 7 50	51	6 50 to 7 50	51	6 00 to 7 25	51	6 00 to 7 00
Jewelers	53	7 00 to 8 50	53	7 00 to 8 50	53	7 00 to 8 50	53	7 00 to 8 00	53	6 50 to 7 50
Marble-cutters	51	7 00 to 7 50	51	7 00 to 7 50	51	7 00 to 7 50	51	6 75 to 7 25	51	6 50 to 7 00
Millers	56	5 00 to 5 20	56	5 00 to 5 20	58	5 00 to 5 20	56	4 80 to 5 00	56	4 80 to 5 00
Millwrights	51	7 00 to 8 00	51	7 00 to 8 00	51	7 00 to 8 00	51	7 00 to 8 00	51	7 00 to 8 00
Paper-rulers	54	7 00 to 7 50	54	7 00 to 7 50	54	7 00 to 7 50	54	7 00 to 7 50	54	7 00 to 7 50
Printers, letter-press, piece-work	54	7 00 to 9 00	54	7 00 to 9 00	54	7 00 to 9 00	54	7 00 to 9 00	54	7 00 to 9 00
lithographers	54	6 00 to 7 00	54	6 00 to 7 00	54	6 00 to 7 00	54	6 00 to 7 00	54	6 00 to 7 00
Ropemakers	56	5 00 to 5 75	56	5 00 to 5 75	56	5 00 to 5 75	56	5 00 to 5 75	56	5 00 to 5 75
Saddlers	51	5 50 to 6 00	51	5 50 to 6 00	51	5 50 to 6 00	51	5 50 to 6 00	51	5 50 to 6 00
Sawyers (in saw-mills)	56	5 75 to 6 00	56	5 75 to 6 00	56	5 75 to 6 00	56	5 75 to 6 00	56	5 75 to 6 00
Sailmakers	54	5 75 to 6 25	54	5 75 to 6 25	54	5 75 to 6 25	54	5 75 to 6 25	54	5 25 to 5 75
Tanners	56	6 50 to 7 00	56	6 50 to 7 00	50	6 50 to 7 00	56	6 50 to 7 00	56	6 50 to 7 00
Tinsmiths	51	5 00 to 5 50	51	5 50 to 5 75	51	5 50 to 5 75	51	5 00 to 5 50	51	5 00 to 5 50
Tailors	54	7 00 to 8 00	54	7 00 to 8 00	54	7 80 to 8 20	54	7 00 to 8 00	54	6 50 to 7 50
Brassfinishers	51	6 50 to 7 00	51	6 50 to 7 00	51	6 50 to 7 00	51	6 00 to 6 50	51	6 00 to 6 50

Carvers and gilders	51	6 00 to 7 00	51	6 00 to 7 00	51	6 00 to 7 00	51	6 00 to 7 00	51	6 00 to 7 00
Laborers, porters, &c.	56	4 00 to 5 00	56	4 00 to 5 00	56	4 00 to 5 00	56	4 00 to 5 00	56	4 00 to 5 00
Railway employés:										
Engine-drivers, freight	60	8 50 to 9 00	60	8 50 to 9 00	60	8 50 to 9 00	60	8 50 to 9 00	60	8 50 to 9 00
Firemen, freight	60	5 50 to 6 00	60	5 50 to 6 00	60	5 50 to 6 00	60	5 50 to 6 00	60	5 50 to 6 00
Engine-drivers, passenger	60	9 00 to 10 00	60	9 00 to 10 00	60	9 00 to 10 00	60	9 00 to 10 00	60	9 00 to 10 00
Firemen, passenger	60	5 75 to 6 25	60	5 75 to 6 25	60	5 75 to 6 25	60	5 75 to 6 25	60	5 75 to 6 25
Brakemen, freight	60	6 00 to 6 50	60	6 00 to 6 50	60	6 00 to 6 50	60	6 00 to 6 50	60	6 00 to 6 50
Brakemen, passenger	60	6 50 to 7 00	60	6 50 to 7 00	60	6 50 to 7 00	60	6 50 to 7 00	60	6 50 to 7 00
Signalmen	60	6 00 to 6 50	60	6 00 to 6 50	60	6 00 to 6 50	60	6 00 to 6 50	60	6 00 to 6 50
Pointsmen	60	5 75 to 6 25	60	5 75 to 6 25	60	5 75 to 6 25	60	5 75 to 6 25	60	5 75 to 6 25
Shunters	60	5 00 to 5 50	60	5 00 to 5 50	60	5 00 to 5 50	60	5 00 to 5 50	60	5 00 to 5 50
Porters, freight	60	4 00 to 5 00	60	4 00 to 5 00	60	4 00 to 5 00	60	4 00 to 5 00	60	4 00 to 5 00
Porters, passenger	60	4 00 to 4 50	60	4 00 to 4 50	60	4 00 to 4 50	60	4 00 to 5 50	60	4 00 to 4 50
Jute and flax workers:										
a Preparing department:										
Jutepickers, men	56	3 25 to 4 00	56	3 25 to 4 00	56	3 50 to 4 50	56	3 50 to 4 50	56	3 50 to 4 00
Jute strikers-up, women	56	2 12 to 2 50	56	2 12 to 2 50	56	2 25 to 3 00	56	2 25 to 3 00	56	2 50 to 3 15
Jutesofteners, young men	56	3 00 to 3 50	56	3 00 to 3 75	56	3 50 to 4 00	56	3 50 to 4 00	56	3 50 to 3 75
Jutepreparers, women	56	2 00 to 2 25	56	2 13 to 2 50	56	2 25 to 2 75	56	2 25 to 2 75	56	2 13 to 2 50
Juteworkers, boys	56	1 75 to 2 00	56	1 75 to 2 00	56	1 75 to 2 13	56	1 75 to 2 13	56	1 75 to 2 13
Flaxcarders, women	56	2 00 to 2 25	56	2 00 to 2 25	56	2 13 to 2 75	56	2 13 to 2 75	56	2 13 to 2 75
Flaxpreparers, women	56	2 13 to 2 38	56	2 13 to 2 38	56	2 25 to 2 75	56	2 25 to 2 75	56	2 25 to 2 75
Foremen	56	6 00 to 7 00	56	6 00 to 7 00	56	6 50 to 7 25	56	6 50 to 7 25	56	6 50 to 7 25
b Spinning department:										
Coarse-jute spinners, women	56	2 25 to 2 50	56	2 25 to 2 50	56	2 50 to 2 75	56	2 50 to 2 75	56	2 50 to 2 75
Fine-jute spinners, women	56	2 40 to 2 80	59	2 40 to 2 80	56	2 50 to 2 90	56	2 50 to 2 90	56	2 50 to 2 90
Coarse-flax spinners, women	56	2 30 to 2 60	56	2 30 to 2 60	56	2 40 to 2 70	56	2 40 to 2 70	56	2 40 to 2 70
Fine-flax spinners, women	56	2 45 to 2 80	56	2 45 to 2 80	56	2 50 to 2 80	56	2 50 to 2 90	56	2 50 to 2 90
Piecers, jute and flax, girls	56	1 75 to 2 00	56	1 75 to 2 00	56	1 90 to 2 13	56	1 90 to 2 13	56	1 90 to 2 13
Shifters, jute and flax, girls	56	2 00 to 2 13	56	2 00 to 2 13	56	2 13 to 2 30	56	2 13 to 2 30	56	2 13 to 2 30
Halftimers, children, 7 to 12	56	45 to 70	56	45 to 70	56	45 to 70	56	45 to 70	56	45 to 70
Jute and flax reelers, piece-work, women	56	3 13 to 3 50	56	3 13 to 3 50	56	3 25 to 3 70	56	3 25 to 3 70	56	3 25 to 3 70
bobbin-winders, piece-work, women	56	3 25 to 3 75	56	3 25 to 3 75	56	3 50 to 3 90	56	3 50 to 4 00	56	3 50 to 4 00
capwinders, piece-work, women	56	3 00 to 3 50	56	3 00 to 3 50	56	3 75 to 4 00	56	3 75 to 4 00	56	3 75 to 4 00
warpers, piece-work, women	56	3 00 to 3 25	56	3 00 to 3 25	56	3 25 to 3 50	56	3 25 to 3 50	56	3 25 to 3 50
Foremen	56	6 00 to 7 00	56	6 00 to 7 00	56	6 50 to 7 00	56	6 50 to 7 00	56	6 50 to 7 00
c Weaving department:										
Single-loom weavers, piece-work, women	56	3 00 to 3 75	56	3 00 to 3 75	56	3 25 to 4 00	56	3 25 to 4 00	56	3 25 to 4 00
Double-loom weavers, piece-work, women	56	3 25 to 4 25	56	3 25 to 4 25	56	3 50 to 4 50	56	3 50 to 4 50	56	3 50 to 4 50
Tenters, piece-work, women	56	6 00 to 6 50	56	6 00 to 6 50	56	6 50 to 7 00	56	6 50 to 7 00	56	6 50 to 7 00
Foremen	56	6 50 to 7 00	56	6 50 to 7 00	56	7 00 to 7 50	56	7 00 to 7 50	56	7 00 to 7 50
d Finishing department:										
Croppers, men	56	4 50 to 5 00	56	4 50 to 5 00	56	4 50 to 5 00	56	4 75 to 5 25	56	4 75 to 5 25
Starchers, piece-work, men	56	6 00 to 6 50	56	6 00 to 6 50	56	6 50 to 6 75	56	6 50 to 7 00	56	6 50 to 7 00
Calendorers, men	56	4 75 to 5 25	56	4 75 to 5 25	56	5 00 to 5 50	56	5 00 to 5 50	56	5 00 to 5 50
Measurers, men	56	4 50 to 5 00	56	4 50 to 6 00	56	4 75 to 5 25	56	4 50 to 5 25	56	4 50 to 5 25
Lappers, men	56	4 75 to 5 25	56	4 75 to 5 25	56	5 00 to 5 50	56	5 00 to 5 50	56	5 00 to 5 50
Packers, men	56	4 75 to 5 25	56	4 75 to 5 25	56	5 00 to 6 00	56	5 00 to 6 00	56	5 00 to 6 00
Foremen	56	6 00 to 7 00	56	6 00 to 7 00	56	6 50 to 7 50	56	6 50 to 7 50	56	6 50 to 7 50

1. *Comparative statement showing the number of hours worked per week, &c.*—Continued.

Occupation.	1878. Per week.		1877. Per week.		1876. Per week.		1875. Per week.		1874. Per week.	
	Hours of labor.	Wages.	Hours of labor.	Wages.	Hours of labor.	Wages.	Hours of labor.	Wages.	Hours of labor.	Wages.
Domestic servants (with board):										
Housemaids .... per year..	......	$65 00 to $80 00	......	$65 00 to $80 00	......	$60 00 to $75 00	......	$60 00 to $75 00	......	$60 00 to $75 00
Cooks, women .... do....	......	80 00 to 100 00	......	80 00 to 100 00	......	80 00 to 100 00	......	80 00 to 100 00	......	80 00 to 100 00
Agricultural laborers (with board):										
Farm-hands experienced .... per year..	60	190 00 to 200 00	60	190 00 to 200 00	60	195 00 to 205 00	60	190 00 to 200 00	60	190 00 to 200 00
ordinary .... do....	60	175 00 to 190 00	60	175 00 to 190 00	60	180 00 to 190 00	60	175 00 to 190 00	60	175 00 to 100 00
Female servants .... do....	60	75 00 to 80 00	60	75 00 to 80 00	60	75 00 to 85 00	60	75 00 to 80 00	60	75 00 to 80 00

COST OF LIVING.

2. *Statement showing the average value of commodities that may be termed the necessaries of life during the five years* 1874–1878, *at Dundee.*

Article	Price	Article	Price
Bread .... per 4-pound loaf..	$0 15	Beef, fresh .... per pound..	$0 24
Butter .... per pound..	30	American .... do......	16
Sugar .... do......	08	Mutton .... do......	16
Tea .... do......	88	Rice .... do......	4
Coffee .... do......	32	Cheese .... do......	14
Ham .... do......	24	Codfish, salted .... do......	06
Eggs .... per dozen..	30	Potatoes .... per 28 pounds..	38
Oatmeal .... per 7 pounds..	28	Milk .... per pint..	04
Flour, American .... do......	28	Pork, salted .... per pound..	13
European .... do......	27	American canned beef .... do......	20

Clothing made of Scotch or English tweeds.—Coats, ordinary, \$9; waistcoats, \$3.50; pantaloons, \$4.50—or, say, \$17 a suit; boots, \$4 a pair.

House-rent.—Per year, including all taxes and, for convenience, water in house, but not including gas: Two-roomed houses, \$48; three-roomed, \$72.50; four-roomed, \$95; six-roomed, \$120.

3. PRESENT CONDITION OF TRADE.

In answer to this point of Department Circular, I have to state that the staple trade of this district is the manufacture of jute and linen fabrics, principally the former, and principally of a coarse kind. This trade at present is in a most depressed condition and has been so for the past four years.

The staple industry having been so long an unprofitable trade has similarly affected all other branches of business more or less, so that the wages of all classes of laborers, it is predicted, must inevitably fall, unless commercial prospects brighten in the mean time, which is not considered probable.

I beg to refer to my annual report for the year ending September 30, 1877, for full particulars as to the condition of trade in this consular district for a number of years back.*

4. CURRENCY.

The average circulation and coin held by the Scotch banks during the four weeks ending Saturday, March 16, 1878, will be seen from the following table:

Banks.	Authorized circulation of notes.	Average circulation during the four weeks ending as above.			Average amount of gold and silver coin held during the four weeks ending as above.
		£5 notes and upwards.	Under £5 notes.	Total.	
Bank of Scotland	£343, 418	£199, 406	£431, 930	£631, 336	£419, 453
Royal Bank of Scotland	216, 451	223, 591	435, 992	659, 584	607, 403
British Linen Company	438, 024	151, 974	353, 688	505, 663	227, 039
Commercial Bank of Scotland	374, 880	213, 277	520, 555	733, 832	495, 828
National Bank of Scotland	297, 024	158, 815	398, 629	557, 444	386, 425
Union Bank of Scotland	454, 346	229, 519	479, 465	708, 984	426, 774
Aberdeen Town and County Bank	70, 133	95, 152	112, 159	207, 312	187, 898
North of Scotland Banking Company	154 319	157, 902	164, 159	322, 062	198, 931
Clydesdale Banking Company	274, 321	163, 533	321, 030	484, 564	340, 679
City of Glasgow Bank	72, 921	212, 847	365, 560	578, 407	548, 699
Caledonian Banking Company	53, 434	36, 482	74, 300	110, 783.	74, 462
Total	2, 749, 271	1, 842, 498	3, 657, 467	5, 499, 971	3, 913, 621

It will be observed that the total average circulation of notes, in every case, far exceeds the issue or authorized circulation fixed by act of Parliament; but this is permitted by law, provided these banks keep in their custody gold specie equivalent to the amount of their overissue. These notes are not, like the Bank of England notes, a legal tender guaranteed by the State; they are, however, on account of the high standing of the Scotch banks, always accepted in Scotland for the value they represent. In England they are regarded as ordinary promissory notes, and are liable to an average discount of 5 per cent. per annum.

* For the report referred to, see Commercial Relations for the year 1877, page 442.

5. Business habits and systems.

Lastly, as to the fifth point of the circular, I am informed that the general method of doing business here is to give a discount of 3 per cent. for cash in seven days, or 2½ per cent. discount and one month's credit. This is almost the invariable rule of doing business in the home trade. In the export trade three, four, and six months' good bills on London are accepted, subject to 1 and 1½ per cent. discount for three and four months' bills respectively. For a six months' bill the goods are sold net.

MATTHEW McDOUGALL.

United States Consulate,
Dundee, April 11, 1878.

GLASGOW.

Report, by Consul Cooper, on labor, wages, and cost of living in Glasgow, and the coin and paper money, of Scotland.

I have the honor to transmit herewith a statement of the rates of wages paid to laborers of different classes at the present time; also a statement showing the aggregate capital, circulation, deposits, &c., of the banks of Scotland on the 15th day of May, 1878.

PAST AND PRESENT RATES OF WAGES.

The rate of wages now paid is about 7 per cent. higher than it was five years ago (except that of miners, which has declined 100 per cent.), but is at present declining, and, if the present stagnation in trade continues, will soon fall even below former rates. In fact, thousands in this city and neighboring towns are gladly working, if given the opportunity, at far lower rates than those herein stated.

COST OF LIVING.

There is yet no corresponding decline in the cost of living, which, to the lower classes, is about the same as in the United States. Meats and fruits are quite beyond the reach of the working classes, being far dearer than they are in the United States. Rent, clothing, bread, sugar, tea, and coffee are about the same in Glasgow as in New York. Whisky (which is considered a positive necessity by the great mass of laborers here, and costs about 300 per cent. more than in the United States), with beer, which latter is comparatively cheap (and as unwholesome as it is cheap), absorbs the larger portion of the laborer's earnings here.

COIN AND PAPER MONEY.

There are eleven banks of issue in Scotland, with their branches, each working under its own special charter. The circulation of each bank is unrestricted. It is only required to redeem its issue in coin, and to hold an amount of coin equivalent to the excess of actual circulation over the authorized circulation.

Only about 5 per cent. of the money in circulation is coin and four-fifths of this is silver. Paper is universally preferred, and gold coin never desired or called for except for special purposes.

Laborers of all classes are paid off in silver, which is in constant demand for change, and sometimes commands a small premium over gold or paper, owing to the fact that a pound note is the smallest denomination issued.

SAMUEL F. COOPER.

UNITED STATES CONSULATE,
Glasgow, June 28, 1878.

Statement showing the rate of wages paid to laborers of different classes at Glasgow.

Occupations.	Wages.			
	Per hour.	Per day.	Per week.	
Ordinary laborers:				
Farm servants, male			$3 05	With board.
female			1 98	Do.
Domestic servants, male			2 50	Do.
female			1 25	Do.
Day-laborers		$0 50 to $0 75	$3 00 to 4 50	
Stevedores		50 to 75	3 00 to 4 50	
Miners	$0 08 to $0 12	72 to 1 08	4 32 to 6 48	
Railway laborers:				
Guards (conductors)			5 00 to 6 00	
Porters			4 00 to 5 00	
Shunters (switchmen)			5 00	
Engine-drivers	10 to 14			
Firemen	06 to 08			
Tracklayers			5 00	
Surfacemen			4 00	
Factory hands:				
Mechanics			7 00	
Dyers			7 00	
Weavers, men			8 00	
women			3 00	
Spinners, women			2 50	
common, women			2 00	
House-building and other trades:*				
Bellhangers	14	1 26	7 56	
Bricklayers	18	1 62	9 72	
laborers	10	90	5 40	
Stonecutters or masons	15	1 35	8 10	
laborers	10	90	5 40	
Carpenters or joiners	15	1 35	8 10	
Gasfitters and plumbers	15	1 35	8 10	
Glaziers	14	1 26	7 56	
Painters	16	1 54	9 24	
Plasterers	18	1 62	9 72	
Slaters	15	1 35	8 10	
Stonecarvers	20	1 80	10 80	
Shoemakers	20	1 80	10 80	
Blacksmiths	15	1 35	8 10	
Tailors	12	1 08	6 48	
Seamstresses	05	45	2 70	
Saddlers	12	1 08	6 48	
Coopers	12	1 08	6 48	
Glassstainers	14	1 26	7 56	
Ropemakers	12	1 08	6 48	
Marble-cutters	18	1 62	9 72	
Jewelers	12	1 08	6 48	
Cabinet-makers and upholsterers			6 00 to 9 00	
Sailmakers			7 00	
Printing and bookbinding:				
Compositors			$8 00	54 hours.
Press-hands			8 00	Do.
Lithographers			7 00	Do.
Stereotypers			8 00	Do.
Binders			7 00	Do.
Edge-gilders			10 00	Do.
Paper-rulers			7 00	Do.

* The consul did not give the wages per day, nor per week, nor the hours which constitute a day's labor for house-building and other trades, simply giving the rates paid per hour. The Department, to facilitate immediate comparison with the rates of wages paid elsewhere, fixed upon the weekly hours of labor for those trades as 54, that being the general weekly labor-time throughout Great Britain.

Statement showing the rate of wages paid to laborers at Glasgow—Continued.

Occupations.	Wages.			
	Per hour.	Per day.	Per week.	
Carriage-makers:				
Body-makers			$8 00	51 hours.
Smiths			9 00	Do.
Wheelers			7 00	Do.
Painters and trimmers			7 00	Do.
Chemical works:				
Ordinary laborers			4 00	Do.
Skilled laborers			6 00	72 hours.
Furnacemen			7 50	Do.
Skilled furnace and chamber attendants			$7 50 to 9 00	Do.
Ship-building:				
Joiners	$0 15	$1 35	8 10	54 hours.
Carpenters	14	1 26	7 56	Do.
Engineers	14	1 26	7 56	Do.
Riveters and caulkers	12	1 08	6 48	Do.
Pattern-makers	15	1 35	8 10	Do.
Painters	15	1 35	8 10	Do.
Smiths	12	1 08	6 48	Do.
Hammermen	08	72	4 42	Do.
Coppersmiths	14	1 26	7 56	Do.
Tinsmiths	12	1 08	6 48	Do.
Brassfinishers	13	1 17	7 02	Do.
Iron-finishers	12	1 08	6 48	Do.
Mechanics	12	1 08	6 48	Do.
Brassmolders	14	1 26	7 56	Do.
Riggers	12	1 08	6 48	Do.
Platers	15	1 35	8 10	Do.
Furnacemen	09	81	4 86	Do.
Machinemen	12	1 08	6 48	Do.
Sawyers	11	99	5 94	Do.
Shipfitters	12	1 08	6 48	Do.
Helpers (various)	08	72	4 32	Do.
Laborers (various)	08	72	4 32	Do.
Boys	$0 02 to 04	$0 18 to 36	1 08 to 2 16	Do.
Carters		1 00	6 00	Do.

Statement showing the aggregate capital, circulation, deposits, &c., of the banks of Scotland on the 15*th day of May*, 1878.

Capital stock paid up	$50,228,900
Surplus, or reserve	23,035,335
Deposits	341,979,385
Authorized circulation	13,746,355
Actual average circulation in April, 1878	28,941,675
Gold held	17,015,665
Silver held	2,932,495
Total	19,948,160

LEITH.

*Report, by Consul Robeson, on the coal-mines and rates of wages paid the miners, in the district of Leith.**

Within my consular district there are a large number of coal-mines worked by individuals and by mining companies. These mines are nearly all situated on the estates of large landowners, and are leased to individuals or companies, and in some cases they are worked by the owners themselves. The usual duration of a coal-lease is thirty-five

* For the rates of wages paid the different tradesmen in Leith, see Mr. Robeson's very interesting report at page 256.

years, and the "lordship" or duty paid by the lessee to the lessor averages 18 cents per ton of 22½ cwt. produced from the mine. There are of course different rates of lordship for different qualities of coal and special conditions as to working certain seams. It is very difficult to estimate the cost of working a coal-mine, as so much depends upon the nature of the particular seam and the extent to which water may be present. Within the last four or five years, however, the cost has been increased by about 15 cents per ton in consequence of certain conditions imposed by recent legislation, such as that there should be two shafts to each pit, and other important regulations regarding ventilation and inspection, and also the employment of boys, &c. During the last few years also the rate of lordships has had a tendency towards increase.

At the pit-head coal is sold at an average of $1.56 per ton of 20 cwt. The cost to the lessee is as follows:

	Per ton of 20 cwt.
Lordship	$0 18
Cost of working	24
raising	24
pumping water	20
Storage, management, &c	16
Average profit	54
Total	1 56

In addition to the ordinary contingencies of working a particular coal, the drawing of water forms a most important element in the cost of working any mine. The least increase in the flow incurs an additional cost, while in some districts, at certain seasons, this cost is so great, that the coal has to be disposed of at almost cost price. Many seams, however, are usually comparatively free from water, and when in these cases the coal is of a soft working quality and stands well in the market, the average profit to the producer is considerably increased.

Coal agents and retailers purchasing at the pit make, as a rule, enormous profits upon their subsequent sales to the public. Taking the average distance as 25 miles over which coal is transported from pits to the centers of disposal, the costs to the coal agents or middlemen and the price paid by the public stand thus:

	Per ton.
Price at the pit	$1 56
Railway carriage (4 cents per ton per mile)	1 00
Storage, cartage, breakages, &c	08
Commissions and discounts	24
Clear profit	84
Cost to the public	3 72

These figures show the estimated average, but at certain seasons the prices over all are very largely increased.

As regards the wages paid to miners, these vary in different districts. They are paid at so much per ton turned out; and this rate is usually fixed as near as possible upon the principle of allowing the miner about $1.20 per day if he were paid by the day. It is considered that a miner is capable of turning out on an average five tons of coal per day, and the wages allowed are from 20 to 36 cents per ton, according to the nature of the seam. Where the seam is difficult to work, he receives the higher wage, and, of course, produces less coal in a working-day. From this wage the miner has, in certain districts in Scotland, to pay the boys for drawing the coal to the pit-mouth, provide his own oil, make a small contribution toward the expense of repairing tools, &c., and also contribute to the medical fund. The usual way is for two miners to work together, and in this way they succeed in averaging a turn-out of ten tons per day, which, at the average remuneration of 28 cents per ton, gives an allowance to each miner of $8.40 cents per week. These wages are at present what they were about seven years ago. Exactly five years ago the price of coal was raised very high, and continued so for about eighteen months. During that time the wages paid to miners averaged $2.50 per day, and in consequence the price of coal became very high, as much as $10 per ton. The profits realized from this increase were, so far as the owners or lessees were concerned, applied toward extending coal operations; and, in the case of the miners themselves, these profits were swallowed up by extravagance, and finally reduced by overcrowding of the trade of miners.

JOHN T. ROBESON.

UNITED STATES CONSULATE,
Leith, July 22, 1878.

WALES.

Report, by Consul Sykes, on the (1) *rates of wages;* (2) *cost of living;* (3) *past and present rates; and* (4) *the present condition of trade, in Wales.*

In response to Department circular of April 11, 1878, I have the honor to report as follows:

1. RATES OF WAGES.

The wages paid to farm-hands in Wales vary considerably in different counties. In those sections which, like Cardiganshire and Carmarthenshire, are still remote from railways, and where the habits and usages of the people are somewhat primitive, the wages paid and the cost of living are lower than in the more progressive parts of the country.

Farm-hands.—It may be roundly stated, however, that farm-hands are paid an average of $1.50 to $3.50 per week, with certain privileges in the way of beer and house-room. Frequently such laborers, when married, are provided with a cottage, and allowed to cultivate their own vegetable garden.

Mechanics and town laborers are paid as follows:

Brickmakerss	per week	$2 50 to $7 50
Engine-fitters	do	6 00 to 10 50
Shipcarpenters	per day	1 62
Shipsmiths	do	1 50
Sawyers	do	1 25
Coopers	do	1 12
Riggers	do	1 50
Boiler-makers	do	1 00 to 1 40
Engine-drivers (engineers) with premiums for merit	do	1 25 to 2 00
Firemen	do	1 00 to 1 12
Laborers	do	66 to 90
Dock-laborers	do	1 00
Painters	per hour	13 to 14
Masons	do	16
Carpenters	do	16
Plumbers	do	15
Plasterers	do	15

2. COST OF LIVING.

The cost of living to the laboring class in towns will probable average \$3 to \$5 per week for man and wife. There is a fair amount of thrift prevailing among this class, who are, however, somewhat given to unnecessary expenditures for jollification, especially those among them who are not of Welsh blood. Welsh laborers are, as a class, thriftier than the English and Irish, who help largely to make up the population of the chief towns in this district.

It should be mentioned, also, for it is an important fact, that the wives of laboring men here fill a more active place in the bread-winning scheme than women do in America. Many go off to their work as regularly as their husbands every morning of their lives. They are also very frequently the treasurers of the marital firm, and help to keep the weekly outlay for jollification as near the minimum as possible. Among the occupations followed by women in this district are some which I think women nowhere else in Great Britain engage in, such as letter-carriers (in lieu of postmen), mussel-diggers, oyster-peddlers, &c. Among the benefit societies, so called, such as Odd-Fellows, Shepherds, &c., is one composed exclusively of women, and peculiar to Wales alone, denominated the "Friendly Sisters." Facts like these are most important in forming an estimate of the social condition of a people.

3. PAST AND PRESENT RATES.

The cost of living in Wales would be somewhat higher now than five years ago were it not for the very potent influence now exerted thereon by American imports, especially of beef, canned meats, canned fruits, and canned vegetables. This influence has not only reduced the cost to consumers of the articles most imported, but it has had the further effect of leading to a spirit of competition among tradesmen—an active bidding for the "nimble sixpence," which has caused a sweeping reduction in the price of every possible article of household use to cash buyers. Of course the poorer classes, who are seldom able to buy on credit, profit by this movement among dealers. The rates of wages have somewhat decreased within the last five years, and the tendency is still downward.

4. PRESENT CONDITION OF TRADE.

Trade throughout the district is in a very depressed condition, and there is no little distress among the laboring classes, owing to lack of employment.

WIRT SIKES.

UNITED STATES CONSULATE,
Cardiff, June 29, 1878.

ITALY.

FLORENCE.

Report, by Consul Crosby, on the (1) *rates of wages;* (2) *cost of living;* (3) *paper money of Italy;* (4) *present state of trade; for the district of Florence.*

I have the honor to acknowledge the receipt of the circular from the Department of State dated April 11, 1878.

By my previous reports Nos. 30, 31, 39, it will be noticed that there exists in this district a general depression in all branches of trade, and a much worse condition of the poorer classes than has existed for many years, although with regard to exports to the United States a certain development has taken place.

1. RATES OF WAGES.

To answer categorically the inquiries contained in the above-mentioned circular, I beg respectfully to submit to the Department the following statements, embracing all the information I have been able to obtain from the chamber of commerce and other reliable sources. I give, first, a statement showing the daily rate of wages usually paid to laborers of every class, with especial reference to agricultural laborers, mechanical laborers, and those upon public works and railways, compared with those prevailing during the past five years:

Occupations.	Daily wages, without board, 1877-'78.	Daily wages without board during the past five years.	Increase.
Blacksmiths	$0 80	$0 75	$0 05
Carpenters	85	80	05
Machinists	1 00	90	10
Masons	75	70	05
Shoemakers	70	60	10
Stonecutters	65	60	05
Straw laborers (women)	17	15	02
Tanners	60	60	02
Tailors	80	75	05
House servants*	65	50	15
French servants*	20	14	06
Experienced hands, winter	40	30	10
summer	60	50	10
Ordinary hands, winter	35	30	05
summer	50	40	10
Common laborers	40	40	10
Tinsmiths	60	60	10

*With board.

2. COST OF LIVING.

Statement showing the cost of living to the laboring class, or the prices paid for the necessaries of life, compared with the cost prevailing during the past five years

Articles.	Prices, 1877, 1878.	Prices for the past five years	Increase.
Flour, wheat .... per pound..	$0 07	$0 06	$0 01
Beef .... do....	18	15	03
Pork .... do....	20	18	02
Lard .... do....	28	25	03
Codfish, dry .... do....	10	08	02
Butter .... do....	30	25	05
Cheese .... do....	28	25	03
Potatoes .... do....	03	02	01
Rice .... do....	07	06	01
Beans .... do....	04	03	01
Milk .... per quart..	06	05	01
Eggs .... per dozen..	19	17	02
Coal .... per ton..	11 00	10 60	40
House rent:			
Four-roomed tenement .... per ½ year..	30 00	40 00	*10 00
Six room tenement .... do....	50 00	60 00	*10 00
Board:			
For men .... per week..	4 00	3 50	50
For women per week .... do.....	3 00	2 60	40

* Decrease, owing to the removal of the capital.

3. PAPER MONEY.

The standard for all negotiations in this consular district is the Italian lira, in paper money, although every bargain with foreign countries takes place in gold francs. The average value of the Italian paper lira for past year may be quoted at $0.1750, being actually of $0.1742, in proportion to the rate of exchange.

In the early days of the Kingdom of Italy the National Bank was the only one entitled to issue paper currency. Afterwards other banking establishments claimed a like privilege, owing to the scarcity of coin, but the inconvenience arising from the issue and unequal value of so many kinds of paper money hindered trade, so that the Government decided finally the establishment of six banking institutions, very much on the principle of our national banking system, with a total secured capital of a milliard of lire, viz: the Italian National Bank of Naples, National Tuscan Bank, Roman Bank, Sicilian Bank, and Tuscan Bank of Credit.

Customs duties are required to be paid in coin.

4. PRESENT STATE OF TRADE.

The prevailing system of commercial transactions between Tuscan and American merchants and manufacturers is by consignment of merchandise to agents in the United States.

Straw hats and straw braids, which constitute the most important item of exports from this district, are sent by steamers from Leghorn or Havre to America, being invoiced at the actual market value, and paid for by drafts on Paris at thirty days, or after sale with a commission to the agent.

Works of art, such as marbles, paintings, alabasters, mosaics, &c., are all sold at the actual cost; wine and olive-oil, usually for cash.

Florence cannot be said to be either a commercial or a manufacturing center when compared with cities of the same size and population in countries like France, England, and some parts of Germany; and although it is making advancement in both directions every year, yet the deplorable state of its finances, high rate of taxation, and general poverty of its inhabitants render the investment of capital here at the present very questionable; yet, under all these adverse circumstances, both the export and import trade with the United States is improving.

J. SCHUYLER CROSBY.

UNITED STATES CONSULATE,
Florence, May 17, 1878.

GENOA.

Report, by Consul Spencer, on the (1) *rates of wages;* (2) *cost of living;* (3) *past and present rates;* (4) *present condition of trade;* (5) *paper currency* (*of all Italy*); *for the district of Genoa.*

In compliance with instructions contained in the Department Circular of the Acting Secretary of State, dated April 11, 1878, I beg leave to submit the following report:

1. RATES OF WAGES.

With regard to the rates of wages usually paid to the laboring classes within the limits of this consular district, I would refer the Department to the tabular statement herewith inclosed, which has been prepared with great care from the most authentic sources of information, both official and otherwise.

2. COST OF LIVING.

The cost of living to the laboring classes differs materially according to the locality, ranging from 12 to 20 cents per day in the rural districts, and from 25 to 35 cents per day in the cities.

The fare of the Italian laborer is usually very simple, consisting of bread, boiled chestnuts, *polenta* (mush), and minestrone, a substantial soup, composed of vegetables, olive-oil, and macaroni. This, with an occasional bottle of ordinary wine, a relish of stockfish or cheese, and at rare intervals, on great festivals or holidays, a dinner of fresh meat, constitutes the homely fare of the Italian laborer or peasant.

3. PAST AND PRESENT RATES.

The cost of living to the laboring classes has fluctuated more or less during the past five years, but, on the whole, has not materially increased. For the rates of wages during the past sixteen years, I would refer again to the accompanying statement.

4. PRESENT CONDITION OF TRADE.

The commercial depression which has prevailed in this district for several years past continues with unabated, if not increased, severity.

During the past year there has been a falling off in Italian commerce of about 17 per cent. Aside from the general causes which have operated to produce a general stagnation of business here as well as elsewhere, there are some special reasons for this temporary decline in Italian commerce. Among these may be enumerated the diminished productions, during the past year, of wine, olive-oil, and almonds, but more especially the crisis which has overtaken the silk industry, in which there has been a falling off of 119,000,000 lire in the imports and of 234,000,000 in the exports.

4. PAPER CURRENCY.

From the last monthly statement of the minister of the treasury, it appears that the total amount of the paper currency in circulation, April

30, 1878, throughout the kingdom, was 1,537,907 lire, and the specie reserve held by the various banks of issue was 128,698,496 lire.

This currency is a legal tender for all debts, both public and private, with the exception of customs duties. At the present date it bears the relation to gold of 92.4 to 100.

O. M. SPENCER.

UNITED STATES CONSULATE,
Genoa, June 19, 1878.

Comparative statement of the average rate of wages per day for the various trades and occupations in the province of Genoa for the years 1870, 1873, and 1878, inclusive.

Trade or occupation.	1870.	1873.	1878.
Agricultural laborers, Piedmont:			
Men: Maximum	$0 70	$0 76	$0 76
Minimum	14	15	16
Women: Maximum	48	58	58
Minimum	08	08	09
Blacksmiths:			
First class	70	76	76
Second class	43	48	58
Third class	20	25	29
Carpenters	65	70	70
apprentices	48	54	54
boys	02½	02½	03
Cabinet-makers	60	....	76
Cotton-dyers:			
Maximum	64	....	54
Minimum	60	....	28
Common laborers*	48	44	46
boys	28	27	28
women	23	24	25
railroads and public works	49	56	58
boys	28	33	34
women	22	25	26
Cotton spinners and weavers: †			
Men	40	58	70
Women	16	19	21
Goldsmiths:			
Maximum	....	....	1 33
Minimum	....	....	12
Hodcarriers	43	42	43
Hatters	....	....	96
Linen-weavers:			
Women: Maximum	24	....	25
Minimum	16	....	16
Girls: Maximum	14	....	16
Minimum	08	....	10
Masons: *			
First class	74	68	74
Second class	58	53	68
Boys	48	25	29
Men servants ‡	....	....	19
Maid servants ‡	....	....	12
Miners (Sardinia):			
Maximum	70	70	74
Minimum	48	52	55
Ropemakers:			
Maximum	....	....	68
Minimum	....	....	38
Shoemakers:			
First class	80	96	81
Second class	33	38	34
Women	46	54	38
Stonecutters	....	....	81
Silkweavers:			
Men: Maximum	38	....	1 95
Minimum	16	....	38
Women: Maximum	38	....	38
Minimum	12	....	10
Seamstresses §	....	....	19
Tailors	....	....	70
Velvet-weavers	58	....	38

* The medium length of a working-day is 10 hours.
† The medium length of a working-day is 12 hours.
‡ With board and lodging.
§ With board.

MESSINA.

Report, by Consul Owen, on the (1) *rates of wages;* (2) *condition of the laboring classes;* (3) *present condition of trade;* (4) *paper money;* (5) *business habits and systems; for the district of Messina, Sicily.*

In reply to the Circular of the Department dated 11th April, 1878, I have the honor to forward the following information, contained in two tabular statements:

1. Rate of wages.

From the Table A it will be seen that the average rate of wages paid to ordinary unskilled laborers is from 30 to 70 cents per day, without food. This class comprises porters, laborers on public works, and men that work out by the day. As most of the agricultural laborers are peasants, residing upon the estate, and receive their compensation from a share of the crop, their wages must be a matter of estimation, depending upon the harvest. These estimates I have received from some of the principal proprietors, and are, I think, correct. There is nothing similar to the "hiring-out" system of the United States and England.

Mechanics command good wages here, and receive from 70 cents to $1 per day of twelve hours. Those employed upon the public works and railways are paid perhaps a little more, but the difference is trifling. Until recently, unskilled mechanics were foreigners, principally French and English; but owing to the high rates of wages asked, nearly all have been discharged and native laborers substituted, with benefit both to themselves and their employers.

The fruit-packing establishments give in the season employment to from 2,000 to 3,000 women, who are preferred for this work by reason of their skill in selecting fruit fit for exportation. They earn from 20 to 30 cents a day of twelve hours. With the exception of the silk-reeling establishments, which employ about 600, this is the only branch of industry where women are employed in large numbers.

The rates of wages and the cost of living to the laboring classes show very little difference during the past five years.

2. Condition of the laboring classes.

The condition of the laboring classes has been very much bettered under the present Government.

The opening of public schools, and the law of the Italian army, withholding the discharge of a soldier until he can read and write, have been productive of good results.

The laboring classes are frugal and industrious; very rarely do you find destitution among them. They are contented with little, and live upon what our workmen would despise. The living expenses of a mechanic with a family of three, including tenement, clothes, &c., amounts to $4.90 per week.

3. Present state of trade.

On account of the unsettled state of affairs in the East, Messina, together with other Mediterranean ports, has suffered; but at the present time trade seems to revive, and the prospect of an abundant harvest gives great encouragement. The business season for Messina is from September to April, during which period fruits, wine, and oil are shipped in large quantities. The exportation of green fruit—lemons and oranges—to our markets, which now take the greatest part of the yield of the island, owes its rise to Mr. John L. Payson, who was United States consul at this port for many years.

At the present time the exportation is increasing. Large orchards are every year being planted, and many who were formerly but growers now compete in the export trade with the regular export merchants.

The essence, extract, acid, and other manufactures that depend upon the fruit crop are also increasing; improvements are being made; and whereas formerly the articles were shipped in a crude state, they are now put on the market ready for use. They command ready sale in all parts of the world. The exportation of crude olive-oil is mostly confined to the North Sea and Baltic ports. The exportation of wine is principally to France.

4. Paper money.

Owing to the system of banking adopted by the Italian Government, there is no means, as I am informed by bankers, of ascertaining the amount of paper money in circulation in the district. Aside from the government issue, the Bank of Sicily, whose headquarters are at Palermo, with branches in the different cities of the island, issues notes from 20 to 1,000 lire in value, subject to a slight discount when used on the continent of Italy. There is no coin in actual circulation, except what is required to pay custom-house dues.

5. Business habits and systems.

As regards business habits and systems of the district, they conform in the main to those adopted in other parts of the world.

Fruit is generally sold on commission, letters of credit being issued from London bankers, where drafts are paid by presentation of consular invoices and authenticated shipping documents. The commission generally charged rarely exceeds 3 per cent.

GEO. H. OWEN.

United States Consulate,
Messina, July 20, 1878.

Rates of wages paid for farm and mechanical labor in consular district Messina, Sicily, in the year 1878.

Occupations.	Wages, without board.	Wages, with board.
Farm laborers:		
Experienced hands, in summer	$0 45	$0 30
winter	65	45
Ordinary hands, in summer	30	20
winter	38	25
Common laborers on farm	30	15
Skilled laborers, by day only:		
Blacksmiths	70	....
Bricklayers or masons	80	....
Cabinet-makers	1 00	....
Carpenters	80	....
Coopers	80	....
Machinists	1 20	....
Painters	1 00	....
Plasterers	80	....
Shoemakers	95	....
Stonecutters	70	....
Tailors	90	....
Tanners	70	....
Tinsmiths	70	....
Wheelwrights	1 00	....

Prices of provisions and groceries in the town of Messina, Sicily, in the year 1878.

Bread	per pound	$0 07
Butter	do	25
Beef, roasting pieces	do	15
soup	do	12
Codfish	do	06
Cheese	do	19
Coffee	do	25
Charcoal	do	01
Eggs	per dozen	17
Fish	per pound	05
Lard	do	13
Milk	per quart	12
Macaroni	per pound	06
Olive-oil	per quart	40
Pork	per pound	11
Potatoes	do	01
Rice	do	04
Sugar	do	09
Starch	do	10
Soap	do	04
Vegetables	do	01
Wine	per quart	08
Average daily expenditures to a skilled laborer		$0 40 to $0 45
Average daily expenditures to a common laborer		10 to 13

PIEDMONT.

Report, by Mr. Noble, consular-agent at Turin, on the (1) *rates of wages;* (2) *past and present rates;* (3) *present state of trade; and* (4) *the paper money of Italy; with inclosures from Piedmontese officials on the same and other subjects; for Piedmont.*

1. RATES OF WAGES.

Agricultural laborers.—Males: Daily wages, say, nine months, and nine hours per day, without maintenance, 24 cents; say nine months, twelve hours per day, without maintenance, 40 cents per day; say three months in harvest-time, fifteen hours per day, without maintenance, 60 to 70 cents per day. Some proprietors, in harvest-time, pay per day 40 to 50 cents, with a bottle of common wine and a dish of soup. In winter-time some laborers are paid 30 cents per day, without maintenance. Females are paid about one-half of the above rates of wages. Youths fourteen to sixteen years of age are paid from $20 to $24 per annum, with board. There are field-hands who receive $18 per annum, with board.

Railroad laborers.—The Great Northern Railway, now run by the National Government, pays about as follows: Males: Ordinary daily laborers are paid from 50 to 60 cents. Engineers: First-class, $42 monthly; second-class, $36 monthly; third-class, $30 monthly, besides a small interest on the economy made on coal (in the quantity fixed by the railway authorities and based on the distance); on the average this bonus amounts to $12 monthly. Chief conductors of trains, $360 to $400 per annum; other conductors of trains, $240 to $280 per annum; other employés on trains, $200 per annum; station-masters, not classed, $800 to $1,000 per annum; station-masters, first-class, $600 per annum; station-masters, second-class, $440 to $500 per annum; station-masters, third-class, $260 to $300 per annum; supervisors of goods, $360 to $480; other employés, according to grade, $240 to $300.

The salaries of all railway employés, on lines run by the Government, who are paid by the month or year, are subject to a rebate, which is put into a common pension-fund, so that, after a certain number of years of continual and faithful service, every one is entitled to an annual pension, based on the amount of salary paid him while in active service. In case of accident or death, when on duty, the widow receives a subsidy.

The Colli Railway, individual property: Laborers, males: Daily wages, 32 to 40 cents; mechanics, 50 to 80 cents per day. Females: 16 cents per day to those who guard the crossings; to those who sell tickets 20 cents per day, staying in service all day and the whole year, but on an average labor 4 or 5 hours. In spare hours they attend to their domestic affairs. This railway allows no pension.

Public works.—Public works are let out to the lowest bidder. Generally speaking, therefore, contractors pay a lower rate of wages than those heretofore noted.

Silkspinners.—Females are paid from 18 to 24 cents per day of 13 hours, with lodging in common, wood and light. Others are paid 24 cents per day of 12 hours, without anything else.

Mechanics: Males, bricklayers, stonemasons, carpenters, smiths, 50, 60, 70, 80 cents, and $1 to $1.20, for 12 hours' work, and according to the season of the year; upon an average, 65 cents per day.

Cooks: Females, $3, $4, and $5 per month; housemaids, $2.50, $3, to $3.50 monthly.

2. Cost of living.

Agricultural laborers spend 16 to 20 cents daily; females, 15 to 16 cents. The agriculturist, both farmer and laborer, lives very economically; hardly knows what fresh meat is, except half a dozen times a year, on state and church festivals, the latter being too numerous for the moral and physical well-being of the laboring classes. Sometimes he eats a little sausage, but the daily food consists of polenta (a kind of mush made from cornmeal. Maize is not so succulent and nourishing as in the United States); rice-bread, where rice grows, soups, made generally of wheat-flour pastes, rice, except in time of garden vegetables, sometimes with a little lard in the soups by way of a luxury, cheese, greens, and chestnuts in their season. Some laborers keep poultry, which is shared with the owner of the land. Agricultural families also have wheat-bread occasionally, which they make at home.

In cities and villages no one makes bread; the baker supplies all with bread and cakes daily. The barns attached to many country dwellings are built two stories high, adjoining the home of the owner. In the upper part of the barn is stored the fodder; in the lower story are the stables for horses and cattle, in which male and female laborers and their children are lodged. There is also a kitchen adjoining the stable, where the laborers cook their food in common, so the heat of the animals serves to keep the humans warm, and consequently not much fuel is used.

There are some farms which are cultivated on shares, generally for one-half of the crop, for particulars of which I refer the reader to the papers annexed to this report.

In Turin the laborer's daily expenses are, say, 16 cents for food, $1\frac{1}{10}$ cents to 3 cents for lodging in a small room, where the laborer has a family—all generally stowed in a single room—wife, children, the latter at a tender age have to work early and late to obtain a scanty subsistence and necessary raiment. It may be assumed that laborers spend one-half of their wages for food.

2. Past and present rates.

During the past five years there has been a gradual advance of at least 15 per cent. in the rates of wages and costs of the necessaries of life.

3. Present state of trade.

Commercial and manufacturing affairs are at present, and have been for five years, quite unsatisfactory; indeed, exportation of manufactured articles has almost ceased, matters going from bad to worse. The causes of such a deplorable condition may be stated as follows: Disturbances owing to the Russo-Turkish war. The political horizon being overspread by clouds indicating threatening coming storms and tempests, capitalists withhold their funds, not wishing to embark in enterprises which may prove ruinous. Another cause quite potent is a standing army of, say, 300,000 men in the vigor of life, being only consumers, not producers, leaving the old people, the youth, the maidens, and the cripples to cultivate the earth and to propagate the race.

4. Paper money.

In Italy there are six banks which have the right to issue paper money, and are not compelled by law to have any reserve in coin. Herewith find annexed statement showing the present situation of these banks, which shows a circulation amounting to $124,854,258; from which must be deducted, amount of gold and silver coin and bullion, $29,287,939; amount of government notes, $28,958,286; making $58,246,225. Total circulation now of the six banks is $66,608,033. Besides, the government has issued notes for $188,000,000. So that the total circulation in paper money is $254,608,033.

The government notes are good for all dues, are legal tender except for duties on imports.

Taking into consideration the amount of coin and bullion in the vaults of the six banks, viz, in round numbers, 146,500,000, the proportion to the paper circulation would be 1.13 per cent. These government notes are guaranteed by the banks, and for such a guarantee pay annually 50 centimes per cent. commission (10 cents for each 100 francs), which, however, will be reduced to 40 centimes from the 20th of June next.

The premium on gold and silver coin (gold mostly) ranges from 9 to 11½ per cent. I have rated the lira, or franc, where it is named, as being 20 cents in giving the rates of wages, &c.

Piedmont is one of the principal seats of industry in Italy. Home-manufactured articles are generally sold on a credit of three or four months. Enterprises in trade, manufactures, mining, when in the hands of Englishmen, German, Frenchmen, and other foreigners in this country seem to result in a greater success than when they are controlled by the sons of this land.

The laborer in this country, being poorly nourished, does not, in my opinion, perform in a given time as much labor as the Englishman or the North American, who are better nourished.

One of the signs of the times here is, that during the past five years there has been a gradual increase of suicides, larceny, and of beggars.

Increasing taxation, a less demand for labor, so many drones—that is to say, military men, priests, and an army of tax-gatherers—that the substance of the people is lessening day by day, and misery from want of food and proper raiment, on the contrary, is daily increasing.

HENRY NOBLE.

United States Consular Agency,
Turin, July 24, 1878.

[Translation of inclosures in Mr. Noble's report.]

1. *Mr. Donalisio, of Fossano, to Mr. Noble.*

1. In the Piedmontese districts of Brá, Cuneo, Carmagnola, Piovani, Savigliano, Saluzzo, and Fossano, the wages paid to farm-hands not permanently employed are as follows: 1.20 lire* per day of 9 working hours, without board; 2 lire per day of 12 working hours (women earn one-half), and from 3 to 3.50 lire per day of 15 hours.

The above rates are for the months of June and July, when heavy work has to be performed, such as reaping and thrashing grain and cutting grass in the meadows. These hands do not find employment for more than nine months in the year.

2. Hands permanently employed on farms receive lodging, fire, light, a portion of land for their own garden, and an allowance of money and provisions amounting to 400 lire. Married men are employed in preference to those who are unmarried, but their wives receive no pay. In case a permanently employed farm-hand is sick for more than five days, he is obliged to furnish a substitute, if the weather is not inclement.

Female hands.—There are female farm-hands permanently employed, who receive 90 lire per annum, with board.

Boys.—Boys between fourteen and sixteen years of age receive from 100 to 120 lire per annum, with board.

3. *Agricultural families working farms on shares.*—The condition of these is preferable to that of those included under No. 2. A farmer cultivating on shares, however, requires some capital, in order to meet expenses and to purchase the implements and cattle required to cultivate and manure the land. When he has sufficient capital for these purposes his gain is greater, and the money thus invested may yield him a return of from 10 to 12 per cent. This class of agriculturists receives one-half of all the productions of the soil and also two-thirds of all the fowls that they raise. They are obliged to furnish two-thirds of the seed used in sowing.

4. A day's board usually costs 80 centimes for a man and 60 for a woman. For extra hands the same. One-third less if they are permanent and reside with the family. In the months of June and July the work to be performed is harder, and board then costs half as much again for both classes. The food furnished in Piedmont is generally good and nourishing; small wine is also commonly allowed.

5. *Atmospheric conditions.*—In the space of five years there is no sensible change in the state of things above described. In the space of ten years hail may do great damage to the crops. The farmer and the landowner, in case of such a misfortune, have nothing to depend upon save the productions of the stable and the fruits and produce of the autumn. The hail usually injures the crops in the months of May, June, and July. In the event of such a disaster, the Government does not remit any portion of the revenue-tax, which in Piedmont is excessive, being equal to 30 per cent. of the gross produce of the soil. This tax of 30 per cent. includes the national, provincial, and communal tax. An extra tax of 5 per cent. is sometimes levied for the purpose of keeping the roads, bridges, canals, &c., in repair, besides the communal tax on horned cattle, and the tax on personal property which is exacted of the cultivator who receives no salary. This tax affects the class described under No. 3.

6. Landowners receive as rent for first-class land 5 per cent. of its value. For second and third class land, 4 and 3 per cent.

First-class meadow land is rented at 220 lire per hectare.†

First-class wheat land is rented at 125 lire per hectare.

First-class vine land is rented at 300 lire per hectare.

Second-class land for the same purposes is rented at 20 lire less per hectare.

Classification.—By first-class land is meant land which is well watered and adapted to the growth of grass, wheat, and hemp. This is alluvial land.

By second-class land is meant such as is not well watered, which is hard, and in which silex or clay predominates. The vine is excepted, which in a clayey and tufaceous soil gives a larger return, inasmuch as it produces grapes of a superior quality, the net yield being 12 and 15 per cent.

7. *Capital and money.*—The negligence of the Government in not taking measures to cause the *credit foncier* to aid the capital invested in agriculture is much to be lamented. Records of mortgages are well established. Whenever landed property changes hands the fact is duly recorded at the expense of both purchaser and seller. All sales of land pay 4½ per cent. ad valorem to the Government; also, ½ per cent. for notarial fees.

The abolition of the ministry of agriculture at Rome, which took place toward the close of the year 1877, shows that all that the Government cares for is to get all it can out of the farmers; as to troubling itself to do anything to aid them, that is not to be

---

* The value of the lire is 19.3 cents.

† An hectare is equal to 2.4711 English acres.

thought of. Yet the amount realized by the Government in the way of taxes on agriculture exceeds one hundred millions of francs; and this, when added to the provincial and communal taxes, makes a grand total of about one hundred and fifty millions of francs.

And although it is now (May 24, 1878) proposed by the Government to re-establish the ministry of agriculture, in compliance with the wishes of the rural proprietors and of the boards of trade, the new minister of agriculture will render no great service to agricultural enterprises for want of assistance from the Government and Parliament. The cause of this indifference is that very few deputies are landowners, whereas there is an abundance of lawyers, scriveners, generals, and bankers, who represent interests of a different character.

The charitable institutions hold a great deal of landed property for which they paid nothing, having come into possession of it through the confessional. These institutions, together with the rich landowners, keep up the nominal value of landed property. If it were not for this, such property would ere this have fallen greatly, to the injury of the middle class and of the small farmers who own the land which they cultivate.

8. *Female operatives.*—Female silkspinners can earn 1.20 lire per day of 12 working hours, without board.

9. Mechanics earn from 2.50 to 3 lire per day, without board.

10. A working week consists of six days. The more important feast days are excepted, such as Ascension Day, Corpus Domini, Pentecost, Christmas, &c., on which no work is done.

11. *Productions.*—In upper Piedmont the following are the staple productions: Wheat, Indian corn, buckwheat, potatoes, millet, beans, oats, rye, hemp, grass, and hay.

In the Alps the staple productions are potatoes, chesnuts, and rye.

G. B. DONALISIO.

FOSSANO, *May* 26, 1878.

---

2. Messrs. Martini, Sola & Co., of Turin, to Mr. Noble.

1. The pay usually given to farm-hands is from 1.25 to 2 lire per day of from eleven to twelve working hours. For these no communal tax is paid, so that board and lodging cost somewhat less.

As to persons employed on railroads, there are mechanics who earn from 4 to 6 lire per day of from 10 to 11 hours; then there are the train-hands and those employed in keeping the road in repair, some of whom earn 60, others 90, and others 120 lire per month. In private establishments masons earn from 1.50 to 3.50 lire per day, carpenters from 1 to 3.35 lire, and blacksmiths from 2 to 3 lire per day. Very superior mechanics do their work by the job, and earn 3, 4, and 5 lire per day.

2. The expenses of living (as regards food) may be moderately estimated at from 3 to 4 lire per day for a family of two or three persons; at from 4 to 6 lire for one of four persons or more; bread of a medium quality, such as is used by mechanics, costing from 50 to 60 centimes per kilogramme; meat, 1.80 to 2 lire per kilogramme; butter, from 2.50 to 3.50 lire per kilogramme; wine, from 20 to 28 lire per half hectoliter; sugar, from 1.40 to 1.80 lire per kilogramme; coffee, from 4 to 5 lire per kilogramme. The price paid for a room is from 12 to 15 lire per month; for two rooms, from 20 to 30 lire; for three rooms, from 25 to 30 lire.

3. It is to be remarked that the wages of mechanics have not been increased at all during the past five years, while the cost of living has been constantly increasing. To bring about an equilibrium, wages should be raised at least 20 or 25 per cent.

4. Commercial and business transactions, moreover, have become considerably reduced in importance of late years. Evidence of this is to be found in the fact that all manufacturers have been obliged to discharge a portion of the hands formerly employed by them, and that many strikes have taken place in the hope of securing higher rates of wages, which it would be very difficult to grant, in view of the inactivity of the market and of the competition which the manufacturer is obliged to sustain. Paper money is a legal tender in Italy, and it may be estimated that the premium on gold and silver has varied during the past five years from 9 to 11½ per cent.

This is a critical time for business; there is very little doing, numerous failures have recently occurred, and money is very scarce; when it is loaned on approved paper, 7 per cent. is the minimum rate paid; sometimes even 12 per cent. is paid, and cases are not unfrequent in which money commands the usurious rate of 25 and even 30 per cent.

5. The hours of labor in factories are usually from 9 to 10 hours for females and from 10 to 12 for men; the wages earned by women may be estimated at one-third less than those earned by men. There are various governmental establishments, such as

those where equipments for the army are manufactured, in which the operatives receive very small wages. They may be classified as follows: Foremen (first class), 5 lire per day; foremen (second clas), 2.75 lire per day; measurers of material, 2.75 lire per day; workmen (first class), 2.25 lire per day; workmen (second class), 2 lire per day.

In other factories, such as paper factories, work is done by the piece, that is to say, portions of work are distributed to both men and women, and each workman, according to his ability, may earn from 3 to 5 lire per day; women, from 1.25 to 1.75 lire per day. In arsenals and establishments where arms are manufactured, a superior class of workmen is required, who earn from 3 to 6 lire per day.

The absinthe and liquor factory of Messrs. Martini, Sola & Co., at Turin, employs about one hundred and fifty hands. The absinthe and liquors made at this factory are used for home consumption, and are also exported. The employés work twelve hours per day; their food costs them 80 centimes each per day, and the price of a small room is 15 centimes per day. Sometimes they work at night, and then their wages are increased.

The price of food is 15 per cent. higher this year than it has been in previous years.

The export trade with America is now very dull on account of the difference between the value of gold and that of the paper money in circulation.

Here in Italy the premium on gold is 10½ per cent., which also has an injurious effect upon trade.

MARTINI, SOLA & CO.

TURIN, *May* 20, 1878.

---

3. *Mr. Raimondo, of Turin, to Mr. Noble.*

THE COLLI RAILWAY BETWEEN TURIN AND RIVOLI.

1. Laborers on railroads, and mechanics employed in the repairing-shops receive their wages fortnightly. Laborers receive from 1.60 to 2 lire, and mechanics from 2.50 to 4 lire per day.

2. The cost of living for the laboring classes varies according to the amount earned by them. A single laboring man can live on 80 centimes per day, while a mechanic may require from 1 to 1.20 lire.

3. The increase in wages and in the price of provisions may be estimated at one-sixth more than the prices paid five years ago.

4. Business is just now in a very unsatisfactory condition, but this is mainly due to the present political situation, and to the Russo-Turkish war which lately came to an end. The increase in industrial activity at Turin and in Piedmont generally has become very apparent. The same thing is observed in many other localities, and it is a good thing for Italy, which was formerly so dependent upon other countries for articles of mechanical construction, that she is now becoming independent of them in this respect.

In Italy there is a redundance of paper money, and confusion prevails even to this day, inasmuch as it has not yet been possible to secure the withdrawal of the paper money issued by every bank in the small towns. The union of the banks is now introducing a paper currency which readily passes throughout the entire kingdom. Meanwhile gold and silver coin are exceedingly scarce, and the difference between the price of gold and that of currency amounts to 10 per cent.

5. This railway is only twelve kilometers in length. It is the only one in Italy that has been built by a single individual, for which reason it bears the name of its builder and present owner, Mr. G. Colli (Colli Railway). As it connects two cities of considerable importance, its business, which consists almost exclusively in the carrying of passengers, is remunerative, although its running expenses amount to 53 per cent. of the gross receipts.

Some women are employed on this road, almost all in the capacity of ticket-sellers. They earn one lira per day.

This railway went into operation September 17, 1871. It gives no holidays to its employés, some of whom have opportunities of adding something to their earnings at the stations, when they are not on duty. The road provides lodgings for a considerable portion of its employés.

LORENZO RAIMONDO,
Engineer and Master of Transportation.

TURIN, *May* 18, 1878.

4. *Replies to various inquiries made by the consular agent of the United States at Turin.*

1. Journeymen shoemakers usually receive their wages at the end of each week.
2. The cost of living for shoemakers varies from 1½ to 2 lire per day.
3. The cost of living is becoming greater every year; articles of prime necessity, however, have not varied in price during the past five years.
4. Business is now at a standstill, owing to the great competition that exists. Paper money is the only kind in circulation, and the price of gold rises and falls with that of the bonds of the Italian 5 per cent. loan.
5. The working hours are from 12 to 14 per day.

NOTE.—Shoemakers work by the piece, and good hands earn from 3 to 4 lire per day.

ROME.

Report, by Consul-General McMillan, on the (1) *rates of wages;* (2) *cost of living;* (3) *past and present rates;* (4) *present state of trade;* (5) *paper money (for Italy);* (6) *business habits and systems; for the city and district of Rome.*

I have the honor to acknowledge the receipt of the Circular under date of April 11, 1878, instructing a report from this district on the wages paid to agriculturists and mechanical laborers, cost of living to same, &c., and I have now to transmit such information as I have been able to obtain touching the five points submitted for inquiry.

1. RATES OF WAGES.

The rates of wages usually paid to laborers of every class, but with more especial reference to agricultural laborers, mechanical laborers, and those upon public works and railways are as follows:

From 26 cents to 60 cents, including lodging but not board, is stated to be the average daily wages paid to agricultural laborers for the entire district. For that portion known as Agro Romano their wages may be calculated at from 55 cents to 60 cents per day, including lodging; throughout the remainder of the district 30 cents per day, including lodging.

The following class of laborers on the large estate of the Agro Romano are paid by the year, lodgings included but no board:

Engaged in raising grain and hay: Overseers, $144; underoverseers, $56; stewards, $66; watchmen and keepers, $54.

Engaged in tending horses and cattle: Head farmers, $126; dairymen, $80.

Engaged in tending sheep and goats: Overseers, $65; shepherds, $24.

Women are largely engaged in field labor in this district, with wages from 12 cents to 22 cents per day, including lodging in some localities; by the year, at from $1.80 to $3 per month, including board and lodging.

Throughout the district, children from twelve to fourteen years of age, working with men and women, in agricultural pursuits, receive the wages usually allowed for women.

Statement No. 1 shows the rates of wages paid to mechanical laborers in this city, compiled from a statistical work that has been prepared by the Paris Exhibition. In a report made by the Chambers of Commerce of Rome on the condition of the laboring classes in the manufactories, 60 cents for men, 30 cents for women, and 5 cents for children, is stated to be the average daily wages paid to this class of laborers in Rome, not including board and lodging. The same report gives 40 cents for men, 20 cents for women, and 5 cents for children, for the remainder of the province.

1. *Statement showing the daily wages paid to mechanical laborers in the city of Rome.**

Trade or occupation.	Amount.	Remarks.
Woolen spinners and weavers:		
Washers and dyers ....per day..	$0 30 to $0 60	No increase in wages during past ten years, as the number of workmen has been greatly superior to the demand, and wages were formerly relatively too high.
Carders ....do.....	40 to 60	
Spinners ....do.....	40 to 60	
Weavers ....do.....	60 to 1 00	
Cotton spinners and weavers:		
Dyers ....per day..	30 to 60	No increase during past ten years for the reasons as above.
Carders ....do.....	40 to 60	
Bobbin-winders ....do.....	10 to 15	
Weavers ....do.....	20 to 60	
Silk spinners and weavers:		
Dyers ....per day..	50 to 60	No increase in wages during past ten years for reasons as above.
Spinners ....do.....	30 to 40	
Weavers ....do.....	60 to 1 00	
Carpenters and joiners:		
Master workmen ....per day..	50 to 70	Wages have increased 40 per cent. within the past ten years.
Assistants ....do.....	40 to 50	
Polishers ....do.....	70	
Sawyers ....do.....	65	
Carpenters' apprentices ....do.....	10 to 30	
Polishers' apprentices ....do.....	40	
Shoemakers:		
Master workmen ....per day..	60 to 1 00	Notable increase in wages during past ten years.
Stitchers ....do.....	30	
Shoemakers' apprentices ....do.....	05 to 20	
Stitchers' apprentices ....do.....	05	
Tailors:		
Cutters ....per month..	15 00 to 30 00	Twenty per cent. increase in wages during past ten years.
Master workmen ....per day..	50 to 90	
Apprentices ....do.....	10 to 30	
Bricklayers and masons:		
Master workmen ....per day..	45 to 60	Slight increase in wages during past ten years.
Assistants ....do.....	35 to 40	
Apprentices ....do.....	35 to 40	
Blacksmiths:		
Master workmen ....per day..	50 to 60	Slight increase in wages during past ten years.
Assistants ....do.....	20 to 35	
Apprentices ....do.....	5 to 15	
Metal founders and machinists:		
Master machinists ....per month..	60 00 to 80 00	Increase of 15 per cent. within past ten years.
Assistant foremen ....do.....	30 00	
Master finishers ....per day..	70 to 2 00	
Master forgers ....do.....	80 to 1 20	
Master founders ....do.....	50 to 1 60	
Master modelers in wood ....do.....	60 to 1 00	
Other hands in general ....do.....	40 to 50	
Apprentices ....do.....	10 to 30	
Stonecutters:		
Sawyers ....per day..	20 to 40	Increase of 20 per cent. within past ten years.
Master workmen ....do.....	60 to 1 00	
House servants (experienced hands):		
Men ....per month..	8 00 to 12 00	Increase of 10 per cent. within past ten years.
Women ....do.....	4 00 to 5 00	

* With the exception of house servants, neither board nor lodging is included in this statement.

With the exception of house servants, neither board nor lodging is included in the above tabular statement. The average day's labor consists of ten hours, with half an hour for dinner in winter, and one and a half hours for dinner and repose in summer.

The following are the wages paid for hands by the Roman Railway Company:

Engineers ....per month..	$30 to $40
Firemen ....do......	16 to 18
Ordinary hands, including lodging ....do......	12
Overseer for hands, including lodging ....do......	18

2. Cost of living.

The cost of living per day to agriculturist laborers of this district may be calculated at from 12 to 20 cents. The ordinary laborer's fare consists of coarse bread and cheese, with raw onions, in the morning; at midday, a substantial soup of vegetables and macaroni, with pork-fat or olive-oil, or a dish of polenta; and bread and cheese, with onions or salad, as the case may be, in the afternoon and evening, sometimes varied by stockfish. Only on very rare occasions mutton or goat's meat and wine are indulged in. The cost of living per day to mechanical laborers in this city is variously estimated at from 30 cents to 50 cents.

The following were the market rates of the principal articles of consumption at Rome during the second week in June, 1878:

Article	Unit	From	To
Flour	per kilogramme	$0 12 to	$0 15
Bread	do	11 to	12½
Macaroni	do	12 to	18
Rice	do	09 to	15
Beans	do		12
Fave	do		06
Lentils	do		15
Potatoes	do	04 to	06
Milk	per liter		08
Butter	per kilogramme	60 to	66
Lard	do		48
Eggs	per dozen	18 to	22
Sugar	per kilogramme	27 to	36
Coffee	do	78 to	96
Olive-oil	per liter	30 to	38
Wine, first quality	do		20
second quality	do		16
third quality	do		08
Vinegar	do	12 to	16
Cheese, Parmesan	per kilogramme	40 to	72
Roman	do	30 to	42
Swiss	do	48 to	60
Codfish	do		24
Beef, first cuts	do		42
second cuts	do		30
third cuts	do		24
Mutton, first cuts	do		42
second cuts	do		30
Lamb, first cut	do		18
second cut	do		12
Kid, first cut	do		18
second cut	do		12
Pork, first cut	do		30
second cut	do		28
third cut	do		26
Ham	do	60 to	72
Petroleum-oil	per liter		16
Firewood	per cart of 600 kilogrammes		3 50
Charcoal	per sack of 39 kilogrammes	78 to	96

3. PAST AND PRESENT RATES.

A considerable advance in wages paid to agricultural laborers and in the cost of living followed immediately on the annexation of this district to the Kingdom of Italy in 1870, but they have not varied materially during the past five years. Dating from 1870, wages paid to agricultural laborers on that portion known as the Agro Romano have increased 40 per cent.; other portions of the district of Rome show an increase of from 20 per cent. to 25 per cent.

Reference may be made to statement No. 1 for the increase in wages paid to mechanical laborers in the city since 1870; with few exceptions the advance is slight, and bears no proportion to the increased cost of living. Immediately after the events of 1870 prices of the principal articles of consumption advanced 25 per cent.; during the past five years they have not varied sensibly.

When Rome became the capital of Italy, owing to the great influx of speculation, government employés, and strangers from all parts of Italy, rents advanced from 75 to 100 per cent., where they still remain.

4. Present state of trade.

The returns of Italian commerce for the quarter ending March 31, 1878, give the following results, compared with the same period of the preceding year:

IMPORTS.

First quarter, 1877	$65,968,727 20
First quarter, 1878	59,232,208 00
Decrease in 1878	6,736,519 20

EXPORTS.

First quarter, 1877	$50,283,545 60
First quarter, 1878	50,239,995 40
Increase in 1878	43,550 20

The custom-house receipts for the same period (1878) were $5,279,447.40 against $4,843,651.60 in 1877; an increase in 1878 of $235,795.80.

The year 1877 was most disastrous to Italian commerce, as will be seen from the following returns compared with 1876:

IMPORTS.

1876	$265,427,460 20
1877	230,860,607 80

EXPORTS.

1876	$243,385,883 20
1877	193,304,708 60

There being a falling off in exports in 1877 of $50,081,174.60 and of $460,603 in custom-house receipts. The depression in trade is to be attributed to a variety of causes, first among which are the Eastern war, the overstocked markets, and the uncertainty attending the ratification of the commercial treaty with France.

As regards the commercial relations of Rome, it cannot be said to be prosperous, although a slight improvement has been manifest during the present year, and exports to the United States have been more active than for several years back. Although Rome is not a great manufacturing center as compared with the industrial importance of cities of its size in Northern Europe, it is one of the principal markets of Central Italy. Its principal articles of export to foreign countries are raw wool, horned cattle, cheese, cereals for seed, raw hides of small animals, such as lambs, kids, and hares, an earth for cement known as pazzolana, statuary, paintings, mosaics, cameos, jewelry, and an infinite variety of minor works of fine art. The limited manufactures of woolen, cotton, and silk are nearly all absorbed at home or in the surrounding rural districts. The same is true of manufactures of boots and shoes, carriages, firearms, and machines and machinery.

Rome, from its historical associations, as the principal seat of classical study of the fine arts, as the capital of Italy, and the seat of the Papacy, attracts a large floating population of all nationalities, constantly renewed, whose expenditures form a very considerable source of wealth, that thus far has not been noted in any statistics. This is especially true of mosaics, cameos, and jewelry, all of which are among its most flourishing industries, and such other works of art as may be carried away directly by the purchaser without having recourse to the ordinary means of shipment. Most European nations have established institutions for the study of the fine arts in Rome, while the United States are represented by 17 sculptors and 18 painters, whose artistic productions are destined almost exclusively for our country.

The following are the chief articles of import into Rome from foreign countries: Dry and smoked fish, petroleum, spirits, sugar, coffee, spices, colored marbles, cast-iron and steel, hardware, hard coal, coke, porcelain, pottery, glass and crystal, medicines, chemical products, paints, kid-gloves, woolen, cotton, linen and hemp, and their respective manufactures, paper, books, machines and machinery, haberdashery, gold, silver, and precious stones.

Imports from the United States consist almost wholly of petroleum, cotton goods, sewing-machines, and agricultural implements and machinery. I have not been able to obtain trustworthy figures of the imports into Rome from the United States, as they are only in part received direct from New York via Glasgow and Leghorn per Anchor Line steamers, and in part through the ports of Genoa, Civita Vecchia, and Naples.

5. PAPER MONEY.

Paper money is a legal tender in Italy for all payments except customs. During the year 1877 the premium on gold raised from 9 per cent. to 12.50 per cent., and from 8 per cent. to 11 per cent. for the 5½ months ending June 15, 1878.

By act of Parliament six of the leading credit establishments form the syndicate for the emission of bank-notes. The syndicate guarantees the government paper money with its united capital and reserve, and in turn is authorized to issue a limited amount of paper money on its own account. Italian paper money is of one uniform type throughout the kingdom. The denominations of bank-notes in circulation are as follows: 50 centimes, 1, 2, 5, 10, 20, 50, 100, 250, 500, and 1,000 lire.

On the 1st of April, 1878, the total of paper money in circulation in Italy amounted to $304,155,396. In this sum the Government figures for $182,000,000 and the syndicate for 122,155,396.20. The small amount of coin reserves (for the syndicate banks, only $25,739,600, on the 1st of January, 1877), must render any attempt at a resumption of specie payments for the present, at least, improbable.

6. BUSINESS HABITS AND SYSTEMS.

Large estates, with the exception of the Agro Romano, are usually let on long leases, of not less than three generations; a small percentage of land is also worked directly by the owner. The estates on the Agro Romano are let on leases of from five to twelve years to middlemen, who in turn sublet in small lots, on shares, for periods of from one to three years; the lessee cultivating for a stipulated amount in kind for every acre under cultivation.

In that which relates to the business habits of the importers and merchants of this city in their relations with foreign countries, I can only offer the following: Contracts in trade are usually paid in acceptance at 90 days, which are returned from London, Paris, or Vienna, as the case may be, to a banker in Rome for collection; cash, in some cases, is paid with the usual discount. All commercial transactions with the various cities and markets of Italy are subject to the same conditions.

In conclusion, I may add that the conditions of the trade have changed sensibly since Rome became the capital of Italy; the barrier that formerly separated this city from the remainder of the peninsula blighted all enterprise and barely enabled a few industries to struggle along in the shadow of protection. The field is now free to all, and although not many new industries have appeared, work in others, with the exception of the textile, has grown in proportion to the increased population.

CHAS. McMILLAN.

UNITED STATES CONSULATE-GENERAL,
Rome, June 25, 1878.

THE NETHERLANDS.

AMSTERDAM.

Report, by Consul Eckstein, on the rates of wages, past and present rates, and the condition of labor, in the district of Amsterdam.

In looking over the archives of the consulate I found the Department Circular of the 11th of April last, addressed to consuls in certain countries, asking them to make inquiries and report in regard to certain points bearing upon the subject of labor and wages and kindred matters. Believing that up to the present no such report has been made from this consulate, and desirous to comply with the requirements and wishes of the Department, I have the honor herewith to make a brief report upon some of the points upon which the Department wishes information. As my knowledge of matters of this character appertaining to this city and consular district is, necessarily, very limited, on account of the short duration of my residence here, I may be allowed to bespeak the kind indulgence of the Department for any defects in the substance or form of this report.

RATES OF WAGES.

Agricultural laborers, who are employed by the year, and who have their homes and receive their subsistence upon the premises of their employers, are paid from $50 to $60 per annum, and usually receive, in addition, two common suits of clothing during the same time.

Farm laborers, hired by the day during the busy seasons, receive from 40 to 50 cents per day.

Florists and nursery laborers, at the city of Harlem and its neighborhood, engaged in raising bulbs or flower-roots, are paid $2.90 per week for nine months in the year and $265 for the other three months.

Female servants are paid from $20 to $60 per annum; but those whose wages are only from $20 to $30 are not living in the houses of their employers altogether, but come early in the morning and leave at about four o'clock in the afternoon.

Hotel servants.—Hotel and restaurant employés, and persons employed in public institutions of every description, are, as a rule, paid very low wages, but this fact is no criterion of the actual condition of this class of laborers, for the well-established custom of giving them *drinkgeld*—drink-money—very often more than makes up for the low wages they receive; in fact, all such persons, including house-servants, males and females, rely more upon the income which they derive from this source than upon the actual wages which they receive from their employers.

Diamond-cutting, or polishing, a trade peculiar to Amsterdam, and carried on to a great extent, has of late years been, as it is now, remarkably prosperous. I am credibly informed that experienced and skillful diamond-cutters earn from $40 to $80 per week. There are said to be more than 1,500 of them in the city. The prosperity of those engaged in this trade dates from the discovery of diamonds at the Cape of Good Hope, as since that time diamond-cutting here has been an almost uninterrupted lucrative employment. Many diamond-cutters have within the last ten or twelve years laid the foundations of splendid fortunes.

The following statement shows the wages paid certain workmen per hour, the working hours being never less but often more than 12 per day: Carpenters, 7 to 10 cents; painters, 6¾ to 9¼ cents; masons, 7 to 10 cents; plumbers, 6½ to 9 cents; paper-hangers, 6½ to 9 cents; blacksmiths, 7 to 10 cents; stucco-workers, 8¾ to 10 cents; shoemakers, best, $6 to $6.60 per week; ordinary and repairers, $2.40 to $3.60; tailors, best, $5.60 to $6.80 per week; ordinary and repairers, $2.40 to $3.60; cigar-makers, when steadily employed, make from $5.20 to $6.80 per week; common railroad laborers and laborers employed on public works and by contractors, receive from 40 to 60 cents per day.

PAST AND PRESENT RATES.

The present rates of wages for nearly all classes of labor are said to be from 25 to 35 per cent. higher than they were five years ago, but the cost of living to the laborer (house-rent, board, and the prices of the necessaries of life) has increased during the same period even more than the wages.

PRESENT CONDITION OF LABOR.

The general condition of the laboring classes is not regarded as being prosperous or even as being satisfactory, as it is only by being extremely economical, frugal, and abstemious that many maintain themselves and families. At the same time there does not seem to be any wide-spread discontent or loudly-expressed complaints. On the contrary, the situation appears to be generally and ungrudgingly accepted by the mass of the laboring classes, and, apparently, they are not in the least impregnated with socialistic or communistic ideas or notions.

A noteworthy item in connection with this city is the fact that all city property has increased in value from 75 to 100 per cent. during the past eight or ten years. This is not, however, indicative of present prosperity in the trade and commerce of Amsterdam, for it is claimed that business just now is very much depressed, although by no means as much so as in other cities of Europe.

D. ECKSTEIN.

UNITED STATES CONSULATE,
Amsterdam, August 14, 1878.

ROTTERDAM.

Report, by Consul Winter, on the (1) *rates of wages;* (2) *cost of living;* (3) *past and present rates;* (4) *specie and paper money* (*Holland*); (5) *present condition of trade; for the district of Rotterdam.*

I have the honor to submit the following report, in response to the Circular from the Department of State, dated April 11, 1878, addressed to consular officers of the United States, and directing them to make inquiries and report in regard to the present price of mechanical and unskilled labor, the cost of living to the laborer, a comparison of the present rates of wages and cost of living with those which prevailed during the past five years, the amount and character of paper money and coin in circulation, with the relation borne by the one to the other, and in regard to the state of trade, &c.

1. Rates of wages.

The rate of wages usually paid to laborers of every class in the Netherlands is comparatively low, especially as compared to the rate of wages paid for mechanical and unskilled labor in the United States.

The usual or average rate of wages paid to agricultural laborers is 30 cents per day, or about $10 per month.

The average rate of wages paid for mechanical labor is shown by the following table:

Machinists	per day..	$0 80 to $1 20
Molders	do....	80 to 1 20
Carpenters	do....	60 to 1 00
Masons	do....	60 to 1 00
Smiths	do....	60 to 1 00
Painters	do....	60 to 1 00
Plasterers	do....	60 to 1 00

The rate of wages paid to porters, jobbers, and common laborers is 40 cents to 60 cents per day

The usual rate of wages paid for mechanical labor upon public works and railways is as follows:

Machinists	per day..	$0 80 to $1 40
Molders	do....	80 to 1 40
Carpenters	do....	60 to 1 10
Masons	do....	60 to 1 10
Smiths	do....	60 to 1 10
Painters	do....	60 to 1 10
Plasterers	do....	60 to 1 10
Plumbers	do....	60 to 1 10

Canal and street masons receive from 80 cents to $1.20 per day. Porters, jobbers, and common laborers receive from 40 cents to 60 cents per day.

2. Cost of living

The cost of living in the Netherlands consumes the wages of the mechanic and laborer. Meat, excepting sausage and chipped beef, is regarded by the mechanic and laboring man as a luxury, and is rarely indulged in except upon extra occasions. Bread, rice, fish, potatoes, and other vegetables constitute the staple articles of food for the laboring classes of the Netherlands.

3. Past and present rates.

A comparison of the present rates of wages paid for labor with those prevailing during the past five years shows an increase in the present rates of from 10 to 15 per cent., and the cost of living has advanced in at least equal proportions.

4. Specie and paper money.

The financial affairs of the Netherlands are evidently in a sound condition. Paper money is legally issued by the Bank of the Netherlands in notes of the following amounts: 1,000, 300, 200, 100, 60, 40, and 25 florins, respectively. The amount of these notes in circulation, according to the last official statement of 27th May, 1878, is 200,100,600 florins, against which the Netherlands Bank holds a reserve of coin and bullion of 114,275,902 florins.

The mint of the Netherlands also issues notes of 10-florin denomination, the total value of which in circulation amounts to 10,000,000 florins. Therefore the total amount of paper money in circulation in the kingdom is 210,100,000 florins.

According to the statement of the 27th of May, above referred to, the total amount of paper money in circulation still remains beneath the maximum amount authorized by 74,490,026.90 florins, and the reserve in coin and bullion exceeds the minimum amount by 29,760,010.76 florins.

Gold coins are issued by the mint of the Netherlands of only one denomination, namely, 10-florin pieces. The total amount of gold coin in circulation, as per last report of the superintendent of the mint, is 147,940,850 florins.

Silver is coined in sums of $2\frac{1}{2}$, 1, $\frac{1}{2}$, $\frac{1}{4}$, $\frac{1}{10}$, and $\frac{1}{20}$ florin, respectively. The total circulation of silver coin is estimated at 100,000,000 florins.

Copper coins in circulation in the kingdom are estimated at 142,000,000 cent pieces, and 110,400,000 $\frac{1}{2}$-cent pieces.

Paper money and silver coin are at par with gold coin and are a legal tender in any sums for both public and private debts.

5. Present condition of trade.

Concerning the present state of trade little can be said that is encouraging, though there are indications of improvement, and the merchants and business men of this consular district have high hopes of a general revival of trade in the near future.

The Netherlands merchants and business men, with their industry and economical business habits, have not felt the general depression of trade and the continued hard times so keenly as those engaged in trade and manufacture in other parts of the commercial world.

JOHN F. WINTER.

United States Consulate,
Rotterdam, July 10, 1878.

SPAIN.

BARCELONA.

Report, by Consul Scheuch, on the commerce and industries; labor and wages; cost of living; and the habits and customs of the working classes, for the province of Catalonia.

FINANCIAL CRISIS.

Barcelona, the commercial capital of Spain, with a harbor second to none in the Mediterranean, an energetic population of 350,000, has been, and is now, experiencing a financial crisis, since the early part of last fall, as never heretofore. Since the commencement of this year the results of the crisis began to be heavily felt by the cotton, wool, and linen manufacturers, the most important industries in Catalonia, and this day there are many of the largest establishments closed entirely and many others running on half-time; and I find that 43,000 persons, formerly employed in these three branches of industry, are to-day without work.

Statement showing the number of cotton and wool fabricants out of employment in the province of Catalonia.

Hand-looms.	Number of persons out of employment.
Wool	4,145
Cotton	9,355
Linen	1,033
Total	14,433

Employing 1¾ persons per loom, including bleaching, dyers, &c.	25,257
Woolen looms, run by steam, 515, at the rate of 1½ workmen per loom	722
Cotton looms, run by steam, 4,921, employing 84 workmen to each 100 looms	4,150
Cotton-spindles, by steam, 188,800, employing 11 men for each 1,000 spindles	2,252
Knitting-machines, with all the finishing, 250, employing 1⅓ each	333
Round looms, 630, at 4 men each	2,520
Looms stopped in Sabadell (10 miles from Barcelona), for the manufacture of cloths, velvets, 959, besides 33,500 spindles, employing in all	4,000
Looms stopped in Olesa (8 miles from Barcelona), for the manufacture of cloths, velvets, and beavers, 147, with 2,700 spindles	400
In Tarrassa (8 miles from Barcelona)	1,800
Looms for the manufacture of silk cravats and handkerchiefs, 768, 2 men per loom	1,536
Looms for velvets, 44, 3 men per loom	132
Total number of working persons, of both sexes, unemployed	43,102

COMMERCIAL STAGNATION.

The exportations and importations during the past eight months have fallen off more than one-half from the corresponding period of last year, and shipping is almost at a standstill. There are this day 80 to 100 vessels lying in the harbor for sale without any buyers, and more than that number are idle, not being able to find cargoes in or outward. The consequence is that thousands of shipcarpenters, sailmakers, calkers, and sailors are unemployed.

PAST AND PRESENT RATES.

Wages paid to artisans and laborers are about the same as last year, but comparing the present prices with those paid five years ago a decline of 25 to 30 per cent. is clearly visible. The trades occupied in construction and building, as carpenters, masons, smiths, &c., resisted a decrease in wages longer than all others, for the reason that capitalists have for the last two years withdrawn as much as possible of their money from investments made in public stocks and commercial and industrial enterprises and invested it in house-building, considering it the safest. For this reason there are now many houses to let, and rents have decreased 25 to 30 per cent.

I now append a list of wages paid to skilled mechanics and laborers in Catalonia and the number of working hours per day:

Rate of wages per diem in the province of Catalonia.

Occupations.	Average daily wages.	Hours of labor.
Blacksmiths	$0 70 to $0 80	10
Bakers	80 to 1 00	*14
Bookbinders	60	10
Bricklayers	85 to 90	9
Cabinet-makers	70	10
Carpenters	80 to 85	10
Coopers	90 to 1 00	9
Corkcutters	70	10
Machinists	1 00 to 1 50	10
Ironfounders	60	10
Painters, house	80	8
Plasterers	1 20	9
Shoemakers	60	12
Stonecutters	1 05 to 1 10	7
Tailors	60	11
Tanners	60 to 70	9½
Tinsmiths	65	10

*Summer.

Factory hands.—Experienced men on cotton, $5 to $5.50 per week; on wool, $6 to $8 per week. Experienced women on cotton, $5 to $5.50 per week; on wool, $3 to $3.50 per week. Children on cotton, $1.40 to $1.80 per week; on wool, $1.40 to $1.80 per week. Women spinners (cotton), $5 to $5.50 per week; daily working hours for all, 10 hours.

Farm laborers.—Experienced hands, 60 to 70 cents per day; ordinary hands, 55 to 60 cents per day; special hands during harvest, $1 to $1.20 per day, 12 working hours.

Female servants (including board), $3 to $5 per month.

COST OF LIVING.

As to the cost of living, there exists a considerable difference between Barcelona and the interior, chiefly due to the municipal consumption tax. For this reason living in Barcelona is exceedingly expensive, many articles costing from 20 to 50 per cent. more than in the country. The Catalonia working people live mostly on greens, beans, potatoes, onions, garlick, codfish (dried), and wine, and although these articles are very cheap in the country, they become dear in this city on account of the high entry-tax imposed on them. The following table shows the present retail prices of groceries and provisions, computed in United States gold:

Provisions:			
Flour, fine	per pound		$0 06¼
extra family	do		07½
Beef, with bone	do		15
without bone	do		18
Veal, with bone	do		15
without bone	do		22½
Mutton, with bone	do		12½
Pork (sale prohibited from May 15 to September 25) in winter	do		21
smoked ham	do		40
Lard	do		19
Butter, fresh	do		40
Codfish, dry	do		09
Cheese, Holland	do		25
Potatoes	do		01¾
Rice, good	do		06½
Beans, white	do		04½
Milk	per quart		11¾
Eggs	per dozen	$0 20 to	25
Groceries:			
Tea	per pound		60
Coffee, superior	do		40
Sugar, good brown	do		10
coffee	do		12½
Soap, common	do	08 to	10
Starch	do	08 to	10
Coal, English	per quintal	40 to	50
Salad-oil, common	per cuartan		1 00
best	do		1 30

B.—100 Catalan pounds = 88.41 English pounds; 100 cuartanes of oil = 90.68 English imp. gallons, or 109.66 English old gallons; 1 Catalan quintal contains 104 pounds Catalan (12 ounces English each).

HOUSE RENT AND CLOTHING.

The average apartments of a Catalonian workman, with a family—wife and three to four children—consists of kitchen and four to five rooms (rather small), for which he pays, in the country, from $8 to $20 per annum; in this city, from $2 to $5 per month.

Clothing is cheap, and the climate being mild and even, during the entire year, workmen dress summer and winter alike, mostly wearing corduroy pantaloons and a Spanish (short) jacket of the same material. Boots or shoes are very seldom seen worn by laborers (men), the sandal (made of twine or grass) being the common foot cover.

HABITS AND CUSTOMS.

As to the habits of the Catalonian laboring class, they are certainly very laborious, and the most sober and frugal I have seen. During my four years' residence here I have never yet met an intoxicated person belonging to that class; yet wine is constantly drunk by the men, women, and children. Not being drunk for enjoyment, it is considered beneficial to health, and taken sparingly but regularly after every meal.

FRED. H. SCHEUCH.

UNITED STATES CONSULATE,
Barcelona, June 20, 1878.

CADIZ.

Report, by Consul Duffié, on the (1) distress among the laboring class; (2) food of the laborers; (3) rates of wages; (4) cost of living; (5) past and present rates; (6) present state of trade; (7) paper money (of Spain); (8) business habits and systems; for the district of Cadiz, embracing the cities of Cadiz, Jerez, and Seville.

In answer to the questions contained in the Circular of the Department of 11th April, 1878, I beg to report as follows:

The unsatisfactory state of trade and the paralyzation of industry, due to divers causes, among which the recent drought may be specially mentioned, have almost put a stop to the demand for labor.

1. DISTRESS AMONG THE LABORING CLASS.

In order to relieve the consequent distress of the laboring class, the Spanish Government has been compelled to turn its attention to the promotion of public works in different parts of the country, and even to supply some districts with sums drawn from the public calamities fund, to be distributed in daily allowances to laborers without work.

The municipal bodies likewise contribute, but are hardly able thoroughly to remedy the evil, being, in general, deeply indebted to contractors, in arrears in the payment of salaries to their own emyloyés, in default toward the general government in the matter of taxes on consumption, which they collect, their credit lost, and, in brief, in a state akin to bankruptcy.

The wages paid in this district are therefore applicable only to such mechanics and laborers as have the good fortune to find temporary employment.

2. FOOD OF THE LABORERS.

In reference to the cost of living to the laboring classes, it may also be stated that no article, foreign or native, comprised in the category of the necessaries of life, fit for food, for drink, for heating, burning, or lighting, escapes a special taxation, styled "Duties on consumption." These duties are levied on certain articles by the State and by the municipal authorities on the rest. They are collected by the municipal officials, who also levy on the articles taxed by the Government an additional tax, now amounting to 50 per cent. of the government dues. The price of every article is thus enhanced to a degree which excludes the laboring classes from all but the commonest vegetable food.

The farm laborers of Andalusia, fed by their employers, are allowed daily three pounds of bread, some oil, and a little vinegar. A portion of the bread is set aside, with the oil and vinegar, to form the two meals of the *gaspacho* served to the farm hands. It consists of bread soaked in water, to which the oil and vinegar are added. It is served hot in winter and cold in summer. Any additions, generally of vegetables, are supplied by the laborer at his own cost. This cheap ration is generally adopted by the working classes that pay their own board.

I may further premise that the three principal cities in my consular district, Seville, Cadiz, and Jerez, are in different conditions of prosperity. Seville is largely on the increase in commerce and industry at the expense of Cadiz, which has steadily declined, and both Seville and Jerez have the advantage over Cadiz of being located in fertile agricultural districts. I now proceed to answer the questions propounded.

3. Rates of wages.

Mechanical laborers are usually paid 40 to 50 cents per working day, according to aptitude; laborers on public works and railways from 40 to 45 cents per day; carpenters, blacksmiths, and masons are paid 80 cents per day; coopers and collarmen (in the wine district), 95 cents; farm laborers, 20 to 25 cents per day, exclusive of board and lodging; vineyard laborers, 50 to 70 cents.

4. Cost of living.

The cost of living to a laborer may be estimated to average 30 cents per diem on scanty rations (from which meat is excluded) and miserable lodgings. In Jerez it may be calculated at 40 cents a day. An item, considered as indispensable as food, is tobacco, smoked in cigarettes; it is calculated at 2½ cents per diem per capita.

5. Past and present rates.

The comparison between the actual rates of wages and the cost of living to the laboring classes and those prevailing during the past five years shows at the outside no particular difference. The higher prices of the necessaries of life, consequent on the duties on consumption, is met by diminished expenditure both in the quantity and quality of the food.

6. Present state of trade.

The present state of trade compares unfavorably, as I have intimated, with former periods. Mechanics, artisans, and laborers lack employment in Cadiz. At Jerez, Sanlucar and Port St. Mary the wine business is paralyzed. A considerable falling off in the demand for sherries from England have induced a fall in prices, and a further decline would threaten ruin to vineyard proprietors.

Seville, which has been steadily improving for the last ten years in industry and commerce, presents a healthier appearance. Attention is there given to the manufacture of soap, leather, common textile fabrics, earthenware, corks, machinery, ornamental iron factories, and corn, flour, and semoline mills.

The licorice factories have been closed since the United States, the chief consumer, laid heavy import duties on the article.

7. Paper money.

The only paper money issued in Spain is the bank-note of the Banco de España, established at Madrid. Its paper has no circulation outside of the capital, and is there often exchanged for coin at 1 to 1½ per cent. discount. The bank has established branch offices in seventeen important cities, of which three—Cadiz, Seville, and Jerez—are within this consular district. In these seventeen towns the bank-notes issued are for the exclusive use of each locality and are nowhere else received, nor discounted except at usurious rates. The bank-notes are of value of 5, 10, 25, 50, and 200 dollars. They circulate in the towns only among the mercantile class, and, when received by the rest of the community, are taken, as a general rule, to the branch office and exchanged for coin.

The average circulation of bank-notes in Madrid amounted in the year 1877 to $20,346,377; and in the seventeen branches, comprising such important centers as Barcelona, Valencia, Seville, Malaga, Jerez, Santander, and Cadiz, to $11,228,977; while the payment of bank-notes during the same period was as follows: In Madrid, $13,723,500, in the branches, $24,043,230.

The average circulation of bank-notes and the payment of the same in 1877 in this consulate district was as follows:

	Average circulation.	Bank-notes paid.
Cadiz	$195, 980	$1, 323, 855
Jerez	284, 263	1, 193, 165
Seville	831, 148	357, 725
Total	1, 311, 391	2, 874, 745

8. BUSINESS HABITS AND SYSTEMS.

The business habits and systems of this district present no particular feature different from those in practice generally in Europe. It may, however, be noticeable that manufacturers allow no discount for cash payments.

A. M. DUFFIÉ.

UNITED STATES CONSULATE,
Cadiz, May 28, 1878.

MALAGA.

Report, by Consul Quarles, on (1) *the rates of wages*; (2) *the cost of living*; (3) *past and present rates*; (4) *present condition of trade*; (5) *the currency*; (6) *the business habits and customs*; *for the district of Malaga.*

I have not replied earlier to the Department circular of April 11, 1878, asking for certain information in regard to the general condition of labor and trade in this consulate, for the reason that information on subjects of this character is extremely difficult to obtain, and that obtained is very imperfect.

1. RATES OF WAGES.

So far as I have been able to ascertain, the rates of wages are as follows, per day:

Carpenters	$0 70 to $0 90
Blacksmiths	70 to 90
Masons	70 to 90
Caulkers	1 25 to 1 50
Shipwrights	1 25 to 1 50
Shoemakers, piece-work	60 to 80
Tailors, piece-work	60 to 80
Hatters, piece-work	60 to 80
Coopers, piece-work	60 to 80
Common laborers	40 to 50
Agricultural laborers, with board and lodging	15 to 20

2. COST OF LIVING.

In regard to the cost of living, it is proper to remark that the laborer in the south of Spain is the most frugal of beings. He rarely or never eats meat. Indeed, it would be impossible for him to do so and live on his earnings, as meat is extremely dear; common fresh meat being worth 20 cents and beef-steak 30 cents per pound. The laborer here generally subsists on fish, rice, beans, and other vegetables. Rice is worth about 12½ cents per pound, fish 5 cents, beans 10 cents, and other vegetables in proportion.

3. Past and present rates.

In regard to the comparison of the present rates with those prevailing during the last five years, so far as I have been able to ascertain, the rate of wages has increased from 10 to 15 per cent., while the cost of living has increased something like 40 per cent. In this disparity between the increase of wages and the increase in the cost of living may be discovered one of the causes of the increase of petty crimes so noticeable in this province.

4. Present condition of trade.

With regard to the state of trade, I have to say that it is far from prosperous. Owing to the many failures which occurred toward the close of last year and the beginning of this, as well as to the depressed state of trade everywhere, business here has almost ceased. It is expected that there will be a revival as soon as the vintage begins, but no one can tell to what extent.

5. The currency.

With regard to the circulating medium, it is proper to say that most of the money here consists of gold and silver, chiefly the latter. Paper money is, however, issued by the Bank of Spain in notes of $5 and upwards. These notes are at par value, and are convertible into specie.

6. Business habits and customs.

With regard to the business habits of the people, I have to say that business, like everything else, is done in that irregular manner so characteristic of the people of this country.

In Malaga there are a great many descendants of English and German families doing business, and therefore one is likely to find more order and method in the manner of doing business here than in other commercial centers of Spain; still many evidences of want of method in business affairs are always to be found. As, however, the business of Malaga is passing more and more into the hands of foreigners, it is reasonable to expect great improvements in this respect.

JOHN F. QUARLES.

United States Consulate,
Malaga, Jule 15, 1878.

SANTANDER.

Report, by Consul Gallo, on (1) *the rates of wages;* (2) *the cost of living;* (3) *past and present rates;* (4) *the paper money; for the district of Santander.*

I acknowledge the receipt of Department Circular of April 11, 1878, and in reply I beg to inform you on the following points:

1. Rates of wages.

The wages usually paid to agricultural laborers are very low, because the agricultural wealth is not important. Women are generally employed for this work. They are paid about 30 cents per day at and about the villages, and 50 cents in the town. Mechanics are paid from 80 cents to $2 per day; laborers on the railways and public works, 40 to 60 cents.

2. Cost of living.

The cost of living to the laboring classes, or the price paid for what may be termed the necessaries of life, is in the same ratio as the wages, and the highest order of working people are able to save something.

3. Past and present rates.

The difference between the present rates and those which prevailed during the last five years has been a slight increase in wages, but the cost of living has increased in the same proportion. Business is almost paralyzed in Santander, although the population and wealth have considerably increased during the past ten years.

4. Paper money.

The paper money in circulation is emitted by the Bank of Spain at Madrid, and the total amount in circulation on December 31, 1877, was 2,635,175 pesetas ($527,000), and the coin, in relation to the notes in circulation, one-third less. The discount at the Bank of Santander and at Madrid varies from 4 to 5 per cent. per annum.

The usual commission in all commercial transactions is 2 per cent.; in merchandise brokerage, 2 per thousand; negotiation of drafts, 1 per thousand.

LUIS GALLO.

United States Consulate,
Santander, May 29, 1878.

SWITZERLAND.

Report, by Consul Montgomery on the (1) *cost of living in Geneva;* (2) *rates of wages throughout Switzerland; and* (3 *and* 4) *food-prices in and financial condition of Geneva.*

1. Cost of living.

The cost of living in Geneva may be stated as somewhat less than the average in the United States, although it must be admitted that it has advanced considerably during the last decade on account of the annual influx of thousands of visitors from all parts of Europe and America, many of whom remain here during the winter for educational and other purposes.

The difference, as compared with our own country, arises not so much from any marked contrast in the price of provisions or articles of domestic use and comfort, as from the three important elements of house-rent, labor, and service, all of which remain at a much lower standard than can be commanded in the United States.

The cost of labor and service in this country presents a very remarkable contrast to that in the United States, and are important features, therefore, in the economical administration of the Government, in the reduced rate of taxation, and the consequent expenses of living. These, in fact, in connection with cheap rents of houses and apartments, and not the price of provisions and the ordinary necessaries of life, many of which can be purchased at lower rates in our own country, are the causes alone which reduce the average cost of living below that in the United States.

2. Rates of wages.

The following statement will demonstrate that the wages throughout Switzerland will average 78 cents per day of 10 hours, viz:

Carpenters, musical-box makers, and tinsmiths	per day	$0 80 to $1 40
Mechanics, skilled	do	2 00 to 2 50
ordinary	do	60 to 1 20
Operatives, male	do	80
female	do	60
Workmen	do	60 to 1 00
Laborers, male	do	50 to 75
female	do	30 to 50
Farm hands, male	do	60 to 75
female	do	40 to 50
Employés, male (in stores)	do	80
female (in stores)	do	30
Masons, joiners, and woodcarvers	do	80 to 1 00

I have introduced these details inasmuch as in these times of "strikes" it is important to know the value of labor in different parts of Europe, so as to be enabled to compare it with the more liberal scale prevailing in our own country.

3. Food-prices.

The following table exhibits the present retail prices of the principal articles of food in the Geneva market, viz:

Beef for roasting	per pound	$0 18
for steaks	do	30
for soup	do	18
Bread, best	do	04
Butter, best	do	36

Candles, best	per pound	$0 28
Gas, per meter cube (3 feet 3 inches cube)		07
Cheese, Swiss	per pound	23
Chickens	per bird	70
Coffee, raw, best	per pound	30
Eggs	per dozen	20
Flour, best	per pound	07
Green corn (in cans)	per can	50
Milk	per liter	05
Mutton, best	per pound	18
Oats	do	08
Wheat	do	08
Rye	do	08
Potatoes	per 100 pounds	1 20
Pork, fresh	per pound	18
salt	do	28
White sugar	do	09
Brown sugar	do	08
Tea, black	do	50
green	do	1 30
Tomatoes	do	05
Turkeys	per 7 or 8 pounds	1 40
Veal	per pound	20
American pressed meat	per can	90
Wood	per cord	18 00
Coke	per ton	10 00

4. Financial condition.

The financial condition of Geneva does not present as flattering or satisfactory an outlook as represented in my last annual report. At that time the city was free from debt, the former indebtedness of 7,000,000 francs having been paid off out of the money left to Geneva in 1873 by the late Duke of Brunswick. At present there is a debt of 3,000,000 francs, contracted this year for the purposes of general improvement, such as opening new streets, building schools and other buildings, &c., while the Canton of Geneva, having a population of about 90,000, is burdened with outstanding obligations of 22,000,000 francs, or $4,246,000. The annual expenses of the city amount to 1,600,000 francs, or $308,800, and those of the canton to 5,500,000 francs, or $1,061,500. Money, however, is abundant, and good paper has been readily discounted during the past year at an average of 3½ per cent. The rate of taxation on productive real estate is 3 per cent. The tax on capital is graduated as follows, viz: Up to 3,000 francs of capital there is no tax; from 3,000 to 50,000 francs of capital there is a tax of 1 franc per thousand; from 50,000 to 250,000 francs of capital there is a tax of 2 francs per thousand; above 250,000 francs of capital there is a tax of 3 francs per thousand.

In addition to the above, there is a personal tax upon domestics, carriages, horses, dogs, and for the cantonal hospital, the aggregate of which is very moderate. As far as can be ascertained, the annual revenue derived in this city and adjoining cantons from American investments amounts to $1,000,000, representing a capital of $15,000,000, of which three-fourths approximately consist of State and railroad bonds, and the remainder United States Government securities.

J. EGLINTON MONTGOMERY.

United States Consulate,
Geneva, October 21, 1878.

APPENDIX TO LABOR REPORTS.

APPENDIX TO LABOR REPORTS.

WAGES AND FOOD PRICES IN NEW YORK AND CHICAGO.

The following correspondence will show the sources from which the Secretary of State received the information which enabled him to give the rates of wages and prices of the necessaries of life in New York and Chicago in the comparative form in which it has been used throughout the Secretary's letter:

The gentlemen who so kindly furnished the information, at considerable inconvenience, are well posted on the subjects on which they treat. Mr. Bartholomew is editor of the American Exporter, besides being editorially connected with the Daily News and other newspapers in New York, has given much study to the labor question, and fully understands the subject; Mr. Thurber, being of the house of Thurber & Co., New York, is necessarily posted on the food-prices and the wants of the working classes, having given much thought to the subject as connected with commerce not only in the United States, but in Europe also; Mr. Scanlan has represented one of the labor districts of Chicago in the Illinois legislature, and has long been identified with the labor interests of that city; so that the information used by the Secretary in his letter in regard to those two cities may be relied upon as correct at the dates on which it was given.

WAGES AND THE PRICES OF THE NECESSARIES OF LIFE IN CHICAGO.

CHICAGO, *December* 2, 1878.

The list, showing the weekly wages paid the several trades in this city, which I inclose, is thoroughly reliable, as I obtained the information personally from both employers and employés. The prices of the necessaries of life I have obtained from the very best representative dealers in Chicago, viz: C. H. Slacks, Charles Curdy, Thomas McEnirey, Pierce & Whettmore, and A. Triggs. These houses are situated in various parts of the city, and are largely patronized by the laboring classes.

As to the wages paid to the trades, as per list herewith, it should be taken into consideration that the same are based on full time, while the real state of the case would show that very few are permanently at work. The only trades that I found fairly employed were bookbinders, cabinet-makers, coppersmiths, and saddlers and harness-makers. These average from nine to twelve months' work in the year.

This fall has been the busiest and best for labor in a number of years.

JOHN F. SCANLAN.

Statement showing the weekly hours of labor and the rates of wages paid at Chicago, November, 1878.

Occupations.	Weekly hours.	Weekly wages (full time).
Blacksmiths	59	$9 00 to $12 00
Bakers	60	8 00 to 12 00
Bookbinders	59	9 00 to 20 00
Shoemakers	59	9 00 to 18 00
Butchers	72	12 00 to 18 00
Cabinet-makers	54	7 00 to 15 00
Coopers	66	6 00 to 15 00
Coppersmiths	60	15 00 to 21 00
Cutlers	60	*6 00
Engravers	54	9 00 to 30 00
Horseshoers	60	15 00 to 21 00
Millwrights	60	12 00 to 21 00
Printers	60	12 00 to 18 00
Saddlers and harness-makers	59	6 00 to 12 00
Sailmakers	60	12 00 to 15 00
Tinsmiths	60	9 00 to 12 00
Tailors	60	6 00 to 18 00
Brassfinishers	60	8 00 to 15 00
Laborers, porters, &c	60	5 52 to 9 00
Bricklayers	60	6 00 to 10 50
Masons	60	12 00 to 15 00
Carpenters and joiners	60	7 50 to 12 00
Gasfitters	60	10 00 to 12 00
Painters	60	6 00 to 12 00
Plasterers	52 to 60	9 00 to 15 00
Plumbers	60	12 00 to 21 00
Slaters	60	12 00 to 18 00

* Average for men, boys, and girls.

Statement showing the retail prices of the necessaries of life, as given by foregoing houses, in Chicago, November, 1878.

Provisions and groceries:

Bread	per pound	$0 04	to	$0 04½
Flour	do	2½	to	04½
Beef, for roasting	do	08	to	12½
for soup	do			05
rump-steak	do	08	to	12½
Corned	do	04	to	07
Veal, fore quarter	do	06	to	10
hind quarter	do	10	to	12
cutlets	do	12½	to	15
Mutton, fore quarter	do	05	to	12½
hind quarter	do	05	to	15
chops	do	10	to	15
Pork, fresh	do	04	to	08
salted	do	06	to	12
bacon	do	07	to	12
ham	do	07	to	15
shoulder	do	04	to	10
sausage	do	06	to	10
Lard	do	06	to	10
Codfish, dry	do	05	to	09
Butter	do	16	to	40
Cheese	do	05	to	16
Potatoes	per bushel	60	to	80
Rice	per pound	05	to	10
Beans	per quart	05	to	09
Milk	do	03	to	06
Eggs	per dozen	10	to	24
Oatmeal	per pound	04	to	05
Tea	do	25	to	1 00
Coffee	do	15	to	40
Sugar	do	07	to	11
Molasses	per gallon	40	to	80
Soap, common	per pound	03	to	08
Starch	do	05	to	10
Coal	per ton	3 00	to	6 75

WAGES AND THE PRICES OF THE NECESSARIES OF LIFE IN NEW YORK.

NEW YORK, *December* 18, 1878.

I send you the list of trades filled out. It required considerable time, the occupations being so scattered in the metropolis, and no one man's word being taken. The *highest prices* (of wages) are obtained by those who represent the trades-unions (printers, for instance, $18 for daytime-work); the lowest, those who are not in the unions, boys of 18 to 20, who do what men are supposed to be capable of (printers, $8.) There are very few trades-unions now in New York. Some of the trades hold regular meetings, but there is scarcely any limit fixed by the organizations as to wages. "Get work where you can and at the best price you can obtain," is the general rule. The only concession regarding hours is quitting at 5 p. m. Saturdays. Ten hours is really a day's work in every trade.

I inclose you some articles which have appeared recently. As managing editor of the New York Daily and Sunday News, in which most of the trades advertise their meetings, &c., I am perhaps as able to judge of the affairs of the workingmen *in general* as any one person in the metropolis.

GEORGE BARTHOLOMEW.

Statement showing the weekly hours of labor and the wages paid in New York and vicinity per week.

Occupations.	Weekly hours.	Weekly wages (full time).
Building trades:		
Bricklayers	59	$12 00 to $15 00
Masons	59	12 00 to 18 00
Carpenters and joiners	59	9 00 to 12 00
Gasfitters	60	10 00 to 14 00
Painters	58	10 00 to 16 00
Plasterers	59	10 00 to 15 00
Plumbers	59	12 00 to 18 00
Slaters	59	10 00 to 15 00
Blacksmiths	60	10 00 to 14 00
Bakers	80	5 00 to 8 00
Bookbinders	60	12 00 to 18 00
Shoemakers	Piece-work.	12 00 to 18 00
Butchers	70	8 00 to 12 00
Cabinet-makers	60	9 00 to 13 00
Coopers	60	12 00 to 16 00
Coppersmiths	60	12 00 to 15 00
Cutlers	60	10 00 to 13 00
Engravers	60	15 00 to 25 00
Horseshoers	59	12 00 to 18 00
Millwrights	60	10 00 to 15 00
Printers	60 / Piece-work.	8 00 to 18 00
Saddlers and harness-makers	60	12 00 to 15 00
Sailmakers	56	12 00 to 18 00
Tinsmiths	60	10 00 to 14 00
Tailors (custom-work, merchant tailors)	Piece-work.	10 00 to 18 00
Brassfounders	60	10 00 to 14 00
Laborers, porters, &c	60	6 00 to 9 00

PRICES OF THE NECESSARIES OF LIFE IN NEW YORK.

NEW YORK, *November* 23, 1878.

Regarding the question of retail prices of the necessaries life, would say that I inclose herewith a schedule of prices, as requested. It will be observed that there is a wide range of prices, as it is a most difficult thing to give a single price where there is both a range in quality and the terms of purchase.

Grocery stores and meat markets which sell exclusively for cash and deal in the lowest quality of articles, will give quite a different range of prices from those which do a credit business and handle better grades. I do not see that you can do better than to take the average, although the lower prices probably represent more nearly the qualities and prices paid by the laboring classes.

There has been a large decline in the prices of all food-products, both at wholesale and retail, during the last ten years, and especially during the last two years. In some cases I do not think the full decline has yet been realized by the retailer, and it is probable that retail prices will in some cases further decline.

The prospects for the future are, that there will be a very low range in the price of all food-products, and, so far as the necessaries of life are concerned, for the future exceedingly low prices will prevail.

While this is not to the interest of the producer, it certainly is to that of the consumer, and is, in some measure, a recompense for the great decline in wages which has taken place.

F. B. THURBER.

Statement showing the retail prices of the necessaries of life in New York and vicinity, as given by H. K. & F. B. Thurber & Co., of New York City, November 1, 1878.

Bread, per loaf	1 pound 6 ounces..	$0 05
Do	1 pound 12 ounces..	08
Do	2 pounds 4 ounces..	10
Flour, per barrel	196 pounds..	$6 50 to 7 50
Beef, for roasting	per pound..	12 to 16
for soup	do	06 to 08
rump-steak	do	14 to 16
corned	do	08 to 12
Veal, fore quarter	do	08 to 10
hind quarter	do	10 to 12
cutlets	do	20 to 24
Mutton, fore quarter	do	09 to 10
hind quarter	do	12 to 14
chops	do	14 to 16
Pork, fresh	do	08 to 10
salted	do	08 to 10
bacon	do	08 to 10
ham	do	08 to 12
shoulder	do	08 to 10
sausage	do	08 to 10
Lard	do	10 to 12
Codfish, dry	do	06 to 07
Butter	do	25 to 32
Cheese	do	12 to 15
Potatoes	per half-peck..	18 to 20
Rice	per pound..	08 to 10
Beans	per quart..	07 to 10
Milk	do	08 to 10
Eggs	per dozen..	25 to 30
Oatmeal	per pound..	04 to 05
Tea	do	50 to 60
Coffee	do	20 to 30
Sugar	do	08 to 10
Molasses	per gallon..	60 to 70
Soap, common	per pound..	06 to 07
Starch	do	08 to 10
Coal	per half-ton..	3 00
Do	per quarter-ton..	1 75
Do	per ton..	5 25

COST OF LIVING IN VARIOUS COUNTRIES.

Extract from the Annual Commercial Report of Consul Potter, of Stuttgart, Germany, for the year 1878.

The following table exhibits the average retail price in different parts of Europe of thirteen principal articles of food, considered of best quality, in the localities named. The figures are obtained from statistics and facts communicated to this consulate by the American consuls residing in the different cities enumerated.

Regarding exports from the United States the table is not particularly useful. It will, however, if made public, answer inquiries almost daily addressed to this consulate by persons in the United States who propose residing temporarily on the Continent. It will also show, generally, that the prices of food in Errope are, on an average, considerably higher than those prevailing in America.

The food-producing capacities of the various countries upon the Continent, as well as of England, cannot be much increased. As an example may be mentioned this kingdom, where every arable acre of land is under thorough cultivation. Questions relating to fuel and timber supply, as well as the climatic and sanitary conditions of the country, will prevent any additional clearing of forest lands. If, therefore, the population should increase to double its present number—as it some time will—the food supply would be no greater than at the present time. The yield of the bread crop of Würtemberg for the present year is bountiful and more than an average, and yet, with a population of little more than 1,800,000, there will be a deficiency in the food supply of about 2,000,000 bushels of wheat, which must be imported from countries that have a surplus. And what is true of this kingdom is substantially true of all continental countries, as also England. As the population of these countries increases, in the same ratio will the demand for food upon the United States, which is the most convenient source of supply, increase. The redundant population of Europe must have food brought to them, or, by emigration, they must seek it where it is produced.

The export trade of the United States in breadstuffs and food of all kinds must, therefore, rapidly increase, until it attains dimensions, even in the near future, which promise to be enormous. With adequate terminal railroad facilities at the great seaports; with a wise distribution of the surplus labor of the country over unoccupied lands; with stability in the administration of national affairs, and with a currency based upon the standard adopted by all commercial nations, and of uniform value at home and abroad, the immediate future of the United States would seem to foreshadow the commencement of an era of unusual prosperity and contentment for all.

Table showing the average retail prices in different parts of Europe of

Country.	City or town.	White bread.	Wheat flour.	Beefsteak.	Chickens.	Veal.
		Per lb.	*Per lb.*	*Per lb.*	*Per lb.*	*Per lb.*
Belgium	Antwerp	$0 04½	$0 05½	$0 22½	$0 20 -$0 25	$0 20
Prussia	Barmen	06¼	07½	18	40	19
England	Bristol	04	06	22	39	22
Ireland	Belfast	04	04¼	21	23	18
Prussia	Berlin	03½	04½	19	20 - 25	18
France	Bordeaux	05	06	30	12½	28
Germany	Brunswick	06	05	17½	22	17
Spain	Cadiz	05	04	18½	20	22½
South Wales	Cardiff	03¼	04	20	31	18
United States	Cincinnati	03¼	03½	15	17	16
Italy	Carrara	07	09	20	20	25
Saxony	Chemnitz	06	06	24	23	19
Do	Coburg	05	06¼	30	18	13
Denmark	Copenhagen	04	04	19	18	17
Prussia	Cologne	07½	06	18¼	21	20
Ireland	Dublin	02½	03	21	15	20½
Prussia	Düsseldorf	09	07	20	24	17
England	Falmouth	04	04½	19	20	19
Italy	Florence	06	06½	17	19	20
Germany	Frankfort-on-the-Main	06½	06	19	24	18
Italy	Genoa	05½	06	20	27	34
Switzerland	Geneva	05½	07	30	35	20
Belgium	Ghent	05	05½	20	31	20
Scotland	Glasgow	04	04½	32	35	20
Spain	Gibraltar	$0 03½- 04¼	03½	13	12½- 20	16
Italy	Leghorn	......	......	......	......	......
Germany	Leipsic	03½- 04	03½	17	26	13½
Portugal	Lisbon	05½	06	16	19	19
England	Liverpool	04	03½	22	22	19
Germany	Mannheim	06	07	22	25	21
England	Manchester	04	05	29	33	18
Italy	Messina	05	05½	13	18	13
Bavaria	Munich	06½	07	21	19	18
Italy	Palermo	06	05	24	22	30
England	Plymouth	05	05	21	28	18
Ireland	Queenstown	05	06	22	17 - 28	22
Italy	Nice	05	05½	25	20	23
England	Sheffield	04	04	22	25	20
Wurtemberg	Stuttgart	07	09	20	18	17½
Sweden	Stockholm	†11	06	08	18	11
Austria	Trieste	03½	04½	16	30	22
Italy	Turin	06½	07	17	15	21
Austria	Vienna	04½	05½	17	20	18
Russia	Warsaw	05	06	15½	20 - 25	08
United States	Boston	04	04½	$0 18- 23	21	16
Do	New York City	03	04	15- 20	19	15

* Ground. † Little used.

thirteen principal articles of food, of the very best quality, October 1, 1878.

Pork, fresh.	Eggs.	Butter, best table.	Cheese.	Coffee.	Tea.	White sugar.	Potatoes.
Per lb.	*Per doz.*	*Per lb.*	*Per lb.*	*Per lb.*	*Per lb.*	*Per lb.*	*Per lb.*
$0 18	$0 11	$0 26	$0 19	$0 36	$0 85	$0 15	$0 02
20	20	31	$0 20– 30	40	$0 60– 1 25	14	01¼
20	22½	30	22	38	68	08	02
16	24	25	17	$0 22– 30	30– 82	07	01
17	14	35	20– 30	52	1 25	13	03½
26	19	40	25	59	1 58	17	02
16	15	31	25	35	60– 1 10	11¾	00¾
20	20	30	15	45	1 00	15	02
16	37	24	20	36	66	10	02
09	18	24	10	27	75– 1 30	09½	00¾
18	24	30	28	20	Not used.	13	04
19	16	19	25	30– 38	80	14	01
15	20	23	25	40	80	11	01
13	17	39	25	43	86	12	02½
17	20½	31	27	50	1 22	13½	01
20	34	38	22	22	50– 1 25	10	02
21	24	32	22	45	50– 1 00	12	01¼
18	20	25	22	40	40– 85	09	01
16	16	30	29	35	1 30	14	01½
18	21	29	20– 30	45	1 00– 1 25	14	01½
32	12	31	18– 36	25– 37	1 10– 1 75	15	02½
18	20	36	22	30	50– 1 30	09	01⅛
20	18	40	25	35	....	17	01
22	32	40	25	40	75	07	01⅓
$0 14– 16	12	$0 25– 40	25– 30	40– 50	30– 90	07	01½
....	....	....	....	....	....	....	....
16	15	25– 36	19	34– 45	68– 1 70	$0 10– 13	02
18	15	41	41	29	87	11	01¼
15	22	32	15	25	25– 87	09	01½
18	16	25	24	30– 40	70– 1 25	12	01
16	24	34	14– 28	30	62– 88	05– 10	01⅓
11	16	23	18	25– 28	Little used.	10	00¾
16	18	25	14– 25	45	45– 1 20	14	01½
18	24	40	19	32	70	15	01
15	21	22	15– 50	17– 34	35– 78	09	01⅓
14	20	30	25	*44	80	08	02
20	16	40	28	43	1 00– 1 20	15	01¾
16	22	30– 35	18	22– 40	1 00	09	01½
17½	18½	22½	20– 30	46	50– 1 25	14½	01¾
10	13	25	18– 24	27	75	12	(‡)
14	14	24½	12– 16	....	35– 1 12	13	01
19	19	24	27	32	Not used.	13½	00¾
21	12	20– 50	19– 25	....	2 00	25	01
08	10– 12	18	23	35– 40	1 00– 3 00	08	03– 04
13	25	30– 65	12	26	75– 1 25	10	02
11	20	25– 35	11	24	50– 1 20	09½	01

†6 cents per cubic foot.

J. S. POTTER.

UNITED STATES CONSULATE,
Stuttgart, November 9, 1878.

ARGENTINE REPUBLIC.

Rates of wages in the Argentine Republic, being an extract from the annual commercial report of E. J. Baker, esq., United States consul at Buenos Ayres.

* * * * * * * *

In regard to wages, the immigration office has published a schedule of what immigrants may hope to get who come to this country. It seems that in some cases the prices are considerably exaggerated, but I give it for what it is worth. Wages are paid in paper money, which is at present at about 30 per cent. discount.

Agriculturists, in harvest-time, receive $60 per month, with board and lodging; during the remainder of the year from $16 to $24 per month, with board and lodging. The following receive board and lodging in addition to their wages, which are monthly: Joiners, $32; bricklayers, $24 to $36; gunsmiths, $16; apothecaries, $48; men cooks, $16 to $24; women cooks, $10 to $20; boiler-makers, $66; carpenters, $24 to $48; seamstresses, $20 to $32; clerks, $10 to $24; typefounders, $60; blacksmiths, $32; men servants, $12 to $20; women servants, $12 to $20; boys and girls, $4 to $12; machinists, $24 to $40; tailors, $24 to $40; saddlers, $24 to $48; typesetters, $32 to $50; gardeners, $32 to $60; shoemakers, $16 to $24.

AUSTRALIA.

THE LABOR MARKET.

[From the Melbourne Argus, October 31, 1878.]

The labor market has not altered materially since last month. In the building trades business is dull, and the action of the tradesmen at the new eastern market building is not likely to encourage business. The bootmaking trade is in a very indifferent condition, several of the leading establishments doing scarcely any work. In the clothing factories the summer orders are about concluded, the work done this spring being considerably below the average. At present there is plenty of work for laborers in the country at shearing and haymaking. In Riverina the rates paid for shearing varies from 16*s.* to 18*s.* per 100, according to locality, the men to find their own rations. In Victoria it is from 12*s.* to 13*s.* per 100. House servants are scarcer, the demand being greater than the supply, which is usually the case at this time of the year, when so many orders are received from the country.

The following are the rates of wages paid:

Domestic servants.—For town: Housemaids, £30 to £36 per annum; female cooks receive from £35 to £60 per annum; male cooks, 30*s.* to 80*s.* per week; nursemaids, £25 to £35 per annum; laundresses, £30 to £40 per annum. For hotels: Cooks, male and female, £50 to £100 per annum; housemaids, £35 to £40 per annum. For stations: First-class married couples for home stations, £70 to £90 per annum; second-class married couples for home stations, with children, £40 to £50 per annum; cooks, £45 to £55 per annum; housemaids, £35 to £40 per annum. For farms: Men cooks, £50 per annum; married couples, £60 to £70 per annum; women servants, £30 to £35 per annum; farming men, 20*s.* per week; milkmen, 20*s.* per week; plowmen, about 20*s.* per week.

Waiters for hotels, 25*s.* to 35*s.* per week; grocers' assistants, 15*s.* to 30*s.* per week; general store assistants, 20*s.* to 40*s.* per week; nursery governesses, £30 to £40 per annum; finishing governesses, £60 to £80 per annum.

Station hands.—Stockmen receive from £60 to £75 per annum; shepherds, 15*s.* to 20*s.* per week; ordinary workingmen, 15*s.* to 20*s.* per week; drovers, 25*s.* to 40*s.* per week; gardeners, 15*s.* to 25*s.* per week.

Building trades.—Stonemasons, 10*s.* per day; plasterers, bricklayers, slaters, 10*s.* per day; carpenters, 10*s.* per day; laborers, 7*s.* per day; pick-and-shovel men, 6*s.* 6*d.* per day. The day's work is eight hours.

Bootmakers.—For riveting children's boots the rate is 6*d.* per pair; boys', 10*d.*; women's, 1*s.*; and men's, 1*s.* 3*d.* The same rates are paid for finishing. In some of the best order shops the rates paid are: Wellingtons, 10*s.*; elastics, 7*s.* 6*d.*; closing, 8*s.* Good hands for ladies' boots are scarce. Higher rates are paid in first and second class "bespoke shops."

Bakers.—First-class workmen (foremen) average £3 per week; second hands, £2 to £2 2s. In the inferior shops the rates are slightly lower.

Butchers.—Shopmen receive from 35s. to 40s. per week; boys, 15s. to 20s. per week; slaughtermen receive from 40s. to 50s. per week; small-goods men (pork butchers) receive 30s. to 40s. per week, with rations; superior men receive more.

Brassfinishers and coppersmiths.—In the engine-fitting shops there is a fair supply of workmen; the wages are from 9s. to 12s. per day. The same rates are paid in the fine brassfinishing shops.

Cabinetmakers.—The earnings of the men employed in this trade are very variable. In some of the best shops in Melbourne the wages paid are as high as £3 10s. per week, while in inferior establishments the men receive from £2 10s. to £3 per week. In the country the wages paid are still less.

Clothing factories.—Where the work is done on the premises, the wages earned are as follows: Tailoresses, from £1 to £1 15s. per week; pressers, £2 to £2 15s. and upwards. From 12s. to £1 is earned at shirtmaking in factory hours, but the greater portion is taken home. Clothing machinists earn from 15s. to 30s. per week in factory hours.

Coopers.—Most of the work in this trade is done by the piece; the wages fixed by the trade are 10s. per day of 10 hours. Tallow casks are made at 5s. to 5s. 6d. for thirds and 4s. 6d. for fourths. Thirds are now most made, there being but little demand for fourths.

Coachbuilders.—Smiths receive from £2 10s. to £3 5s. and £4 per week. A few hands earn as high as £4 per week. Body-makers: Most of this work is done by the piece. The average earnings of good hands are from £2 10s. to as high as £4 per week. Wheelers: Most of this work is done by the piece. The wages made are from £2 10s. to £3 10s. per week. Painters receive from 9s. to 12s. per day. Trimmers get from £2 10s. to £3 10s. per week. Visemen earn from £1 10s. to £2 per week. The rate of labor in this trade is 10 hours per day.

Drapers.—In all the best establishments well-qualified drapers' assistants earn from £2 10s. to £4 per week. Carpet salesmen obtain about the same rates. Upholsterers, £2 10s. to £3 and £4 per week. Mantle-makers, 15s. to 20s. per week. Milliners from 35s. to £3 10s. per week. Needlewomen and dressmakers from 15s. to 20s. per week.

Gardeners.—The men in this trade are not at all well paid. In situations near town the rates are from 30s. to 40s. per week, without rations. The rates with rations are 15s. to 20s. Very good men get 25s. per week.

Hatters.—Body-makers get 18s. to 20s. per dozen for regulars, and 12s. to 14s. per dozen far low crowns. Finishers get 22s. to 24s. per dozen for silk hats; 20s. per dozen for pull-over; and 12s. to 14s. per dozen for low crown. Shapers are paid, for regulars, 12s. per dozen; for Anglesea, 9s. per dozen over $\frac{5}{8}$ths; and 6s. per dozen for plain shape; low-crown Anglesea, 8s. per dozen; over $\frac{5}{8}$ths, 6s. per dozen; under $\frac{5}{8}$ths, 4s. per dozen.

Iron trades.—Fitters receive from 9s. to 12s. per day; turners from 10s. to 13s. per day; boiler-makers and platers from 12s. to 13s. per day; riveters from 9s. to 11s. per day; blacksmiths from 10s. to 13s. per day; hammermen from 7s. to 8s. per day; and molders from 10s. to 12s. and 13s. per day.

Jewelers.—In the manufacturing jewelers' establishments the workmen receive from £2 15s. to £3 15s. For the finer work the wages range higher. Good tradesmen can get full employment.

Miners.—The average rates for miners is £2 per week for surface miners, and £2 5s. for underground work; in some deep, wet mines £2 10s. is paid. In some outlying districts higher rates are obtained, but only by a few men.

Navvies.—The rate paid the men employed on the Government railways is 6s. 6d. per day.

Painters and glaziers.—Fair tradesmen receive 9s. per day. This trade is fully supplied.

Plumbers and gasfitters receive £3 per week of eight hours per day.

Printers, &c.—The rate paid in this trade is 1s. per 1,000. In manufacturing stationers' establishments lithographers are paid £2 10s. to £3 15s. per week; binders, £2 to £3 per week, paper-rulers, £3 to £3 10s. per week. The demand for labor in these trades is limited, and is at present fully supplied. Good head men get higher rates in the binding and lithographing departments.

Stevedores' men, &c.—Lumpers' wages are 12s. per day at present. There is a good deal of business doing. Engineers in tugboats and donkey-engine drivers receive £18 per month.

Shipcarpenters.—The rate paid in this trade is 13s. per day of eight hours. Work is irregular.

Sailors on board ocean-going ships and steamers receive £4 10s. per month. In coasting vessels the rate is £5 per month. Men receive £6 per month in coasting steamers. Trimmers get £7 and firemen £9 in coasting steamers. In vessels foreign bound from Melbourne the rate is the same as in coasting vessels.

Saddlers.—Really good tradesmen are scarce, but second-class workmen are plentiful enough. The earnings are about £2 15*s.* per week. The commoner sorts of work are not paid for so well, and wages vary from 25*s.* to 35*s.* per week. The work in this trade is nine hours per day.

Tanners and curriers.—Beamsmen receive 40*s.* to 50*s.* per week; shedsmen, 42*s.* to 45*s.* per week; tanners, 38*s.* to 45*s.* per week. Time, ten hours per day. Curriers at piece-work can earn from 50*s.* to 70*s.* per week.

Tailors.—In a few first-class establishments the rate paid is 1*s.* per hour. In others the rate is 10*d.* per hour. In second-class shops the earnings are from £2 10*s.* to £3 per week. In factories the rates vary, the men being often paid by the piece. Where wages are paid, the rate is 40*s.* per week in factory hours.

Tinsmiths earn from £2 to £3 per week; ironworkers, £2 10*s.* to £3 per week; galvanizers, £3 per week. Most of the work in this trade is done by the piece.

Watchmakers.—The general rate of wages in this trade is £2 10*s.* to £4 per week, though some of the superior workmen get as high as £5.

STRIKES.

[From the Melbourne Argus, October 31, 1878.]

Early in the month a strike occurred among the workmen employed on the Oakleigh and South Yarra Railway. The contractors, Messrs. Higgins, announced that the men employed at the South Yarra end of the line would be taken on at 6*s.* 6*d.* per day till they could select the experienced workmen, whom they purposed to pay the full wage for railway laborers, namely, 7*s.* per day. The men, thinking if once they commenced to work at the lower rate they would never get the full price, refused to go to work at all unless at 7*s.* per day. The dispute lasted two or three days, and eventually the contractors selected known workmen, to whom they paid the full rate, and the strike ceased.

A strike of a more complicated nature occurred among the bricklayers employed on the new eastern market buildings on the 5th instant. The bricklayers employed on the building petitioned the contractors, Messrs. J. Nation & Co. for a half-holiday on Saturday afternoons. The contractors refused to grant the concession, as it would be an injustice to the large number of bricklayers' laborers employed on the building, who could ill afford to lose the half a day's pay per week. The bricklayers declined to consider the laborers, and left work on Saturday afternoon, the 5th October. When they returned to work on Monday morning, Messrs. Nation & Co. informed them that if they did not conform to the rules of the Eight Hours' Society, namely, eight hours work per day, they need not go to work. The men refused to accept these conditions, and since then have been idle. The usual tactics were then employed by the men. Pickets were posted round the building to prevent any men who wished to take on work on the contractors' terms from doing so. A meeting of the Contractors' Association has been held, and it was resolved that a vote of the whole of the tradesmen should be taken on November 1 as to whether there should be a general half-holiday throughout the building trade, upon which vote the contractors will take their stand. The workmen in the different trades have decided, however, to have nothing to do with a vote of that description, and the question remains as it was before. Messrs. Nation & Co. have about sixteen bricklayers who have taken on work since the strike began.

AMERICAN IMMIGRATION AND WAGES IN NEW SOUTH WALES.

[The following remarks on immigration from the United States to, and the list showing the rates of wages in, New South Wales are so appropriate to the completion of this volume, that they are inserted herein as taken from Consul Williams's annual report in Commercial Relations for 1877, pp. 467–473. The report is dated Sidney, October 1, 1877.]

IMMIGRANTS FROM THE UNITED STATES.

From what I can learn there are but few native-born Americans among the passengers, and I have felt glad that such was the case, as I hear of a good deal of disappointment and dissatisfaction among those who have arrived. Several have applied to me for assistance to return, after, as they said, endeavoring to get work both in town and country, and if they had met with encouragement I should, without doubt, have had many more. I have no doubt of there being plenty of employment for all who may come. but to me there appears to be no properly arranged system for bringing employers and laborers together; no such place as a central intelligence office, where employers can make known their wants and their wages (if not themselves in town), and to which persons seeking employment could resort with some degree of confidence that they would obtain good information and advice. There is no provision made for sheltering and feeding the immigrants on their arrival, and if they are without money and do not obtain immediate employment, they are reduced to sad straits. Several have told me that they were without food and were sleeping in the parks, but some of the same men afterward obtained work. Several, I am told, enlisted in the permanent-defense force of the colony as a last resort. Employers here generally look for written certificates of character, which persons coming from the United States could not well give, and even if they could, the writers would be no better known than the person presenting them. Again, there is a bitter hostility on the part of the laboring classes to all immigration promoted by the public funds, and the new arrivals meet with anything but a sympathetic reception from their own class. Indeed, this hostile feeling is shaping into a labor-defense association, intended to embrace the whole colony, for the purpose of bringing political pressure to bear upon the Government through the legislature for the purpose both of restricting immigration and introducing a protective tariff.

In my opinion, any man who is tolerably comfortable where he is will do well to remain, rather than come here with the hope of bettering his condition.

RATES OF WAGES.

The following return (official) shows the current prices paid in the month of December, 1876, for labor in some of the principal trades of the Colony of New South Wales, which of course vary somewhat in different districts:

Coalminers (the demand for miners at present is not great, and in many cases the men are only employed half-time), $2.43 to $3.65 per day; compositors 24 to 26 cents per 1,000; stonemasons, $2.67 per day; stonemasons' laborers, $1.94 per day; plasterers, $2.92 per day; plasterers' laborers, $1.94 per day; bricklayers, $2.92 per day; bricklayers' laborers, $1.94 per day; painters, $2.19 to $2.43 per day; saddlers, $10.94 to $13.38 per week; tailors (paid by the piece) can average about $14.60 to $17 per week; shoemakers (paid by the piece) can average about $14.60 to $17 per week; iron-turners, 30 to 32 cents per hour; carpenters, 30 cents per hour; engine fitters, 28 to 33 cents per hour; coppersmiths, 32 to 36 cents per hour; general fitters, 26 to 31 cents per hour; blacksmiths, 28 to 38 cents per hour; blacksmiths' strikers, 18 to 22 cents per hour; ironmolders, 30 to 34 cents per hour; boiler-makers, 28 to 32 cents per hour; pattern-makers, 28 to 32 cents per hour; boiler-makers' assistants, 16 to 22 cents per hour; general laborers in iron-works, 14 to 16 cents per hour; brassmolders, 28 to 32 cents per hour; carriage and wagon builders, 26 to 32 cents per hour; carriage-painters, 20 to 28 cents per hour; sawyers, in mill, 20 to 30 cents per hour; brassfinishers, 22 to 30 cents per hour; machine men, in fitting-shop, 22 cents per hour.

The foregoing trades connected with the iron and engineering departments work eight hours a day, with one or two breaks.

The following quotations are exclusive of rations or board, in town or country, which are not charged for:

Married couples for stations, $268 to $316 per annum; farmlaborers, $170 to $220 per annum; bullock-drivers, $195 to $253 per annum; horse-team drivers, $195 to $316 per annum; boundary-riders, $195 to 253 per annum; stockmen, $195 to $365 per annum; shepherds, $170 to $230 per annum; roadmakers, $253 to $316 per annum; grooms, $195 to $253 per annum; gardeners, $195 to $253 per annum; gardeners (in town), $252 to $316 per annum; blacksmiths (country), $365 to $487 per annum; bakers, $7.30 to $14.60 per week; butchers, $12.16 per week; cooks (private houses), $156 to $253 per annum; cooks (hotels), $252 to $316 per annum; laundresses, $156 to $219 per annum; house and parlor maids, $127 to $170 per annum; general female servants, $127 to $220 per annum; nursemaids, $97 to $170 per annum; grooms and coachmen (in town), $220 to $316 per annum; useful boys on stations, $78 to $146 per annum.

Current rate of wages, without board or lodging:

Wheelwrights (country), $14.60 to $17 per week; railway-laborers, $1.70 to $2.16 per day; brickmakers, $3.47 per 1,000; potters, $12.16 per week; tinsmiths, $2.19 per day; galvanized-iron workers, $2.45 to $2.92 per day. (The two trades last mentioned work ten hours to the day.)

Lumpers and wharf laborers:

Day-work for handling general cargo, 24 cents per hour; day-work for handling coal, 30 cents per hour; night-work, 36 cents per hour; plumbers, $2.43 per day; gasfitters, $2.43 per day. (These two trades last mentioned work eight hours to the day.) Coopers (on odd jobs), $2.92 per day; coopers, on piece, as follows: Wine-casks, $5.46 per ton; oil-casks, $4.87 per ton; tierces, 85 cents each; hogsheads, $1.33 each; ten-gallon kegs, 73 cents each; five-gallon kegs, 48 cents each; two-gallon kegs, 42 cents each.

HOUSE-RENT.

Small cottages in Sydney and suburbs, 3 or 4 rooms and kitchen, $1.94 to $2.92 per week; small houses, 3 or 4 rooms, with kitchen, &c., $3.40 to $4.80 per week; other larger houses from $4.80 per week upward; board and lodging for single men, from $3.40 to $4.80 per week.

NOTE BY THE CONSUL.—The above rates of wages are without doubt the maximum, and the rates for rents the minimum, while, at the same time, the dwellings let to laborers are of a very inferior character generally.

AUSTRIA-HUNGARY.

Report, by Consul Phelps, on the wages of railroad employés in Bohemia.

I have the honor to report that during my late journey from Liverpool to Prague I was surprised at the interest shown by all classes whom I met in the recent "railroad strikes" in the United States. In England, Belgium, Germany, and Austria I was spoken to in regard to them by educated and uneducated, by professors and by laboring men. They were regarded as a real convulsion, as a war upon capital, and as a culmination of agrarian violence long expected from a republican government. The scenes of tumult were fully portrayed in all the pictorial papers of Europe in sensational style.

In view of these incidents, it has occurred to me that it might be of interest to present a statement of the rates of wages paid by the railroad companies of Bohemia, and also a statement showing the cost of living, which I have the honor to inclose.

CHARLES A. PHELPS.

UNITED STATES CONSULATE,
Prague, October 25, 1877.

Statement showing the rates of wages of Bohemian railroad employés.

Employés.	Wages.	Rent.	Compensation.	Compensation for saving fuel and oil.	Extras.
Engineers .... per annum..	$245 00 to $360 00	$64 00 to $73 00	For 23,800 kilometers, $141 00	$30 00	
Firemen .... do......	145 00 to 182 00	45 00 to 55 00	For 23,800 kilometers, 70 00	14 00	2,000 kilos of coal.
First conductors .... do......	203 00 to 227 00	55 00 to 64 00	For 44,600 kilometers, 138 00	....	Service-dress and 2,000 kilos of coal.
Second conductors .... do......	126 00 to 182 00	45 00 to 55 00	For 39,600 kilometers, 104 00	....	(same as above)
Watchmen and switchmen .... do......	120 00 to 158 00	Lodgings.	....	....	
Chief engineers for construction and architects.... do......	524 00 to 997 00	....	....	....	

PER-DIEM WAGES.

Blacksmiths and locksmiths, 45 to 68 cents; carbuilders, 45 to 55 cents; boiler-makers and cabinet-makers, 55 to 68 cents; painters, 45 to 65 cents; laborers, 40 cents; apprentices, 23 cents.

FOOD-PRICES IN PRAGUE.

Wheat-flour 18 to 19 kreuzers per kilogramme; rye-flour, 15 to 16 kreuzers per kilogramme; beef, 64 kreuzers per kilogramme; beans, 22 kreuzers per liter; pease 25 kreuzers per liter; lentils, 19 kreuzers per kilogramme; beer, ordinary, 8 kreuzers per liter; beer, Pilsen, 22 kreuzers per liter; coal, 45 to 62 kreuzers per 50 kilogrammes; petroleum (American), 28 kreuzers per kilogramme.

CHINA.

MEMORANDUM ON THE CURRENCY OF CHINA.

By George F. Seward, United States minister.

It is well known that the Chinese Government do not issue coins of silver or gold, and that the pieces called by them "ch'ien," by the English "cash," and the French "sapeque," from the Portuguese "sapeca," which are made of copper variously alloyed, are the only ones in use among them. They are circular, and have square holes at the center, which are used for stringing them together. They are cast and not minted.

The places and mode of casting cash are regulated by imperial statutes. Models are given out by the board of revenue at Peking. The standard weight is one mace (ch'ien) each, and the value, by government standard, is the one-thousandth part of a tael of silver of the treasury scale. (Staunton's Penal Code, sec. 118.) The casting of cash is under the control of the provincial governors, subject to the orders of the board of revenue, and theoretically care is taken that the issues shall be so managed that the supply shall be sufficient to meet the demands of the people, and not so great as to cause their depreciation relatively to silver.

A coin, if it can be called such, which is cast and not minted, will as a matter of course be counterfeited. One made of a metal so base as copper, with alloys of a still baser sort, will be peculiarly liable to be counterfeited on the one hand and debased on the other. In this connection the following remarks, taken from the Commercial Guide of Dr. Williams, will be found pertinent:

"Within the last few years the Government have taken strong measures to suppress the private manufacture of cash, but in vain. The capacity of the governors is strongly exemplified in its gross adulteration since the time of Kianghsi, about one hundred and fifty years ago. It is debased in the coarsest manner with iron dust and sand, and presents a gritty appearance to the eye. In the reign of Taokwang (1821–'51), it became so bad that it would not remunerate forgers to counterfeit it. In the reign of Hsienfung (1851–'61), iron cash and paper notes were substituted for the copper cash."

The currency of Peking gives special evidence of the irregularities which have marked its history. By a curious fiction every piece of cash is called two. Without being able to trace out the cause of this, I have supposed that when the cash in use at a given period had been debased in value about one-half, an effort was made to correct matters by issuing coin of standard merit, and ordering that each piece of the new issue should be taken as equal to two pieces of the old. The new issue in time became debased and confused with the old, until there was no recourse for the people but to call one cash two, irrespective of the issue.

Still later, copper tokens of ten, twenty, &c., cash were issued, and these are now in circulation. They were never, however, of standard value. In 1869 one ten-cash piece was worth about three of the single cash pieces of varying issues which were in circulation, and 525 of them were required to purchase a tael of silver. As each piece represented ten cash, and as every piece of cash was doubled by the custom already referred to, 10.500 nominal cash were equal to a tael. Their value has decreased relatively to silver since then, and at times 18.000 nominal cash are required to purchase a tael. The paper tiao of the city represents 1.000 nominal cash, while in theory a tiao or string of cash should be equal to a tael.

In 1853–'54 an effort was made to force the iron cash spoken of above upon the people of the city, but it signally failed. "It was thrown away about the walls and by-ways, no one even thinking it worth the trouble of picking up."

It would seem, indeed, that the capital city and the north of China generally have suffered more from irregular practices affecting the currency than the more southern districts. It is said that many iron cash are in circulation in Chihli, Shansi, and Shensi, and that an effort has been made in each considerable town to preserve a standard of value by counting more or less of the actual cash as equal to a tiao, so that the custom of the place must be known before the person who has bought articles to any given value can tell how many actual pieces of money he is to pay for them.

At the ports open to foreign trade and in the southern provinces generally the actual cash are counted and so passed for the purposes of a currency, but their intrinsic value varies, not only as between the ports, but at the several ports. From statements made by the consuls of the United States to the legation in the year 1873 I have derived the following results as to the value of the average cash of each port relatively to the Haikwan or customs tael.

	Tael.	Cash.
At Newchwang	1 =	1,900
At Shanghai	1 =	1,800
At Chinkiang	1 =	1,960
At Ningpo	1 =	1,868
At Foochow	1 =	1,605
At Amoy	1 =	1,736
At Swatow	1 =	1,668

Assuming these figures to be approximately correct, a range of relative values amounting to nearly 20 per cent. is shown.

Mr. Kingsmill, writing at Shanghai about ten years ago, said:

"Taking carefully picked cash, coined before 1820, such as are known in the market as "Hankow picked," the average weight is rather less than 1.00 ch'ien Slightly below this is what is known as "Chinkiang cash," weighing from .940 to .043. Far below either is the ordinary currency in Shanghai. Taking a sample rather above than below what is known as fair quality, we will probably find it composed as follows:

Fair to good (in numbers)	500
Japanese and foreign	300
Debased of last two emperors	200
	1,000

"The average weight is about ch'ien 780 only."

The same writer shows that at Hankow, under circumstances which created special demand, cash varied in value relatively to silver as follows:

	Cash.		Taels.
1863	1,000	=	0.750
1864	1,000	=	0.795
1865	1,000	=	0.805
1866	1,000	=	0.785
1867	1,000	=	0.650

The tael quotations given show the averages of the years, but in 1865 the price ran up so high that 88½ tael cents were required to buy 1,000 cash; a range of relative value as compared with the price stated for 1867 of more than 33⅓ per cent.

Mr. Wylie, of Shanghai, states that the cash of the 17th century were made of copper, zinc, lead, and tin, in the following proportions:

Copper	50.00
Zinc	41.50
Lead	6.50
Tin	2.00
	100.00

Mr. Kingsmill, following these figures, estimates the cost of making 1,000 cash, weighing 1 ch'ien each, as follows:

	Taels.
Copper, at 15 taels per picul	0.46875
Zinc, at 5.20 taels per picul	0.12453
Lead, at 5 taels per picul	0.02031
Tin, at 15 taels per picul	0.02250
Say Shanghai taels	0.63609

Assuming 6 per cent. to be sufficient to defray the cost of coinage (casting), we arrive at about taels 0.675, as the price at which the Chinese Government could issue such cash. At the standard of 1,000 cash to the tael, the profit of the Government would amount to more than 30 per cent.

We find, therefore, these facts existing:

1st. That cash vary greatly in weight and fineness.

2d. That their value, as compared with silver, is not constant.

3d. That they are not worth, when issued of standard weight and fineness, more than 70 per cent. of their nominal value.

As a permanent standard of value, then, the copper coinage of this empire is unsatisfactory in the extreme. It is, nevertheless, the currency which is used in all the ordinary transactions of the people. The laborer receives his wages in it; the farmer calculates in it the out-turn of his crops; the small consumers and small producers, whose aggregate demands and supplies make up the great markets, find in it an index of the rise and fall of price. It can be shown even that at given times copper cash appear to have a more stable purchasing power than silver, and an argument raised to sustain the proposition, which has been advanced over and again, that it forms "the virtual monetary unit."

In passing, it may be remarked that the evils of an unstable currency are not now felt for the first time. It is said that in the Sung dynasty (960 to 1127 A. D.), cash were made "so small that they were called geese eyes, and so thin that they would swim upon the water," and every one has read what Marco Polo wrote of the vast issues of paper money by the Mongols, who reigned between 1280 and 1368 A. D. They found "rag money" in the land which they had conquered, and while extending issues here, carried the practice into Persia, where paper of the sort is still called by the Chinese name, "Ch'aou." It has been stated that they abused the power to make money to such an extent that the discontent of the people due to this cause did more than anything else to bring about their downfall.

When we turn from this statement of the unsatisfactory character of the copper currency to deal with the facts in regard to the use of silver, we meet again with much that is singular and confusing.

At the foreign customs, duties are demanded according to the Haikwan scale, and payments at the ports named below made in local taels are received at the following rates:

Newchwang	100 Haikwan taels = 103.50 local taels.
Tientsin	100 Haikwan taels = 105.00 local taels.
Chefoo	100 Haikwan taels = 104.40 local taels.
Hankow	100 Haikwan taels = 108.75 local taels.
Kiukiang	100 Haikwan taels = 106.31 local taels.
Chinkiang	100 Haikwan taels = 104.21 local taels.
Shanghai	100 Haikwan taels = 111.40 local taels.
Ningpo	100 Haikwan taels = 111.40 Shanghai scale tales.

South of Ningpo duties are generally paid in dollars. So nearly as I have been able to learn, local taels are valued, relatively to the Haikwan standard, as follows:

Amoy	100 Haikwan taels = 110.00 local taels.
Tamsui	100 Haikwan taels = 110.00 local taels.
Taiwan	100 Haikwan taels = 111.37 local taels.
Swatow	100 Haikwan taels = 110.00 local taels.

At Foochow two local taels are used, one by foreign, the other by native merchants. One hundred Haikwan taels are equal to 100.50 of the former and 101.45 of the latter.

At several, if not all the ports, there are other taels known besides the Haikwan and the local commercial taels. One of these is called the "Kuping" or treasury tael. It is not constant, however, with the Haikwan tael, as will be seen from the following table:

Tientsin	100 Haikwan taels = 103.40 kuping taels.
Hankow	100 Haikwan taels = 101.01 kuping taels.
Shanghai	100 Haikwan taels = 101.65 kuping taels.
Foochow	101 Haikwan taels = 101.14 kuping taels.

In a dispatch addressed by Prince Kung, on the 9th of April, 1877, to the foreign ministers at Peking, he said: "All payments to and from the provinces are made in Kuping taels of pure silver."

The table shows that the Haikwan tael is better than the Kuping, and the provincial officers doubtless get the benefit of the difference.

It is suggestive of the lax ideas of currency and administration generally prevailing in China, that at one port foreigners of one nationality pay their dues at the customs at a rate different from that exacted of other foreigners, and that at several ports different rates are exacted of natives from those demanded from foreigners.

At Peking, Dr. Williams found five scales used for weighing silver, the tael of each weighing respectively, 548, 541, 552, 539, and 579 grains.

But while there seems to be and is much confusion, matters are not so bad as they appear. It is a fact that the weight of the Kuping tael has been very constant for the last 200 years. The catty of this scale has been quoted at Peking as follows:

	Grammes.
In 1580, by Le Compte	596.044
In 1769, by Clerc	596.800
In 1822, by Timkowski	595.345
In 1841, by Kupffuer	595.135

It is also reported as follows:

	Grammes.
At Soochow, in 1779, by Collas	598.976
At Shanghai, in 1857, by Wylie	596.800

The same thing seems to be true in regard to the scale used at Canton for weighing silver, as will be seen from the following authorities:

	Grammes.
In 1710, Williams	601.104
In 1779, Collas	601.328
In 1710, Milburn	601.190
In 1828, Thompson	600.658
In 1845, Rondot	600.432
In 1847, Carvalho	601.112
In 1857, Rondot	*600.432

In view of the constancy for long periods of the scales indicated, it may very well be supposed that the Chinese throughout the empire are acquainted with a standard scale, the Kuping for instance, and that the variation of local scales from the standard is clearly defined and understood.

The actual scales or balances used by the Chinese are more or less well made. Those oftenest seen in shops, &c., have a brass beam suspended from a standard, and two brass basins carried by brass chains. It cannot be supposed that they are very sensitive and accurate. Others of a finer sort are made in the same way, the beam being of ebony or ivory, and the basins of brass, suspended by silken cords. Others are fashioned like our steelyards. These all would be condemned, of course, in assay-offices or mints in Europe or America.

Chinese assays of silver are equally defective. The process at Peking appears to be a simple one, in which the borate of soda is used with or without lead, according to the proportion of alloy. At Shanghai, niter and lead are used with white sand, and at the last moment of the melting process a piece of the white oxide of arsenic is thrown in to give splendor to the metal. Cupellation and the use of acids are not known.

The trade-dollar was declared by the assay of 1873 to be .8961 fine, instead of .900. While this is a wider deviation than is allowed in the mints of Europe or America for "toleration" or "remedy," it is so close that I have suspected that it was based on the well-known standard of the coin. In the same year I endeavored to have an assay made at Shanghai, but found many unnecessary difficulties raised. At the assay of the Hongkong dollar, the result obtained was a fineness of .8944. An allowance was then made of $\frac{6}{1000}$ for silver remaining incorporated with the lead, and the dollar declared to be .900 fine. This assay was made in the presence of the assayer of the Hongkong mint, who exhibited also the foreign process of assaying. It is reported that the Chinese were highly interested in the skillfulness displayed in the process.

After the assay of the Hongkong dollar a proclamation was issued, declaring that 111.1.1 taels' weight of that coinage should be held equal to 100 Haikwan taels, and after the assay of the trade-dollar, it was in the same way declared that 111.9 taels, weight of the American coin should be held equal to 100 taels, a proportion not justified by the actual fineness of the coin nor by the fineness declared by the assay. I am informed, however, that 103 taels' weight of dollars are frequently accepted as equal to 100 taels Haikwan.†

* This scale is probably the Kuping, but I am not able at the moment to verify the point.

† The inspector-general of customs has given me a memorandum on the weight and fineness of the Haikwan tael. According to this, it should weigh 1 ounce 4 pennyweights 3.84 grains troy, say, 589.84 grains, or 37.578 grammes. The Haikwan catty would be, therefore, 601.248 grammes, or something more than the Canton and Kuping catties. An assay of the trade-dollar was made at Canton in 1873. The assayers declared that 100 trade-dollars weighed 72.68 taels by the Haikwan standard. At an earlier assay 100 Hongkong dollars were declared to weigh 71.92 taels. The actual weight of the trade-dollar is 420 grains; that of the Hongkong dollar, 416 grains. The tael, at these rates, would be 577.875 and 578.402 grains, and the catty, 599.216 and 599.766 grammes.

Haikwan silver is supposed to be perfectly pure. Foreign dollars are accepted by

Chinese assaying establishments are called kungkoo. They are not found in all the cities of the empire, nor even in many of the most important. Mr. Billequin, professor of chemistry in the Imperial College of this city, is of the opinion that very little silver is refined here. In a report of the United States consul at Newchwang, made in 1870, he states that "there is no kungkoo here. Any one who chooses, may fabricate ingots of silver, and the only check upon such persons is their fear to lose their reputation for honesty."

The commissioner of customs at Chefoo reported in the same year that "serious inconvenience, delay, and losses have resulted to foreign merchants from the quantity of inferior sycee in circulation. To remedy this, a kungkoo has been established, but the country buyers refuse to recognize it, and suspension of business with the interior has resulted." In 1865, the commissioner at Hankow wrote: "In the early days of this port the demand for sycee was so sudden and extensive that Shanghai was unable to supply standard sycee in sufficient quantities. It thus arose that sycee of an inferior quality was transmitted to this port, and on its being found that adulterated silver was accepted as equivalent to standard, the practice, originally exceptional, became the rule, and sycee, depreciated to the extent of two, three, or even four mace per shoe, was regularly manufactured for the Hankow market. About two years ago an attempt was made to establish a kungkoo, or assay office, which was unsuccessful, and the failure was followed by an enormous increase in the depreciation of silver. It was not, however, until the present month that an assay office, duly recognized by the Chinese and the consular authorities, was opened."

In the absence of assay offices the Chinese rely upon the *touch*. Le Compte, writing in 1790, says what is equally true at this day: "They are so expert in guessing at the goodness of any piece of silver by looking on it only, that they are seldom mistaken, especially if it be melted after the manner practiced by them. They know the goodness in three ways; by the color, by small holes which are made in melting, and by the small circles which the air makes on the surface of the metal when it cools. If the color be white, the holes small and deep, if the circles be many and those close and very fine, especially toward the center of the piece, then the silver is pure; but the more it differs from these three indications, so much the more alloy it has."

While it appears that uncertainties arising from the multiplicity of standards, the imperfect construction of scales, and the defective means of testing the quality of silver must prove a great source of annoyance to those who have occasion to use the metal, in one way and another fairly accurate results seem to be reached. This is the case at least as between the open ports. There is, of course, frequent occasion to remit bullion from the northern and riverine ports to Shanghai. I am informed that such remittances almost invariably result according to the expectations of shippers.

It follows from what has been said that, however defective may be the test of silver and of the scales by which it is weighed, no such failures attend its use for purposes of a currency as have been experienced in the case of the copper currency already described.

That silver is the real standard of value is well understood by the Chinese. We have seen that a cash is supposed to be the one-thousandth part of a tael of silver. This is the declaration of the Government and indicates the view taken by it. But cash pass among the people for just so much as they consider them worth, having regard to their intrinsic value and their convenience as a medium of exchange. The Government, recognizing its failure to keep the coin up to standard, have accepted the action of the people, and receive cash in payment of taxes only at the exchange current among them. The dues collected at the foreign customs are in silver, and remittances from the provinces to the capital are in silver or in banker's bills calling for silver.

The penal code provides that soldiers and citizens shall not use in their houses any utensils of copper, saving such as are permitted by the law, and that any excess shall be given over to the Government at a stated price in silver. Importations of copper from Yunnan are similarly not to cost more than a stated price in silver.

What has been said will indicate the position of cash and silver in the Chinese currency. It remains to speak of gold.

---

the Haikwan standard only with an allowance which gives a result in pure silver. It is not likely that in estimating the value of silver otherwise current the proportion of alloy is arrived at and reported with equal care. In point of fact, as might be expected, Haikwan silver is not up to the assumed standard. On the 19th of June, 1876, thirty-five ingots of Canton silver, said to be of the Haikwan standard, were assayed at the Osaka mint. Thirteen of these proved to be .9820 fine; seventeen, .9835; two, .9800; and three, .9845. On the 13th fourteen shoes were assayed, resulting as follows: Two, .9865; eight, .9860; two, .9855; and two, .9850. It thus appears that Haikwan silver contains really about $1\frac{1}{2}$ per cent. of base metal, and that 109.5 taels' weight, about, of dollars, 900 fine should be held equal to 100 taels of Haikwan silver. An officer formerly connected with the Canton customs informs me that the bullion received there is cast into 10-tael ingots for transmission to the capital, and that these ingots are of about 98 touch.

It cannot be doubted that the latter forms a part of the currency, but this is true only to a limited extent. It is more properly a merchandise, which is bought and sold in the market.

The tendency throughout Asia is to place a lower relative value upon gold than prevails in Europe and America. In China this tendency has been a normal one, and not the result of legislation, for in one sense gold and silver are equally articles of commerce, that is to say, neither has been coined. The case has been different in Japan, gold and silver having been long coined there. At the date of Commodore Perry's treaty, gold, judged by the face value of coins in circulation, was worth only five times as much as silver. It is understood that the Government received the whole production of the mines, and as no considerable import or export of the precious metals was allowed, it was able to establish their relative value by decree.

Quotations of these metals in China and Japan must be received with the reservation that one cannot be sure how far pure gold has been weighed against pure silver. I think that, as a rule, the gold is purer than the silver.

Rondot gives the following table:

Years.	City.	Gold.	Silver.
1285		1	10
1375		1	4
1779	Peking	1	17½
1810	Canton	1	10
1821	Peking	1	21
1844	Canton	1	17
1845	......do	1	16

These quotations are so widely and irregularly at variance, that their accuracy may be greatly questioned. It is the general fact, however, which is in point, and regarding this the two following quotations are sufficient:

Le Compte, writing in 1690, says: "Europeans make a good market of gold, because in China a pound of it bears but the same proportion to a pound of silver as 1 to 10, whereas among us it is 1 to 15." Sir George Staunton, writing a century later, made the following statement: "In general, the value of silver has borne a much greater proportion to that of gold in China than in Europe, excepting when an extraordinary demand for the latter by foreign merchants has increased the rate of it."

I have been at some pains to collect statistics of the relative values of the metals for recent years. The general result shows that while the markets have been sensitive to the European demand, there have been some wide fluctuations. The lowest quotation in the last 30 years is 1 to 12.8 (at Shanghai, in 1855); the highest is 1 to 17.5 (at Peking, in August, 1876).

There is here an exchange for the purchase and sale of gold, at which the price is determined for the day. Whether similar exchanges may be found in other cities I do not know. I imagine, however, that there is relatively more gold in circulation at Peking than at other leading points, for the reason that a great deal of trade with Mongolia, Central Asia, and Siberia centers here, bringing in that metal, and that persons of the official class coming here for greater or less periods find it more convenient to carry than silver. There is a constant flow of gold in commerce from the northern ports to Shanghai and the south, but the quantity of it so moved is not great.

Paper obligations of one kind and another take an important place in the currency of the empire. None of this, so far as I know, is issued or sanctioned by the Government, and all issues which are intended for currency purposes are to be classed as "shinplaster" paper, as the American term is. Probably, however, 75 per cent. of the smaller business of Peking is transacted with such paper. In some cities, as at Shanghai, for instance, it is never seen. Foochow has long enjoyed prominence in the use of paper money, and it is likely that the practice followed here and in that city will be found to exist in many others. One author says: "Bank-notes, payable to bearer, are in use throughout the empire, and are issued by the great houses of business, and accepted in all the principal towns." At Shanghai, by far the greater part of the merchandise purchased by Chinese from foreigners is paid for by orders drawn by the native bankers on themselves, and having usually ten days to run. Formal bills of exchange drawn by bankers in one city upon those in others are greatly used. At times a considerable part of the revenue transmitted to Peking from other parts of the empire has been sent up in this way.

It may be assumed, I think, that paper in its different forms takes the place of silver and cash in the transaction of business generally to a very considerable extent, and that this result is largely due to the facts that cash are inconvenient to handle, and that the use of silver is attended with difficulties not met with where a coinage system exists.

The failure of the Chinese to coin precious metals is due to a variety of reasons. Du Halde says quaintly: "It is easy to judge that there would be many debasers of money in China if silver was coined, since the small pieces of copper are so often counterfeited." Dr. Williams says: "Silver and gold coin were both used in China at different periods of her ancient history, but never have been issued by the present or any modern dynasty. A consciousness of their inability to maintain the standard alloy and weight throughout their vast domain, and a knowledge of the facility with which the coins could be counterfeited, combined with their ignorance of the advantages of a gold and silver currency, and a disposition to meddle with the coinage, explains why the Manchus have never attempted to circulate silver coins." Issues of silver, moreover, could be made only at or near the intrinsic value of the metal used. Upon such issues the Government could make but small profit, while, as we have seen, the profit upon issues of cash is very great.

It cannot be supposed, however, that the Chinese are different from other people in their need for and their capacity to appreciate a currency convenient in form and based on value. The Mexican dollar is much used at Shanghai, and it is always at a premium. Two years ago it ran up in a few months from 72.5 to 82.4 per cent. of the local tael, a range of 10 per cent. nearly, in the relative value of silver conveniently coined and silver as bullion. Twenty years ago the Carolus dollar came to be at par with the tael. At Canton, dollars, although passed by weight, are generally, as we have seen, at a small premium over bullion. In this city they pass freely, but at a slight discount. At Tientsin, as I am informed, they have sometimes been in such demand that it would pay to import them from Shanghai. Experience shows, as I believe, that if the supply of foreign dollars were constant and sufficient, they would come to be the money of account at all the open ports.

In making this statement, I am aware that it involves the proposition that the Government would have no serious difficulty in establishing a mint and in putting out coins of determined value. They would need only to offer such money to their people to have it accepted. It would not be necessary to declare it legal tender, but, on the contrary, better that this should not be done, saving in respect of customs dues. At first, doubtless, it would be regarded with suspicion, as anything is in China which is strange. The readiness of the Government to receive it would commend it greatly to the people, and their freedom to receive or to reject it would dispel doubt. The absence of legal-tender laws would prevent any movement to debase the coin, for so soon as debased the people would discover and reject it. Well-executed coins would be so difficult to counterfeit as to prevent danger of this kind. In point of fact, all the reasons would exist for the acceptance of such coins which have induced the acceptance so widely of certain foreign coins and many more besides.

That great opposition to the establishment of a mint must be expected is manifest. Foreign bankers appear to prefer to have the currency in its present irregular and uncertain condition, doubtless because they make a profit from it. How much more native bankers and money-changers and receivers of the revenue and disbursing officers will strive to uphold the existing system may be readily imagined.

It is well known, however, that the Chinese central authorities and some of their leading provincial officers are alive to the evils of the present system, and disposed to introduce remedies, and it may be predicted with safety that a coinage system will be adopted within a near period; I do not say within five or ten years, or attempt to anticipate the date. It is coming to be a felt want, and such wants create their remedy.

It is evident that no step short of the establishment of a mint can effect a radical improvement of the currency. Gold and silver must be coined in order to be convenient for use, and such coins must be authoritatively issued, in order to be accepted without hesitation or doubt. The object to be kept in view, then, is the establishment of a mint and nothing less.

It may be possible, however, to correct some of the evils of the existing currency. I think that we are fairly entitled to ask:

1st. That the Government shall declare in what tael the customs and other dues payable by foreigners are to be discharged. It appears from Prince Kung's dispatch that the action of provincial officers in demanding such payments by a higher scale than the Kuping is a departure from the established rule of the Government in regard to the receipt and disbursement of the public moneys.

2d. The standard tael having been decided upon, its exact equivalent in grains troy and grammes should be declared. Looking to the inferiority of native scales, there can be no certainty in passing bullion until this has been done.

3d. The purity of the silver of the standard tael should also be declared. There is no such thing in China, or elsewhere for that matter, as silver 1,000 fine, and it is necessary to have a standard purity declared, not only in order to effect certainty in passing bullion, but also in determining the equivalent values of the foreign coins in circulation.

4th. The values of local taels relatively to the standard tael should be restated and declared.

5th. The values of foreign coins should be restated and declared.

It is not necessary, as I think, to enter upon an extended argument to show that the steps mentioned above are of much importance, or to explain why silver only is spoken of. All that has preceded in this paper indicates that silver is the real standard of value in China; that much uncertainty exists in its use, and that, if effort is to be made to improve matters without a radical departure from the existing system, the suggestions made are perhaps those which, if carried out, would offer the best results.

It is not necessary, either, to point out the treaty stipulations which would justify the effort to effect such an improvement of the currency. When foreign nations agreed with China for the payment of duties upon merchandise imported and exported by their people, it is not to be supposed that they imagined that the unit of the currency was an unknown quantity, or that they can be satisfied to have a situation continue which does not give uniform results.

It is desirable, of course, to proceed toward the accomplishment of reforms in this country, or in any other, within existing lines of administration. Perhaps a leading merit of the suggestions advanced lies in the fact that it would not be necessary to bring any new instrument of administration into use. It would be quite possible for this Government to direct its provincial officers to take steps in concert with the foreign customs establishment to bring about all the reforms indicated.

There can be no doubt, moreover, that steps so taken would prove an advance toward the ultimate object. They would expose more clearly the faults of the existing system, and they would break down in some measure the interests which are upholding it. All considerations, then—those of the immediate interests of commerce, and those which look to the ultimate and complete reformation of the currency to the advantage of all, to that of the native indeed, far more than to the foreigner—indicate that it will be wise to prosecute this business with all appropriate earnestness.

GEORGE F. SEWARD.

PEKING, *February* 20, 1878.

DANISH DEPENDENCIES.

LABOR AND LABOR LAWS IN ST. CROIX.

[Although the following report from the United States consul at St. Thomas was not written in answer to the Department's labor circular, the subject treated of is so intimately connected with labor, and helps to elucidate a most peculiar and, happily, abnormal condition thereof, a condition in such marked contrast to that reported from any other country—that its insertion in the appendix to this volume was considered allowable, if not necessary, to complete the entire view of the rounds of labor, this making the lowest round given in this volume, with the exception of that reported from Egypt, which will be found in its proper place in this appendix also, and the United States undoubtedly the highest.]

UNITED STATES CONSULATE,
St. Thomas, October 22, 1878.

I have to report that on the 1st of October a riot commenced in St. Croix, and was not quelled until all of the business portions of the town of Frederiksted and the works and dwellings on some fifty of the largest sugar estates were burned, as well as a large quantity of sugar, molasses, rum, and provisions, and several hundred acres of sugar-cane.

The riot was principally caused by the general dissatisfaction of the laborers with the law regulating their labor, which, although enacted as a provisional law, has been in force from their emancipation in 1848 to the present time. I inclose herewith a copy of the law. By reference to it you will see—

1. That the laborer must, on the 12th of October of each year, contract to labor for the ensuing year.

2. That if he intends to leave the estate on which he is working at the expiration of the year, he must notify his employer during the month of August of his intention. Failing to do this, he is held to have renewed his contract for another year, and cannot leave the estate.

3. That the highest wages that a first-class laborer is allowed to receive for his work from sunrise to sunset, for five days in each week, is 75 cents, from which 25 cents is deducted for his week's ration, consisting arbitrarily of six quarts of corn-meal and five herrings, also a physician's fee of three cents; leaving a balance in actual cash of 47 cents, or $24.44 for a year's work consisting of 260 days.

4. That he is subject to various fines and forfeitures of wages, which may be imposed by the employer or overseer.

These are the principal provisions of the law that the laborers claim are unjust and oppressive.

The home government has endeavored several times to induce the local government to repeal the same; but its efforts have been successfully resisted, not only by the local government, but by the planters.

Some two years ago the home government made a grant of money to be used in building sugar factories on the island. They were to be operated under the management and control of the Government, and the large number of laborers required could not be advantageously employed under a yearly contract, as the law requires a condition to be inserted in the grant specifying that the labor law should be abolished within three years from the time the first factory was ready to commence work. One of the factories was completed about the first of this year; but after a few months' trial proved a failure, and work was suspended. While in operation, the laborers employed were paid from 25 to 50 cents per day, in violation of law. These laborers, by exhibiting the wages they received to their comrades on the estates, increased the dissatisfaction with the law regulating their wages.

The open disregard of the law by the government officials, santioned as it was by the governor of the island, led the laborers to believe that the law would be abolished on the expiration of the then existing contracts, September 30. They took the precaution, however, in August, to give the necessary notice of their intention to leave the estates on which they were at work, and made no selection of ground for garden cultivation, as they had universally done before.

By custom the laborers have been allowed the 1st, 2d, and 3d of October to select the estates on which they desired to work for the ensuing year and to make all necessary arrangements. These days are regarded by them as holidays, and great numbers of them spend the same in town. There they meet the planters, or their agents, who, for a small bonus or bribe, procure from them their written acknowledgment from their former employers that the proper notice of their intention to leave their employ has been given, as prescribed by law, the simple possession of wheih is legal evidence of contract.

These who desire to leave the island try to get away during these three days. I say try, for as a rule they do not succeed, on account of obstacles thrown in the way to prevent them. The supply of labor is not equal to the demand, and if they can be prevented from leaving during the three days specified, they are saved to the planter for another year. This is not a very difficult thing to do, as no vessels leave the island for ports other than St. Thomas, and these vessels are owned by citizens of the island who are more or less interested in estates.

By law no vessel is allowed to carry a passenger from the island unless he is provided with a passport duly issued by the policemaster, the legal cost of which is 33 cents to St. Thomas and $1 to the islands. The local law of St. Thomas not permitting any one to be landed who has no means of support, or, in other words, who cannot deposit $15 with the policemaster as a guarantee for two weeks' support, the policemaster, by an arbitrary order to the policemasters at St. Croix, required them to collect from all laborers coming to St. Thomas a sufficient amount to pay their passages to other islands before issuing them a passport. The amount fixed in pursuance of this unwarranted order was about $10.

Many of the laborers are natives of the English islands, and it is impossible for them to get home without first coming to St. Thomas. Should one have been fortunate enough to have saved enough money out of his earnings to make this deposit, the chances are that he will find no vessel in port to take him away.

On the 1st of October some five or six hundred men and women congregated, as customary, in Fredericksted. They were disappointed to learn that the "labor law" was to remain in force another year at least, and that they must select their masters as usual. Those who wanted to leave the island could not get away owing to the requirements at the police office and the absence of vessels in port. The latter commenced to drink freely, and, in their intoxicated condition, were bitter in their denunciations of the officials, planters, owners of vessels, and the law. They accused the officials of charging them $10 for a passport, while a white man could get one for 33 cents, and the planters and owners of vessels with having entered into an agreement to keep the vessels away from the port.

Late in the afternoon a policeman attempted to arrest one for boisterous language. The man declared that he had done nothing to be arrested for, and would not submit to it. The policeman struck him on the head with his club, knocking him senseless. He was at once taken to the hospital, and his companions, believing him to be dead, spread the report throughout the town that he had been killed. The excitement among the laborers became intense, and they threatened to avenge his death on the policeman.

After being fully convinced that the man was not dead, and being assured by Du Bois, English consular agent, that if they would go home and select twelve of their number to come to him the following day to state their grievances, he would go with them to the governor and see what steps could be taken in their behalf, they became pacified and consented to leave town.

As they were about to do so, two mounted policemen, with swords drawn, rode in among them, striking right and left. Instantly the air was full of stones and sticks hurled at the policemen, who beat a hasty retreat and sought refuge in the fort. An assault was at once made on the fort, during which a planter by the name of Fountaine, who bore the name of being a very hard master, rode up with his revolver in hand and threatened to kill the next man who threw a stone. The next one thrown knocked him mortally wounded from his horse, having hit him on the head.

The entire police force of the town was in the fort, as well as the police-master and several officials. The rioters, not being able to beat the doors down, and several having been shot by the besieged parties, made a rush for the customs-house and stores and residences of such parties as were particularly obnoxious to them, which they forced open, saturated their contents with kerosene, and applied the match.

They continued at their work during the entire night, occasionally making an assault upon the fort.

The families of the white men living in the town took refuge in the churches and residences of the ministers and on board of a ship lying in the harbor, soon after the general rioting commenced. In going to places of safety, they had to pass through bands of the rioters, none of whom offered to molest them in any way. This action on the part of the rioters shows conclusively that they did not intend to take life. Had they so intended, every man, woman, and child in the town was completely in their power. The only persons they might have killed were the police-master and his men.

By sunrise the entire business portion of the town was in ashes, as well as many private residences. Nothing whatever was saved except a few small articles of wearing apparel or furniture taken charge of by house-servants. The books belonging to the consulate were saved, but the seals and other property were burned.

Shortly after sunrise a detachment of one officer and twenty-five soldiers, sent from Christiansted, entered the town. The firing of a few volleys was sufficient to clear the town. The riot commenced between two and three o'clock on the 1st, and the soldiers arrived about six o'clock on the morning of the 2d, some fifteen hours after its commencement. Christiansted is fifteen miles from Frederiksted. I have often driven from one town to the other in one hour and a half. Light spring-wagons were used to transport the soldiers; therefore the delay was not caused by a fatiguing march.

As the officer had seen no indications of a disturbance in the country he concluded that the riot was over, and sent two of his men unarmed to a plantation some two miles distant to feed his horses.

The rioters, when driven out of town, collected near by, and hearing that the two soldiers were on the plantation, went there, captured and killed them.

They then sent messengers to the different estates to tell what they had done, and to urge all to join them in their struggle for their freedom, and to threaten all who did not do so with death.

As the planters commenced to flee to town the demoralization among the laborers became general. The ranks of the rioters were increased until probably they numbered six or eight hundred, and then commenced the work of burning the buildings on the estates. The officer was bottled up in the fort, having used all his ammunition; therefore the rioters met with no resistance whatever.

On the morning of the 2nd I received the following telegrams from Mr. Willard, consular agent at Christiansted, viz:

First. Government unable to open communication with Frederiksted. Mob moving towards Christiansted. Send armed vessel, if possible.

Second. If any assistance can be had, send it here. Frederiksted in ashes. Mob still advancing towards Christiansted. Several prominent citizens murdered.

On receipt of these telegrams I repeated the substance of same to the Department. The English and French consuls telegraphed for armed vessels to protect English and French and also American interests.

The telegrams received here created the impression that the blacks contemplated the murder of the whites and the overthrow of the government.

Hearing that Governor Garde had chartered a steamer and was going to St. Croix with fifty soldiers, all the force available here, I asked permission to go over on the steamer which was chartered.

The steamer left here at one o'clock in the afternoon and arrived at Christiansted at five o'clock. The soldiers were safely landed by half past eight, only three hours and a half after arrival. The people in the town were in the wildest state of excitement and terror. The planters and their families had sought refuge there, and those who had not arrived were reported murdered. The rioters were reported to be six or eight thousand strong and steadily advancing towards the town, destroying all property as they came. All places of apparent safety were filled with women and children.

The reports were so exaggerated and conflicting, that it was impossible to form any correct idea as to the true state of affairs. One report was evidently true, and that was that the estates were being burned. The fires could be distinctly seen from the town.

The governor issued a proclamation declaring the island in a state of siege, a copy of which I inclose, and proceeded to organize for the defense of the town. The regular troops under his command numbered about 80, and the volunteer force organized numbered about 100, making an available force of 180 men.

The rioters continued, undisturbed, to burn estates during the entire night of the 2d, and by daylight on the 3d were within a few miles of the town.

At nine o'clock, after the troops had taken coffee, the governor started with them to attack the rioters, or rebels, as they are called. At an estate called Anna's Hope, about two and a half miles from town, about a dozen rioters were found. They had broken open the provision cellar, and seven of the number were locked up in the manager's house eating their breakfast when the troops arrived. The door was broken down and they were all shot to death in the house.

This was telegraphed as a bloody engagement, in which 200 were killed, the troops being victorious. The line of march after this battle was again taken up for Frederiksted. After proceeding about a mile, a large steam-plow was found in the road. Two men from an estate near by were called to remove it. After doing so they were accidentally shot.

No more of the rebels were seen or encountered until their arrival at an estate called Carleton, about two miles from Frederiksted. Here the bodies of the two soldiers killed on the previous day were found lying by the side of the road. To avenge their death an attack was made on the laborers, who were in their quarters, and some fifteen or twenty were killed. After this heroic exploit the troops marched triumphantly into Frederiksted.

Great must have been the disappointment of the governor in not having encountered more than a dozen rioters, although he had marched over the ground where they were reported to be thousands strong.

The volunteers, composed principally of planters and overseers, seeing that there was not the least show of resistance on the part of the rioters, became very brave, and commenced to go from estate to estate searching for those who had been engaged in the riot. Many of them were found at home as unconcerned as if nothing had happened. They were either summarily shot or arrested and imprisoned in the fort. At night the governor returned with his forces by sea and the volunteers by land. During the night a few more estates were burned.

On the 4th two men-of-war arrived, one English and one French. The former anchored off Frederiksted and the latter in the harbor of Christiansted.

Notwithstanding the arrival of these vessels, and the fact that no rioters could be found assembled together, women and children continued to flee to St. Thomas whenever an opportunity offered.

The volunteers again went into the country, where they killed and arrested many of the rioters. As those killed or arrested were all on the estates where they belonged, the riot might safely have been considered ended.

On the 5th the governor issued an order creating a court-martial for the trial of the prisoners, a copy of which I inclose. This court is still in session. To date, twelve of the rioters have been sentenced to death by it and have been executed. They did not deny their participation in the riot and died like martyrs. For several days the planters continued to kill and arrest those accused of having been engaged in the riot. I estimate, from the best information I can get, the number of killed to be 250. The hospitals are filled with the wounded and the prisons hold about 270. There is no doubt but that many were killed who had taken no active part in the riot. At first the planters were so enraged that they were not particular in requiring proof of guilt before they shot. If evidence was necessary, no difficulty was found in procuring it. By placing a gun at the head of some laborer who had remained on the estate and threatening him with instant death if he did not give the names of the parties who destroyed it, they succeeded in getting the names of the men they wanted to kill. The unlucky owners of the names given have no one who will take enough interest in them to prove their innocence if they were so.

The method of obtaining evidence in the courts is somewhat similar. If the accused does not confess his guilt of the offense charged satisfactorily to the judge, or if a witness does not testify as he is wanted to, the court official standing near *persuades* the accused or witness with a rattan to confess or testify as desired. This method of obtaining confessions and evidence is daily practiced in the police courts of both islands.

I inclose herewith a list of the estates burned, together with a map of the island, on which I have marked the same.

The Plymouth arrived at Christiansted on the 16th and on the 18th came to St. Thomas for coal. By request of the governor the captain goes to Frederiksted to-day, where he will remain for several days, perhaps until the arrival of a Danish man-of-war, which is said to be on the way.

Notwithstanding the laborers are at work as peaceably as ever, a general apprehension is felt that they will again attempt to accomplish what they failed to do by their first effort, that is, the repeal of the "labor law."

I regret to say that there are many citizens on the island who would not hesitate to demand that the Danish Government should keep a large force of troops on the island, and to accept the moral support of the men-of-war of foreign nations, in order that they might have the services of the laborer without paying him an equivalent for it. As it is well known to the laborers that a law had been passed stipulating that the labor act must be repealed within three years, one of which had expired, and that officials sent out by the home Government, with the knowledge of the governor and courts, had openly violated the letter and spirit of the said act, during the year, by paying much higher wages to the employés of the factory than it allowed to be paid, and for doing which planters had previously been fined, they had good reason to suppose that the act would not be enforced after the 1st of October. It is undeniable that if the officials had, instead of violating the law in question, secured its immediate repeal, which they could easily have done, there would have been no riot, and consequently no destruction of property.

The sufferers by the riot, as well as nine-tenths of the white inhabitants, openly accuse the governor and other officials with maladministration, as follows:

1st. That they created discontent among the laborers by violating the law.

2d. That they dismantled the forts at Frederiksted and King's Hill, and removed the troops to Christiansted against their protest, thereby leaving them entirely unprotected.

3d. That the officials should have asked for assistance as soon as they saw there would be trouble.

4th. That prompt action, even after the arrival of the governor with re-enforcements, would have saved the estates.

5th. That the governor permitted their works to be destroyed in order to force them to use the factory to grind their cane and manufacture their sugar.

I understand that on these grounds they propose to claim indemnity for their losses. One of the planters so told the governor, who at once had him arrested and confined in jail. Another is being prosecuted by the courts for having done the same.

I estimate the property destroyed to be worth at from $750,000 to $1,000,000. The general estimate of citizens of the island is more than twice the latter amount.

In a few months the works on the estates will be in as good condition as before, and if the labor law is repealed, as it should be, the island will soon recover from its loss, and all danger of a repetition of the riot will have passed for years to come.

I am, &c.,

V. V. SMITH.

[Inclosures to Consul Smith's report.]

Provisional act to regulate the relations between the proprietors of landed estates and the rural population of free laborers.

I, Peter Hansen, Knight Commander of the Order of Dannebrog, the King's Commissioner for and officiating Governor-General of the Danish West India Islands, make known:

That whereas the ordinance dated 29th July, 1848, by which yearly contracts for labor on landed estates were introduced, has not been duly acted upon; whereas the interest of the proprietors of estates, as well as of the laborers, requires that their mutual obligations should be defined; and whereas on inquiry into the practice of the island, and into the private contracts and agreements hitherto made, it appears expedient to establish uniform rules throughout the island for the guidance of all parties concerned, it is enacted and ordained:

PARA. 1. All engagements of laborers now domiciled on landed estates and receiving wages in money, or in kind, for cultivating and working such estates, are to be continued as directed by the ordinance of 29th July, 1848, until the first day of October of the present year; and all similar engagements shall in future be made, or shall be considered as having been made, for a term of twelve months, viz, from the first of October till the first of October year after year.

Engagements made by heads of families are to include their children between five and fifteen years of age, and other relatives depending on them and staying with them.

PARA. 2. No laborer engaged as aforesaid in the cultivation of the soil shall be discharged or dismissed from, nor shall be permitted to dissolve, his or her engagement before the expiration of the same on the first of October of the present or of any following year, except in the instances hereafter enumerated:

A. By mutual agreement of master and laborer before a magistrate.

B. By order of a magistrate, on just and equitable cause being shown by the parties interested.

Legal marriage, and the natural tie between mothers and their children, shall be deemed by the magistrate just and legal cause of removal from one estate to another. The husband shall have the right to be removed to his wife, the wife to her husband, and children under fifteen years of age to their mother, provided no objection to employing such individuals shall be made by the owner of the estate to which the removal is to take place.

PARA. 3. No engagement of a laborer shall be lawful in future unless made in the presence of witnesses, and entered in the day-book of the estate.

PARA. 4. Notice to quit service shall be given by the employer, as well as by the laborer, at no other period but once a year, in the month of August, not before the first nor after the last day of the said month. An entry thereof shall be made in the day-book, and an acknowledgment in writing shall be given to the laborer.

The laborer shall have given or received legal notice of removal from the estate where he serves before any one can engage his services. Otherwise, the new contract to be void, and the party engaging or tampering with a laborer employed by others will be dealt with according to law.

In case any owner or manager of an estate should dismiss a laborer during the year without sufficient cause, or should refuse to receive him at the time stipulated, or refuse to grant him a passport when due notice of removal has been given, the owner or manager is to pay full damages to the laborer and to be sentenced to a fine not exceeding $20.

PARA. 5. Laborers employed or rated as first, second, or third class laborers, shall perform all the work in the field, or about the works, or otherwise concerning the estate, which it hitherto has been customary for such laborers to perform, according to the season. They shall attend faithfully to their work, and willingly obey the directions given by the employer or the person appointed by him. No laborer shall presume to dictate what work he or she is to do, or refuse the work he may be ordered to perform, unless expressly engaged for some particular work only. If a laborer thinks himself aggrieved, he shall not therefore leave the work, but in due time apply for redress to the owner of the estate or to the magistrate.

It is the duty of all laborers, on all occasions and at all times, to protect the property of his employer, to prevent mischief to the estate, to apprehend evildoers, and not to give countenance to or conceal unlawful practices.

PARA. 6. The working days to be as usual, only five days in the week, and the same days as hitherto. The ordinary work of estates is to commence at sunrise and to be finished at sunset every day, leaving one hour for breakfast and two hours at noon from 12 to 2 o'clock.

Planters who prefer to begin the work at 7 o'clock in the morning, making no separate breakfast-time, are at liberty to adopt this plan, either during the year or when out of crop.

The laborers shall be present in due time at the place where they are to work. The list to be called and answered regularly; whoever does not answer the list when called, is too late.

PARA. 7. No throwing of grass or of wood shall be exacted during working-hours, all former agreements to the contrary notwithstanding; but during crop the laborers are expected to bring home a bundle of longtops from the field where they are at work.

Cartmen and crook-people, when breaking off, shall attend properly to their stock, as hitherto usual.

PARA. 8. During crop the mill-gang, the crook-gang, boilermen, firemen, stillmen, and any other person employed about the mill and the boiling-house, shall continue their work during breakfast and noon hours, as hitherto usual; and the boilermen, firemen, magass-carriers, &c., also during evening hours after sunset, when required; but all workmen employed as aforesaid shall be paid an extra remuneration for the work done by them in extra hours.

The boiling-house is to be cleared, the mill to be washed down, and the magass to be swept up, before the laborers leave the work, as hitherto usual.

The mill is not to turn after six o'clock in the evening, and the boiling not to be continued after ten o'clock, except by special permission of the governor-general, who then will determine, if any, and what, extra remuneration shall be paid to the laborers.

PARA. 9. The laborers are to receive, until otherwise ordered, the following remuneration:

A. The use of a house, or dwelling-rooms, for themselves and their children, to be built and repaired by the estate, but to be kept in proper order by the laborers.

B. The use of a piece of provision ground, thirty feet in square, as usual, for every first and second class laborer, or, if it be standing ground, up to fifty feet in square. Third-class laborers are not entitled to, but may be allowed, some provision ground.

C. Weekly wages at the rate of 15 cents to every first-class laborer, of 10 cents to every second-class laborer, and of 5 cents to every third-class laborer for every working-day.

Where the usual allowance of meal and herrings has been agreed on in part of wages, full weekly allowance shall be taken for 5 cents a day, or 25 cents a week.

Nurses losing two hours every working-day shall be paid at the rate of four full working-days in the week.

The wages of minors to be paid, as usual, to their parents, or to the person in charge of them.

Laborers not calling at pay-time personally, or by another authorized, to wait till next pay-day, unless they were prevented by working for the estate.

No attachment of wages for private debts to be allowed, nor more than two-thirds to be deducted for debts to the estate, unless otherwise ordered by the magistrate.

Extra provisions occasionally given during the ordinary working-hours, are not be claimed as a right nor to be bargained for.

PARA. 10. Work in extra hours during crop is to be paid as follows:

To the mill-gang and to the crook-gang for working through the breakfast-hour one stiver, and for working through noon two stivers per day.

Extra provision is not to be given, except at the option of the laborers, in place of the money or in part of it.

The boilermen, firemen, and magass-carriers are to receive for all days when the boiling is carried on until late hours a maximum pay of 20 cents per day. No bargaining for extra pay by the hour is permitted.

Laborers working such extra hours only by turns are not to have additional payment.

PARA. 11. Tradesmen on estates are considered as engaged to perform the same work as hitherto usual: assisting in the field, carting, potting sugar, &c. They shall be rated as first, second, and third class laborers, according to their proficiency. Where no definite terms have been agreed on previously, the wages of first-class tradesmen, having full work in their trade, are to be 20 cents per day. Any existing contract with tradesmen is to continue until October next.

No tradesman is allowed to keep apprentices without the consent of the owner of the estate. Such apprentices to be bound for no less period than three years, and not to be removed without the permission of the magistrate.

PARA. 12. No laborer is obliged to work for others on Saturdays, but if they choose to work for hire, it is proper that they should give their own estate the preference. For a full day's work on Saturday there shall not be asked for, nor given more than—

Twenty cents to a first-class laborer, 13 cents to a second-class laborer, 7 cents to a third-class laborer.

Work on Saturday may, however, be ordered by the magistrate as a punishment to the laborer for having absented himself from work during the week for one whole day or more, and for having been idle during the week; and then the laborer shall not receive more than his usual pay for a common day's work.

PARA. 13. All the male laborers, tradesmen included, above 18 years of age, working on an estate, are bound to take the usual night-watch by turns, but only once in ten days, notice to be given before noon to break off from work in the afternoon with the nurses and to come to work next day at eight o'clock. The watch to be delivered in the usual manner by nightfall and by sunrise.

The above rule shall not be compulsory, except where voluntary watchmen cannot be obtained at a hire the planters may be willing to give to save the time lost by employing their ordinary laborers as watchmen.

Likewise, the male laborers are bound, once a month, on Sundays and holidays, to take the day-watch about the yard and to act as pasturemen, on receiving their usual pay for a week-day's work. This rule applies also to the crook-boys.

All orders about the watches to be duly entered in the day-book of the estate.

Should a laborer, having been duly warned to take the watch, not attend, another laborer is to be hired in the place of the absentee, and at his expense; not, however, to exceed 15 cents. The person who willfully leaves the watch, or neglects it, is to be reported to the magistrate and punished as the case merits.

PARA. 14. Laborers willfully abstaining from work on a working-day are to forfeit their wages for the day; and will have to pay over and above the forfeit a fine, which can be lawfully deducted in their wages, of 7 cents for a first-class laborer, 5 cents for a second-class laborer, and 3 cents for a third-class laborer.

In crop, on grinding days, when employed about the works, in cutting canes or in crook, an additional punishment will be awarded for willful absence and neglect by the magistrate, on complaint being made.

Laborers abstaining from work for half a day, or breaking off from work before being dismissed, to forfeit their wages for one day.

Laborers not coming to work in due time, to forfeit half a day's wages.

Parents keeping their children from work shall be fined instead of the children.

No charge of house-rent is to be made in future on account of absence from work or for the Saturday.

PARA. 15. Laborers willfully abstaining from work for two or more days during the week, or habitually absenting themselves, or working badly or lazily, shall be punished as the case merits, on complaint to the magistrate.

PARA. 16. Laborers assaulting any person in authority on the estate, or planning or conspiring to retard or to stop the work of the estate, or uniting to abstain from work, or to break their engagements, shall be punished according to law on investigation before a magistrate.

PARA. 17. Until measures can be adopted for securing medical attendance to the laborers, and for regulating the treatment of the sick and the infirm, it is ordered:

That infirm persons unfit for any work shall as hitherto be maintained on the estates where they are domiciled, and be attended to by their next relations.

That parents or children of such infirm persons shall not move from the estate, leaving them behind, without making provision for them to the satisfaction of the owner or of the magistrate.

That laborers unable to attend to work on account of illness, or on account of having sick children, shall make a report to the manager or any other person in authority on the estate, who, if the case appears dangerous and the sick person destitute, shall cause medical assistance to be given.

That all sick laborers willing to remain in the hospital during their illness shall there be attended to at the cost of the estate.

PARA. 18. If a laborer reported sick shall be at any time found absent from the estate without leave, or is trespassing about the estate, or found occupied with work requiring health, he shall be considered skulking and willfully absent from work.

When a laborer pretends illness and is not apparently sick, it shall be his duty to prove his illness by medical certificate.

PARA. 19. Pregnant women shall be at liberty to work with the small gang as customary, and, when confined, not to be called on to work for seven weeks after their confinement.

Young children shall be fed and attended to during the hours of work at some proper place at the cost of the estate.

Nobody is allowed to stay from work on pretense of attending a sick person, except the wife and the mother in dangerous cases of illness.

PARA. 20. It is the duty of the managers to report to the police any contagious or suspicious cases of illness and death, especially when gross neglect is believed to have taken place, or when children have been neglected by their mothers, in order that the guilty person may be punished according to law.

PARA. 21. The driver or foreman on the estate is to receive in wages four and a half dollars monthly, if no other terms have been agreed on. The driver may be dismissed at any time during the year with the consent of the magistrate. It is the duty of the driver to see the work duly performed, to maintain order and peace on the estate during the work and at other times, and to prevent and report all offenses committed. Should any laborer insult or use insulting language towards him during or on account of the performance of his duties, such person is to be punished according to law.

PARA. 22. No laborer is allowed without the special permission of the owner or manager to appropriate wood, grass, vegetables, fruits, or the like, belonging to the estate, nor to appropriate such produce from other estates, nor to cut canes, or to burn charcoal. Persons making themselves guilty of such offenses shall be punished according to law with fines or imprisonment with hard labor; and the possession of such articles not satisfactorily accounted for shall be sufficient evidence of unlawful acquisition.

PARA. 23. All agreements contrary to the above rules are to be null and void, and owners and managers of estates convicted of any practice tending willfully to counteract or avoid these rules, by direct or indirect means, shall be subject to a fine not exceeding $200.

Government House, St. Croix, 26th January, 1849.

P. HANSEN.

Ordinance containing further provisions relative to the second section of the ordinance of the 26th of January, 1849, for Saint Croix, &c.

We, Frederik the Seventh, by the grace of God King of Denmark, the Vandals and the Goths, Duke of Sleswick, Holsteen, Stormarn, Ditmarsh, Lauenborg, and Oldenborg, make known:

On the report of our minister of finance, who has laid before us the deliberation of the colonial council in our West India possessions, on a draft of ordinance abrogating the provisions contained in the 2d section of the ordinances of the 26th of January, the 18th of May, and the 13th of June, 1849, concerning marriage being a legal cause for dissolving contracts for agricultural labor, we most graciously decree:

The provisions contained in the 2d section of the ordinances of the 26th January, 1849, for St. Croix, of the 18th May, same year, for St. Johns, and of the 13th June, same year, for St. Thomas, relative to the dissolution of contracts of labor on account of marriage, shall in future be interpreted thus: that only in the case of marriage being entered during the course of the year of contract it shall be considered to establish a claim to have the contract dissolved on the conditions therein mentioned, and in such cases the party who intends to move to another estate shall give notice at least three weeks previous to the marriage ceremony.

To which all concerned have to conform.

Given at our Castle Christiansborg the 22d of February, 1855, under our royal hand and seal.

[L. S. R.] FREDERIK R.

ANDRÆ.

Ordinance concerning medical attendance on the landed properties in the islands of St. Croix and St. Johns.

We Frederik the Seventh, by the grace of God King of Denmark, the Vandals and the Goths, Duke of Sleswick, Holsteen, Stormarn, Ditmarsh, Lauenborg, and Oldenborg, make known:

On the report of our minister of finance, who has laid before us the deliberation of the colonial council in our West India possessions, on a draft of ordinance concerning medical attendance at the sugar estates, we most graciously decree:

§ 1. When the owner of any estate or landed property in St. Croix engages a physician to attend the laborers and their familes residing on the property (comprising all persons of the laboring class who, with the consent or knowledge of the owner, are domiciled or reside on the estate), and furnishes them with the requisite medicines, he shall be entitled to collect from every such individual 3 cents (2 stivers) per week as a contribution towards the expenses, invalids, and children under the age of 12 years, excepted. If the owner has not engaged any physician, he, or the person who on his behalf at the time represents him on the property, shall nevertheless be bound, in cases of disasters or of dangerous illness, to procure medical aid; if, and in what manner, the expenses arising therefrom are to be refunded by the individual concerned, or by the parents or master of the individual concerned, shall in every case be decided by the police-master according to equity.

§ 2. In the island of St. Johns all owners of estates shall pay to the physician that will be appointed by His Majesty the King an annual remuneration for attendance and traveling expenses of 75 cents (to be paid quarterly) for each of the laborers and their families (comprising each individual of the laboring class who with the consent or knowledge of the owner is domiciled or resides on the estate), and, besides, they shall furnish them with medicines. No deduction from the laborers' wages can be made for reimbursing these expenses.

To which all concerned have to conform.

Given at our Castle Christiansborg the 22d of February, 1855, under our royal hand and seal.

[L. S. R.] FREDERIK R.

ANDRÆ.

EGYPT.

AGRICULTURAL AND LABORING CLASSES.

[The following extract from a report by the agent and consul-general of the United States at Cairo (see Commercial Relations for 1877), is inserted in the appendix to this volume, in order to give as complete a view as possible of the condition of labor in the several countries. As a marked contrast to the condition of labor in the United States, this view of the condition of the agricultural classes in Egypt cannot fail to impress our people with a deep sense of thankfulness for the innumerable comforts and blessings which are the result of our more advanced civilization and of that form of government whose aim is the happiness of the people.]

Condition of the rural or fellaheen classes.—The rural districts of Egypt present a strange anomaly. The richest and most productive lands in the world are occupied and cultivated by a people in extreme poverty, living in mud or unburnt brick hovels, little, if any, better than those of the barbarians of Central Africa.

The black slaves brought from the interior are as intelligent and, in everything that pertains to modern civilization, little if at all inferior to the native rural population of Egypt, and so far as relates to their treatment and physical comforts, they are quite as well off and equally contented.

Of the two and sometimes three crops annually produced, only enough is left the fellah for his scantiest subsistence. With the price of all kinds of provisions higher than in the United States, his circumstances are such as not to permit him to consume on an average to exceed five cents' worth of food a day. Everything not required for his actual physical necessities is taken in one manner or another for taxes, and if the amount demanded is not forthcoming, the whip is freely used until it is paid. This instrument is in fact indispensable to the collector of taxes.

The tax agent demands the taxes of the sheiks of the small villages, and if the required sum is not paid, the sheik is whipped and sent away to procure the money; and chagrined, if not smarting from his own punishment, he does not fail to repeat the same process upon the fallahs under his jurisdiction. Sometimes when there is a deficiency in the payment of the amount required in a particular district, the tax agent summons all the sheiks to meet him at some designated place, and such as do not produce the sums demanded are whipped, and the process is afterward repeated from time to time until the money is paid.

The manner of procedure above described and occasional imprisonment are the ordinary means of enforcing the payment of delinquent taxes.

The sheiks sometimes suffer more than their share of the punishment. This arises from their relations to those under them. Their appointment is somewhat democratic, and their continuance in office to a certain extent a matter of sufferance. The older and chief men of the village designate one of their number to act as sheik, and if he were not sufficiently inspired with a sense of his duty to his constituents to resist the payment of taxes to the extent of subjecting himself to an occasional flogging, he would have very little excuse for punishing those under him, and a poor chance for continuance in his position, which is one of great power in his little community.

The idea of the fellah is that if he pays freely the amount asked, for which, in fact, he rarely has sufficient money, more will be demanded under the belief that he is able to pay it, and that in any event he will finally be punished. There is probably some truth in this, for the rule that governs many of the subcollectors is to take all they can find, and the sum demanded by the Government is often so large that, with the good will and the most strenuous efforts of all parties, it could only be procured with the greatest difficulty.

The time of collecting taxes is very irregular, and they are often demanded long before due, and in sums greatly in excess of those authorized by law. In the latter respect there are great abuses on the part of the subordinate officers and sometimes the sheiks. The Government often demands of the provincial governor a certain sum to be paid within a fixed number of days, and in order to obtain it, he is compelled to resort to measures that would be regarded as excessively severe in any Christian country.

The products of Egypt.—Notwithstanding the little apparent inducement, the fellah labors faithfully, and the land produces, if not to its maximum capacity, as nearly as it would be likely to do if it were cultivated according to the modes of more enlightened countries. The products per acre are very large. This will be readily seen when we consider the fact that the land of Egypt (not including Nubia) capable of cultivation has an area only of about one-sixth of that of the State of New York, and that from this small territory about 5,000,000 of people receive their support and pay annual taxes to the amount of $50,000,000.

Irrigation.—While the land produces thus bountifully, the labor required in its cultivation is proportionally great.

The tillable land of Egypt consists of the delta of the Nile and a narrow valley extending from Cairo southward This valley is generally from one to ten miles wide, though for 150 miles above Cairo it has a width of from ten to thirty miles. Both the delta and the valley, except so far as the former borders on the Mediterranean, are bounded on all sides by mountainous deserts, and for more than 2,000 miles from its mouths the river has not the smallest tributary. It rolls on toward the sea, unlike other rivers, constantly decreasing in volume. As there are no rains of any practical importance, it sustains all vegetation, and all the inhabitants of Egypt and all its herds drink its waters. It is to this country the source of life, and should its flow be stopped, every plant, shrub, and tree would wither and die in less than three months, and the whole land become as uninhabitable as the Great Sahara. The millions of native inhabitants, who have never drunk any other water, await its accustomed annual rise with more solicitude than a northern farmer awaits the return of spring.

The facts above stated are known to most well-informed persons, but comparatively few know or have anything more than the vaguest conception of the amount of labor required to conduct the waters of this great river and raise and distribute them, at precisely the right time and in the required quantities, upon every acre of cultivated land.

For two or three months in the year a considerable portion of the country may be irrigated by the natural rise of the river, but, with the exception of certain sections, the water is not permitted to flow freely over the land. It is taken from the river and conducted by canals alongside the fields where it is to be used and then let upon the different parcels of land, if it is sufficiently high, and if not, it is raised by some of the various modes employed for that purpose. Small embankments prevent the water from running on to other lands that may not at the time be in a condition to receive it. In fact, the processes of overflowing the lands, plowing, sowing, and harvesting are often being carried on simultaneously in adjoining fields.

When the land is sufficiently irrigated, the water is shut off or the pumping discontinued.

The process of irrigation is required to be repeated several times before the maturity of the crop, the quantity of water depending very much upon the kind of product. Rice requires a large amount of water, and wheat, oats, and rye much less.

There are in Egypt 8,406 miles of irrigating canals, of which 1,897 miles are navigable. There are also great dikes along the river and its various delta branches to prevent their overflow, and innumerable small ditches and embankments everywhere throughout the country.

In consequence of the muddiness of the waters of the Nile, the canals require frequent cleanings, and the high waters injure the dikes and render it necessary to repair them each year. The greatest amount of labor is, however, that required in raising the water from the river and canals to the level of the lands. Dipping, drawing, and pumping are processes going on nearly the whole year, and more than half of all the irrigation is done by these means. The water is raised from one or two feet to twenty, and sometimes more, according to the location of the land and the height of the river. A single case will illustrate the amount of labor required in this mode of irrigation. Those who have made the ascent of the Nile for any considerable distance above Cairo will have seen along its banks people in considerable numbers raising water by means of the shadoof. This is simply a leather basket-shaped bucket attached to a pole suspended in the same manner as the ordinary well-sweep. The sweep is very short and the bucket of water balanced by a mud weight. The instrument is of the rudest character, but by this means water is raised to the height of eight or nine feet with considerable rapidity. If the water is to be raised twenty feet, one man close to the river raises it four or five feet into a basin made of clay in the side of the bank, and from this point two men, each with a bucket, raise it about eight feet to a similar basin, and two others in the same manner to the required height, whence it is conducted by small earth-sluices to the required place, often a considerable distance from the river. It requires the constant working of these five shadoofs for forty-eight hours to water one feddan (acre). This, by changing once in four or six hours, would require ten men, each of whom would apply twenty-four hours' labor to the watering of one acre. The process requires repeating at least three times for each crop. Thus the labor required for the irrigation of one acre would be 720 hours, or 72 days of ten hours each.

This is an extreme case; still a very large amount of irrigation is done all along the banks of the river where the water is required to be raised in this manner to a height of from sixteen to twenty feet.

The labor is of the severest kind, and the fellah, with nothing except a cloth around his loins, is compelled to apply himself to his task with all the energy at his command.

In the delta and some parts of Upper Egypt, the water, being taken from the river at some distance above the point where it is used, is kept for a considerable portion of the year on very nearly the same level as the land. If, however, it has to be raised at all, it requires at least fifteen days to the acre.

When the water is raised only a few feet, the more ordinary method is that of the sakia, a rude machine propelled by oxen, cows, and horses, and sometimes camels and donkeys, and which raises the water by means of earthern jars attached to an endless rope-chain passing over a vertical wheel.

There are a few steam-pumps, but fuel is too expensive and labor too cheap to permit of their general use. The number employed is about 400, and these are mostly in Lower Egypt. They are used principally on large estates, but in some instances by those who irrigate the lands of the small farmers at a fixed price per acre. This is generally where cotton is produced, which requires watering once in eight or ten days throughout the season. The water has ordinarily to be raised but a few feet, and the quantity required each time when the watering is so frequent is much less. The usual price paid per acre is a half cantar of cotton, which is at the present time equivalent to $7.50.

Price of labor.—It is only the low price of farm labor that renders it practicable to cultivate lands requiring so much irrigation. The price differs in the various provinces. The following table is compiled from a semi-official report published in 1873, and, so far as I can learn, the present price of labor does not materially differ from that then paid.

Statement showing the number of agricultural laborers in the different moudirichs of Egypt and the average price of labor per day in 1873.

Name of moudirich.	Laborers owning or leasing lands.	Common field laborers.	Total agricultural laborers.	Average price of labor per day.
Minié and Bénimazar	....	11, 602	....	$0 13¼
Esné	28, 899	5, 860	34, 739	12½
Dahaklieh	....	4, 000	....	10
Galyoubieh	....	20, 909	....	10
Ghirgeh	....	....	100, 000	10
Manoufieh	47, 430	12, 000	59, 430	10
Sharkieh	57, 000	43, 000	100, 000	07½
Kéné	....	22, 688	....	06¼
Assiout	19, 091	10, 396	29, 487	05⅝
Behera	18, 495	4, 252	22, 747	06¼

It appears from this statement that in 1873 there were in four moudirichs 80,536 common field laborers, whose average pay was from 5⅝ to 7½ cents a day, and that the price exceeded 10 cents a day in but two moudirichs, having only 17,462 common laborers. The average price of the different moudirichs was 9 cents a day, but the average price of all the laborers was much less, being only 7½ cents.

It must not be understood that the laborer is also furnished with food. He provides this himself, so that the prices above named are the whole cost of the labor.

Even at these low prices the laborer does not find constant employment. He is only hired by the day at such times as his services are required. He is also subject to a personal tax, which, though small, represents from ten to twenty-five days' labor.

In addition to the agricultural laborers mentioned in the above table, there were employed at the same time 1,735 gardeners, who were distributed as follows: Cairo, 700; Alexandria, 414; Rosetta, 373; in the rest of Egypt, 248. Their average daily pay was 3 piasters, or 15 cents.

Agricultural implements.—Labor-saving machines and improved agricultural instruments are of little value in a country where labor is only worth from six to ten cents a day, and all attempts to introduce American machines or agricultural tools will only result, in the future as in the past, in absolute failure.

The shadoof and tàbout, the latter being a simple basket worked by two men, are the cheapest means for raising water in most parts of Egypt; and the most economical mode of constructing canals, dikes, and roads is that now employed, which consists of loosening the earth with a kind of mattock, and filling, with the same instrument and the hands, rude baskets, which are carried on the heads of boys and girls from eight to fourteen years old to the desired place. The same principle applies to all kinds of agricultural implements.

The rudest and cheapest are the best adapted to the present condition of Egypt. A spade or shovel that would cost ten or more days' labor would be of little value in the hands of a barefooted, half-naked fellah; and, were he accustomed to its use, he could not afford the luxury of an instrument the cost of which would nearly equal the value of all his household effects.

GERMANY.

CO-OPERATIVE SOCIETIES.

[Referred to in the report of the consul-general at Frankfort-on-the-Main, at page 157.]

*Report, by Consul-General Lee, on the formation, principles, benefits, and present extent of the co-operative societies of Germany.**

It is a notable fact that, notwithstanding the decline of labor prices, their present cheapness, the discharges of factory operatives, the advance in the cost of living, and the perpetual agitation of the socialists, there have been neither recently nor for many years past any serious labor strikes or troubles. Labor, with all its hardships, and

* From Commercial Relations for 1877, page 280.

they are many, appears to be complacent, contented, and even prosperous. There must be some potent cause for this, and a careful consideration of the subject leads me to the conclusion that the great system of co-operation, which had its origin in Germany about eighteen years ago, and has had its principal growth within the last ten years, is the chief resolvent of this labor problem. It would be impossible to give an adequate review of this system within the compass of this report. That task must be reserved for future occasions affording better adaptations of time and space. A few salient features only may now be mentioned.

The founder, chief organizer, and present head of the system is Dr. Schulze-Delitzsch, an eminent member of the Prussian Parliament. It arose from no pressure of social disturbances or political agitations, but began and grew from a careful and systematic study of economical principles. It is a system of self-help, as distinguished from State help on the one hand and communal absolutism on the other. It was therefore opposed alike by the bureaucratic and the socialistic elements; the first jealous of all freedom of association, and the latter of all social organization stopping short of political dominion. The first of these forces soon relaxed its opposition, however, for it was directly seen that nothing could more effectually preserve the equilibrium of labor-capital and money-capital, and so set social agitators at defiance, than the organic growth of the self-helping principle.

The leading purpose of the system is that of affording labor direct access to capital by converting labor into a basis of credit. It proceeds from the idea that credit may be created by association; that while an individual artisan cannot borrow the necessary capital to make himself an independent producer, an association of artisans can do so, and that such an association, converting itself in turn into a lender, may obtain the minimum of risk and maximum of security in its transactions by confining its loans to its own members. Lenders and borrowers being virtually the same persons, the former must have the most accurate information possible as to the reliability of the latter, and may have the further advantage of retaining their loans perpetually within the range of their inspection. An additional diminution of risk is obtained by making the members of the association liable for its entire debts and the whole association liable for the debts of each member. So important is this principle of mutual liability, that it has been called the keystone of the whole system.

The first association of this kind established in Germany was organized by Dr. Schulze-Delitzsch, in 1851, at Delitzsch, a small town of Prussian Saxony. This pioneer society is the model from which the multitude of credit banks that now cover the face of the empire have been formed. The statutes of its organization were substantially as follows:

1. That all self-helping, industrious persons in regular employment may be eligible to membership.
2. Capital to be acquired by subscriptions of members and by loans.
3. Business to be kept strictly within advances to members.
4. Capital stock owned by the association never to be less than 10 per cent. of the borrowed stock, and to be raised as soon as practicable to 50 per cent.
5. A reserve fund of 6 per cent. of the owned capital and 10 per cent. of the borrowed to be maintained by a contribution of 20 to 25 per cent. of net profits.
6. Shares to be of equal amounts, proportionate to the number of members, and each member to have one share only.
7. Gains and losses to be distributed in proportion to money paid in.
8. Loans to be made mainly on personal security of members, but mortgage may be taken.
9. Rate of interest to be uniform for all, and to depend on state of the money market.
10. Management to be representative, and subject to control of the members in their general meetings. The managing body is a standing committee, or executive council, responsible to the general meeting; in the larger associations, the management is vested in the unlimitedly liable directors, who choose a board of control.

On these foundations, with such improvements as time and experience have developed, multitudes of credit societies have sprung into existence in all parts of the empire, affording the German laborer a practical school of business, a safe deposit, and profitable investment for his earnings, a wholesome and contenting incentive to toil, and the ability to borrow money on equal terms with the millionaire.

It must not be supposed, however, that the credit societies constitute the whole of the German co-operative system. They are the peculiarly German part of the system, but it also includes raw material and store unions, productive associations, or unions for the production and sale of finished wares, building unions, consumption unions, or associations for the purchase and sale of the necessaries of life, and others, whose recent origin indicates the movement of the co-operative principle into new fields.

As early as 1863 a national union was formed of the different co-operative societies then existing, with Dr. Schulze-Delitzsch as anwalt, or presiding counselor. At the present time about three-fourths of all the societies belong to this union and send their annual balance-sheets to the central office. The general union is subdivided into thirty-four provincial unions, each with its own president and staff, and all under the direction of the national anwalt. The legislative powers of the national union are vested in a general convention of delegates from the different societies, which meets once a year, and for which the business is prepared by the standing committee of the union, consisting of the presidents of the subunions.

The most recent of these conventions was held at Wiesbaden, beginning on the 3d of September last, Dr. Schulze-Delitzsch presiding. According to the reports of the eminent anwalt on that occasion, there now exist 2,830 credit societies, 743 special commercial societies, 1,049 co-operative stores, and 64 building societies, making a total of 4,686 co-operative associations. As there are probably many more not yet heard from at the central office, the actual number will not fall short of 4,800, with an aggregate membership of 1,400,000.

Of the 2,830 credit banks now in operation, 1,037 are in German Austria, 1,120 in Prussia, 160 in Saxony, 136 in Bavaria, 105 in Würtemberg, 101 in Baden, 59 in Hesse, and the remainder scattered through the smaller States. From balance-sheets furnished to the anwalt, it appears (see table appended to this report) that 806 of these societies contained at the close of last year 431,216 members, and that their advances during that year amounted to 508,463,073 thalers,* a sum sufficient to mitigate, at least, the prevailing money stringency. The amount of capital owned by members of these 806 societies was, including reserves, 23,536,097 thalers, and of credits, 79,604,474. There was a large increase of active capital and cash deposits during the year, while at the same time there was an encouraging decrease of the loans on mortgage. The amount of discounts during the year was 323,288,631 thalers; a large increase, indicating a corresponding increase of business. The losses were less than in 1875, being only one mark to 416 thalers (23¾ cents to $297). Eighteen societies closed up their affairs during the year, four of them being declared bankrupt. Others of the 18 failed through speculations in violation of their statutes of organization, and others through the dishonesty of managers, who were not kept under strict surveillance. Considering the protracted depression of business and the severity of the ordeal it has applied to all banking enterprises, the number of failures has been remarkably small.

Statistics of 702 credit societies show that 75,396, or 21.8 per cent., of their members are agriculturists, 3.8 per cent. manfacturers, and of the remainder over 20 per cent. miscellaneous workmen. Reports from 180 productive societies show that 36,628 of their members, or 51.2 per cent., are workingmen, 18.2 per cent. tradesmen of fixed positions, and 10.4 per cent. teachers, physicians, officials, and other professional persons. The proportion of working people in some of the other co-operative organizations is probably still greater.

A table accompanies this report giving a statistical review of the consumption societies from 1864 to 1876, inclusive.

ALFRED E. LEE.

UNITED STATES CONSULATE-GENERAL,
Frankfort-on-the-Main, November 1, 1877.

---

*Thaler = about 72 cents

Statement showing the progress of the union co-operative credit societies in Germany from 1859 to 1876.

Year.	Number of societies which have sent in balance-sheets.	Number of members of the societies.	Sums advanced and renowals granted.		Own capital.				Borrowed funds.					Average in per cent. showing the difference between own and borrowed funds.
			Total amount.	Average sum for each society.	Amounts due to members.	Reserve.	Total amount of both.	Average sum for each society.	A. From private persons.	B. From banks and societies.	C. Saving deposit.	Total amount from columns A, B, C.	Average sum for each society.	
			Thalers.	*Thalers.*	*Thalers.*	*Thalers.*	*Thalers.*	*Thalers.*	*Thalers.*		*Thalers.*	*Thalers.*	*Thalers.*	*Per. ct.*
1859	80	18,676	4,131,436	51,642	246,001	30,845	276,846	3,460	501,795		512,350	1,014,145	12,676	27.50
1860	133	31,603	8,478,489	63,748	462,012	66,845	528,857	3,976	1,069,833		1,322,494	2,392,327	17,987	22.10
1861	188	48,760	16,876,009	89,766	799,375	107,238	907,213	4,825	1,983,441		2,649,036	4,632,477	24,641	19.50
1862	243	69,202	23,674,261	97,425	1,199,545	132,893	1,332,438	5,483	3,441,033		2,747,577	6,188,610	25,467	21.10
1863	339	99,175	33,917,248	100,053	1,803,203	218,047	2,021,250	5,962	5,641,820		3,416,220	9,058,040	26,719	22.30
1864	455	135,013	48,147,495	105,818	2,959,296	293,461	3,252,757	7,148	7,401,317		5,355,265	12,756,582	28,036	25.40
1865	498	169,595	67,509,903	135,682	4,442,879	409,679	4,852,558	9,744	11,154,579		6,502,197	17,656,776	35,455	27.40
1866	532	193,712	85,010,145	159,793	5,773,106	556,398	6,329,504	11,897	10,646,394	522,617	8,726,518	19,895,529	37,397	31.80
1867	570	219,258	102,026,152	178,993	6,847,031	660,054	7,507,085	13,170	12,335,960	975,709	11,378,570	24,690,239	42,316	30.40
1868	666	256,337	139,247,793	209,080	9,365,502	865,055	10,231,457	15,362	16,309,078	1,178,367	16,221,592	33,709,037	50,614	30.30
1869	735	304,772	181,602,100	247,078	12,078,464	1,175,138	13,253,602	18,032	19,658,859	1,989,661	21,053,863	42,702,383	58,098	31.03
1870	740	314,656	207,618,287	280,565	13,449,152	1,214,175	14,663,327	19,815	20,136,670	2,360,040	23,502,443	45,999,162	62,161	31.87
1871	777	340,336	241,331,151	310,593	15,530,620	1,505,689	17,036,309	21,925	32,027,913	2,165,160	24,610,177	58,803,280	75,679	28.97
1872	807	372,742	354,519,200	439,305	19,515,767	1,857,762	21,373,529	26,485	41,747,927	4,283,432	31,157,372	77,188,731	95,649	27.69
1873	834	399,741	446,733,015	535,651	23,250,531	2,281,284	25,531,815	30,613	56,145,748	4,383,177	32,891,198	93,420,123	112,014	27.33
1874	815	411,143	451 908,394	554,488	25,711,589	2,479,783	28,191,372	34,590	59,686,384	3,686,272	38,439,274	101,811,930	124,923	27.68
1875	815	418,251	498,549,479	611,717	27,847,336	2,809,327	30,656,663	37,616	64,858,584	4,409,705	40,087,672	109,355,961	135,037	27.85
1876	806	431,216	508,463,073	630,847	29,625,380	3,338,342	32,963,722	40,898	66,116,411	4,720,142	40,654,307	111,490,860	138,326	29.57

To show the progress between the years 1859 and 1876 the sums for these two years are reduced to United States dollars:

Year														
1859	80	18,676	$2,949,845	$36,872	$175,644	$22,023	$197,668	$2,470	$358,281		$365,817	$724,099	$9,050	....
1876	806	431,216	363,042,634	430,424	21,152,521	2,383,576	23,536,097	29,201	47,207,117	3,370,181	29,027,175	79,604,474	98,764	....

Statement showing the progress of the union co-operative consumption societies in Germany from 1864 to 1876.

Year.	Number of societies known at the central office.	Number of societies which have sent in balance-sheets.	Number of members.	Receipts from sales during the year.	Amount due to members.	Reserve.	Debts contracted.	Debts from the societies on goods bought on credit.	Sums due by members for goods sold on credit. Total.
				Thalers.	*Thalers.*	*Thalers.*	*Thalers.*	*Thalers.*	*Thalers.*
1864...	97	38	7, 709	267, 589	21, 433	4, 912	16, 951	12, 636	5, 750
1865...	157	34	6, 647	308, 461	22, 226	2, 767	16, 529	18, 948	5, 225
1866...	199	46	14, 083	826, 598	46, 982	6, 058	51, 062	29, 394	9, 275
1867...	316	49	18, 884	967, 974	72, 186	11, 160	72, 070	44, 060	10, 897
1868...	555	75	33, 656	2, 124, 141	156, 244	25, 179	125, 717	68, 272	11, 425
1869...	627	109	42, 283	2, 375, 417	208, 717	40, 857	115, 342	80, 295	14, 106
1870...	739	111	45, 761	3, 002, 620	272, 935	50, 408	182, 126	155, 760	20, 077
1871...	827	143	64, 517	4, 507, 658	529, 857	73, 842	268, 976	209, 658	32, 444
1872...	902	170	72, 622	5, 219, 849	558, 377	86, 135	419, 781	248, 180	23, 186
1873...	973	189	87, 504	7, 294, 136	804, 709	117, 688	688, 593	308, 391	23, 425
1874...	1, 089	178	90, 088	7, 530, 831	898, 407	142, 611	723, 547	268, 007	26, 802
1875...	1, 034	179	98, 055	7, 568, 321	970, 755	167, 803	809, 862	291, 948	41, 473
1876...	1, 049	180	101, 727	8, 126, 137	1, 015, 364	185, 466	890, 805	334, 729	47, 574

To show the progress between the years 1864 and 1876 the sums for these two years are reduced below into United States dollars:

1864 ..	97	38	7, 709	$191, 058	$15, 303	$3, 507	$12, 103	$9, 022	$4, 105	19
1876...	1, 049	180	101, 727	5, 802, 061	724, 969	132, 422	636, 033	238, 996	33, 967	49

LABOR, CO-OPERATIVE SOCIETIES, AND BANKING IN GERMANY.

The following very interesting report on the condition of labor, co-operative societies, and various statistics concerning their workings, banking and monetary statistics for the German Empire, comprised part of the annual commercial report for the year 1878, of the consul-general at Frankfort-on-the-Main, but being more properly related to labor and labor statistics, is inserted in this Appendix; nothing appearing in the body of this work but those reports which were sent to the Department of State in special form in answer to the trade Circular issued by the Department:

LABOR.

Official tables have been recently published showing the classification of laborers and distribution of employments throughout the empire, but as these tables contain manifest inaccuracies, they can only be taken for approximate truth. They represent that the total number of establishments in the empire employing laborers is 2,936,572, and that the entire number of persons employed, including owners, directors, and other attaches, is 5,362,078 males and 1,105,492 females; making a total of 6,467,570 persons. From the same tables it appears that in Prussia 28.4 per cent. of the people are engaged in agriculture and kindred pursuits; 30.4 per cent. in mining and mechanic arts; 8.9 per cent. in trade and commerce; 21 per cent. in what may be called personal service; 1.3 per cent. in the army and navy; 4 per cent. in various other professions; and 6 per cent. in no special business or employment. Of the population of the other German States, 29.7 per cent. are engaged in agriculture; 32.7 per cent. in mining and mechanic industry; 8.9 per cent. in trade; 17.3 per cent. in personal service; 1.2 per cent. in military service; 4.2 per cent. in the professions; and 6 per cent. in no special employment.

The rates of wages have declined rather than increased during the past twelve months. In the mining districts of Westphalia this decline has been especially notable, and in some parts of Southern Germany it has amounted to 5 and even 10 per cent. Nowhere is an advance reported. Many manufacturing establishments have reduced the number of their workmen, and the unemployed population of the cities and towns is unusually large. All are willing to work, however, though it be for nominal wages or a bare support, and the spectacle of gangs of idle vagrants roving from place to place, and living by begging or plunder, is not tolerated and seldom or never seen.

Increased discontent among the laboring classes is noticeable, owing to increased socialist agitations, but the signs of this discontent have been almost entirely political, and no strikes or violent measures have been resorted to. At the same time the government, both local and general, has addressed itself in many ways to the mitigation of industrial distress. Public kitchens, for instance, have been established all over the country, where working people may buy substantial food at the lowest possible prices. An imperial law forbids the employment of children under sixteen years of age in factories, and makes the owner of a factory responsible to his employés for any injury caused to them by culpable accident. To insure the enforcement of these and other laws for the protection of factory operatives, government officials are charged with the inspection, from time to time, of the various establishments.

Distribution of labor and professional employments in the German Empire.

Kind of employment.	Number of establishments.	Number of persons employed.		Total.
		Males.	Females.	
Gardening (for trade and art purposes)	13, 072	21, 966	2, 927	24, 893
Fisheries	15, 636	19, 143	480	19, 623
Mining	7, 893	421, 125	11, 984	433, 109
Ceramic industry	51, 235	246, 256	18, 883	265, 139
Metal works	164, 328	404, 137	16, 308	420, 445
Machinery	83, 635	304, 552	3, 153	307, 705
Chemical industry	8, 640	45, 876	5, 863	51, 739
Heating and lighting	8, 947	39, 113	3, 205	42, 318
Textile industry	380, 918	610, 764	314, 693	925, 457
Paper and leather	56, 614	157, 770	29, 404	187, 174
Woodcutting, &c	245, 703	443, 285	20, 248	463, 533
Food and liquors	241, 694	600, 653	92, 625	693, 278
Furnishing and dressing	755, 616	662, 785	386, 685	1, 049, 470
Building	234, 334	482, 616	3, 381	485, 997
Polygraphic industries	8, 108	48, 823	7, 029	55, 852
Art industries	5, 534	12, 810	373	13, 183
Trade	420, 129	540, 449	119, 539	659, 988
Transportation	74, 655	129, 018	4, 801	133, 819
Hotels, inns, &c	159, 881	170, 937	63, 911	234, 848
Total	2, 936, 572	5, 362, 078	1, 105, 492	6, 467, 570

CO-OPERATIVE SOCIETIES.

In my annual report for last year reference was made to the co-operative system of Germany as a mediatory agency between labor and capital, and some account was given of the history and operations of the co-operative societies down to the latest period for which statistics could be obtained. Further observation has confirmed the opinions then expressed as to the efficiency of those societies in preventing and neutralizing labor discontents. Perhaps no better proof could be given of the stability and usefulness of these associations than the success with which they have withstood the business depression which has broken down so many well-grounded enterprises, and in spite of which they have steadily increased in numbers, in membership, in profits, and in the extent of their operations. The system has, moreover, extended itself to other portions of the continent, and in Italy and Belgium the credit banks have become sufficiently numerous to form general unions and hold general congresses. The German union, to which it is believed all the societies of the empire will ultimately attach themselves, comprises about 1,100 societies, constituting thirty-two subordinate provincial unions, all under the presidency of Mr. Schulze-Delitzsch, the founder of the system.

The Austrian societies having about a year ago separated from the union, the statistics for the year 1877, which here follow, refer, unlike those for 1876, to the German societies only.

As appears from tabulations hereto appended, the number of co-operative or self-helping societies in the German Empire officially known to the general administration is 3,123, of which 1,827 are credit, 622 productive, 624 consumé, or provision supplying, and 50 building societies. The total number, as stated in the tabulations for 1876, was 4,686; but this included 1,606 Austrian societies, now not counted.

Many societies have made no report to the central office, and, including these, the total number in the empire cannot be much short of 3,300, containing about 1,000,000 members. The aggregate transactions of these societies during the year is estimated at 2,200,000,000 marks, or, say, $50,000,000. These 3,300 societies have an aggregate capital invested in shares and reserve funds of 150,000,000 to 160,000,000 marks, besides about 400,000,000 marks in the form of interest-bearing loans. They contribute about 25,000 marks per annum to educational purposes, and are represented in the press by several well-edited journals devoted to their interests.

During the year 74 new societies were organized and 40 were liquidated, making a net increase of 34. Only 5 were declared bankrupt, and of these part have been reorganized.

The credit, or loan, societies continue to hold the first place in the system. Of these 929 have reported balances, showing aggregate advances for the year amounting to 1,500,000,000 marks; a sum which, distributed among the masses, must afford very material relief in a time of financial stringency. The issues on account current during the year amounted to 515,988,709 marks and the receipts to 497,693,970, leaving outstanding 134,463,963, or 20 per cent. more than the year before. These credits, as extended under the safeguards of the system, are considered perfectly safe. The total transactions for the year exceed by about 25,000,000 marks those of 1876. The deposited funds amounted at the close of the year to abut 351,000,000 marks, and the proportion of capital to deposits was about 2 per cent. better than the year before. In 1876 the issues on mortgage were 11,533,512 marks; in 1877 they were 12,665,635. Strenuous efforts have been made to reduce these mortgage transactions, but thus far with only relative success. The 929 reporting societies contain, as will be seen, nearly 470,000 members.

The productive, or raw-material producing, societies have increased in membership but have slightly declined in number. The reduction in the cost of raw material which they have effected is estimated at from 10 to 20 per cent.

An appended table shows the operations of the consumé, or provision-furnishing, societies from 1864 to 1877, inclusive. Reports from 202 of these societies show nearly 100,000 members, and sales during the year amounting to nearly 26,000,000 marks. Nearly three-fourths of them have reduced their business to a strictly cash basis, and the credits outstanding at the end of the year were trifling. The debts for goods purchased were less than 25 per cent. of the capital, and the reserves amounted to 20 per cent. of the capital shares. Owing to the depression of business, the number of consumé societies has decreased, especially in Saxony, Brandenburg, and the Grand Duchy of Baden, but no losses of any consequence have occurred. On the contrary, handsome dividends have been realized even by the butcher and baker societies, which were experimental.

The building societies have also diminished in number during the year. Many of them were established in flush times, when rents were high, and the real-estate market active. The financial stringency has, therefore, obliged some of them to go into liquidation, but no serious losses have occurred. Thirty per cent. of the members of these societies are laborers.

Comparative view of operations of the co-operative loan societies of the German Empire from 1859 to 1877, inclusive

1. Year.	2. No. of societies that have reported balances.	Societies enumerated in column 2.												7. Percentage of funds owned to other funds.
		3. Members.	4. Advances and prolongations.		5. Funds owned.				6. Deposits and credits.					
			a. Total.	b. Average per society.	a. Shares of members.	b. Reserves.	c. Total of a and b.	d. Average per society.	a. Loans from private persons.	b. Credits from banks and societies.	c. Savings deposits.	d. Total from a to c.	e. Average per society.	
			Marks.	Marks.	Marks.	Marks.	Marks.	Marks.	Marks.		Marks.	Marks.	Marks.	Pr. ct.
1859....	80	18,676	12,394,308	154,926	738,003	92,535	830,538	10,380	1,505,385		1,537,050	3,042,435	38,028	27.50
1860....	133	31,603	25,435,467	191,244	1,386,036	200,535	1,586,571	11,928	3,209,499		3,967,482	7,176,981	53,961	22.10
1861....	188	48,760	50,628,027	269,298	2,398,125	321,714	2,721,639	14,475	5,950,323		7,947,108	13,897,431	73,923	19.50
1862...	243	69,202	71,022,783	292,275	3,598,635	398,679	3,997,314	16,449	10,323,099		8,242,731	18,565,830	76,401	21.10
1863....	339	99,175	101,753,844	300,150	5,409,609	654,141	6,063,750	17,886	16,925,460		10,248,660	27,174,120	80,157	22.30
1864....	455	135,013	144,442,485	317,454	8,877,888	880,383	9,758,171	21,414	22,203,951		16,065,795	38,269,746	84,108	25.40
1865....	498	169,595	202,709,709	407,046	13,328,637	1,229,037	14,557,674	29,232	33,463,737		19,506,591	52,970,328	106,365	27.40
1866....	532	193,712	255,030,435	479,379	17,319,318	1,669,194	18,988,512	35,691	31,939,182	1,567,851	26,179,554	59,686,587	112,191	31.80
1867....	570	219,358	306,078,456	536,979	20,541,093	1,980,162	22,521,255	39,510	37,007,880	2,927,127	34,135,710	74,070,717	129,948	30.40
1868 ..	666	256,337	417,743,379	627,240	28,096,506	2,597,865	30,694,371	46,066	48,927,234	3,525,101	48,664,776	101,127,111	151,842	30.30
1869....	735	304,772	514,806,327	741,233	36,235,392	3,525,414	39,760,806	54,095	58,976,577	5,968,983	63,161,589	128,107,149	174,294	31.03
1870....	740	314,656	622,854,861	841,695	40,347,456	3,642,525	43,989,981	59,445	60,410,037	7,080,120	70,507,329	137,997,486	186,483	31.87
1871....	777	310,336	723,993,453	931,779	46,591,860	4,517,067	51,108,927	65,775	90,083,829	6,495,480	73,830,531	170,409,840	227,037	28.97
1872....	807	372,742	1,063,557,600	1,317,915	58,547,301	5,573,286	64,120,587	79,455	125,243,781	12,850,296	93,472,116	231,566,193	286,947	27.69
1873....	834	399,741	1,340,199,045	1,606,953	69,751,593	6,813,852	76,595,445	91,839	168,437,244	13,149,531	98,673,594	280,260,369	336,042	27.33
1874....	815	411,443	1,355,725,182	1,663,464	77,134,767	7,439,349	84,574,116	103,770	179,059,152	11,058,816	115,317,822	305,435,790	374,769	27.60
1875...	815	418,251	1,495,648,437	1,835,131	83,542,008	8,427,981	91,969,989	112,848	194,575,752	13,229,115	120,263,016	330,164,901	405,111	27.85
1876....	806	431,216	1,525,389,219	1,892,542	88,878,139	10,015,027	98,891,166	122,694	198,349,234	14,160,425	121,962,922	334,472,581	414,978	29.57
1877....	929	468,652	1,550,402,483	1,668,894	98,635,583	12,065,410	110,700,993	119,161	200,285,582	17,141,659	124,591,862	351,019,103	377,846	31.54

Comparative view of the results of the co-operative consumé societies from 1864 to 1877.

1. Year.	2. Members of societies known to the administration.	3. Number of societies which have struck balances.	4. Number of members.	5. Amount of sales during year.	6. Balances of members.	7. Reserve funds.	8. Loans taken.	9. Debts for merchandise bought on credit.	10. Debts of members for credit granted. Amount.	10. Debts of members for credit granted. Societies.
			Results of societies mentioned in column 3.							
				Marks.	*Marks.*	*Marks.*	*Marks.*	*Marks.*	*Marks.*	
1864	07	38	7, 709	802, 767	64, 299	14, 736	50, 853	37, 908	17, 250	19
1865	157	31	6, 647	925, 383	66, 678	8, 292	49, 587	56, 844	15, 675	17
1866	199	46	14, 083	2, 479, 794	140, 946	18, 174	153, 186	88, 182	27, 825	14
1867	316	49	18, 884	2, 903, 922	216, 558	33, 480	216, 210	132, 180	32, 691	14
1868	555	75	33, 656	6, 372, 423	468, 732	75, 537	377, 151	204, 816	34, 275	24
1869	627	100	42, 286	7, 126, 251	626, 151	122, 571	346, 020	240, 885	42, 318	30
1870	739	111	45, 761	9, 007, 860	818, 805	151, 224	546, 378	467, 280	60, 231	27
1871	827	143	64, 517	13, 522, 974	1, 589, 571	221, 526	806, 028	628, 074	97, 332	51
1872	902	170	72, 622	15, 659, 547	1, 675, 131	258, 405	1, 259, 343	744, 540	69, 558	57
1873	073	189	87, 504	21, 882, 408	2, 414, 127	353, 064	2, 065, 770	025, 173	70, 275	53
1874	1, 089	178	90, 088	22, 592, 493	2, 695, 221	427, 833	2, 170, 641	804, 021	80, 406	53
1875	1, 034	179	98, 055	22, 704, 963	2, 912, 261	503, 409	2, 429, 585	875, 844	124, 419	56
1876	1, 049	180	101, 727	24, 378, 410	3, 046, 093	556, 398	2, 672, 415	1, 004, 186	142, 722	49
1677	....	202	99, 862	26, 503, 379	3, 109, 532	671, 519	2, 564, 148	899, 163	158, 113	54

Every bank of issue is required to redeem its notes in gold, or its equivalent, on presentation, and to issue new notes for damaged ones. The right of issue can be acquired only by a special law, and the withdrawal and cancellation of notes can take place only with the concurrence of the federal council. Banks of issue, other than the Imperial Bank, cannot offer their notes outside of the State from which they derive their privilege unless they fulfill all the conditions required of the Imperial Bank, in which case they may exchange their notes in Berlin or Frankfort-on-the-Main. Such banks are also forbidden to accept bills of exchange, to buy or sell on time, or to extend their credit to time transactions. They are required to publish a complete statement of their condition four times per month, and an annual report not more than three months from the close of the calendar year. When a bank loses or surrenders its right of issue, the Imperial Bank may increase its circulation an equivalent amount. Issues exceeding the reserves are taxed 5 per cent.

The Imperial Bank has an original capital of 120,000,000 marks, divided into 40,000 shares, issued in the names of the holders. Its general supervision is vested in a curatorium, consisting of the imperial chancellor and four other members, one of whom is named by the Emperor, and the other three by the Bundesrath. The shareholders, who are personally responsible for the obligations of the bank, constitute a general assembly, with a central committee of fifteen members, which meet at least once a month. The special control is exercised by three members chosen for one year by this commission. The empire reserves the right on the 1st of January, 1891, and, on one year's notice, at intervals of ten years thereafter, either to dissolve the bank or to acquire its shares at their nominal value. The bank is authorized to conduct the following transactions: Purchase and sale of gold and silver in bars and coins; discount of bills of exchange running not more than three months, and bearing at least two solvent and well-known signatures; discount of obligations of German States and municipalities running not more than three months from date of the transaction; loans for not longer than three months, on deposit of satisfactory securities; purchase and sale of specified securities to an amount regulated by the general bank directory; collection of accounts on behalf of private individuals, corporations, or the Government; purchase and sale on commission of precious metals and all kinds of securities under fixed regulations; custody and administration of valuable trusts; reception of deposits, with or without interest; the total amount of deposits on interest not to exceed the total capital and reserves.

The bank must cover one-third of its issue by reserves in current German money, gold in bars, or foreign coins of the value of 1,392 marks per pound; the remaining two-thirds must be covered by discounted bills of exchange having not more than three months to run. The bank (and its branches) must redeem its notes in current money of the empire on presentation, and is exempt from all income or license taxes. Net profits are disposed of as follows: An ordinary dividend of 4½ per cent. of the original capital to the shareholders; 20 per cent. to the reserves, so long as they do not equal one-quarter of the original capital; remainder, half to the shareowners and half to the imperial treasury, except when the dividend to shareowners amounts to 8 per cent., in which case the surplus beyond that goes one-quarter to the shareowners and three-quarters to the treasury. If the net profit does not amount to 4½ per cent. of the original capital, the deficiency is taken from the reserves.

The dividends declared by the banks of issue for the year 1877 amounted to about one and a half million marks (16 per cent. less than the previous year). They were, in percentages, as follows:

	1877.	1876.
Five old Prussian banks	4.6	6.5
Four North German banks	4.7	5.5
Three Saxon banks	5.7	7.7
Three South German banks	5.2	4.9
Frankfort banks	6.7	6.7
Bavarian banks	8.0	8.0

The condition of these banks at the close of September, 1878, is stated as follows: Stock capital, in marks, 268,332,000; reserves, 29,929,000; notes in circulation, 858,944,000; circulation not covered by securities, 253,712,000; current deposits, 136,181,000; deposits on call, 52,216,000; sundry liabilities, 8,739,000; coin on hand, 555,673,000; notes of the empire, 33,885,000; notes of other banks, 16,274,000; loans, 90,212,000; securities, 18,859,000; sundry assets, 61,366,000; note reserves, 131,288,000.

The transactions of the Reichsbank for the present year will not be officially made known until some time next spring. The statements for 1877, recently published, show transactions for that year amounting, in marks, to 13,726,266,800 at the main office in Berlin, and at the branches to 33,815,353; making a total of 47,541,619,800 marks. This total exceeds by 10,856,989,200 marks that of the previous year. The average bank rates during the year were 4½ per cent. for exchange and 5½ for loans. The owners of the bank shares were:

December 31, 1876.	Shares.	December 31, 1877.	Shares.
6,803 Germans, owning..........	29,033	6,346 Germans, owning..........	28,959
1,374 foreigners, owning........	10,967	1,425 foreigners, owning........	11,041
	40,000		40,000

The deposits reached their highest amount, 42,367,000, January 15, and their lowest amount, 14,665,000, December 31. The average note circulation during the year was 694,929,000 marks; an excess over the previous year of 10,062,000. On the 31st of December, 1877, the paper circulation comprised the following amounts and denominations:

	Marks.
7,679 ten-thaler notes..	290,370
9,712 twenty-five thaler notes..	728,400
1,803 fifty-thaler-notes...	270,300
2,996 hundred-thaler notes...	898,800
397 five-hundred-thaler notes...	595,500
3,664,772 hundred-mark notes...	366,477,200
237,397 five-hundred-mark notes......................................	118,698,500
227,863 thousand-mark notes..	227,863,000
Total..	715,822,070

The operations of the bank during the year may be stated as follows:

	Marks.
Average amount of coin and bullion held.................................. (or 75.27 per cent. of paper circulation.)	523,104,000
Reserves at close of the year..	14,145,583
Real estate..	15,628,600
Gold coin and bullion...	71,853,097
Deposits..	555,406,414
Domestic bills remitted..	2,944,711,874
Domestic bills collected...	2,714,979,453
Foreign bills bought...	20,204,383
Foreign bills sold..	18,430,126
Total transactions in bills of exchange..................................	3,851,121,579
Total loans..	553,277,880
Loans outstanding at end of the year.....................................	65,420,480
Interest collected on loans..	2,682,191
Transactions in gold bars and foreign gold coins........................	220,047,636
Expenses of bank administration..	5,517,538
Net profits..	10,770,229

Dividend to shareholders 6.29 per cent. against 6¼ per cent. in 1876.

The transactions of the imperial branch bank at Frankfort-on-the-Main during the year are stated as follows:

	Marks.
Loans on securities..	3,213,300
Bills of exchange (total)..	745,778,300
Money transfers with other banks..	14,549,100
Current accounts (Giro-Verkehr)...	3,652,843,300
Deposits..	2,000
Transactions with Imperial and State treasuries........................	97,761,800
Total..	4,514,147,800

During the last twelve months banking has shared in the general depression. Capitalists have been content with moderate rates of interest, and the private rate of discount has generally been much lower than the bank rate. In Breslau transactions have been small, especially in bank and railway shares. In Cologne, where the money transactions of a large mining and manufacturing district are carried on, the depressed state of those industries has restricted business.

In Frankfort-on-the-Main banking has not been more prosperous than last year. No new banks have been established, and none have been suspended or liquidated. The bank rate of discount has ranged from 4 to 5 per cent., and the private rate from 2 to 4½ per cent. The favorite continental investments have been the preferred 3 and 5 per cent. Government railway securities, and the 4, 4½, and 5 per cent. State obligations of Bavaria, Prussia, and Würtemberg. The principal new loans placed in this market during the year were those of the three governments just named. A new Prussian loan, it is expected, will shortly be issued.

The amount of United States securities held here has diminished during the year, considerable quantities having been sent home for redemption or on account of the silver agitation. The prices, however, are from 1 to 3 per cent. higher than last year, and our national bonds continue to stand in the foremost rank of favorite investments.

ALFRED E. LEE.

UNITED STATES CONSULATE-GENERAL,
Frankfort-on-the-Main, November 1, 1878.

PRISON LABOR IN GERMANY.

[Supplementary to the report of Consul Stanton, of Barmen.]

In view of the repeated complaints from all sides of the injurious effect of the labor of criminals on various branches of manufacture, a committee was appointed to inquire what this effect was. I give below the opinions on the subject expressed by the Barmen and Hagen Boards of Trade:

In answering the question, in what manner the employment of criminals, *i. e.*, the assignment of their working power for manufacturing purposes to the highest bidder, affects the labor of freemen injuriously, the fact is not to be lost sight of that the prisoners are not exclusively employed in their acquired trades, but without exception are employed in the manufacture of the article which the prison authorities have contracted for.

In the prisons, for instance, which compete with manufacturers of hardware, there are employed in—

Werden, on locks	104, of which	63 are smiths by trade.
Münster, on locks	67, of which	28 are smiths by trade.
Cologne, on locks	60, of which	11 are smiths by trade.
Benninghausen, on locks	64, of which	28 are smiths by trade.
Ratibor, on locks	135, of which	16 are smiths by trade.
Cologne, on chains	58, of which	8 are smiths by trade.
Düsseldorf, on chains	32, of which	6 are smiths by trade.
In all	520, of which	160 are smiths by trade.

According to this, but about 30 per cent. of the prisoners have been employed in a trade they had previously acquired, and since in the different prisons a few specialties in locks only are made, most unfavorable results for this branch ensue.

Now, as no branch of manufacture can flourish without due regard for the laws of supply and demand, it follows that every arbitrary increase of production must be prejudicial to the interests of free labor, and the injurious effects of an arbitrary increase of the workmen in a branch of manufacture by 360 criminals can hardly be estimated. The production of locks in Cologne, Werden, and Münster is so great as to make this article virtually a monopoly of those prisons.

For a certain amount of daily labor, which is clearly determined, contractors pay in the undermentioned prisons the following rates of wages:

In Benninghausen, 50 pfennige, or about 12 cents.
In Cologne, 60 pfennige, or about 14 cents.
In Werden, 70 pfennige, or about 16½ cents.
In Münster, 80 pfennige, or about 19 cents.
In Düsseldorf, 60 to 70 pfennige, or about 14 to 16½ cents.
In Ratibor, 80 pfennige, or about 19 cents.

Besides these advantages, the contractors have the free use of all apprentices until the prisoners have thoroughly mastered the work to be done, or on the average from six to twelve months.

It is difficult to draw an accurate comparison between the labor of freemen and criminals, but taking a day's wages as a standard, and assuming that a criminal produces half as much as a freeman, although this is a low estimate, since the use of machinery places skilled and unskilled labor nearly on a par, the daily wages of a criminal amount to but 80 or 100 pfennige, or not 50 per cent. of the amount which must be paid to free labor, and the contractor has moreover the free use of shops, heat, light, and in some prisons of steam in consideration of a small remuneration for coal; while if against this the cost of free labor, together with that of factories, repairs, interest, &c., be placed, it becomes perfectly plain that contractors for prison labor are secure from all competition.

A proof of this is afforded in the official reports of the Ratibor prison, where, according to which reports, the contractors, having but a few years ago introduced the manufacture of hardware, have conquered the markets of Silesia, Prussia, Pomerania, and

Saxony. They underbid every competitor, and where free labor enters the lists against them it inevitably succumbs, for prison contractors are in a position to sell much cheaper than they do. If it be opposed that the products of free labor are of much superior quality, this advantage is more than balanced by the cheap prices of prison wares.

Whilst ordinarily the competition of criminals is bad enough, in times of depression and business stagnation the effect is simply ruinous, for the terms of the contract forbidding any limitation of the production, contractors, in order to realize, are compelled to throw their goods at any price on the already overstocked markets, which in the district of Hagen has resulted in the utter ruin of many branches of hardware.

Again, whilst the prison wares are sufficiently well known at home, and consequently less fatal to the reputation of the products of free labor, they have a very different effect in foreign markets. Abroad they are known as German wares, and undermine the good name of that country's products. The best example of this is the article of chains, which was formerly an important article of export to all transatlantic lands, and which now, in consequence of the competition of the Cologne prison, are scouted in all foreign markets.

The prescriptive quality of a chain is strength, which depends not only on the excellence of the material, but also on the proper welding of each link, *i. e.*, the perfect union of the ends of the links. The manipulation is an excessively difficult one, requiring long practice, since it is dependent not only on great mechanical dexterity, but also on the knowledge of the degree of heat and the seizure of the proper moment. Externally it is generally impossible to determine whether a welding has succeeded or not; wherefore, a badly-welded chain is not to be distinguished with certainty from a well-made one, which fact renders this article one of confidence entirely.

If it be considered that of the 58 criminals employed on chains in Cologne but 8 had formerly learned the trade, it is not to be wondered at that the article produced by no means satisfies the demands as to strength which are made on it, or that the above-mentioned result should ensue. Externally the prison-made chains are not to be distinguished from the products of free labor, and both receive the same condemnation. English chains, on the contrary, being less polished, are easily recognizable, and although in this respect the German wares have the advantage, the English article, on account of the bad experience had in Cologne chains, are invariably preferred in foreign markets.

The necessity for employing criminals is duly admitted, but the system at present in vogue is injurious to the trading community. It is thought it would be better were the prisoners employed in the manufacture of articles for their own needs, or that such work only should be done in prisons as could not conflict with mercantile enterprise, such as what is needed for the prisons, province, or community, or in the partial manufacture of articles which, before entering into consumption, should be finished by free labor. It is also suggested that the criminals be employed on public works, such as highways, canals, fortifications, &c.

It is also believed that a systematic grouping of the prisons, after the performance of certain work, and the assignment of the criminal to the prison his trade most fits him for, would soon enable the prisons to manufacture every article needed by them.

EDGAR STANTON.

UNITED STATES CONSULATE, *September* 20, 1878.

GREAT BRITAIN.—ENGLAND.

FACTORY ACT.

The following is the English factory act referred to by Consul Shepard in his report (see page 197) on labor and wages in Bradford and vicinity:

A. D. 1877.

A BILL to consolidate and amend the law relating to factories and workshops.

Be it enacted by the Queen's most Excellent Majesty, by and with the advice and consent of the Lords Spiritual and Temporal, and Commons, in this present Parliament assembled, and by the authority of the same, as follows:

Preliminary.

1. This act may be cited as the factory and workshop act, 1877.

2. This act shall come into operation on *the first day of January, one thousand eight hundred and seventy-eight*, which day is in this act referred to as the commencement of this act: Provided that at any time after the passing of this act, any appointment, regulation, or order may be made, any notice issued, form prescribed, and act done which appears to a secretary of state necessary or proper for the due execution of this act at the commencement thereof.

Part I.

GENERAL LAW RELATING TO FACTORIES AND WORKSHOPS.

(1.) *Sanitary provisions.*

3. Every factory and every workshop shall be kept in a cleanly state and free from effluvia arising from any drain, privy, or other nuisance.

A factory or workshop shall not be so overcrowded while work is carried on therein as to be injurious to the health of those employed therein, and shall be ventilated in such a manner as to render harmless, so far as is practicable, all gases, vapors, dust, or other impurities generated in the course of the manufacturing process or handicraft carried on therein that may be injurious to health.

A factory or workshop in which there is a contravention of this section shall be deemed not to be kept in conformity with this act.

4. Where it appears to an inspector under this act that any act, neglect, or default in relation to any drain, watercloset, earthcloset, privy, ashpit, water-supply, nuisance, or other matter in any factory or workshop is punishable or remediable under the law relating to public health, but not under this act, that inspector shall give notice in writing of such act, neglect, or default to the sanitary authority in whose district the factory or workshop is situate, and it shall be the duty of the sanitary authority to make such inquiry into the subject of the notice, and take such action thereon, as to that authority may seem proper for the purpose of enforcing the law.

An inspector under this act may, for the purposes of this section, take with him into a factory or a workshop a medical officer of health, inspector of nuisances, or other officer of the sanitary authority.

(2.) *Safety.*

5. With respect to the fencing of machinery in a factory the following provisions shall have effect:

(1.) Every hoist or teagle near to which children or young persons are liable to pass or to be employed, and every fly-wheel directly connected with the steam or water or other mechanical power, whether in the engine-house or not, and every part of a steam-engine and water-wheel, shall be securely fenced; and

(2.) Every wheel-race not otherwise secured shall be securely fenced close to the edge of the wheel-race; and

(3.) Every part of the mill-gearing shall either be securely fenced or be in such position or of such construction as to be equally safe to every person employed in the factory as it would be if it were securely fenced; and

(4.) All fencing shall be constantly maintained in an efficient state while the parts required to be fenced are in motion by the action of steam, water, or other mechanical power for any manufacturing process.

A factory in which there is a contravention of this section shall be deemed not to be kept in conformity with this act.

6. Where an inspector considers that in a factory any part of the machinery of any kind, moved by steam, water, or other mechanical power to which the foregoing provisions of this act with respect to the fencing of machinery do not apply, is not securely fenced, and is so dangerous as to be likely to cause bodily injury to any person employed in the factory, he shall serve on the occupier of the factory a notice requiring him to fence the part of the machinery which he so deems to be dangerous.

The occupier, within *fourteen days* after the receipt of the notice, may serve on the inspector a requisition requiring the matter to be referred to arbitration, and thereupon the matter shall be referred to arbitration, and two skilled arbitrators shall be appointed, the one by the inspector and the other by the occupier, and the provisions of the companies clauses consolidation act, 1845, with respect to the settlement of disputes by arbitration, shall, subject to the express provisions of this section, apply to the said arbitration.

If the arbitrators or their umpire decide that it is unnecessary or impossible to fence the machinery alleged in the notice to be dangerous, the notice shall be canceled, and the occupier shall not be required to fence in pursuance thereof, and the expenses of the arbitration shall be paid as the expenses of the inspectors under this act.

If the occupier does not appoint an arbitrator within *fourteen days* after he served on the inspector the requisition requiring the matter to be referred to arbitration, or if neither the arbitrators nor the umpire decide that it is unnecessary or impossible to fence the machinery alleged in the notice to be dangerous, the occupier shall securely fence the said machinery as required by the notice, or by the award of the arbitrators or umpire if it modifies the notice, and the expenses of the arbitration shall be paid by the occupier of the factory, and shall be recoverable from him by the inspector in the county court.

Where the occupier of a factory fails to comply within a reasonable time with a notice or award under this section, or fails to keep the machinery mentioned in such notice or award securely fenced as thereby required, the factory shall be deemed not to be kept in conformity with this act.

For the purpose of this section and of any provisions of this act relating thereto, "machinery" shall be deemed to include any driving band or strap.

7. Where an inspector observes in a factory that any grindstone, worked by steam, water, or other mechanical power, is in itself so faulty or is fixed in so faulty a manner as to be likely to cause bodily injury to the grinder using the same, such inspector shall serve on the occupier of the factory a notice requiring him to replace such faulty grindstone, or to properly fix the grindstone fixed in the faulty manner, and the provisions of this act with respect to the notice requiring dangerous machinery to be fenced and arbitration thereon shall apply in like manner as if they were re-enacted in this section with the necessary modifications.

Where the occupier of a factory fails to comply within a reasonable time with a notice or award under this section, or fails to keep the grindstone mentioned in such notice or award in such a state and fixed in such manner as not to be dangerous, the factory shall be deemed not to be kept in conformity with this act.

8. A child shall not be allowed to clean any part of the machinery in a factory while the same is in motion.

A child, young person, or woman shall not be allowed—

(1.) to clean any part of the mill-gearing in a factory while the same is in motion for the purpose of propelling any part of the manufacturing machinery; nor

(2.) to work between the fixed and traversing part of any self-acting machine while the machine is in motion by the action of steam, water, or other mechanical power.

A child, young person, or woman allowed to clean or to work in contravention of this section shall be deemed to be employed contrary to the provisions of this act.

(3.) *Employment and meal hours.*

9. A child, young person, or woman shall not be employed in a factory or a workshop, except during the period of employment fixed by the occupier in pursuance of this act and specified in the notice affixed in the factory or workshop.

10. With respect to the employment of young persons and women in a textile factory the following regulations shall be observed:

(1.) The period of employment, except on Saturday, shall be a period of *twelve* consecutive hours, inclusive of meal hours, and either shall begin at *six o'clock* in the morning and end at *six o'clock* in the evening, or shall begin at *seven o'clock* in the morning and end at *seven o'clock* in the evening; and

(2.) The period of employment on Saturday shall begin either at *six o'clock* or at *seven o'clock* in the morning; and

(3.) Where the period of employment on Saturday begins at six o'clock in the morning, such period—

(*a.*) If not less than *one hour* is allowed for meals, shall end at *one o'clock* in the afternoon as regards employment in any manufacturing process, and at *half past one o'clock* in the afternoon as regards employment for any purpose whatever; and

(*b.*) If less than *one hour* is allowed for meals, shall end at at *half an hour after noon* as regards employment in any manufacturing process, and at *one o'clock* in the afternoon as regards employment for any purpose whatever; and

(4.) Where the period of employment on Saturday begins at *seven o'clock* in the morning, such period shall end at *half past one o'clock* in the afternoon as regards any manufacturing process, and at *two o'clock* in the afternoon as regards employment for any purpose whatever; and

(5.) There shall be allowed for meals during the period of employment for young persons and women in the factory—

(*a.*) on every day, except Saturday, not less than *two hours*, of which *one hour* at the least, either at the same time or at different times, shall be before *three o'clock* in the afternoon; and

(*b.*) on Saturday, not less than *half an hour;* and

(6.) A young person or woman shall not be employed continuously for more than *four hours and a half*, without an interval of at least *half an hour* for a meal.

11. With respect to the employment of children in a textile factory, the following regulations shall be observed:

(1.) Children shall not be employed except on the system either of employment in morning and afternoon sets, or of employment on alternate days only;

(2.) The period of employment for a child in a morning set shall, except on Saturday, begin at the same hour as if the child were a young person, and end at *one o'clock* in the afternoon, or, if the dinner time begins before *one o'clock*, at the beginning of dinner time; and

(3.) The period of employment for a child in an afternoon set shall, except on Saturday, begin at *one o'clock* in the afternoon, or any later hour at which the dinner time terminates, and end at the same hour as if the child were a young person; and

(4.) The period of employment for a child in a morning or afternoon set on Saturday shall begin and end at the same hour as if the child were a young person; and

(5.) A child, whether employed in a morning or afternoon set, shall not be employed on Saturday in *two successive weeks*, nor on Saturday in any week, if on any other day in the same week he has been employed for more than *five hours*; and

(6.) When a child is employed on the alternate day system, the period of employment for such child and the time allowed for meals shall be the same as if the child were a young person, but the child shall not be employed on *two successive days*, and shall not be employed on the same day of the week in *two successive weeks*; and

(7.) A child shall not be employed continuously for any longer period than he could be if he were a young person without an interval of at least *half an hour* for a meal.

12. With respect to the employment of young persons and women in a non-textile factory, and of young persons in a workshop, the following regulations shall be observed:

(1.) The period of employment, except on Saturday, shall (save as is in this act specially excepted) be a period of *twelve consecutive hours*, inclusive of meal hours, and either shall begin at *six o'clock* in the morning and end at *six o'clock* in the evening, or shall begin at *seven o'clock* in the morning and end at *seven o'clock* in the evening; and

(2.) The period of employment on Saturday shall (save as is in this act specially excepted) begin at *six o'clock* in the morning or at *seven o'clock* in the morning, and end at *two o'clock* in the afternoon; and

(3.) There shall be allowed for meals during the period of employment in the factory or workshop—

(*a.*) on every day except Saturday not less than *one hour and a half*, of which *one hour* at the least, either at the same time or at different times, shall be before *three o'clock* in the afternoon; and

(*b.*) on Saturday not less than *half an hour;* and

(4.) A young person or a woman in a non-textile factory and a young person in a workshop shall not be employed continuously for more than *five hours* without an interval of at least *half an hour* for a meal.

13. With respect to the employment of children in a non-textile factory and a workshop, the following regulations shall be observed:

(1.) Children shall not be employed except either on the system of employment in morning and afternoon sets, or, in a factory or workshop in which the actual hours of work of young persons and women, exclusive of meal hours, are restricted to *ten hours* a day, on the system of employment on alternate days only; and

(2.) The period of employment for a child in a morning set on every day, including Saturday, shall begin at the same hour as if the child were a young person, and end at *one o'clock* in the afternoon, or, if the dinner time begins before *one o'clock*, at the beginning of dinner time; and

(3.) The period of employment for a child in an afternoon set on every day, including Saturday, shall begin at *one o'clock* in the afternoon, or at any later hour at which the dinner time terminates, and end at the same hour as if the child were a young person; and

(4.) A child shall not be employed in *two successive weeks* in a morning set, or in *two successive weeks* in an afternoon set; and

(5.) When a child is employed on the alternate-day system the period of employment for such child and the time allowed for meals shall be the same as if the child were a young person, but the child shall not be employed in any manner on *two successive days*, and shall not be employed on the same day of the week in *two successive weeks;* and

(6.) A child shall not be employed continuously for any longer period than he could be if he were a young person without an interval of at least *half an hour* for a meal.

14. In a workshop in which a young person or a child is employed a woman shall not be employed except during the same period and subject to the same restrictions as if she were a young person; and the regulations of this act with respect to the employment of young persons in a workshop shall apply accordingly to the employment of women in that workshop.

In a workshop in which no young person or child is employed—

(1.) The period of employment for a woman shall, except on Saturday, be a period not exceeding *twelve hours*, inclusive of meal hours, between *six o'clock* in the morning and *nine o'clock* in the evening, and shall on Saturday be the period between *six o'clock* in the morning and *two o'clock* in the afternoon; and

(2.) There shall be allowed to a woman for meals during the period of employment on any day except Saturday not less than *one hour and a half*, and on Saturday *half an hour*.

15. In a workshop which is a dwelling-house and in which the family only of the occupier living in that dwelling-house are employed, the foregoing regulations of this act with respect to the employment of women young persons and children shall not apply, and in lieu thereof the following regulations shall be observed:

(1.) A child, young person, or woman shall not be employed in the workshop except during the period of employment fixed by the occupier in accordance with this section;

(2.) The period of employment for young persons and women shall, except on Saturday, be a period not exceeding *twelve hours*, inclusive of meal hours, between *six o'clock* in the morning and *nine o'clock* in the evening, and shall on Saturday be the period between *six o'clock* in the morning and *two o'clock* in the afternoon; and

(3.) There shall be allowed to every woman and young person for meals during the period of employment on any day except Saturday not less than *one hour and a half*, and on Saturday *half an hour*; and

(4.) The period of employment for a child shall be a period not exceeding *six hours and a half* between *six o'clock* in the morning and *one o'clock* in the afternoon, or between *noon* and the hour of *eight* in the evening, or (on Saturday) of two in the afternoon, and for the purpose of the provisions of this act respecting education, such child, shall be deemed, according to circumstances, to be employed in a morning or afternoon set; and

(5.) A child shall not be employed continuously for more than *five hours* without an interval of at least *half an hour* for a meal.

16. With respect to meals the following regulations shall (save as is in this act specially excepted) be observed in every factory and workshop:

(1.) All children young persons and women employed therein shall have the time allowed for meals at the same time in the day; and

(2.) A child young person or woman shall not during any part of the time allowed for meals in the factory or workshop, be employed in the factory or the workshop, or be allowed to remain in a room in which a manufacturing process or handicraft is being carried on.

17. The occupier of a factory or workshop may from time to time fix within the limits allowed by this act, and shall (save as is in this act specially excepted) specify in a notice affixed in the factory or workshop, the period of employment, the times allowed for meals, and whether the children are employed on the system of morning and afternoon sets, or of alternate days.

The period of employment and the times allowed for meals in the factory or workshop shall be deemed to be the period and times specified in the notice affixed in the factory or workshop, and all the children in the factory or workshop shall be employed either on the system of morning and afternoon sets or on the system of alternate days according to the system for the time being specified in such notice;

Provided that a change in the period of employment and in the times allowed for meals, or in the system of employment of the children shall not be made, until after the occupier has served on an inspector and affixed in the factory or workshop notice of his intention to make such change, and shall not be made oftener than *once a quarter*, unless for special cause allowed in writing by an inspector.

18. A child under the age of *ten years* shall not be employed in a factory or a workshop.

19. A child young person or woman shall not (save as is in this act specially excepted) be employed on Sunday in a factory or workshop.

(4.) *Holidays.*

20. The occupier of every factory and workshop shall allow to every child young person and woman employed therein the following holidays; that is to say,

(1.) The whole of Christmas Day, and either the whole of Good Friday, or, if it is so specified by the occupier in the notice affixed in the factory or workshop, of the next public holiday under the holidays extension act, 1875; and in addition

(2.) *Eight* half holidays in every year, but a whole holiday may be allowed in lieu of any *two* such half holidays; and
(3.) At least half of the said half holidays or whole holidays shall be allowed between the *fifteenth day of March* and the *first day of October* in every year; and
(4.) Cessation from work shall not be deemed to be a half holiday or whole holiday, unless a notice of the half holiday or holiday has been affixed in the factory or workshop for at least the whole period of employment on the last previous work day; and
(5.) A half holiday shall comprise at least *one half* of the period of employment for young persons and women some day other than Saturday.

A child, young person, or woman who—
(1.) on a whole holiday fixed by or in pursuance of this section for a factory or workshop, is employed in the factory or workshop; or
(2.) on a half holiday fixed in pursuance of this section for a factory or workshop, is employed in the factory or workshop during the portion of the period of employment assigned for such half holiday

shall be deemed to be employed contrary to the provisions of this act.

(5.) *Education of children.*

21. The parent of a child employed in a factory or in a workshop shall cause that child to attend some certified efficient school (which school may be selected by such parent) as follows:
(1.) The child, when employed in a morning or afternoon set, shall on each work day of every week, during any part of which he is so employed, be caused to attend for at least one attendance (as defined for the time being by a secretary of state with the consent of the education department), between the hours of *eight* in the morning and *six* in the evening; and
(2.) The child, when employed on the alternate day system, shall be caused to attend school for at least *two* attendances (as defined for the time being by a secretary of state with the consent of the education department), between the hours of *eight* in the morning and *six* in the evening on each work day preceding each day of employment in the factory or workshop:

Provided that—
(1.) A child shall not be required by this act to attend school on Saturday or on any holiday or half holiday allowed by or in pursuance of this act in the factory or workshop in which the child is employed; and
(2.) The non-attendance of the child shall be excused on every day on which he is certified by the teacher of the school to have been prevented from attending by sickness or other unavoidable cause, also when the school is closed during the ordinary holidays or for any other temporary cause; and
(3.) Where there is not within the distance of *two miles*, measured according to the nearest road, from the factory or workshop in which the child is employed or from the residence of the child a certified efficient school which the child can attend, attendance at a school temporarily approved in writing by an inspector under this act, although not a certified efficient school, shall for the purposes of this act be deemed attendance at a certified efficient school until such certified efficient school as aforesaid is established, and with a view to such establishment the inspector shall immediately report to the education department every case of the approval of a school by him under this section.

A child who has not in any week attended school for all the attendances required by this section shall not be employed in the following week, until he has attended school for the deficient number of attendances.

The education department shall from time to time by the publication of lists or by notices, or otherwise as they think expedient, provide for giving to all persons interested information of the schools in each school district which are certified efficient schools.

22. The occupier of every factory or worshop in which a child is employed shall on *Monday* in every week after the first week in which such child began to work therein, or on some other day appointed for that purpose by an inspector, obtain from the teacher of the certified efficient school attended by the child, a certificate (according to the prescribed form and directions) respecting the attendance of such child at school in accordance with this act.

The employment of a child without obtaining such certificate as is required by this section shall be deemed to be employment of a child contrary to the provisions of this act.

The occupier shall keep every such certificate for *two months* after the date thereof if the child so long continues to be employed in his factory or his workshop, and shall produce the same to an inspector when required during that period.

23. The principal teacher of a certified efficient school attended by a child employed in a factory or workshop may apply in writing to the occupier of the factory or workshop to pay a weekly sum specified in the application not exceeding *twopence a week*, and not exceeding *one-twelfth* part of the wages of the child, and after that application the occupier, so long as he employs the child, shall be liable to pay to the applicant while the child attends his school the weekly sum specified in the application, and the sum may be recovered as a debt, and the occupier may deduct the sum so paid by him from the wages payable for the services of the child.

24. When a child of the age of *thirteen years* has obtained from a person authorized by the education department a certificate of having attained such standard of proficiency in reading, writing, and arithmetic, or of previous due attendance at a certified efficient school, as hereinafter mentioned, that child shall be deemed to be a young person for the purposes of this act.

The standards for the purposes of this section shall be such as may be from time to time fixed for the purposes of this act by a secretary of state, with the consent of the education department, and the standards so fixed shall be published in the London Gazette, and shall not have effect until the expiration of at least *six months* after such publication.

Attendance at a certified day industrial school shall be deemed for the purposes of this section to be attendance at a certified efficient school.

(6.) *Certificates of fitness for employment.*

25. In a factory a child or young person under the age of *sixteen years* shall not be employed for more than *seven*, or if the certifying surgeon for the district resides more than *three miles* from the factory *thirteen*, working days, unless the occupier thereof has obtained a certificate, in the prescribed form, of the fitness of such child or young person for employment in that factory.

A certificate of fitness for employment for the purposes of this act shall be granted by the certifying surgeon for the district, and shall be to the effect that he is satisfied, by the production of a certificate of birth or otherwise, that such child or young person is of the age named in the certificate of fitness, and that such child or young person has been personally examined by him and is not incapacitated by disease or bodily infirmity for working daily for the time allowed by law in the factory named in the certificate.

26. In order to enable occupiers of workshops to better secure the observance of this act, and prevent the employment in their workshops of children and young persons under the age of *sixteen years* who are unfitted for that employment, an occupier of a workshop is hereby authorized to obtain, if he thinks fit, from the certifying surgeon for the district, a certificate of the fitness of children and young persons under the age of *sixteen years* for employment in his workshop, in like manner as if that workshop were a factory, and the certifying surgeon shall examine the children and young persons, and grant certificates accordingly.

27. Where an inspector is of opinion that any child or young person under the age of *sixteen years* is by disease or bodily infirmity incapacitated from working daily for the time allowed by law in the factory or workshop in which he is employed, he may serve written notice thereof on the occupier of the factory or workshop, and the occupier shall not continue for more than *seven days* after the service of such notice to employ such child or young person (notwithstanding a certificate of fitness has been previously obtained for such child or young person), unless the certifying surgeon for the district has, after the service of the notice, personally examined such child or young person and has certified that such child or young person is not so incapacitated as aforesaid.

28. All factories and workshops in the occupation of the same occupier, and in the district of the same certifying surgeon, or any of them, may be named in the certificate of fitness for employment, if the surgeon is of opinion that he can truly give the certificate for employment therein.

The certificate of birth (which may be produced to a certifying surgeon) shall either be a certified copy of the entry in the register of births, kept in pursuance of the acts relating to the registration of births, of the birth of the child or young person (whether such copy be obtained in pursuance of the elementary education act 1876 or otherwise), or be a certificate from a local authority within the meaning of the elementary education act 1876, to the effect that it appears from the returns transmitted to such authority in pursuance of the said act by the registrar of births and deaths that the child was born at the date named in the certificate.

Where a certificate of fitness for employment is to the effect that the certifying surgeon has been satisfied of the age of a child or young person, otherwise than by the production of a certificate of birth, an inspector may, by notice in writing, annul the surgeon's certificate if he has reasonable cause to believe that the real age of the child or young person named in it is less than that mentioned in the certificate, and thereupon that certificate shall be of no avail for the purposes of this act.

When a child becomes a young person a fresh certificate of fitness must be obtained.

The occupier shall, when required, produce to an inspector at the factory or workshop in which a child or young person is employed the certificate of fitness of such child or young person for employment which he is required to obtain under this act.

(7.) *Accidents.*

29. Where there occurs in a factory or a workshop any accident which either—

(*a.*) Causes loss of life to a person employed in the factory or in the workship, or

(*b.*) Causes bodily injury to a person employed in the factory or the workshop, and is produced either by machinery moved by steam water or other mechanical power, or by explosion or escape of gas, steam or metal, and is of such a nature as to prevent the person injured by it from returning to his work in the factory or workshop within *forty-eight hours* after the occurrence of the accident,

written notice of the accident shall forthwith be sent to the certifying surgeon for the district, stating the residence of the person injured, or the place to which he may have been removed, and if such notice is not sent the occupier of the factory or workshop shall be liable to a fine not exceeding *five pounds.*

If any such accident as aforesaid occurs to a person employed in an iron mill or blast furnace, the actual employer of the person killed or injured shall immediately report the same to the occupier, and in default shall be liable to a fine not exceeding *five pounds.*

A notice of an accident of which notice is required by section sixty-three of the explosives act, 1875, to be sent to a government inspector, need not be sent to the certifying surgeon in pursuance of this section.

30. Where a certifying surgeon receives in pursuance of this act notice of an accident in a factory or a workshop, he shall send a copy of such notice to an inspector by the first post after the receipt thereof, and shall with the least possible delay proceed to the factory or workshop, and make a full investigation as to the nature and cause of the death or injury caused by that accident, and shall within the next *twenty-four hours* send to the inspector a report thereof.

The certifying surgeon, for the purpose only of an investigation under this section, shall have the same powers as an inspector, and shall also have power to enter any room in a building to which the person killed or injured has been removed.

There shall be paid to the said surgeon for the investigation such fee, not exceeding *ten* nor less than *three shillings*, as a Secretary of State considers reasonable, which fee shall be paid as expenses incurred in the execution of this act.

PART II.

SPECIAL PROVISIONS RELATING TO PARTICULAR CLASSES OF FACTORIES AND WORKSHOPS.

(1.) *Special provisions for health in certain factories and workshops.*

31. For the purpose of securing the observance of the requirements of this act as to cleanliness in every factory and workshop, all the inside walls of the rooms of such factory or workshop, and all the ceilings or tops of such rooms, whether such walls, ceilings, or tops be plastered or not, and all the passages and staircases of every such factory or workshop, if they have not been painted with oil once at least within *seven years*, shall be limewashed once at least within every successive period of *fourteen months*, to date from the period when last limewashed; and if they have been so painted, shall be washed with hot water and soap once at least within every successive period of *fourteen months*, to date from the period when last washed.

A factory or workshop in which there is a contravention of this section shall be deemed not to be kept in conformity with this act.

Where it appears to a secretary of state that in any class of factories or workshops, or parts thereof, the regulations in this section are not required for the purpose of securing therein the observance of the requirements of this act as to cleanliness, or are by reason of special circumstances inapplicable, he may if he thinks fit, by order made under this part of this act, grant to such class of factories or workshops, or parts thereof, a special exception that the regulations in this section shall not apply thereto.

32. Where a bakehouse is situate in any city, town, or place containing, according to the last published census for the time being, a population of more than *five thousand persons*, all the inside walls of the rooms of such bakehouse, and all the ceilings or tops of such rooms, whether such walls, ceilings, or tops be plastered or not, and all the passages and staircases of such bakehouse, shall either be painted with oil or be limewashed, or partly painted and partly limewashed; where painted with oil there shall be three coats of paint, and the painting shall be renewed once at least in every *seven years*, and shall be washed with hot water and soap once at least in every *six months;* where limewashed, the limewashing shall be renewed once at least in every *six months.*

A bakehouse in which there is any contravention of this section shall be deemed not to be kept in conformity with this act.

33. Where a bakehouse is situate in any city, town, or place containing, according to the last published census for the time being, a population of more than *five thousand persons*, a place on the same level with the bakehouse, and forming part of the same building, shall not be used as a sleeping place, unless it is constructed as follows; that is to say,

Unless it is effectually separated from the bakehouse by a partition extending from the floor to the ceiling; and

Unless there be an external glazed window of at least *nine superficial feet in area*, of which at least *four and a half superficial feet* are made to open for ventilation.

Any person who lets or occupies, or continues to let or knowingly suffers to be occupied, any place contrary to this section, shall be liable to a fine not exceeding, for the first offense, *twenty shillings*, and for every subsequent offense *five pounds.*

34. If in a factory or workshop where grinding, glazing, or polishing on a wheel, or any process is carried on by which dust is generated and inhaled by the workers to an injurious extent, it appears to an inspector under this act that such inhalation could be to a great extent prevented by the use of a fan or other mechanical means, the inspector may direct a fan or other mechanical means of a proper construction for preventing such inhalation, to be provided within a reasonable time; and if the same is not provided, maintained, and used, the factory or workshop shall be deemed not to be kept in conformity with this act.

35. A child, young person or woman shall not be employed in any part of a factory in which the wet-spinning of flax, hemp, jute, or tow is carried on, unless sufficient means be employed and continued for protecting the workers from being wetted, and, where hot water is used, for preventing the escape of steam into the room occupied by the workers.

A factory in which there is a contravention of this section shall be deemed not to be kept in conformity with this act.

(2.) *Special restrictions as to employment, meals, and certificates of fitness.*

36. A child or young person shall not, to the extent mentioned in the first schedule of this act, be employed in the factories or workshops or parts thereof named in that schedule.

Notice of the prohibition in this section shall be affixed in a factory or workshop to which it applies.

37. A child, young person, or woman shall not be allowed to take a meal or to remain during the time allowed for meals in the parts of factories or workshops to which this section applies; and a child, young person, or woman allowed to take a meal or to remain in contravention of this section shall be deemed to be employed contrary to the provisions of this act.

Notice of the prohibition in this section shall be affixed in a factory or workshop to which it applies.

This section applies to the parts of factories or workshops named in part one of the second schedule of this act.

Where it appears to a secretary of state that by reason of the nature of the process in any class of factories or workshops or parts thereof not named in the said part of the said schedule, the taking of meals therein is specially injurious to health, he may, if he thinks fit, by order made under this part of this act extend the prohibition in this section to the said class of factories or workshops or parts thereof.

If the prohibition in this section is proved to the satisfaction of a secretary of state to be no longer necessary for the protection of the health of children, young persons, and women in any class of factories or workshops or parts thereof to which the prohibition has been extended by an order, he may, by an order made under this part of this act, rescind the order of extension, without prejudice nevertheless to the making of another order at a future period.

38. In print works and bleaching and dyeing works, the period of employment for a child, young person, and woman and the time allowed for meals shall be the same as if the said works were a textile factory, and the regulations of this act with respect to the employment of children, young persons, and women in a textile factory shall apply accordingly as if print works and bleaching dyeing works were textile factories; save that nothing in this section shall prevent the continuous employment in the said works, without an interval of *half an hour* for a meal, of a child, young person, or woman for the period allowed by this act in a non-textile factory.

39. In a workshop to which this section applies, a child or young person under the age of *sixteen years* shall not be employed for more than *seven*, or, if the certifying surgeon for the district resides more than *three miles* from the workshop, *thirteen working days*, unless the occupier thereof has obtained a certificate in the prescribed form of fitness of such child or young person for employment in that workshop, and the provisions of this act with respect to certificates of fitness for employment shall apply in like manner as if that workshop were a factory.

This section applies to the workshops specified in part two of the second schedule to this act.

Where it appears to a secretary of state that by reason of special circumstances affecting any class of workshops not named in the said part of the said schedule, it is expedient, for protecting the health of the children and young persons under the age of *sixteen years* employed therein, to extend this section to such class of workshops, he may, if he thinks fit, by order made under this part of this act, extend this section accordingly.

If the prohibition in this section is proved to the satisfaction of the secretary of state to be no longer necessary for the protection of the health of children and young persons under the age of sixteen years employed in any class of workshops to which this section has been extended by an order, he may, by order made under this part of this act, rescind the order of extension, without prejudice nevertheless to the making of another order at a future period.

(3.) *Special exceptions relaxing general law in certain factories and workshops.*

(a.) *Period of employment.*

40. In the factories and workshops or parts thereof to which this exception applies the period of employment for young persons and women, if so fixed by the occupier and specified in the notice, may, except on Saturday, begin at *eight o'clock* in the morning and end at *eight o'clock* in the evening, and may on Saturday begin at *eight o'clock* in the morning and end at *four o'clock* in the evening; and the beginning of the period of employment for a child in a morning set and the end of the period of employment for a child in an afternoon set may be altered accordingly.

This exception applies to the factories and workshops and parts thereof specified in part one of the third schedule of this act.

Where it is proved to the satisfaction of a secretary of state that the customs or exigencies of the trade carried in any class of factories or workshops or parts thereof, either generally or when situate in any particular locality, require the extension thereto of this exception, and that the extension can be made without injury to the health of the children young persons and women affected thereby, he may by order made under this part of this act extend this exception accordingly.

41. Where it is proved to the satisfaction of a secretary of state that the customs or exigencies of the trade carried on in any class of factories or workshops or parts thereof, either generally or when situate in any particular locality, require that the special exception hereafter in this section mentioned should be granted, and that such grant can be made without injury to the health of the young persons and women affected thereby, he may by order made under this part of this act grant to such class of factories or workshops or parts thereof, a special exception that the period of employment for young persons and women therein, if so fixed by the occupier and specified in the notice, may on any day, except Saturday, begin at *nine o'clock* in the morning and end at *nine o'clock* in the evening, but in such case the period of employment for a child shall end at *eight o'clock* in the evening or some earlier hour.

42. The regulations of this act with respect to the employment of young persons in textile factories shall not prevent the employment in the part of a textile factory in which a machine for the manufacture of lace is moved by steam, water, or other mechanical power, of any male young person above the age of sixteen years between *four o'clock* in the morning and *ten o'clock* in the evening, if he is employed in accordance with the following conditions, namely:

(*a.*) Where such young person is employed on any day before the beginning or after the end of the period of employment for young persons under *sixteen years* of age or women in the factory, his hours of actual work on that day shall not exceed *nine hours*; and

(*b.*) Where such young person is employed on any day before the beginning of the period of employment for young persons under *sixteen years* of age or women in the factory, he shall not be employed on the same day after the end of that period; and

(*c.*) Where such young person is employed on any day after the end of the period of employment for young persons of *sixteen years* of age or women in the factory, he shall not be employed next morning before the beginning of such period of employment.

If young persons under the age of *sixteen years* or women are not employed in the factory, the period of employment for the purpose of this exception shall mean such period as can, under this act, be fixed for the employment of such young persons and women in the factory, and notice of such period shall be affixed in the factory.

43. The regulations of this act with respect to the employment of young persons in non-textile factories or workshops shall not prevent the employment in the part of a bakehouse in which the process of baking bread is carried on of any male young person above the age of *sixteen years* between *five o'clock* in the morning and *nine o'clock* in the evening, if he is employed in accordance with the following conditions, namely:

(*a.*) Where such young person is employed on any day before the beginning or after the end of the period of employment for young persons under *sixteen years* of age or women in the bakehouse, his hours of actual work on that day shall not exceed *nine hours;* and

(*b.*) Where such young person is employed on any day before the beginning of the period of employment for young persons under *sixteen years* of age or women in the bakehouse, he shall not be employed after the end of that period on the same day; and

(*c.*) Where such young person is employed on any day after the end of the period of employment for young persons under the age of *sixteen years* or women in the bakehouse, he shall not be employed next morning before the beginning of such period of employment.

If young persons under the age of *sixteen years* or women are not employed in the bakehouse, the period of employment for the purpose of this exception shall mean such period as can under this act, be fixed for the employment of such young persons and women in the bakehouse, and notice of such period shall be affixed in the bakehouse.

Where it is proved to the satisfaction of a secretary of state that the exigencies of the trade carried on in bakehouses, either generally or when situate in any particular locality, require that the special exception hereafter in this section mentioned should be granted, and that such grant can be made without injury to the health of the male young persons affected thereby, he may by order made under this part of this act grant to bakehouses, or to bakehouses situate in the said locality, a special exception permitting the employment of male young persons of *sixteen years* of age and upwards as if they were no longer young persons.

44. Where it is proved to the satisfaction of a secretary of state that the customs or exigencies of the trade carried on in any class of factories or workshops, either generally or when situate in any particular locality, require some other day in the week to be substituted for Saturday as regards the hour at which the period of employment for children young persons and women is required by this act to end on Saturday, he may by order made under this part of this act grant to such class of factories or workshops, a special exception, authorizing the occupiers of every such factory and workshop to substitute by a notice affixed in the factory or workshop some other day for Saturday, and in such case this act shall apply in such factory and workshop in like manner as if the substituted day were Saturday, and Saturday were an ordinary work day.

45. In the process of Turkey red dyeing, nothing in part one of this act shall prevent the employment of young persons and women on Saturday until *half past four o'clock* in the afternoon.

46. Where it is proved to the satisfaction of a secretary of state that the customs or exigencies of the trade carried on in any class of factories or workshops, either generally or when situate in any particular locality, require that the special exception hereafter in this section mentioned should be granted, he may by order made under this part of this act grant to such class of factories or workshops a special exception, authorizing the occupier of any such factory or workshop to allow all or any of the half holidays, or whole holidays in lieu of them, on different days to any of the children young persons and women employed in his factory or workshop, or to any sets of such children young persons and women, and not on the same days.

47. Where the occupier of a factory or workshop is a person of the Jewish religion, the regulations of this act with respect to the employment of young persons and women shall not prevent him—

(1.) If he keeps his factory or workshop closed on Saturday until sunset, from employing young persons and women on Saturday from after sunset until *nine o'clock* in the evening; or

(2.) If he keeps his factory or workshop closed on Saturday both before and after sunset, from employing young persons and women one hour on every other day in the week (not being Sunday), in addition to the hours allowed by this act, so that such hour be at the beginning or end of the period of employment, and be not before *six o'clock* in the morning or after *nine o'clock* in the evening.

48. No penalty shall be incurred by any person in respect of any work done on Sunday in a factory or workshop by a young person or woman of the Jewish religion, subject to the following conditions:

(1.) The occupier of the factory or workshop shall be of the Jewish religion; and

(2.) The factory or workshop shall be closed on Saturday and shall not be opened for traffic on Sunday; and

(3.) The occupier shall not avail himself of the exception in this part of this act for the employment of young persons and women on Saturday evening, or for an additional hour during any other day of the week.

Where the occupier avails himself of this exception, this act shall apply to the factory or workshop in like manner as if Sunday were Saturday and the Saturday were Sunday.

(b.) *Meal hours.*

49. The provisions of this act which require that all the children young persons and women employed in a factory or workshop shall have the time allowed for meals at the same time in the day shall not apply in the cases mentioned in part two of the third schedule to this act.

The provisions of this act which require that a child young person and woman shall not, during any part of the time allowed for meals in a factory or workshop, be employed in the factory or the workshop, or be allowed to remain in a room in which a manufacturing process or handicraft is being carried on, shall not apply in the cases and to the extent mentioned in part two of the third schedule to this act.

Where it is proved to the satisfaction of a secretary of state that in any class of factories or workshops, or parts thereof, it is necessary by reason of the continuous nature of the process, or of special circumstances affecting such class, or of any temporary or special emergency affecting the business carried on in such class, to extend thereto the exceptions in this section or either of them, and that such extension can be made without injury to the health of the children young persons and women affected thereby, he may by order made under this part of this act extend such exceptions or exception accordingly.

(c.) *Overtime.*

50. The regulations of this act with respect to the employment of young persons and women, shall not prevent the employment in the factories and workshops or parts thereof to which this exception applies, of young persons, if upwards of *fourteen years* of age, and of women for *fourteen hours* (inclusive of meal hours), on any one day, if they are employed in accordance with the following conditions, namely:

(1.) The period of employment shall end at *eight o'clock* in the evening, or if such period begins at *seven o'clock* or any later hour in the morning, at *nine o'clock* in the evening; and

(2.) Where the time allowed for meals under the said regulations of this act is less than *two hours* during the period of employment, there shall be allowed an additional *half an hour* for a meal after the hour of *five* in the evening; and

(3.) Any such young person or woman shall not be so employed on the whole for more than *five days* in any one week, nor for more than *forty-eight days* in any period of *twelve months*.

This exception applies to the factories and workshops and parts thereof specified in part three of the third schedule to this act.

Where it is proved to the satisfaction of a secretary of state that in any class of factories or workshops or parts thereof, it is necessary, by reason of the nature of the business depending on the weather or the seasons of the year, or by reason of any special emergency affecting the business, to employ young persons and women in manner authorized by this exception, and that such employment will not injure the health of the young persons and women affected thereby, he may, by order made under this part of this act, extend this exception to such factories or workshops or parts thereof.

51. If in any factory or workshop or part thereof to which this exception applies, the process in which a child, young person, or woman is employed is in an incomplete state at the end of the period of employment of such child, young person, or woman, the provisions of this act with respect to the period of employment shall not prevent such child, young person, or woman from being employed for a further period not exceeding *thirty minutes:*

Provided that the hours of actual work of such child, young person or woman in that week do not exceed the total number of hours for which such child, young person, or woman would have been permitted to actually work if this exception did not apply.

This exception applies to the factories and workshops specified in part four of the third schedule to this act.

Where it is proved to the satisfaction of a secretary of state that in any class of factories or workshops or parts thereof the time for the completion of a process cannot by reason of the nature thereof be accurately fixed, and that the extension to such class of factories or workshops or parts thereof of this exception can be made without injury to the health of the children young persons and women affected thereby, he may by order made under this part of the act extend this exception accordingly.

52. Nothing in this act shall prevent the employment of young persons and women so far as is necessary for the purpose only of preventing any damage which may arise from spontaneous combustion in the process of Turkey red dyeing, or from any extraordinary atmospheric influence in the process of open-air bleaching.

53. The regulations of this act with respect to the employment of young persons and women shall not prevent the employment in the factories and workshops and parts thereof to which this exception applies of women for *fourteen hours* (inclusive of meal hours) on any one day, if they are employed in accordance with the following conditions, namely:

(*a.*) The period of employment shall end at *eight o'clock* in the *evening*, or if such period begins at *seven o'clock* or any later hour in the morning, at *nine o'clock* in the evening; and

(*b.*) There shall be allowed an additional *half an hour* for a meal after the hour of *five* in the evening; and

(*c.*) Any such woman shall not be so employed on the whole for more than *five days* in any one week, nor for more than *ninety-six days* in any period of *twelve months.*

This exception applies to the factories and workshops and parts thereof specified in part five of the third schedule to this act.

Where it is proved to the satisfaction of a secretary of state that in any class of factories or workshops or parts thereof, it is necessary by reason of the perishable nature of the articles or materials which are the subject of the manufacturing process or handicraft to employ women in manner authorized by this exception, and that such employment will not injure the health of the women employed, he may, by order made under this part of this act, extend this exception to such factories or workshops or parts thereof.

(d.) *Nightwork.*

54. Nothing in this act shall prevent the employment in factories and workshops to which this exception applies of male young persons when upwards of *fourteen years* of age during the night, if they are employed in accordance with the following conditions:

(1.) The period of employment shall not exceed *twelve consecutive hours* (inclusive of meal hours), and shall begin and end at the hours specified in the notice; and

(2.) The provisions of part one of this act with respect to the allowance of time for meals to young persons shall be observed with the necessary modifications as to the hour at which the times allowed for meals are fixed; and

(3.) A male young person employed during the night shall not be employed during any part of the *twelve hours* preceding or succeeding the period of employment; and

(4.) A male young person shall not be employed on more than *six nights*, or in the case of blast furnaces or paper mills *seven nights*, in any *two weeks.*

The provisions of this act with respect to the period of employment on Saturday, and with respect to the allowance to young persons of eight half holidays in every year, or of whole holidays in lieu of them, shall not apply to a male young person employed in day and night turns in pursuance of this exception.

This exception applies to the factories and workshops specified in part six of the third schedule to this act.

Where it is proved to the satisfaction of a secretary of state that in any class of factories or workshops or parts thereof it is necessary, by reason of the nature of the business requiring the process to be carried on throughout the night, to employ male young persons at night, and that such employment will not injure the health of the male young persons employed, he may by order made under this part of this act extend this exception to such factories or workshops or parts thereof.

55. In a factory or workshop in which the process of printing newspapers is carried on not more than *two nights* in the week, nothing in this act shall prevent the employment of a male young person of *sixteen years* of age and upwards at night during not more than *two nights* in a week, as if he were no longer a young person.

56. In a factory or workshop in which the making of glass is carried on, nothing in this act shall prevent any male young person of upwards of *fourteen years* of age from working according to the accustomed hours of the factory or workshop, if he is employed in accordance with the following conditions, namely:

(1.) The total hours of the periods of employment shall not exceed *sixty* in any one week; and

(2.) The periods of employment (inclusive of meal hours) for any such young person shall not exceed *fourteen hours* in *four* separate turns per week, or *twelve hours* in *five* separate turns per week, or ten hours in six separate turns per week, or any less number of hours in the accustomed number of separate turns per week, so that such number of turns do not exceed *nine*; and

(3.) Such young person shall not work in any turn without an interval of time not less than one full turn; and

(4.) There shall be allowed to such young person during each turn (so far as is practicable) the same intervals for meals as are required by this act to be allowed in any other non-textile factory or workshop.

(4.) *Special exception for domestic and certain other workshops.*

57. The provisions of this act, which relate—

(1.) To the cleanliness (including lime-washing, painting, and washing), or to the overcrowding, or ventilation of a workshop; or,

(2.) To all children young persons and women employed in a workshop having the time allowed for meals at the same time in the day, or during any part of the time allowed for meals being employed or being allowed to remain in any room; or,

(3.) To the affixing of any notice or abstract in a workshop; or, specifying any matter in the notice; or,

(4.) To the allowance of any holidays to a child young person or woman; or,

(5.) To the sending notice of accidents;

shall not apply to a workshop

(1.) In which no young person or child is employed; or,

(2.) Which is a dwelling-house, and in which the family only of the occupier living in that dwelling-house carry on the handicraft:

Provided that nothing in this section shall exempt a bakehouse from the provisions of this act with respect to cleanliness (including limewashing, painting, and washing).

(5.) *Supplemental as to special provisions.*

58. Where it appears to a secretary of state that the adoption of any special means or provision for the cleanliness or ventilation of a factory or workshop is required for the protection of the health of any child young person or woman employed in pursuance of an exception under this part of this act, either for a longer period than is otherwise allowed by this act, or at night, he may by order made under this part of this act direct that the adoption of such means or provision shall be a condition of such employment.

59. Where an exception has been granted or extended under this part of this act by an order of a secretary of state, and it appears to a secretary of state that such exception is injurious to the health of the children young persons or women employed in, or is no longer necessary for the carrying on of the business in the class of factories or workshops or parts thereof, to which the said exception was so granted or extended, he may by an order made under this part of this act rescind the grant or extension, without prejudice to the making of another order at a future period.

60. Where a secretary of state has power to make an order under this part of this act, the following provisions shall apply to that order:

(1.) The order shall be under the hand of the secretary of state and shall be published in the London Gazette, and shall come into operation at the date of the publication in the London Gazette of the order, or at any later date mentioned in the order:

(2.) The order may be temporary or permanent, conditional or unconditional, and may extend a provision prohibition or exception, grant an exception, or rescind a previous order, either wholly or partly:

(3.) The order shall be laid before both Houses of Parliament, and if either House of Parliament, within *forty days* after the same has been so laid before it, resolve that such order ought to be annulled, the same shall after the date of such resolution be of no effect, without prejudice to the validity of anything done in the mean time under such order or to the making of any new order:

(4.) The order, while it is in force, shall, so far as is consistent with the tenor thereof, apply as if it formed part of the enactment which provides for the extension or grant or otherwise for making the order.

61. An occupier of a factory or workshop, not less than *seven days* before he avails himself of any special exception under this part of this act, shall (except in the case of a workshop to which the provisions of this act with respect to notices do not apply) affix in his factory or workshop and serve on an inspector notice of his intention so to avail himself, and whilst he avails himself of the exception shall keep the notice so affixed.

The notice so affixed shall specify the hours for the beginning and end of the period of employment, and the times to be allowed for meals to every child young person and woman where they differ from the ordinary hours or times.

An occupier of a factory or workshop shall enter in the prescribed register, and report to an inspector, the prescribed particulars respecting the employment of any child young person or woman in pursuance of any exception.

Where the occupier of a factory or workshop avails himself of an exception under this part of this act, and a condition for availing himself of such exception (whether specified in this part of this act, or in the order granting or extending the exception) is not observed in that factory or workshop, then

(1.) If such condition relates to the cleanliness, ventilation, or overcrowding of the factory or workshop, the factory or workshop shall be deemed not to be kept in conformity with this act; and

(2.) In any other case a child young person or woman employed in the factory or workshop, in alleged pursuance of the said exception, shall be deemed to be employed contrary to the provisions of this act.

Part III.

ADMINISTRATION, PENALTIES, AND LEGAL PROCEEDINGS.

(1.) *Inspection.*

62. A secretary of state from time to time may appoint such inspectors (under whatever title he may from time to time fix), and such clerks and servants as he may, with the approval of the treasury, think necessary for carrying into effect the execution of this act, and may assign to them their duties, and may constitute a principal inspector with an office in London, and may regulate the cases and manner in which they or any of them are to execute and perform the powers and duties of inspectors under this act, and *may award such salaries as he, with the consent of the treasury, thinks proper, and* may remove such inspectors, clerks, and servants.

All salaries paid to inspectors, clerks, and servants appointed under this act, and all expenses incurred by them or by a secretary of state in the execution of this act, shall be paid out of moneys provided by Parliament.

Notice of the appointment of every such inspector shall be published in the London Gazette.

A person who is the occupier of a factory or workshop or is directly or indirectly interested therein or in any process or business carried on therein or in a patent connected therewith, or is employed in or about a factory or workshop, shall not act as an inspector under this act.

An inspector under this act shall not be liable to serve in any parochial or municipal office.

Such annual report of the proceedings of the inspectors under this act as the secretary of state from time to time directs shall be laid before both Houses of Parliament.

A reference in this act to an inspector refers, unless it is otherwise expressed, to an inspector appointed in pursuance of this section, and a notice or other document required by this act to be sent to an inspector shall be sent to such inspector as a secretary of state may from time to time, by declaration published in the London Gazette or otherwise as he thinks expedient for making the same known to all persons interested direct, and the inspector named in such declaration shall be deemed to be for the purposes mentioned in the declaration the inspector of the district.

63. An inspector under this act shall for the purpose of the execution of this act have power to do all or any of the following things, namely:

(1.) To enter, inspect, and examine at all reasonable times by day and night any factory and workshop and every part thereof when he has reasonable cause to believe that any person is employed therein, and to enter by day any place which he has reasonable cause to believe to be a factory or workshop, and to take with him on every such entry a certifying surgeon and any constable whom he may need to assist him, and any other officer whom he is authorized by this act to take into a factory or workshop; and

(2.) To require the production of the registers certificates notices and documents kept in pursuance of this act, and to inspect, examine, and copy the same; and

(3.) To make such examination and inquiry as may be necessary to ascertain whether the enactments of this act and the enactments for the time being in force relating to public health are complied with, so far as respects the factory or workshop and the persons employed therein; and

(4.) To enter any school in which he has reasonable cause to believe that children employed in a factory or workshop are for the time being educated; and

(5.) To examine either alone or in the presence of any other person, as he thinks fit, with respect to matters under this act, every person whom he finds in a factory or workshop, or such a school as aforesaid, or whom he has reasonable cause to believe to be or to have been within the preceding *two months* employed in a factory or workshop, and to require such person to be so examined and to sign a declaration of the truth of the matters respecting which he is so examined; and

(6.) To exercise such other powers as may be necessary for carrying this act into effect.

The occupier of every factory and workshop his agents and servants, shall furnish the means required by an inspector as necessary for an entry inspection examination or inquiry under this act in relation to such factory and workshop.

Every person who wilfully delays an inspector in the exercise of any power under this section, or who fails to comply with a requisition of an inspector in pursuance of this section, or who conceals or prevents or attempts to conceal or prevent a child young person or woman from appearing before or being examined by an inspector, shall be deemed to obstruct an inspector in the execution of his duties under this act.

Where an inspector is obstructed in the execution of his duties under this act in a factory or workshop, the occupier of that factory or workshop shall be liable to a fine not exceeding *five*, or where the offence is committed at night *twenty*, pounds.

64. Every inspector under this act shall be furnished with the prescribed certificate of his appointment, and on applying for admission to a factory or workshop shall, if required, produce to the occupier the said certificate.

Every person who forges or counterfeits any such certificate, or makes use of any forged, counterfeited, or false certificate, or personates the inspector named in any such certificate, or falsely pretends to be an inspector under this act, shall be guilty of a misdemeanor, and be liable on conviction on indictment to be imprisoned for any period not exceeding *three months, with or without hard labor.*

(2.) *Certifying surgeons.*

65. Subject to such regulations as may be from time to time made by a secretary of state, an inspector may from time to time appoint a sufficient number of legally qualified medical practitioners to be certifying surgeons for the purposes of this act, and may from time to time revoke any such appointment.

Every appointment and revocation of appointment of a certifying surgeon may be annulled by a secretary of state upon appeal to him for that purpose.

A surgeon who is the occupier of a factory or workshop, or is directly or indirectly interested therein or in any process or business carried on therein or in a patent connected therewith, shall not be a certifying surgeon for that factory or workshop.

A secretary of state may from time to time make rules for the guidance of certifying surgeons, and for the particulars to be registered respecting their visits, and for the forms of certificates and other documents to be used by them.

66. A certificate of fitness for employment shall not be granted for the purposes of this act, except upon personal examination of the person named therein.

A certifying surgeon shall not examine any child or young person for the purposes of a certificate of fitness for employment, or sign any such certificate elsewhere than at the factory or workship where such child or person is or is about to be employed, unless the number of children and young persons employed in that factory or workshop are less than *ten*, or unless for some special reason allowed in writing by an inspector.

If a certifying surgeon refuses to grant for any person examined by him a certificate of fitness for employment, he shall when required give in writing and sign the reasons for such refusal.

67. With respect to the fees to be paid to certifying surgeons in respect of the examination of, and grant of certificates of fitness for employment for, children and young persons in factories or workshops the following provisions shall have effect:

(1.) The occupier may agree with the certifying surgeon as to the amount of such fees:

(2.) In the absence of any such agreement the fees shall be those named in the following scale:

When the examination is at a factory or workshop not exceeding one mile from the surgeon's residence.	2*s.* 6*d.* for each visit and 6*d.* for each person after the first *five* examined at that visit.
When the examination is at a factory or workshop more than one mile from the surgeon's residence.	The above fees and an additional 6*d.* for each complete *half mile* over and above the *mile.*
When the examination is not at the factory or workshop but at the residence of the surgeon, or at some place, day, or hour appointed by the surgeon for the purpose, and published in the prescribed manner.	6*d.* for each person examined.

(3.) The occupier shall pay the fees at the time at which the surgeon signs the certificates, or at any other time that may be directed by the inspector.

(4.) The occupier may deduct the fee or any part thereof, not exceeding in any case *threepence*, from the wages of the person for whom the certificate was granted.
(5.) A secretary of state may from time to time, if he think it expedient, alter any fees fixed by this section.

(3.) *Miscellaneous.*

68. Every person shall, within *one month* after he begins to occupy a factory, serve on an inspector a written notice containing the name of the factory, the place where it is situate, the address to which he desires his letters to be addressed, the nature of the work, the nature and amount of the moving power, and the name of the firm under which the business of the factory is to be carried on, and in default shall be liable to a fine not exceeding five pounds.

69. Where an inspector, by notice in writing, names a public clock, or some other clock open to public view, for the purpose of regulating the period of employment in a factory or workshop, the period of employment and time allowed for meals for children young persons and women in that factory or workshop shall be regulated by that clock, which shall be specified in the notice affixed in the factory or workshop.

70. The occupier of every factory and the occupier of every workshop in which a child or young person under the age of *sixteen years* is prohibited by or in pursuance of this act from being employed without a certificate of fitness for employment, shall keep in the prescribed form and with the prescribed particulars registers of the children and young persons employed in that factory or workshop, and of their employment, and other matters under this act.

The occupier of a factory or workshop shall send to an inspector such extracts from any register kept in pursuance of this act as the inspector may from time to time require for the execution of his duties under this act.

Where by reason of the number of children and young persons employed in a workshop (other than one above in this section mentioned), or otherwise, it seems expedient to a secretary of state so to do, he may order the occupier of that workshop to keep a register under this section, with power to rescind such order, and while such order is in force this section shall apply to that workshop in like manner as if it were a factory.

In the event of a contravention of this section in a factory or workshop, the occupier of the factory or workshop shall be liable to a fine not exceeding *forty shillings*.

71. There shall be affixed at the entrance of every factory and workshop, and in such other parts thereof as an inspector may for the time being direct, and be constantly kept so affixed in the prescribed form and in such position as to be easily read by the persons employed in the factory or workshop—
(1.) The prescribed abstract of this act; and
(2.) A notice of the name and address of the prescribed inspector; and
(3.) A notice of the name and address of the certifying surgeon for the district; and
(4.) A notice of the clock (if any) by which the period of employment and time for meals in the factory or workshop are regulated; and
(5.) Every notice and document required by this act to be affixed in the factory or workshop.

In the event of a contravention of this section in a factory or workshop, the occupier of the factory or workshop shall be liable to a fine not exceeding *forty shillings*.

72. Any notice, order, requisition, summons, and document under this act may be in writing or print, or partly in writing and partly in print.

Any notice, order, requisition, summons, and document required or authorized to be served or sent for the purposes of this act may be served and sent by delivering the same to or at the residence of the person to whom it is addressed, or where addressed to the occupier of a factory or workshop by delivering the same or a true copy thereof to the agent of the occupier or some person in the factory or workshop; it may also be served or sent by post by a prepaid letter, and if served or sent by post shall be deemed to have been served and received respectively at the time when the letter containing the same would be delivered in the ordinary course of post, and in proving such service or sending, it shall be sufficient to prove that the notice, order, requisition, summons, or document was properly addressed and put into the post, and the same when required to be served on or sent to the occupier of any factory or workshop shall be deemed to be properly addressed if addressed to the occupier of such factory or workshop at the factory or workshop, with the addition of the proper postal address, but without naming the person who is the occupier.

(4.) *Public establishments.*

73. A factory or workshop shall not be exempted from the provisions of this act by reason that it belongs to the Crown, or that the articles manufactured therein, or otherwise the subject of any manufacturing process or handicraft therein, being the property of the Crown, are not intended for sale.

Provided that in case of any public emergency it shall be lawful for a secretary of state to exempt any such establishment from any of the provisions of this act during the period named by him.

(5.) *Penalties.*

74. If a factory or workshop is not kept in conformity with this act, the occupier thereof shall be liable to a fine not exceeding *ten pounds*.

The court of summary jurisdiction, in addition to or instead of inflicting such fine, may order certain means to be adopted by the occupier, within the time named in the order, for the purpose of bringing his factory or workshop into conformity with this act; the court may, upon application, enlarge the time so named, but if, after the expiration of the time as originally limited or enlarged by subsequent order, the order is not complied with, the occupier shall be liable to a fine not exceeding *one pound for every day* that such non-compliance continues.

75. If any person suffers any bodily injury in consequence of the occupier of a factory having neglected to fence any machinery required by or in pursuance of this act to be securely fenced, the occupier of the factory shall be liable to a fine not exceeding *one hundred pounds*, the whole or any part of which may be applied for the benefit of the injured person, or otherwise as a secretary of state determines.

Provided that the occupier of a factory shall not be liable to any fine under this section if an information against him for not fencing the part of the machinery by which the bodily injury was inflicted has been heard and dismissed previous to the time when the bodily injury was inflicted.

76. Where a child, young person, or woman is employed in a factory or workshop contrary to the provisions of this act, the occupier of the factory or workshop shall be liable to a fine not exceeding *three*, or if the offence was committed during the night, *five pounds* for each child young person or woman so employed.

A child, young person, or woman who is not allowed time for meals as required by this act, or during the time allowed for meals is employed in the factory or workshop or allowed to remain in any room in contravention of the provisions of this act, shall be deemed to be employed contrary to the provisions of this act.

77. The parent of a child or young person shall—

(1.) If such child or young person is employed in a factory or workshop contrary to the provisions of this act, be liable to a fine not exceeding *twenty shillings* for each offence, unless it appears to the court that such offence was committed without the consent, connivance or wilful default of such parent; and

(2.) If he neglects to cause such child to attend school in accordance with this act, be liable to a fine not exceeding *twenty shillings for each offence*.

78. Every person who forges or counterfeits any certificate required for the purposes of this act (for the forgery or counterfeiting of which no other punishment is provided), or gives or signs any such certificate knowing the same to be false in any material particular, or utters or knowingly makes use of any certificate so forged, counterfeited, or false as aforesaid, or utters or knowingly makes use of as applying to any person any certificate which does not so apply, or personates any person named in any certificate, or wilfully connives at the forging, counterfeiting, giving, signing, uttering, making use, or personating as aforesaid, shall be liable to a fine not exceeding *twenty pounds*, or to imprisonment for a term not exceeding *three months, with or without hard labour*.

Every person who wilfully makes a false entry in any register, notice, certificate, or document required by this act to be kept, or wilfully makes or signs a false declaration under this act, or knowingly makes use of any such false entry or declaration, shall be liable to a fine not exceeding *twenty pounds*, or to imprisonment for any term not exceeding *three months, with or without hard labour*.

79. Where an offence for which the occupier of a factory or workshop is liable under this act to a fine, has in fact been committed by some agent, servant, workman, or other person, such agent, servant, workman, or other person shall be liable to the same fine as if he were the occupier.

80. Where the occupier of a factory or workshop is charged with an offence against this act, he shall be entitled upon information duly laid by him to have any other person whom he charges as the actual offender brought before the court at the time appointed for hearing the charge; and if, after the commission of the offence has been proved, the occupier of the fa tory or workshop proves to the satisfaction of the court that he had used due dilligence to enforce the execution of the act, and that the said other person had committed the offence in question without his knowledge, consent, or connivance, the said other person shall be summarily convicted of such offence, and the occupier shall be exempt from any penalty.

When it is made to appear to the satisfaction of an inspector at the time of discovering the offence, that the occupier of the factory or workshop had used all due diligence to enforce the execution of this act, and also by what person such offence had been committed, and also that it had been committed without the personal consent, connivance or knowledge of the occupier, and in contravention of his orders, then the inspector shall proceed against the person whom he believes to be the actual offender in the first instance, without first proceeding against the occupier of the factory or workshop.

81. A person shall not be liable in respect of a repetition of the same kind of offence from day to day to any larger amount of fines than the highest fine fixed by this act for the offence, except—

(*a.*) where the repetition of the offence occurs after an information has been laid for the previous offence; or

(*b.*) where the offence is one of employing two or more children young persons or women contrary to the provisions of this act.

(4.) *Legal proceedings.*

82. Save as is otherwise provided by this act, all offences under this act shall be prosecuted, and all fines under this act shall be recovered, on summary conviction before a court of summary jurisdiction in manner provided by the summary jurisdiction acts.

A summary order may be made for the purposes of this Act by a court of summary jurisdiction in manner provided by the summary jurisdiction acts.

All fines imposed in pursuance of this act shall, save as otherwise expressly provided by this act, be paid into the exchequer.

The court of summary jurisdiction, when hearing and determining a case arising under this act, shall be constituted either of two or more justices of the peace in petty sessions sitting at a place appointed for holding petty sessions, or of some magistrate or officer sitting alone or with others at some court or other place appointed for the administration of justice, and for the time being empowered by law to do alone any act authorised to be done by more than one justice of the peace.

Where any proceeding is taken before a court of summary jurisdiction with respect to an offence against this act alleged to be committed in or with reference to a factory or workshop, the occupier of that factory or workshop, and the father son or brother of such occupier, shall not be qualified to act as a member of such court.

83. If any person feels aggrieved by a conviction or order made by a court of summary jurisdiction on determining an information or complaint under this act, he may appeal therefrom; subject, in England, to the conditions and regulations following:

(1.) The appeal shall be made to the next practicable court of general or quarter sessions for the county or place in which the cause of appeal has arisen, holden not less than *twenty-one days* after the decision of the court from which the appeal is made:

(2.) The appellant shall, within *ten days* after the decision of the court, give notice to the other party and to the court of summary jurisdiction of his intention to appeal, and of the ground thereof:

(3.) The appellant shall, within *three days* after such notice, enter into a recognizance before a justice of the peace, with *two* sufficient sureties, conditioned personally to try such appeal, and to abide the judgment of the court thereon, and to pay such costs as may be awarded by the court, or shall, if such appeal is against an order or against a conviction whereby only a sum of money is adjudged to be paid, give such other security by deposit of money with the clerk of the court of summary jurisdiction or otherwise as the justice may allow:

(4.) The appellant, after entering into such recognizance or giving such other security as aforesaid, shall forthwith give notice in writing thereof to the other party:

(5.) The clerk of the court of summary jurisdiction shall, seven days at least before the sessions, transmit to the clerk of the peace the recognizance duly signed by the justice, or if such other security as aforesaid is taken a certificate thereof signed by such justice or clerk:

(6.) Where the appellant is in custody the justice may, if he think fit, on the appellant entering into such recognizance or giving such other security as aforesaid, release him from custody:

(7.) The court of appeal may adjourn the appeal, and upon the hearing thereof may confirm, reverse, or modify the decision of the court of summary jurisdiction, or remit the matter to the court of summary jurisdiction with the opinion of the court of appeal thereon, or make such other order in the matter as the court thinks just:

(8.) The court of appeal may make such order as to costs to be paid by either party as the court thinks just:

(9.) Whenever a decision is reversed by the court of appeal the clerk of the peace shall indorse on the conviction order or other adjudication a memorandum that the same has been so reversed, and whenever any copy or certificate of such conviction order or other adjudication is made, a copy of such memorandum shall be added thereto, and shall be sufficient evidence that the conviction order or other adjudication has been reversed, in every case where such copy or certificate would be sufficient evidence of such conviction order or other adjudication:

(10.) Every notice in writing required by this section to be given by an appellant may be signed by him or his attorney on his behalf, and every such notice and every recognizance and certificate mentioned in this section may be transmitted by the post in the ordinary way.

84. The following provisions shall have effect with respect to proceedings for offences and fines under this act:

(1.) The information shall be laid within *two months*, or, where the offence is punishable at discretion by imprisonment, or is a breach of the provisions of this act with respect to holidays, within *three months* after the commission of the offence:

(2.) The description of an offence in the words of this act, or as near thereto as may be, shall be sufficient in law:

(3.) Any exception, exemption, proviso, excuse, or qualification, whether it does or not accompany the description of the offence in this act, may be proved by the defendant, but need not be specified or negatived in the information, and if so specified or negatived, no proof in relation to the matters so specified or negatived shall be required on the part of the informant:

(4.) It shall be sufficient to allege that a factory or workshop is a factory or workshop within the meaning of this act without more; and

(5.) It shall be sufficient to state the name of the ostensible occupier of the factory or workshop or the title of the firm by which the occupier employing persons in the factory or workshop is usually known:

(6.) A conviction or order made in any matter arising under this act, either originally or on appeal, shall not be quashed for want of form, and a conviction or order made by a court of summary jurisdiction against which a person is authorized by this act to appeal shall not be removed by certiorari or otherwise, either at the instance of the Crown or of any private person, into a superior court, except for the purpose of the hearing and determination of a special case.

85. If any person is found in a factory, except at meal times, or while all the machinery of the factory is stopped, or for the sole purpose of bringing food to the persons employed in the factory between the hours of *four and five o'clock* in the afternoon, such person shall, until the contrary is proved, be deemed for the purposes of this act to have been then employed in the factory:

Provided that yards, playgrounds, and places open to the public view, schoolrooms, waiting rooms, and other rooms belonging to the factory in which no machinery is used or manufacturing process carried on, shall not be taken to be any part of the factory within the meaning of this enactment.

Where a child or young person is, in the opinion of the court, apparently of the age alleged by the informant, it shall lie on the defendant to prove that the child or young person is not of that age.

A declaration in writing by a certifying surgeon for the district that he has personally examined any person employed in a factory or workshop in that district, and believes him to be under the age set forth in the declaration, shall be admissible in evidence of the age of that person.

A copy of a conviction for an offence against this act purporting to be certified under the hand of the clerk of the peace having the custody of such conviction to be a true copy shall be receivable as evidence, and every such clerk of the peace shall, upon the written request of an inspector and payment of a fee of *one shilling*, deliver to him a copy of the conviction so certified.

Part IV.

DEFINITIONS, SAVINGS, APPLICATION TO SCOTLAND AND IRELAND, AND REPEAL.

(1.) *Definitions.*

86. For the purposes of this act, unless the context otherwise requires—

"Manufacturing process" as respects a factory, and "handicraft" as respects a workshop, means any manual labour exercised by way of trade or for purposes of gain in or incidental to the making any article or part of an article, or in or incidental to the altering, repairing, ornamenting, finishing, or otherwise adapting for sale any article; and

"Factory" means any premises within the same close or curtilage in which or in any part of which any manufacturing process is carried on with the aid of steam, water, or other mechanical power; and

A part of such premises which is used solely for the purpose of a dwelling-house or for any purpose other than the said manufacturing process or some works incidental to or connected with the said manufacturing process shall not by reason only of its being within the same close or curtilage be deemed to be part of the factory, but save as aforesaid every part of such premises shall be deemed to be part of the factory, although not containing any machinery; and

"Textile factory" means, subject as hereinafter mentioned, any factory in which there is carried on the preparing, manufacturing, or finishing, or any process incident to the manufacture of cotton, wool, hair, silk, flax, hemp, jute, or tow, either separately or mixed together, or mixed with any other material or of any fabric made thereof; and

"Non-texile factory" means any factory not a texile factory; and "workshop" means any premises, room, or place in which any handicraft is carried on by any person, and which is not a factory as before defined, and to which and over which the employer of such persons has the right of access and control; and

A part of any such premises, room, or place which is used solely for the purpose of a dwelling-house shall not be deemed to be part of the workshop; and

Any premises or place shall not be excluded from the definition of a factory or a workshop by reason only that the same are or is in the open air.

Any part of a factory or workshop may be taken to be a separate factory or workshop within the meaning of this act.

87. In this act, unless the context otherwise requires—

"Bakehouse" means any premises room or place in which bread, biscuits, or confectionery are baked from the baking or selling of which a profit is derived:

"Blast furnace" means any blast furnace or other furnace or premises in which the process of smelting or otherwise obtaining any metal from the ores is carried on:

"Bleaching and dyeing works" means any premises room or place in which the processes of bleaching, beetling, dyeing, calendering, finishing, hooking, lapping, and making up and packing any yarn or cloth of any material, or the dressing or finishing of lace, or any one or more of such processes, or any process incidental thereto, are or is carried on:

"Iron mill" means any mill, forge, or other premises or place in which any process is carried on for converting iron into malleable iron, steel, or tin plate, or for otherwise making or converting steel:

"Pit-bank" means any premises or place in which the dressing of ore obtained from a mine within the meaning of the metalliferous mines regulation act, 1872, is carried on, whether such premises do or do not form part of the mine within the meaning of that act:

"Print works" means any premises room or place in which persons are employed to print figures, patterns, or designs upon any cotton, linen, woollen, worsted, or silken yarn, or upon any woven or felted fabric, not being paper:

"Public laundry" means any premises room or place in which the business of washing articles of wearing apparel, sheets, towels, or other articles is carried on for profit:

"Quarry" means any premises or place, not being a mine, in which persons work in getting slate, stone, coprolites, or other minerals:

"Rope works" means any ropery, ropewalk, or rope work in which machinery moved by steam water or other mechanical power is not used for drawing or spinning the fibres of flax hemp jute or tow, but only for laying or twisting or other process of preparing or finishing the lines twines cords or ropes, and which has no internal communication with any buildings or premises forming or forming part of a textile factory within the meaning of this act, except such as is necessary for the transmission of power:

"Shipbuilding yard" means any premises or place in which any ships, boats, or vessels used in navigation are made, finished, or repaired:

Any premises or place shall not be excluded from a definition in this section by reason only that the same are or is in the open air.

88. Where a part of any premises within the same close or curtilage defined by this act to be a textile factory is used solely for the purpose of the manufacture of goods made entirely of any material other than those enumerated in the definition of textile factory, such part shall be deemed not to be a textile factory, but shall be deemed, according to circumstances, to be a non-textile factory or a workshop.

Hat manufactories, paper mills, and rope works shall not be deemed for the purposes of this act to be textile factories, but shall be deemed, according to circumstances, to be non-textile factories or workshops.

Blast furnaces, bleaching and dyeing works, and print works shall be deemed for the purposes of this act to be non-textile factories, whether the manufacturing process is or is not carried on with the aid of steam water or other mechanical power.

This act shall apply to a pit-bank, public laundry, quarry, and shipbuilding yard in like manner, if the work therein is carried on with the aid of steam water or other mechanical power, as if the same were a non-textile factory, and if the work therein is carried on without such aid, as if the same were a workshop.

89. A child young person or woman who works in a factory or workshop, whether for wages or not, either in a manufacturing process or handicraft, or in cleaning any part of the factory or workshop used for any manufacturing process or handicraft, or in cleaning or oiling any part of the machinery, or in any other kind of work whatsoever incidental to or connected with the manufacturing process or handicraft, shall, save as is otherwise provided by this act, be deemed to be employed therein within the meaning of this act.

90. "Certified efficient school" in this act means a public elementary school within the meaning of the elementary education acts, 1870 and 1873, and any workhouse school in England certified to be efficient by the local government board, and also any elementary school which is not conducted for private profit, and is open at all reasonable times to the inspection of Her Majesty's inspectors of schools, and requires the like attendance from its scholars as is required in a public elementary school, and keeps such registers of those attendances as may be for the time being required by the education department, and is certified by the education department to be an efficient school.

91. In this act, unless the context otherwise requires—

"Child" means a child under the age of *fourteen years:*

"Young person" means a person of the age of *fourteen years*, and under the age of *eighteen years:*

"Woman" means a woman of *eighteen years* of age and upwards:

"Parent" means a parent guardian or person having the legal custody of or the control over a child or young person, or having direct benefit from the wages of a child or young person:

"Treasury" means the commissioners of Her Majesty's treasury:

"Secretary of state" means one of Her Majesty's principal secretaries of state:

"Education department" means the lords of the committee of the privy council on education:

"Sanitary authority" means an urban or rural sanitary authority within the meaning of the public health act, 1875:

"Person" includes a body of persons corporate or unincorporate:

"Week" means the period between midnight on Saturday night and midnight on the succeeding Saturday night:

"Night" means the period between *nine o'clock* in the evening and *six o'clock* in the succeeding morning:

"Prescribed" means prescribed for the time being by a secretary of state:

"Summary jurisdiction acts" means the act of the session of the eleventh and twelve years of the reign of Her present Majesty, chapter forty-three, intituled "An act to facilitate the performance of the duties of justices of the peace out of sessions within England and Wales with respect to summary convictions and orders," and any acts amending the same:

"Court of summary jurisdiction" means any justice or justices of the peace, metropolitan police magistrate, stipendiary or other magistrate, or officer, by whatever name called, to whom jurisdiction is given by the summary jurisdiction acts or any acts therein referred to:

"Mill-gearing" comprehends every shaft, whether upright, oblique, or horizontal, and every wheel, drum, or pulley by which the motion of the first moving power is communicated to any machine appertaining to a manufacturing process.

(2.) *Savings.*

92. Where in any factory the owner or hirer of any machine or implement moved by steam water or other mechanical power, in or about or in connection with which machine or implement children young persons or women are employed, is some person other than the occupier of the factory, and such children, young persons, or women are in the employment and pay of the owner or hirer of such machine or implement, in any such case such owner or hirer shall, so far as respects any offence against this act which may be committed in relation to such children young persons or women, be deemed to be the occupier of the factory.

93. Nothing in this act shall extend—

(1.) To any young person, being a mechanic, artisan, labourer, working only in repairing either the machinery in or any part of a factory or workshop; or

(2.) To the process of gutting salting and packing fish immediately upon its arrival in the fishing boats.

94. The provisions of section ninety-one of the public health act, 1875, with respect to a factory, workshop or workplace, not kept in a cleanly state or not ventilated or overcrowded, shall not apply to a factory or workshop which is subject to the provisions of this act relating to cleanliness, ventilation and crowding.

95. Any enactment or document referring to the factory acts, 1833 to 1874, or to the workshop acts, 1867 to 1871, or any of them, or to any enactment thereof, shall be construed to refer to this act and to the corresponding enactment thereof.

(3.) *Application of act to Scotland and Ireland.*

96. The provisions of this act shall, in the case of a factory or workshop in Scotland or Ireland, be modified as follows: that is to say,

(1.) Shall apply during *twelve months* after the commencement of this act to children of the age of *nine years* and upwards, as if they were of the age of *ten years;* and

(2.) Shall not prevent a child who, before the commencement of this act, is lawfully employed in any factory or workship as a child under the age of *nine years,* or any child who during the *twelve months next after the commencement of this act* is lawfully employed in any factory or workshop as a child under the age of *ten years,* from continuing to be employed in a factory or workshop in like manner as if the child were above the age of *ten years;* and

(3.) Shall apply during *twelve months* after the commencement of this act to children of the age of *thirteen years* and upwards as if they were young persons; and

(4.) Shall not prevent a child, who before the expiration of *twelve months* after the commencement of this act is lawfully employed in a factory or workshop as a young person, from continuing to be employed in a factory or workshop as a young person.

97. In Scotland or Ireland where the age of any child is required to be ascertained or proved for the purposes of this act, or for any purpose connected with the elementary education or employment in labour of such child, any person, on presenting a written requisition in such form and containing such particulars as may be from time to time prescribed by a secretary of state, and on payment of such fee, not exceeding *one shilling,* as a secretary of state from time to time fixes, shall be entitled to obtain—

(1.) In Scotland an extract under the hand of the registrar under the act of the seventeenth and eighteenth years of Her present Majesty, chapter eighty, and any acts amending the same, of the entry in the register kept under those acts; and

(2.) In Ireland a certified copy under the hand of the registrar or superintendent registrar under the registration of births and deaths (Ireland) act of the entry in the register under that act of the birth of the child named in the requisition.

98. In the application of this act to Scotland—

(1.) "Certified efficient school" means any public or other elementary school under government inspection:

(2.) In lieu of Christmas Day, and either Good Friday or the next public holiday under the holidays extension act, 1875, there shall be allowed as a holiday to every child, young person and woman employed in a factory or workshop the whole of *two days* separated from each other by an interval of not less than *three months,* one of which shall be a day set apart by the Church of Scotland for the observance of the sacramental fast in the parish in which the factory or workshop is situate, or some other day substituted for such day as aforesaid by the occupier specifying the same in the notice affixed in the factory or workshop:

(3.) "Sanitary authority" means the local authority under the public health (Scotland) act, 1867:

(4.) "Medical officer of health" means the medical officer under the public health (Scotland) act, 1867, or where no such officer has been appointed, the medical officer appointed by the parochial board:

(5.) The "companies clauses consolidation act, 1845," means the companies clauses consolidation (Scotland) act, 1845:

(6.) "Summary jurisdiction acts," means "the summary procedure act, 1864," and any acts amending the same:

(7.) "Court of summary jurisdiction" means the sheriff of the county or any of his substitutes:

(8.) "Education department" means the lords of the committee of the privy council appointed by Her Majesty on education in Scotland:

(9.) "County court" means the sheriff court:

(10.) All matters required by this act to be published in the London Gazette shall (if they relate exclusively to Scotland) instead of being published in the London Gazette, be published in the Edinburgh Gazette only:

(11.) "Misdemeanor" means crime and offence:

(12.) "Information" means petition or complaint:
(13.) "Informant" means petitioner, pursuer, or complainer:
(14.) "Defendant" means defender or respondent:
(15.) "Clerk of the peace" means sheriff clerk:
(16.) All offences under this act shall be prosecuted and all penalties under this act shall be recovered under the provisions of the summary jurisdiction acts at the instance of the procurator fiscal or of an inspector under this act:
(17.) The court may make and may also from time to time alter or vary, summary orders under this act on petition by such procurator fiscal or inspector presented in common form:
(18.) All fines under this act in default of payment, and all orders made under this act failing compliance, may be enforced by imprisonment for a term to be specified in the order or conviction, but not exceeding *three months:*
(19.) It shall be no objection to the competency of an inspector to give evidence as a witness in any prosecution for offences under this act, that such prosecution is brought at the instance of such inspector:
(20.) Every person convicted of an offence under this act shall be liable in the reasonable costs and charges of such conviction:
(21.) All penalties imposed and recovered under this act shall be paid to the clerk of the court, and by him accounted for and paid to the Queen's and lord treasurer's remembrancer, on behalf of Her Majesty's exchequer, and shall be carried to the consolidated fund:
(22.) All jurisdictions, powers, and authorities necessary for the purposes of this section are conferred on the sheriffs and their substitutes:
(23.) Any person may appeal from any order or conviction under this act to the court of justiciary, under and in terms of the act of the twentieth year of the reign of His Majesty King George the Second, chapter forty-three, or under any enactment amending that act, or applying or incorporating its provisions or any of them, with regard to appeals, or to the court of justiciary at Edinburgh under and in terms of "The summary prosecutions appeal (Scotland) act, 1875."

99. In the application of this act to Ireland—
(1.) "Certified efficient school" means any national school:
(2.) "Sanitary authority" means an urban or rural sanitary authority within the meaning of the public health (Ireland) act, 1874, and any act amending the same:
(3.) "Medical officer of health" means the medical sanitary officer of the sanitary district:
(4.) Any act authorised to be done or consent required to be given by the education Department under this act shall be done and given by the lord lieutenant or lords justices of Ireland, acting by and with the advice of the privy council in Ireland:
(5.) "County court" means the civil bill court:
(6.) "Summary jurisdiction acts" means within the police district of Dublin metropolis, the acts regulating the powers and duties of justices of the peace for such district, or of the police of such district, and elsewhere in Ireland the petty sessions (Ireland) act, 1851, and any act amending the same:
(7.) A court of summary jurisdiction when hearing and determining an information or complaint in any matter arising under this act shall be constituted within the police district of Dublin metropolis of one of the divisional justices of that district sitting at a police court within the district, and elsewhere of a stipendiary magistrate sitting alone, or with others, or of *two or more* justices of the peace sitting in petty sessions at a place appointed for holding petty sessions:
(8.) Appeals from a court of summary jurisdiction shall lie in the manner and subject to the conditions and regulations prescribed in the twenty-fourth section of the petty sessions (Ireland) act, 1851, and any acts amending the same:
(9.) All fines imposed under this act shall, save as is otherwise expressly provided by this act, be applied in the manner directed by the fines act (Ireland), 1851, and any act amending the same:
(10.) The provisions of section nineteen of the public health act, 1866, or of any enactment substituted for that section, with respect to any factory, workshop, or workplace, not kept in a cleanly state, or not ventilated, or overcrowded shall not apply to any factory or workshop which is subject to the provisions of this act with respect to cleanliness, ventilation, and overcrowding:
(11.) All matters required by this act to be published in the London Gazette shall, if they relate exclusively to Ireland, instead of being published in the London Gazette, be published in the Dublin Gazette only.

(4.) *Repeal.*

100. The acts specified in the fourth schedule to this act are hereby repealed from and after the commencement of this act to the extent in the third column of that schedule mentioned:

Provided that—

(1.) All notices affixed in the factory in pursuance of the acts hereby repealed shall, so far as they are in accordance with the provisions of this act, be deemed to have been affixed in pursuance of this act; and

(2.) All inspectors, subinspectors, officers, clerks, and servants appointed in pursuance of the acts hereby repealed shall continue in office as if they had been appointed in pursuance of this act; and

(3.) All certifying surgeons appointed in pursuance of any act hereby repealed shall be deemed to have been appointed in pursuance of this act; and

(4.) All surgical certificates granted in pursuance of any act hereby repealed shall have effect as certificates of fitness for employment granted in pursuance of this act, and all registers kept in pursuance of any act hereby repealed shall, until otherwise directed by a secretary of state, be deemed to be the registers required by this act; and

(5.) Any order made by the secretary of state in pursuance of any enactment hereby repealed for granting any permission or relaxation to any factories or workshops may, if the secretary of state so direct, continue in force for a period not exceeding *three months* after the commencement of this act; and

(6.) The standard of proficiency fixed by the education department in pursuance of any enactment hereby repealed shall be deemed to have been fixed in pursuance of this act; and

(7.) A child exempted by section eight of the elementary education act, 1876, from the provisions of section twelve of the factory act, 1874, shall, on attaining the age of *thirteen years*, be deemed to be a young person within the meaning of this act.

(8.) This repeal shall not affect—

(*a.*) Anything duly done or suffered under any enactment hereby repealed; or

(*b.*) Any obligation or liability incurred under any enactment hereby repealed; or

(*c.*) Any penalty or punishment incurred in respect of any offence committed against an enactment hereby repealed; or

(*d.*) Any legal proceeding or remedy in respect of any such obligation, liability, penalty, or punishment as aforesaid, and any such legal proceeding and remedy may be carried on as if this act had not passed.

SCHEDULES.

FIRST SCHEDULE.

Factories or workshops in which employment of young persons and children is restricted.

1. In a part of a factory or workshop in which there is carried on—
The process of silvering of mirrors by the mercurial process; or
The process of making white lead,
a young person or child shall not be employed.

2. In the part of a factory or workshop in which the process of melting or annealing glass is carried on, a child or female young person shall not be employed.

3. In a factory or workshop in which there is carried on—
(*a.*) The making or finishing of bricks or tiles not being ornamental tiles; or
(*b.*) The making or finishing of salt,
a girl under the age of *sixteen years* shall not be employed.

4. In a part of a factory or workshop in which there is carried on—
(*a.*) Metal grinding, or
(*b.*) The dipping of lucifer matches,
a child shall not be employed.

5. In fustain cutting a child under the age of *eleven years* shall not be employed.

SECOND SCHEDULE.

SPECIAL RESTRICTIONS.

PART ONE.—*Places forbidden for meals.*

The prohibition on a child, young person, or woman taking a meal or remaining during the time allowed for meals in certain parts of factories or workshops applies to the parts of factories and workshops following; that is to say,

(1.) In the case of a factory or workshop where glass is made, to any part of such factory or workshop in which the materials are mixed; and

(2.) In the case of any factory or workshop where flint glass is made, any part of that factory or workshop in which the work of grinding, cutting, or polishing is carried on; and

(3.) In the case of any factory or workshop, to any part of the factory or workshop in which the making of lucifer matches or any process incidental to the making of lucifer matches (except that of cutting the wood) is usually carried on; and

(4.) In the case of a factory or workshop where earthenware of any description is made or finished, to any part of the factory or warehouse known or used as dippers house, dippers drying room, or china scouring room.

PART TWO.—*Certificates of fitness in workshops.*

The provision prohibiting the employment of children and young persons under the age of *sixteen years* unless the occupier has first obtained a certificate of their fitness for employment applies to every workshop (other than one which is a dwelling-house where the family only of the occupier living in that dwelling-house carry on the handicraft) in which any of the following handicrafts is carried on, namely,

(*a.*) The making or finishing of earthenware (except bricks and tiles not being ornamental tiles):

(*b.*) The making of lucifer matches:

(*c.*) The making of percussion caps:

(*d.*) The making of cartridges (other than the manufacture of paper or other material for the cases of the cartridges):

(*e.*) The printing of a pattern in colours upon sheets of paper:

(*f.*) Fustian cutting:

(*g.*) The founding or casting of any metal:

(*h.*) The making of glass:

(*i.*) The manufacture of tobacco:

(*j.*) Letter-press printing:

(*k.*) Bookbinding; or,

(*l.*) The making of India-rubber or gutta percha, or of any article made wholly or partly of India-rubber or gutta percha.

THIRD SCHEDULE.

SPECIAL EXCEPTIONS.

PART ONE.—*Period of employment.*

The exception respecting the employment of children, young persons, and women between the hours of *eight* in the morning and *eight* in the evening, and on Saturday between the hours of *eight* in the morning and *four* in the afternoon applies to any factory or workshop or part thereof in which any of the following manufacturing processes or handicrafts are carried on; that is to say,

(*a.*) Letter-press printing:

(*b.*) Lithographic printing:

(*c.*) Book-binding:

(*d.*) Turkey-red dyeing:

(*e.*) The making of any article of wearing apparel

(*f.*) The making of furniture hangings:

(*g.*) Artificial flower making:

(*h.*) Bon-bon and Christmas present making:

(*i.*) Valentine making:

(*j.*) Fancy-box making:

(*k.*) Envelope making:

(*l.*) Almanac making:

(*m.*) Playing-card making:

(*n.*) Machine ruling:

(*o.*) Biscuit making:

(*p.*) Firewood cutting:

(*q.*) Job dyeing:

(*r.*) Aërated water making; and also

to a part of a factory or workshop which is a warehouse not used for any manufacturing process or handicraft, and in which persons are solely employed in polishing, cleaning, wrapping, or packing up goods.

PART TWO.—*Meal hours.*

The cases in which the provisions of this act as to meals being allowed at the same time in the day are not to apply are—

(1.) The case of children, young persons, and women employed in the following factories and workshops;

Blast furnaces,

Iron mills,

Paper mills; and

Any factory or workshop in which the process of making glass or of letter-press printing is carried on; and

(2.) The case of male young persons employed in that part of any print works or bleaching and dyeing works in which the process of dyeing or open-air bleaching is carried on.

The cases in which and the extent to which the provisions of this act as to a child, young person, of woman during the time allowed for meals being employed or being allowed to remain in a room in which a manufacturing process or handicraft is being carried on, are not to apply are—

(1.) The case of children young persons and women employed in the following factories and workshops; that is to say,

Iron mills,

Paper mills; and

Any factory or workshop in which the process of making glass (save as otherwise provided by this act), or of letter-press printing is carried on; and

(2.) The case of a male young person employed in that part of any print works or bleaching and dyeing works in which the process of dyeing or open-air bleaching is carried on to this extent that the said provisions shall not prevent him, during the time allowed for meals to any other young person or to any child or woman, from being employed or being allowed to remain in any room in which any manufacturing process is carried on, and shall not prevent, during the time allowed for meals to such male young person, any other young person or any child or woman from being employed in the factory or allowed to remain in any room in which any manufacturing process is carried on.

PART THREE.—*Overtime.*

The exception with respect to the employment of young persons if upwards of *fourteen years* of age and women for *fourteen hours* a day applies to the factories and workshops and parts thereof in which any of the following manufacturing processes or handicrafts are carried on; that is to say:

(*a.*) Letter-press printing;
(*b.*) Lithographic printing;
(*c.*) Book-binding;
(*d.*) Open-air bleaching or Turkey-red dyeing;
(*e.*) An open air process in rope works;
(*f.*) Glue making;
(*g.*) The making of any article of wearing apparel;
(*h.*) The making of furniture hangings;
(*i.*) Artificial flower making;
(*j.*) Bon bon and Christmas present making;
(*k.*) Valentine making;
(*l.*) Fancy box making;
(*m.*) Envelope making;
(*n.*) Almanack making;
(*o.*) Machine ruling;
(*p.*) Playing card making;
(*q.*) Biscuit making;
(*r.*) Firewood cutting;
(*s.*) Job dyeing; and
(*t.*) Aërated water making; and
(*u.*) The making or finishing of bricks or tiles not being ornamental tiles; and also to a part of a factory or workshop which is a warehouse not used for any manufacturing process or handicraft, and in which persons are solely employed in polishing, cleaning, wrapping, and packing goods.

PART FOUR.—*Additional half hour.*

The exception with respect to the employment of a child young person or woman for an additional thirty minutes where the process is in an incomplete state applies to the factories and workshops following; (that is to say,)

(*a.*) Bleaching and dyeing works;
(*b.*) Print works;
(*c.*) Iron mills in which male young persons are not employed during any part of the night;

(*d.*) A factory or workshop in which the process of founding or casting any metal is carried on, and in which male young persons are not employed during any part of the night; and

(*e.*) Paper mills in which male young persons are not employed during any part of the night.

PART FIVE.—*Overtime for perishable articles.*

The exception with respect to the employment of women for *fourteen hours* a day for *ninety-six days* in a year applies to a factory or workshop or part thereof in which any of the following processes is carried on; namely,

The process of making preserves from fruit,
The process of preserving or curing fish, or
The process of making condensed milk.

PART SIX.—*Night work.*

The exception with respect to the employment of male young persons when upwards of *fourteen years* of age during the night applies to the factories and workshops following; (that is to say,)

(*a.*) Blast furnaces,
(*b.*) Iron mills,
(*c.*) A factory or workship in which the process of letter-press printing is carried on,
(*d.*) Paper mills, and
(*e.*) Oil and seed crushing mills.

FOURTH SCHEDULE.

Acts repealed.

Session and chapter.	Title of act.	Extent of repeal.
42 Geo. 3., c. 73	An act for the preservation of the health and morals of apprentices and others employed in cotton and other mills and cotton and other factories.	The whole act.
3 & 4 Will. 4., c.103.	An act to regulate the labour of children and young persons in the mills and factories of the United Kingdom.	The whole act.
7 & 8 Vict., c. 15.	An act to amend the laws relating to labour in factories.	The whole act.
9 & 10 Vict., c. 40.	An act to declare certain ropeworks not within the operation of the factory acts.	The whole act.
13 & 14 Vict., c. 54.	An act to amend the acts relating to labour in factories.	The whole act.
16 & 17 Vict., c. 104	An act further to regulate the employment of children in factories.	The whole act.
19 & 20 Vict., c. 38	The factory act, 1856	The whole act.
24 & 25 Vict., c. 117.	An act to place the employment of women, young persons, youths, and children in lace factories under the regulations of the factories acts.	The whole act.
26 & 27 Vict., c. 40.	The bakehouse regulation act, 1863	The whole act.
27 & 28 Vict., c. 48.	The factory acts extension act, 1864......	The whole act.
29 & 30 Vict., c. 90.	The sanitary act, 1867.....................	The following words (so far as unrepealed) in section nineteen, "not already under the operation of any general act for the regulation of factories or bakehouses."
30 & 31 Vict., c. 103.	The factory acts extension act, 1867......	The whole act.
30 & 31 Vict., c. 146.	The workshop regulation act, 1867	The whole act.
33 & 34 Vict., c. 62.	The factory and workshop act, 1870	The whole act.
34 & 35 Vict., c. 19.	An act for exempting persons professing the Jewish religion from penalties in respect of young persons and females professing the said religion working on Sundays.	The whole act.
34 & 35 Vict., c. 104.	The factory and workshop act, 1871......	The whole act.
37 & 38 Vict., c. 44.	The factory act, 1874	The whole act.
38 & 39 Vict., c. 55.	The public health act, 1875	The following words in section ninety-one, "not already under the operation of any general act for the regulation of factories or bakehouses."
39 & 40 Vict., c. 79.	The elementary education act, 1876	Section eight and the following words in section forty-eight, "the factory acts, 1833 to 1874, as amended by this act, and includes the workshop acts, 1867 to 1871, as amended by this act, and".

CHILDREN IN FACTORIES IN ENGLAND.

The following is the workshop-regulation act in relation to children employed in factories in England, and a page showing the form of schoolmasters' certificate, from "School certificate book," referred to in the report of Consul Shepard, of Bradford, at page 197.

[This book is to be forwarded to the school, for signature by the schoolmaster, every Friday morning.]

WORKSHOP REGULATION ACT.

The occupier of a workshop in which any child is illegally employed is liable to a penalty not exceeding £3 for each child illegally employed.

The occupier of a workshop is required to obtain weekly a certificate of the attendance of every child employed in his workshop.

The parent of any child in any way illegally employed is liable to a penalty not exceeding 20*s*. for each child illegally employed.

FACTORY ACT.—(7 VICT., CAP. 15.)

School certificate

I hereby certify that the undermentioned children, employed in the factory of —— ——, situated in —— ——, have attended the school kept by me at ——.—— for the number of hours and at the time on each day specified in the columns opposite to their names during the week ending on Saturday, the —— day of——, one thousand eight hundred and seventy —, and that the causes of absence stated are true, to the best of my belief.

Name of child.	Monday.		Tuesday.		Wednesday.		Thursday.		Friday.		Causes of absence.
	*Time.		*Time.		*Time.		*Time.		*Time.		
	From—	To—	From—	To—	From—	To—	From—	To—	From—	To—	

(Signed.) —— ——, Schoolmaster, the —— day of ——, 187–.

* When the schooling begins or ends at a half-hour, the half hour will be most conveniently inserted in figures, thus: 8½—11½, or 1½—4½, in the time columns.

Enter the names of the children who attend the forenoon school and those who attend the afternoon school separately.

ENGLISH TRADE WORKING RULES.

The following (6) trade-working rules and (2) master-builders' statements are those referred to in the report of the consul-general of Liverpool, at page 217, in the following manner: "To any one investigating the condition of labor in his country, I think these rules will afford much valuable information."

I.

LIVERPOOL MASTER BUILDERS' ASSOCIATION.

Working rules of the Liverpool, Birkenhead, and district house-painters.

1. RATE OF WAGES.

On and after 1st of March, 1878, efficient house-painters and those who are also paper-hangers to be paid at the rate of 7½*d*. per hour.

2. Overtime.

That all time worked, at the request of the employer, after one o'clock on Saturdays, and from 9.30 p. m. to 6 a. m. on other days, shall be paid for as time-and-a-half.

No overtime will be allowed unless the employer previously authorizes the men to make it.

3. Hours of work.

To commence work, from the 1st March to the 1st November, each morning at six o'clock, except on Monday, when they shall commence at seven o'clock, and leave off work each day at half past five, except on Saturday; and on that day to leave off at half past twelve o'clock. One hour for dinner and half an hour for breakfast to be allowed each day, except Saturday, when half an hour shall be allowed for breakfast. From 1st November to 1st March the working hours to be regulated as trade will allow. If any workman is late in the morning, he shall not commence work till 8.30 a. m.

4. Pay time.

All men working at jobs above 30 minutes' walk from the employer's place of business shall leave work in time to reach the pay-table at one o'clock on Saturday; if paid at the job, to work until 12.30.

5. Boundary.

The boundary in Liverpool shall be taken at a radius of one mile and a half from St. George's Hall as a center, and in Birkenhead at one mile and a half from Charing Cross as a center, beyond which walking-time shall be allowed in the first quarter only at the rate of three miles an hour, but men to walk back in their own time. This rule applies only to men sent from the shop, and not to men engaged and paid at the job.

6. Country jobs.

All men sent out to a country job shall have their traveling expenses paid going and returning, or if discharged or sent back to the shop, and 2*s.* 6*d.* per week for lodgings; any allowance beyond this to be by special arrangement.

7. Union and non-union men.

That operative society men shall not be allowed to interfere with or molest in any way non-society men who may be employed along with them, or *vice versa.*

8. Use of employer's tools and plant.

That no workman shall be allowed to use any brushes or other tools or plant belonging to his employer without first obtaining his consent thereto; neither shall any workman be allowed, under any circumstances, to work for another employer, or any one else, when his regular employer requires his services.

9. Smoking.

That no smoking shall be allowed on the jobs, and any man found offending against this rule shall be liable to instant dismissal.

10. Insobriety.

Any workman leaving his work and going for intoxicating liquors will be considered to have canceled all claim for expenses and wages due for work executed that day; also, any man found in a state of intoxication at his work shall not be paid for any work executed that day and also be liable to instant dismissal, at the option of his employer.

11. Apprentices.

That all boys coming into the trade, after date of these rules, shall be legally bound within three months of the time of coming into the shop, and serve not less than five years.

12. Time sheets.

Every workman must send in his time-sheet, made up to Thursday night, properly filled up and signed by himself and also by the foreman of the job, when one is appointed, not later than Friday noon; or, if working in the country, the sheets must be posted not later than the first post on Friday morning, or otherwise he will forfeit his right to be paid to time as per Rule 3.

13. Workmen's responsibility for tools and plant.

That each man shall leave in the hands of his employer not less than one and a half days' wages, as provided by Rule 12, which shall be given up to him on leaving his employment on condition that all his employer's tools are given up in a satisfactory state, and all damage or deficiency made good, reasonable wear and tear excepted. Each workman shall also be held responsible for all tools entrusted to his care, and shall make good any damage or deficiency.

WM. TOMKINSON, JUN'R,
President.
W. KNOX, *Secretary.*

——— ———, *Employer.*

6 LORD STREET,
Liverpool, May, 1878.

II.

LIVERPOOL MASTER BUILDERS' ASSOCIATION.

Carpenters' and joiners' trade rules, as agreed to by the employers and operatives, to come into operation on 1st May, 1877.

1. HOURS OF WORK.

The ordinary hours of work shall be 55 hours per week, apportioned as follows: On Monday morning from 7 a. m. to half past 5 p. m., with half an hour for breakfast and one hour for dinner; on Tuesday, Wednesday, Thursday, and Friday, from 6 a. m. to half past 5 p. m., with half an hour for breakfast and one hour for dinner; and on Saturday from 6 a. m. to half past twelve p. m., with half an hour for breakfast. But for the four winter months—November, December, January, and February—where artificial light is not provided, the ordinary hours of work shall be 47½ hours, from 7 a. m. to 5 p. m. on the first five days, and from 7 a. m to half past 12 p. m. on Saturday, with meal hours the same as in summer. No reduction to be made when men cannot see the full time.

2. RATE OF WAGES.

Wages shall be paid by the hour at the average rate of 8¼*d.* per hour, or £1 17*s.* 10*d* per week of 55 hours; but for the four winter months, where artificial light is not provided, the average rate of wages shall be 9*d.* per hour, or £1 15*s.* 7½*d.* per week of 47½ hours.

3. STARTING TIME.

Starting time on Monday shall be at 7 a. m., 8.30 a. m., and 1 p. m.; on Tuesday' Wednesday, Thursday, and Friday at 6 a. m., 8.30 a. m., and 1 p. m.; on Saturday, 6 a. m. and 8.30 a. m. But for the four winter months, where artificial light is not provided, the starting time in the morning to be 7 o'clock instead of 6 o'clock a. m. Seven a. m. may be considered a starting time, when the first hour has been lost—not as a recognized rule, but as an exceptional convenience.

4. OVERTIME.

All overtime made by the request of the employers to be paid by the hour, at time and a quarter up to 10 p. m., on the first five days of the week; all overtime after 10 p. m. to be time and a half. On Saturday all overtime to be time and a half; on Sunday, Good Friday, and Christmas Day double time.

5. BOUNDARY.

The boundary shall be taken at a radius of one and a half miles from St. George's Hall as a center, beyond which walking-time shall be allowed in the first quarter at the rate of three miles an hour; but men to walk back in their own time. For shops outside the above radius the boundary shall be taken at a radius of one and a half mile from each employer's shop as a center. This rule applies only to men sent from the shop, and not to men engaged and paid at the job.

6. COUNTRY JOBS.

All men sent out to a country job shall have their traveling expenses paid going and returning, if discharged, or sent back to the shop, and 3*s.* per week for lodgings. Any allowance beyond this to be by special arrangement.

7. PAY TIME.

All men working at jobs above 30 minutes' walk from their employer's place of business shall leave work in time to reach the pay-table at 1 o'clock, if paid on Saturday, or at 6 o'clock, if paid on Friday; if paid at the job, to work the same as in the shop. If pay is not commenced at the above times, overtime to be charged at the ordinary rate.

8. AUTHORITY OF EMPLOYERS.

Each employer shall conduct his business in any way he may think advantageous in all details of management, not infringing the individual liberty of the workmen

9. HOT WATER AND LOCK-UP PLACE.

That the employers provide hot water for workmen's meals; also a lock-up place in buildings for workmen's tools where the magnitude of the work renders it necessary.

10. NOTICE OF DISMISSAL.

That, before discharging outside men, notice be always given them previous to leaving-off time, or the employer to forfeit two hours' pay.

11. ALTERATION OF RULES.

Six months' notice in writing (to expire on the 1st of May) shall be given on both sides of any alteration in the foregoing rules, stating full particulars, and the party receiving the notice shall reply to it within one month, either by giving a counter notice or otherwise; and, if necessary, a deputation of six working joiners shall be appointed to meet six employers, to endeavor to come to an understanding, failing which, both parties shall refer the question back to their respective general meetings, and propose arbitration; and if a majority on both sides are in favor of arbitration, then a court shall be formed as follows:

12. PUBLIC COURT OF ARBITRATION.

The court shall consist of six employers and six working joiners, who shall have power to come to terms, and whose decision shall be binding on both parties; but, if unable to agree, they shall proceed to appoint an umpire, to be mutually agreed upon, who shall act as sole referee, and whose decision shall be the decision of the court, and shall be equally binding on both parties.

SAMUEL H. HOLME,
THOMAS HAIGA,
THOS. S. WYNSON,
WILLIAM AITT,
WM. TOMPKINSON, JR.,
EDW'D HUGHES,
Of the Liverpool Master Builders' Association.
H. McMILLEN,
TOM BROOKSBANK,
GEORGE MASSEY,
JOHN COGLEY,
JOHN PATTINSON,
THOMAS WATT,
Of the Amalgamated and General Union Societies of Carpenters and Joiners.

Witness to the signatures of the above:
W. KNOX,
Secretary to the Liverpool Master Builders' Association.
6 LORD STREET, *Liverpool.*

III.

LIVERPOOL MASTER BUILDERS' ASSOCIATION.

Bricklayers' trade rules, arranged between the master builders and operative bricklayers of Liverpool, 8th May, 1877, to come into operation on 17th May, 1877.

1. SUMMER RULE.

From the 1st day of March to the 31st day of October (both inclusive) the following regulations shall be observed: Work to commence on Monday morning at 7 a. m. and terminate at half past 5 p. m., allowing half an hour (from eight o'clock to half past) for breakfast, and one hour (from twelve to one) for dinner. Starting times to be 7 a. m., 8.30 a. m., and 1 p. m.

Work to commence on Tuesday, Wednesday, Thursday, and Friday, respectively, at 6 a. m. and terminate at half past 5 p. m., allowing half an hour (from eight o'clock to half past) for breakfast and one hour (from twelve to one) for dinner. Starting times to be 6 a. m., 8.30 a. m., and 1 p. m.

Work to commence on Saturday at 6 a. m. and terminate at half past 12 p. m., allowing half an hour (from eight o'clock to half past) for breakfast. Starting times to be 6 a. m. and 8.30 a. m.

Wages to be paid at the rate of 9*d.* per hour on and after the 17th May, 1877.

2. WINTER RULE.

From the 1st day of November to the last day of February (both inclusive) the following regulations shall be observed: Work to commence on Monday, Tuesday, Wednesday, Thursday, and Friday, respectively, at 7 a. m. and terminate at 5 p. m., with meal hours the same as in summer. Starting times to be 7 a. m., 8.30 a. m., and 1 p. m.

Work to commence on Saturday at 7 a. m. and terminate at half past 12 p. m., with breakfast half-hour, same as in summer. Starting times to be 7 a. m. and 8.30 a. m.

Wages to be paid at the rate of 9*d.* per hour.

3. OVERTIME.

All overtime made by the request of the employers to be paid by the hour at time-and-a-quarter up to 10 p. m. on the first five days of the week; all overtime after 10 p. m. to be time-and-a-half. On Saturday all overtime to be time-and-a-half; on Sunday double time.

4. BOUNDARY.

The boundary shall be taken at a radius of one and a half miles from St. George's Hall as a center, beyond which walking distance will be allowed in the first quarter at the rate of three miles an hour; but no walking time to be allowed in the second quarter, and men to walk back in their own time, except when going to the shop for wages, then walking time to be allowed to the boundary. This rule to apply only when men are sent from the shop.

5. COUNTRY JOBS.

At country jobs, where the employer, instead of walking time, undertakes to pay lodgings, the allowance for lodging money shall be 2*s.* 6*d.* per week; and, if wages are paid on the job, no walking time shall be allowed except when first sent out and when sent home; but if wages are paid in the shop, then walking time shall be allowed in on Saturday to the boundary and out on Monday from the boundary, in accordance with Rule No. 4. The payment of wages at the job or in the shop to be at the option of the employer.

6. TRAVELING EXPENSES AND TIME.

If, instead of allowing walking time, the employer undertakes to pay traveling expenses, then the train or other conveyance which leaves Liverpool nearest 7 a. m. on Monday morning, and leaves the station in the vicinity of the work nearest 12.30 p. m. on Saturday, shall be taken in those cases where wages are paid in the shop; but if wages are paid on the job, then the traveling expenses only to be allowed when sent out to a job and when sent home.

7. PAYMENT OF WAGES.

If wages are not paid by half past one o'clock on Saturday, time may be charged at the same rate as if working, and no wages shall be paid in a public house or beer house.

8. AUTHORITY OF EMPLOYERS.

Each employer shall conduct his business in any way he may think advantageous in the matter of letting piece-work, taking apprentices, using machinery and implements, employment of society or non-society men, employment of town or country bricklayers, and in all details of management not infringing the individual liberty of the workmen.

9. ALTERATION OF RULES.

Six months' notice, in writing (to expire on 1st May), shall be given on either side of any alteration in the foregoing rules, stating full particulars, and the party receiving the notice shall reply to it within one month, either by giving a counter notice or otherwise; and, if necessary, a deputation of six working bricklayers shall be appointed to meet six employers to endeavor to come to an understanding, failing which, both parties shall refer the question back to their respective general meetings, and propose arbitration; and if a majority on both sides are in favor of arbitration, then a court shall be formed as follows:

10. COURT OF ARBITRATION.

The court shall consist of six employers and six working bricklayers, who shall have power to come to terms, and whose decision shall be binding on both parties; but, if unable to agree, they shall proceed to appoint an umpire, to be mutually agreed upon, who shall act as sole referee, and whose decision shall be the decison of the court, and shall be equally binding on both parties.

WILLIAM LITT, *President*,
W. KNOX, *Secretary*,
Of the Liverpool Master Builders' Association.
JOSEPH POVEY, *President*,
SAMUEL WEBSTER, *Secretary*,
Of the Liverpool Operative Bricklayers Society.

6 LORD STREET, *Liverpool.*

IV.

MASONS' TRADE RULES,

Arranged between the master builders and operative stonemasons of Liverpool on the 24th April, and to come into operation on 1st May, 1876.

1. WAGES AND WORKING TIME.

The current rate of wages for efficient workmen to be ninepence per hour all the year round, and the time to be worked as follows: From the 1st day of February to the 10th day of November, inclusive, from 7 o'clock in the morning to half past 5 in the afternoon; and from the 11th day of November to the 4th day of December from 7 in the morning to 5 in the afternoon; and from December 5 to January 10, inclusive, from half past 7 to half past 4; and from the 11th day of January to the 1st day of February, from 7 o'clock in the morning to 5 o'clock in the afternoon (Saturdays in each case excepted, when work shall cease at 12 o'clock throughout the year), and pay to commence not later than 12.30 p. m. on Saturdays.

2. MEAL HOURS.

Breakfast-time to be from 8.30 to 9 a. m.; dinner-time to be from 12 noon to 1 p. m.

3. WORK SHEDS.

In yards or other jobs the nature and extent of which render the demand reasonable, sheds shall be erected. The operatives, in conjunction with the masters, to have a voice in directing where a dispute exists relative to the erection of sheds. In the event of any disputes a deputation of two employers and two workmen not connected with the work in question to form a committee to decide whether such demand is reasonable; and any employers refusing to erect sheds, if this committee decide that the demand is reasonable, to pay half the time lost by his men through the non-erection of such sheds.

4. OVERTIME.

All overtime made by the request of the employers to be paid by the hour at time and a quarter up to 10 p. m. on the first five days of the week. All overtime after 10 p. m. to be time and a half. On Saturdays all overtime to be time and a half; on Sunday and Chrismas Day double time.

5. APPRENTICES.

Boys entering the trade on no account to exceed 16 years of age, and to be bound until the age of 21 years. No boy to work longer than three months without being legally bound.

6. ALTERATION OF RULES.

Six months' notice in writing (to expire on the 1st of May) shall be given by either party of any alteration in the foregoing rules, stating full particulars; and the party receiving the notice shall reply to it within one month either by giving a counter notice or otherwise; and, if necessary, a deputation of six working masons shall be appointed to meet six employers to endeavor to come to an understanding, failing which, both parties shall refer the question back to their respective general meetings and propose arbitration, and if a majority on both sides are in favor of arbitration, then a court shall be formed as follows:

7. Public court of arbitration.

The court shall consist of six employers and six working masons, who shall have power to come to terms, and whose decision shall be binding on both parties; but if unable to agree, they shall proceed to appoint an umpire who shall be mutually agreed upon, who shall act as sole referee, and whose decision shall be the decision of the court and shall be equally binding on both parties.

D. RADCLIFFE, *President.*
W. KNOX, *Secretary,*
Of the Liverpool Master Builders' Association.
BENJAMIN MARSH,
President Stonemasons' Society.
ROBERT IRVING,
Secretary of the Operative Stonemasons' Society.

V.

Liverpool Master Builders' Association.

Plasterers' trade rules, to come into operation on 7th May, 1877.

1. Hours of work.

The ordinary hours of work shall be 49½ hours per week, apportioned as follows: Every morning from 7 a. m. to 5.30 p. m., with half an hour for breakfast and one hour for dinner; and on Saturday from 7 a. m. to 12 at noon, and half an hour for breakfast. But for the four winter months, November, December, January, and February, the ordinary hours of work shall be 47 hours—from 7 a. m. to 5 p. m. on the first five days, and from 7 a. m. to 12 at noon on Saturday, with meal hours the same as in summer.

2. Starting time.

Starting time every day shall be at 7 a. m., 9 a. m., and 1 p. m., excepting Saturday, when it shall be 7 and 9 a. m. only.

3. Rate of wages.

Wages shall be paid by the hour, at the average rate of 9*d.* per hour all the year round.

4. Authority of employers.

Each employer shall conduct his business in any way he may think advantageous in all details of management, not infringing upon the individual liberty of the workmen or these general rules.

5. Overtime.

All overtime made by the request of the employers shall be paid by the hour, at the following rates, viz: Full time and a quarter up to 10 p. m. on the first five days; after 10 p. m. time and a half; on Saturdays all overtime to be time and a half.

6. Boundary.

The boundary shall be taken at a radius of one and a half miles from St. George's Hall as a center, beyond which walking time shall be allowed, in the first quarter only, at the rate of three miles an hour, but men to walk back in their own time. This rule applies to men only sent from the shop, and not to men engaged and paid at the job.

7. Country jobs.

All men sent out to a country job shall have their traveling expenses paid going and returning, if discharged or sent back to the shop, and 2*s.* 6*d.* per week for lodgings; any allowance beyond this to be by special arrangement.

8. Pay time.

All men working at jobs above thirty minutes' walk from their employer's place of business shall leave work in time to reach the pay-table at 12.30 p. m. if paid on Saturday, or at 6 o'clock if paid on Friday; if paid at the job, to be paid at 12 noon.

9. Alteration of rules.

Six months' notice in writing (to expire between the 1st May and 1st August) shall be given on both sides of any alteration in the foregoing rules, stating full particulars; and the party receiving the notice shall reply to it within one month, either by giving a counter notice or otherwise; and, if necessary, a deputation of six working plasterer, shall be appointed to meet six employers to endeavor to come to an understandings failing which, both parties shall refer the question back to their respective general meetings and propose arbitration; and if a majority on both sides are in favor of arbitration, then a court shall be formed as follows:

10. Public court of arbitration.

The court shall consist of six employers and six working plasterers, who shall have power to come to terms, and whose decision shall be binding on both parties; but, if unable to agree, they shall proceed to appoint an umpire, to be mutually agreed upon, who shall act as sole referee, and whose decision shall be the decision of the court, and shall be equally binding on both parties.

WILLIAM LITT, *President,*
W. KNOX, *Secretary,*
Of the Liverpool Master Builders' Association.
CHARLES LEAF, *President,*
THOS. REILLY, *Secretary,*
Of the Operative Plasterers' Society.

It was agreed that these rules come into operation on the 7th day of May, 1877.

VI.

Wirral Branch of the Liverpool Master Builders' Association.

Carpenters' and joiners' trade rules, as agreed to by the employers and operatives, to come into operation on 1st May, 1877.

1. Hours of work.

The ordinary hours of work shall be 55 hours per week, apportioned as follows: On Monday morning from 7 a. m. to half past 5 p. m., with half an hour for breakfast and one hour for dinner; on Tuesday, Wednesday, Thursday, and Friday, from 6 a. m. to half past 5 p. m., with half an hour for breakfast and one hour for dinner; and on Saturday from 6 a. m. to half past 12 p. m., with half an hour for breakfast. But for the four winter months—November, December, January, and February—where artificial light is not provided, the ordinary hours of work shall be 47½ hours—from 7 a. m. to 5 p. m. on the first five days, and from 7 a. m. to half past 12 p. m. on Saturday, with meal hours the same as in summer. No reduction to be made when men cannot see the full time.

2. Rate of wages.

Wages shall be paid by the hour at the average rate of 8¼*d.* per hour, or £1 17*s.* 10*d.* per week of 55 hours; but for the four winter months, where artificial light is not provided, the average rate of wages shall be 9*d.* per hour, or £1 15*s.* 7½*d.* per week of 47½ hours.

3. Starting time.

Starting time on Monday shall be 7 a. m., 8.30 a. m., and 1 p. m.; on Tuesday, Wednesday, Thursday, and Friday, at 6 a. m., 6.30 a. m., 7 a. m., 8.30 a. m., and 1 p. m., and on Saturday, 6 a. m., 6.30 a. m., 7 a. m., and 8.30 a. m. But for the four winter months, where artificial light is not provided, the starting time to be 7 a. m. (instead of 6 a. m.), 8.30 a. m., and 1 p. m.; 6.30 a. m. and 7 a. m. are not recognized as starting times, but allowed for the convenience of the workmen.

4. Overtime.

All time worked at the request of the employers after 5.30 p. m. on the first five days of the week to be paid at the following rates: Time and quarter for the first four hours; double time after, up to starting time next morning. On Saturday all time worked after 12.30 to be paid time and half up to 5 p. m., and double time after; on Sundays, Christmas Day, and Good Friday double time.

5. Boundary.

That the boundary shall be taken at a radius of one and a half miles from Charing Cross as a center, and all men employed within this boundary shall work the same as in the workshops; but if employed at any job beyond this boundary, workmen to be at the boundary at the time stated for starting and leaving off in these rules.

6. Payment of wages.

All employers to commence to pay not later than ten minutes after leaving-off time. All men working at outside jobs to be at the pay-table not later than ten minutes after leaving-off time, unless paid at the job. If not paid within half an hour, overtime to be charged at the above rate (Rule 4).

7. Dismissal or leaving employ.

Two hours' notice shall be given by the employer or workman of an intention to put an end to the service, and in default either party shall forfeit and pay to the other two hours' wages. Such notice to be given, in all cases, so as to expire at the termination of the day's work.

8. Country jobs.

All men sent to country jobs shall have their traveling expenses paid going and returning once a week, together with 3*s*. per week lodging money within a radius of ten miles; beyond this to be by special agreement.

9. Piece work.

No piece-work to be allowed in any class of work except stairs or staircases.

10. Apprentices.

All apprentices, after a month's trial, to be legally bound for not less than five years.

11. Hot water and lock-up place.

Employers to provide hot water for workmen's meals; also a lock-up place for the protection of workmen's tools.

12. Authority of employers.

Each employer shall conduct his business in any way he may think advantageous in all details of management, not infringing the individual liberty of the workmen.

13. Alteration of rules.

Six months' notice in writing (to expire on the 1st of May) shall be given on both sides of any alteration in the foregoing rules, stating full particulars, and the party receiving the notice shall reply to it within one month, either by giving a counter notice or otherwise; and, if necessary, a deputation of four working joiners shall be appointed to meet four employers, to endeavor to come to an understanding, failing which, both parties shall refer the question back to their respective general meetings, and propose arbitration; and if a majority on both sides are in favor of arbitration, then a court shall be formed as follows:

13. PUBLIC COURT OF ARBITRATION.

The court shall consist of four employers and four working joiners, who shall have power to come to terms, and whose decision shall be binding on both parties; but, if unable to agree, they shall proceed to appoint an umpire, to be mutually agreed upon, who shall act as sole referee, and whose decision shall be the decision of the court, and shall be equally binding on both parties.

HENRY FISHER,
WILLIAM H. FORDE,
JAMES HARKNESS & SON,
ALEX'R BLEAKLEY,
Of the Wirral Branch of the Liverpool Master Builders' Association.
THOS. GEO. KNIGHT,
DAVID SMAIL,
RICHARD POTTER,
JAMES DAVIES,
Of the Birkenhead Branch of the Amalgamated Societies of Carpenters and Joiners.

Witness to the signatures of the above:
W. KNOX,
Secretary to the Wirral Branch of the Liverpool Master Builders' Association.

6 LORD STREET, *Liverpool.*

VII.

NATIONAL ASSOCIATION OF MASTER BUILDERS OF GREAT BRITAIN.

Comparative statement (for the first six months of 1878) showing the hours worked per week and the rate of wages per hour in the various branches of the building trade in the undermentioned towns.

Town.	Masons.				Bricklayers.				Carpenters and Joiners.			
	Summer.		Winter.		Summer.		Winter.		Summer.		Winter.	
	Hours worked per week.	Rate of wages per hour.	Hours worked per week.	Rate of wages per hour.	Hours worked per week.	Rate of wages per hour.	Hours worked per week.	Rate of wages per hour.	Hours worked per week.	Rate of wages per hour.	Hours worked per week.	Rate of wages per hour.
Aberdeen	51	7½ and 8	45	7½	none employed.				51	7½	45	7½
Ashton-under-Lyne	49½	9	47	9	54½	9	....	9	54½	8	54½	8
Alderley Edge	49½	8¼	43½	8¼	54½	8	46½	8	54½	32s. wk	54½	32s. wk
Bradford	49½	35s. wk	44	33s. wk	49¾	35s. wk	44	33s. wk	49½	8	49½	8
Bristol	54	8	48	8	54	8	48	8	54	7½	48	7½
Barnsley	49¾	36s. wk	lt-dk	36s. wk	49¾	36s. wk	lt-dk	36s. wk	50	7½ and 8	50	7½ and 8
Barrow	54	8½	44	8½	54½	39s. wk	48½	36s. wk	54	8	49	8
Bolton	48½	9¾	43½	9¾	49½	39s. wk	47	36s. 6d wk	48½	8⅞	48½	8⅞
Birmingham	54	9	48	9	54	8½	50	8½	54	8½	50	8½
Cambridge	56½	7 to 7½	56½	7 to 7½	56¼	6 to 7½	56¼	6 to 6½	56½	6 to 7	56½	6 to 7
Coventry	56½	7½	51	7½	56½	7½	51	7½	56½	7½	51	7½ and 8
Cardiff	54	8	50½	8	54	8	50½	8	54	7½	50½	7½
Cirencester	56½	26s. wk	56½	26s. wk	56¼	26s. wk	56½	26s. wk	56½	24s.–25s.	56½	24s.–25s.
Cheadle	49½	9	48½	9	49½	8¾	44½	8¾	54½	8	52	8
Chichester	58	7	48	7	58	6	48	6	58	6	48	6
Crewe	54½	8	54½	8	54½	8	54½	8	51½	7	54½	7
Chatham	56½	7½ to 8	54	7½ to 8	56½	7 to 8	54	7 to 8	56½	7 to 7½	54	7 to 7½
Doncaster	49½	8	{ 49½ s { 47½ b	} 8 } 8¼	49½	8	47½	8	49½	8	{ 49½ s { 47½ b	} 8 } 8⅜
Droylsden	49½	9	47	9	54½	10	47	10	52	8¼	47	8¼
Devizes	57½	5 to 7	57¼	5 to 7	57½	5 to 6	57½	5 to 6	57½	5 to 6	57½	5 to 6
Dorchester	65	6	48	6	65	5	48	5	65	5	65	5
Derby	....	....	....	....	....	....	....	....	....	....	....	....
Dudley	54	8	54	8	54	7½	54	7½	54	7½	54	7½
Darlington	49½	9	44	9	49¼	36s. wk	lt-dk	34s. wk	50	8	50	8

Guildford	56½	7	50½	7	56½	7	50½	7	50½	7	50½	7
Holmfirth									50½	27s.–31s.	lt-dk	27s.–31s.
Hartford	54	7¼	54	7½	55¼	7	53	7	55½	7	53	7
Inverness	57	8	40	8					57	7	40	7
Lancaster	49½	8¼	44	8½	49½	9	49½	9	54	7¼	54	7½
Liverpool	49½	9	41¼	9	55	9	47¼	9	55	8¼	47½	9
London	52½	9	48	9	52½	9	48	9	52½	9	52½	9
Leeds	48½	9			50	8½		8½	50	8	50	8
Lewes	61	7 to 8	53 to 55	7 to 8	61	6	53 to 55	6	61	6	53 to 55	6
Leicester	54	9	54	9	56	8	50½	8	56	8		
Lincoln	53½	8	53½	8	53½	34s. wk	47½	31s. wk	54	7¾	54	7¼
Leith and Edinburgh	51	9	45	9	51	10	48	10	51	8¼	45	8½
Manchester	49½	9	41½	9	54½	10	47	10	52	8½	47	8¼
Northampton	54	8	51	8	54	7½	51	7½	54	7½	51 to 54	7½
Newport	54	7½	50½	7½					54	7	54	7
North Shields	50	8½	47	8½	50	8⅓	47	8½	50	8⅓	50	8½
Nottingham	52	9	42	9	54	8	42	8	54	8½	42	8¼
Oxford	53	8	53	8	54	7½	53¼	7½	54	8	54	8
Preston	49½	39s. wk	lt-dk	35s. 9d. wk	49½	39s. wk	lt-dk	36s. wk	49½	35s. wk	49¼	35s. wk
Plymouth	56½	7	51	7	56⅓	7	51	7	56½	6½ be 5 r	51	6½ be 5 r
Runcorn	55½	36s. wk	49½	33s. wk	55½	8⅓	48	8½	55½	7¼	55½	7¼
Southampton	56¼	7	56½	7	56½	6¾ & 7	56	6½ & 7	56½	7	56½	7
St. Helen's	48½	36s. wk	43½	33s. wk	54	9	46½ to 49	9⅓	54	8¼	54	8¼
South Shields	50	36s. wk	lt-dk	33s. wk	50	36s. wk	lt-dk	32s. wk	50	8½	50	8½
Southport												
Sunderland	50	9	43½	9	50	36s. wk	43¼	33s. wk	50	8¼	50	8¼
Taunton	59½	4½ to 5½	59¼	4½ to 5½	59½	4½ to 5½	59½	4½ to 5½	59½	4½ to 5½	59½	4½ to 5½
Wolverhampton	54	8½	50½	8½	54	8	50½	8	54	8	54	8
Walsall	56½	9	56½	9	56½	8	50½	8	56½	8	56½	8
Wigan	48½	36s. wk	46	34s. 6d. wk	49½	9	47	9	49½	8	49½	8
Wakefield	49¼	36s. wk	lt-dk	33s. wk	49½	33s. wk	lt-dk	31s. wk	49½	7½	49½	7½
Winchester	60	7	54	7	60	4s. 6d. dy	54	4s. 6d. dy.	60	4s. 6 dy	60	4s. 6d. dy
Warrington	49	9	49	9	54½	9	50	9	54½	8	49¼	8¼
York	49½	8½	41½	8¾	53	8	47	8	53	7½	53	7½

Abbreviations.—dy, day; lt-dk, light to dark; s, shop; b, building; wk, week; sq, square; be, best; r, rough; hr, hour.

Comparative statement showing the hours worked per week and the rate of wages per hour in the various branches of the building trade, &c.—Continued.

Town.	PLASTERERS.				SLATERS.				PLUMBERS.			
	SUMMER.		WINTER.		SUMMER.		WINTER.		SUMMER.		WINTER.	
	Hours worked per week.	Rate of wages per hour.	Hours worked per week.	Rate of wages per hour.	Hours worked per week.	Rate of wages per hour.	Hours worked per week.	Rate of wages per hour.	Hours worked per week.	Rate of wages per hour.	Hours worked per week.	Rate of wages per hour.
Aberdeen	51	8	45	8	51	7	45	7	51	7½	45	7½
Ashton-under-Lyne	49½	8¾			49½	8¾			54½	8	43	8
Alderley Edge	54½	36s. wk	46½	36s. wk	54½	30s. wk	46½	27s. wk	54½	30s. wk	49½	30s. wk
Bradford	49½	33s. wk	49½	33s. wk	50	32s. wk	50	32s. wk	49½	7¾	49½	7¾
Bristol	54	7½	48	7¼	54	7½	48	7½	54	7½ to 8	48	7½ to 8
Barnsley	49½	8¾	44	8¾	50	8½	50	8½				
Barrow	54½	38s. wk	47	35s. wk	54½	38s. wk	47	35s. wk	54	8	54	8
Bolton	48½	36s. wk	41	33s. wk	48½	33s.–36s.	lt-dk	33s.–36s.	48½	35s. wk	48½	35s. wk
Birmingham	51	8½	50	8½		Piece-work.			56½	8½	50½	8½
Cambridge	56½	7 to 8	56½	7 to 8	70	6½ to 7	¾ time.	6¼ to 7		6¼ to 7¼		6½ to 7½
Coventry	56½	7½	51	7½	56½	7½	51	7½	56½	7¾	51	7½
Cardiff	54	7½	50½	7½	54	7½	50¾	7½	54	7	50½	7
Cirencester	56½	24s.–30s.	56½	24s.–30s.	56½	24s.–30s.	56½	24s.–30s.	56½	27s.–30s.	56¼	27s.–30s.
Cheadle	54½	8	47	8	49½	8	44½	8	54½	7½	52	7½
Chichester	58	6	48	6	58	6	48	6	58	8	48	8
Crewe	54½	6s. dy	54½	6s. dy	54½	8½	54½	8½	54½	32s. wk	54½	32s. wk
Chatham									56½	7 to 7½	54	7 to 7½
Doncaster	49½	8	47¼	8	49½	8	47½	8	54	7	54	7
Droylsden	52	8½	47	8½					52	8½	47	8½
Devizes	57½	6 to 7	57¼	6 to 7	37½	6 to 7	57½	6 to 7	57½	6 to 6½	57½	6 to 6½
Dorchester	65	5	48	5	65	5	48	5	65	5¼	48	5¼
Derby												
Dudley	54	7½ to 8	54	7½ to 8	54	7½	54	7½	54	8	54	8
Darlington	49½	39s. wk	lt-dk	36s. wk	50	8¾			53	7¾	53	7¾
Guildford	56½	7	50½	7	Piece-work.		3s. to 3s.3 sq		56½	8	56½	8
Holmfirth												
Hartford	55½	8½	53	8½	55½	7	53	7	55½	7	53	7
Inverness	57	7	40	7	57	8	40	8	57	5½	57	5½
Lancaster	54½	7½	50	7½	54½	7½	50	7½	54	7	54	7
Liverpool	49½	9	47	9	49½	9	47	9	55	8½	47½	9
London	52½	9	48	9	52½	10	48	10	52½	10	48	10
Leeds	49½	8½	49½	8½	50	8½		8¾	50	7½	50	7½

Lewes	61	8	53 to 55	8	done by bricklayers.				61	7	53 to 55	7
Leicester	56½	8	48	8					56	7½	56	7½
Lincoln	53½	8	47½	8	54	8	47½	8	54	7½	47½	7½
Leith and Edinburgh	51	10	42	10	51	8	48	8	51	8	51	8
Manchester	48½	36s.6d. wk	40½	33s. wk	54½	8½			52	8½	47	8½
Northampton	54	7½	51	7½	54	7½	51	7½	54	7½ to 8	51 to 54	7½ to 8
Newport	54	7½	50½	7½	54	7½	50½	7½	54	7	54	7
North Shields	50	8⅝	50	8¼								
Nottingham	54	9							54	9	54	9
Oxford	54	8	53½	8	54	8	53½	8	54	8 to 9	54	8 to 9
Preston	49½	36s. wk	lt-dk	36s. wk	49½	36s. wk	lt-dk	36s. wk	49½	34s. wk	49½	34s. wk
Plymouth	54	7	53½	7	56½	7	51	7	54	25s. wk	50	25s. wk
Runcorn	54	8½	46½	8½	55½	7¾	49½	7¾	55½	36s. wk	48	36s. wk
Southampton	56¼	7	56	7	56½	7	56	7	56½	7 and 8	56½	7 and 8
St. Helen's	54	8½	54	8½	54	32s. wk	54	32s. wk	54	8	54	8
South Shields	50	36s. wk	lt-dk	33s. wk	50	36s. wk	50	36s. wk	54	34s.6d. wk	54	34s.6d. wk
Southport												
Sunderland	50	36s. wk	46	33s. wk	50	36s. wk	46	36s. wk	50	33s. wk	50	33s. wk
Taunton	59½	4½ to 5½	59½	4½ to 5½	59¼	4½ to 5½	59½	4½ to 5½	59½	5 to 6	59½	5 to 6
Wolverhampton	54	8	50½	8					54	8	54	8
Walsall	56½	8	50¼	8					56½	8	56½	8
Wigan	49½	8	47	8	49½	32s. wk or 7 hr	47	32s. wk or 7 hr	49½	8	47	8
Wakefield	50	8 to 8½	50	8 to 8¼	49½	8½	lt-dk	8½	49½	28s. wk	49½	28s. wk
Winchester	60	7	54	7	piece-work.				60	7	54	7
Warrington	54½	36s. wk	50	33s. wk	54½	7½	50	7½	54½	8	54½	8
York	53	8	41	8								

Abbreviations.—dy, day; lt-dk, light to dark; s, shop; b, building; wk, week; sq, square; be, best; r, rough; hr, hour.

Comparative statement showing the hours worked per week and the rate of wages per hour in the various branches of the building-trade, &c.—Continued.

Town.	Painters. Summer. Hours worked per week.	Painters. Summer. Rate of wages per hour.	Painters. Winter. Hours worked per week.	Painters. Winter. Rate of wages per hour.	Masons' laborers. Summer. Hours worked per week.	Masons' laborers. Summer. Rate of wages per hour.	Masons' laborers. Winter. Hours worked per week.	Masons' laborers. Winter. Rate of wages per hour.	Bricklayers' laborers. Summer. Hours worked per week.	Bricklayers' laborers. Summer. Rate of wages per hour.	Bricklayers' laborers. Winter. Hours worked per week.	Bricklayers' laborers. Winter. Rate of wages per hour.	Plasterers' laborers. Summer. Hours worked per week.	Plasterers' laborers. Summer. Rate of wages per hour.	Plasterers' laborers. Winter. Hours worked per week.	Plasterers' laborers. Winter. Rate of wages per hour.
Aberdeen	51	7	45	7	54	4½ and 5	48	4½ and 5		not gi	von.		54	4½ and 5	48	4½ and 5
Ashton-under-Lyne	57	9	39	9	49½	5¾	47	5¾	54½	6	......	6	49½	6½	......	......
Alderley Edge	54½	7	44	7	49½	5⅓	43½	5½	54½	24s. wk	46½	21s. w	54½	27s. wk	46½	24s. wk
Bradford	49½	7	49½	7	49½	25s. wk	44	24s. wk	49½	25s. wk	44	24s. wk	49½	......	49½	......
Bristol	54	7 to 7½	48	7 to 7½	54	4¾	48	4¾	54	4⅓	48	4¾	54	4¾	48	4¾
Barnsley	49½	7½	49½	7½	49¾	26s. wk	lt-dk	24s. wk	49¾	25s. wk	lt-dk	24s. wk	49¾	25s. wk	lt-dk	24s. wk
Barrow	54	8	44	8	54	......	44	......	54⅛	28s. wk	48¼	26s. wk	54½	28s. wk	47	26s. wk
Bolton	55½	8	39	8	48¼	5¼ to 5½	43½	5¼ to 5½	49½	28s. wk	47	26s. wk	48½	28s. wk	41	26s. wk
Birmingham	56½	7½	50½	7½	54	6½	48	6½	54	6	50½	6	54½	6½	50	6½
Cambridge	......	5 to 6½	......	......	......	4	......	......	......	3¾	......	......	......	4	......	......
Coventry	56½	6¾	51	6¾	56½	5	51	5	56½	4¾	51	4¾	56½	4¾ and 5	51	4¾ and 5
Cardiff	54	6½ to 7	50½	6½ to 7	54	4 to 5¼	50½	4 to 5¼	54	4 to 5½	50½	4 to 5½	54	4 to 5½	50½	4 to 5½
Cirencester	56½	22s.–27s.	56½	22s.–27s.	56¼	16s.–18s.	56½	16s.–18s.	56½	16s.–18s.	56½	16s.–18s.	56¼	16s.–18s.	56½	1[?]s.–18s.
Cheadle	54	7¼	44	7½	49½	5	48½	5	49½	5½	44½	5½	54	5	47½	5
Chichester	58	6	48	6	58	4	48	4	58	4	48	4	58	4	48	4
Crewe	54½	7	54½	7	54½	6	54½	6	54½	5	54¼	5	54½	6	54½	6
Chatham	50½	6¾ to 7	54	6¼ to 7	56½	4½	54	4½	56½	4½	54	4½	......	......	......	......
Doncaster	54	7	44	7	49½	5 13/16	47½	5 13/16	49½	5 13/16	47½	5 13/16	49½	5 13/16	47½	5 13/16
Droylsden	......	......	......	......	49½	6	47	6	54½	6¼	47	6¼	52	6¼	47	6¼
Devizes	57½	5 to 5½	57½	5 to 5½	57½	3½	57½	3½	57½	3½	57½	3½	57½	3½	57½	3½
Dorchester	65	5	60	5	65	3½	48	3½	65	3¼	48	3¼	65	3¼	48	3¼
Derby	......	......	......	......	......	......	......	......	......	......	......	......	......	......	......	......
Dudley	54	6½	54	6½	54	4½ to 5	54	4½ to 5	54	4½ to 5	54	4½ to 5	54	5	54	5
Darlington	52½	6½	39	6½	49½	26s. wk	lt-dk	24s. wk	49½	26s. wk	lt-dk	24s. wk	49½	26s. wk	lt-dk	24s. wk
Guildford	56½	6½	50½	6½	56½	4	50½	4	56½	3½ to 4	50½	3½ to 4	56½	3½ to 4	50½	3½ to 4
Holmfirth	......	......	......	......	......	......	......	......	......	......	......	......	......	......	......	......
Hartford	55½	7	53	7	55½	4⅓	53	4½	55½	4½	53	4½	55½	5½	53	5½
Inverness	57	6	35	6	60	4¼	40	4¼	......	......	......	......	60	4¼	40	4¼
Lancaster	54	7	54	7	49¼	5¾	44	5¾	49½	5½	49½	5½	54½	5¾	50	5½
Liverpool	55	7¼	47½	7½	49½	......	41½	......	......	......	......	......	......	......	......	......
London	52½	10	48	10	52½	6¼	48	6¼	52½	5¾	48	5¾	52½	5¾	48	5¾
Leeds	56	7	......	7	50	6	......	6	50	6	......	6	49½	6¼	49¼	6¼

Lowes	64	6	53 to 55	6	61	3½ to 4	53 to 55	3½ to 4	61	3½ to 4	53 to 55	3½ to 4	61	3½ to 4	53 to 55	3½ to 4
Leicester	......	7½	......	7½	54	6	54	6	......	5 to 5½	......	5 to 5½	......	5¼	......	5¼
Lincoln	56	7	47½	7	53½	5	47½	5	53½	4¾	47½	4¾	53½	5	47½	5
Leith and Edinburgh	51	7½	40	7½	51	6	45	6	51	6½	48	6½	51	6	42	6
Manchester	55½	7¾	40	7¾	52	6	47	6	54½	5¾	49½	5¾	52	5¾	47	5¾
Northampton	60	7	45	7	54	4½	51	4½	54	4¼	51	4½	54	5	51	5
Newport	54	6	54	6	54	4	50½	4	......	......	......	......	54	4½	50½	4½
North Shields	......	......	......	......	50	5¼	47	5	50	5¼	47	5	50	5¼	50	5¼
Nottingham	......	......	......	......	50	6½	42	6½	54	5½	42	5¼	54	5½ and 6	54	5½ and 6
Oxford	54	6 to 7½	53½	6 to 7½	53	4½	53	4½	54	4¾	53½	4½	54	4½	53½	4½
Preston	49½	7½	lt-dk	7½	49½	24s. wk	lt-dk	24s. wk	49½	26s. wk	lt-dk	24s. wk	49¾	4s. 6d. dy	lt-dk	4s. 6d. dy
Plymouth	50	5½	46	5½	56½	4¼ to 4½	51	4¼ to 4½	50½	4¼ to 4½	51	4¼ to 4½	54	4¼	53½	4¼
Runcorn	55½	28s. wk	48	28s. wk	......	......	......	......	55½	5½	48	5½	54	5½	46½	5½
Southampton	56½	6 to 7	56	6 to 7	56½	4 and 4½	56½	4 and 4½	56½	4 to 4½	56	4 and 4½	56½	4 and 4½	56	4 and 4½
St. Helen's	54	7½	54	7½	54	4¾	54	4¾	54	6	46½ to 49	6½	54	6	54	6
South Shields	50	36s. wk	50	36s. wk	50	23s. wk	lt-dk	23s. wk	50	23s. wk	lt-dk	23s. wk	50	23s. wk	lt-dk	23s. wk
Southport	......	......	......	......	......	......	......	......	......	......	......	......	......	......	......	......
Sunderland	53	33s. wk	48	30s. wk	50	23s. wk	43½	22s. wk	50	23s. wk	43½	22s. wk	50	23s. wk	43½	22s. wk
Taunton	59½	4 to 5	59½	4 to 5	59½	4	59¼	4	59½	3 to 4	59½	3 to 4	59¼	3 to 4	59½	3 to 4
Wolverhampton	54	7¼	54	7½	54	5½	50½	5½	54	5	50½	5	54	5	50½	5
Walsall	56½	6½	56½	6½	56½	6	50½	6	56½	4¾	50½	4¾	56½	6	50½	6
Wigan	49½	8	47	8	49½	6½	47	6½	49½	6½	47	6½	49½	5¼ to 6½	47	5¼ to 6¼
Wakefield	......	7	......	7	49½	22s.–23s.	lt-dk	22s.–23s.	49½	22s.–23s.	lt-dk	22s.–23s.	50	6½	50	6½
Winchester	60	4s.–4s. 6d.	54	4s. –4s. 6d.	60	3s. 4d. dy	54	3s. 4d. dy	60	2s. 8d. –3s.	54	2s. 8d. –3s.	60	2s. 8d. –3s.	54	2s. 8d. –3s.
Warrington	54½	7½ and 8	54½	7½ and 8	49	21s.–23s.	49	21s.–23s.	54½	6	50	6	......	......	......	......
York	......	......	......	......	53	5¼	47	5¼	53	5½	47	5¼	53	5½	41	5¼

Abbreviations.—dy, day; lt-dk, light to dark; s, shop; b, building; wk, week; sq, square; be, best; r, rough; hr, hour.

W. KNOX, *Secretary, 6 Lord Street, Liverpool.*

VIII.

NATIONAL ASSOCIATION OF MASTER BUILDERS OF GREAT BRITAIN.

Tabular statement of the state of trade and the labor market.

Town.	State of trade.	In what branch.	Supply of labor.	In what branch.	Demands (if any) from operatives.
Aberdeen	Fair, but prospects not bright.	All	Good	In all branches, and abundant in joiners, plumbers, and painters.	
Ashton-under-Lyne	Quiet	do	Fair	All	
Alderly Edge	Very quiet, and not good prospects.		Bricklayers, good; masons and plasterers not equal to the demand; other branches moderate.		Bricklayers want 1*d.* per hour additional, making 9*d.*, to come into operation 1st May.
Burslem	Rather dull	All	Plentiful	All	
Birmingham	Very bad	do	Largely in excess	do	
Bradford	Quiet	do	Plentiful	do	
Bristol	Fairly good	All except masons, bricklayers and plumbers, who are slack.	Sufficient	do	Plasterers have made a demand for 1*d.* an hour, to commence 1st June, 1878.
Barnsley	Very bad	All	Plentiful	do	
Barrow	Depressed	do	Ample	All except slaters and plumbers, of whom supply is poor.	
Bolton	Very slack	do	Plentiful	All	
Cambridge	Fair average	do			
Coventry	Flat, with good prospect	do	Plentiful	All	A notice for an advance from the bricklayers' laborers of ½*d.* per hour, but not expected to be pressed.
Cardiff	Slack	do	Ample	All except plumbers	Carpenters, joiners, and plasterers have made a demand of ½*d.* per hour, to come into force 1st and 13th May respectively, but subject to arbitration.
Cirencester	Fair; little fluctuation	do	Sufficient	All except joiners, in which good hands are scarce.	
Cheadle	Moderately good	do	Ample in masons, joiners, and slaters, and sufficient in other branches.		Demand by plasterers' laborers of 1*d.* per hour.
Chichester	Dull	do	Sufficient	All	
Crewe	Middling	do	Good	do	
Darlington	Depressed	do	Greater than demand	do	
Doncaster	Pretty good	do	Plentiful, except plasterers rather scarce.		
Droylsden	Dull	All except plasterers, which is fair.	Plenty	All	

Devizes	Bad	All except bricklayers, carpenters, joiners and plasterers, which are moderate.	do	do	
Dorchester	do	All except carpenters and joiners, who are pretty good.	Good	do	
Dudley	Fair	All	Ample	do	
Guildford	Dull	do	Plenty		
Holmfirth	do	Carpenters and joiners	do	Carpenters and joiners	
Hartford	Slack	All	Good	All	
Inverness	Good	In all but plumbers and painters, which are fair and indifferent respectively.	Plentiful	In all but plasterers and slaters, who are scarce.	Plumbers agitating for reduction of hours and advance of wages, but no action taken on either side. Painters made a demand for 1*d.* an hour, and have been locked out in consequence for nearly a fortnight.
London	Slack	All	Good	All	Masons have been thirty weeks on strike for 1*d.* an hour and reduction of 2½ hours in time, but are now applying for work; carpenters and joiners also demand 1*d.* an hour.
Leicester	Depressed	do	Ample	do	Plasterers have given notice of demand for 1*d.* an hour, to commence 22d April.
Liverpool	Dull, with no prospect of improvement.	do	Plentiful	do	Painters demand advance of 1*d.* per hour from 1st April, 1878.
Lancaster	Dull	In all except masons	do	do	Masons 2*s.* per week and 3 hours less time, from 1st May, 1878; joiners 2*s.* per week and 4½ hours less time, from 1st May, 1878; plasterers and slaters, 1*d.* an hour from 1st April, 1878.
Lewes	Depressed	All	Short	do	
Leith & Edinburgh	Rather dull, but fair prospect.	do	Plentiful	do	
Lincoln	Moderate	do	Abundant	do	
Leeds	Depressed	do	Plentiful	do	Notice of 1*d.* per hour advance from bricklayers, and also to leave 12 instead of 12.30 Saturdays, and also walking time at 3 miles an hour for jobs more than 1 mile from Wellington station, instead of 1½ miles as now; also demand from plasterers of ½*d.* per hour, to commence 1st April.
Manchester	Generally slack	All branches except plasterers.	Ample	All, plasterers excepted	
Northampton	Dull	All except carpenters, joiners, plasterers, plumbers, painters, and plasterers' laborers, which are moderate.	Good	Except plasterers, moderate.	Plasterers demand 1*d.* per hour from 25th April, but are not at all likely to succeed in their demand.
Newport	Very bad	All	Plentiful	All	

Tabular statement of the state of trade and the labor market.—Continued.

Town.	State of trade.	In what branch.	Supply of labor.	In what branch.	Demands (if any) from operatives.
Nottingham	Bad	All	Plentiful	All	Bricklayers have given notice of demand for advance of 1*d.* per hour and alteration of time; plumbers have given notice of demand for ½*d.* an hour, to commence April 1st next; bricklayers' laborers have given notice of demand for ½*d.* an hour advance.
Oxford	Dull	do	Abundant	do	Masons have made a demand of ½*d.* per hour, from 1st June, 1878, but are not at all likely to succeed.
Preston	Slack	All but masons, bricklayers, and their laborers, who are moderately busy, and painters very slack.	Plentiful	do	Painters have given notice of demand for 1*d.* an hour, to commence on March 1, 1878.
Plymouth	do	All but plasterers, plumbers, and plasterers' laborers good, and painters indifferent.	do	All except plumbers and painters, which are good.	Painters have given notice of demand for ½*d.* an hour, and 6*d.* per day extra for country money.
Runcorn	Moderate, and prospects not bright.	All	Sufficient	All	Carpenters and joiners demand ½*d.* per hour advance from 1st May, 1878, and reduction of time of half an hour.
Southampton	Slack	All but painters, which branch is much depressed.	Scarce	All but painters, of whom pretty fair supply.	
St. Helen's	Good	All but masons, bricklayers, slaters, painters, masons and bricklayers' laborers moderate.	Excessive	All but carpenters, joiners, plasterers, plumbers, and bricklayers' laborers, in which it is moderate.	
South Shields	Bad	All	Large	All	
Sunderland	Slack	do	Plentiful	do	
Taunton	do	do	Sufficient	do	
Wolverhampton	Depressed	do	In excess of demand	All except plasterers and slaters, who are only equal to the demand.	
Walsall	do	All except masons, plumbers, and masons' laborers good.	Greatly in excess of demand.	All except plumbers and painters, who are only equal to demand.	
Wigan	Rather slack	All	In excess of demand	All	Plasterers demand 1*d.* an hour from 1st May, 1878.
Wakefield	Slack	All but plasterers and painters, who are moderate.	Plentiful	do	Bricklayers demand 3*s.* per week advance from 1st May.
Winchester	Not generally good	All	do	do	

Warrington					Carpenters and joiners demand 6*d*. per day country money for distances of 2 miles from boundary, to come into operation 1st May; plasterers demand same wages as now received—for 48½ hours in summer and 41½ in winter—to come into operation 2d April.
York	Bad	Except masons and bricklayers, good; carpenters and joiners, fair; plasterers, good.	Good	All	

SCOTLAND.

Report, by Consul-General Badeau, of London, on the failure of the City of Glasgow Bank.

Referring to the recent failure of the City of Glasgow Bank, Scotland, which has of course been known in the United States from the date of its occurrence, I have the honor to state that it is difficult in these days, when every circumstance connected with such an event is telegraphed almost from hour to hour, to be certain that a report on the subject is not completely forestalled and useless when it arrives at the Department. There seem, however, to be some results of this failure which may possibly not have been caught up in the returns sent across the wires—results which elevate the misfortune into a commercial event, and make it worthy of consideration in the United States as well as in Great Britian. Some of these could not be perceived at first, and are only appreciated after full knowledge is obtained, and a calmer judgment has been able to consider them. Even now all is not entirely clear, but enough is known for some account of them to be offered.

The City Bank of Glasgow was one of the commercial institutions of Scotland most trusted by the community where it existed, as is evident by the fact that its £100 shares sold for £240 the day before the failure. It had 133 branches, with 750 employés, and for fifteen years its dividends had been steadily increasing from 5 per cent. in 1863, until in 1877 they had reached 12 per cent. The character of the directors stood high; the transactions of the bank were considered irreproachable; and on the 1st October its current deposits amounted to £2,500,000.

On that day, October 1, it stopped payment. The affairs of the bank were at once subjected to an investigation by competent accountants, who have since reported a deficiency of £5,190,983, in addition to the capital stock of £1,000,000. This deficiency was caused in the main by the acceptance by the directors of bad securities; securities of such a character that, when they were examined by the banks which were consulted before the stoppage, it was decided to be inexpedient to render the assistance applied for.

This great disaster at once affected the entire commercial community of Great Britain. Something very like a panic occurred. The Bank of England's rate went up from 5 to 6 per cent.; runs were made on other banks; several other large failures occurred both in Scotland and in England, though none of anything like the importance of that which was their cause; and the general depression in trade which had previously existed was enhanced. These effects have not yet disappeared, but it is believed that the worst has been experienced. The banks, without exception, have so far been able to stand the run made against them, and though uneasiness still exists and possibly more failures may occur, the gloomiest apprehensions at first entertained in some quarters have happily not been realized.

There are, however, two points of view from which this calamity appears to differ from or to transend any that has recently occurred. The bank was one of unlimited liability, and the stockholders have already been called upon to make good the losses of the creditors to the extent of five times their original investments. The number of really wealthy stockholders is said to be small; the great majority being persons of limited means, principally clergymen and other professional men, farmers, tradesmen, or women, whose little fortunes were all invested in this institution. These, of course, are utterly unable to meet the demand upon them, and, in most cases, can with difficulty pay what amounts to the first value of the stock. They are ruined absolutely; while the loss, heavier in amount though hardly more severe in reality, falls upon a comparatively few, who are reduced in one day from affluence to poverty. It has been estimated that a score and a half of stockholders under the call mentioned must furnish millions. When the reply to this first call is exhausted, another is to be made upon those who have anything left, and so on till the debt is liquidated or the stockholders are all pennyless.

Those taking stock to a large extent were doubtless aware of their liabilities and chose to incur the risk, which, however, probably seemed remote, but among the smaller investors many women and persons unused to practical business, it is believed, were utterly ignorant that they were liable for any sum beyond their original investment. Universal sympathy has been expressed for these, and it is proposed to raise a fund by subscription to relieve in some degree the suffering which the failure has occasioned.

But, besides this distressing feature of the present calamity, there is another which provokes comment and commiseration. According to English law, trustees investing in such stocks are personally liable as if they were the actual investors, while the beneficiaries of the trust, who in this case have been the recipients of the large dividends yielded by the stock, are free from any liability. This state of the law comes upon the unfortunate trustees with crushing force. Their liability is also unlimited, and many who have been acting for others, and often receiving no personal benefit from their labors, will now be obliged, if they can, to make good a loss from which those for whom they act may not suffer at all. The only possible remedy of the trustees will be against the beneficiaries, and this depends entirely upon the wording of the deed of trust, which in many instances does not provide for such an emergency.

The conduct of the directors, who are answerable for all, is hardly susceptible of explanation. They appear in the first instance to have advanced large sums to their friends and connections in business on securities which no business man should have accepted, and over £5,790,000 of which the accountants value at only £1,521,000; and when this conduct could no longer be fairly and honorably concealed, to have entered upon a system of false returns to the Government and false accounts generally, which lasted for years, until finally it could no longer be maintained without exposure. When the bank applied for relief and was obliged to submit its books to examination the character of the securities was at once apparent and occasioned the refusal of aid, upon which its downfall followed. Then came the investigation of accounts, which has disclosed the state of affairs described.

There seems to be some doubt as to whether the directors who are implicated in these transactions benefited individually by them or whether it was in the first place only to assist friends and business connections, that they displayed the fatuity of accepting utterly insufficient securities. The principal persons concerned have been arrested and will be held answerable to the courts.

ADAM BADEAU.

UNITED STATES CONSULATE-GENERAL,
London, November 1, 1878.

NETHERLANDS.

Report, by Mr. Birney, minister resident of the United States at the Hague, on labor and the laboring classes of the Netherlands.

* * * * * * *

In the present antagonism between capital and labor in the United States, I cannot aid your inquiries better than by giving facts in regard to the price of labor and the condition of laborers in Holland.

In this country, upon an area of somewhat more than 20,000 English square miles, there live four millions of people. There perhaps cannot be found elsewhere an equal number occupying a similar area in which a larger amount of wealth has been accumulated in individual ownership, and in which the operatives or producers are more contented, and in possession of more of the ordinary needs of life, and less embarrassed by debt.

The average compensation of laborers in Holland does not exceed one-third of the average compensation of the same class in the United States. (I may note here that when I speak of prices, it will be more convenient to the reader to use the terms of the United States currency, the Holland florin, or its 100 cents, being of the same value as 40 cents United States.) The ordinary workman in this country receives from 40 to 60 cents per day, according to the number of hours in which he may have worked. It will not be amiss to remark that the difficulty which has often threatened to be serious in the United States has been satisfactorily solved here by paying the workman by the hour, and giving him the privilege to work as many hours as he pleases. The result is, that the time of work, instead of being less than ten hours, is almost invariably in excess. Some continue at work ten, some eleven, some twelve, and others even thirteen or fourteen hours. During the summer months there are eighteen hours of daylight in this latitude. They can commence the working-day at five or six o'clock in the morning, rest for breakfast between seven and eight, rest for second meal between twelve and one and a half, and the third time between four and five, quitting at any time before dark, which does not set in at that season until nine or nine and a half o'clock. That I may speak reliably, I have before me the time-book of the superintendent of the workmen of a large brick building being constructed for one of the government departments. The highest rate to the bricklayers is 7.20 cents per hour; others received from 5.20 cents to 6 cents per hour. So that, for a day of ten hours, the best received 72 cents, the inferior 52 cents, and at the same rate for additional hours, many of them making fourteen hours per day. Men employed in sweeping the streets of the city receive 40 cents per day. Farm hands in the country receive less. Nor is this low rate of compensation confined to those called laborers. It pervades all callings. The policemen of the city are paid from $2.80 to $4 per week; letter-carriers are paid at the same rate; well-trained men-servants who speak more than one language offer their services for from $8 to $10 per month; female cooks, for from $3 to $4 per month; housemaids, for from $2.50 to $3.50 for the same time. An experienced coachman hires for $15 per month, and supports himself, wife, and child upon this sum.

Efficient merchant-clerks receive $300 to $600 per annum; school teachers in academies receive from $400 to $500, and the rector or principal of the chief high school in the city receives $1,100 per annum. The annual allowance for members of Parliament is $800, and for ministers of state or cabinet officers $5,000 per annum. Barristers are regarded as at the top of the profession when their receipts reach $8,000.

Sitting one day at dinner with a very intelligent and prominent officer of the government, I inquired of him how it was possible for employés to live upon such meager wages. "Possible!" said he; "they live very well; and experience has shown that the laborers have more saved, as a general rule, at the end of the year at the present rate than when the compensation was higher.

After many inquiries and some consideration given to the subject, I infer that the laboring population maintain themselves by the low rates of compensation for the following reasons:

1. They are accustomed to a careful economy. If their wages are only $3 per week, they will live within that amount by denying themselves indulgence in the more costly articles. For purposes of revenue the Government treats meat and sugar as luxuries, and a tax is assessed upon so much of these articles as may be consumed within the country. They are therefore very sparingly used by workingmen. Meat is of higher price here than in the United States, and this price is kept up by the demand in the London market, where all that Holland can spare finds ready sale. On account of cheap labor, vegetables and other products of the farm sell very low. The cheaper grains are used for bread. The laboring man obtains his rent at a reasonable rate. As he lives chiefly in towns and cities, he takes an apartment or so much space as he actually needs for his family. Rents are low, because the taxes upon real estate are very moderate. In his dress he adopts the style and material that has been in use for many years. This can be made up at home, without resort to the shops. If he is employed on damp ground, he uses the wooden instead of leather shoes. Many articles he uses are as much lower in price than the same articles in the United States as the rate of his wages is lower than those given there. This difference in price may be illustrated by an example. Holland and the United States each import the stock or body of the silk hat from the same country. When you go into a store here to buy the article, after it has passed through the hands of the operatives, you will be charged only $2.80 for the best quality, but you may pay for a similar article in the cities of the United States the sum of $8; and a like disparity will be found in the price of linen goods and other articles of ordinary wearing apparel.

2. Their economy is promoted by the careful preparation and prompt execution of the laws of their country.

All the laws are prepared and proposed by the ministers of state, having each in his department the responsibility of the conduct of the Government. They propose nothing for which they do not anticipate the approval of a majority of both branches of the legislative assembly. When a bill is introduced, it is subject to all the amendments that may occur to any of the members. If, after being thus thoroughly considered, it passes into law, it is duly respected by all concerned, and its provisions are thoroughly and efficiently executed. The consequence of this care is that but few laws are passed, and those already passed are not frequently altered by amendments. All subordinates who have any share in their administration are faithful in their application. The result is that litigation is diminished in a remarkable degree.

Judges and magistrates are selected discreetly and from men of solid character and ripe experience. Certainty in the execution of the law is so invariable, that very few of the minor differences among men find their way into the courts. Disagreements between employers and employés have ready solution without the aid of attorneys or magistrates. The costs and fees of frivolous actions are in this way saved. In the city of the Hague, having a population of 100,000, there are only about a dozen lawyers who subsist upon practice at the bar.

3. The laboring population do not incur the expense of time and money connected with the excitement of political strife. Political elections here proceed as quietly as any other matter of business. Candidates for office are selected from men so well known to electors, that scarcely any one deems it necessary to give them any more information than they already have. Processions, mass-meetings, and addresses to crowds are not in fashion. The Government, in regulating the extent of suffrage, has regard to the protection of property, by making the right dependent upon a property qualification. Every citizen in the Hague who pays taxes equal to $20 can vote; and every citizen in Amsterdam who pays taxes equal to $50 votes. So that the limitation is affected by the size of the city in which the voter exercises the privilege of suffrage. In the country it is as low as $8. By long usage a candidate here has nothing to do with urging his own claims for office. A member of Parliament may be elected from

any one of the districts of the realm, but he never appears in the district with the view of canvassing. To do so would only jeopardize his prospects of success.

As the non-voter is not occupied with the effort to gain office for himself or in hearing the harangues of others who would secure it, he devotes the time and money thus saved to the making of his tenement more comfortable. He cultivates and ornaments the patch of ground he may have about it. There is scarcely a house in Holland whose windows or surroundings are not decorated with flowers.

As offices are not used for partisan purposes, those who may be in office do not lose time in the apprehension of being suddenly ejected. The clerk of the first house of Parliament resigned a few days since, having served that body in the same capacity for thirty-five years. His deputy, who had been with him for twenty-five years, was made his successor. The register of deeds for this district has been in that office for forty years. One of the public printers has been in the service of the Government for sixty-six years. Of the city board, or common council, of the Hague, seven members have been in office since 1851, having been re-elected at each successive election during that period. A public dinner was recently given to them in commemoration of their quarter-century service. In a town near by the postmaster holds the office that has been held by members of the same family for over one hundred and fifty years, his father, grandfather, and great-grandfather having been his predecessors. The present incumbent has had uninterrupted possession during the last twenty-five years. These instances show either that there is no great pressure on the part of outsiders, or that the appointing power is not moved by the clamor of applicants so long as the incumbent is competent and faithful.

4. There is economy in the steadiness of habit and pursuit. The business in which a young man has been trained is generally his business for life. He does not readily change from one pursuit to another. He is content with moderate gains without risk. Failure in business is a lasting stigma; so much so, that it descends from father to son and to grandson. The man who should fail in this country cannot well set up again. His business career is ended.

Instances are numerous in which employés have remained with their employers for twenty-five or thirty years and even longer. A large portion of the population, though constantly coming in contact with people from all parts of the world, retain the same habits, customs, and style of dress which their ancestors for many generations had. This saves the expense arising from change of fashion and change of material.

It is owing to this steadiness of pursuit and carefulness in regard to business obligations that what are called *crises*, or revulsions, in the commercial world do not occur in Holland. There are periods when business is said to be less active or profitable than at other times, sympathizing in this respect with the countries with which she has trade. Banks are conducted frugally, with no attempt at display or show, and consider that they are doing well if they realize from 3 to 4 per cent. per annum. One of the best-informed gentlemen of Holland tells me that during the past forty-four years there has not been an instance of a failure among the banks of the country. A defaulting officer would not be tolerated. The currency has for a great while been perfectly sound, the paper of the banks during the past sixty years being at all times equal in value to gold.

A large portion of the Government debt, contracted years ago by the war with Belgium and other such extraordinary occurrences, bears only 2½ per cent. interest. The Government could at any time raise from its own citizens all the money it could need at from 3 to 4 per cent. interest.

5. There is economy to all the people in the fact that the State is moderate and discriminating in its method of assessing taxes. It seeks to draw its revenues chiefly from the productive property, making its assessments light upon what is yielding no income. For example, although the tax upon an unproductive city lot may be small, yet if the owner gives notice that he is ready to put buildings upon it, the lot will be exempted from taxation for seven years; and when the building is completed, if at any time it is unoccupied or tenantless, on application of the owner there will be an abatement of the tax. Taxes are rated upon houses by the number of doors, windows, and chimneys, for by this method the more costly dwellings, owned by the wealthy, pay proportionably a higher tax.

While the Government thus gathers its revenues by moderate assessments, it is in return prompt in extending protection to person and property. An efficient police is maintained not only in the cities, but throughout the country. A trespasser upon land will be at once arrested and made to suffer the penalty. The division-line of the owner is as inviolable as the walls of his mansion. The largest possible freedom is allowed to every one so long as he is well disposed, but so soon as a violation of the law is threatened the most summary treatment is dealt out. Not long since there were indications of a formidable riot in Amsterdam, caused by the suppression of a noisy holiday. The Government at the capital, upon the requisition of the burgomaster of that city, dispatched a military force, that at once quelled the disturbance.

6. There is economy in the mode of building that saves property from destruction by fire. Since my residence here I have not heard a fire-alarm, nor have I seen the gathering of an engine company. The only fire that I can obtain any account of during the past fifteen months was the burning of the inside of a small confectionery-shop, caused by the breaking of a gas-pipe. The buildings are constructed of brick or stone, and the roof covered with tile, that cannot burn. I have not seen a wooden dwelling in Holland. Incendiarism is unknown. If it should occur, efforts would not cease till the perpetrator should be discovered, and so severely punished as to discourage the crime.

In corroboration of the above statement it may be mentioned that the cost of insurance against loss by fire is almost nominal. It does not average more than the half of 1 per cent. And even at this rate insurance companies are very profitable, realizing from 12 to 16 per cent.

On two occasions since I have been here the soot in one of the chimneys of my residence took fire and made more than the usual smoke issue from the top; but before any of my household were aware that anything unusual was happening the police were ringing hurriedly at the door, with fire-extinguishers in their hands.

Having thus referred to some of the causes which appear to be aids in enabling this people to prosper with a scale of low compensations, I may add generally that no compression is used on the part of the Government to promote this condition of moderation. Each individual appears to possess the largest possible personal liberty. The people are more than usually good-humored, kind, and courteous. There is a very noticeable absence of the rougher element that is conspicuous in some countries. Strikes and trades-unions seem to have no existence. The Government assumes scarcely any responsibility in the direction of sumptuary laws. It does not direct what the subject shall eat or drink, It has adopted no license-law regulating the use or sale of intoxicating liquors. Any citizen may engage in the business of vending liquors, wholesale or retail, without prohibition. The business is taxed like other forms of business. Nor does it take charge of the domestic relations, in so far that it makes no provisions for actions at law for breach of promise to marry. It furnishes no redress by what are called actions of *crim. con.* So far as the State is concerned, marriage is treated as a civil contract, and divorce is granted on proof of violations of its terms.

While the Government is thus liberal in regard to the personal rights of its subjects, it is very successful in the management of its internal or fiscal affairs. It projects and carries on public works with a success not surpassed by individual enterprise. "It has ordered and controlled the building of a sufficient number of lines of railroads to accommodate the business of the country. It operates these by the agency of companies, who are joint stockholders; and although it has fixed the tariff of travel at a rate not exceeding one cent per mile for third-class passengers, which forms 75 per cent. of the whole amount of travel, yet it has not suffered a deficiency, and on the trunk-routes distributes satisfactory dividends." Pilfering by officials rarely, if ever, occurs. It grants no free passes, and when an officer of the road wishes to give his friends a ride or an excursion, he pays for the tickets as he would if he had no connection with the road. The greatest possible care is taken to avoid accidents. At every road-crossing a guard attends upon the passing of every train. A telegraph-bell notifies the guard from the last station of the approach of each train. He then closes the gate, and renders it impossible for ordinary vehicles to cross the track when the train is passing.

The Government, through its post-office department, delivers by carriers, for two cents each, letters to every house in the kingdom—not only in the cities, but in the entire country. The report of the receipts and expenditures of this department, laid before me by the postmaster-general of Holland, embracing the time between the years 1849 and 1877, shows that for each year the receipts have been largely in excess of the expenditures. Take, for example, the year 1876. The receipts were $1,308,025.78, the expenditures were $865,690.19, giving to the State a profit of $442,345.59. The excess on the side of profit has been about in the same proportion during the past twenty-five years.

The Government provides throughout the realm the best of wagon-roads. They are paved with stone or a very hard clinker brick. They are kept in perfect repair by a force that is constantly traversing them for that purpose. As the heavy freight is more cheaply carried by canal, the roads are better preserved. The streets of the city in which this is written are swept within every twenty-four hours, and the sweepings are sold for nearly enough to pay the expense. They are used for fertilizing the farming-land.

The Government maintains an army of 60,000 men, besides 23,000 in one of the colonies. The soldiers are well clothed and fed while under training, but receive but nominal pay.

The State relies upon religious societies for the care of the poor within their districts. It has no general system of houses or farms for paupers.

As to education, the obligation the Government assumes is to require municipalities to provide abundant schools for all youth between the ages of six and twelve years. The option remains with the municipality whether to make tuition free or to charge a moderate rate.

After this cursory statement of the price of labor and what the Government is enabled to do for the people on an economical basis, it is not for me to discuss further the causes of this stable condition of affairs. Suffice it to say that, within the range of my observation, the inhabitants, as a whole, of no county appear more prosperous, more comfortable, or more contented.

The prices of nearly all commodities are placed upon their merits, without artificial props, and the markets of all the world are accessible for the introduction of whatever may be cheapest and most needed.

JAMES BIRNEY.

LEGATION OF THE UNITED STATES,
The Hague, September 30, 1877.

INDEX.

SECRETARY'S LETTER.

LABOR CIRCULAR.

BELGIUM.

(See, also, index to Secretary's letter.)

CANADA.

DENMARK.

(See, also, index to Secretary's letter.)

FRANCE.

(See, also, index to Secretary's letter.)

GERMANY.

(See, also, index to Secretary's letter.)

GREAT BRITAIN AND IRELAND.

ENGLAND.

(See, also, index to Secretary's letter.)

IRELAND.

(See, also, index to Secretary's letter.)

SCOTLAND.

(See, also, index to Secretary's letter.)

WALES.

ITALY.

(See, also, index to Secretary's letter.)

THE NETHERLANDS.

(See, also, index to Secretary's letter.)

SPAIN.

(See, also, index to Secretary's letter.)

SWITZERLAND.

APPENDIX.

www.ingramcontent.com/pod-product-compliance
Lightning Source LLC
Chambersburg PA
CBHW032305280326
41932CB00009B/703
9783337291235